KT-194-221

THE ROUGH GUIDE TO

London
Restaurants

2001 EDITION

There are more than one hundred and
fifty Rough Guide travel, phrasebook,
and music titles, covering destinations
from Amsterdam to Zimbabwe, languages
from Czech to Vietnamese, and musics
from World to Opera and Jazz

Rough Guides on the Internet

www.roughguides.com

Rough Guide Credits

Text editor: Samantha Cook; **Series editor**: Mark Ellingham
Production: Michelle Draycott, Helen Ostick, Ed Wright, Derek Wilde
Photography: Giles Stokoe

Publishing Information

This third edition published November 2000 by
Rough Guides Ltd, 62–70 Shorts Gardens, London WC2H 9AH.

Distributed by the Penguin Group

Penguin Books Ltd, 27 Wrights Lane, London W8 5TZ
Penguin Putnam, Inc., 375 Hudson Street, New York 10014, USA
Penguin Books Australia Ltd, 487 Maroondah Highway,
PO Box 257, Ringwood, Victoria 3134, Australia
Penguin Books Canada Ltd, 10 Alcorn Avenue,
Toronto, Ontario, Canada M4V 1E4
Penguin Books (NZ) Ltd, 182–190 Wairau Road,
Auckland 10, New Zealand

Typeset in Bembo and Helvetica to an original design by Henry Iles.
Printed in Spain by Graphy Cems.

Maps based upon Ordnance Survey mapping with the permission of The
Controller of Her Majesty's Stationery Office,
© Crown copyright, Licence No. 43361U

© Charles Campion,608pp includes index
A catalogue record for this book is available from the British Library.
ISBN 1-85828-605-0

THE ROUGH GUIDE TO

London Restaurants

2001 EDITION

Written and edited by

Charles Campion

Additional research and reviews

George Theo, Margaret Clancy, Jan Leary,
Samantha Cook and Julie Sanderson

Pubs and Bars

George Theo

About Rough Guides

Rough Guides have always set out to do something different. Our first book, published in 1982, was written by Mark Ellingham. Just out of university, travelling in Greece, he took along the popular guides of the day but found they were all lacking in some way. They were either strong on ruins and museums but went on for pages without mentioning a beach or taverna, or so conscious of the need to save money that they lost sight of Greece's cultural and historical significance. Also, none of the books told him anything about Greece's contemporary life – its politics, its culture, its people and how they lived.

So, with no job in prospect, Mark decided to write his own guidebook, one which aimed to provide practical information that was second to none, detailing the best beaches and the hottest clubs and restaurants, alongside interesting accounts of sights both famous and obscure, and up-to-the-minute information on contemporary culture. It was a guide that encouraged independent travellers to find the best of Greece, and was an immediate success, getting shortlisted for the Thomas Cook travel guide award, and encouraging Mark and a few friends to expand the series.

The Rough Guide list grew rapidly and the letters flooded in, indicating a much broader readership than anticipated, but one which uniformly appreciated the Rough Guide mix of practical detail and humour, irreverence and enthusiasm. Things haven't changed. The same writers who began the series are still the caretakers of the Rough Guide mission today: to provide the most reliable, up-to-date and entertaining information to independent-minded travellers of all ages, on all budgets.

Rough Guides now publish more than a hundred and fifty titles, written and researched by a dedicated team based in Britain, Europe, the USA and Australia. We have also created a unique series of phrasebooks, along with an acclaimed series of music guides, and a best-selling pocket guide to the Internet. We also publish comprehensive travel information on our Web site: www.roughguides.com

About the Author

Charles Campion is an award-winning food writer and restaurant reviewer. He writes a restaurant column for *ES*, the *London Evening Standard* magazine, which won him the Glenfiddich "Restaurant Writer of the Year" award, and contributes to radio and TV food programmes, as well as a variety of magazines including *Bon Appetit* in the USA. His most recent book publication was *Real Greek Food*, which he wrote with chef Theodore Kyriakou.

Before becoming a food writer, Charles worked in a succession of London ad agencies and had a spell as chef-proprietor of a hotel and restaurant in darkest Derbyshire.

Help Us Update

We've tried to ensure that this third edition of *The Rough Guide to London Restaurants* is as up to date and accurate as possible. However, London's restaurant scene is in constant flux: chefs change jobs; restaurants are bought and sold; menus change. There will probably be a few references in this guide that are out of date even as this book is printed – and standards, of course, go up and down. If you feel there are places we've underrated or overpraised, or others we've unjustly omitted, please let us know: comments or corrections are much appreciated, and we'll send a copy of the next edition (or any other Rough Guide if you prefer) for the best letters. Please address letters to Charles Campion at:

Rough Guides, 62–70 Shorts Gardens, London WC2H 9AH or
Rough Guides, 4th Floor, 375 Hudson St, New York, NY 10014.

Or send email to: mail@roughguides.co.uk

Contents

Introduction	x

Getting off the fence: xii
   the best food in London

Best Newcomers; Chinese & Southeast Asian; French;
New-Style Indian; Old-Style Indian; Italian; Middle Eastern;
(Gastro) Pub; Vegetarian; Budget; Extravagance;
Neighbourhood; Restaurant Set Lunch

London map	xvi
Central London map	xviii
Underground map	xx

Central London

Bloomsbury & Fitzrovia	3
Chinatown	17
Covent Garden & Holborn	29
Euston & King's Cross	45
Kensington	53
Knightsbridge & Belgravia	61
Marylebone	69
Mayfair & Bond Street	81

Paddington & Edgware Road	93
Piccadilly & St James's	103
Queensway & Westbourne Grove	119
Soho	129
South Kensington	157
Victoria & Westminster	165
Waterloo & The South Bank	177

The City & East London

Brick Lane & Spitalfields	187
The City	197
Clerkenwell	211
Docklands	221
Hackney & Dalston	229
Hoxton & Shoreditch	239
Further East	247

Forest Gate, Newbury Park, West Ham

North London

Camden Town & Primrose Hill	255
Hampstead & Golders Green	265
Highgate & Crouch End	279

Holloway & Highbury	287
Islington	297
Maida Vale & Kilburn	309
St John's Wood & Swiss Cottage	317
Stoke Newington	325
Wembley	335
Further North	343
Haringey, Hendon, Kingsbury, Willesden	

South London

Battersea	353
Brixton & Camberwell	361
Clapham & Wandsworth	369
Greenwich & Blackheath	379
Kennington & Vauxhall	385
Putney	393
Tower Bridge & Bermondsey	401
Wimbledon & Southfields	415
Further South	423
Bromley, Croydon, Epsom Downs, Forest Hill, Herne Hill, Norbury, Tooting, West Dulwich	

West London

Barnes & Sheen	439
Chelsea	447
Ealing & Acton	461
Earl's Court	471
Fulham	477
Hammersmith & Chiswick	485
Notting Hill	495
Richmond & Twickenham	515
Shepherd's Bush & Olympia	525
Southall	533
Further West Greenford, Hampton, Surbiton	543

Indexes

Index of restaurants by name	551
Index of restaurants by cuisine	568
Index of pubs and bars	579

Introduction

Welcome to the third edition of The Rough Guide to London Restaurants. If you used the first two, you will have noticed that the guide continues to grow – while still, we hope, staying pocketable. This edition has been extensively revised and as well as re-assessing all the previous entries we have added a wide selection of new establishments. But the way we have organised the book has stayed the same. Anyone who has lived or worked in London knows that, while it may seem like one big metropolis to the outsider, it is really a series of villages. If you live in Clapham, you know about Clapham and Battersea, and maybe Brixton or Chelsea, while Highgate or Shepherd's Bush are far-off lands. And vice versa. Yet almost every other restaurant guide is divided up by cuisine, which assumes that this is your first criterion when choosing a place to eat. It shouldn't be. If you're meeting friends in Chiswick your best options might be Italian or Modern British; in Wembley or Tooting they might be Indian. But you want to know about that oddball great restaurant, too: whether it's an interesting newcomer like the *Station Grill* in Kennington, or a bargain Sri Lankan like the *Palm Palace* in Southall. This book divides London into five geographic sections (Central; City & East; North; South; West) and then breaks these down into the **neighbourhoods**, with restaurants arranged alphabetically in each section. Keep this guide handy and it will tell you where to eat well from Soho to Southall.

There is one significant change to the 2001 edition. At the end of each neighbourhood section we have added a short directory of convenient **pubs and bars**. This is not an attempt to put the beer pundits out of business, but rather to make this *Rough Guide to London Restaurants* even more useful than previous editions. For many, part of the ritual of eating out is to meet for a drink before or after the meal. But where –

especially if it is your first visit to a particular restaurant – should you arrange to meet? The reviews in the new "drinking" pages will give you some pointers, and to make your choices even simpler we have included all our selected pubs and bars on the neighbourhood maps.

Another important thing to note about the 350 or so restaurants selected and reviewed in this book is that they are all **recommended** – none has been included simply to make up the numbers. There are some very cheap places and there are some potentially pretty expensive places, but they all represent good value. The only rule we have made for inclusion is that it must be possible to eat a meal for £35 a head or less. In some of the *haute cuisine* establishments, that will mean keeping to the set lunch, while in some of the bargain eateries £35 might cover a blow-out for four. This guide reviews restaurants for every possible occasion from quick lunches to celebratory dinners. It also covers many different kinds of food, some fifty cuisines in all, and even more in reality, as for simplicity we have used "Indian" and "Chinese" as catch-all terms.

Prices and credit cards

Price is one of the most difficult areas for any restaurant guide to master. Every review in this book has at the top of the page a **spread of two prices** (eg £12–£40). The first figure relates to what you could get away with: this is the minimum amount per person you are likely to spend on a meal here (assuming you are not a non-tipping, non-drinking skinflint). The second relates to what it would cost if you don't hold back. Wild diners with a taste for fine wines will leave our top estimates far behind, but they are there as a guide. For most people, the cost of a meal will lie somewhere within the spread.

For a more detailed picture, each review sets out the prices of various dishes. At some time in the guide's life these specific prices (and indeed the overall price spreads) will become out of date, but they were all accurate when the book left for the printer. And even in the giddy world of restaurants, when prices rise or prices fall, everyone tends to move together. If this book shows one restaurant as being twice as expensive as another, that is likely to remain.

The reviews also keep faith with original menu spellings of dishes, so you'll find satays, satehs and satés – all of which will probably taste much the same. Hieroglyphics have been kept to a minimum, so opening hours and days are spelled out, as are the credit cards accepted. Where reviews specify "all major credit cards accepted", that means at least Amex, Diners, Mastercard and Visa. Acceptance of Visa and Mastercard usually means Switch and Delta, too; we've specified the odd exception, but if you're relying on one card it's always best to check when you book.

Getting off the fence . . .

Every restaurant reviewed in this book is wholeheartedly recommended . . . but it would be a very strange person who did not have favourites, so here are some of my "six of the bests".

Best Newcomers

New End, Hampstead & Golders Green	p.275
Nosh Brothers, Notting Hill Gate	p.506
Osteria d'Isola, Knightsbridge & Belgravia	p.64
Parade, Ealing & Acton	p.467
Tabla, Docklands	p.226
Al Waha, Queensway & Westbourne Grove	p.122

Best Chinese and Southeast Asian

Aroma II, Chinatown   p.19
Fung Shing, Chinatown   p.21
Huong Viet, Hackney & Dalston   p.234
Jen, Chinatown   p.22
Mandarin Kitchen, Queensway & Westbourne Grove   p.125
Mr Kong, Chinatown   p.24

Best French

Aubergine, Chelsea   p.449
Chez Bruce, Clapham & Wandsworth   p.372
Orrery, Marylebone   p.75
The Station Grill, Kennington & Vauxhall   p.390
The Square, Mayfair & Bond Street   p.90
La Tante Clare, Knightsbridge & Belgravia   p.66

Best New-Style Indian

Café Spice Namaste, Prescot Street, The City   p.203
Planet Spice, Further South – South Croydon   p.431
Quilon, Victoria & Westminster   p.172
Le Raj, Further South – Epsom Downs   p.432
Sarkhel's, Wimbledon & Southfields   p.419
Zaika, Chelsea   p.458

Best Old-Style Indian

The Brilliant, Southall   p.535
Ma Goa, Putney   p.398
Monty's, Ealing & Acton   p.465
Omi's, Southall   p.538
Palm Palace, Southall   p.539
Tabaq, Clapham & Wandsworth   p.377

Best Italian

Assaggi, Notting Hill		p.499
Del Buongustaio, Putney		p.396
Grano, Hammersmith & Chiswick		p.491
Osteria d'Isola, Knightsbridge & Belgravia		p.64
Vasco & Piero's Pavilion, Soho		p.151
Zafferano, Knightsbridge & Belgravia		p.67

Best Middle Eastern

Abu Ali, Paddington & Edgware Road		p.95
Alounak, Queensway & Westbourne Grove		p.121
Al Waha, Queensway & Westbourne Grove		p.122
Fairuz, Marylebone		p.73
Mohsen, Earl's Court		p.475
Ranoush, Paddington & Edgware Road		p.100

Best (Gastro) Pub

The Anglesea Arms, Hammersmith & Chiswick		p.487
The Eagle, Clerkenwell		p.215
The Engineer, Camden Town & Primrose Hill		p.258
The Havelock Tavern, Shepherd's Bush & Olympia		p.529
St John's, Holloway & Highbury		p.294
The Salusbury, Maida Vale & Kilburn		p.314

Best Vegetarian

Bah Humbug, Brixton & Camberwell		p.363
Carnevale, Hoxton & Shoreditch		p.242
Fiction, Highgate & Crouch End		p.282
The Gate, Hammersmith & Chiswick		p.490
Kastoori, Further South – Tooting		p.427
Roussillon, Victoria & Westminster		p.174

Best Budget Meal

Al Duca, Piccadilly & St James's	p.108
Café España, Soho	p.134
Gastro, Clapham & Wandsworth	p.374
Huong Viet, Hackney & Dalston	p.234
Palm Palace, Southall	p.539
The Toucan, Soho	p.150

Best Extravagance

Assaggi, Notting Hill	p.499
Defune, Paddington & Edgware Road	p.97
Fung Shing, Chinatown	p.21
The Square, Mayfair & Bond Street	p.90
La Tante Clare, Knightsbridge & Belgravia	p.66
Zaika, Chelsea	p.458

Best Neighbourhood Restaurant

No.77 Wine Bar, Hampstead & Golders Green	p.267
Brula Bistrot, Richmond & Twickenham	p.517
Miraggio, Fulham	p.481
Parade, Ealing & Acton	p.467
The Station Grill, Kennington & Vauxhall	p.390
The Salusbury, Maida Vale & Kilburn	p.314

Best Value Set Lunch

Gordon Ramsay, Chelsea	p.454
The House, Chelsea	p.455
Orrery, Marylebone	p.75
The Real Greek, Hoxton & Shoreditch	p.244
The Square, Mayfair & Bond Street	p.90
La Tante Clare, Knightsbridge & Belgravia	p.66

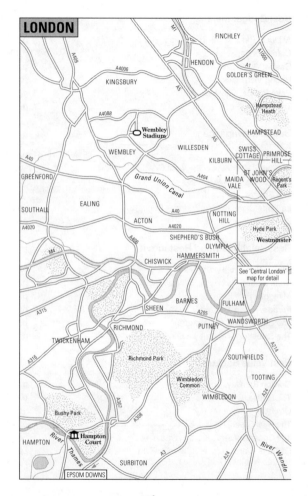

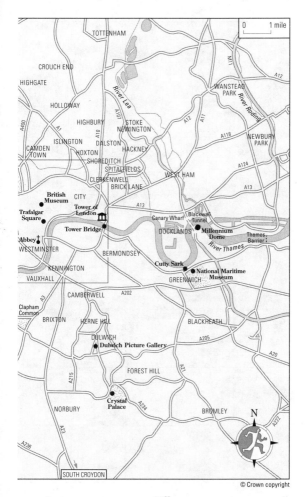

0   1 mile

TOTTENHAM

CROUCH END

HIGHGATE

HOLLOWAY

HIGHBURY

ISLINGTON

CAMDEN TOWN

HOXTON

SHOREDITCH

CLERKENWELL

CITY

British Museum

Trafalgar Square

Tower of London

Tower Bridge

Abbey

WESTMINSTER

KENNINGTON

VAUXHALL

BERMONDSEY

DALSTON

HACKNEY

STOKE NEWINGTON

SPITALFIELDS

BRICK LANE

WEST HAM

WANSTEAD PARK

NEWBURY PARK

River Lea

River Roding

Canary Wharf

DOCKLANDS

Blackwall Tunnel

Millennium Dome

Thames Barrier

River Thames

Cutty Sark

National Maritime Museum

GREENWICH

Clapham Common

CAMBERWELL

BRIXTON

HERNE HILL

DULWICH

Dulwich Picture Gallery

FOREST HILL

NORBURY

Crystal Palace

BLACKHEATH

BROMLEY

N

SOUTH CROYDON

© Crown copyright

xvii

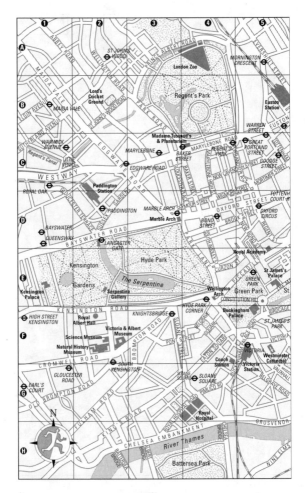

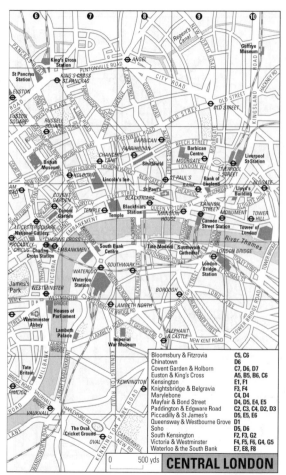

Bloomsbury & Fitzrovia	C5, C6
Chinatown	D6
Covent Garden & Holborn	C7, D6, D7
Euston & King's Cross	A5, B5, B6, C6
Kensington	E1, F1
Knightsbridge & Belgravia	F3, F4
Marylebone	C4, D4
Mayfair & Bond Street	D4, D5, E4, E5
Paddington & Edgware Road	C2, C3, C4, D2, D3
Piccadilly & St James's	D5, E5, E6
Queensway & Westbourne Grove	D1
Soho	D5, D6
South Kensington	F2, F3, G2
Victoria & Westminster	F4, F5, F6, G4, G5
Waterloo & the South Bank	E7, E8, F8

0   500 yds

CENTRAL LONDON

© Crown copyright

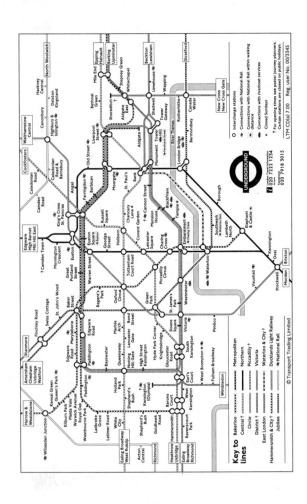

Central

Bloomsbury & Fitzrovia 3

Chinatown 17

Covent Garden & Holborn 29

Euston & King's Cross 45

Kensington 53

Knightsbridge & Belgravia 61

Marylebone 69

Mayfair & Bond Street 81

Paddington & Edgware Road..93

Piccadilly & St James's...103

Queensway & Westbourne Grove...................................119

Soho..129

South Kensington 157

Victoria & Westminster..165

Waterloo & The South Bank 177

Bloomsbury
& Fitzrovia

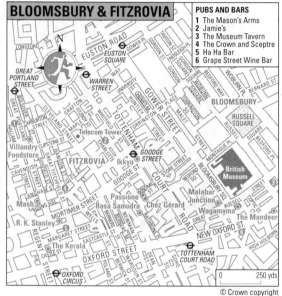

BLOOMSBURY & FITZROVIA

PUBS AND BARS
1 The Mason's Arms
2 Jamie's
3 The Museum Tavern
4 The Crown and Sceptre
5 Ha Ha Bar
6 Grape Street Wine Bar

© Crown copyright

CENTRAL

Chez Gérard

8 Charlotte St, W1 ✆020 7636 4975	⊖ Goodge Street
Mon–Fri noon–3pm & 6–11.30pm, Sat 6–11.30pm,	
Sun noon–3pm & 6–10.30pm	All major credit cards
www.sante-gcg.com	

When the inner prompting shouts for steak frîtes you can't do better than turn to Chez Gérard. Though today there are more than a dozen branches of this popular brasserie spread throughout London, the Charlotte Street branch is the original and, some say, the best. When it opened, twenty years ago, this type of French restaurant – where the steak is good and the frîtes are fabulous – was a novelty in London; today, Chez Gérard feels reassuringly old-fashioned. Along with the fine steak frîtes, you'll find salade Périgourdine, French onion soup, snails and crème brûlée. The bread is crusty, the service Gallic, and they serve decent red wine. It's not cheap, but the food is always good, and in summer you can eat al fresco at one of the pavement tables.

Start with rock oysters (£6.20 for six; £9.30 for nine; £12.40 for twelve), chicken liver pâté with toasted brioche (£4.50), or, for a real belt of nostalgia, a dozen snails in garlic butter (£5.30). The steaks come in all shapes and sizes – Châteaubriand and côte de boeuf are both for two people (£31 and £22.95 respectively). There's a 9oz fillet steak (£15.95) and entrecôte (£12.65). This is also one of the few places in London where you can get onglet (£9.75), a particularly tasty French cut. Everything from the grill comes with pommes frîtes and sauce Béarnaise. There is also space on the grill for salmon, sea bass and chicken, and on the menu for a couple of vegetarian options. But don't kid yourself; you're here for the steak frîtes. Salad, side orders of vegetables, desserts – including tarte Tatin (£4.50) – and a decent selection of regional French cheeses (£4.25) are nicely in tune with the Gallic ambience. So too are the house wines (£9.50), which are so good that you can almost disregard the wine list.

There is also a very sound menu prix fixe available from Monday to Saturday evening, and all day Sunday – just £16.95 for three courses.

BLOOMSBURY & FITZROVIA ⑪ JAPANESE

Ikkyu

67a Tottenham Court Rd, W1 ✆020 7636 9280	⊖ Goodge Street
Mon–Fri noon–2.30pm & 6–10.30pm, Sun 6–10.30pm	All major credit cards

Busy, basic and full of people eating reliable Japanese food at sensible prices – all in all, Ikkyu is a good match for any popular neighbourhood restaurant in Tokyo. What's more, it is hard to find, which adds to the authenticity. Down the steps and through the twine fly screen and you've made it. The first shock is how very busy the place is – you are not the first person to discover what must be about the best-value Japanese food in London.

Nigiri sushi is good here and is priced by the piece – tuna (£2), yellow tail (£2.10), salmon (£1.70), mackerel (£1.40) or cuttlefish (£1.70). Or there's sashimi – which runs all the way from mackerel (£4.50) to sea urchin (£13), with an assortment for £13.50. Alternatively, start with soba, cold brown noodles (£3.60) – delicious. Then allow yourself a selection of yakitori, either a portion of assorted (£5), or mix and match from tongue, heart, liver, gizzard or chicken skin, all at £1 a stick. You will need a good many skewers of the grilled chicken skin which is implausibly delicious. Moving on to the main dishes, an order of fried leeks with pork (£7.20) brings a bunch of long onion-flavoured greens which may well be chives, although not so pungent, strewn with morsels of grilled pork. Whatever the green element is, it is certainly not leeks. Or there's grilled aubergine (£3.40), or rolled five vegetables with shrimp (£7.70), which is like a Swiss roll made with egg and vegetable with a core of prawn.

Ikkyu's menu rewards experimentation as it has a good many delicious secrets, though the Japanese-favoured drink, shouchu and soda (£3.50), is perhaps not among them – shouchu is a clear spirit which tastes like clear spirit and the addition of soda does little to make it palatable. Asahi and Kirin beers (both £2.70) are a much better choice. Another doubtful order would be fermented soya beans topped with a raw egg (£3.10), which in Japan is thought to be the perfect way to start the day, but is unlikely to woo you away from cornflakes.

CENTRAL

The Kerala

15 Great Castle St, W1 ℗020 7580 2125	⊖ Oxford Circus
Daily noon–3pm & 5.30–11pm	All major credit cards

In 1935 Gough Brothers opened a wine bar, Shirref's, 15 Great Castle Street, at which time such establishments were something of a novelty; Shirref's stood the test of time and became a favourite watering hole for musicians and actors working around the corner at the BBC in Portland Place. At the end of the 1980s it was taken over by David Tharakan and continued to prosper – a good deal of wine was consumed and there was even a short menu of pub food favourites. The big changes came at the end of 1997, when David's wife Millie took over the kitchen and changed the menu. Shirref's started to offer Keralan home cooking, with well-judged, well-spiced dishes at bargain-basement prices. Since then The Kerala restaurant – because this is what it has now become – has gone from strength to strength.

To start with, you must order a platoon of simple things: cashew nut pakoda (£2), potato bonda (£2), lamb samosa (£2), chicken liver masala (£2.75), mussels ularthu (£2.75). These are honest dishes simply presented and at a price which encourages experimentation. Thereafter the menu is divided into a number of sections – Syrian Christian specialities from Kerala, Coastal seafood dishes, Malabar biryanis, vegetable curries, and special dosas. From the first, try erachi olathiathu (£4.25): this is a splendid dry curry of lamb with coconut. From the second, try meen and mango vevichathu (£4.95), which is kingfish cooked with the sharpness of green mango. From the biryanis, how about chemmin biryani (£5.25), prawns cooked with basmati rice? Avial (£2.75) is a mixed vegetable curry with yoghurt and coconut. The breads are fascinating: try the lacy and delicate appams (two for £1.90), which are made from rice flour and steamed.

This is a very friendly place, completely at odds with the hectic rush of nearby Oxford Street. The people who run the Kerala are intensely proud of their country and its cuisine, and will be happy to help you discover glorious new dishes. The Kerala would be good value in the suburbs, but being hidden behind Oxford Circus makes it a contender for bargain of the age.

£12–£25

Malabar Junction

107 Great Russell St, WC1 ©020 7580 5230	✆ Tottenham Court Road
Daily noon–3pm & 6–11.30pm	All major credit cards except Diners

The cuisine at Malabar Junction is that of Kerala – the home province of the proprietor – and it is served up from two entirely separate kitchens and brigades of chefs, vegetarian and non-vegetarian, kept completely separate to comply with religious requirements. However busy it may be down in the kitchens, though, inside the restaurant all is calm. This is a top-quality Indian restaurant, fully licensed, with a spacious dining room with comfortable chairs and a conservatory roof, none of which elegance is hinted at by the rather unprepossessing frontage at the Tottenham Court Road end of Great Russell Street.

Kerala is the spice centre of India, and all the Malabar dishes tend to be spicy and nutty – curry leaves, cinnamon, coconut, chilli and cashew nuts prevail. There is also a good deal of fish. To start with, try the spinach vadia (£3) – small chickpea doughnuts made with spinach and ginger, deep-fried and served crunchy with two dipping sauces of yoghurt and tamarind. Or there's uppuma (£3.30), a kind of eastern polenta – semolina fried in ghee with onions, spices and cashew nuts. The poori masala (£2.50) takes the form of two balloon-shaped, puffed breads with a potato cake that's not a million miles from bubble and squeak. For a main course, try some fish or seafood: the fish moilee (£7.50) runs the gamut of cinnamon, cloves, cardamom, green chillies, garlic, coconut and curry leaves, while the Cochin prawn curry (£8) is more tomatoey with huge prawns. Chicken Malabar (£6) applies much the same Keralan spice palate to chicken. From the array of vegetable dishes, try avial (£3.50), a combination of all sorts of vegetables but with a host of woody and aromatic spices, and a plate of green bananas (£4), tangy and delicious.

You'll also find all the traditional Southern Indian vegetarian favourites listed on the menu here – rava dosa (semolina pancake), uthappam (crisp lentil pancake) and iddly (rice and lentil cakes). This may well be the perfect restaurant for any mix of vegetarians and fish (or meat) eaters.

The Mandeer

8 Bloomsbury Way, WC1 ✆020 7242 6202	✪ Holborn/Tottenham Court Road
Mon–Sat noon–3pm & 5–10pm	All major credit cards (evenings only)

This is the second address for the Mandeer restaurant, but don't get the impression that Ramesh and Usha Patel are flighty – it was their first move in forty years. The Mandeer Ayurvedic Vegetarian restaurant is something of an institution. From its old premises just off Tottenham Court Road smiling staff dished up very cheap, very good, very worthy Gujarati food, to everyone from penniless students to religious devotees. Nowadays the new Mandeer stands next to the Centre for Tibetan Studies in Bloomsbury Way, and it is full of much the same clientele as before. The food is just as good, too, and just as good value as it ever was. The most expensive dish on the menu is a thali, at £14.70, which brings you an absolute feast of Gujarati and Maharashtran cooking: a well-balanced meal on a tray, featuring pilau rice, two purum puri, kadhi, dry potato, bhindi, aubergines, beans, two kachori, raita and papadom. There's a beer and organic wine list for the weak of spirit, but no smoking – as you'd expect of a "medicinal" restaurant.

You can easily eat for a lot less – but there is much to tempt. Crisp, plump samosas (£2.60) are served with date and tamarind chutney. Batata vada (£2.60) are mini-hand-grenades of spicy mashed potato, deep-fried. Kachori (£3.85) are a revelation – deep-fried pastries filled with split mung beans, redolent of cinnamon and cloves. Breads are wholemeal and delicious – puris (two for £1.20), chapattis with ghee (two for £1.40) and parathas (£1.25). Bhindi (£5.60), from the Gujarati section of the menu, is a rich, dry curry of okra. The "beans of the day" (£4.50) may be anything from chickpeas to aduki beans. Panir mattar (£5.50) is cubes of Indian cheese with peas in a much-reduced garlic and onion sauce. These are good concentrated flavours, no wading through anonymous and wishy-washy sauces. Desserts are Indian and very sweet in the main, although the shrikand (£2.50) – a strained yoghurt with saffron and cardamom – is pleasantly tangy.

Turn up at lunchtime and part of the dining room becomes a self-service buffet – good food, very low prices, cash only. There's a display board with the dishes on it: try the masala dosa with soup (£4.50), and add a samosa (60p), or batata vada (60p). As you might expect, it's busy.

BLOOMSBURY & FITZROVIA ⑭ MODERN EUROPEAN

Mash

19–21 Great Portland St, W1 ℂ020 7637 5555	⊖ Oxford Circus
Mon–Sat noon–3pm & 6–11.30pm	All major credit cards

Mash is certainly modern – and it will probably go on looking modern for the next twenty years. Like its antecedent in Manchester, London Mash combines a brewery with bar, deli and restaurant. The brewery stands at the back of the low and busy bar, and the deli, always busy, is open for breakfast and sells takeaway packed lunches. Occasionally a restaurant has an indefinable something which guarantees it success: London Mash has been full since the day it opened and if you like the buzz (and the crowds of other people who like the buzz) you will be happy here. There are moments when the food is very good and it seldom slips much below okay. There is a wood-fired oven, and a wood-fired grill. And lots and lots of wood-fired food.

The reasonably priced starters range from the Italian charcuterie plate (£6.50/£11), to ceviche of salmon, cucumber and tomato salsa with an avocado dressing (£6) and baked goats' cheese, plum tomato, roast aubergine and crostini with herb mustard vinaigrette (£6). To follow, there are pizzas, pasta, salads, fish from the wood-fired grill, mains and sides. Pizzas are of the new breed, with toppings such as confit duck, plum sauce, cucumber and bok choi (£9.90), or natural smoked haddock, spinach, free-range egg, crème fraîche and smoked Cheddar (£9.90); pastas likewise, with such varieties as aubergine and ricotta tortelloni with a roasted pepper sauce (£10). And then there is a section of fish dishes from the wood-fired oven – grilled marlin steak with crushed new potatoes, wilted spinach and tapenade (£14) or whole roasted sea bass with green olive caper mayonnaise (£15.50). Or how about rolled grilled rump of lamb steak, ragout of peppers, lima beans and Swiss chard (£13)? If dishes such as these sing out to you, you'll be very happy here, as they are confidently cooked and well presented.

The four beers made on the premises are probably an acquired taste – though anyone drinking enough of the fruit beer to acquire a taste for it deserves some sort of commendation for fortitude. There's a decent wine list, if you don't get along with the beer. On Saturday the Mash Brewer's Brunch combines a brewery tour with tutored tasting and brunch.

CENTRAL

Passione

10 Charlotte St, W1 ✆020 7636 2833	⊖ Goodge Street
Mon–Fri 12.30–2.30pm & 7–10.30pm, Sat 7–10.30pm	All major credit cards

You may not have heard of Gennaro Contaldo, but you will certainly have heard of his protégé Jamie Oliver, aka the Naked Chef, whose scooter-driving, drum-bashing antics keep a swathe of middle England foodies firmly glued to their television screens when they could be out having a nice dinner. Many of Oliver's "revolutionary" methods stem from the time he spent working as a commis in a brigade headed by Contaldo. That was in the days before 1999 when Contaldo achieved his ambition and opened his own place, Passione. This is a good restaurant. Simplicity, an unpretentious feel to the place, seasonal ingredients and a great deal of care and ability in the kitchen, are sure bets when it comes to eating. Be sure not to miss the splendid breads, including Contaldo's fabled focaccio, which the Naked One is always banging on about.

You owe it to yourself to have four courses here, and the portions are geared towards being able to manage such a splurge – how nice it is to have four delicious platefuls and not feel overstuffed. The menu changes frequently and is admirably seasonal. Antipasti may include petto d'anatra affumicata con rucola e pera (£7.50), which is smoked duck breast with rocket and pear; or zuppa di lenticchie (£6), a plain lentil soup; or insalata di funghi famigliola buona con aglio, peperoncini, olive e prezzemolo (£8), a stunning salad of cold mushrooms. Then there are pastas and risotti – tagliatelle con tartufo (£9/£11) is suffused with the heady scent of truffles, while risotto all'accetosella (£9/£11) has the tasty tang of wild sorrel. Mains are rich and satisfying: cotoletta di vitella in padella con parmigiano e salsa di tartufo servito con spinach (£16) is a veal chop cooked under a rich layer of cheese, with a truffled sauce and one concession to health – a side order of spinach. Or maybe sarago con salsa di pomodoro freschi e olive servito con patatine (£13.50) tempts? It's a simple dish of precisely cooked sea bream with a fresh tomato sauce. The service is slick here; this is a place where they understand the art of running a great restaurant.

Puddings (all £5.50) are serious stuff, though it has to be said that the delicious gelato passione, a swirl of zesty limoncello ice with a splash of wild strawberry folded into it, is for all the world a grown-up's raspberry ripple.

Rasa Samudra

5 Charlotte St, W1 ℂ020 7637 0222	⊖ Goodge Street
Mon–Sat noon–3pm & 6–11pm	All major credit cards except Diners

Rasa Samudra is the latest in a long line of restaurants to occupy this site. After many years as a smart English fish restaurant, it was most recently an haute cuisine establishment where the cooking was good enough to win a Michelin star – just after the chef responsible had been let go! Amid murmurings about a "doomed site", the Charlotte Street knife and fork brigade sat back and waited to see what would happen next. It takes a brave man to start another restaurant under such scrutiny and just such a man is Mr Das, who already had two notable South Indian restaurants – Rasa W1 (see p.88) and Rasa (see p.332). The food served at Rasa Samudra would be more at home in Bombay than in London, consisting as it does of sophisticated Southern Indian fish dishes – a million miles from curry-house staples.

At first glance the menu may seem heart-stoppingly expensive, partly due to a strange, exclusively British, prejudice that no curry should ever cost more than a fiver even if made from the kind of top-quality ingredients that are worth £15 in a French restaurant. Note, however, that all the more expensive choices – which are often based on fish, usually the most pricey of ingredients – come complete with accompaniments. This makes them substantial enough to allow all but the greediest of diners to dispense with starters, except perhaps for the samudra rasam (£5.95), a stunning shellfish soup, or the array of pappadoms, pappar-vardi and achappam (£4) plus wicked pickles (£2.50). For main course, koonthal olathiathu (£9.95), squid cooked with onion, curry leaves, ginger and fresh coconut, is well offset by pooris (£2.50) and spicy potatoes (£5.25) as side dishes. Other good choices include crab varuthathu (£12.95) – crab cooked dry with ginger – and arachu vecha aavoli (£10.95), which is pomfret cooked with shallots, red chillies and tamarind, well complemented by the beetroot curry (£6.25) and a cha-pati. The cooking is well judged and the spices well balanced.

If you are still nervous of the bill, don't be: the food is worth it. Try lunch – three courses for £14.95 (seafood) or £10.95 (vegetarian).

R.K. Stanley

6 Little Portland St, W1 ✆020 7462 0099	⊖ Oxford Circus
Mon–Fri noon–11.30pm, Sat 6–11.30pm	All major credit cards

www.rkstanley.co.uk

Beer and sausages: at first glance a prescription for German restaurant hell . . . a noisy bierkeller with over-cheerful waitresses serving over-large portions. Think again. R.K. Stanley is a highly successful celebration of two of Britain's culinary strengths, presented in a stylish, modern take on an upmarket American diner; the service is swift and friendly, and good-value pricing belies its location just north of Oxford Street. The food is well cooked and tasty, and the inspiration for the sausages comes from all over the globe. Prices are lowered by a pound or two for the main courses between 6pm and 7pm, in order to encourage early dining.

The centrepiece of the menu is a selection of different sausages, all of which are freshly made on the premises. Bratwurst (£7.95) comes with choucroute, grilled bacon, caramelised pears, and champ mash, while game sausage (£8.95) comes with wine-scented cabbage, mustard mash, glazed parsnips and pancetta. Pork sausages include the Thai sausage (£7.50), which comes with noodles, choi sum and spicy vegetables, and the delightful Simple Stanley (£7.25) – a home-made pork sausage served with onion gravy, spinach and champ mash. The Caribbean-style jerk sausage (£7.95) is hotter, served with plantain, chilli peppers and sweet-potato mash. There is even a lamb sausage that comes with kale, glazed carrots and parsnip mash (£8.95). Nigel Slater's white bean vegetarian sausages (£6.95) are, on the face of it, a very strange idea. The starters include a splendid plate of house savouries, cured meats, chutneys and pickle (£5.50 or £9.95 for two), and steamed mussels with Stilton cream (£5.50). There is also a small selection of alternative mains for sausaphobics – and reliable puddings at under £5.

You should drink ale, lager, stout or porter here. There are dozens of interesting bottled ales on offer, ranging from Shepherd Neame's Spitfire – smooth and soft (£3.75) – to Fraoch Heather ale, which is brewed with hand-picked flowering shoots of heather (£4.20). Or try Stanley's Stout from the keg (£2.70 a pint). The bottle prices might seem high but you get some fine brews – and experimenting with rare beers is a lot cheaper than trying fine wines.

Villandry Foodstore

170 Great Portland St, W1 ✆020 7631 3131   ⊖ Great Portland Street

Daily 8.30am–10pm   Amex, Mastercard, Visa

Both foodstore and restaurant serving breakfast, elevenses, lunch, tea and dinner, Villandry *began in more fashionable but cramped surroundings in Marylebone High Street. Its success brought the need for larger premises and, thus installed in Great Portland Street, a handsome foodstore gives onto a modern, rather stark, dining room. Passing displays of some of Europe's most extravagant ingredients may jangle the nerves and alarm the wallet, but if you're serious about your food, and you have time to wait for careful preparation,* Villandry *won't disappoint.*

The menu changes daily, so you won't necessarily find all – or indeed any – of the dishes mentioned here. But as you'd expect at the back of a foodstore that caters for the well-heeled sector of the foodie faithful, ingredients are scrupulously chosen and prepared with care. At its best this kind of "informal" menu is surprisingly demanding on the cook – and exact cooking is crucial to ostensibly simple dishes. To start you may be offered a butterbean, rosemary and pancetta soup (£5), a vegetarian salad of beetroot, blood orange, toasted hazelnuts and chicory (£5.50), poached tiger prawns with aioli (£7.50), or a small dish of sautéed lamb kidneys with lentils and mustard (£6.50). Main courses are often hugely impressive: roast shoulder of lamb, sweet potatoes, spinach and chilli (£13.25), whole lemon sole with new potatoes, watercress and herb butter (£13.50), Gloucester Old Spot confit with mashed swede and red cabbage (£14), sea bass en papillote, with Pernod, fennel and lemon (£14.50). Desserts include moist chocolate cake (£5.50) and, as you'd expect from the array in the shop, there's an extensive if expensive cheeseboard (£9.50) served with terrific walnut and sourdough breads.

Wine prices, like the food, are distinctly West End, though there are house selections from £11 – Villandry features a range of wines from Legrand filles et fils. Overall, standards are high, and the balancing both of flavours and of the menu itself suggests that the kitchen brigade know what they're doing and are not afraid to buck the trends. Lunch prices are a tad easier on the wallet.

Wagamama

4 Streatham St, WC1 © 020 7323 9223	⊖ Tottenham Court Road
Mon–Sat noon–11pm, Sun 12.30–10pm	All major credit cards

www.wagamama.com

Wagamama has been trendy – and packed – since the day it opened, and its popularity shows no signs of falling off. Which is fair enough: this is as good a canteen as you'll find, serving simple, and generally rather good, Japanese food at very reasonable prices. What it's not is a place for a relaxed or intimate meal. The basement interior is cavernous and minimalist, and diners are seated side by side on long benches. At regular eating times, you'll find yourself in a queue lining the stairway (there are no reservations). When you reach the front, you're seated, your order is punched into a hand-held computer, then the code numbers for your dishes are written on the low-tech placemat in front of you – a legacy of the day when the radio-ordering system failed. There's beer and wine available, as well as free green tea.

Dishes arrive when they're cooked, so a party of four will be served at different times. This system doesn't favour sharing – what you order is yours. Generally that means ordering a main dish – noodles in soup, fried noodles or sauce-based noodles – or a rice dish. Plus a side dish (which can also be pressed into service as sort of starters). The mains include a splendid chilli beef ramen (£7.35), slivers of sirloin steak in a vat of soup with vegetables and noodles (it's good etiquette to slurp these); yasai katsu curry (£5.35), boiled rice with a light curry sauce and discs of deep-fried vegetables; and ebi katsu (£4.96), very tasty deep-fried king prawns with chilli and garlic sauce. A couple of interesting sides are gyoza (£3.70) – chicken dumplings, fried and delicious – and the rich, pan-fried noodles known as yaki soba (£4.85). If this all sounds confusing, that's because it is: to enjoy Wagamama you'll need to go with the flow.

It's not often that a restaurant offers a glossary that includes its own name. Wagamama is described as "Willfulness or selfishness: selfishness in terms of looking after oneself, looking after oneself in terms of positive eating and positive living." It seems to work here and at the numerous other branches scattered around town.

The Crown & Sceptre

26–27 Foley St, W1   ✆020 7307 9971

There's often a party atmosphere here, with revellers enjoying drinks served in capacious jugs and buckets. You get £1 off a four-pint jug, and six bottles in a bucket for the price of five. Fuller's London Pride, Staropramen and Caffrey's are the on-tap favourites here.

Grape Street Wine Bar

224a Shaftesbury Ave, WC2   ✆020 7240 0686

Tucked away off the beaten track, this cosy cellar bar offers a very well-priced selection of wines. It's a quiet oasis where you can recharge before braving the wilder excesses of the area.

Ha Ha Bar

43–51 Great Titchfield St, W1

✆020 7580 7252

This huge, bright, modern lounge bar attracts a mixed crowd who drink and chill in equal proportions. It's very female-friendly and relaxed, offering a varied mix of wines, beers, spirits, mixers and coffees. Plenty of newspapers and magazines to read as well.

Jamie's

74 Charlotte St, W1   ✆020 7636 7556

A favourite haunt of advertising people, this popular modern wine bar offers an excellent selection of reasonably priced wines as well as bottled beers and spirits. Usually there's plenty of room, but it gets crowded and noisy between 6pm and 8pm, when it caters to the after-work crowd.

The Mason's Arms

58 Devonshire St, W1   ✆020 7580 6501

A small and welcoming pub in traditional style. Pavement tables and hanging baskets give a country feel to what is essentially a watering hole for local workers enjoying John Smith's, Courage Directors and Theakston.

The Museum Tavern

cnr Great Russell St
   and Museum St, WC1   ✆020 7242 8987

Very much a tourist landmark, this old pub has been here since 1760. Its genuine old mirrors and fittings give it huge charm, and its list of famous drinkers includes Karl Marx. Theakston's Old Peculiar, Charles Wells' Bombardier and Greene King Abbot Ale on tap.

Chinatown

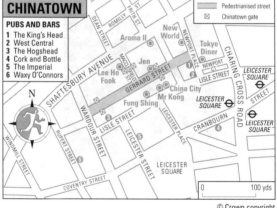

CHINATOWN

PUBS AND BARS

1 The King's Head
2 West Central
3 The Hogshead
4 Cork and Bottle
5 The Imperial
6 Waxy O'Connors

Pedestrianised street
⊠ Chinatown gate

N

0   100 yds

© Crown copyright

Aroma II

118 Shaftesbury Ave, W1 ⓒ020 7437 0370	⊖ Leicester Square/Piccadilly Circus
Daily noon–11.30pm	All major credit cards

www.aromares.co.uk

Ken and Kitty Lee, the people behind Aroma II, have an unusually long track record on the Chinese restaurant scene. Previously at Aroma I and before that at Harbour City, they now run this bright, modern restaurant, a comfortable place if somewhat fussy in decor. The menu is exhaustive, sweeping from trad dishes to some rather interesting and authentic Mandarin treats which hail from Peking. But, not to be left out, there are also Cantonese specialities, barbecued meats, and traditional hand-pulled noodles that are well worth investigation.

The breadth of the menu at Aroma II means that it is targeted directly at you whatever kind of meal you are after. For a bargain lunch you can't do better than the noodles: stir-fried hand-pulled noodle with seafood or king prawn (both £6.80), Singapore fried rice noodle (£4), or braised soft egg noodle with shredded pork and mushroom (£7). For a no-holds-barred banquet, there is braised shark fin superior (£48), braised abalone with oyster sauce (£18), or even braised sea slug and spring onions with shrimp roe (£12.80). Perhaps the best strategy is to make up an order that combines the cheapest and the most expensive, and includes dishes you know and love along with more adventurous options. So have the sautéed squid and scallop in five-spice salt and pepper (£9.50), and the braised duck in plum sauce (£6.50), but save room for the deep-fried marinated pork chitterling (£7.50), a dish of crispy tubes whose pungent flavours wouldn't be out of place in rural France. Or you could team prawns Kung Po (£8.80) with bang bang chicken (£5.50), and play baked eel fillet with spicy salt and pepper (£9) as your adventure.

This is one of the more accessible of London's finer Chinese restaurants, and staff are happy to give advice. Or go for one of the well-judged set menus – the seafood option (£22 per person for two) brings fish slice and crabmeat soup, sautéed lobster with hand-pulled noodles, stir-fried king prawn and scallops, fish in garlic sauce, Kung Po squid, braised mushrooms and rice.

£10–£25

China City

White Bear Yard, 25a Lisle St, WC2 ⑦020 7734 3388	⊖ Leicester Square
Mon–Sat noon–midnight	All major credit cards

White Bear Yard lies off Lisle Street to the north. You'll see a large gate and an archway; go through the arch, cross the courtyard, and you'll come to a large glass-fronted Chinese restaurant which seats 500 diners on three floors. Go early and you will see the restaurant transform from cavernously empty to bustling and packed. The service is "Chinatown-brusque" but a combination of good flavours, large portions, and sensible pricing keeps the clientele coming back for more. The menu stipulates a minimum charge of £10 per person, but don't be put off – this is not an expensive restaurant and you have to go some to spend much more than a tenner.

Both home-style dishes and less familiar exotic dishes are good here – this is a place in which to spread your wings and try something new. Naturally the menu includes sweet and sour pork, platters of mixed appetisers, and crispy duck with attendant pancakes, but why not start instead by trying the mixed seafood with fish straw soup (£3.50), which is something like that old workhorse crabmeat and sweetcorn soup but altogether more delicate. Whatever fish straw may be (and you cannot tell from the evidence in the bowl), it is certainly delicious. Then sample some chicken – steamed with ginger and spring onion sauce (£8.50), it produces astonishingly rich flavours and satisfying chunks of meat. Alternatively, look in the section on hot-pot dishes. Mixed seafood with bean curd in hot pot (£7) is a casserole containing fresh scallops, huge prawns, crisp mangetout and bean curd, all in a terrific sauce. The simpler dishes are good too; try the fried ho fun with beef, dry (£4.50) – a very comforting concoction of wide noodles with tender beef and a rich brown sauce. And to see something green on the table and so appease your conscience, order choi sum in oyster sauce (£4.50).

"Seasonal price" are words to strike fear into the heart of even the most experienced diner. At China City you'll find them alongside the lobster dishes. These include deep-fried lobster with garlic and chilli, and baked lobster with cheese and garlic. Ask the price, you'll get a straightforward answer – and it may just prove surprisingly accessible.

Fung Shing

15 Lisle St, WC2 ℭ020 7437 1539   ⊖ Leicester Square

Daily noon–11.30pm   All major credit cards

Fung Shing was one of the first restaurants in Chinatown to take cooking seriously. Twenty or so years ago, when it was still a dowdy little place with a mural on the back wall, the kitchens were run by the man acknowledged to be Chinatown's number one fish cook – chef Wu. When he died in 1996 his sous chef took over. The restaurant itself has changed beyond recognition and now stretches all the way from Lisle Street to Gerrard Street, ever bigger and ever brassier. The menu is littered with interesting dishes – the fish is still very fine – and portions are large. And, while the prices creep ever upwards, Fung Shing still offers really good value.

By Chinese restaurant standards the menu is not huge, topping out at around 160 dishes, but the food has that earthy, robust quality which you only encounter when the chef is absolutely confident of his flavours and textures – whatever the cuisine. To start, ignore the crispy duck with pancakes (half for £10.50) – good but too predictable – and the lobster with noodles (£18 a pound, with noodles £2 extra) – too expensive. Turn instead to the steamed scallops with garlic and soya sauce (£2.40 each); nowhere does them better. Or the spare ribs – with chilli and garlic (£7.50) or barbecued (£7.50). The prosaically named mixed meat with lettuce (£8.50), is also good – a wonderfully savoury dish of mince with lettuce-leaf wraps. You could also happily order mains solely from the chef's specials: stewed belly pork with yam in hot pot (£9.50), crispy spicy eel (£10.95), cold spice- and herb-boiled chicken with jellyfish (half £14) – suspend your doubts, for it's amazingly delicious. The other dishes are good too – the perfect Singapore noodle (£6), crispy stuffed baby squids with chilli and garlic (£8.95), braised aubergine with black bean sauce (£7).

The Fung Shing is a class act, but what makes it doubly successful is the unusually (for Chinatown) gracious and patient service. This is a place where you can ask questions and take advice with confidence.

£15–£50

Jen

7 Gerrard St, W1 ©020 7287 8193	⊖ Leicester Square
Mon–Sat noon–3am, Sun noon–10.30pm	All major credit cards

Jen burst onto the scene during 1998. The restaurant is bright, light and, although the first gloss is begining to wear off, it still looks pretty sharp. The menu proclaims that the restaurant's objective is to serve "the best Hong Kong style food available", and for once this is no idle boast. Only navigate your way past the five pages of very dull set menus and you'll find yourself among some interesting dishes. What's more, the service is friendly, the cooking is adept and the prices are accessible. This is a very good place to broaden your knowledge of Chinese cuisine.

Start with deep-fried squid in spicy peppercorn salt and garlic (£6) – perfectly cooked squid coated in a mixture redolent of chilli. Or treat yourself to a whole crispy soft-shell crab in the same sauce (£4.50 each) – delicious. You eat the whole thing: just bite some off and chomp it up. Or perhaps this will be the place you first try ducks' tongues, pepper-flavoured ducks' tongues (£4.50) – if ducks' tongues were bigger and less fiddly to eat then they would be a candidate for dish of the century. Take a look at the fish and seafood listings – fried fresh scallops with sautéed mashed shrimps and pear (£9.80), a thoroughly successful combination of flavours. Fresh fish is prepared seven different ways, and there's a vast range of fish (£8.50–£16): three kinds of carp, Dover sole, sea bass, salmon, turbot, snapper, eel, catfish. Perhaps some veg? Asparagus poached in bouillon (£5.50) is served wonderfully crunchy. Quick-fried neck of lamb with Peking scallion (£7.50) is as tender as you could wish for, and rich without being greasy.

You may not feel quite ready for the double boiled Chinese mushroom, fish maw and chicken claws soup (£12 for four people; order in advance). But make yourself a promise when you come to Jen: order one dish that is an outlandish experiment, something you have never had before, or even dreamed of . . . you may be surprised how much you enjoy it.

Lee Ho Fook

4 Macclesfield St, W1 ©020 7734 0782   ⊖ Leicester Square

Daily 11.30am–11pm   Cash only

Encouraged by the glowing reports in the guidebooks, lots of tourists set out to eat at the Macclesfield Street Lee Ho Fook but never actually manage to find it. This is a genuine Chinese barbecue house – small, spartan, cheap and the food is good of its kind – but it is not so helpful as to have a sign in English. Thus, many potential non-Chinese diners find themselves at the larger, grander, more tourist-friendly Lee Ho Fook around the corner in Gerrard Street. These, then, are the directions: Macclesfield Street runs from Shaftesbury Avenue in the north to Gerrard Street in the south; on the west side there is a backstreet called Dansey Place and, on the corner with a red and gold sign in Chinese characters and a host of ducks hanging on a rack, is Lee Ho Fook. Inside there's a chef chopping things at a block in the window, and four or five waiters. Sit down and you get tea, chopsticks and a big bottle of chilli sauce placed in front of you. Tables are shared and eating is a brisk, no-nonsense business.

The main focus of the short menu is an array of plated meals – a mound of rice with a splash of soy sauce "gravy" and a portion of chopped barbecued meat balanced on top. Choose from lean pork loin, crisp, fatty belly pork, soya chicken or duck (all £4.10), or suckling pig (£6.50). You can also mix and match – half pork, half duck, say – or order a "combination" of mixed roast pork, soya chicken, and duck with rice (£5.60). Some choose to order the meats without rice – perhaps a whole duck (£18) or a portion of suckling pig (£7). There's also a thriving takeaway trade – a whole duck costs £14, a half £7.50.

Because of the specialised nature of this place, the other menu items are all too easily overlooked. Try adding a plate of crisp vegetables in oyster sauce (£3.80) to your order. And, before the main event, perhaps choose a bowl of won ton soup (£2.20) or the even more substantial won ton noodle soup (£2.80). A recent extension into the shop next door will double the number of seats to forty and provide room downstairs for swish new toilets.

£7–£20

Mr Kong

21 Lisle St, WC2 ℂ020 7437 7923   ⊖ Leicester Square

Daily noon–3am   All major credit cards

You have to wonder whether the eponymous Mr Kong flirted with the idea of calling his restaurant King Kong. Despite its marathon open hours, at all regular mealtimes it's full of satisfied customers who would support such an accolade. Going with a party of six or more is the best plan when dining at Mr Kong: that way you can order, taste and argue over a raft of dishes. You can share, and if there's something you really don't like you can exile it to the other end of the table; if there's something wonderful, you can call up a second portion. It's a canny strategy which means that you can never be caught out.

There are three menus here: the main menu (5 pages and 160 or so dishes), the "Chef's Specials" (70 more), and the "Today's Chef's Specials" (10 more). The main menu is rather safety-first, but sliced pork, salted egg and vegetable soup (minimum of two £2.10 each), something of a house speciality, is worth a try. It's very good and rich, and the salted egg tastes pleasantly cheesy. Then try deep-fried crispy Mongolian lamb (£6.50) from "Today's": very crisp breast of lamb that comes with a lettuce-leaf wrap – but avoid the accompanying shin sauce, which is very sickly. Also from "Today's" there is braised shin of beef with fresh lotus root in hot pot (£6.50). Then turn to the "Chef's Specials" for sautéed dragon whistlers with dried scallops (£11), made with fresh pea shoots. Back to the main menu for a good, spicy Singapore noodle (£4.20), Kon Chin king prawn (£7.50), an interesting prawn dish in a spicy tomatoey sauce, and Chinese broccoli in oyster sauce (£4.60) – dark green, crunchy and delicious. On the "Chef's Specials" you'll find steamed fresh razor clam with garlic "seasonal price"; when available that's about £2.50 each. They're tender, well flavoured and worth every penny. Order a couple per person by way of an extravagance.

Portions are generous and, even when dishes contain exotic ingredients, prices are reasonable. Just ignore the decor, which falls somewhere between ordinary and grubby.

£6–£18

New World

1 Gerrard Place, W1 ℂ020 7734 0396	⊖ Leicester Square
Daily 11am–midnight	All major credit cards

When the 1990s saw the arrival of the mega-restaurants – giant 200- and 300-seater emporiums – the proprietors of this long-established Chinese restaurant were right to feel aggrieved, and ask what all the fuss was about. The New World seats between 400 and 600 depending on how many functions are going on at any one time. This is probably the largest single restaurant in Europe and it can comfortably swallow up a couple of huge Chinese wedding parties as well as getting on with the daily business of feeding thousands of people. When you arrive you invariably have to wait in a sort of holding pen just inside the door until the intercom screeches with static and you are sent off to your table. The menu, leather-bound and nearly twenty pages long, features everything you have ever heard of and quite a lot you haven't. In any case, you don't need it – go for the dim sum, which are served every day from 11am until 6pm.

The dim sum come round on trolleys. First catch the eye of a waiter or waitress with a bow tie to order drinks and then you're at the mercy of the trolley pushers. Broadly speaking the trolleys are themed: one has a lot of barbecued meat, another is packed with ho fun – the broad noodles – another with steamed dumplings, another with soups, another with cheung fun – the long slippery rolls of pastry with different meats inside – and so on. A good mix would be to take siu mai (£1.50) and har kau (£1.50) from the "steamers" trolley. Then char sui cheung fun (£2.35), a long roll with pork. Then some deep-fried won ton (£1.50) – little crispy parcels with sweet sauce. Or perhaps try something exotic like woo kwok (£1.50) – deep-fried taro dumplings stuffed with pork and yam. And something filling like char sui pow (£1.50) – steamed doughnuts filled with pork – or nor mai gai (£2.35) – a lotus-leaf parcel of glutinous rice and meats.

If you arrive after 6pm, you're on your own: there are literally hundreds of dishes on the main menus. However, Chinese functions apart, New World is really best as an in-and-out dim sum joint. It's about eating – and not, as the sticky carpet immediately declares, design and fripperies.

Tokyo Diner

2 Newport Place, WC2 ℗020 7287 8777   ⊖ Leicester Square

Daily noon–midnight   All major credit cards

Tokyo Diner offers conclusive proof that you needn't take out a second mortgage to enjoy Japanese food in London. Stacked up on three floors of a block that clings to Chinatown's silk skirts, this is a friendly eatery that shuns elaboration in favour of fast food, Tokyo-style. The place was actually set up by a Nipponophile Englishman, but the kitchen staff are all Japanese, and its Far Eastern credentials bear scrutiny. The decor, crisp and minimalist, leaves the food to do the talking, which it does fluently if the number of Japanese walk through the doors are any indication. If you don't know your teppanyaki from your kamikaze, or your sushi from your sumo, you'll be glad of the explanatory notes on the menu. When your food arrives, pick a set of chopsticks, snap them apart – the menu recommends that you rub them together to rid them of splinters – and get stuck in.

Top seller is the soba noodle soup (£4.90), thin brown buckwheat noodles in a soya broth, which is pleasant, filling and very popular with the drop-by lunchtime trade. Don't be afraid of slurping it – as the menu explains, slurping is okay. Or try the set lunch in a bento box: this comprises rice, noodles, sashimi and your choice of teriyaki, all for around £10. The bento will dispel once and for all the misconception that Japanese food is just for picking at, though watch out for the little green mound of wasabi which will blow your head off if you're not careful (it should be mixed with soy sauce in a saucer and used to dunk a morsel into). If you don't have appetite enough for a full-on bento box, skip the curries (as the menu admits, they're a bit like school food) and head straight for the sushi and sashimi. They too come in "sets" and, if you like sushi, try the nigiri set (£7.50) – very good value.

To wash it all down, the Japanese beer, Asahi (£1.99), is good – or there's complimentary Japanese tea. For a special treat try the rich, sweet plum wine (£2.99 for 125ml), which is surprisingly moreish and quite delicious.

The Cork & Bottle

44–46 Cranbourn St, WC2   ✆020 7734 7807

Tucked between a sex shop and a take-away kebab place, this cellar wine bar is worth searching out. It offers an unusual list of rarer New World wines (including the legendary Cloudy Bay Sauvignon) at low prices, plus a selection of twenty or so by the glass. It's cosy and cramped and delightfully unhurried.

The Hogshead

5 Lisle St, WC2   ✆020 7437 3335

The decor of this new themed venue skilfully mixes the traditional and the modern, and the scrubbed pale wood gives both the ground floor and the quieter upstairs bar a light, airy, youthful feel. Beers change regularly: there's always something unusual on offer, such as the Wolf Brewery's Coyote Bitter and the dangerously rich Granny Wouldn't Like It. A welcome addition to the area.

The Imperial

5 Leicester St, WC2   ✆020 7437 6573

A quiet, traditional local in the heart of the West End. It's been modernised, but sympathetically, and the air conditioning makes it cool and un-smoky. There's Courage, Directors and Guinness Extra Cold on tap and a friendly mix of people, many of whom work in the bars nearby.

The King's Head

48 Gerrard St, W1   ✆020 7437 5858

Bang in the heart of Chinatown, this straightforward Courage pub is busy and smoky and a popular hangout for the Chinese community. The absence of beer pumps on the bar feels slightly odd, but it's comfortable, and a convenient meeting place.

Waxy O'Connors

14–16 Rupert St, W1   ✆020 7287 0255

This labyrinthine cellar bar runs right through from one street to another, taking its Gothic-Medieval theme with it. The decor – church pulpits, gravestones, tiling and potted trees – is striking, and the beer is good: Caffrey's, Murphy's, Beamish and Guinness.

West Central

29–30 Lisle St, W1   ✆020 7479 7980

A massive, cool and dark venue that attracts a noisy young crowd drinking bottled beers and alco-pops. The DJs and 2am licence keep the ground floor bar bouncing, but there's a quieter upstairs bar more conducive to chatting. There are theme nights as well – Wednesday is singles night.

CENTRAL

Covent Garden & Holborn

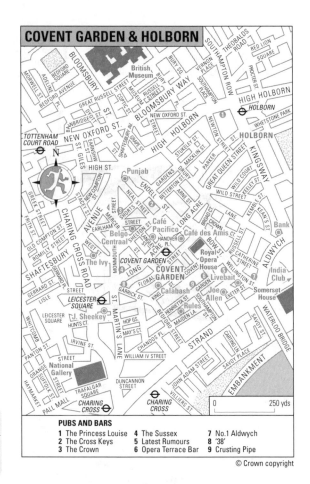

COVENT GARDEN & HOLBORN

PUBS AND BARS

1 The Princess Louise 4 The Sussex   7 No.1 Aldwych
2 The Cross Keys   5 Latest Rumours   8 '38'
3 The Crown   6 Opera Terrace Bar   9 Crusting Pipe

© Crown copyright

Bank

1 Kingsway, corner of Aldwych, WC2 ©020 7234 3344	⊖ Holborn
Mon–Fri 7–11.30am, noon–3pm & 5.30–11.30pm,	
Sat & Sun 11.30am–3.30pm & 5.30–11.30pm (Sun 10pm)	All major credit cards
www.bankrestaurant.co.uk	

A good many foodists believe that this restaurant is the closest London gets to recreating the all-day buzz and unfussy cuisine of the big Parisian brasseries. Bank opens for breakfast (Continental, Full English, or Caviar), lays on brunch at the weekend, does a good-value pre-theatre (5.30–7pm) and lunch prix fixe (both are £13.90 for two courses, £17.50 for three), has a bustling bar . . . and then there's the other matter of lunch and dinner for several hundred. Whatever the time of day, the food is impressive, especially considering the large numbers of people fed, and if you like things lively you will have a great time. If you're leaving after 10pm, incidentally, and want a taxi, go for the cabs arranged by the doorman; black cabs are rare as hen's teeth around here after the Drury Lane theatres empty.

The menu changes seasonally, so dishes may come and go. Start with something simple – simple to get wrong, that is – a Caesar salad (£6.75), say, or a smoked haddock and ricotta tart (£6.50); or push the boat out with a well-made terrine of foie gras and confit duck with beetroot chutney (£9.50). Or go for shellfish. Bank is owned by one of London's leading catering fishmongers, so crustacea such as cold lobster in shell (half £13.95, whole £26.50) or dressed crab and avocado dressing (£12.50) should be reliable. The fish dishes are equally good, from the ambitious – red mullet, wok fried greens and tamarind dressing (£12.50) – to the traditional – Bank fish and chips, featuring halibut, mushy peas and tartare sauce (£18.50). Meat dishes are well-prepared brasserie fare, such as grilled calves' liver, sage and onion mash (£16.50), and glazed belly of pork with Chinese cabbage (£12.50). Puds include sticky toffee pudding, vanilla ice cream (£5.90), and gateau Opera with coffee sauce (£4.50).

When Bank first opened many diners felt uneasy about the ceiling decoration – a modernist extravaganza of suspended armoured glass – and the tables around the edge were always the first to fill. Thankfully, and as the insurance company predicted, the ceiling is safe and no one seems to worry any more.

Belgo Centraal

50 Earlham St, WC2 ✆020 7813 2233   ⊖ Covent Garden

Mon–Thurs noon–11.30pm, Fri & Sat noon–midnight, Sun noon–10.30pm

Restaurant closed but beerhall open 3–5.30pm   All major credit cards

www.belgo.restaurants.com

The Belgians invented mussels, frîtes and mayonnaise – and Belgo has done all it can to help the Belgian national dish take over London. The Belgo group's flagship restaurant is a massive metal-minimalist cavern accessed by riding down in a scissor-powered lift. Turn left at the bottom and you enter the restaurant (booked seats), turn right and you get seated in the beerhall where diners share tables. With 95 different beers, some at alcoholic strengths of 8–9%, it's difficult not to be sociable.

Belgo offers the best mussels in town and no mistake. A kilo of classic moules marinière served with frîtes and mayonnaise (£10.95) is fresh and clearly cooked then and there. Other varieties of moules on offer include Blonde/bacon, with Leffe beer and bacon; Moutarde, with grain mustard; and Provençale, with tomato, herbs and garlic (all £12.95). And there are many alternatives for the non-mussel eater. Try carbonnade Flamande (£9.95) – beef braised in Geuze beer with apples and plums and served with frîtes; or waterzooi à la Gantoise (£9.95) – chicken cooked with a vegetable julienne in a light sauce. There are also five different asparagus dishes, rôtisserie chickens and whole Canadian lobsters for £17.95. Desserts, as you might expect, are strong on Belgian chocolate. They include, among many others, crème brûlée aux fraises (£3.95), and traditional Belgian waffles with ice cream, cream and chocolate sauce (£4.75). Belgo delights in special offers, too. There's a £5 lunch – boar sausages with Belgian mash and a beer, or half a kilo of mussels and salad. The Belgo Complet (£16.95), always available, comprises a mini salade Liègoise followed by a kilo of moules served with frîtes, and a choice of Hoegaarden beer, soft drink or ice cream.

Belgo offers value, atmosphere and very sound food. But it's the awesome beer list that makes it a must-visit. There are other branches at Belgo Noord, 72 Chalk Farm Rd, NW1 (✆020 7267 0718), and Belgo Zuid, 124 Ladbroke Grove, W10 (✆020 8982 8400).

Café des Amis

11–14 Hanover Place, off Long Acre, WC2 ©020 7379 3444   ⊖ Covent Garden

Mon–Sat 11.30am–11.30pm   All major credit cards

www.cafedesamis.co.uk

This is the reincarnation of an old-established restaurant, just around the corner from the newly resurrected Opera House. Where once it was Gallic shabby, all is now bleached, blond wood. All is modern, all is clean and bright. The resuscitated menu sits uneasily with its French section headings – "Les plats", "Les poissons" – as it ranges across the globe, through Thai fishcakes, Malaysian noodles, polenta fritters and tuna carpaccio. The old clientele, many of whom used to have half a meal before the opera, and a dessert in the interval, are in shock. However, from a food point of view, there's only good to report. In the hands of a predominantly French team, the old bistro menu has been shaken into the new millennium. Service is efficient and friendly, while the set menus, served all day, are a real bargain – two courses £12.50, three courses £15.

You might start with a dish like terrine of chorizo, black pudding and pork fillet with kumquat chutney (£6.25). Or there's peppered goats' cheese with moscato and cardamom, roasted pear and walnut croûte (£5.75). Between starters and mains you'll find dishes that can be served as either – Caesar salad (£4.95/£7.95); wild mushroom risotto (£5.85/£9.95); char-grilled tuna Niçoise with quail eggs and anchoyade (£8.25/£12.50). The main courses run the gamut from rump of lamb with potato and pumpkin gratin, roasted garlic and thyme jus (£14.25) to salmon fillet poached in vegetable minestrone with pesto aioli (£12.50); or roast fillet steak wrapped in prosciutto with potato rosti, baby beetroot and port jus (£16.95). The set menu (three courses £15) features starters like squid bisque with croutons and rouille; mains like fillet of plaice with cumin crust, mint tabbouleh, oregano and fresh basil; and desserts such as chocolate truffle cake with sauce Anglaise. The cooking is well judged, the presentation on the plate is good, and the prices are reasonable.

The winebar/bar under the restaurant is as dark and cavernous as the restaurant above is light and bright . . . and so it should be!

Café Pacifico

5 Langley St, WC2 ©020 7379 7728	⊖ Covent Garden
Mon–Sat noon–midnight, Sun noon–11pm	All major credit cards except Diners

www.cafepacifico-laperla.co.uk

The salsa is hot at Café Pacifico – both types. As you are seated, a complimentary bowl of searing salsa dip with corn chips is put on your table. As you eat, hot salsa music gets your fingers tapping. The atmosphere is relaxed and you're soon in the mood for a cold Tecate (£2.70) or Negro Modelo (£2.80) beer. There are nine Mexican beers, a good selection of wines and dozens of cocktails. Parties can enjoy a pitcher of Margaritas to serve eight people for £27.95. But Pacifico's tequila list is the highlight. There are more than sixty varieties, ranging from £2.50 to £100 a shot, and including some very old and rare brands.

The menu is a lively mixture of old-style Californian Mexican and new Mexican, so, while favourites like fajitas, flautas and tacos dominate, there are also some interesting and unusual dishes. Portions are generous and spicy, and many main courses come with refried beans and rice. Refried beans at Café Pacifico are smooth and comforting, and just the thing to balance the spicy heat. Try nachos rancheros (£7.75, £6.75 vegetarian) for starters and enjoy a huge plate of corn chips with beans, cheese, guacamole, onions, sour cream and olives. Excellent for sharing. Taquitos (£4.25) – filled fried baby tacos – are very tasty, too, as are smoked chicken quesadillas (£5.25) – flour tortillas with chicken, red peppers and avocado salsa. Main courses include degustación del Pacifico (£9.50), which includes a taste of almost everything. The burrito especial (£8.95) gives you a flour tortilla filled with cheese and refried beans covered with ranchero sauce and a choice of roast beef, chicken or ground beef. Roast beef is slow-cooked and falling-apart tender. Look out for their modern Mexican dishes like fillet of beef in ancho-chipotle cracked pepper gravy (£11.95) – these are available from 6pm.

Café Pacifico has been a place to party since 1978 and claims to be London's oldest Mexican restaurant. And, yes, they do have a bottle of mescal with a worm in it.

Calabash

The Africa Centre, 38 King St, WC2 ©020 7836 1976	⊖ Covent Garden
Mon–Fri noon–2.30pm & 6-10.30pm, Sat 6–10.30pm	All major credit cards

The Calabash is a very cool place, in the old-fashioned, laid-back sense of the word. The restaurant, deep within the bowels of the Africa Centre, is at once worthy, comfortable and cheap. The same complex features a splendidly seedy bar, a live music hall, and African arts and crafts for sale. The food is genuine and somewhat unsophisticated, and the menu struggles bravely to give snapshots of the extraordinary diversity of African cuisine. They manage dishes from North, East and West Africa, as well as specialities from Nigeria, Ivory Coast, Senegal and Malawi. So if you're looking for a particular dish you may be out of luck. However, if you want a cheerful atmosphere, a small bill, and wholesome, often spicy and usually unfamiliar food, the Calabash is worth seeking out.

Starters include familiar dishes like avocado salad and hummus (both £2.20) along with interesting offerings such as aloco (£2.30) – fried plantain in a hot tomato sauce – and sambusas (£2.95), a vegetarian cousin of the samosa. Those with an enquiring palate will pick the gizzards (£2.95) – a splendid dish of chicken gizzards served in a rich, spiky pepper sauce. Grilled chicken wings (£2.60) are less exotic but very good nonetheless. Main courses are marked according to origin. From Nigeria comes egusi (£6.95), a rich soup/stew with spinach, meat, and dried shrimps thickened with melon seed. Yassa (£6.50) is grilled chicken from Senegal, while doro wot (£6.95) is a pungent chicken stew from East Africa, served with injera, the soft and thin sourdough bread. From Malawi there is nyamam yo phika (£7.75), a rich beef stew made with sweet peppers and potatoes and served with rice. Drink whichever of the African beers is in stock at the time you visit.

One of the best dishes, simply called "chicken" (£6.25), takes the form of superb fried chicken served with fried plantain, sweet potato chips, mixed salad and ferocious hot sauce. The chef who handles the frying is a master craftsman who manages to get the outside perfectly crisp and the inside perfectly tender. Order this to get an inkling of what the Colonel has been striving for all these years.

India Club

143 Strand, WC2 ✆020 7836 0650   ⊖ Charing Cross

Mon–Sat noon–2.30pm & 6–10pm   Cash or cheque only

When the India Club opened in 1950, the linoleum flooring was probably quite chic; today it has a faded period charm. Situated up two flights of stairs, sandwiched between floors of the grandly named Strand Continental Hotel (one of London's cheaper hotels), the Club is an institution, generally full, and mostly with regulars, as you can tell by the stares of appraisal given to newcomers. The regulars, in love with the strangely old-fashioned combination of runny curry and low, low prices, don't mind paying a £4-a-year membership fee for the right to buy cold bottles of Cobra beer from the hotel reception downstairs – they quite understand the inflexibility of English licensing arrangements. These stalwart customers can be split into two categories: suave Indians from the nearby High Commission, and a miscellany of folk from the BBC World Service, hanging on precariously to their old Central London base down the road in Bush House.

The food at the India Club predates any London consciousness of the different spicings of Bengal, Kerala, Rajasthan or Goa. It is Anglo-Indian, essentially, and well cooked of its kind, although to palates accustomed to more modern Indian dishes it is something of a symphony to runny sauce. Mughlay chicken (£4.80) is a wing and a drumstick in a rich brown, oniony gravy, garnished with two half hard-boiled eggs, while scampi curry is runny and brown with fearless prawns swimming through it (£5.80). Masala dosai is a well-made crispy pancake with a pleasantly sharp-tasting potato filling (£2.90). Dhal is yellow and . . . runny (£2.90). The mango chutney is a revelation: thick parings of mango, each three inches long, chewy and delicious (40p). Breads – paratha (£1.50), puris (two for £1.30) – are good, while the rice is white and comes in clumps (£1.80).

You should heed the kindly warning of your waiter about the chilli bhajis (£2.50), a dish as simple as it is thought-provoking. Long, thin, extra-hot green chillies are given a thick coating of gram flour batter and then deep-fried until crisp. These are served with a coconut chutney that has a few more chopped chillies sprinkled through it. Eating this actually hurts. Console yourself by remembering that, however bad, chilli burn lasts only ten minutes.

The Ivy

1 West St, WC2 ℂ020 7836 4751	⊖ Leicester Square
Daily noon–3pm (Sun 3.30pm) & 5.30pm–midnight	All major credit cards

The Ivy is a beautiful Regency-style restaurant, built in 1928 by Mario Gallati, who later founded Le Caprice. It has been a theatreland and society favourite ever since – Noël Coward was a noted regular – and never more so than today. The staff, it is said, notice recessions only because they have to turn fewer people away. And that's no joke: The Ivy is booked solid for lunch and dinner, right through the week. Its clientele include a lot of face-familiar actors and media folk, and to get a booking it helps to proffer a name of at least B-list celebrity. That said, there are tables to be had here if you book far enough ahead – or try at very short notice – or if you ask after a table in the bar area (nice enough, if your legs aren't over-long). It's also less busy for the weekend lunch – three courses for a bargain £16.50 plus £1.50 service charge, with valet parking thrown in.

And once you're in? Well, first off, whether you're famous or not, the staff are charming and unhurrying. Second, the food is pretty good. The menu is essentially a brasserie list of comfort food – nice dishes that combine simplicity with familiarity and which are invariably well cooked. You could spend a lot here without restraint; surprisingly little if you limit yourself to a single course and pud. You might start with marinated anchovies (£7.75); or the famous risotto nero (£7.50), black with squid ink; or the eggs Benedict (£5.75/£10.75). Then there's kedgeree (£10.25) and corned beef hash with double fried egg (£9.50), and well-made versions of classic staples: calves' liver and bacon (£16.75), the Ivy hamburger with dill pickle and club sauce (£9), shepherd's pie (£10.75), salmon fishcakes (£11.75). Even the vegetable section is enlivened with homely delights like bubble and squeak (£2.75) and medium-cut chips (£3). For dessert you might turn to Bakewell tart (£5.50) or Eton mess (£9.50), or perhaps finish with a savoury such as Welsh rarebit (£5.75).

The Ivy's present incarnation is the result of a 1990 makeover which meticulously restored the wood panelling and leaded stained glass. It also involved a roll call of British artists. Look around and you may notice works by, among others, Howard Hodgkin, Peter Blake, Tom Phillips and Patrick Caulfield.

£17–£55

J. Sheekey

28–32 St Martin's Court, WC2 ©020 7240 2565	⊖ Leicester Square
Mon–Sat noon–3pm & 5.30pm–midnight,	
Sun noon–3.30pm & 5.30pm–midnight	All major credit cards

Sheekey's is one of a handful of restaurants which had shambled along since the War – the First World War – and then in the late 1990s was taken over by the team behind The Ivy and Le Caprice (see p.37 and p.106). After a good deal of redesign and refurbishment it emerged from the builders' clutches as J. Sheekey, with much the same attitudes and style as its senior siblings, but still focused on fish. The restaurant may be new, then, but it certainly seems old, and its series of interconnecting dining rooms gives it an intimate feel. The cooking is accomplished, the service is first-rate, and the fish is fresh – a good combination!

The long menu presents a seductive blend of plain old-fashioned classic fish cuisine – lemon sole belle meunière (£16.25) – with more modernist dishes – peppered blue-fin tuna with Italian barley and herb salsa (£14.75). There are always hand-written dishes on the menu, "specials" which change on a weekly basis. To start with there are oysters, crabs and shellfish, plus everything from jellied eels (£4.75) and potted shrimps (£9.75) to seared rare tuna (£8.50) and char-grilled razor clams with chorizo and broad beans (£8.75). Main courses, like roasted scallops with crab and samphire risotto (£18.50), and wing of skate Grenobloise (£13.75), are backed up by herb crusted cod (£13.25) and Sheekey's fish pie (£9.50). Puddings go from spotted dick with vanilla custard (£5.25) to red fruit soup (£5.50).

The set menus are good value. At the weekend, lunch costs just £9.75 for two courses or £13.50 for three (plus a £1.50 cover charge in the main dining room). You could tuck into Italian black figs with Parma ham, then escalope of salmon with mixed courgettes and tomato vinaigrette, and finish with chocolate and Grand Marnier tart. In a further bid to make life at the weekend hassle-free, the restaurant operates a valet parking system on Sunday.

Joe Allen

13 Exeter St, WC2 ℗020 7836 0651	⊖ Covent Garden
Mon–Fri noon–12.45am, Sat 11.30am–12.45am,	
Sun 11.30am–11.30pm	All major credit cards except Diners

By some inexplicable alchemy Joe Allen continues to be the Covent Garden eatery of choice for a wide swathe of the acting profession. It is a dark place, resolutely untrendy, and continues to dish up American comfort food. So saying, you can never have anything better than exactly what you want, and, if your heart is set on a Caesar salad, chilli con carne or eggs Benedict, this is a great place to come. Joe Allen also has a splendid attitude to mealtimes: the à la carte runs all day so you can have lunch when you will; there's a special menu offering two courses for £11 and three for £13 (noon–4pm), and a pre-theatre menu which takes over between 5pm and 6.45pm Monday to Saturday (two courses £13, three courses £15).

The food is the kind of stuff that we are all comfortable with. Starters include salmon and cod fishcake with grain mustard sauce (£5.50), chopped chicken liver (£5), and bang bang chicken (£6). They are followed on the menu by a section described as salads/eggs/sandwiches, in which you'll find some of Joe Allen's strengths – Caesar salad (£4.50), roast chicken salad with penne, cherry tomatoes and pesto dressing (£8), and eggs Joe Allen (£8), a satisfying combination of poached eggs, potato skins, Hollandaise sauce, and spinach. Main courses range from grilled swordfish with Niçoise salad and citrus dressing (£13), through barbecue spare ribs with rice, wilted spinach, black-eyed peas and corn muffin (£11), to pan-fried calves' liver with bubble and squeak and red onion marmalade (£12.50). The side orders are most attractive – mashed potatoes with gravy (£2.50), broccoli with toasted almonds (£2.50). And the desserts are serious – go for the brownie (£4.50) with hot fudge sauce as an extra (£1.50).

Joe Allen is also home to its very own urban legend. The hamburger is very highly rated by aficionados everywhere, but you have to be "in the know" to order one, as it has never been listed on the menu.

£20–£50

Livebait Restaurant & Bar

21 Wellington St, WC2 ℗020 7836 7161	⊖ Covent Garden
Mon–Sat noon–3pm & 5.30–11.30pm	All major credit cards
www.sante-gcg.com	

This large, bustling restaurant is an offshoot of the original Livebait, 41 The Cut, SE1 (℗020 7928 7211), behind Waterloo station, and there is now a third, at 175 Westbourne Grove, W11 (℗020 7727 4321). You'll find the same black-and-white tiling and rather cramped diner booths in each. Things have calmed down a bit since the early days – when the kitchen was all eccentricity – and some of the wilder combinations of ingredients have been tamed. The emphasis, however, remains on superb crustacea and fish so fresh you expect to see it flapping on the slab. The breads are still a feature and service is friendly. The hand of big business is apparent, but the Livebait ethos is so irrepressible that this remains one of the most succesful fish restaurants in town.

As an amuse-gueule you get a few fresh prawns to munch on along with the amazing Technicolor breads – anything from red bread made with beetroot to yellow bread made with tagine. If you continue with seafood, you've any number of treats to choose from – vast crevettes with mayonnaise (£2.65 each), whole Dorset brown crabs, cracked with mayonnaise (£7.75 each), winkles, cockles, clams, oysters – maybe it is best to go for it, and have the two-tier shellfish platter (£25.95), and if someone else is paying add a supplementary half-lobster (pushing the price up to £48.50). The cooked starters are often complex: they might include such combinations as oriental fishcakes with glass noodle salad, chilli jam and deep fried won tun (£5.75), or seared marlin Niçoise salad with quail eggs and coriander pesto (£6.50). If you are not hugely hungry, you'd do well to order one for starter and another for your main course. Which is not to knock the mains, which are equally original, with such offerings as char-grilled swordfish, roasted garlic and herb mash, and onion rings with lime chutney (£16.60) or pan-roasted cod with Parma ham, minted pea puree, wild mushroom, tarragon cream sauce (£14.75).

Livebait's food is exciting and the wine list is carefully chosen. But the wide range of beers is a particular delight.

Punjab

80–82 Neal St, WC2 ℂ020 7836 9787	⊖ Covent Garden
Daily noon–3pm & 6–11.30pm	Amex, Mastercard, Visa
www.punjab.co.uk	

In 1951 Gurbachan Singh Maan moved his fledgling Indian restaurant from the City to new premises in Neal Street in Covent Garden, his plan being to take advantage of the trade from the nearby Indian High Commission. It was a strategy that has worked handsomely. Today his grandson Sital Singh Maan runs what is one of London's oldest curry houses, though one which has always been at the forefront of new developments – in 1962 the Maan family brought over one of the first tandoor ovens to be seen in Britain, and in 1989 they added the then exotic chicken jalfrezi to their repertoire. Despite these forays into fashion, the cuisine at the Punjab has always been firmly rooted where it belongs . . . in the Punjab. This is a Sikh restaurant, as you'll realise straightaway from the imposing, turbaned waiters.

Punjabi cuisine offers some interesting, non-standard Indian dishes, so start by ordering from among the less familiar items on the menu. Kadu and puri (£2.10), for instance, a sweet and sharp mash of curried pumpkin served on a puri; or aloo tikka (£2.10), which are described as potato cutlets but arrive as small deep-fried moons on a sea of tangy sauce; or chicken chat (£2.60), diced chicken in rich sauce. To follow, try the acharri gosht (£7.50) or the acharri murgha (£7.80) – the first is made with lamb, and the second with chicken. The Maan family are very proud of the acharri: the meat is "pickled" in traditional Punjabi spices and as a result both meat and sauce have an agreeable edge of sharpness. Chicken karahi (£7.10) is good, too – rich and thick. The anari gosht (£7.50) combines lamb with pomegranate, while from the vegetable dishes, channa aloo (£4) offsets the nutty crunch of chickpeas with the solace of potatoes. For refreshment, turn to a satisfyingly large bottle of Cobra lager (£3.60), which originated in Bangalore but is now rather more prosaically "brewed in Bedford".

On the menu you'll also find benaam macchi tarkari (£7.50), a "nameless fish curry, speciality of chef". This curry may be nameless but it is certainly not flavourless, with solid lumps of boneless white fish in rich and tasty gravy.

£25–£65

Rules

35 Maiden Lane, WC2 ✆020 7836 5314   ⊖ Covent Garden

Mon–Sat noon–11.30pm, Sun noon–10.30pm   All major credit cards

Info@rules.co.uk

The Americans have a word for it. When something is so very clichéd that it starts to parody itself they rather unkindly refer to it as "schlock". Rules could be "schlock" but for one essential saving grace – all the fixtures and fittings and studied eccentricities that look as if they have been custom-made in some modern factory to bemuse punters are real. Rules is the genuine article, a very English restaurant that has been taking its toll of tourists for two hundred years. Charles Dickens, John Betjeman, H.G. Wells, Thackeray, Graham Greene, King Edward VII. . . just a few of the celebs who have revelled in Rules. In 1984 the restaurant passed into the hands of John Mayhew who sourced some of its game from his estate – Lartington Hall Park in the High Pennines – and in 1997 brought in David Chambers as head chef. Rules' proud boast is: "We specialise in classic game cookery". Indeed they do, but now the restaurant has become more of a bustling brasserie than the mausoleum it once was.

First of all you should note that Rules is open from noon till late, which is very handy when circumstances dictate a four o'clock lunch. There is also a competitive pre-theatre offer – £19.95 for two courses. Start with a good carpaccio of venison with a poached egg and baby vegetables set in jelly (£9.95), a mussel and scallop soup with saffron (£6.95), or an outstanding terrine of foie gras and pigeon with walnut and raisin bread (£10.95). Go on to game in season, whatever the time of year: you'll find something good here. The menu changes with the season but, aside from game, the steak and kidney pudding with mash (£15.95) is a banker. As is the grilled Dover sole for two (£37.90) and the Aberdeen Angus roast rib of beef for two (£39.90). Also noteworthy is the poached Finnan haddock in a mussel and saffron sauce (£17.95). Puddings are merciless – treacle sponge or sticky toffee (both £6.25). And there are even savouries: Welsh rarebit, and Scotch woodcock with fresh anchovies (both £6.25).

All this in a beautiful Victorian setting. Should you face entertaining out-of-town relations, foreign visitors in search of something old and English, or even yourself, Rules is a good place to indulge your nostalgia to the full.

38

1–3 Long Acre, WC2   *©*020 7836 7794

With its picture windows and sharp corner position, Bar 38 gives great views of the bustle outside. It's young and noisy, with John Smith's and Beck's on draught served in tall narrow glasses. A good cocktail and wine selection, with two-pint cocktail pitchers at £10. Occasional door policy when it gets full.

The Cross Keys

31 Endell St, WC2   *©*020 7836 5185

A wonderfully cluttered old pub with Marten's Pedigree on draught. Outside seating in summer and a good blend of older Covent Garden residents and new young workers give this pretty venue a friendly feel.

The Crown

43 Monmouth St, WC2   *©*020 7836 5861

Overlooking the Seven Dials crossroads in the heart of Covent Garden, this charming pub offers Adnams, Burton and Tetley's on tap as well as a very warm welcome.

Crusting Pipe

27 The Market, WC2   *©*020 7836 1415

A spit-and-sawdust, olde-worlde-style basement wine bar, which opens onto the piazza interior and has outside tables in summer. A well-chosen list of wines and port, but no beers or spirits.

Latest Rumours

33–35 Wellington St, WC2   *©*020 7836 0038

With cocktails and shooters called things like Suffering Bastard, Slippery Nipple and Blow Job, it's no surprise that this corner bar is not a place for a quiet drink. Come with a raucous crowd.

The Lobby Bar, No 1 Aldwych

1 Aldwych, WC2   *©*020 7300 1070

Located in a hotel lobby, this spacious, modern designer bar attracts a fashionable crowd, many of them from the City. A huge sculpture of a rower graces its vaulted space and, though there's no dress code, people tend to dress up. A great place to people watch, while sipping pricey cocktails and good wines.

Opera Terrace Bar

The Opera Terrace,
Covent Garden Piazza   *©*020 7379 0666

A little hard to find, but worth the effort, this upstairs bar overlooks the piazza and offers a good selection of wines and bottled beers with competitively priced champagnes. There's an outdoor terrace open in summer, but even in winter the glass walls give it a light, modern feel. A good place for a celebration.

The Princess Louise

208 High Holborn, WC1   *©*020 7405 8816

Graced with lovely decorative mouldings, this Sam Smith's pub offers its own Sovereign and Old Brewery bitters, the latter at £1.64 a pint. A close-knit crowd of regulars have made it their own, but it's a friendly place for all that.

The Sussex

20 St Martin's Lane, WC2   *©*020 7836 1834

A traditional pub with Courage Best, Directors and Theakston on draught. Popular in summer, when its many pavement tables allow a huge throng to gather and watch the world go by. There's also a cellar bar with a spiral staircase that you'll need to be sober to negotiate.

Euston &
King's Cross

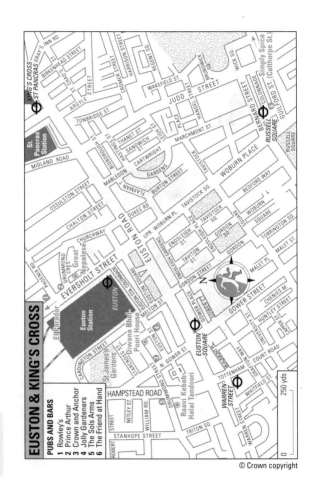

EUSTON & KING'S CROSS

PUBS AND BARS

1 Rowley's
2 Prince Arthur
3 Crown and Anchor
4 Jolly Gardeners
5 The Sols Arms
6 The Friend at Hand

© Crown copyright

Diwana Bhel-Poori House

121 Drummond St, NW1 ℂ020 7387 5556	⊖ Euston
Daily noon–11.30pm	All major credit cards

All varnished pine and shag-pile carpets, the Diwana Bhel-Poori House puts you in mind of a late-70s Wimpy bar. Only the Indian woodcarvings dotted around the walls give the game away – that and the heady scent of freshly blended spices. It's a busy place, with tables filling up and emptying at a fair crack, though the atmosphere is convivial and casual rather than rushed. There's no licence, so you can bring your own beer or wine (corkage is free) and a full water jug is supplied on each table. This, the low prices (the costliest dish will set you back £6.20), a chatty menu listing "tasty snacks", and fast, friendly service combine to create a deceptively simple stage for some fine Indian vegetarian cooking. There's even a set lunch buffet at £4.50.

Starters are copious, ladled out in no-nonsense stainless steel bowls. The dahi bhalle chat (£2.30) is a cool, yoghurty blend of chickpeas, crushed pooris and bulghur wheat, sprinkled with "very special spices". The dahi poori (£2.30) is a fragrant concoction of pooris, potatoes, onions, sweet and sour sauces and chilli chutney, again smothered in yoghurt and laced with spices. Stars of the main menu are the dosas, particularly the flamboyant paper dosa (£4.30), a giant fan of a pancake with coconut chutney, potatoes and dhal nestling beneath its folds. Also superb is the house speciality, thali annapurna (£6), a feast of dhal, rice, vegetables, pickles, side dishes, mini bhajees and your choice of pooris or chapattis – divine but unfinishable, especially if you make the mistake of ordering some monstrously proportioned side dishes as well.

Whatever feast you put together, do leave room for dessert, as there's a heavenly kulfi malai (£1.70) to dig into – a creamy pyramid of frozen milk flavoured with kevda, nuts and herbs. A rich but less sweet-toothed option is the shrikhand (£1.60), a Western Indian dish with cheese, spices and herbs counteracting the sugar. Alternatively, try the Kashmiri falooda (£2.20) – cold milk with china grass and rose syrup topped with ice cream and nuts. Though strictly speaking a drink, this is surely pudding enough for anyone.

EUSTON & KING'S CROSS ⑪ SPANISH

El Parador

245 Eversholt St, NW1 ☏020 7387 2789   ⊖ Mornington Crescent

Mon–Thurs noon–3pm & 6–11pm, Fri noon–3pm & 6–11.30pm,

Sat 6–11.30pm, Sun 7–10.30pm   All major credit cards

El Parador is a small, no-frills Spanish restaurant and tapas bar – slightly stranded in the quiet little enclave around Mornington Crescent, between King's Cross and Camden. It serves very tasty tapas at very reasonable prices and has a friendly, laid-back atmosphere, even on busy Friday and Saturday nights. It's a good place to spend a summer evening, with a lovely garden out the back, though this is no secret and the sought-after tables here should be booked in advance.

As ever with tapas, the fun part of eating here is choosing several dishes from the wide selection on offer, and then sharing and swapping with your companions. The plates are small, so allow yourself at least two or three tapas a head – more for a really filling meal – and go for at least one of the fish or seafood dishes, which are treats. Highlights include chipirones picantes (£3.90), baby squid sautéed with chilli; gambas salteadas (£4.60), nice fat tiger prawns, pan-fried with parsley and hot paprika; tortilla de bacalao (£4.20), made with salt cod. Carnivores shouldn't miss out on the jamón Serrano (£4.60), delicious Spanish cured ham, or the salchichas de Navarra (£3.70), sausages that are at once smoked, herby and spicy. Also good is cordero a la plancha (£4.20), grilled lamb with rosemary and olive oil. The numerous vegetarian tapas include judias saltedas (£4), green beans sautéed with braised leeks, red peppers and wine; paella del Parador (£3.60), a vegetable paella with peas, corn and green beans, and buñuelos de patatas (£3.50), mashed potato cooked with sun-dried tomatoes, cumin and Manchego cheese. Desserts keep up the pace. Marquesa de chocolate (£3) is a luscious, creamy home-made chocolate mousse; flan de naranja (£2.80) is really good orange crème caramel.

Try a glass of the dry Manzanilla (£2) to start or accompany your meal. It's a perfect foil for tapas. Or delve into El Parador's strong selection of Spanish wines. Enjoyable choices include Muga crianza '97 (£14.50), a smooth white Rioja, and the Guelbenzu crianza '95 (£14), a rich and fruity red.

CENTRAL

Great Nepalese

48 Eversholt St, NW1 ©020 7388 6737	⊖ Euston/Euston Square
Mon–Sat noon–2.45pm & 6–11.30pm,	
Sun noon–2.30pm & 6–11.15pm	Amex, Diners, Mastercard, Visa

This bit of London behind Euston station is distinctly seedy, and the shops that are neighbours to the Great Nepalese offer strange products for probably quite strange people. Inside the restaurant, however, everything is reassuringly normal, if a little old and faded, like the giant wall photo showing the Queen and Prince Philip standing with the five living Gurkha holders of the Victoria Cross. This is a place that manages to combine friendly and homely service with authentic Nepalese food and, in case your nerve falters, the menu also has a buffer zone littered with standard curry house favourites like chicken tikka masala and lamb rogan josh – the latter helpfully subtitled "a very popular lamb curry".

Don't order the lamb curry unless feeling profoundly unadventurous. It may be a very nice, popular lamb curry but the authentic Great Nepalese dishes are nicer still. Start with masco bhara, a large frisbee-shaped doughnut. It is made from black lentils, but without their black skins, so the result is a nutty-tasting, fluffy white mass with a crisp outside. It comes with a bowl of curry gravy for dipping (£3.35 plain, £3.75 with a hidden core of shredded lamb). Or try haku choyala (£3.60), diced mutton with garlic, lemon juice and ginger. It's spicy and agreeably sharp. For mains, the staff direct you to the dumba curry (£4.70), a traditional Nepalese-style curry, reliant on the same rich gravy as the masco bhara, or the chicken ra piaj (£4.80), with onions and spices. Both are highly recommended. Another very typical Nepalese dish is the butuwa chicken (£4.85). It combines ginger and spices with garlic and green herbs and is delicious. And if you like dhal, you shouldn't miss the kalo dal (£2.85), nutty and dark with black lentils.

A single note of caution. Beware the Coronation rum from Kathmandu. This firewater was first distilled in 1975 for the coronation of his majesty King Birendra Bir Bikram Shah Deva, and it comes in a bottle shaped like a glass kukri. You probably have to be a Gurkha to appreciate its finer points.

EUSTON & KING'S CROSS ⓉⒷ **INDIAN**

Raavi Kebab Halal Tandoori

125 Drummond St, NW1 ©020 7388 1780   ⊖ Euston/Euston Square

Daily 12.30–10.30pm   All major credit cards

This small restaurant has been a fixture for more than 25 years, during which time Drummond Street has become one of the main curry centres of London. Competition here is more than just fierce, it is ludicrous, as well-established vegetarian restaurants compete to offer the cheapest "eat-as-much-as-you-can" lunch buffet. It is lucky that vegetables are so cheap. But the Raavi is not just about bargain prices – or vegetables, come to that. It specialises in halal meat dishes, especially grills, and on the menu claims to offer "probably the best grilled and cooked items in London". And indeed, when you fancy tucking into an item, this is a great place to come.

The grills here are good but hot – hot enough for the wildest chilli head. Seekh kebab (£2), juicy and well flavoured, is straight from the charcoal grill in the doorway – and hot. Chicken tikka (£2.10) is hot. Mutton tikka (£2.20) is hot. And with the kebabs comes a khaki-coloured dipping sauce that is sharp with lemon juice, strongly flavoured with fresh coriander and, as you'd expect, hot with fresh chillies. Lamb quorma (£4.25) is not so fierce: a rich sauce with fresh ginger and garlic topped with a sprinkle of shaved almonds. Chicken daal (£3.25) brings chunks of chicken on the bone, thoroughly delicious, bobbing on a sea of savoury yellow split-pea dhal. Nan breads (90p) are light and crispy. In 1999, a new arrival, nihari (£4.50) – the traditional breakfast dish of slow-cooked curried mutton – dislodged haleem from its spot as best-seller here. Haleem (£3.20) is a dish whose origins are shrouded in mystery. Some say that it was invented in the Middle East, which is certainly where it is most popular today; other devotees track it back to Moghul kitchens. The recipe is arduous. Take some meat and cook it, add four kinds of dhal, a good deal of cracked wheat, and two kinds of rice, plus spices. Cook for up to seven hours, then add some garam masala. The result is a gluey slick of smooth and spicy glop from which any traces of the meat have all but disappeared.

And how does it taste? You'd be hard pushed to be more enthusiastic than "not bad".

Simply Spice

53 Calthorpe St, WC1 ©020 7833 9787	⊖ King's Cross/Farringdon
Mon–Fri & Sun noon–2.30pm & 6–10.30pm, Sat 6–10.30pm	All major credit cards

On the face of it you wouldn't class the Holiday Inn as a mould-breaking hotel chain, but their King's Cross hotel just opposite the Post Office's Mount Pleasant Sorting Centre has something special. In 1998 they opened the hotel restaurant to non-residents. In the morning the 160-seat dining room is full of breakfasting businessmen; later, as if by magic, it turns into a first-rate Indian restaurant. The woman in charge of the kitchens – Manjula – has an enviable track record – she used to be head chef of Café Indiya in the City (see p.202). The food at Simply Spice reflects her love of regional dishes, and you'll find all manner of interesting Goan specialities along with sound service and surprisingly comfortable surroundings.

Start with the Andhra fried chicken (£3.95), a dry dish with the distinctive taste of curry leaves and a welcome bite of chilli. Or there are chote nargis (£3.95), miniature scotch eggs made with quails' eggs and a well-spiced mincemeat mixture. The chicken tikka (£6.95) – which is always a test of a tandoor chef – is very tender and well judged. Moving on to the main dishes, imldaar batak (£8.50) is outstandingly successful – a duck breast cooked in a tamarind sauce, sharp, hot and tangy all at the same time; it's exceedingly good. Also good is the dahiwala lamb (£8.50), its sauce made from yoghurt thickened with chickpea flour. Or the famous chicken xacutti (£7.95), which is a classic dish involving the careful balancing of 21 different spices. But the star turn harks back to Manjula's time in Goa – a genuine pork vindaloo, rich, chilli-hot and most authentic. For anyone who prefers their food less incendiary, the biryani (£9.95) is to be recommended: try it made with either lamb or chicken and served with a bowl of yoghurt.

Vegetarians will be impressed with the chole bhatura (£5.95) – two discs of fried wholemeal bread topped with a small mountain of curried chickpeas. Could this famously spicy Punjabi snack be the shape of hotel food to come?

Crown & Anchor

137 Drummond St, NW1   ©020 7255 9871

This modernised, scrubbed wooden pub has a young and fresh feel. The drinkers are mainly students and nurses, enjoying the Staropramen and Grolsch on tap.

The Friend at Hand

4 Herbrand St, WC1   ©020 7837 5524

A pub since 1797, this friendly venue boasts T.S. Eliot as a past regular. It is now favoured by tourists, nurses and students from nearby London University, who eagerly down the well-pulled pints of Courage, Directors and Theakston. It's tucked behind Russell Square station and worth the search.

The Jolly Gardeners

69 Coburg St, NW1   ©020 7383 2141

Landlords Roisin and Peter give a warm welcome at this friendly little local. It's as cosy and relaxed as someone's sitting room. Greene King IPA, Old Speckled Hen and Courage Best are the favourites on tap.

Prince Arthur

80–82 Eversholt St, NW1   ©020 7387 2165

Genuine neighbourhood pub that pulls in a friendly crowd of local residents who enjoy Boddingtons, Flowers IPA and Whitbread Best. The honey-coloured wood panelling gives the place a retro feel.

Rowley's

162 Eversholt St, NW1   ©020 7383 0925

A comfortable, family-run Free House close to Euston mainline train station with Tetley's, Calder's Cream Ale and Fuller's London Pride the favourites on tap. Go with a distinctive hat or cap and donate it to the great collection that lines the walls.

The Sols Arms

65–68 Hampstead Rd, NW1   ©020 7387 3721

A capacious, traditional-style venue, this pub attracts a mixed crowd of local office workers and shoppers from Tottenham Court Road who want a quiet pint of Courage Best, Directors or John Smith's. The drinking area is extended by the pavement tables, which are sheltered by an overhang from the building above.

Kensington

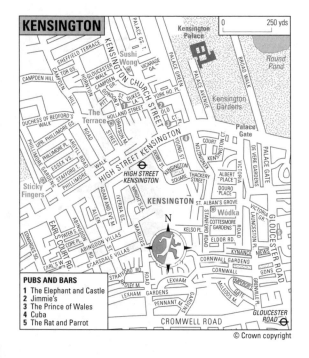

KENSINGTON

PUBS AND BARS

1 The Elephant and Castle
2 Jimmie's
3 The Prince of Wales
4 Cuba
5 The Rat and Parrot

© Crown copyright

£8–£25

Sticky Fingers

1a Phillimore Gardens, W8 ℂ020 7938 5338	⊖ High Street Kensington
Mon–Sat noon–11.30pm, Sun noon–11pm	All major credit cards

www.stickyfingers.co.uk

It should be enough to strike fear into the heart of any sophisticated diner. A hamburger restaurant which is the pride and joy of a wrinkly rocker. But take heart. The food at Bill Wyman's Sticky Fingers is very good indeed. If there are times when you feel like the burger, the whole burger and nothing but the burger, or when your kids demand the same, then visit Sticky Fingers and you'll be well satisfied. Go in any other mood and the foreground music, the rock memorabilia and the waves of excited children may prove a bit much.

Sticky Fingers make an effort to tempt adults and kids alike with their starters: barbecue chicken wings (£4.25), deep-fried potato skins with sour cream and chives (£3.25) or cheese and bacon (£3.75), half a rack of spare ribs (£4.95), guacamole with corn chips (£3.95). To follow they offer pasta dishes, or specials like a char-grilled English lamb steak (£8.95) or herb-crusted salmon fillet (£10.95). There are New York-style sandwiches – house club (£7.95) is a multi-layered delight of chicken, crisp bacon, tomato and so forth. There are even salads: Caesar (£6.95), or bang-bang chicken (£7.95). But this is all high-class, inter-national-hotel food and you are here for the real stuff: the burgers. The burgers weigh in at 6oz. They are cooked to order, and the cook listens to what you say – medium turns out medium, and rare is suitably rare. They come in a good soft sesame seed bun. There's a choice of cheese – blue, Swiss and American – and a choice of dressing on the side salad: herb, balsamic, blue cheese, Thousand Island, honey mustard or mayon-naise. Pick from a char-grilled burger (£7.25); bar-b-q burger (£7.75); cheeseburger (£7.75); cheese and bacon burger (£8.25); and the sticky stack (£10.95), which is a double burger with cheese, crisp bacon and fried onions.

For the studiously eccentric, Sticky Fingers also purvey a decent lamb burger (£7.75). Better, though, to opt for the Beggar's Banquet, which is available for parties of six or more at £10.95 per person – "a spectacu-lar feast of whole roast chicken, ribs, bar-b-q chicken wings, salsa, guacamole, corn chips, coleslaw, huge salad, garlic bread, and piles of crispy fries". Quite so.

£15–£35

Sushi Wong

38c–d Kensington Church St, W8 ℂ020 7937 5007   ⊖ High Street Kensington

Mon–Fri noon–2.30pm & 6–10.30pm, Sat noon–10.30pm,

Sun 6–10.30pm   All major credit cards

Sushi Wong is the kind of name you either love or hate, but whichever side you take you have to concede that it is certainly slick – just like this deceptively sized restaurant. On the ground floor there's a modernist Japanese restaurant-cum-sushi-bar seating about 25 people. Downstairs there's a teppanyaki table and room for a further sixty diners. Looking in from the street it's hard not to admire the stark bright-yellow and blue colour scheme, and the tables, each topped with ground glass backed by a blue neon tube. In the face of all this brightness and modernity, the service is so low-key that it almost seems timid, but Sushi Wong is a confident and efficient place for all that.

Sushi is delicious here. Ordering the sushi matsu set (£19) brings a round lacquer tray with six pieces of salmon or tuna roll flanked by ten pieces of sushi various – the chef's selection. The fish is fresh, the wasabi strong, the gari delicious and the sushi well prepared. A good array at a fair price. The menu emphasises hosomaki (roll sushi), ranging from edo (£4.20) – crab meat, salmon and cucumber – to "Kensington roll" (£3.80), which is a crispy salmon and asparagus concoction "specially made for Kensington dwellers!" There is also a wide range of à la carte selections: starters like agedofu dengkaku (£3.90), deep-fried soft-shell crab (£6.20), yakitori (£4.90), and age-gyoza (£4), which are deep-fried dumplings. Mains include stir-fried lobster tail (£10.80), chicken teriyaki (£8.80), pork tonkatsu (£8.80), and the Sushi Wong tempura selection (£12.80), which includes king prawns, fish and vegetables. Among the noodle dishes you'll find nabeyaki udon (£7.50) and Sushi Wong ramen (£6.50) – egg noodles with chicken, prawns, egg and vegetables in miso broth.

The set menus make life simpler. The Geisha gets you five courses for £23. The Sakura gets you sashimi, tempura, salmon steak or beef teriyaki, rice and miso soup, and dessert for £26. There's also a seven-course Sushi Wong Dinner (£36). Or book one of the hibashi tables for a teppanyaki dinner cooked in front of you – five courses for £33.

The Terrace

33c Holland St, W8 ©020 7937 3224	⊖ High Street Kensington
Mon–Sat noon–2.30pm & 7–10.30pm, Sun 12.30–3pm	All major credit cards

The Terrace is a small, modern restaurant hidden among the residential streets north of Kensington High Street. Its dining room is small, but as the name proclaims there is a terrace fronting onto the street where a handful of tables await any diners who have the nerve to brave the British weather. The food is simple, seasonal and modern. Presentation is unfussy and the standard of cooking is generally high; elsewhere you would probably expect the prices to be a tad lower, but here – in Kensington on the way to Holland Park – they represent quite decent value.

The menu changes regularly. Starters like warm smoked haddock brandade with beef tomato salad and majoram dressing (£8.50) are well executed, while the pan-fried foie gras (£11), a huge portion of liver served with caramelised pears, is an impressive bargain of a dish but not to be trifled with. Or there's a scallop and red onion marmalade tart (£8.50), served with a wild leaf salad and an orange and thyme beurre blanc. The Terrace salad (£5) could be anything from a competently made Caesar to a combination of grilled spiced aubergines, plum tomatoes and goats' cheese. Soups veer towards the exotic, such as watercress and lime with crème fraîche (£5). At first glance the main courses look like standard fare – cod, tuna, chicken, lamb – but they're all made from fresh ingredients which deliver good strong flavours. Pan-fried fillet of pork with an apple and ginger purée with melted Gorgonzola, Pommery mustard sauce (£14.50) is particularly good; roast rack of grass-fed Welsh lamb comes with a herb and mustard crust, potato gratin and mint Béarnaise (£19.50). Or there's char-grilled blue-fin tuna (£18.50), accompanied by a Niçoise salad, and a fine wild mushroom risotto (£10.50), which comes with a splash of truffle oil and plenty of Parmesan. The dessert section ranges from chocolate mousse with vanilla cream (£5.50), via gooseberry fool (£5.50), to raspberry crème brûlée (£5.50).

Regulars are easily spotted: they're the ones tucking into the excellent-value (and constantly changing) set lunches – £12.50 for two courses, £14.50 for three.

Wódka

12 St Albans Grove, W8 ⓒ020 7937 6513   ⊖ High Street Kensington

Mon–Fri 12.30–2.30pm & 7–11pm, Sat & Sun 7–11.15pm   All major credit cards

Wódka is a restaurant which lies in wait for you. It's calm, and bare; the food is better than you might expect, well cooked, and thoughtfully seasoned. The daily lunch menu represents extremely good value at £10.90 for two courses and £13.50 for three, a large proportion of the dishes being refugees from the evening à la carte. Where, you wonder, is the streak of madness that helped the Polish cavalry take on German tank regiments with sabres drawn? On the shelves behind the bar, that's where – in the extensive collection of moody and esoteric vodkas which are for sale both by the shot and by the carafe.

The soups are tasty for starters: zur (£3.90) is a sour rye and sausage soup, while the parsnip soup (£4.50) is rich and creamy. Blinis are also the business: they come with smoked salmon (£6.90), aubergine mousse (£4.90), foie gras (£8.90) or 40 grams of oscietra caviar (£19). A lunchtime selection will get you all except the caviar. Also good is the kaszanka (£5.25) – grilled black pudding with one salad of fresh green leaves and another made from lentils, onions and white beans. For a main course, the fish cakes (£9.90) with leeks and a dill sauce are firm favourites with the regulars (many of whom are from nearby Penguin Books). When partridge is available, it is roasted and served with a splendid mash of root vegetables – the mashed potato is also worthy of special praise. Puddings tend to be of the oversweet, underimaginative gateaux variety, but the vodka will ensure that you won't be worrying about that.

Consider the vodka list with due attention – there is a host of them: Zubrówka (made with bison grass); Okhotnichya (for hunters); Jarzebiak (that's rowan berries); Cytrynówka (lemon); Sliwowica (plum); Sliwówka (plum, but hot and sweet); Czarna Porezecka (blackcurrant); Ananas (pineapple); Krupnik (honey, and served hot); Roza (rose petals); Goldwasser (made with flakes of gold and aniseed); Soplica (which is a mystery). They cost from £2.25 to £2.75 a shot, and from £33.90 to £37.90 per 50cl carafe. Remember this simple test: pick any three of the above names and say them quickly. If anyone shows signs of understanding, you need another shot.

Cuba

11–13 High St Kensington,
W8   ✆020 7938 4137

Latin-themed bar and dance venue with salsa and samba classes and sexy club nights till 2am. Upstairs, above all the action, drinkers enjoy wicked cocktails, and there's a good selection of cold Mexican beers.

The Elephant & Castle

40 Holland St, W8   ✆020 7368 0901

Ablaze with lovely baskets and window boxes this unspoilt little local has won the London in Bloom awards countless times. With its outside tables, this is a haven of peace in Ferrari territory, with Bass, Fuller's Bitter and London Pride among other beers.

Jimmies Wine Bar

18 Kensington Church St,
W8   ✆020 7937 9988

Jimmies is a lively basement wine bar with an excellent drinks selection, DJs on Monday and Tuesday and live music Wednesday to Saturday. It's popular, and often loud. You'll pay £3 on the door after 10.30 pm, but it's open until 1am.

The Prince of Wales

8 Kensington Church St, W8 ✆020 7937 0867

A tiny bow window belies the size of this T & J Barnard pub, with its long interior – the frontage is so small you could easily walk past it. Once inside, however, you'll find an oasis of calm in the frantic Kensington High Street area. Courage Directors on draught.

The Rat & Parrot

25 Gloucester Rd, SW7   ✆020 7589 0905

This cavernous venue, a Scottish and Newcastle standard, attracts a noisy young crowd. Plenty of space, lots of tables and a brasserie-like atmosphere with locals reading newspapers and simply hanging out. A good pint of Guinness too.

Knightsbridge & Belgravia

KNIGHTSBRIDGE & BELGRAVIA

PUBS AND BARS
1 The Grenadier
2 The Fifth Floor Bar
3 The Nag's Head
4 The Wilton Arms
5 The Chelsea Bar at the Millennium
6 The Turk's Head
7 The Gloucester

© Crown copyright

£28–£50

The Fifth Floor

5th Floor, Harvey Nichols, Knightsbridge, SW1 ⓒ020 7235 5250	⊖ Knightsbridge
Mon–Fri noon–3pm & 6.30–11.30pm,	
Sat noon–3.30pm & 6.30–11.30pm, Sun noon–3.30pm	All major credit cards
www.harveynichols.co.uk	

Harvey Nichols is practically a synonym for upmarket fashion – *the* place where Ab Fabbers come to shop. Its Knightsbridge store has many floors, a couple of restaurants, a rather notorious bar (B- and sometimes A-list celeb shoppers in need of refreshment), a cafe, a conveyor-belt sushi bar, and a very smart food hall and wine department. The Fifth Floor restaurant is the smartest of the lot, and you would rightly infer that it is not cheap. What you get for your money, however, is very accomplished cooking, attentive but not overbearing service, fine wines and good times. The dining room is a large one, separated from the lively bar by nothing more formidable than a velvet rope. The menu is long and interesting, and as well as the à la carte there is a three-course prix fixe lunch menu which offers half a dozen choices for each course at a surprisingly accessible price – £23.50.

The main menu is broadly seasonal, and it is left to the daily specials to introduce game, mushrooms, spring vegetables, and the new season's this and that. The cooking is satisfying and the flavours are pronounced – there is nothing wishy-washy here. Among the starters you'll find Henry's black bean soup (£6.50) – tasty, rich and satisfying. Another star dish is deep-fried oysters and belly pork, soy and yuzu dressing (£9). Or there's potato thyme and Taleggio "tarte fine" (£8), or Lincolnshire duck, smoked eel and dandelion salad (£8.25). Fish mains may include salt cod fish cakes with pepper and lemon aioli (£14.50), whole Dover sole with brown shrimps and verjuice (£19.75), or roasted scallops with "Sri Lankan" spiced lentils and a spring onion salad (£19.75). Meat mains generally feature good classic dishes like grilled veal chop with Rocquefort butter (£18) or fillet of beef Vigneronne (£19.50). Puddings are suitably greed-inspiring.

As you would expect from a restaurant that is fifty feet from its own smart wine department, there's a pretty smoky wine list. And, for after dinner, 28 different Cognacs ranging from Hennessy VS (£6 a measure) to the very grown-up Richard Hennessy (£110 a measure).

£20–£45

Osteria d'Isola

145 Knightsbridge, SW1 ✆020 7838 1099   ⊖ Knightsbridge

Mon–Fri noon–2.30pm & 6–10pm, Sat noon–3.30pm & 6–10pm,

Sun noon–2.30pm & 6–9pm   All major credit cards

There are two restaurants at this swanky Knightsbridge address: upstairs there is Isola, which is exceedingly smart, and downstairs there is the Osteria d'Isola, which is less formal and accommodates a large bar that breathes life into the space. In the kitchen (which serves both venues) is a highly regarded Frenchman called Bruno Loubet. So far so good; nice place, great chef. Most critics and commentators then go on alarmingly about the perils of expecting a Frenchman to cook Italian food. Why? There are enough Englishmen cooking good French food. And Bruno Loubet is an outstanding chef. So, service is friendly. The dining room is comfortable. Prices are tolerable. There's a wood-fired oven. The food is delicious. And the chef is French. Carry on.

The menu changes regularly to reflect the seasons and what's good at the market. It is a four-stage affair, with antipasti, pasta, secondi, and dolci. Start with a classic like vitello tonnato (£6.50), which is well made, and a large portion; or insalata di mozzarella di bufala e pomodori (£7); or carpaccio (£6.50). Pasta dishes might be pasta e fagioli (£5.50) – the classic bean and pasta soup – or ravioli di barbabietola e salvia (£7/£11) – ravioli with roast beetroot ricotta, sage and horseradish. You won't find better in Italy. Main course dishes might include a Livornese fish stew (£15), osso buco alla Milanese (£15), or a whole sea bass which has been roasted in the wood -fired oven (£39 for two). Or how about the insalata di barbabietola e arancia (£14) – a pork knuckle served with a beetroot and orange salad? Puds are equally Italian – as always tiramisù (£6), plus dangerous delicacies like panettone pudding (£6). The bread is good here. The wine list is extensive and delves deeply into far corners of Italy; gratifyingly, there is a huge range served by the glass.

At lunch they offer a deal which proves both intriguing eating and very good value indeed. This "taste of Osteria" gets you eight different antipasti followed by dessert for just £15.

Pizza on the Park

11 Knightsbridge, SW1 ©020 7235 5273	⊖ Hyde Park Corner
Mon–Sat 8.15am–midnight, Sat 9.30am–midnight,	
Sun 9.30am–11.30pm	All major credit cards

For Pizza on the Park read Pizza on the Road – busy Knightsbridge flows like a river between Hyde Park and the forecourt tables that front this popular restaurant. Happily, things improve greatly inside, where palms, woodwork, white tiles and spotlights conjure the elegant ethos of Pizza Express, the chain to which this place once belonged.

Fans of Pizza Express will find the evening menu reassuringly familiar. Aficionados will make straight for the dough ball starter – £1.95 worth of deliciously crusty, warm bread dipped in garlic butter. You can be sure your pizza toppings will be fresh, as they're laid out for your inspection in big glass bowls along the back of the dining room, adding a cheery splash of colour to the whole affair. This is one place where they're not afraid to go heavy on the anchovies, capers and olives. If those ingredients take your fancy, then opt for the Napoletana (£7.10), the Neptune (£7.95), the Capricciosa or the Four Seasons (both £7.75). For those in need of a touch more fire, the American Hot (£7.75) is a classic, laden with pepperoni and green pepper. When choosing the Quattro Formaggi (£7.25), it's worth remembering that this seriously cheese-laden affair is dauntingly rich. Of the handful of pasta offerings, the rich, creamy cannelloni (£7.25) makes an excellent alternative to pizza. Puddings are generous – the apple pie (£4.25), which actually tastes home-made, is a real winner.

But that's where similarities to Pizza Express end. Pizza on the Park also offers a choice of all-day breakfasts from 8.15am: a Continental (£4), which features a pastry, orange juice and a hot drink, and an English (£4.95), which brings eggs, tomato, mushroom, toast and coffee. Alternatively, should you saunter in around 3.15pm, you can enjoy a three-course afternoon tea (£6.95) or various snacks. Visit on a Sunday and you can listen to live jazz as well. If you can't wait that long, the downstairs restaurant has a jazz band every night, but you pay a charge for the privilege.

£35–£120

La Tante Clare

Wilton Place, SW1 ℂ020 7823 2003   ⊖ Hyde Park Corner

Mon–Fri noon–2.30pm & 7–11pm, Sat 7–11pm   All major credit cards

At the end of 1998 Pierre Koffman gathered up his kitchen brigade and moved them all to a new location within the purlieus of the Berkeley Hotel in Knightsbridge. How the owners of this hostelry must have rubbed their hands with glee – now they had not only Vong on one flank, but also Koffman on the other. The Michelin people, however, showed their disapproval of restaurants gadding about like this, and promptly docked Tante Clare a star. As things have settled down, the new Tante Clare has found form and is as sublime as ever. Perhaps it is his Gascon heritage, but Koffman's food pulls off an amazing treble whammy: it is sophisticated but earthy and rich in flavour; dishes are both elegant and satisfying; things look good but they taste better. There is only one way to find out how he does it, and that is to go and eat. Every chef with aspirations should try the set lunch here – £28 for three courses, coffee and petits fours.

What an amazing deal: there are two choices for both starter and main, so you might find yourself agonising between a salade Niçoise – a large bowlful with small potatoes and runny egg, marinated tuna, capers, and anchovies – and a chicken liver parfait with Sauternes jelly. Choosing the main is no easier – herb-crusted cod versus perfect rack of lamb with ratatouille. If these dishes sound simple, that is because they are. They are also perfectly judged, strongly flavoured, well balanced and well presented. Come back at dinner and prices move briskly upwards. There are usually five starters, five fish and six meats on offer. Starters like soupe de morue aux truffes (£24), and coquilles St Jacques rôties à l'encre (£21.50), pave the way for filet à la graine de moutarde et pâtes fraîches (£31), suprême de canard de Challan, jus à l'os et cuisse confite (£29), and canon d'agneau, épinards à la Bohémienne (£27). Or perhaps you should try Koffman's signature dish – the pied de cochon farci aux morilles (£27) – and see the fabled dish from which so many chefs have drawn inspiration for so long.

The service here is slick and unobtrusive; the petits fours are good and the puddings are amazing; there's a minimum charge of £50 a head in the evening; there's a 12.5% service charge, and there's a wine list that starts sensibly and ends up stratospheric. All in all this is the real thing. So start saving now and treat yourself.

Zafferano

15 Lowndes St, SW1 ©020 7235 5800	⊖ Knightsbridge
Mon–Sat noon–2.30pm & 7–11pm,	
Sun noon–2.30pm & 7–10.30pm	All major credit cards

Zafferano is a very exciting place to eat. The decor is a touch bleak, service is quick and slick, but the food . . . well, the food is amazing. This is what Italian food is like when it is trying very hard – not too precious, rooted firmly in tradition, with wonderful natural combinations of tastes and textures. Unsurprisingly, everyone who is anyone has noticed this restaurant, so booking ahead has become a necessity. It is worth the wait. Zafferano sticks to good-value fixed-price menus: two or three courses at lunch Monday to Friday (£18.50 and £21.50), and two, three or four courses at Saturday and Sunday lunch and every dinner (£29.50, £35.50 and £39.50). This is the perfect place to recognise Italian instincts, enjoy a pasta course – and go for the four!

The menu changes each season and is "tinkered" with every month or so. There is also a list of four or five daily seasonal specials, which almost invariably include some fish dishes. The lunchtime menu is a shortened version of the dinner menu and the few dishes which attract a supplement tend to be fish and crustacea, which seems fair enough. The kind of antipasti you can expect are sformato di patate con pancetta and Taleggio (layered potatoes and pork belly with Taleggio cheese); insalata di spada al verde (swordfish and yellow bean salad with olive oil and herbs); and mozzarella di bufala (buffalo mozzarella with baked aubergine). On to the pastas and risotti: ravioli di borragine (borage parcels with herbs and olive oil), taglioni al nero di seppia (black fresh egg pasta with cuttlefish), risotto alle ortiche (nettle risotto). Or there's sometimes a splendid and simple saffron risotto. Then the mains, always well balanced and always well cooked. Look out for anatra arrosto con farro al balsamico (roast duck with pearl spelt and balsamic vinegar), and coda di rospo salsa di noci, capperi e barbe di frate (baked monkfish with a walnut and caper sauce).

For pudding, shun the cheesecake, the polenta cake, the chocolate soufflé torte with liquorice ice cream, the caramel parfait with rum molasses sauce. . . they are all delicious, but not quite so delicious as the tiramisù!

The Fifth Floor Bar

5th Floor, Harvey Nichols, SW1 ℭ020 7235 5000

Favourite haunt of the rich and gorgeous, with a long cocktail list (that often gets ignored in favour of champagne by the glass), and chichi Japanese crackers instead of peanuts. You don't have to eat in the restaurant to drink here, but it makes a good place to start the night if you are. Credit cards are de rigueur.

The Gloucester

187 Sloane St, SW1 ℭ020 7235 0298

An unpretentious and welcome pub in a sea of chic and expensive shops. There's plenty of room, as the deceptively small frontage masks a long, cool and dark interior. Courage Directors and Best on tap.

The Grenadier

18 Wilton Row, SW1 ℭ020 7235 3074

Nestled in a labyrinth of pretty private mews, this picturesque pub is much visited by sightseers. Come the evening it gets quite noisy with a crowd of local hoorays, but there's a Guardsman's box to hide in. Courage Best and Directors are the favourites on tap.

Millennium Knightsbridge

17 Sloane St, SW1 ℭ020 7235 4377

This stylish hotel bar makes an excellent meeting place if you like things ultra-modern. There's a great range of classic cocktails, comfortable leather sofas and very attentive service. Perfect for de-stressing after work and before dinner.

The Nag's Head

53 Kinnerton St, SW1 ℭ020 7235 1135

A delightfully old-fashioned Free House. Open fires burn in real old iron ranges, there's a curious low bar that doubles as a table, and you can get Adnams, London Pride and Benskins on draught. It's tucked away, but well worth seeking out.

The Turk's Head

10 Motcomb St, SW1 ℭ020 7245 0131

This small, friendly backstreet local offers Fuller's London Pride, Staropramen and Bass on draught. It's quiet, in a nice residential street – *very* Knightsbridge.

The Wilton Arms

71 Kinnerton St, SW1 ℭ020 7235 4854

Small and cosy, this traditional Whitbread pub is very much a local, incongruously tucked just behind swanky Knightsbridge. There's a nice conservatory at the back.

Marylebone

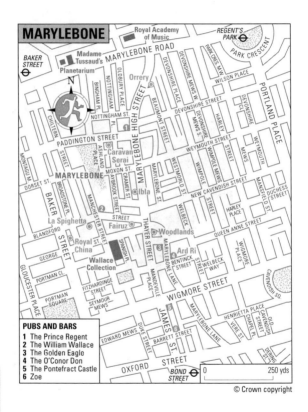

MARYLEBONE

PUBS AND BARS
1 The Prince Regent
2 The William Wallace
3 The Golden Eagle
4 The O'Conor Don
5 The Pontefract Castle
6 Zoe

0   250 yds

© Crown copyright

Ard Ri

At the O'Conor Don pub, 88 Marylebone Lane, W1 ©020 7935 9311   ⊖ Bond Street

Mon–Fri noon–2.30pm & 6–10.30pm   Amex, Mastercard, Visa

The Ard Ri Dining Room is above the O'Conor Don – and the pub downstairs (see p.79) is where you should begin your eating experience. It's a large, crowded and jolly place and serves one of London's finest pints of draught Guinness. When you have taken enough fuel on board, make your way upstairs. The decor in the dining room is comfortable, homely and unpretentious. There's a fireplace – with a real fire in season – and tables and chairs assembled from various junk shops that probably call themselves antique dealers.

The food is simple and good, and the new chef, appointed in 1999, has continued to balance the homely with more studiously fashionable dishes. Service is friendly. The main menu changes monthly to reflect the seasons and creates a fine balance between modern Irish dishes on the one hand and traditional Irish meals on the other. Thus as starters you might choose half a dozen fresh Irish Cuan oysters (£6.75), home-cured salmon with pickled cucumber (£4.95), or Caesar salad with crisp bacon (£5.50). For main courses, traditional Irish lamb stew (£9) and beef and Guinness casserole with mash (£9) rub shoulders with poached fillet of salmon with champ and creamed leeks (£8.95). Home-made fish cakes come with a light lemon sauce (£8.20), and you can have a large bowl of mussels with chips (£8.80). There are some serious steaks, too, including a 16oz Scotch T-bone with chips, mushrooms, onion and tomato. The side orders (all £2.50) provide rich pickings: scallion champ, Colcannon and soda bread (95p).

Puddings – stuffed baked apple with fresh cream (£3.50), warm Guinness cake with fresh cream (£3.50), and baked rhubarb with custard (£3.50) among them – are backed by a good all-Irish cheeseboard (£4.95) which is well worth sampling. There is also a section of large dishes called "As you like it" which must be ordered 36 hours in advance and come for a minimum of two people – whole lobster, fore rib of beef, game, leg of lamb, beef Wellington. Good simple food bought fresh and cooked to order – most promising.

£14–£27

Caravan Serai

50 Paddington St, W1 ✆020 7935 1208   ⊖ Baker Street

Mon–Sat noon–3pm & 6–11pm, Sun noon–3pm & 6–10.30pm   All major credit cards

Caravan Serai lays claim to having been the first genuine Afghan restaurant in London. It is still owned by Kahlil Nayebkhail, the man who set it up in 1975, and nothing very much has changed since then. The decor is still single-mindedly devoted to all things Afghan; the seats are still made from Eastern carpets and kelims; there are still Afghan posters on the walls to demonstrate what a beautiful place the country can be, and the door is still guarded by a pair of life-size, china, Afghan hounds. About the only thing missing is the wreckage of a burnt-out Russian helicopter.

Just who has borrowed from whom (and exactly when the exchange took place) is a bit of a mystery, but a glance at the menu reveals the strong links between Afghan, Indian and Middle Eastern cuisines. You'll see a good many familiar spices, healthy dollops of yoghurt, and a tandoor in the kitchen. There are also some delicate and unexpected touches. Ashak (£4.95), billed as a national dish, is a kind of leek ravioli filled with minced lamb and lentils; it comes with a seasoned yoghurt sauce. You could also try ravioli filled with spiced minced lamb as a first course, or mashawa (£4.95), soup made from strained yoghurt, chickpeas and kofta meatballs. The list of main courses is split between kebabs and curries. Try the kebab-e-murgh (£6.45), which is marinated chicken grilled and served with a strangely pungent cherry sauce. Perhaps the kohi lawangi (£10.75) described as a "Traditional Afghan mountain dish roast shoulder of lamb" appeals? Or there's lawabee subzi gosht chalaw (£8.95), a tender lamb and spinach curry with chalaw rice, which is not a million miles from pillau rice. You must try the simplest staple – mash palaw (£2.85), a food-combiner's dream. It's a dish of rice plus lentils and is surprisingly good.

Caravan Serai opens out onto the street, which makes it a good choice in fine weather. There's a set lunch at £6.95, and for the hungry a four-course feast in the evenings, which is reasonably priced at £16.95.

Fairuz

3 Blandford St, W1 ℂ020 7935 9311	⊖ Bond Street
Daily noon–11pm	All major credit cards

Squeezed in between Stephen Bull on one side and a hip and groovy bistro on the other, Fairuz happily carries on doing its own thing, which is Lebanese cooking. As you open the front door, jolly souk music, the smell of Eastern spices and the warmly lit mud-coloured room assault and beguile the senses.

The menu is set out in traditional style. There's an epic list of mezze, both hot and cold, to start, followed by a selection of charcoal grills and a couple of oven-baked dishes. You can leave the selection up to the restaurant and order a set mezza (minimum two people, £14.95 per head), or a set menu (minimum two people, £24.95 per head) which combines a mezza with a mixed grill "specially made to regret being a vegetarian", with a glass of fiery arak thrown in. The set mezza delivers eight or ten little dishes, plenty for lunch or a light supper. But if you prefer to make your own selection, the menu lists 39 different mezze for you to choose from. Particularly recommended are the wonderfully fresh and herby tabbouleh (£3.95), the warak inab (£3.75), which are stuffed vine leaves, the hummous Beiruty (£4), and makanek (£4.75), or spicy lamb sausages. Even that most dangerously indigestible of delicacies, the felafel (£3.75), is fine here. Main course grills are generous and well prepared. Kafta khashkhash (£9.95) – lamb minced with parsley and grilled on skewers – is unexpectedly delicate and fragrant, but stands up well against its accompanying chilli sauce, while the shish taouk (£9.95) – chicken marinated in garlic and lemon – really *is* finger-licking good. Round off your meal with excellent baklava (£3.50), and real Turkish coffee (£2).

Fairuz is a comfortable place, full of sleek and contented Marylebonians. It's not the most authentic, cheapest or the best Lebanese food that you'll eat in town (best head to the nearby Edgware Road for that). But the ambience at Fairuz is better suited to novice Westerners – the staff are friendly and helpful, and the wine list, though short, is offered willingly. If you can, get there early to secure one of the nook and crannyish tent-like tables.

£18–£35

Ibla

89 Marylebone High St, W1 ©020 7224 3799	⊖ Baker St/Regent's Park
Mon–Sat noon–2.30pm & 7–10.15pm	Amex, Mastercard, Visa

At first glance Ibla looks unpromising – not helped by retaining the odd shade of green that somehow suited the previous occupant, the upmarket deli-restaurant Villandry (now transplanted to Great Portland Street – see p.14). But persevere – it will be worth it. Along with well-laid dining tables at the front, there is a nod to the shop-like premises with a small attempt to sell smart packets of pasta and the like. If possible, ask for a table in the back room, a pretty yet functional square space painted beetroot red, and settle down for some excellent Italian food.

The menu – uncompromisingly Italian – changes weekly and works on a set-price basis. You choose from the à la carte and pay £23 for two courses or £27 for three. There is also a special set lunch with limited choice (just a couple of options for each course) – two courses cost £15 and three cost £18. Starters may include courgette flowers and crab, with tomato and basil sauce; marinated red mullet with orange, fresh chilli and mango; or asparagus, rocket and Parmesan salad. Primi piatti are often inspired – fish ravioli with home-made bottarga; cannelloni of rabbit ragout, Taleggio and truffle sauce; or quail risotto with wild mushrooms. Main courses split into piatti di pesce and piatti di carne – the former along the lines of grilled sea bass with grilled vegetables and balsamic sauce, or monkfish fillet with sweet tomatoes, mussels and clams. Piatti di carne might be grilled pork fillet with stuffed aubergines and tomato sauce, or roast breast of duck, with timbale of ham and chickpeas, lemon and fig sauce. The less Italian-sounding dishes, such as salmon with herb crust, are in general less interesting, but the chef really knows his stuff and all will be zingily fresh, well seasoned and perfectly presented. Puddings are good, though they do suffer somewhat from coming at the end of a filling Italian meal.

Picky diners might take issue with the all-Italian wine list, which will be confusing to anyone but a connoisseur, and the service, which has more attitude than you might enjoy. But on the positive side, the staff are perfectionists, and will only take as many customers as the kitchen can cope with. This is no bad thing, as after all, a kitchen that's not over-stressed is a kitchen that is at its best.

£29–£90

Orrery

55 Marylebone High St, W1 ⓒ020 7616 8000	⊖ Baker Street/Regent's Park
Mon–Sat noon–3pm & 7–11pm, Sun 7–10.30pm	All major credit cards

www.conran.com

There is no doubt that Sir Terence Conran has gone to great lengths in order that the public don't see a "formula" in his restaurants – there are large ones, small ones, short ones, tall ones; Italian, French, British; loud music, no music. Even so, Orrery stands out. This is a very good restaurant indeed, driven by a passion for food, and the mainspring is the head chef Chris Galvin. It may be part of a large group, but they still change the menu daily if need be. Centralised buying might make economic sense, but Orrery still cherishes its own small local suppliers, going for large, line-caught, sea bass above their smaller farmed cousins, and selecting the best poulet noir, Bresse pigeon and Scottish beef. The service is slick and friendly, the dining room is beautiful, the cheeseboard has won prizes, the wine list is exhaustive. And the cooking is very good indeed. All of the above is reflected in the bill. For once, you do get what you pay for.

What a pleasure to see such a short menu – simple starters like wild mushroom consommé (£7.50), a first-rate terrine of foie gras served with Sauternes jelly and toasted brioche (£16.50), or cannelloni of Dorset crab, tomato, tarragon and Banyuls dressing (£11.50). Mains feature well-judged combinations of flavours: jarret de veau with glazed carrots, pommes purée and Madeira jus (£19.50), Bresse pigeon with cèpes, Savoy cabbage shallots and Burgundy jus (£19.50), tronçon of turbot with bourguignonne garnish (£19.50). Presentation is ultra-chic, flavours are intense; this is serious stuff. Puddings span the range from the classic – crème brûlée (£6.50) – to the nouvelle – carpaccio of pineapple with basil sorbet (£6.50).

One way to eat well here is to rely heavily on the set menus – the three-course menu du jour is £23.50. Sunday dinner – three courses – costs £28.50 including a glass of champagne. The Menu Gourmand (which must be ordered by the entire table) brings six courses, coffee and petits fours for £60, rising to £90 when you opt for the specially matched glasses of wine. A stress-free bargain.

Royal China

40 Baker St, W1 ©020 7487 4688	⊖ Baker Street/Bond Street
Mon–Sat noon–11pm, Sun 11am–10pm	
Dim sum served daily until 5pm	¯All major credit cards except Diners

Like its elder sibling – at 13 Queensway, W2 (©020 7221 2535) – this branch of the Royal China is a black-and-gold palace. The effect is a kind of "cigarette-packet chic" and smacks of the 1970s. But don't let that put you off. The food is not as expensive as the decor would have you believe, the service is efficient and brisk rather than that special kind of rude and brisk you may encounter in Chinatown, and the food is really good. One knowledgeable chef-critic describes the Royal China's sticky rice wrapped in a lotus leaf as the "best ever".

You could eat well from the Royal China's full menu, but it is the dim sum here that is most enticing. Like everything else in the Royal China, the small booklet that holds the dim sum menu is bound in gold. It goes from "Today's Chef Special", through dim sum, to lunchtime noodle and rice dishes. The most famous dim sum here is the roast pork puff (£1.80) – unusual, in that it is made from puff pastry, very light and with a sweetish char sui filling. From the "specials", try the lobster dumpling (£3.50) and Thai-style fish cake (£2.30), both of which are tasty. Also worth noting are prawn and chive dumpling (£2.20), pork and radish dumpling (£1.80), and seafood dumpling (£2.20) – or a selection of three. The glutinous rice in lotus leaves (£3) really is the best ever – rich and not too "gamey". Two parcels come in each steamer. The Royal China cheung fun (£2.70) is another sampler providing one of each filling – prawn, pork and beef. They take their cheung fun seriously here, with a total of eight variants including mushrooms and dry shrimp (£3). The fried rice dishes and the noodles are well priced (£5-7).

This may well be the place finally to take the plunge and try chicken's feet. Spicy chicken feet (£1.80) come thickly coated in a rich, spicy goo and to be frank this sauce is so strong that – were it not for the obvious claw shapes – you could be eating almost anything.

£25–£40

La Spighetta

43 Blandford St, W1 ©020 7486 7340	⊖ Bond Street/Baker Street
Mon–Fri noon–2.15pm & 6.30–10.30pm,	
Sat noon–2.15pm & 6.30–11pm, Sun 6.30–10.30pm	Amex, Mastercard, Visa

Walk past La Spighetta and you could be forgiven for thinking that this is the least popular small pizza and pasta joint in London. You will see five or six tables, generally deserted, and you'll be lucky if there is a member of staff within sight. But venture inside and down the stairs and you will discover a large basement restaurant buzzing with activity. At lunchtime there is the Marylebone office crowd (advertising, Marks & Spencer staff); at dinner it's more local (young professionals). The decor is more practical than elegant, with bare table tops, terracotta and cream walls, and banquette seating, while the kitchens are open-plan, with a magnificent pizza oven dominating the room. But it's the food – well cooked and well priced – that you're here for.

Even if you had planned to drop in for just a bowl of pasta, it's worth considering La Spighetta's first courses. Carpaccio di spada affumicato con insalata di finocchi al limone (£6.50) is a light, fresh and simple dish of smoked swordfish, while mozzarella di bufala con melanzane grigliate (£6) reminds you what mozzarella really can taste like. A smallish choice of pastas and a full list of pizzas follow, alongside some main courses. But the pastas and pizzas are so good that you'd be advised to stick to them. Especially good are the linguine alle vongole e peperoncino (£7.50), which is dressed with fine olive oil and actually tastes of clams, and the tagliatelle di castagne con funghi ed erbe (£7.50), a flavoursome chestnut pasta. Pizza Napoli (£7) really tastes of tomato, anchovies and capers, while the chef's pizza (£8) is a well-judged combination of mozzarella, rocket, fresh tomato, Parmesan and Parma ham. The other mains are standard Italian restaurant fare – fegato di vitello con zucchine brasate all erbe (£9.50), say, or tonno alla griglia con rucola e pomodoro (£9.50). Puddings are classics and workmanlike. If you have room, try the tiramisù (£6).

La Spighetta is the perfect local pizza and pasta joint – simple food at sensible prices, a good buzz most times of night, and no real need to book. If it has a fault, it's that the service is a bit rushed and can be forgetful. But at these prices, that's hardly a gripe.

Woodlands

77 Marylebone Lane, W1 ✆020 7486 3862   ⊖ Bond Street

Daily noon–2.30pm & 6–10.30pm   All major credit cards

The Marylebone Lane branch of this South Indian vegetarian restaurant group has been trading for some years, ignored by many locals simply because of the vegetarian tag – but adored by all those who have been through the doors. The interior is rather classier than most local Indian restaurants, with simply decorated white walls, adorned with a few Indian artefacts, and a huge skylight rendering electric light unnecessary during the day. Large tables are built for comfort rather than practicality, giving diners plenty of room for their food, but making it very awkward to get in and out without disturbing the table next door. There are more Asian faces in this restaurant than English, and even on a Monday lunchtime the room is filled with chatter and laughter. Other branches at 37 Panton St, SW1 (✆020 7839 7258) and 402a High Rd, Wembley (✆020 8902 9869).

The food is as dramatic to look at as it is delicious to eat. Kick off with a masala dosa (£4.25), a great cone of pancake resembling nothing so much as a nun's wimple, with a well-spiced potato and onion filling, served with an excellent coconut chutney and sambar. Or try the tomato and onion uthappam (£3.95), an Indian version of a pizza made with lentils. Follow it with a thali – the mini thali (£9.95) includes all that you are likely to want, and the price includes a popadom and dessert; the Delhi royal thali (£10.95) offers even more. The breads are well made, especially the chappati (£1.95 for two) and the lachadar paratha (£2.95 for two), and if you can possibly manage it you should leave room for pudding. The jaggary dosa (£2.75) is sweet-toothed heaven and the gajjar halwa (£2.75) is better than most.

Service is very helpful, and if you don't really know your way around South Indian food they will help you get your bearings. If you ask for guidance they won't let you order too much or eat things in the wrong order. It is also an ideal place to take someone who has dietary difficulties, as ingredients used here are generally obvious and, if you have doubts about the suitability of a dish for a wheat, nut or even dairy allergy, the staff will generally know the answer.

The Golden Eagle

59 Marylebone Lane, W1   ℅020 7935 3228

A tiny, well-kept Free House with a cosy feel. Brakspear's Bitter, Shepherd Neame and Fuller's London Pride are the favourite draughts. Live piano on Thursday and Friday.

The O'Conor Don

88 Marylebone Lane, W2   ℅020 7935 9311

Newly refurbished, but sympathetically, this is probably the oldest of London's Irish pubs. Guinness, Extra Cold Guinness and Harp lager brewed in Ireland are on offer here, as well as a good selection of Irish whiskeys. It purports to offer a real Irish atmosphere as well.

The Pontefract Castle

71 Wigmore St, W2   ℅020 7486 4941

Lively, modern pub on three floors. The first and second have the feel of a mezzanine balcony, and there's an additional cellar for private parties. Big-screen sport, a spiral staircase and a young, enthusiastic crowd make it noisy and fun. Grolsch, Staropramen and Caffrey's on tap.

The Prince Regent

71 Marylebone High St, W1   no phone

Situated on a corner, with big picture windows, this bright pub combines the best of the old and new, with wooden floors and brass inside, and aluminium cafe tables on the pavement outside. A mixed crowd drinks Caffrey's, Fuller's London Pride, Grolsch and Staropramen on draught.

The William Wallace

44 Blandford St, W1   ℅020 7935 5963

Stained-glass leaded windows and a mock Tudor theme make this pub stand out, and with McEwans 80/-, 70/-, and Deuchars Caledonian IPA on offer you will detect a slight Scottish feel. For the record, the 70/- and 80/- stand for the cost per bushel of barley that the beer was brewed from.

Zoe

St Christopher's Place,
3–5 Barrett St, W1   ℅020 7224 1122

A brightly coloured cocktail bar that opens onto the Barrett Street piazza. Bottled beers, wines and half-price Happy Hour (5.30–7pm) cocktails attract the young Selfridges shoppers; later in the evening, a sophisticated clubber crowd gathers. There are pavement tables with overhead heaters.

Mayfair
& Bond Street

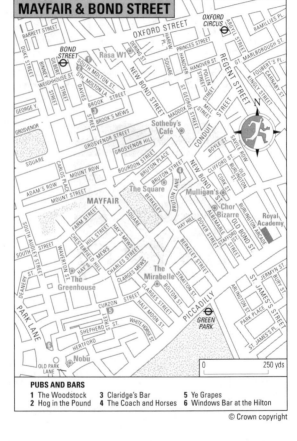

MAYFAIR & BOND STREET

PUBS AND BARS

1 The Woodstock
2 Hog in the Pound
3 Claridge's Bar
4 The Coach and Horses
5 Ye Grapes
6 Windows Bar at the Hilton

© Crown copyright

Chor Bizarre

16 Albemarle St, W1 ©020 7629 9802 or 8542   ⊖ Green Park

Mon–Sat noon–3pm & 6–11.30pm, Sun 6–10.30pm   All major credit cards

Chor Bizarre is something of a novelty in London as one of a handful of Indian restaurants that has a "head office" in India. Indeed the London Chor Bizarre is a straight copy of the one in the Broadway Hotel in Delhi. Its name is an elaborate pun (Chor Bazaar translates as "thieves' market") and, like the Delhi branch, the London restaurant is furnished with an amazing clutter of Indian antiques and bric-a-brac. Every table, and each set of chairs, is different and you may find yourself dining within the frame of an antique four-poster bed. The food is similarly eccentric, but very well prepared and strikingly authentic. Care is taken over the detail, and wine expert Charles Metcalfe has devised a striking wine list. Chor Bizarre does, however, carry the kind of price tag you'd expect of Mayfair.

Start with simple things such as pakoras (£4.50), which are tasty vegetable fritters, or samosas (£4.50), which are fresh, full of potato and peas, and served with fine accompanying chutneys. Kebabs are taken seriously here, too: gilawat ke kebab (£6) is a Lucknow speciality made with lamb. Gazab ka tikka (£11), a best-seller in Delhi, is a kind of chicken tikka de luxe. Then, for your main course, choose dishes like baghare baingan (£8), a Hyderabadi dish combining aubergine, peanuts and tamarind. Or one of the dum pukht dishes, where the food is cooked slowly in a sealed pot – the chooza dum pukht (£14) is made with chicken. Breads are also impressive, including an excellent naan (£2.50), pudina paratha (£2.75), which is a mint paratha, and stuffed kulcha (£2.75) – choose from cheese, potato or mince.

The many imposing set menus are a good way to tour the menu without watching your wallet implode. South Indian Tiffin (£24) features chicken Chettinad, Kerala prawn, porial, and sambal, served with rice and Malabari parathas on a banana leaf. Kashmiri tarami (£24) is a copper platter with goshtaba, mirchi korma, rajmah, al Yakhni, tamatar chaaman and nadru haaq on rice, preceded by a starter of dry-cooked lamb ribs. Or there is the Royal Repast (£24, or £22 vegetarian) – two starters, one item from the tandoor, two non-vegetarian main courses, three vegetarian mains, two breads, rice, two desserts and coffee!

£20–£45

The Greenhouse

27a Hay's Mews, W1 ℂ020 7499 3331	⊖ Green Park
Mon–Fri noon–2.30pm & 6.30–11pm, Sat 6.30–11pm,	
Sun noon–3pm & 6.30–10pm	All major credit cards

www.capitalgrp.co.uk

Make your way down an alleyway, just around the corner from the cabbies' favourite Mayfair petrol stop, and you find yourself walking under a long canopy into the reception of The Greenhouse. For somewhere located on the ground floor of a rather nasty Mayfair apartment block, this is a remarkably attractive restaurant. The room has a light, spacious feel and the gardening theme is brought home with topiary bushes, flowerpots and picture windows. It's all classic, country English – stable and a little staid, but undeniably well done. And in 1999 the Michelin-bespangled Paul Merrett took over as head chef.

The Greenhouse offers a good-value lunch at £19.50 for two courses, £22.50 for three, which might comprise potage of potato, bacon and cabbage followed by John Dory, pork, or salt cod fish cakes, and a choice of three desserts. Ordering from the carte brings more ambitious starters, like terrine of salmon with field mushrooms, potato, caper and saffron vinaigrette (£10.50), or cream of Puy lentil and smoked bacon with sautéed foie gras (£9.50), or perhaps herb-crusted goats' cheese on vinaigrette of wild mushrooms (£10.50). Main courses rely on top-quality ingredients and are seasonally inspired, but Merrett has brought a whiff of exoticism to the seasoning and spicing – roast fillet of beef on crisp noodles and bok choi with a miso and coriander broth (£18.50), pan-fried sea bass on sag aloo, onion bhajee, tomato pickle (£18.50), roasted rump of lamb on sweet potatoes, with smoked aubergine and a spiced roasted pepper and pine nut jus (£18.50). And then there are more classical dishes, like roast fillet of hare on braised cabbage with celeriac cream (£18.50), or pot-au-feu of black-leg chicken with root vegetables, smoked bacon and bone marrow dumplings (£18.50). Puddings follow the same principles: apple and blackberry pie with custard contrasts with baked rice pudding, spiced apple mash and butterscotch sauce (all at £7).

There's a "semi-traditional" three-course Sunday lunch for £22.50. The Greenhouse proprietors are Mr and Mrs Levin, and suitably enough they offer as house wine Le Vin de Levin – very drinkable, and excellent value at £13.25.

The Mirabelle

56 Curzon St, W1 ©020 7499 4636	⊖ Green Park
Mon–Fri noon–2.30pm & 6–11.30pm, Sat & Sun 6–10.30pm	All major credit cards

Anyone hoping to open their own restaurant should have lunch at The Mirabelle. It's not just the touch of Marco Pierre White (London's own culinary Rasputin); the whole operation is superlative. Forgive them the mind-numbingly arrogant and extensive wine list – which climaxes with an 1847 vintage Chateau d'Yquem at £30,000 – and concentrate on the food, which is quite reasonably priced for such haute cuisine. The ingredients are carefully chosen. The presentation on the plate is stunning. The surroundings are elegant, and the service attentive. There's a very elegant bar, too, which really does invite a pause for a drink before and maybe after a meal. Go on, splash out – it truly is worth it.

Start with a classic – omelette "Arnold Bennett" (£8.95). It's no wonder that Arnold liked these so much – they're rich, buttery and light, made with smoked haddock. Or there's Bayonne ham with celeriac rémoulade (£10.50). Or a risotto of saffron Milanaise (£8.50). Step up a level for some triumphant foie gras "en terrine" dishes: with green peppercorns, gelée de Sauternes, and toasted brioche (£16.95), or "parfait en gelée" with toasted Poilane bread (£8.95). Believe it or not these two are actually bargains. For a fishy main course, how about fillet of red mullet, ratatouille Provençale, and sauce tapenade (£14.50)? Or the classical grilled Dover sole served on the bone with sauce tartare and Jersey royals (£25). In the meat section there's braised pork cheeks with spices and fresh ginger, and étuvée of spring vegetables (£13.50). Or there is calves' liver and bacon (£14.50), or an Aberdeen Angus ribeye with fresh snails, pommes frites and sauce Béarnaise (£15.50). Puddings (all at £7.50) are deftly handled. The star is chocolate fondant with bitter chocolate sorbet.

Choose the set lunch, and don't let the wine list sneak up on you (there's a decent enough Montes Sauvignon Blanc for £16), and you could be enjoying a fine meal of salade frisée Lyonnaise, pajarski of wild salmon with sorrel, lemon tart, and finally coffee, for a very reasonable price. Three courses go for £17.95, two courses £14.95 (both 45p cheaper on Sundays). It's a steal.

£24–£45

Mulligan's

13–14 Cork St, W1 ©020 7409 1370	⊖ Piccadilly Circus
Mon–Fri noon–3pm & 6.30–9.30pm, Sat 6.30–9.30pm	All major credit cards

You could be forgiven for overlooking the downstairs restaurant at Mulligan's, as the upstairs bar is inviting and lively. But squeeze down the narrow spiral staircase at the front and you find a calm haven of white tablecloths. Mulligan's styles itself as a restaurant with a pronounced Irish flavour rather than as an Irish restaurant. Dishes veer towards the modern rather than traditional, and have been adapted for a cosmopolitan palate. More business-crowd at lunchtime, it livens up in the evenings with devotees out for the craic.

There is a seasonally changing and seasonally inspired à la carte menu. Starters may include black- and white-pudding tart, poached egg and crispy red onions (£4.50); pressed rabbit and wood pigeon terrine with kumquat marmalade (£6.25); or perhaps a salad of Dublin Bay prawns, lamb's leaf lettuce and papaya (£6.90). Main courses feature dishes like traditional Irish stew with pickled red cabbage (£9.95), Irish beef fillets with pink peppercorn mash and green beans (£15.50), fillet of haddock with crispy potatoes and rosemary-roasted cherry tomatoes (£13) and roast breast of pheasant stuffed with walnut mousse and redcurrant jus (£14). Puddings include lemon tart with orange sorbet (£4.50), gooseberry crumble with cream (£4.50), and a rather un-Irish hot chocolate fudge brownie with chocolate and toffee sauce (£4.75). A sound option is cheese – Cashel blue, Porter cheddar, and Ardrahan with grape chutney and biscuits (£4.95). Wines range from the mid-priced to the dear; there will be few surprises for any stray regulars from Balls Brothers wine bars, as Balls Brothers own Mulligan's and they share the list.

Ingredients at Mulligan's are sourced from Ireland when possible, and service has a friendly charm and disdain for time. The upstairs offers oysters throughout the year – rock oysters from Strangford Lough with house dressings (£7.90/£14.80) or oysters Kilpatrick (£8.50/£16), and the only draught beer is – yes, you guessed it – Guinness. But Mulligan's is also a must if you're an Irish whiskey fan. They boast 23 different types, from the run-of-the-mill to the old and rare at £7.50 a tot – and not a drop of Scotch.

£30–£95

Nobu

19 Old Park Lane, W1 ©020 7447 4747	⊖ Hyde Park Corner
Mon–Fri noon–2.15pm & 6–10.30pm, Sat 6–10.30pm	All major credit cards

It's hard to know just what to make of Nobu. On the face of it, a restaurant owned by Robert de Niro, Drew Nieporent and Matsuhisa Nobuyuki sounds like the invention of a deranged Hollywood producer. And then there is the cocoon of hype: the restaurant is exclusive, it's within the mega-cool Metropolitan hotel, it's amazingly expensive, it's full of famous people. As is often the case with hype, some of the above is gossip and some is gospel, but which is which? Don't worry about it: concentrate on the food, which is innovative and superb. Ingredients are fresh. Flavour combinations are novel and inspired. Presentation is elegant and stylish. See for yourself – breeze in for the lunchtime bento box, which includes sashimi salad, rock shrimp tempura, black cod, oshitashi, vegetable spicy garlic, assorted sushi and miso soup, all for £25.

Chef Matsuhisa worked for many years in Peru, and South American flavours and techniques segue into classical Japanese dishes – some of the dishes here puzzle even stalwart Japanese foodies and certainly defy classification. There are lists of Nobu "special appetisers" and "special dishes"; the problem is where to begin. Tiradito "Nobu" style (£10.50) is a plate of wafer-thin scallop slices, each topped with a dab of chilli, half a coriander leaf and a citrus dressing (£10.50) – delicate and utterly delicious. The sashimi is terrific; salmon is sliced and just warmed through to "set" it before being served with sesame seeds (£10) – the minimal cooking makes for a superb texture. The black cod with miso (£19.50) is a grandstand dish – a piece of perfectly cooked, well-marinated fish presented with an elaborate banana-leaf canopy. Other inspired dishes are the rock shrimp tempura (£8.75), and the dessert spring roll full of chocolate goo.

Nobu is probably the only place in London where none of the customers fully understands the menu. No one on their first visit could hope to make sense of it. For once it is no cop-out to opt for the omakase (or chef's choice) menu, which costs £70 in the evenings and £40 at lunchtime. Do not be intimidated, book your table well in advance and settle back for a really stunning and unusual gastronomic experience.

£12–£40

Rasa W1

6 Dering St, W1 ©020 7629 1346 ⊖ Bond Street

Mon–Sat noon–3pm & 6–11pm, Sun 6–11pm · All major credit cards

Rasa W1 is a multiple contradiction: a Keralan restaurant that is pricey, elegant, fashionable, upmarket, and still strictly vegetarian. When they opened in 1998, the management proudly claimed that this was the only non-smoking Indian restaurant in Britain. Rasa is a place completely at ease with itself and with good reason – this is an off-shoot of the hugely successful Rasa in Stoke Newington (p.332), and it continues the tradition of superb cooking and friendly service that has kept North London diners blissfully happy for the last few years. The menu is littered with unfamiliar and homely dishes and they are all worth investigation. Lean heavily on the sound advice available.

Start with the pre-meal snacks (£4) and you will never be satisfied by a few curling popadoms again. Five different variations on the popadom theme are accompanied by seven fresh chutneys. Of the snacks, the acchappam is a fascinating three-dimensional honeycomb affair, while the chena upperi are root vegetable crisps. The chutneys, too, are stunning – there's a garlic pickle of genuine virulence and what is described by Das the proprietor as "Mum's special" – a terrific concoction made from sharp green mangoes. Don't miss these. Highlights on the starters menu are banana boli (£4.25) – deep-fried plantain fritters; Mysore bonda (£4.25) – potato, ginger and curry-leaf cakes; and cashew nut pakoda (£4.25) – a kind of peanut brittle made with cashews. With the main courses (which in the evenings are served the traditional way, on banana leaves), try as many of the different rices as possible: tamarind, lemon and coconut (all £3.75). The curries are fascinating and unusual. Cheera parippu curry (£6.25) is made with spinach, toor dall, garlic cheese and tomatoes; bagar baingan (£6.25) is rich with aubergines; moru kachiathu (£6.25) is an unusual combination of sweet mangoes and green bananas. Also look out for the nadan parippu (£6), which is a Keralan lentil curry.

Going for the set menu often seems like an easy option, but this is one place where you'd be foolish not to consider it. The Kerala feast costs a not insubstantial £22.50 a head, but brings waves of dishes, each one seemingly better than the last. There are also likely to be a few off-menu delights – Mum's specials – which really *are* special.

Sotheby's Café

34–35 New Bond St, W1 ©020 7293 5077	⊖ Bond Street
Mon–Fri 9.30–11.30am, noon–3pm & 3–4.45pm (tea)	All major credit cards

If you like the idea of eating in an art collection attached to a famous auction house, and rubbing shoulders with international art dealers and collectors, you will enjoy Sotheby's Café. Quintessentially English, it manages to retain an air of peace despite being sited on one side of the main hall of Sotheby's. For once, mumblings about an oasis of calm are entirely appropriate. The Café is also that rarity among London restaurants nowadays – a place where you can get a proper English afternoon tea.

The lunch menu is short and changes daily with seasonal variations. Warm asparagus with citrus butter (£5.95) is very fresh and there's a good tang of lemon in the butter, while the Vichyssoise (£4.50) is smooth, creamy and subtle. Grilled cod with warm salad of cannellini beans, leeks, radicchio and citrus dressing (£12.95) is delicate – and the accompaniments do not overpower the very fresh and just-cooked cod. Lobster club sandwich (£10.55) makes for an ideal light lunch, the large chunks of fresh lobster served in a club sandwich with fresh mayonnaise but has proved so popular that it's worth ordering it in advance. Puddings include strawberry ice cream, fresh strawberries and lemon biscuits (£4.50) and a delightfully fresh-tasting pear and almond tart with clotted cream (£4.50). There is also a large range of teas, herbal teas and other infusions. Wines are chosen by Serena Sutcliffe, who runs Sotheby's wine auction department, and are well suited to the dishes that they accompany.

For afternoon tea you can choose dishes like Welsh rarebit (£4.25), Dumfries smoked salmon with brown bread (£7.25), and chicken club sandwich (£6.50). There are also set tea menus at £4.95 and £9.90; the latter includes cucumber and ham and egg sandwiches and home-made cakes. Breakfast extends to Scottish smoked salmon and scrambled eggs with toast (£7.25), but sadly no bacon and eggs. Whatever time of day, visitors who come just for the food are made very welcome – there's no pressure to feel that you need to go home with a paperweight or an old master. However, in keeping with the reverential atmosphere, a notice whispers "please, no smoking or mobile phones".

£25–£110

The Square

6–10 Bruton St, W1 ⓒ020 7795 7100   ⊖ Green Park

Mon–Fri noon–3pm & 7–11pm, Sat 6.30–11pm,

Sun 6.30–10pm   All major credit cards

Hooray! Finally The Square gets into this, the third edition of the guide. A recent change in the way that they do things means that you can try Phillip Howard's astonishingly good food for under £35 a head, and we can include this excellent restaurant among our selections. Formerly there was a serious à la carte menu in the evening and a separate (and equally serious) à la carte at lunch. Now the main menu is available at both lunch and dinner and a special set lunch menu offers two choices for each course at the bargain price of £20 for two courses and £25 for three. This makes the kitchen's life a little easier – no switching from menu to menu – and the customer's life happier – a stunning cheap lunch *and* the full Monty available at lunchtime. The new system also gives Phillip Howard the chance to try out dishes before putting them on the main menu.

This is very serious restaurant. Service is suave, silent and effortless. Dishes use the very best seasonal produce. Seasoning is on the button. Presentation is elegant. The wine list seems boundless in scope and soars to the very topmost heights (where mortals dare not even ask the price). Go for lunch and experience real excellence. For £20 you might have Salade Niçoise with gulls' eggs, or a salmon and herb fish cake with samphire; followed by either crisp red mullet with pesto noodles and sauce vierge or roast chicken with truffle creamed potato. Add the extra fiver and go on to fondant of chocolate with white chocolate ice cream. In the evening three courses cost £45. You get to choose from nine starters – stand-outs are jelly of oysters and langoustine with sour cream caviar and cucumber; the velouté of truffles with wild mushroom tortellini and Parmesan; pea and ham soup with pig's trotter, morels and sweetbreads. Then nine mains, which may include loin of monkfish with a vinaigrette of shellfish and clam and anchovy beignet; roast halibut with pea purée, button onions and lardons; roast fillet of beef with a sauté of snails and foie gras. Howard is an able man and Michelin's two-star measure of his worth is an under-estimate. Dishes are deceptively simple, honest, and very, very good to eat.

There's also a six-course "taster" menu for £65 (for the entire table only). Book now. This is one treat you will never regret.

Claridge's Bar

Brook St, W1   ✆020 7629 8860

Refined and muted, this expensive venue is everything a luxury bar should be. The wonderful atmosphere, stylish deco design, attentive service, aristocratic nibbles and massive selection of wines, cocktails and spirits make it worth the cost. There's champagne at £200 a bottle if you're in the mood. Not a place for jeans and trainers.

The Coach & Horses

5 Bruton St, W1   ✆020 7629 4123

A tiny, island-site venue done out in mock Tudor outside and warm wood inside. Its quaint charm attracts lots of tourists, but a lively crowd of Bond Street shoppers and Mayfair locals crank up the accent a bit. Courage Directors. Closed on Sun.

Hog in the Pound

28 South Molton St, W1   ✆020 7493 7720

A big corner pub with pavement seating. It's a predominantly younger crowd of drinkers here, getting a few in after a hard day's serving people in the shops. You can get Courage Best and Directors, but it's more of a lager pub, with Fosters and Kronenbourg being the big hits.

Windows at the Hilton

London Hilton,
  22 Park Lane, W1   ✆020 7208 4021

Go early for a window table and enjoy the view from the highest bar in London. It's a good place for people-watching, too. There's a classic list of cocktails at around £8 a go and beers at £4, along with the usual hotel-style list of spirits. The resident pianist gives the place something of a 70s feel.

The Woodstock

11 Woodstock St, W1   ✆020 7408 2008

This small, traditional pub, just off Oxford Street, offers Abbot Ales, Theakston, guest beers and a good wine selection. It's comfortable and quiet, and an oasis of calm in this hectic area.

Ye Grapes

16 Shepherd Market, W1   ✆020 7499 1563

Established in 1882, this very picturesque Free House is a great place to stand and watch the world go by. With its country-pub atmosphere, it draws a mixed crowd who happily select from the Flowers IPA, Wadworth's 6X , Fuller's London Pride, Hoegaarden, Boddingtons and wide choice of other drinks.

Paddington &
Edgware Road

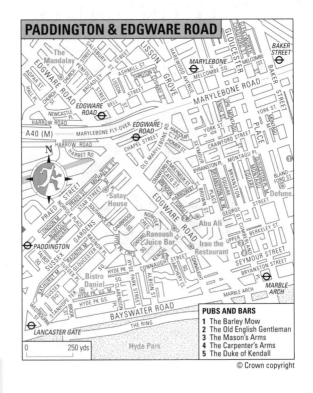

PADDINGTON & EDGWARE ROAD

PUBS AND BARS
1 The Barley Mow
2 The Old English Gentleman
3 The Mason's Arms
4 The Carpenter's Arms
5 The Duke of Kendall

© Crown copyright

0   250 yds

Hyde Park

CENTRAL

Abu Ali

136–138 George St, W1 ©020 7724 6338   ⊖ Marble Arch

Daily 9.30am–midnight   Cheque or cash only

You can only suppose that in the Lebanon going out to eat is man's work. That certainly seems to be the case around the Oxford Street end of the Edgware Road, where you'll find Abu Ali's bustling cafe. This is an authentic place: the Lebanese equivalent of a northern working man's club, a bit spartan in appearance, with honest, terrific-value food, and pavement tables, where men gather to smoke a pipe or two and discuss the world. Although you are unlikely to find many Lebanese women here, female diners get a dignified welcome. There's nothing intimidating about the place or its clientele.

You will want a selection of starters. Tabouleh (£2) is bright green with lots of fresh parsley, lemon juice, oil, and only a little cracked wheat – it even tastes healthy. Hommos (£2.50) is rich and spicy, garnished with a few whole chickpeas and Cayenne pepper. Warak inab (£3) are stuffed vine leaves served hot or cold, thin and pleasantly sour. Kabis is a plate of tangy salt and sour pickles – cucumber, chillies and red cabbage – that comes free with every order. For main dishes there's kafta billaban (£5.50) – minced lamb kebabs served hot under a layer of sharp yoghurt and with a sprinkling of pine kernels. Or there's kibbeh bissiniyeh (£5), which is a strange dish: a ball of mince and pine kernels coated with a layer of mince and cracked wheat, then baked until crispy in the oven. The plain grilled meats are also good: try the boned-out poussin – farrouge moussahab (£6). To drink, there is mint tea (£2) – a Lipton's teabag and a bunch of fresh mint in every pot – or soft drinks.

Inside and outside Abu Ali's, the air is full of the sweet scent of bubble pipes. They cost £5 a go, and you can have either apple or strawberry. The long strands of black tobacco are mixed into a squelchy mess with chopped fruit and then covered with a piece of foil, on top of which is placed a chunk of blazing charcoal – you are on your way to clouds of sweet-smelling smoke. Some of the cognoscenti take this procedure a step further and replace the water through which the smoke bubbles with ice and Appletise. It certainly makes for a perfumed environment from which to watch the world go by.

£15–£50

Bistro Daniel

26 Sussex Place, W2 ©020 7723 8395   ⊖ Paddington

Mon–Fri noon–2.30pm & 6.30–10.30pm,

Sat 7–10pm   All major credit cards except Diners

Bistro Daniel is the baby brother of Daniel Gobet's smarter restaurant, Amandier. The bistro occupies the basement while the restaurant is on the ground floor. Both are dedicated to French gastronomy with a Provençal bias and they share the same kitchen. Daniel served in the kitchens of Mon Plaisir before opening his own place, La Ciboulette in Chelsea, which gained an enviable reputation in a very short space of time. Both establishments were resolutely French; Bistro Daniel, while offering accomplished cooking, introduces some less traditional touches. It is an informal restaurant and the cool basement makes for an intimate atmosphere.

Starters include salade of Cabécou cheese (£4.70), which is a Brie-like goats' cheese, lightly grilled and runny; feuillete of snails with garlic butter sauce (£5.30); a rich and dark crab and fish soup, with creamy rouille and croutons (£4.95), and gnocchi with tomato pistou sauce (£4.70). Main courses include blanquette of veal, basmati rice and tarragon sauce (£10.90) – light but satisfying with a tart yet creamy sauce. There's also bouillabaisse des Calanques rouilles (£11.50); confit of duck leg with Puy lentils (£11.50); pan-fried scallops with tagliatelle and garlic parsley butter sauce (£11.50); and pan-fried salmon with Puy lentils (£10.80), which is crisp on the outside and just cooked inside. Side dishes of gratin Dauphinoise, pommes frites, and carrots with cumin seeeds (all £2) are generous and tasty. Puddings include nougat glacé (£4.50), banana and coconut tartlette (£4.50), and chocolate brownie (£4.50).

Bistro Daniel shares a wine list with the Amandier restaurant upstairs. So you can venture all the way from sensible to serious; listed here are wines as grand as Bâtard Montrachet Grand Cru for £110 or even a Château Latour at £350 if the fancy takes you and your wallet concurs. There's a daily set lunch at £9.95 for two courses and £12.95 for three – an economical way to taste the sophisticated dishes of Amandier.

Defune

61 Blandford St, W1 ℂ020 7935 8311	⊖ Marble Arch
Mon–Sat noon–2.30pm & 6–10.30pm	All major credit cards

For a restaurant renowned for serving some of London's best sushi, Defune is a remarkably unpretentious place – the elderly bar stools, Formica counter and Japanese rock music in the background give no clues as to the quality of the food. The bill, on the other hand, does. Defune serves exceedingly grown-up sushi and if you are a novice you would be well advised to go and practise somewhere that is rather cheaper. When you're ready for Defune, sit at the midpoint of the counter and watch the two sushi chefs pirouette from fish to fish. This is great theatre, as they present the sushi portions to diners with a synchronised exclamation – "Hai!" (Don't make the mistake of putting your beer on the top ledge of the counter as the sushi is served straight onto it.) Pour a little soya sauce from the elegant china flagon into the saucer in front of you; add as much of the super-fiery wasabi as you like, then take your wooden chopsticks, dip the piece of sushi in the sauce and eat it. There are usually two pieces per portion. In between sushi, clean the palate with a morsel of the gari – pickled ginger – which is also plonked on the counter. It is unreservedly delicious.

Start by asking to see the sushi menu, which is a look-and-point series of pictures with prices, then off you go. Sake (salmon; £4.80) is rich and smooth; if you like smoked salmon you'll like this. Maguro (tuna; £5) is meaty in texture. Ebi (cooked shrimp; £4.80) are rather bland, but amaebi (raw sweet shrimp; £7.20) áre delicious. Anago (eel; £7.20) rather surprisingly comes hot off the grill and with a special sauce, while the suzuki (sea bass; £4.80) is fresh-tasting and the hotate (fresh scallops; £6.20) are splendidly sweet. Maki toro is a roll sushi, made from fine scrapings of tuna meat from just beneath the skin and served up with pickles (£4.80).

Some of the sushi are a touch more testing. Uni (£8.20), which is sea urchin either from Iceland or Chile – there's a subtle difference in taste – is one of the most extraordinary textures you'll ever encounter. Miru-gai, giant clam (£6.20) – beaten to death on the counter in front of you – combines an agreeable texture with a less agreeable taste.

CENTRAL

£19–£55

Iran the Restaurant

59 Edgware Rd, W2 ℂ020 7723 1344   ⊖ Marble Arch

Daily noon–midnight   All major credit cards

In comparison with the very basic cafes and very glitzy eateries that are its neighbours, Iran the Restaurant reeks of sophistication. The interior is not over-gaudy, the staff are helpful, and the food is simple, tasty and freshly cooked. It's difficult to put your finger on just what makes one restaurant hospitable and another merely acceptable, but at Iran the Restaurant they manage to put you completely at your ease, however unfamiliar the cuisine may be to you. But it is not a cheap night out – prices are better suited to sleek Middle Eastern wallets. You do pay for the largely considerate service – the portions are not huge; sometimes the better dishes run out; prices are West End; and there is a 15% service charge added – but all in all it is usually worth it.

The first thing to do is marvel at the bread chef. In pride of place is a special oven dedicated to making Iranian bread (£2), which is about the size of a tea towel, thin and chewy, and with crisp edges. It is full of perforations courtesy of a tool that looks like a cross between hedgehog and rolling pin. The oven is so hot that it cooks the bread in about 35 seconds. It is very, very good. Accompany it with some torshi litteh (£3.95) – mixed pickles. Plus halim bademjon (£3.95) – aubergines with dried yoghurt, fried onions and mint. The tapula salad (£3.95), a parsley-rich tabbouleh, is good, too. Borani is also tempting (£3.95), a tasty mix of spinach with fried onion and yoghurt. Go on to something from the grill. The lamb here is very well cooked and not greasy: kebab barg (£10.95), fillet with grilled tomato, and kebab koobideh (£9.95), minced lamb kebabs, stand out. Then there is a section of koresht dishes. At least one of you should order the koresht fesenjon (£11.95), a chicken dish with a delicious sauce made from walnuts, pumpkin and pomegranate. Vegetarians, or anyone who wants to accompany their grilled meats, can order a portion of this sauce on its own (£7.95).

If the wine list here were a car, it would be a Ferrari. It goes from Beaujolais Villages, Domain Soitel (£13.75), to Château Margaux 1981 (£444.50) in the space of just eight bottles.

The Mandalay

444 Edgware Rd, W2 ©020 7258 3696	⊖ Edgware Road
Mon–Sat noon–2.30pm & 6–10.30pm; closed bank holidays	All major credit cards

www.bcity.com/mandalay

In the Edgware Road desert – north of the Harrow Road but south of anything else – Gary and Dwight Ally, Scandinavian-educated Burmese brothers, have set up shop in what must be an ex-greasy spoon. The resulting restaurant is rather bizarre, with just 28 seats, the old sandwich counter filled with strange and exotic ingredients, and greetings and decoration in both Burmese and Norwegian. Gary is in the kitchen and smiley, talkative Dwight is front of house.

The Ally brothers have perhaps correctly concluded that their native language is unmasterable by the English, so the menu is written in English with a Burmese translation – an enormous help when ordering. But the food itself is pure unexpurgated Burmese and all freshly cooked. The local cuisine is a melange of different local influences, with a little bit of Thai and Malaysian and a lot of Indian, and a few things that are distinctly their own. To start there are popadoms (two for £1.20) or a great bowlful of prawn crackers (£1.90), which arrive freshly fried and sizzling hot (and served on domestic kitchen paper to soak up the oil). First courses range from spring rolls (from £1.90 for two), and samosas (£1.90 for four), to salads like raw papaya and cucumber (£3.90), or fermented tea leaf (£3.90), which is a great deal better than it sounds. There are soups, noodle soups and all manner of fritters as well. Main courses are mainly curries, rice and noodle dishes, with plenty of ginger, garlic, coriander and coconut, and using fish, chicken and vegetables as the main ingredients. The cooking is good, flavours hit the mark, portions are huge, and only a handful of dishes costs over £6.50. Vegetable dishes are somewhat more successful than the prawn ones, but at this price it's only to be expected.

Even with its eccentric setting, tiny room and rigorous no-smoking policy, The Mandalay has built up a loyal following over the years. The tables are minuscule and the acoustics are good, so be careful what you talk about and keep your ears open – you are just as likely to sit next to a dustman as an expat Burmese diamond dealer.

£5–£15

Ranoush Juice Bar

43 Edgware Rd, W2 ℂ020 7723 5929   ⊖ Marble Arch

Daily 9am–3am   Cheque and cash only

Ranoush is a Lebanese bar-style restaurant on busy Edgware Road, with counter service and room for just a few tables. The decor, which is all black marble and stainless steel, is smart, and whatever time of the day you pop in there will always be people queueing up for the superb array of vegetables and shawarma – the heir apparent to a doner kebab. After midnight the place buzzes, as clubbers and late-night revellers pile in to recharge their batteries. Towards the back, a juice bar serves up an impressive selection of freshly squeezed fruit drinks. This is the place to come for a superior takeaway; to sit down to a great-value meze; or to finish off a wild night by rehydrating with a timely belt of vitamins and minerals in a long, cool fruit juice.

Once inside, pay for your food at the till and take your receipt to the food counter. Ranoush's popular mixed meze (£9) is a generous plate piled high with six different portions of goodies. You can take your pick from wonderfully fresh offerings, which usually include mousakaa bizeit (fried aubergine cooked with tomato sauce, onions and chickpeas), batata harra (cubes of potatoes fried with garlic and coriander), sambousek (pastry filled with minced meat and pine kernels), pickles, Lebanese salad, hummus and falafel. Round it off with a helping of lamb or chicken – both moist and piping hot. If you haven't got the appetite for such a feast, you might go for a straightforward chicken shawarma (£3), served with just the right amount of relish and tomatoes – absolutely delicious. Then there are the sweet pastries – a whole counter devoted to baklawa and the like. Especially good are the lady fingers, small cubes of almond pastry (four for £1).

Ranoush isn't licensed, but you're unlikely to hanker after booze once you've tasted their juices. The freshly squeezed banana, mango, melon and pineapple varieties (£1.50) are all good, but the king of the range is the Ranoush fruit cocktail (£1.75). This is a creamy, refreshing blend of all of the above, and will send you singing into the night, however washed up and partied out you felt upon arrival.

Satay House

13 Sale Place, W2 ©020 7723 6763	⊖ Paddington
Daily noon–3pm & 6–11pm	All major credit cards

Why is it that starters always seem to have the edge on main courses? This depressingly accurate rule of thumb can be explained in part by the fact that you get to the starters first – when your appetite is still a contender. The Satay House breaks this rule. Here the starters are pretty pedestrian and the satay, for which the establishment was named, particularly ordinary. But do not be downcast, for the main courses are spectacularly good. Simply adjust your expectations and ordering policy to suit. This is also one of the few Malaysian restaurants in London that is actually Malaysian-run (most are owned by Chinese restaurateurs cashing in on something new), and in consequence the Satay House attracts a knowledgeable Malaysian clientele. Service is friendly, and the light, bright dining room is usually full.

Order the satay (£4.80 for six sticks) if you must – the sauce is chunky but under-seasoned. It's much better to make a start elsewhere on the menu, perhaps with a murtabak (£5) off the bread list; this is an eggy Malaysian bread wrapped around minced meat and served like a small plump pillow, with bright orange, sweet pickled onions – it is very delicious indeed and the onions have an almost addictive quality. Continue with nasi lemak (£6.50), rice cooked in coconut milk topped with crisp whole peanuts, still in their little red jackets, and slivers of deep-fried anchovy. You could also go for one of the excellent noodle dishes – mee, mee hoon, or kway teow goreng (£5) – with meat, prawns, egg and vegetables. Among the main dishes, standouts include the rendang daging (£6) – beef cooked for days and served almost dry but spectacularly tender – and the ayam goreng beriada (£5.20) – chicken pieces on the bone covered in chilli paste and fried. Try some specials, too: an order of sambal belacan (£2.90) produces fiercely salty and fishy chillies, fish paste and cucumber. Cincalok (£2.50) brings you shrimps in a fiery sauce from Malacca.

The Malaysian customers drink odd fluorescent-coloured drinks made from sugar cane, or soya beans, or lychees, or guava, or else dark brown tea with condensed milk and ice. Happy experimenting.

The Barley Mow

8 Dorset St, W1 ©020 7935 7318

This classic old pub, built in 1791, offers a cosy panelled interior with Adnams, Tetley's, and Marstons Pedigree among others. Snug booths open directly onto the bar. It's a favourite among advertising folk.

The Carpenter's Arms

12 Seymour Place, W1 ©020 7723 1050

Very popular and friendly Free House with Caledonian 80/- Ale, Websters Yorkshire Bitter and a good selection of whiskies. In addition there's Stonehenge Best Bitter and Fuller's London Pride. Spirit doubles are £1.70. It's young and very lively – not a place for a quiet drink.

The Duke of Kendall

38 Connaught St, W2 ©020 7723 8478

A comfortable neighbourhood local, this narrow corner triangular pub has a warm, family atmosphere. In addition to favourite ales like Theakston's Bitter, John Smith's and Beck's on draught, they do a decent house champagne for a mere £15.35.

The Mason's Arms

51 Upper Berkeley St, W1 ©020 7723 2131

The cellars of this historic pub were used to house prisoners before they were taken to Tyburn (now Marble Arch) to be hanged. Today they make an excellent place to keep the Badger Brewery's IPA, Tanglefoot and Champion ales.

The Old English Gentleman

132 Edgware Rd, W2 ©020 7723 6433

Festooned with greenery and fringed with pavement tables, this roomy Free House has old-world charm and eccentric decor. Ales on tap include Shepherd Neame's Spitfire and Czech Budweiser Budvar.

Piccadilly
& St James's

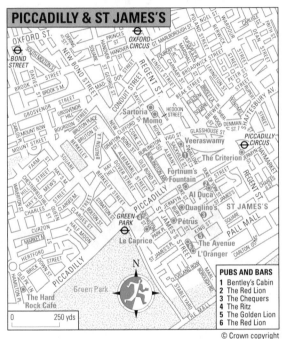

PICCADILLY & ST JAMES'S

PUBS AND BARS
1 Bentley's Cabin
2 The Red Lion
3 The Chequers
4 The Ritz
5 The Golden Lion
6 The Red Lion

© Crown copyright

The Avenue

7–9 St James's St, SW1 ©020 7321 2111	⊖ Green Park
Mon–Thurs noon–3pm & 5.45pm–midnight, Fri & Sat noon–3pm	
& 5.45pm–12.30am, Sun noon–3.30pm & 7–10.30pm	All major credit cards
www.theavenue.co.uk	

The Avenue was one of the first banker-led restaurants in London – owner Chris Bodker got a bunch of City chums to join him in setting up the kind of restaurant where he and they would choose to eat. The result is a stark yet stylish barn of a place, with white walls and pale cherry-wood chairs, and an enormous video wall of moving images around the bar seating area. Entrance is through a glass door, part of a great glass plate fronting the restaurant, and greeting is by designer-clad hosts. Inside it's very noisy, with a really upbeat atmosphere. There is not much subtlety about this place – wear your choicest clobber to feel most at home and do not be afraid to gawp.

Cooking is well executed and the menu is a fashionable mix of English and Italian. First courses are generally salads and pastas: tomato and mozzarella salad (£5.95), gravlax with spinach and mustard salad (£6.50), or a leek and truffle cheese tortellini (£6.25/£11), offered in two sizes to give more choice to vegetarians, who may otherwise feel the choice here is a little cramped. Main courses are generally more substantial, and lean towards nursery food: fish fingers (£11.75), smoked haddock fish cake with mustard sauce (£12.95), or calves' liver with lentils and Tuscan salami (£15), which is a posh liver and bacon with mash. Anyone watching their weight might like to try the rare seared tuna with red onion and parsley salad (£15.50). And for those with a traditionalist bent there's pork loin and belly with parsnip mash (£14.95). Puddings – white chocolate "cannelloni" with mixed berries (£5.75), lemon curd cheesecake (£5.75) and sticky toffee pudding with cream (£5.75) – are generally unchallenging, and will appeal to those with a seriously sweet tooth.

The Avenue is huge, so even if you haven't booked it's likely you'll get a table for dinner. Call to check if there have been any cancellations. At lunchtime there's a good set menu at £17.50/£19.50 for two/three courses; the same menu is available pre- or post-theatre (5.45–7.30pm and 10.15pm–midnight) at £14.50/£16.50.

£25–£55

Le Caprice

Arlington House, Arlington St, SW1 ✆020 7629 2239   ⊖ Green Park

Daily noon–3pm (Sun 4pm) & 5.30pm–midnight   All major credit cards

No socialite in London worth their salt is not a regular at this deeply chic little restaurant behind the Ritz – everyone from royalty downwards uses it for the occasional quiet lunch or dinner. That's not because they'll be hounded by well-wishers or because photographers will be waiting outside. They won't. This restaurant is discreet enough to make an oyster seem a blabbermouth. It's not even particularly plush or comfortable, with black-and-white tiled floor, big black bar, and cane seats. What keeps Le Caprice full day in, day out is its personal service, its very good, properly prepared food . . . and a bill that holds no surprises.

The much-copied menu is enticing from the first moment. Plum tomato and basil galette (£6.75) is simplicity itself, but with decent ingredients that taste of what they should. Crispy duck comes with watercress salad (£8.75); dressed Cornish crab with landcress (£13.75) is so fresh and clean it makes you wonder why other restaurants can't manage this. In season there's usually game, such as a grouse salad with elderberries (£13.50) – perfectly hung breast of grouse with tender salad leaves. Or perhaps char-grilled squid with Italian bacon (£13.50) tempts; or char-grilled ribeye steak with fried onion rings and herb butter (£18.75); or deep-fried haddock with minted pea purée, chips and tartare sauce (£14.75). If you are still up for pudding, try the sherry trifle with summer fruits (£5.75) or the blackberry summer pudding (£6.50) to see just what classic English puds are about. In the winter there is an array of more solid rib-stickers.

Expense aside, the only trouble with Le Caprice is the struggle to get a table. It is so permanently booked up that they only really accept reservations from people they know, or people who book well in advance. If you are able to plan far enough ahead, you should go just for the experience, otherwise you'll have to befriend a regular. But this has its advantages, too. The fly-by-night fashion people won't be found here and it's almost too chic and grown-up to find hip designer wear. All you need to look the part is a Continental tan, a little jewellery, Italian clothes, and a few old-fashioned laughter lines.

The Criterion Brasserie

224 Piccadilly, W1 ©020 7930 0488	⊖ Piccadilly Circus

Mon–Sat noon–2.30pm & 6–11pm,

Sun noon–3pm & 6–10.30pm	All major credit cards except Diners

The Criterion is one of London's most beautiful restaurants. Covered up and used as a shop for decades (it was a 24hr Boots branch for years) in its latest incarnation it has been restored to its full-on belle-époque glory. Areas are divided by swags of muslin and classical arches, and the impossibly high ceiling is decorated with gold mosaics and flower-like lamps. And a trip to the loos is de rigueur, simply to be able to walk the whole length of the room to view the romantic paintings on the walls. Tables are laid with linen and silver in a modern version of traditional perfection and are set far apart from each other. Diners are a mix of young romantic couples, middle-aged gourmets and a few business people clearly plotting the next billion-pound deal. All of them hope that, while Marco Pierre White doesn't cook here personally, he's keeping an eye on the food.

Start with the warm salad of smoked eel, bacon and pommes sautées with creamed horseradish (£8.95), or the risotto with crab, clams and parsley (£8.95), and you will see how a reputation is earned. Main courses are no less cleverly created from simple combinations of highest-quality ingredients – ingredients that have been put together in such a way that each enhances the other. Try caramelised wing of skate with lemons and capers, salad of new potatoes and rocket, jus à la Parisienne (£14.50), or sautéed calves' liver and bacon with garlic mash and shallot gravy (£14.95) – you won't eat liver or skate this good in many other places. Puddings, which all come in at £6.95, include sticky toffee pudding with beurre Café de Paris; tarte fine of bananas with sauce caramel; passionfruits and banana sorbet; truffle au chocolat; and a tarte Tatin of apples with cinnamon (for two). You'll find that overindulgence seems strictly necessary.

The Criterion doesn't come cheap. With wines up to £225 on the ordinary list (there is a fine wine list at much higher prices) you could blow your monthly salary here, but there are some bargains too. The daily set lunch at £14.95 for two courses and £17.95 for three is exceptional value considering the quality and venue. Booking for dinner is essential.

£20–£40

Al Duca

4–5 Duke of York St, SW1 ✆020 7839 3090   ⊖ Piccadilly Circus

Mon–Thurs noon–2.30pm & 6–10.30pm, Fri noon–2.30pm & 6–11pm,

Sat 12.30–3pm & 6–11pm   All major credit cards except Diners

This restaurant is a most welcome addition to the West End scene. High-quality, sophisticated food, agreeable setting, slick service . . . and all at prices that represent real value. What you get here seems to be far more than you pay for. It's unlikely, however, that Al Duca makes a loss – it's part of talented restaurateur Claudio Pulze's mini-group. What seems more likely is that prices elsewhere may be a tad higher than they should be. The formula here is a simple one – at lunch two courses cost £15.50, three £18.50, and four £21.50. In the evening the prices go up to £18, £21, and £24. A four-course dinner for £24 within stumbling distance of Piccadilly. . .? More like this please.

Anyone who eats out regularly in London might feel cynical about such an offer, doubtful that the cooking and portion sizes could remain uncompromised by the low prices. But do not think London, think Italy. Such regularly changing menus are commonplace there. There are usually six starters at Al Duca: dishes like poached egg with organic polenta and Fontina cheese, or salad of spinach, goats' cheese and roasted red onions. Then there are six dishes under the heading pasta: boccoli alla bolognese, linguine with clams, reginette with peas and bacon. Followed by six main courses: roast cod with beans, swordfish, chicken, rib eye steak. Finally, six desserts ranging from an indulgent tiramisù to a classic, simple plate of fresh pear and Pecorino cheese. The standard of cooking is high, with dishes bringing off that difficult trick of being both deceptively simple and satisfyingly rich. The home-made pasta and polenta are fresh and good. The fish is perfectly cooked. Overall there is much to praise here, and the slick service and stylish ambience live up to the efforts in the kitchen.

As seems to be the case with every "all-in" menu, the dreaded supplements do put in an appearance, but they are on the small side and seem fair – £2 extra for the rib eye steak, £2.50 for a starter made with fillet of wild boar.

Fortnum's Fountain

181 Piccadilly, W1 ✆020 7973 4140	⊖ Piccadilly Circus/Green Park
Mon–Sat 8.30–11.30am breakfast, 11.30am–3pm lunch,	
3–5.30pm tea, 5.30–8pm dinner	All major credit cards

The main entrance to Fortnum's Fountain Restaurant is at the back of the store on the corner of Jermyn Street. This makes it a draw for those working and shopping in the surrounding area, though the core clientele of this rather traditional English restaurant are well-to-do retired folk who use Fortnum & Mason to shop, or wish that they still could. The Fountain reflects their taste and is utterly dependable, delivering just what you expect – and indeed hope for – in its well-prepared, very English, breakfasts, lunches, teas and early dinners. The ingredients, as you'd expect of London's smartest and most old-fashioned food shop, are top-class. And the Fountain itself is a very pretty room, with classical murals all around.

The Fountain is deservedly famous for its selection of Fortnum's teas and coffees accompanied by splendid teas and ice cream sundaes, and on any given afternoon you will see small children being treated to their idea of heaven by elderly relatives. And beware, the splendid knicker-bocker glory (£4.95) has a terrifying ability to turn even grumpy middle-aged men into small children. But the restaurant also serves a very decent breakfast – the full English, called Fortnum's Farmhouse Breakfast (£12.95) is rather better than that found in many hotels; the kippers with brown toast (£7.50) gladden the heart – and more formal lunch and dinner menus. The mains reflect the ingredient-buying power of the food department and tend to be straightforward. The excellent smoked salmon is a real treat (£8.75/ £13.95), as are the steak and kidney, and chicken and mushroom, pies (£10.95). There are also classic simple dishes like grilled Dover sole (£18.75), and peppered char-grilled rump steak and chips (£10.95). Hidden on the afternoon menu you'll find a section headed "savouries" – club sandwich with chips (£10.75); Welsh rarebit with back bacon or poached egg (£7.95); or Highland scramble (£9.25) with smoked salmon. Now you're talking!

The restaurant is always busy, and though they turn tables you will not be hurried. The downside is that there is no booking. That's great for shoppers, but anyone on a schedule should avoid the lunchtime peak.

The Hard Rock Café

150 Old Park Lane, W1 ✆020 7629 0382 — ⊖ Hyde Park Corner

Daily 11.30am–12.30am (Sat 1am) — All major credit cards

www.hardrock.com

The Hard Rock Café is a genuine celebration of rock'n'roll, which makes its location, in Hyde Park's trad hotel strip, all the more strange. Perhaps it was chance, or clever marketing, as the bulk of the cafe's customers are tourists. Whatever the reason, this is the original Hard Rock Café, here since the 70s, and the original theme restaurant (and, as such, a hard act to follow). The queue to get in is legendary – there is no booking and you will find a queue almost all day long, every day of the year – and it kind of adds to the occasion. Once in, there is a great atmosphere, created by full-on rock music, dim lighting, and walls dripping with rock memorabilia. The Hard Rock food is not bad, either, predominantly Tex-Mex and burgers.

They like their paperwork here. As well as three separate menus – one in the shape of a life-size guitar; another that lists seasonal specials; and a bar menu which also lists the merchandise available, should you be in any doubt – there is a memorabilia catalogue, the Hall of Fame, which displays the floor plan of this rock'n'roll museum. The menus are peppered with rock'n'roll vocabulary. B.B. wings (boneless bodacious wings – £5.25) are graded classic rock (medium) or heavy metal (hot). The burgers (£7.25) knock spots off those at the high-street chains and cover the spectrum from natural veggie burger (£7.25) to "pig sandwich" (£7.35). Among the Tex-Mex dishes, the grilled fajitas (£11.55) are pretty good. Choose from chicken, beef or vegetarian; all come with bits and pieces for parcelling up with sour cream and guacamole. Puddings are self-indulgent; the hot fudge brownie (£4.25) elevates goo to an art form.

Check out the "Elvis stairs" at the back (they're actually the lower-floor fire escape), where there's even a copy of this junk-food lover's last will and testament. Why are there no Internet reports of the King being sighted here? It's just the sort of place he would like.

£28–£45

Momo

25 Heddon St, W1 ©020 7434 4040   ⊖ Piccadilly Circus/Oxford Circus

Mon–Fri noon–2.30pm & 7–11.30pm, Sat 7–11.30pm,

Sun 7–10pm   All major credit cards

Momo is an attractive and very trendy Moroccan restaurant, tucked away in a backwater off Regent Street. For dinner, you usually have to book at least a week in advance, and to opt for an early or late sitting. If you apply for the late shift, be prepared for a noisy, nightclub ambience, especially on Fridays and Saturdays. The design of the place is clever, with bold geometric kasbah-style architecture, decked out with plush cushions and lots of candles. Downstairs there's an even more splendid-looking Moorish bar, annoyingly reserved for members only – a shame, as Momo is the kind of place where you could happily carry on the evening, especially if you're booked in for the earlier (7–9pm) of its two dining slots.

Whenever you arrive, get into the mood with a Momo special (£6), a blend of vodka, lemon juice and sparkling water, topped with a pile of chopped mint. While you're downing that, you can check out the starters. Briouat de légumes croquants aux herbes fraîches (£5.50) are mouthwatering little parcels of paper-thin pastry filled with vegetables, while salade Méchouia (£6.25) is grilled peppers, tomatoes, cumin and coriander. Or you might try sardines rôties à la chermoula (£6.50), roast sardines stuffed with parsley, garlic, cumin and lemon. For main course, there are seven tagines to choose from – North African-style stews served in a large clay pot. Try the duck (£16) – not something you'd find in Morocco, but delicious all the same. Alternatively, opt for cous cous – brochette de poulet (£13) combines the staple with marinated spicy chicken and a pot of vegetables; cous cous Méchoui (£16.50) adds roasted spiced lamb. Or treat yourself to the Fès speciality of pastilla (£12.50), a super-sweet pigeon pie in millefeuille pastry. Desserts (all around £5) include a pastilla made with fruit; oranges in cinnamon and orange blossom water (plain but effective); or cous cous saffae – a sort of pudding with raisins, almonds and cinnamon.

Finally, don't miss a trip to the toilets downstairs – the men's urinal is an installation of some beauty.

£28–£65

L'Oranger

5 St James's St, SW1 ℗020 7839 3774   ⊖ Green Park

Mon–Fri noon–2.30pm & 6–11pm, Sat 6–11pm   All major credit cards

From the outside, L'Oranger looks like a very expensive French restaurant dedicated to expense-account diners. And, while it's not cheap, the inclusive menus bring serious cooking within reach. At lunch you pay £20 for two courses or £24.50 for three. Dinner is set at £37 for three courses. For your money you can expect modern Provençal cooking of a high standard. The saucing leans towards light olive oil bases rather than the traditional "loadsa-cream" approach and, for cooking of this quality, it is most competitively priced.

Starters may include Provençale chickpea soup; open ravioli of lamb and tomatoes; lamb consommé; steamed salmon boudin stuffed with a mousse of scallops with Niçoise leeks; braised Swiss chard served in a veal broth with bone marrow and herbs. They are beautifully realised and well-judged combinations of flavours. For main courses try roasted duck magret with fondant potato and foie gras sauce – delicious and not as rich you might imagine. There's also roasted monkfish tail rolled in black pepper and crushed with spinach in sauce Antiboise (tomato, basil and pistou); canon of lamb with braised fennel, artichoke and confit of tomato; pan-fried fillet of sea bass with courgettes and tomato, black olive vinaigrette and basil (£3 supplement), and roasted loin of pork wrapped in bacon and sage with confit of celery. Puddings include lemon and thyme crème caramel, warm chocolate fondant, and baked apple pudding with orange zest. It's one of those menus where you want everything, even though some of the more elaborate dishes carry a small supplement. Side dishes of vegetables in season are also served. The wine list is encyclopedic, starting at £16 for a Chardonnay and going up to £450 for a bottle of La Tâche de la Romanée-Conti. But there's plenty of good choice at the lower prices.

L'Oranger is refined and elegant with attentive service, but a relaxed and unstuffy atmosphere. There's also a secret outside courtyard, which is open at dinner only, and a private function room for twenty. The set prices policy turns what would be an expensive treat menu into accessible dining. More restaurants copy please . . .

Pétrus

33 St James's St, SW1 ©020 7930 4272	⊖ Green Park
Mon–Fri noon–2.45pm & 6.45–10.45pm, Sat 6.45–10.45pm	All major credit cards

St James's, which once used to bristle with stuffy clubs for English gentlemen, has achieved a new role as something of a restaurant centre. As the older restaurants – some of which, like Prunier's and Overton's, had been around since the war – upped sticks, so modern establishments arrived, and now despite the terrible shortage of parking there's a small coterie of restaurants offering fine dining. This has not been a simple transformation. The first restaurant on this particular site, 33, opened to fanfares in 1996, but never quite made it, and at the beginning of 1999, after a serious refurb, it reopened with new owners, as Pétrus. The transition was given added spice by the fact that the head chef of the new restaurant had previously been in charge at L'Oranger, just down the road (see opposite for a view on the establishment he left behind).

There have been question marks about the service here, tales of an off-hand approach, but everyone is in agreement that head chef Marcus Wareing is a very skilled cook indeed. Dishes have a grand intensity of flavour, presentation is aimed squarely at the tyrefolk inspectors, and each dish is a well-balanced affair – both in terms of taste and texture. Even more miraculous, dishes here have a quirk of originality about them. Meals are straightforwardly priced at three courses for £35. Starters are often elaborate and "haute cuisine" – sautéed sea scallops served with a chestnut cream; mosaic of confit chicken with foie gras, new potatoes and wild mushrooms; red mullet pan-fried, aubergine caviar, peas and fèves à la crème. Main courses may include a pavé of brill and sautéed scallops with a confit of leeks and sauce matelote; roasted loin of venison and potato rosti, with a fricassee of peas and girolles; or braised halibut with baby leeks and sliced truffle, served with a horseradish velouté. The puddings and pastrywork are accomplished – apple and date crisp with crème fraîche ice cream and caramel sauce; or Earl Grey tea cream with raisin biscuits, Chantilly and vanilla butter sauce.

There's a terrific set lunch – how about salmon and langoustine ravioli with lobster bisque, then poached guinea fowl with braised cos lettuce on a wild mushroom velouté, and finally summer fruit clafoutis with vanilla ice cream?. . . And for £22? Outstanding.

£22–£50

Quaglino's

16 Bury St, SW1 ©020 7930 6767	⊖ Green Park
Mon–Sat noon–3pm & 5.30pm–midnight, Sun 5.30–11pm	All major credit cards

www.conran.com

In 1929 Giovanni Quaglino opened a restaurant in Bury Street which became an instant success. He was a daring innovator – and is reputed to have been the first person to serve hot dishes as hors d'oeuvres. The thing his new restaurant had above all else was glamour. When Sir Terence Conran redesigned and reopened Quaglino's more than sixty years later, his vision was essentially the same. Love it or loathe it, Quaglino's is glamorous, and when it first opened it attracted a glamorous and sophisticated crowd. Inevitably, with such a huge restaurant, that early exclusivity is a fading memory (and all the better for it), but Quag's still has what it takes: the elegant reception, the sweeping staircase into the bar which overlooks the main restaurant, and then another one down to restaurant level. However shy you are, you'll still get a buzz from making an entrance here.

The menu is simple, classy and brasserie-style with very little to scare off the less experienced diner. Given the size of the restaurant it is best to go for the simpler dishes that need less finishing and exactitude – with this number of people to feed, the head chef is not going to have a chance to get to every plate. The fabulous display of seafood at the far end of the restaurant makes it tempting to stick to the plateau de fruits de mer (£28.50 per person), which is as good as you would hope, or lobster mayonnaise (£29). Fish and chips (£12.50) is served with home-made chips and tartare sauce and is excellent, while entrecôte Béarnaise (£16.50) is a treat when served, as it is here, properly cooked. Puddings are straightforward and fine, too.

Quaglino's staff can be brusque – but then marshalling large numbers of glamour-seekers is a testing enough job to make anyone a little tetchy. You can avoid this altogether by staying in the bar, which offers highlights from the menu – including all the seafood. Furthermore Quaglino's is open late, which makes it perfect for a genuine after-theatre dinner.

Sartoria

20 Savile Row, W1 ✆020 7534 7000	⊖ Piccadilly Circus/Oxford Circus
Mon–Sat noon–3pm & 6.30–11.30pm, Sun 6–10.30pm	All major credit cards

www.conran.com

The mounting pressure to find restaurant sites in the West End has put the squeeze on all sorts of real estate – hence Sartoria, a modern building on the corner of Savile Row which Sir Terence Conran has wrested from the grip of the tailoring fraternity. It is a handsome space – long and stylish – and makes a few low-key design references to tailoring (beyond the name). There's a glass wall between the dining area and the wine store and part of the restaurant can be used as a salle privé; the walls here have glass cases full of half-finished suits complete with pins and chalk marks. When Sartoria first opened the menu was littered with Italian dishes so authentic as to be quite obscure. Since those early days, however, dishes have become more accessible and prices have eased somewhat. This is good cooking and the kitchen uses high-quality ingredients.

The à la carte changes twice a day and has many sections – antipasti, pasta, risotto all make an appearance before it finds its way to pesce, carne and contorni. Start with mozzarella di bufala chargrilled Trevise and marjoram (£10.50); salumi misti, "a selection of cured meats from the Valle d'Aosta" (£9.50); or, rather winningly, Salcombe crab with herbs, olive oil and lemon (£12). Move on to the pasta section – fettucine may come with Scottish girolles when they are in season (£16). The risottos are good – risotto of squid, zucchini and basil (£15.50) appeals particularly. Scallops come with aubergine caponata and rosemary (£19), while the pan-fried cod is served with clams and pancetta (£17.50). On a meatier note there is saddle of venison with kale, zucca and salsa verde (£18.50). The cheeseboard is an all-Italian affair – Pecorino, Gorgonzola, Brescianella – all at £5.50. On the dessert menu there's another star turn – blood orange polenta cake (£6.50).

For the wine list here you'd better be sure your tailor equips you with deep pockets. "Super Tuscans" are well represented, along with all manner of other noble Italian bottles. For the cautious, house wine runs at £14 a bottle – and it's not at all bad. Try it with the set lunch, which is available on Saturdays: £16.50 for two courses, £19.50 for three and, sportingly, £24.50 for four.

Veeraswamy

Victory House, 101 Regent St, W1 ℂ020 7734 1401   ⊖ Piccadilly Circus

Mon–Sat noon–2.30pm & 5.30–11.30pm,

Sun noon–3pm & 5.30–10.30pm   All major credit cards

www.realindianfood.com

Veeraswamy is Britain's oldest-surviving Indian restaurant, founded in 1927 by Edward Palmer following a successful catering operation at the British Empire Exhibition. Its next owner was Sir William Steward, who pulled in the rich and famous throughout the postwar boom – their numbers included the king of Denmark, whose penchant for a glass of Carlsberg with his curry is said to have first established the link between Indian food and beer. The latest owner is Namita Panjabi (who also owns Chutney Mary – p.451), and she has swept Veeraswamy into the modern era. The old and faded colonial decor has gone, along with the old and faded dishes. In their place there's an elegant, fashionable restaurant painted in the vibrant colours of today's India, and an all-new menu of bold, modern, authentically Indian dishes of all kinds – from street food to regional specialities. It's a bit of a shock to find an Indian restaurant like this – but a pleasant one. You do, however, need to adjust your pattern of ordering. Main dishes come as a plate, with rice and sometimes vegetables. They're not designed for sharing – and you definitely need one each.

Street food makes great starters: pani puri (£4.50), rich with tamarind, or ragda pattice (£4.50), spiced potato cakes with chickpea curry. Or there's machli ki tikki (£5.20) – fish cakes – or fresh oysters exquisitely stir-fried with Keralan spices (£8). The main dish curries are well spiced and with a depth of flavour. Plum dopiaza (£12) is a lamb curry with chillies, caramelised onions and plums; or try lobster curry with fresh turmeric and raw mango (£16.50); or Mysore chilli chicken with coconut and fresh herbs (£12). The biryanis are a revelation, too – particularly good is the Andhra green biryani (£12), a dish of lamb and rice cooked slowly in a sealed pot with lots of green herbs and nuts. Vegetarian dishes are also grandstand affairs and include such as guchhi biryani (£14) – morels stuffed with paneer cheese and then slowly cooked with rice.

Like its sister restaurant, Chutney Mary, Veeraswamy does an excellent Sunday lunch – £15 for three courses.

Bentley's Cabin

11–15 Swallow St, W1   ✆020 7734 4756

A cross between a wine bar and a pub, with a couple of games machines, this cellar venue is simple and accessible. It's off the beaten track, so doesn't get as crowded as the more central places, and it offers a wide range of wines, beers and spirits.

The Chequers

16 Duke St, St James's, SW1 ✆020 7930 4007

A proper little local right in the heart of tourist West End, this old pub is simple and unpretentious. Expect a nicely pulled pint of Courage Directors, Theakston's Bitter, Fosters or Kronenbourg 1664 in a welcoming atmosphere.

The Golden Lion

25 King St, SW1   ✆020 7930 7227

This quaint, bow-fronted old pub has been here for more than 100 years. It's tiny and full of charm, retaining the character of a real neighbourhood local in the heart of Piccadilly. Bass Red Triangle is the favourite on tap.

The Red Lion

23 Crown Passage, SW1   ✆020 7930 4141

One of London's oldest village inns – it's been here for more than 300 years – the Red Lion has heaps of character. It's tiny, panelled and comfortable and well worth a stop. More than thirty different malt whiskies as well as Courage Directors and Adnams Bitter.

The Red Lion

2 Duke of York St, SW1   ✆020 7930 2030

Genuine old Victorian gin palace with elegant etched mirrors, polished wood and a great ceiling. It's used mostly by local workers – few people live around here – with a sprinkling of photo-snapping tourists. Enjoy Fuller's London Pride, Adnams Bitter and Marstons Pedigree.

The Ritz

Ritz Hotel, Piccadilly, SW1   ✆020 7493 8181

Expensive, elegant and chic, The Ritz lives up to its name more now than ever before. Enjoy mixers, cocktails or wine at high prices in the lounge area and revel in one of the most luxurious atmospheres around. It's waiter service. No trainers, no jeans and for men, jacket and tie. Don't even try to get in without them.

Queensway &
Westbourne Grove

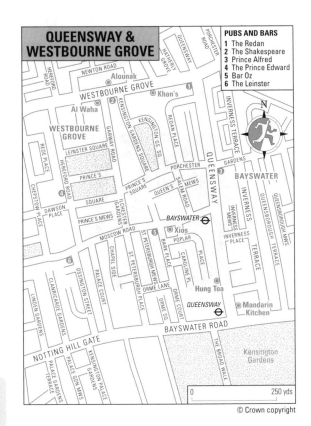

QUEENSWAY & WESTBOURNE GROVE

PUBS AND BARS
1 The Redan
2 The Shakespeare
3 Prince Alfred
4 The Prince Edward
5 Bar Oz
6 The Leinster

N

PORCHESTER ROAD

QUEENSWAY

HATHERLY GROVE

NEWTON ROAD

Alounak

WESTBOURNE GROVE

Khan's

HEREFORD ROAD

Al Waha

INVERNESS TERRACE

WESTBOURNE GROVE

GARWAY ROAD

KENSINGTON GARDENS SQUARE

KENSINGTON GS. SQ.

REDAN PLACE

LEINSTER SQUARE

REDE PLACE

HEREFORD ROAD

PRINCE'S

PORCHESTER GARDENS

QUEENSWAY

BAYSWATER

CHEPSTOW PLACE

SQUARE

PRINCE'S SQUARE

PRINCE'S MEWS

DAWSON PLACE

QUEEN'S

SALEM ROAD

MEWS

ILCHESTER GARDENS

INVERNESS PLACE

INVERNESS MEWS

INVERNESS

QUEENSBOROUGH TERRACE

QUEENSBOROUGH MWS.

BAYSWATER

Xios

MOSCOW ROAD

ST. PETERSBURGH MEWS

POPLAR

BARK PLACE

CAROLINE PL.

INVERNESS PLACE

The Leinster

CHAPEL SIDE

ST. PETERSBURGH PLACE

ORME LANE

Hung Toa

CLANRICARDE GARDENS

OSSINGTON STREET

PALACE COURT

ORME COURT

ORME SQ.

QUEENSWAY

Mandarin Kitchen

LINDEN GARDENS

BAYSWATER ROAD

NOTTING HILL GATE

PALACE GARDENS TERRACE

KENSINGTON PALACE GARDENS

KENSINGTON PALACE GDN MWS

THE BROAD WALK

Kensington Gardens

0   250 yds

© Crown copyright

CENTRAL

120

£8–£20

Alounak

44 Westbourne Grove, W2 ©020 7229 0416   ⊖ Bayswater/Queensway

Daily noon–midnight   All major credit cards

Westbourne Grove has always had a raffish cosmopolitan air to it, which makes it the perfect home for this, the second branch of Alounak – actually the third, if you count its early years in a Portakabin opposite Olympia station. Don't be put off by the dated sign outside: this place turns out really good, really cheap Iranian food. The welcoming smell of clay-oven-baked flat bread hits you the moment you walk through the front door, creating a sense of the Middle East that's enhanced further by the gentle gurgling of a fountain, and the strains of Arabic music.

The sizeable contingent of Middle Eastern locals dining here testifies to the authenticity of the food on offer. As an opening move, you can do no better than order the mixed starter (£8.40), a fine sampler of all the usual dips and hors d'oeuvres, served with splendid freshly baked flat bread. And then follow the regulars with some grilled meat, which is expertly cooked. Joojeh kebab (£6.90) is melt-in-the-mouth baby chicken, packed with flavour. The kebab koobideh morgh (£6.90) is a tasty kebab made from minced chicken "reassembled" into long cylinders. As you would expect from a Middle Eastern restaurant, lamb dishes feature heavily. A good way to try two-in-one is to order the chelo kebab koobideh (£9.10), marinated lamb fillet coupled with minced (lamb) kebab, which is deliciously rich and oniony. For those with an inquisitive bent there is the innocuous-sounding "mixed grill' (£26), which brings a vast platter best summed up as grilled everything. It's worth looking out for the daily specials: especially good on a Tuesday, when they offer zereshk polo (£6.20), a stunning chicken dish served on saffron-steamed rice mixed with sweet and sour forest berries.

Round things off with a pot of Iranian black tea (£3), sufficient for six and served in ornate glass beakers. Infused with refreshing spices, it does a great job of cleaning the palate, leaving you set for a finale of select Persian sweets. Beware, however, of musty-tasting yoghurt drinks with unpronounceable names.

£10-£35

Al Waha

75 Westbourne Grove, W2 ©020 7229 0806   ⊖ Bayswater/Queensway

Daily noon–midnight   All major credit cards except Diners

Anissa Helou, who has written the definitive book on Lebanese cuisine, nominates Al Waha as London's best Lebanese restaurant. And after cantering through a few courses here you will probably agree with her. Lebanese restaurants are all meze-obsessed and Al Waha is no exception. What is different, however, is the way in which the chef at Al Waha is obsessive about the main course dishes as well. The restaurant moved here from Piccadilly in 1999, and has settled in well.

When you sit down a dish of fresh crisp crudités will be brought to the table. It includes everything from some quartered cos lettuce through to a whole green pepper. Get the healthy eating part over early. As always with Middle Eastern food choosing is the problem – there are 22 cold starters and 24 hot ones. Go for a balance and always include one that you have never had before – hummus (£2.75) is good here; tabbouleh (£3.75) is heavy on the parsley; the kabees (£2.75) are moreish if you like the Lebanese style of heavily salted (and so *very* salty) pickles. The foul moukala (£3.75) is good, despite its name; it's a dish of broad beans with garlic, coriander and olive oil. From the hot section try manakeish bizaatar (£3.50), which is a freshly baked mini-bread topped with thyme, like a de luxe pizza, or maybe haliwat (£4.25), a dish of grilled sweetbreads with lemon juice and herbs. Or there's batata harra (£3.50), which is potatoes with garlic and peppers. The makanek ghanam (£4.25) are tiny Lebanese lamb sausages, like a very refined cocktail sausage. For main courses, grills predominate. These are all spanking fresh and accurately cooked – tasty choices include shish taouk (£8.50), made with chicken, and samakeh harrah (£14), with sea bass. Star turn is kafta khashkhash (£8.50), a superb cylinder of minced lamb with parsley, garlic and tomato. The bread here is fresh and delicious. Drink the good Lebanese beer or the very good Lebanese wines.

Al Waha's greatest strength is in its superb home-style dishes of the day. Monday means dajaj mahshi: stuffed chicken with rice and pine nuts. Tuesday gets you a good artichoki mozat, which is lamb stewed with artichoke bottoms. Friday is fish – sayadieh, a fillet of fish cooked with herbs and rice. They are all priced at £8.50.

Hung Toa

51 Queensway, W2 ©020 7727 5753   ⊖ Bayswater/Queensway

Daily 11am–11pm   Cash and cheques only

It is easy to find the Hung Toa: just look out for the much larger New Kam Tong restaurant, and two doors away you'll see this small and spartan establishment. They're actually part of the same group, as is another restaurant over the road (which is where all those singularly appetising ducks hanging up in the windows of the three establishments are roasted). The reason to choose the Hung Toa above its neighbours is if you fancy a one-plate (or one-bowl) meal. Despite a long and traditional menu, featuring mainly Cantonese and Szechwan dishes, its strengths lie in its barbecued meat with rice, noodle dishes and noodle soups. All attract the hungry and are keenly priced.

The very first thing on the menu is delicious – hot and sour soup (£1.70). Uncannily enough, this is both hot (fresh red chillies in profusion) and sour. There are also a dozen different noodle soups – priced between £4 and £4.50. Then there are twenty dishes that go from duck rice (£4) to shrimps and egg with rice (£4.90). Plus about thirty noodle, fried noodle, and ho fun dishes from £2.60 to £5.70. The fried ho fun with beef (£4) is a superb rich dish – well-flavoured brisket cooked until melting, on top of a mountain of ho fun. And the barbecued meats displayed in the window are very tasty, too – rich, red-painted char sui, soya duckling, crispy pork and duck – all shuttled across from the kitchens over the road.

Towards the front of the menu, and hailing from Canton, you'll find a succession of congee dishes. Congee is one of those foods people label "interesting" without meaning it. It is a thick, whitish, runny porridge made with rice: stunningly bland and under-seasoned, but tasting faintly of ginger. Plunge in at the deep end, and try thousand years egg with sliced pork congee (£4). As well as containing pork, there's the "thousand year" egg, the white of which is a translucent chestnut brown and the yolk a fetching green, but inscrutably tastes rather like an ordinary hard-boiled egg. Pundits will tell you that far from being a thousand or even a hundred years old, these eggs acquire their bizarre, slightly cheesey taste after being buried for just one hundred days.

Khan's

13–15 Westbourne Grove, W2 ©020 7727 5420   ⊖ Bayswater

Mon–Thurs noon–3pm & 6-11.45pm,

Fri–Sun noon–midnight   All major credit cards

If you're after a solid, inexpensive and familiar Indian meal, Khan's is the business. This restaurant, in busy Westbourne Grove, is a long-standing favourite with students and budget-wary locals, who know that the curries here may be the staples of a thousand menus across Britain, but they're fresh, well cooked and generously portioned. Just don't turn up for a quiet evening out. Tables turn over in the blink of an eye, service is perfunctory (this isn't a place to dally over the menu), and it's really noisy. Try to get a seat in the vast, echoey ground floor, where blue murals stretch up to high ceilings – it feels a bit like dining in an enormous swimming pool. The basement is stuffier and less atmospheric. Wherever you sit, be prepared to be fed briskly and hurried on your way.

There are some tasty breads on offer. Try the nan-e-mughziat (£1.60), a coconut-flavoured affair with nuts and sultanas, or the paneer kulcha (£1.45), bulging with cottage cheese and mashed potatoes. You might also kick off with half a tandoori chicken (£2.75), which is moist and well cooked, or a creditable chicken tikka (£3.80). For main dishes, all those curry house favourites are listed here – meat madras or vindalu (£3.20), prawn biryani (£5.25), chicken chilli masala (£3.20), king prawn curry (£6.20) – and they all taste unusually fresh. Especially good is the butter chicken (£4.70), while, for lovers of chicken tikka masala, the murgh tikka masala (£3.70) will appeal. There's a typical array of vegetable dishes, too: bhindi (£2.70), sag aloo (£2.60), and vegetable curry (£2.60). Desserts include kulfi (£2.15), chocolate bombe (£1.60) and various ice creams – or you could try the lemon or orange delight (£1.70). A pint of lager will set you back £1.90, and there's a small selection of wines; a bottle of Chardonnay costs £8.50, or you can get a glass of house white or red for £1.60.

Cast your eye around the tall, tiled ground floor and front windows and you'll find enough architectural clues to confirm that this was once a Kardomah coffee bar.

Mandarin Kitchen

14–16 Queensway, W2 ©020 7727 9012	⊖ Queensway
Daily noon–11.30pm	All major credit cards

London has its fair share of French fish restaurants, and there are famous English fish restaurants, so why does it seem odd to come across a Chinese fish restaurant? Part of the mystique of the Mandarin Kitchen, which you'll find at the Kensington Gardens end of Queensway, is the persistent rumour that they sell more lobsters than any other restaurant in Britain. (When questioned about this myth, the management will confirm that they regularly have 100-lobster days!) This is a large restaurant, busy with waiters deftly wheeling four-foot-diameter table tops around like giant hoops as they set up communal tables for large parties of Chinese who all seem to be eating . . . lobster. What's more, as the menu observes, "we only serve the finest Scottish wild lobsters, simply because they are probably the best in the world".

Whatever you fancy for the main course, start with as many of the steamed scallops on the shell with garlic soya sauce (£1.80 each) as you can afford. They're magnificent. Then decide between lobster, crab or fish. If you go for the lobster, try ordering it baked with green pepper and onion in black bean sauce (it is priced at about £15 per pound depending on the season), and be sure that you order the optional extra soft noodle (£1.20) to make a meal of it. The crab is tempting, too. Live crabs are shipped up here from the south coast, and a handsome portion of shells, lots of legs and four claws baked with ginger and spring onion is a pretty reasonable £12. Fish dishes require more thought – and an eye to the per-pound prices. The menu lists "the fish we normally serve" as sea bass, Dover sole, live eels, live carp, monkfish, Chinese pomfret and yellow croaker. Sea bass comes steamed whole at £17–19 per pound depending on season. The roast eel fillets with garlic and chilli (£7.90) are notable, and strongly flavoured. The monkfish (£9.90) is meaty and delicious.

After seafood, the never-ending menu wanders off down a road of old favourites, and even features a number of veal dishes such as roasted veal chop with Mandarin sauce (£9.90) – so a seafood allergy is no reason for you to miss out.

£15–£30

Xios

47 Moscow Rd, W2 ©020 7243 0606   ⊖ Bayswater

Mon–Sat 6pm–midnight, Sun noon–midnight   All major credit cards

This little patch of streets tucked away to the west of Queensway is something of a hidden delight. You'll find Greek corner shops, a good pâtissier-cum-coffee shop, the Orthodox church, and Xios. The Nicolaou family run one of the teeming tourist hotels in this part of town, but in 1997 Mrs Tzeni Nicolaou decided to realise a long-cherished ambition to open her own restaurant, which she did, naming it Xios after the island of her birth. It's a small, patriotically blue and white, family restaurant where everyone looks up at you when you enter – not with a hostile stare but with a warm welcome. The food is unfussy and has Greek rather than Cypriot roots. As is so often the case with family restaurants, you should pounce on any daily specials and ask for, and put your trust in, their advice.

There is a £1 per person cover charge here. Unlike most cover charges – which are eminently resentable – this seems fair enough as it brings with it a basket of good bread, a saucer of limpid green olive oil, a dish of salty home-made pickles and some Kalamata olives: the very combination you need to assist in casting an eye over the menu. Start with a few meze: melitzanosalata (£2.90) is a smoky, creamy aubergine dip with a tiny bite of garlic – quite excellent. Or order feta (£2.90) with confidence: this will bring a slab of rich, well-flavoured cheese, a long way from the insipid mass-produced stuff. Try some grilled sardines (£3.20/£8.50) and a loukaniko spicy sausage (£3.20). Then on to grilled meats – skewers of lamb (£9.50), pork (£8.80) or lamb cutlets (£11.50). House specialities include youvetsi (£9.20), a dish of pasta nibs with lamb and tomato, and a serious moussaka (£8.70). In a family restaurant like this where Tzeni Nicolaou rules the kitchen as well as everything else, house specialities carry more weight than elsewhere, and often prove to be the best option.

The wine list majors in Greek wines, and very good some of them are too. A little decanting and label-hiding and you could use these to play unkind tricks on wine experts – start with the Grand Reserve "Naoussa", which is made by Boutari and delivers astonishing quality for just £15 a bottle.

Bar Oz

51 Moscow Rd, W2　　　Ⓒ020 7229 0647

As its name suggests, this lively bar is a big hit for anyone from down under. Club flyers and Aussie contact mags like *TNT* and *Southern Cross* are piled high, and the talk is of bar work and travel. A great place to meet people if you are planning a trip. Bottled Aussie lagers like Crown, Carlton, Castle and Victoria by the neck are the favourites. There's big-screen sport.

The Leinster

57 Ossington St, W2　　　Ⓒ020 7243 9541

A modernised, blonde-wood pub, this venue attracts a young crowd of locals who enjoy big-screen TV and a fairly noisy atmosphere. There is a large upstairs gallery bar with a spiral stair-case and plenty of room. Favourites on tap include Bass Red Triangle, Grolsch and Carling lager.

Prince Alfred

112 Queensway, W2　　　Ⓒ020 7229 1474

Converted from an old pub, this bright, lounge-bar-style venue has a youthful, scrubbed look. It's comfort-able, with a separate table seating area and plenty of standing bar room. Tetley's and Courage Directors are the ales on tap, but bottled beers are more popular.

The Prince Edward

73 Princes Square, W2　　　Ⓒ020 7727 2221

A big, comfortable bar that's been sym-pathetically updated. Pavement tables overlook the square, and staff and cus-tomers are friendly. Ales on tap are from the Badger Brewery and include Dorset Best, Tanglefoot and Champion. Plus there's an Irish American ale called Dempsey's if you like that sort of thing. A downstairs bar hosts the odd music evening.

The Redan

1 Westbourne Grove, W2　　　Ⓒ020 7229 2993

One of a dying breed, the Redan pulls a regular, local crowd who congregate to smoke ruminatively and reminisce about the old days. It's a real old pub with plenty of character, and characters. Courage Directors, Theakston's Best and XB are the favourites here.

The Shakespeare

65 Westbourne Grove, W2　　　Ⓒ020 7229 2233

Loud and lively, this traditionally deco-rated pub boasts six games machines, a juke box and a pool table. It's not for those who want a quiet pint. It is, how-ever, very friendly and welcoming. Courage Directors and Theakston's Bitter on tap.

Soho

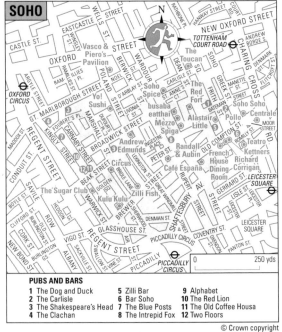

SOHO

PUBS AND BARS

1	The Dog and Duck	5	Zilli Bar
2	The Carlisle	6	Bar Soho
3	The Shakespeare's Head	7	The Blue Posts
4	The Clachan	8	The Intrepid Fox

9	Alphabet
10	The Red Lion
11	The Old Coffee Housa
12	Two Floors

© Crown copyright

CENTRAL

Alastair Little

49 Frith St, W1 ℂ020 7734 5183	⊖ Leicester Square
Mon–Fri noon–3pm & 6–11pm, Sat 6–11pm	All major credit cards

This restaurant was Alastair Little's first, opened back in those days when the London eating public was moving hesitantly out of a world where visiting an Italian restaurant meant gasping at the size of the peppermills and the clever way that the straw-wrapped chianti flasks had been transformed into lamps. The sparse decor and unfussy, modern lines of Little's Frith Street joint seemed little short of revolutionary at the time – today, the place looks much the same as every other trendy eatery. Most importantly, Alastair Little was the man who showed us a new style of Mediterranean food: simple, strong flavours, fresh produce, joyful meals. And today his two restaurants continue to fly the flag for these admirable values (you'll find the other one reviewed on p.498).

Unlike the decor, the menu changes twice a day. Not radically, although there may be one extra starter or main course to choose from at dinner. Pricing is simple – at lunch £25 buys you three courses, or two courses plus coffee; at dinner £33 gets you three courses. The wine list is a largely sub-£30-a-bottle affair with a sprinkling of more ambitiously priced famous names. The menu runs the gamut – the charcuterie may come from Spain, and there will be French classics mixed in with resolutely Italian dishes – but everything is seasonal. Starters may include a rich bourride of seafood, with lots of chunky fish and a delicious sauce, or that old dinner party faithful, beloved of Delia Smith – Piedmontese peppers. Or how about grilled pigeon breast, French beans, sautéed potatoes and pancetta? The main courses are in a similar vein, featuring roast breast of chicken with peas, broad beans and button onions, or calves' liver persillade with potato cake. And, perhaps most accomplished of all, roast plaice steak with mash and shrimp sauce. It's a difficult business, cooking a large tranche of plaice – the fish has to be really fresh to stop it disintegrating into mush. The sweetish sauce served here is a wonderful accompaniment for this good white fish.

To end your meal there are splendid puds like panna cotta with apricot sauce or bitter chcolate tarte with espresso ice cream – but how much better to call for a plate of British cheeses with oatcakes.

£20–£35

Andrew Edmunds

46 Lexington St, W1 ℗020 7437 5708	⊖ Oxford Circus
Mon–Fri noon–3pm & 6–11pm, Sat 1–3pm & 6–11pm,	
Sun 1–3pm & 6–10.30pm	All major credit cards

Andrew Edmunds' wine bar, as it is called by Soho locals, has been an institution in the area for some fifteen years, a long time when you consider how speedily so many restaurants come and go. It all started when the lease on the wine bar next door to his print gallery became vacant and he decided that, as he wanted to go on eating there himself, he should take it on. The restaurant now has a loyal band of regulars who like the imaginative bistro-style dishes. It's cosy, dark and very crowded: a place where people wave to friends across the room.

The menu changes daily and combines solid favourites with bright new ideas, so that regular diners can either comfort themselves with the familiar or head off into the unknown. Start with skate wing rillettes with crème fraîche, cucumber and fried capers (£4.75) – a remarkably accomplished way to deal with skate – or the creamy, rich duck liver pâté and tomato cruda (£4.25). Main courses include stalwarts like lamb casserole with saffron rice (£9.50) and roast guinea fowl with mustard sauce, green vegetables and roast garlic (£9.50), or lighter ideas like roast flat mushrooms with egg noodles, vegetable julienne and peanut dressing (£7.50) and seared swordfish steak with black-eyed beans, French beans and chilli oil (£10). The lamb is rich, robust and deeply satisfying, and the huge mushrooms are tender, sweet and flavoursome. Puddings include chocolate mousse cake (£3.50), the ubiquitous tiramisù (£3.50), and plum and almond tart (£4). The first two are ruinously rich, the last crisp, sharp and nutty.

Wines are a passion with Andrew Edmunds. The constantly changing broker-bought list is long and special and, because of his policy of not marking up much, you get massive bargains in the higher-priced wines, especially French and Californian. Many are at not much more than wine shop prices. There is an additional list of halves of sweet wines as well. Daily special wine offers are chalked on a blackboard and there are excellent sherries and other aperitifs. Expect to pay a bit more and get much more. Booking, especially for the tiny upstairs dining room, is essential.

busaba eathai

106–110 Wardour St, W1 ©0800 316 9950	⊖ Piccadilly Circus
Mon–Thurs noon–11pm, Fri & Sat noon–11.30pm,	
Sun noon–10pm	All major credit cards except Diners

busaba (their decision to dispense with a capital letter, not ours!) occupies a West End site that was once a bank – you remember the days when banks were conveniently positioned all over the place? Former customers stumbling into 106 Wardour Street would be more than a little surprised by the dark, designery, and implacably trendy Thai eatery that is now bedded in. One of the gents behind this new establishment is the brains behind the original Wagamama (see p.15), and regulars there will find all sorts of echoes and resonance at busaba eathai. There's the same share-a-table and no bookings policy – there's the same half-cod philosophy "sanuk is busaba's living ethos. Based upon traditional Bhuddist values . . ." – you need read no further. The place is saved by serving pretty decent Thai food at low prices and with consummate lack of pretension. For all the fake zen this is a jolly and energetic restaurant and you will probably have a very good time.

Food, grouped into categories, veers towards one-pot dishes. Vegetarians are particularly well served. If you want starters you need to peruse the side dishes – choose from such things as a good green papaya salad (£4.50), or po-pea jay (£2.90), which are vegetable spring rolls, or fish cakes (£3.90), or Thai calamari (£3.90), which are not everyone else's calamari. There are four curries: yellow prawn (£7.90), green chicken (£5.90), green vegetable (£5.90), and red salmon (£6.50). You'll find genuine Thai veg like pea aubergines with sweet basil and lime leaves, although these dishes do tend to be on the sweet side. On to the noodles section, which lists pad Thai (£5.90), Thai beef laksa (£6.90), and phad kwetio (£5.50) – a stir-fry of rice sticks with chicken, chilli, onion, sweet basil and fried shallots. On to stir-fries: salmon sweet and sour (£5.90), duck with pickled vegetables in black bean sauce (£7.50), squid khuen chai stir-fry (£5.90), which is baby squid with Chinese celery and curry powder.

The power juice phenomenon has reached busaba. Nam polamai (£3.50) is organic, and combines carrot, apple and celery with dandelion and nettle extract – just the thought of it should be enough to make you repent all those hard days and long nights.

Café España

63 Old Compton St, W1 ©020 7494 1271 ⊖ Piccadilly Circus/Tottenham Court Road

Daily noon–midnight   Mastercard, Visa

Situated as it is at the heart of Soho's pink strip, at the Wardour Street end of Old Compton Street, and nestled among the hard-core shops and video stores, Café España is a remarkably balanced restaurant. From the outside it looks rather small and shabby – not very prepossessing at all, in fact, and much like the more tourist-focused trattorias. But once through the door, tripping over the dessert trolley, you can sense you're in for something good. You'll be greeted by a friendly maître d' and led up the stairs to join a hubbub of hungry Soho folk with a nose for a bargain.

The menu does give a nod to the trattoria with a short list of pastas, but it is Spanish, not Italian cooking that you should be going for here – and if you are anything less than seriously hungry, it's best to stick with the tapas. Mejillones a la marinera (£3.95) delivers enough mussels for a small main course; a portion of tortilla (£4) is the size of a saucer and is likely to be cooked especially for you; ordering the jamón Serrano (£5.25) brings a decent portion at a price you'd be hard to match wholesale. For something more substantial there's plenty of choice, mostly in the form of simple grills. Try chuletas de cordero a la brasa (£8.95) – lamb chops; higado de ternera (£7.95) – calves' liver and bacon; or rodaballo a la plancha (£11.50) – grilled turbot. Or there are the traditional paellas – Valenciana and marinera (£19.50, to feed two) – though these are slightly less exciting. Service is swift, if a little harassed. Keeping food prices this low means a rapid turn-around of custom, but the waiters are nonetheless friendly and polite. And given the number of people in the place, you can be sure that whatever you are eating is freshly prepared – the volume of ingredients they get through must be huge.

To enjoy Café España to the maximum, go mob-handed and allow yourself the luxury of running amok with the tapas selections, before pouncing on the paella. But be warned: it is very unwise to try and recreate the glorious abandon of your last Iberian holiday here – the sangria is a dark and dangerous West End concoction that is really quite horrid.

Centrale

16 Moor St, W1 ©020 7437 5513   ⊖ Leicester Square/Tottenham Court Road

Mon–Sat noon–9.45pm   Cash and cheques only

In a grid of streets full of bottom-dollar belly-fillers, Centrale stands out, with an idiosyncratic charm beloved by its clued-in regulars. Don't be misled by its down-at-heel exterior – there's something special about sweeping through the plain glass door and sliding into one of its cracked vinyl banquettes, forced into cosy, chatty proximity with strangers across a narrow red Formica table. Maybe it's the tininess of the place, maybe it's the crush of students, maybe it's just the cappuccino in smoked-glass cups, but Centrale is not only effortlessly friendly but also strangely glamorous. Odd, really, when this is basically a place to line your stomach with cheap pasta before going on to a pub or club.

Centrale's menu is artless – orange juice (80p) appears as a starter – and the portions are substantial. Appetisers include home-made minestrone (£2), salame (£3.50), and pastina in brodo (£2) – short pasta snippets in a clear, slightly oily soup. There's a fair spread of diner staples to follow, including pork chop (£4.50) and fried scampi (£4.50), each partnered by an inevitable sprinkling of chips, but the main event here is the pasta. The bolognaise dishes – spaghetti, tagliatelle, rigatoni and ravioli (all £3.50) – are equally dependable, adequately spicy and chewily meaty, and the lasagna al forno (£4) reassuringly button-popping, but the specials list holds more adventurous temptations. Standouts include the spaghetti vongole (£4.25), with its shoal of baby clams in a garlic, chilli and tomato sauce, and the rigatoni Alfredo (£4), a pungent swirl of cream, mushrooms, cheese, tomato and lots and lots of garlic. Rather than a small salad (£1.50), a side order of spinach (£2) adds a pleasantly slippery counterpoint to the solid bulk of the pasta.

The menu gives up the ghost a bit when it comes to dessert, sticking to just three old favourites: banana split (£1.50), apple pie (£1.50) and ice cream (£1.20), the last being a tripartite scoop of chocolate, strawberry and vanilla. Still, you're not here for puds. You're here for a fix of cheap food – and cheap wine. There's no licence, so you can bring your own bottle for 50p corkage (£1 for a big bottle). You'll find a couple of off-licences just around the corner in Old Compton Street.

SOHO ⑪ MODERN BRITISH

Circus

1 Upper James St, W1 ©020 7534 4000	⊖ Oxford Circus
Mon–Fri noon–3pm & 5.45pm–midnight, Sat 5.45pm–midnight	All major credit cards

www.circusbar.co.uk

The little sister to big, brash Avenue in St James's (see p.105), Circus can be a tad intimidating. You'll be greeted by a doorman in Armaniesque clothes and, supposing you're a bona fide diner, shown to your table in the colour-draining dining room. Chairs are dressed in neutral suede, walls in white, floor and customers in black. There's a pretty serious aura about it all. Even the name of the restaurant refers to its location, between Oxford and Piccadilly circuses, and not to any frivolous entertainment. That said, the seriousness applies equally to the preparation of the food, which is impressive. The kitchen has the sense to buy decent ingredients and not muck about with them too much, which perfectly suits the punters – an unhealthy mix of record company executives, PR and television people.

The menu changes with the seasons and allows you to keep within your own expense account or to humble that of your host. You can start with Jerusalem artichoke and watercress soup (£4.75), pan-fried risotto with smoked haddock and soft-poached egg (£5.95) – or, if collecting favours, the Iranian beluga (£50) with sour cream and fluffy blinis. Follow with seared tuna with wakame and cucumber (£12.50), a classic 90s dish, prettily presented and full of East/West flavours. Heartier food includes chicken chasseur (£11.50), in its own way just as trendy. The less fashion-conscious are not ignored, and there may well be a roast rump of lamb with courgettes and tomatoes (£15.50). After toying with deeply groovy puddings in 1999 the desserts are now much more retro – chocolate brownie with caramelised banana ice cream (£5.95), or posh rhubarb and custard (£5.25). The wine list tries to encompass all the world's major wine-making areas and is set out by type rather than region.

Annoyingly, the Japanesey bar downstairs becomes a members-only club during the evening, which means that if you are the first of your party to show up, you'll have to sit at your table like a lemon. Arrive very early or very late, however, and you get a bargain: the pre- and post-theatre menus (5.45-7.15pm & 10.45pm-midnight, only in the bar), get you two courses for £10.50 and three for £12.50.

CENTRAL

£22–£45

French House Dining Room

49 Dean St, W1 ©020 7437 2477	⊖ Leicester Square
Mon–Sat noon–3pm & 6–11.15pm	All major credit cards

The French House Dining Room is a small room above the bar of the popular French House pub. It has high ceilings, wooden floors and large windows which overlook the corner of Dean Street and Old Compton Street. Despite its cosy size (around thirteen tables), the restaurant has a light, airy feel and the enormous mirror at one end of the room creates a nice sense of space. Part of the fun of eating here is to be in the heart of Soho, yet feel worlds away from the strip shows and noisy cafes. The French House is a sister restaurant of St John in Clerkenwell (see p.219) and shares its fondness for traditional British dishes and ingredients.

Choosing is made easy by the short, sharp menu, which changes daily. The dishes all look simple and restrained – you have to keep a soft spot in both your heart and appetite for anywhere that serves Welsh rarebit (£4.40) – but don't be fooled; the restaurant's pig motif is a correct indication of how much it is possible to eat here. There are usually four or five starters to pick from, such as leeks gribiche (£5); duck neck, watercress and cabbage (£5.50); mussels and clams (£6), or squid and aioli (£5.50). Main dishes are hearty and presented with a lot of care. Try grey mullet, Jerusalem artichoke and olives (£12.50), or poached chicken with turnips and dumplings (£12.50), or pork belly, lentils and green sauce (£12.50). And while there's always something serious like veal tongue, potato and mustard (£12), there's usually also a veggie choice, such as roast fennel and goats' cheese (£9.50). Vegetables are basic and wholesome: new potatoes (£4), sprouting broccoli (£3) and green salad (£4) all taste very fresh. And there's a choice of four or five puddings; you might go for the traditional treacle tart (£4.20), or the blood orange ice cream (£5.20).

The pub used to be called the York Minster, but during World War II, when it became the unofficial headquarters for the Free French Army (it's claimed that General de Gaulle was a regular), they changed the name. The French has a particular quirk: it only serves beer in half-pint glasses.

SOHO Ⓣ PIZZA/BURGERS

Kettners

29 Romilly St, W1 ☎020 7734 6112   ⊖ Leicester Square

Daily noon–midnight   All major credit cards

Owned by Soho restaurateur Peter Boizot, the man who introduced pizza to Britain in the 1960s, Kettners is modelled on a Pizza Express restaurant, but with a champagne bar attached. Over the years it's built up a loyal following that starts out an evening in the bar for some excellent champagne, then moves on to a pizza in the restaurant across the hall. Going to the bar beforehand (or indeed the restaurant after) isn't obligatory. But do at least one or the other. Kettners is a gorgeous old restaurant and part of the fabric of Soho.

The pizzas are amongst the best in London, their crusts biscuit-thin and crispy, their topping thick, rich and tasty. What more could you ask from a pizza? If you don't want one at all, however, there are additional choices like Kettners special hamburger (£7.75), chilli con carne (£6.70) and sausage mash and onion gravy (£6.85). Given that you'll probably spend a tenner or more on champagne (you could pay up to £865 for a twenty-bottle Nebuchadnezzar of Pol Roger) in the bar, this makes for a delightful paradox of cheap staple food and expensive luxury drink. The pizza list includes the usuals like American hot (£8.75), Margherita (£7.50) and Napoletana (£8.10), plus unusual ideas like the King Edward (£7), which has a potato base. As in Pizza Express, the Veneziana (£8.10) comes with onions, capers, olives, pine kernels, sultanas, mozzarella and tomato, and every time you buy one 50p is passed on to Pizza Express who run the Venice in Peril Fund – this initiative will soon have reached the £1 million mark.

A trip to Kettners isn't just for the pizzas – though they're good, you're here as much for the venue. Decorated in belle époque Baroque, the building was founded as a grand hotel in 1867 by Auguste Kettner, chef to Napoleon III. Stories also have it that the hotel was used by the then King Edward VII to woo and bed his mistress. Upstairs rooms sport numbers to remind you of the racy past and some can be booked for private parties of between eight and eighty. The main restaurants, however, don't accept bookings and you are advised to get there early.

CENTRAL

£10–£30

Kulu Kulu

76 Brewer St, W1 ✆020 7734 7316	⊖ Piccadilly Circus
Mon–Fri noon–2.30pm & 5–10pm,	
Sat noon–3.45pm & 5–10pm	Mastercard, Switch, Visa

Kulu Kulu is a conveyor-belt sushi restaurant which pulls off the unlikely trick of serving really good sushi without being impersonal or intimidating. It is light and airy and there are enough coat hooks for a small army of diners. The only thing you could quibble about is the rather low stools, which are so heavy they feel fixed to the floor – anyone over six feet tall will find themselves dining in the tuck position favoured by divers and trampolinists. The atmosphere is Japanese utilitarian. In front of you is a plastic tub of gari (the rather delicious pickled ginger), a bottle of soy, and a small box containing disposable wooden chopsticks. After that, as they say at Bingo, it's eyes down, look in, and on with the game.

The plates come round on the kaiten, or conveyor, and are coded by design rather than colour, which could prove deceptive: A plates are £1.20, B plates are £1.80, and C plates are £2.40. All the usual sushi favourites are here, and the fish is particularly fresh and well presented. Maguri – tuna – is a B; Amaebi – sweet shrimp – is a C; Hotategai – scallops – is a C, and very sweet indeed. Futomaki – a Californian, cone-shaped roll with tuna – is a B. The wasabi/eye-watering factor, however, is a bit hit or miss. Just as you're wishing for a bit more wasabi, you bite into something that makes you long for a bit less. As well as the sushi, the conveyor parades some little bowls of hot dishes – one worth looking out for combines strips of fried fish skin with a savoury vegetable purée (it counts as an A). The bowl of miso soup is also an A. To drink, there is everything from Oolong tea (£1.50) through Kirin beer (£2.60) to Urku shochu – a particularly dangerous Japanese white spirit (£1.80).

Kulu Kulu also offers a range of set options which represent excellent value and take the strain off keeping your eye fixed on the conveyor belt. They include mixed sashimi (£10) and mixed tempura (£8.60). Look behind the bar and you may see a stack of cardboard cases which contain sake supplies. It is strange but true that one of the premium sakes is made in the Rocky Mountains – in America!

SOHO ⑰ MODERN BRITISH

Mezzo

100 Wardour St, W1 ©020 7314 4000	⊖ Piccadilly Circus

Mon–Thurs noon–3pm & 6pm–midnight,

Fri & Sat noon–3pm & 6pm–1am*, Sun 12.30–3pm & 6–11pm

*Last food orders 1am except crustacea bar (open to 3am)	All major credit cards

When Sir Terence Conran unveiled Mezzo in 1995, people came to look at it just because it was there, and just because it was so . . . big. Nobody had opened a restaurant in London with space for 600 diners in decades, and this was on a grand scale, encompassing a bar, an "informal" ground-floor restaurant (Mezzonine), and a full-on restaurant (Mezzo) at the bottom of a sweeping staircase with a stage for performers. All of these areas have been busy ever since. This is not a place for a quiet night out. The restaurant tables are packed close and there's a fashionable mayhem of noise. But if you like a buzz with your food, Mezzo has few rivals – and the food, considering the huge numbers of covers, is pretty good.

The Mezzo menus send out different signals for each session. Thus you can have three courses of a short pre-theatre menu for £15.50; a set Sunday brunch menu of three courses for £15.50; a weekday two-course set lunch for £12.50 or three courses for £15.50. Or you can spend a good deal more ordering à la carte. Whichever you go for, expect a mix of trad favourites and novel twists – you may see dishes like confit duck leg with braised endive (£14) vying for attention with Portobello mushroom with garlic snails and bacon (£15.50). But things can get a lot more elaborate, and grandstand dishes may include foie gras terrine, Sauternes and Bramley jelly (£12), monkfish saltimbocca (£19 for two), or roast sea scallops, leeks and rock oyster sauce (£16.50). Beware the cost of veg: a side order of French beans is not cheap at £3.50. And leave space for the puds, which are rich and greed-provoking: pain perdu, poached pear, and chocolate ice cream (£5.50), apricot Vacherin with vanilla cream (£5.50), tarte Tatin with crème fraîche (£6).

Mezzo has live music every evening, mostly jazz, and often great. You pay a £5 charge for a seat to watch the shows – not bad value if that's what you're here for.

CENTRAL

Pollo

20 Old Compton St, W1 ©020 7734 5917	⊖ Leicester Square
Daily noon–midnight	Cash or cheque only

You won't find haute cuisine at Pollo, but you do get great value for money. As at its neighbouring rival, Centrale (see p.135), this is comfort food, Latin-style – long on carbohydrate and short on frills. Sophistication is in short supply, too – the interior design begins and ends with the lino floors and tatty pictures – but no matter: devotees return time and again for the cheap platefuls of food and the friendly, prompt service. Diners are shoehorned into booths presided over by a formidable Italian mama who tips you the wink as to what you should order. Downstairs there's more space, but you still might end up sharing a table.

The spotlight of Pollo's lengthy menu falls on cheap, filling pasta in all its permutations. Tagliatelle, rigatoni, ravioli, pappardelle, tortelloni and fusilli are all available. Your choice is basically down to the pasta type, as most of them are offered with the same selection of sauces. The tortelloni salvia (£3.60), which comes with a wonderfully sagey butter sauce, is very good, as is the tagliatelle melanzana (£3.40), whose rich tomato sauce is boosted by melt-in-the-mouth aubergine. Meat courses are less successful; anchovies, for instance, are few and far between in the bistecca alla pizzaiola, steak in capers and anchovy sauce (£5.80). But vegetarians are very well catered for here. Meat-free highlights include spaghetti aglio, olio e peperoncino (£3.30), a hot mix of garlic, olive oil and chilli. Meanwhile, a hearty plateful of gnocchi (£3.60) would curb even the most flamboyant appetite. Then there are pizzas, perhaps not the elegant wood-fired-oven type that are all the rage, but solid and substantial like the Regina (£3.90), a hammy, cheesy, mushroomy kind of experience. There is even a selection of risotti to choose from (all £3.50). A carafe of house wine is a bargain at £5.95; and so are the puddings, at £1.60. After a substantial hit of pasta, the imposing portion of tiramisù is a challenge for even the greediest diner.

As if Pollo wasn't cheap enough as it is, it offers the same menu as takeaway; on which all the pasta dishes cost just £3.

£12–£38

Randall & Aubin

16 Brewer St, W1 ✆020 7287 4447	⊖ Piccadilly Circus
Mon–Sat noon–11pm, Sun 4–10.30pm	All major credit cards

Formerly a butcher's, Randall & Aubin is now a self-proclaimed champagne-oyster bar, as its seafood counter and champagne buckets groaning with flowers suggest – but it's also a rôtisserie, sandwich shop and charcuterie to boot. It's the oysters that draw you in, along with the 1900s shop decor, with its original white tiles, cleverly adapted with French and American diner touches – cool marble table tops and high stools that look characterful, if not exactly lending themselves to relaxed dining. But that's part of the plan: Randall's serves good food, speedily, for folk without a lot of time. In the summer, the huge sash windows are opened up, making this a wonderfully airy place to eat – especially if you grab a seat by the window.

There's an extensive menu: an eclectic choice of starters roaming the globe from soupe de poisson (£3.90), to Japanese fish cakes (£5.95), and smoked salmon and caviar blinis (£8.75). Main courses range from "original" Caesar salad (£5.85), through spit-roast herbed chicken (£8.50) and sausage and mash with onion gravy (£8.75), to sirloin steak with sauce Béarnaise and pommes frites (£11.50). There are also some interesting accompaniments, such as pommes Dauphinoise (£2.50) or ratatouille (£2.75). If you don't mind crowds, drop in for a hot filled baguette (£5.70–£6.70) at lunchtime: the salt beef, sauerkraut and gherkin variety, served with pommes frites (£6.70) is authentic. Also available in the evening, the baguettes provide an inexpensive yet satisfying meal. The fruits de mer list offers well-priced seafood, ranging from dressed crab at £7.75 to delicious, pan-fried scallops with caramelised fennel and sauté chilli potatoes (£12.50), and whole roast lobster, garlic butter and pommes frites (£22). Puddings all cost £3.95 and range from tarts and brûlées to the more adventurous pear and caramel galette or chocolate truffle cake. Many of these dishes are also on the inexpensive takeaway menu, which makes for exciting picnicking.

Hard-core traditionalists with a penchant for chewing gobbets of resilient rubber which taste remarkably like the aroma of pumped-out bilge water will relish the fresh whelks with lemon and vinegar (£6.50).

£17–£45

The Red Fort

77 Dean St, W1 ⓒ020 7437 2115   ⊖ Leicester Square/Tottenham Court Road

Mon–Sat noon–3pm & 5.30–11.45pm,

Sun noon–3pm & 6–11pm   All major credit cards

www.redfort.co.uk

For a long while The Red Fort was the only Indian establishment in Soho serving authentic Indian food. It forged a reputation for regional dishes, accurate spicing and a comfortable – even luxurious – setting (which underwent yet another refurb in the summer of 2000), while the rest of Soho's curry houses purveyed simple dishes to the crowd that stumbled in at closing time. Since then, many others have offered aspirational and regional Indian cuisine, and getting a table at The Red Fort is no longer difficult, nor costly providing you stick to the buffet lunch at £14.95 per person (available until 3pm). But the buffet is really a pale shadow of The Red Fort's freshly cooked dishes and it's best to splash out, going with enough friends to get a good tour of the menu.

Start with the galuti kebab (£5.95), which is minced lamb with rose petals and kewra essence. Or machli-e-kebab (£5.95), salmon marinated in carom seeds. Or a familiar dish, chicken tikka (£11.95), fresh from the tandoor. Then move on to some favourites: crab masala (£11.95), fresh crab cooked with hot spices and curry leaves; rogan josh (£10.95), lamb cooked on the bone, which is the key to getting a really rich gravy. Or maybe korma-e-Avadh, lamb cooked in a mild sauce with poppy seeds (£12.95). Then there are a number of dum dishes, in which each dish is cooked in a sealed pot to trap all the flavour and aroma. Try murg dum handi (£12.95), chicken with chillies, coriander and saffron; or jhinga-dum-nisha (£16.95), prawns in a smooth sesame seed sauce. Anyone feeling both indecisive and extravagant can opt for the Red Fort Selection – for £35 per head you get a complete banquet all the way from an array of starters to an array of puds.

If you look up from your table, it's likely that you will recognise various exalted diners from the House of Commons or the Lords – don't rub your eyes and blame it on the spicy food. The Red Fort has a "Parliamentary Privilege Club" which gives special terms to more than 1000 MPs and peers. It seems that the honourable members are just as keen as everyone else both on going for a curry and on claiming a discount.

£28–£75

Richard Corrigan at The Lindsay House

21 Romilly St, W1 ℂ020 7439 0450 — ⊖ Leicester Square

Mon–Fri 12.30–2.30pm & 6–11pm, Sat 6–11pm — All major credit cards

Even among chefs – not usually held to be overly calm and level-headed people – Richard Corrigan is regarded as something of a wild man. He arrived at this deservedly Michelin-starred restaurant in Soho via a spell bringing haute cuisine to a dog track in the East End, and at The Lindsay House he seems to have found his niche. The restaurant is split into a series of small rooms, the service is attentive, and the food is very good indeed. The menus are uncomplicated and change regularly to keep in step with what is available at the market. Dinner means a choice of seven starters, six main courses and six puddings and costs £42, while at lunch the line-up is a tad smaller, as is the price – a real bargain at £23 for three courses.

Only a fool would try to predict what dishes Richard Corrigan will have on his menu tomorrow, but you can be sure that they will combine unusual flavour combinations with verve and style. Starters surprise – a lightly jellied tomato consommé, ewe's cheese, avocado and basil – or are lusciously opulent – ravioli of foie gras and suckling pig, leek and tarragon. Or there are combinations that seem familiar but come with a twist, like smoked eel with apples, fennel and chorizo. Main courses follow the same ground rules, so you might be offered a slow-roasted shin of veal with watercress, kidney and mushroom, or monkfish wrapped in cured ham, with choucroute, brown shrimp and red wine. The puddings soar towards dessert lover's heaven with such as chocolate fondant, confit kumquats, thyme and orange sorbet, or soft meringue with roast strawberry vanilla ice cream. The wine list is extensive and expensive.

If there is one thing that marks out the cuisine at the Lindsay House, it is Corrigan's love affair with offal. Sweetbreads, kidneys, and tongue all find their way onto the menu, in dishes that perfectly illustrate his deft touch with hearty flavours.

Soho Soho

11–13 Frith St, W1 ✆020 7494 3491   ⊖ Leicester Square/Tottenham Court Road

Restaurant Mon–Fri noon–3.30pm & 5.30-11.30pm, Sat 5.30–11.30pm

Rôtisserie Mon–Sat noon–12.30am   All major credit cards

www.sante-gcg.com

Soho Soho, the Provençal restaurant in Frith Street, was always intended by its owners Groupe Chez Gérard to be their Soho flagship, a trick it never quite accomplished until 1999 when the arrival of a new chef brought changes to both menu and restaurant. On the ground floor, spilling out onto the pavement in fine weather you find the rôtisserie. Upstairs is the more serious restaurant, so, depending on your mood, either may suit. Downstairs you'll get more bistro-like food, which is generally cheaper than the meals served by its grander sibling – moules marinières (£4.95/£7.50), entrecôte Béarnaise (£12.95), or an omelette au jambon et champignon (£7.50). But it is the first floor where Soho Soho shows its potential – there's good cooking with judicious use of spices and seasoning, good friendly service and a menu that still has its roots in Provence. This place is unlikely to have the Michelin men falling over themselves to scatter stars and plaudits but a busy, happy crowd shows that it hits the spot with the public.

The menu is not over-long, with nine choices of first course and eleven mains, but it covers a lot of ground, and the restaurant is busy enough to reassure you that everything will be freshly cooked. First courses range from parfait de foie gras et de volailles (£6.25) to ravioli de crabe, étuvée de poivrons rouges (£6.50). Crème de moules au fenouil (£4.50) is a light mussel and fennel soup which is rather better than the terrine de légumes de Provence (£5.20), but both are above average. There's an attractive-looking loup de mer entier en papillote (£35 for two), and the confit de canard, lentilles du Puy aux lardons (£12.50) is served as you would expect in a restaurant in Paris – rare for England. Aile de raie rôtie, sauce ravigotte (£11.95) – skate wing with caper and anchovy mayonnaise – is delicious; selle d'agneau grillée (£13.50), served properly pink, comes with a melting tarragon butter.

The only niggles are the haricots verts (£2.50), which are on the crunchy side, and the slight predictability about the puds and wine list.

£15–£28

Soho Spice

124–126 Wardour St, W1 ✆020 7434 0808   ⊖ Leicester Square/Piccadilly Circus

Mon–Thurs 11.30am–12.30am, Fri & Sat 11.30am–3am,

Sun 12.30–10.30pm   All major credit cards

Soho Spice is the new face of Indian restaurants. It's large – seating 100 in the restaurant and 40 in the bar – and takes bookings only for parties of six or more. It's busy, with loud music and late opening at the weekends. The decor is based around a riot of colour. And it is very, very successful. Which must be mainly down to the food, which is an equally large step from curry house staples – the main menu featuring contemporary Indian cuisine and a regularly changing special menu showcasing dishes from particular regions. What's more, when you order a main course it comes on a thali – with pulao rice, naan, dhal and seasonal vegetables of the day – which makes ordering simple and paying less painful.

On the main menu there are starters like nargisi kebab (£3.75), small lamb rissoles each stuffed with cheese and then deep-fried. Or try palak plyazee (£2.95), which is a sort of crisp spinach and onion bhaji. Or there's chicken millennium (£3.50), which the unkind would say bears a passing resemblance to last year's dish, "chicken chat" – a simple stir-fry. Main courses represent good value, given their accompaniments. Good choices are the chukanderi champ (£11.95), spicy lamb chops marinated with beetroot; or achaari murg ka tikka (£9.95), a dish of chicken marinated overnight in pickling spices and cooked in the tandoor. Or how about the Bengal fish curry (£10.95), fillets of tilapia cooked with tomatoes and onions and given bite by mustard seeds? Desserts offer a nice range of kulfis (£2.95) – an Indian ice cream made with boiled milk – and that sweetest of comfort foods, gulab jamun (£3.95), a dumpling soaked in rose syrup.

The special regional menu changes every month – so on one visit it may be recipes from Rajasthan and on the next you'll find dishes from Bengal. For example, when the chosen region was the North West Frontier there were starters like gilafi kebab – lamb dumplings with pearl onions and button mushrooms. Mains included the celebrated murg malai Peshwari, a kebab of chicken breast and cheese, and Kandhari pasanda, lamb with onions, tomatoes, almonds and saffron. A three-course set meal costs £15.95 including tea or coffee.

Spiga

84–86 Wardour St, W1 ✆020 7734 3444   ⊖ Leicester Square

Sun–Tues noon–3pm & 6–11pm,

Wed–Sat noon–3pm & 6pm–midnight   All major credit cards

Spiga has an impeccable pedigree. It comes from the same stable as Aubergine, L'Oranger and Zafferano and has that piece of kit that identified any 1990s Italian restaurant as serious – a wood-fired oven. However, despite its credentials, you don't need to pay a king's ransom to eat here, nor do you have to dress up. This is a pleasantly casual affair, the atmosphere is lively – sometimes the music is too lively – and the look is cool. Spiga may have cut the prices but they haven't cut corners: the tableware is the latest in Italian chic.

Menus change monthly, with occasional daily specials, but there's a definite pattern. Starters will get you in the mood. The buffalo mozzarella is served with marinated peppers, olives, capers and basil (£6). Or try something like the cozze affumicate (£6/£9), which are home-smoked mussels, or the legumi griglia (£5.50/£7.50). But the home-made pasta course is where it's really at. What's good is that, like the starters, most pasta dishes come in large or small portions. Think Italian and enjoy an extra course, such as gnocchi di ceci scamorza e pomodorini (£6/£8), or ravioli neri ripieni di zucchine e salmone (£6.50/£9), a tasty dish of black ravioli with zucchine and salmon in a fresh tomato sauce. Then consider a pizza – thin crust, crispy and the size of a dustbin lid. Gorgonzola e speck (£8.50) is good, as is al pesce spada (£8.50), topped with swordfish, capers and shallots and a tomato sauce. Alternatively, main courses offer up char-grilled and pan-fried dishes, like merluzzo con olive neri e pomodorini (£13.50), which teams cod with black olives and cherry tomatoes, or palliard di pollo con patate e spinaci (£12), a simple but good char-grilled chicken breast. And, if you aren't already full, the pudding section is well worth a look, too. Highlights include a wickedly indulgent lemon and mascarpone tart (£5.50) and an excellent tiramisù (£5.50).

Full marks to the person who can identify the weirdly thought-provoking loofah-like objects hanging on the walls.

£32–£60

The Sugar Club

21 Warwick St, W1 ℭ020 7437 7776	⊖ Piccadilly Circus
Daily noon–3pm & 6–11pm	All major credit cards

After a triumphant spell just off Portobello Road, in 1998 The Sugar Club moved to these elegant premises in Soho. Much larger. Much more stylish. Much more blond wood. But still the same passionate, exciting and well-executed food. The menu here typifies all that is best about the irreverent attitudes of all those eclectic Antipodean chefs – ingredients from all over the world are brought together with panache. A starter may be composed from a careful selection of top-quality Spanish foods, and then a main course may have Japanese ingredients as its mainspring. Done well (and it has been done very well at The Sugar Club), this approach is terrifically exciting.

Some of the finest starters at The Sugar Club are assemblies. Eating these feels rather as if you had helped yourself to a plateful of goodies from a fabulously well-stocked fridge. Witness the Garroxta cheese with Leon Iberico chorizo, Serrano ham, piquillo peppers, guindilla chillies, Marcona almonds and caper berries (£8.90): a thoughtful selection of rich cheese, soft peppers, crunchy almonds. Or there are simpler arrays like grilled scallops with sweet chilli sauce and crème fraîche (£12.50), or tuna sashimi salad with avocado, sea kale and roast peanut-ginger dressing (£9.80). Fish is either from the other side of the world, or given accompaniments that makes it look as if it is, like pan-roast sea trout on shaved fennel, crisp lotus root and baby spinach with chickpea, cumin and wasabi tobiko salad (£19.80). Or try roast Trelough duck breast on braised hijiki and buckwheat noodle salad with pickled bean shoots, enoki and caramelised chilli dressing (£16.90). Vegetarians are well served by dishes such as baked globe artichoke, buffalo mozzarella and wild mushrooms with rum- and honey-braised black beans, wilted spinach and sumac (£14.80). And the desserts make even the most experienced puddingist roll over in ecstasy – coffee, dark chocolate and caramel ice cream terrine with cardamom and cherry sauce (£6.50). Bliss.

For recreation, watch elegant and fashionably thin diners as they nibble just one forkful of the mustard mash (£3.50) side dish, and then another, and . . . Peter Gordon no longer heads up the kitchen here, but his books are on sale to remind us how things once were.

Teatro

93–107 Shaftesbury Ave, W1 ©020 7494 3040	⊖ Leicester Square
Mon–Fri noon–3pm & 6–11.45pm, Sat 6–11.45pm	All major credit cards

Eating at Teatro is an appropriately theatrical experience. After the rather intimidating and industrial street-level entrance it's up the metal stairs to reception, where the atmosphere starts to feel a touch friendlier. You then head along the curved corridor, past the members' bar, into the open and elegant dining room. This restaurant has celebrity owners (Lee Chapman and Leslie Ash) and celebrity customers (not only hiding in the members' bar but plying the knife and fork in the main arena). Given all these potential complications, the food is remarkably good and not too extravagantly priced. Indeed there's a two-course prix fixe lunch for £15.50 (plus an iniquitous £1.50 cover charge), or you can have three courses for £18 (£19.50 when marked up).

The menu changes seasonally and offers a mix of old favourites and updated classics. Thus you might find starters like shellfish bisque with Calvados (£7.50), or Belgian endive salad with blue cheese and honey dressing (£7.50), or ravioli of pumpkin with walnut cream and shaved Pecorino (£8.50/£12.75), vying with Teatro salade Niçoise (£7.50/£15). There is even a pleasing extravagance that takes the plat du jour approach to new heights – foie gras du jour (£11.25). Main courses, more or less equally divided between fish and meat, have novel accompaniments. So you might find a herb-crusted sea bass teamed with braised salsify and basil dressing (£19.25), or a grilled fillet of swordfish with spiced lentils and gaufrette chips (£17.50). The pan-fried marinated venison comes with a celeriac choucroute and dried cherry sauce (£17.50), while the roast organic chicken is set off nicely by the lemon confit and fettuccine (£15.50). More simply, there may be a roast veal cutlet with a green salad and sauce Béarnaise (£17.95). The standard of cooking is high and the standard of presentation higher still. The wine list runs from an eminently reasonable French Chardonnay at £11 to a rather more pocket-challenging 1969 Château Pétrus at £325.

Desserts (all £6.50) bring off the difficult trick of being both elegant and satisfying at the same time. The baked rice pudding with Seville orange marmalade and pistachio biscuits covers all the bases: just one taste will make you feel like a celebrity.

£7–£14

The Toucan

19 Carlisle St, W1 ©020 7437 4123	⊖ Leicester Square/Tottenham Court Road
Mon–Sat 11am–11pm	Mastercard, Visa (over £10)
www.thetoucan.co.uk	

When they opened The Toucan the proprietors' first priority was to approach Guinness and ask if they could become a stockist. They explained that they wanted to open a small bar aimed single-mindedly at the drinking public, just like the ones they had enjoyed so much in Dublin. Guinness replied that, providing they could shift two barrels a week, they'd be happy to put them on the list. Neither party imagined that within a couple of years the order would be more like thirty barrels a week! It's an impressive intake, but then The Toucan is an impressive place, serving home-made, very cheap, very wholesome and very filling food, along with all that Guinness. Its success has meant expansion from the original hot, dark, cellar premises to include the ground floor – and the establishment of a Toucan Two at 94 Wimpole St, W1 (©020 7499 2440).

Start with six Galway Bay oysters (£7), or the vegetable soup with bread (£2). Go on to a large bowl of Irish stew with bread (£4.50), or Guinness pie and champ (£5.50) – champ is a kind of super-charged Irish mashed potato with best butter playing a leading role alongside the spring onions. It features in a couple of novelty items – you can have chilli and champ (£4.95), or ratatouille and champ (£3.75) – these two are also available with rice. The JPs (jacket potatoes) come with various fillings, and there's an array of sandwiches. There's also a great-value smoked salmon plate (£6). One thing to bear in mind if you've come here hungry: there are times when The Toucan becomes so packed with people that you can scarcely lift a pint. At those times, all attempts at serving food are abandoned.

Of course, if things have got out of hand, you could spend a happy evening at The Toucan without actually eating. As some Irish sage once remarked, "There's eating and drinking in a pint of Guinness." And if it's a chaser you're after, then be aware that The Toucan also makes a feature of Irish whiskies – including the exotic and stratospherically expensive Middleton Rare. If you have to ask how much it costs, you cannot afford it.

£20–£32

Vasco and Piero's Pavilion

15 Poland St, W1 ©020 7437 8774	⊖ Oxford Circus
Mon–Fri noon–3pm & 6–11pm, Sat 7–11pm	All major credit cards

Very much a family-run restaurant, the Pavilion has been a Soho fixture for the past twenty years. But there's nothing old or institutional about the cooking or decor. Vasco himself cooks for his regulars and the establishment has long been a favourite with diners who appreciate the best family cooking, fairly simple, and with top-class ingredients. Dishes are biased towards Umbrian cuisine. Customers include the great and the good, and the Pavilion's modern yet comfortable atmosphere guarantees them anonymity. The restaurant's new sibling – Caffe Umbria, 108 Heath St, NW3 (©020 7431 4969) – is in the hands of Vasco's son Paul.

There's an à la carte menu at lunchtime only, but the basic deal at the Pavilion is that you choose either two courses for £16.50 or three for £19.50. Given the quality, freshness of ingredients and attention to detail this proves exceptional value. A starter of carpaccio of roast pink lamb, rucola and Parmesan is a moreish and clever variation on traditional carpaccio. Duck salad, mixed leaves, mostarda di Cremona is plate-wipingly good, with the duck shreds crispy yet moist. Pastas (all home-made) are excellent, too, particularly the spaghettini with fresh tomato and basil – perfectly cooked and with a sauce that is prepared from fresh ingredients and tastes like it. For carnivores, however, there is nothing to beat the calves' liver with fresh sage – paper-thin liver that literally melts in the mouth with just a hint of sage, and crisp vegetables that have been cooked at that moment rather than reheated. Puddings continue the quality. A panna cotta that is gelatinously creamy, a praline semi-freddo that is rich and soft as well as being crunchy, and a torta della Nonna that reveals buttery sponge pastry and custard – flavours that remind you of bread and butter pudding and ambrosia. There is a good selection of the less usual Italian wines and good Italian pudding wines, too.

The Pavilion hosts occasional, special, dinners celebrating Italian regional food. A quick phone call gets you on the mailing list for details.

Yo!Sushi

52 Poland St, W1 ©020 7287 0443	⊖ Oxford Circus/Piccadilly Circus
Daily noon–midnight	All major credit cards

www.yosushi.co.uk

When Yo!Sushi burst upon the scene it was to fanfares and a tidal wave of publicity. This was an event beyond just another kaiten (conveyor-belt) sushi bar. Robotic sushi-makers, robotic drinks trolleys, video screens – not many restaurants credit "sponsors" like ANA, Sony and Honda. In among all this there is even some food, and, though purists may shudder, it's more consistent than the hype would have you suspect.

Plates are marked in lime (£1.50), blue (£2), purple (£2.50), orange (£3) and pink (£3.50): when satiated you call for a plate count, and your bill is prepared. You sit at the counter with a little waiters' station in front of you – there's gari (pickled ginger), and there's soy, and wasabi, little dishes and a forest of wooden chopsticks. Kirin beer costs £3; small warm sake £3; and unlimited Japanese tea is £1. You're ready to begin. Yo!Sushi claim to serve more than 100 sushis, so be leisurely and watch the belt – and, if in doubt, ask. The nigiri sushi range from fruit and crabstick (both £1.50) to salmon, French bean and mackerel (at £2); on to tuna, prawn and squid (at £3) and so on up to yellowtail and fatty tuna which carry the warning that they are "as available" and a pink price tag of £3.50. There are about twenty different maki rolls (with vegetarians well catered for) at all prices. The seven different sashimi and seven different gunkan all command orange and pink prices. As do the handrolls – which are nori funnels, Californian-style. Dining at Yo!Sushi does call for some restraint and deft mental arithmetic – the tower of brightly badged empty plates building up in front of you can end up costing more than you expected.

Yo!Sushi is at the forefront of restaurant merchandising and no age group is safe. There are Yo!Sushi T-shirts, fleeces, coats, and even baby-gros. Webbists can even buy badged mouse mats. You'll find other branches of Yo!Sushi within The Fifth Floor Food Market at Harvey Nichols (Knightsbridge), in Selfridges on Oxford Street, and deep within the O2 centre on the Finchley Road.

Zilli Fish

36–40 Brewer St, W1 ℂ020 7734 8649	⊖ Piccadilly Circus
Mon–Sat noon–11.30pm	All major credit cards

Bright, brittle and brash, Zilli Fish is a companion to Aldo Zilli's other Soho venues, Signor Zilli, 40 Dean St, W1 (ℂ020 7734 3924) and the Zilli Bar next door. In a hectic, young atmosphere it serves a modern Italianate fish menu to London's media workers and the rest of the Soho crowd. Tables are close and everything is conducted at a racy pace. Not ideal for a secret conversation or for plighting your troth unless you want the whole place to cheer you on.

The menu starts with the modestly entitled section, "what we are famous for". These are dishes like fillet of monkfish wrapped in speck and roasted, served with grilled vegetables and a pesto dressing (£16.50); hand-pressed spaghetti chitarra with jumbo prawns, tomato, basil, garlic and red chilli (£14.90); and salmon fillet filled with crab and ginger served with a lime sauce (£14.50). Char-grilled swordfish served on Caesar salad (£15.90) proves an excellent flavour alliance. Hot fish and cool salad is a difficult combination, but one that Zilli Fish does well. Dishes like whole pound (lb) lobster, grilled with garlic butter and herbs and served with chips (£19.90), demonstrate admirable restraint. From the side orders, wild rocket and Parmesan salad is simple but well made (£5.90). While the list is dominated by fish, there are daily specials with some modern Italian vegetarian and meat items, from risotto with wild and field mushrooms and white truffle oil (£9.90) to roast suckling pig with apple sauce (£16.50). Puddings include an espresso crème brûlée (£6) – coffee lovers take note: with its soft creamy interior, it's like eating double cream cappuccino. Very moreish. Strawberries with limoncello liqueur and pistachio ice cream (£6) is a refreshing way to eat a sometimes dull fruit.

Aldo Zilli has built up a popularity in Soho which guarantees that his bar and restaurants are almost always packed. Zilli Fish offers good food, but also good fun. In keeping with so many restaurants nowadays, Signor Zilli is quite happy to give away his secrets. Signed copies of Aldo's latest book are always available in the restaurant.

Alphabet

61–63 Beak St, W1   ✆020 7439 2190

Ultra-stylish and young, this minimal bar is a good place to chill out during the day. At night, it fills with a pre-club crowd enjoying cocktails, mixer drinks and bottled beers. Don't even think of going in if you're over thirty.

Bar Soho

23–25 Old Compton St, W1   ✆020 7439 0439

This noisy, bright bar hosts a young, up-for-it crowd who like their music loud and their pleasure lively. Mixer drinks and bottled beers are the favourites here. A late licence (1am Mon–Thurs, 3am Fri & Sat) means that it gets busier and busier as the night draws on, and they sometimes levy a club entrance fee at the door.

The Blue Posts

18 Kingly St, W1   ✆020 7734 1170

An old two-storey pub in the heart of Soho, the Blue Posts is a local home from home for people who have worked around here for years. Its charm is in its friendly unpretentiousness. Enjoy Flowers Original and IPA and Wadworth's 6X.

The Carlisle

2 Bateman St, W1   ✆020 7479 7951

The Carlisle is a favourite among Soho's creative elite. It's nicely modernised, but in traditional style, and offers a friendly welcome to everyone. Favourites include Bass Red Triangle, Fuller's London Pride and Guinness.

The Clachan

34 Kingly St, W1   ✆020 7734 2659

This is a lovely old Victorian-style pub with etched glass and screens, ornate panelling and lots of nooks and corners. The street it's in is narrow and dark and so it tends to get overlooked. Predominantly enjoyed by local after-work drinkers who favour Timothy Taylor's and Greene King IPA.

The Dog & Duck

18 Bateman St, W1   ✆020 7437 4447

This tiny pub is very much a Soho landmark, partly because it has been here for ever, and partly because it's always full with lively media folk. Genuine tiles, a real cosy fireplace and Tetley's, Hook Norton and Timothy Taylor's beers add to the charm.

The Intrepid Fox

97–99 Wardour St, W1   ✆020 7287 8359

Gothic style is alive and well at the Fox. You'll see more amazing fashions and pierced body parts here than anywhere else in this very popular Soho landmark. Famous old rock posters line the walls and it has real character. Enjoy Murphy's, Grolsch and Dry Blackthorn Cider.

The Old Coffee House

49 Beak St, W1   ✆020 7347 2197

It doubtless was a coffee house once, but it's now a very welcoming public house, with just a few traditional pictures and posters telling you its history. Regulars opt for draught Beck's, Marstons Pedigree and Courage Directors.

The Red Lion

14 Kingly St, W1   *©020 7734 4985*

Separate saloon and public bars distinguish this comfortable small pub. It's a nice old place with a well-worn darts area, favourite seats for regulars and an open fire that burns real fuel as opposed to gas. Samuel Smith's Old Brewery Bitter is the favourite ale on tap.

The Shakespeare's Head

29 Great Marlborough St, W1 *©020 7734 2911*

Right on the corner of Carnaby Street, this traditional pub gets more than its fair share of tourists. Brave them, and the crowds of Soho regulars standing on the wide pavement outside, to enjoy a decent pint of Courage Best or Directors.

Two Floors

3 Kingly St, W1   *©020 7439 1007*

Red leather sofas and a clubby atmosphere make this youthful bar feel like an extension of a trendy living room. As its name suggests, there are two floors where you can enjoy mixer drinks, cocktails and bottled beers like Red Stripe, Rolling Rock and Stella.

Zilli Bar

40 Dean St, W1   *©020 7734 1853*

They say that if you sit in Zilli's for long enough you're bound to meet someone you know, or at least recognise. It's very much a film and TV place and gets busy with an evening crowd sharing gossip and enjoying Aldo Zilli's good wine list and bar snacks. Bottled beers, wines and mixer drinks are the order of the day.

South Kensington

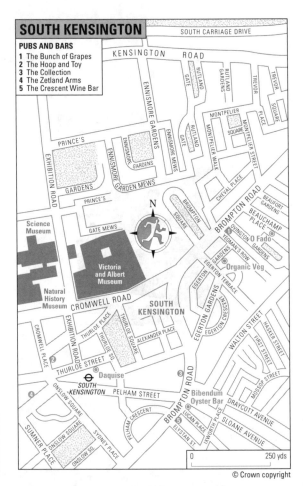

SOUTH KENSINGTON

PUBS AND BARS
1 The Bunch of Grapes
2 The Hoop and Toy
3 The Collection
4 The Zetland Arms
5 The Crescent Wine Bar

SOUTH CARRIAGE DRIVE

KENSINGTON ROAD

RUTLAND GATE
RUTLAND GARDENS
TREVOR
MONTPELIER SQUARE
MONTPELIER PLACE
MONTPELIER STREET
MONTPELIER WALK
RUTLAND GATE
RUTLAND GARDENS

ENNISMORE GARDENS
ENNISMORE GARDENS MEWS
ENNISMORE GARDENS
ENNISMORE MEWS

PRINCE'S GARDENS
EXHIBITION ROAD
PRINCE'S

CHEVAL PLACE

BROMPTON SQUARE

BROMPTON ROAD
BEAUFORT GARDENS
BEAUCHAMP PLACE

N

Science Museum

GATE MEWS

Victoria and Albert Museum

Natural History Museum

QUINTON GARDENS
YEOMAN'S ROW
O Fado
EGERTON GARDENS
EGERTON TERRACE
Organic Veg

CROMWELL ROAD

SOUTH KENSINGTON

EGERTON GARDENS
EGERTON CRESCENT
EGERTON GARDENS

WALTON STREET
FIRST STREET
HASKER STREET

CROMWELL PLACE
EXHIBITION ROAD
THURLOE PLACE
THURLOE STREET
THURLOE SQUARE
ALEXANDER PLACE

Daquise
SOUTH KENSINGTON
PELHAM STREET

BROMPTON ROAD

Bibendum Oyster Bar

MOSSOP STREET
DRAYCOTT AVENUE
SLOANE AVENUE

ONSLOW SQUARE
ONSLOW SQUARE
PELHAM CRESCENT

LUCAN PLACE
WALTON PLACE

SUMNER PLACE
ONSLOW SQUARE
SYDNEY PLACE
PELHAM PLACE

BROMPTON ROAD
ELYSTAN ST

0 _____ 250 yds

© Crown copyright

Bibendum Oyster Bar

Michelin House, 81 Fulham Rd, SW3 ☎020 7589 1480	⊖ South Kensington
Mon–Sat noon–10.30pm, Sun noon–10pm	All major credit cards
www.bibendum.co.uk	

Bibendum Oyster Bar is one of *the* places to eat shellfish in London. The 1911 building, a glorious tiled affair that was a former garage for the French tyre people, is Conranised throughout, but the oyster bar is in what looks like the old workshop on the ground floor and they've done precious little to it. On the old forecourt stand two camionettes: one is used as a shellfish stall, selling lobsters, oysters and crabs to the good people of Chelsea; the other is a flower stall, with lilies, ginger flowers and roses rather than carnations. It all looks rather quaint but it's very attractive, and it gives a much-needed initial splash of colour, which stays with you in the plain oyster bar – cream walls, marble tables, stone floor.

The menu is a shellfish lover's heaven. Here you'll find three different types of rock oysters (£7.50–£8 per half-dozen); you can choose your favourite or order a selection to find out the difference. The crab mayonnaise (£9) comes in the shell, giving you the enormous fun of pulling it apart and digging through the claws. Or you can have it done for you in a crab salad (£9.50) – probably just as good, but not nearly so satisfying. If you're really hungry, there's a particularly fine plateau de fruits de mer (£24.50 per head, minimum two people), which has everything – crab, clams, langoustine, oysters, prawns and shrimps, as well as winkles and whelks. There is plenty of choice for those less inclined to use claw crushers, though surprisingly there is practically nothing that uses this wealth of crustacea in hot dishes. Instead there are simple classics – vitello tonnato (£10), or grilled duck with orange and watercress salad and Cumberland sauce (£12). The daily, set menu follows the same lines – grilled chicken breast with chorizo and potato salad (£12), Greek salad with hummus and pitta bread (£9). Desserts are simple and seasonal – raspberries and Jersey cream (£5.50), a selection of cheeses (£5.50), and the inevitable crème brûlée (£5.50).

Given the nature of the place, there's a really sensible wine list, mostly given over to white wine and champagne, with a decent smattering of half-bottles and wines by the glass.

£8–£25

Daquise

20 Thurloe St, SW7 ℭ020 7589 6117   ⊖ South Kensington

Daily 11.30am–11pm   Mastercard, Visa

Daquise is more old-fashioned than you could possibly imagine. High ceilings, murky lighting, oilcloth table covers, charming service, elderly customers – the full Monty. During the day it serves coffee, tea and rather good cakes to all comers, breaking off at lunchtime and in the evening to dispense Polish home cooking, Tatra Zwiecka beer, and shot glasses of various vodkas. Several novels have been completed here by penniless writers seeking somewhere warm to scribble – buying a cup of coffee gets you a full ration of patience from the management. The food is genuine, although it is sad to see that the occasional, seasonal "wild mushroom stew" fell off the menu in 1999, and that the magnificent "herrings with potato" became the almost as good "herrings with bread". Portions are serious here, but prices are very reasonable, even if you don't take advantage of the hospitality to while away the day.

Start with Ukrainian barszcz (£2.50), rich and red, or the new starter, herrings with bread (£3.50) – the herring fillets are amazingly good here. Thick cut, pleasantly salty, and with a luxurious smooth texture. Go on to the kasanka (£6), a large buckwheat sausage (a cousin to black pudding) made using natural skins. Or, for the fearless, there is giant golonka (£8.80), a marinated pork knuckle which has been boiled and is served with horseradish sauce. Also welcome back an old friend, Vienna schnitzel with a fried egg on top (£9.50). And it is hard not to be tempted into ordering an extra dish of potato pancakes (£5.50), which are large, flat and crispy and come with sour cream or apple sauce. The other side-dish options are a strange sauerkraut (£1.50), served cold and very mild; cucumbers in brine (£1); and kasza (£1.60), the omnipresent buckwheat. For purists there's also that classic Central European dish, simply cooked trout (£8.50).

Every now and then a speculator proposes to redevelop this entire chunk of Thurloe Street. On such occasions the locals and regulars band together to defend the Daquise. Thankfully, so far they've always won.

O Fado

45–50 Beauchamp Place, SW3 ℂ020 7589 3002   ⊖ Knightsbridge

Daily noon–3pm & 6.30pm–1am   All credit cards except Diners

O Fado seems somewhat out of place in the chic environs of Beauchamp Place; in a street lined with some very pretentious establishments this Portuguese restaurant flies the flag for simpler things. O Fado is owned, staffed and largely frequented by Portuguese, though the waiters also need to speak Japanese, or at least refer to the food glossary on the wall when taking orders from the regulars who come here for the seafood. Pretty in pink and bedecked with hand-painted azulejos, it is quite a romantic restaurant, seductively lit with a few nooks and crannies that are bagged quickly – so book well ahead.

The menu and wine list are exhaustive. Favourite dishes among Japanese diners include octopus salad (£6.50), and arroz de marisco (£25 for two), the Portuguese take on paella. But those wanting to get in the mood for their summer holiday should try the crisp and salty grilled sardines (£3.50) or caldo verde soup (£2.60), followed by a spicy piri piri chicken and fries (£7.90) that should send French chefs scuttling for their cooking manuals. Finish off with pasteis de nata (95p each): custard tarts Portuguese-style. More sophisticated options are the shellfish crêpe with brandy sauce (£4.60), or mussels with a twist – served in olive oil and coriander together with the usual wine and garlic (£5.50). Popular with Portuguese families for Saturday lunch is cozido a Portuguesa, a bean and sausage stew (£9.50). Give them a day's notice and bring five friends. Bacalhau a cataplana (£9.80) is a dish of salt cod and clams, pressure-cooked in a rich tomato sauce, and surprisingly delicious. Look out for daily specials such as suckling pig (£15) but ask the price first, as they can prove expensive. If you still have room after the sumo-wrestler portions, try the arroz doce (£2.80), rice pudding – it's wonderful. The tarta da laranja (£2.80), a moist, eggy orange cake, and the pudim flan (£3.20), cream caramel, and molotof (£3.20) – not a bomb but an egg-white soufflé – are all good as well. To accompany your meal, try the Borba VQPRD 1996: delicious, and a snip at £11.90.

This place is called O Fado for a reason: mid-evening the house singer begins the haunting, lyrical strains of fado ballads, with guitar accompaniment, and diners listen appreciatively if they know what's good for them. It's all a lot quieter at lunchtime.

SOUTH KENSINGTON ⑩ CHINESE/VEGETARIAN

Organic Veg

8 Egerton Gardens Mews, SW3 ℂ020 7584 7007   ⊖ South Kensington

Mon–Sat noon–2.30pm & 6–11.15pm,

Sun noon–2.30pm & 6–11pm (winter only)   Cash only

Organic Veg is a no-smoking, Szechwan, vegetarian, Chinese restaurant tucked away in a quiet little mews in South Kensington. The name is perhaps the third that the place has adopted in as many years. Venture down some fairly unprepossessing steps and you find yourself in a dark and homely sort of place. The walls are rag-rolled yellow, the tablecloths are red and some of the furnishings are a little scuffed around the edges. For a tête-à-tête, book one of the two cubbyholes at the back. During the week the place is fairly quiet, and the staff are helpful and charming. Fellow Buddhists have opened an establishment on similar lines called Organic Thai, 10 Greek St, W1 (ℂ020 7287 3713).

If you're the sort of person who has found themselves longing for vegetarian crispy duck, you need look no further: here it is on the menu. But even the most confirmed flesh-eater is likely to be pleasantly surprised by the taste sensations on offer here. The cook serves up imaginative "assimilations" of chicken- fish- and meat-based dishes, and everything tastes light and fresh. Good starters include a veggie dim sum (£3.50) – five fat soya dumplings filled with cabbage, Chinese leaf, Chinese mushroom, fresh ginger and water chestnut. You could also kick off with sesame "prawns" (£4.50), or spring rolls (£3.50), which are crispy and golden, or the yin yang seaweeds (£3), marinated in ginger, onions and sesame. The aromatic crispy veg duck (£7.50) makes for a good mid-course. The "duck" is strips of tofu and looks a bit like an omelette: roll it up in a pancake and it works well. For mains, go for the meatier-sounding dishes. Crispy chilli veg "beef" (£6.50) is spicy and delicious (the "beef" here is strips of soya). Also good is "squid" in black bean sauce (£5.90) – very squid-like creations made of rice. Then there's veg "chicken" and cashew nuts (£5.90), with the soya "chicken" marinated in soy sauce and mixed with golden cashew nuts. For pudding, try the mango sorbet (£3.50) – refreshing and quite luxurious.

Don't ask for the wine list – there isn't one. But you can have a glass of sound house white or red for £3. And there's Chinese beer on offer – Tsing-tao – at £3 a glass.

CENTRAL

The Bunch of Grapes

207 Brompton Rd, SW3   ©020 7589 4944

Dating back to 1770, this unpretentious and friendly pub still has its old snob screens. It's owned by Scottish and Newcastle, so you get Directors and Theakston among others. Conveniently placed for the South Kensington museums and for shopping in Knightsbridge as well.

The Collection

264 Brompton Rd, SW3   ©020 7225 1212

This fashionable, dress-up and chat-up bar is an excellent place to drink cocktails and meet new people. It's young and noisy and gets very crowded, but they boast that they can mix almost any cocktail on the planet (there are 49 to start with on the bar list). It's open in the evenings only, and there's a door policy when it gets crowded later on.

The Crescent Wine Bar

99 Fulham Rd, SW3   ©020 7225 2244

Deservedly much praised, this ground-floor and basement wine bar boasts more than 200 wines on its list, with 23 by the glass. There is also a good selection of Armagnacs, Cognacs and Calvados. Equally good as a place to start your evening or to enjoy coffee and digestifs afterwards.

The Hoop & Toy

34 Thurloe Place, SW7   ©020 7589 8360

Established here in 1790, this pub features Theakston and Abbot Ale on draught. There's a separate cellar wine bar downstairs with its own entrance. It's the nearest pub to South Ken tube, so it can get crowded with people using it as a meeting point.

The Zetland Arms

2 Bute St, SW7   ©020 7589 3813

A spacious, traditional pub – it used to be run by Sid Chaplin, Charlie's brother – with plenty of room and a relaxed atmosphere. Courage Directors and Kronenbourg on draught and a games room upstairs if you get bored. It's called the Zetland because of the Danish influence in the area when it was built in the 1850s.

Victoria & Westminster

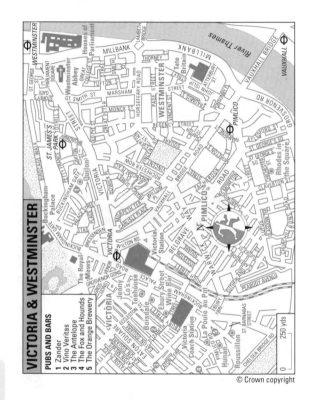

VICTORIA & WESTMINSTER

PUBS AND BARS

1 Zander
2 Vino Veritas
3 The Antelope
4 The Fox and Hounds
5 The Orange Brewery

© Crown copyright

0   250 yds

Boisdale

15 Eccleston St, SW1 ©020 7730 6922	⊖ Victoria
Mon–Sat noon–1am	All major credit cards
www.boisdale.co.uk	

Boisdale is owned by Ranald Macdonald, who is next in line to be the Chief of Clanranald, and if that information gives you a premonition of what the restaurant is like you are probably thinking along the right lines. This is a very Scottish place, strong on hospitality, and with a befuddlingly large range of rare malt whiskies. Fresh produce – correction, fresh Scottish produce – rules wherever possible, and it is no wonder that the clubby atmosphere and reliable cooking makes this a haven of choice for local businessmen, who are also likely to be found in the ultra-Scottish back bar, home to the formidable malt whisky collection. There is also a Boisdale jazz bar and cigar club next door.

There are three Boisdale menus, one of which is admirably simple – for £12.90, diners choosing the "haggis menu" can enjoy leek and potato soup with truffle oil, followed by roast MacSween's haggis with mash and neeps. By way of glossary: MacSween of Edinburgh is a famous haggis-maker, and haggis devotees spend hours arguing whether they or Lindsay Grieve of Hawick makes the ultimate haggis. Either way, haggis itself is still sheep's innards and oatmeal, a sound peasant dish. Neeps is the Scottish term for what everyone else calls swede. Or there's the "Boisdale" menu – a choice of six starters and seven mains for £17.45 (yes, just like the rebellion!). Starters range from salad of smoked Highland venison and pistachio to the slightly less Scottish tagliatelle with fines herbes pesto. Main courses veer from Scotch salmon, through smoked haddock and cod fish cakes, to Scotch sirloin steak Béarnaise with pommes frites.

The à la carte includes a good many luxury ingredients: as well as foie gras, and oysters, there's spiced potted lobster with rocket and warm toasted brioche (£9.50). Commendably, the mains feature fresh fish of the day, fresh offal of the day, and today's roast game. Plus fillet of Aberdeen Angus beef roast with a Lanarkshire blue sauce (£18.90). Sensibly enough, you can mix and match these menus as you work towards an after-dinner malt.

VICTORIA & WESTMINSTER ⓥ MODERN EUROPEAN

Ebury Wine Bar and Restaurant

139 Ebury St, SW1 ©020 7730 5447   ⊖ Victoria

Daily noon–3pm & 6–10.30pm (Sun until 10pm)   All major credit cards

Ebury Street may call itself a wine bar, but the food is not the kind of stuff that springs to mind when wine bars are mentioned. The regulars – from those swingeingly expensive houses in Belgravia and the offices around Victoria – come for a bottle of decent claret in the front area or to eat at the restaurant out the back. They overlook the rather chintzy decor and the closely packed tables, they will even overlook the somewhat uncomfortable chairs. They pitch up for the food, and to enjoy the rather old-fashioned but undeniably friendly service.

The food is well cooked, adventurous and always interesting – in an almost radical counterpoint to the decor. The menu changes regularly, but starters might include crab remoulade (£6); or a chicken and pancetta terrine (£4.75); or spicy fish cakes with peanuts and sweet chilli cucumber (£6). Rare meats like kangaroo, ostrich and emu all make the occasional guest appearance, and there is a magnificent "plate of savouries" (£6.75) offering a complete tour around tastes and textures. Then there's a menu section devoted to salads – in tune with the local customers – offering the likes of salad of chicken livers, new potatoes and goats' cheese (£5.50), or the laconically named Ebury chopped salad (£5). The more orthodox (only slightly more orthodox!) main courses are also inventive: grilled mackerel with Mediterranean garnishes (£11.50); red onion tarte Tatin (£9.50); lamb meatloaf in pancetta on an artichoke purée (£11); seared kangaroo loin with Thai spices (£16); Cumberland sausages with mash and onion gravy (£9.75). These are good dishes, well presented and made with well-chosen ingredients.

Desserts are equally moody – such as figs poached in Shiraz (£5). And a dish that has a generation of chefs arguing over who invented it first – the Mars bar spring roll (£4) aka the deep-fried Mars bar – which was probably (it's worth stressing the "probably" as there's a good deal of debate around the subject) first devised some years ago by Josh Hampton, who's in charge of the kitchens here.

CENTRAL

Hunan

51 Pimlico Rd, SW1 ©020 7730 5712	⊖ Sloane Square
Mon–Sat noon–2.30pm & 6–11.30pm	All major credit cards except Diners

The Hunan is the domain of Mr Peng. As you venture into his restaurant you put yourself into his hands, to do with what he will. It is rather like being trapped in a 1930s B-movie. You order the boiled dumplings . . . and the griddle-fried lettuce-wrapped dumplings turn up, "because you will like them more". And most likely you will. Probably at least ninety percent of Mr Peng's regular customers have given up the unequal struggle, submitting themselves to the "feast" – a multi-course extravaganza, varied according to the maestro's whims and the vagaries of the market, that might include pigeon soup or a dish of cold marinated octopus, or goose . . . This fine food and attentive service is matched by the Hunan's elegant surroundings – but be warned: the prices are Pimlico rather than Chinatown.

If you want to defy Mr Peng and act knowledgeable, you could actually try asking for the griddle-fried lettuce-wrapped dumplings (£4.80), which are exceedingly delicious, or the platter of assorted hot appetisers (£12 for two) – a triumph, with crispy bits of chicken, stuffed mushrooms, deep-fried green beans in peppery chilli, spare ribs, crispy seaweed and other goodies, all piping hot and strewn higgledy-piggledy across the plate in a delicious lucky dip. Alternatively, try the camphor-wood-and-tea-smoked duck (£18 for a half, £33 for a whole): once again, this dish is as interpreted by Mr P, so as well as a southwestern Chinese version of crispy duck (with pancakes etc) there's a sweet and sourish sauce (apparently his regulars felt that it was "too dry" without). Other standouts include spicy-rich beef in Hunan sauce (£6), and stir-fried squid "any style" (£7), which is accurately cooked.

However, for all but the strongest wills, resistance is useless and you'll probably end up with what is described on the menu as "Hunan's special leave-it-to-us-feast – minimum two persons, from £25 a head. We recommend those not familiar with Hunan cuisine to leave it to the chef Mr Peng to prepare for you his favourite and unusual dishes." Quite so.

Jenny Lo's Teahouse

14 Eccleston St, SW1 ℗020 7259 0399   ⊖ Victoria

Mon–Fri 11.30am–3pm & 6–10pm, Sat noon–3pm & 6–10pm   Cash or cheque only

Jenny Lo's Teahouse in Victoria is the complete opposite of those typically stuffy, overdesigned Chinese restaurants. This place is bright, bare and utilitarian – and stylish and fashionable, too. From the blocks of bright colours and refectory tables to the artifice of framing the emergency exit sign like a picture over the door, this is a somewhat smart – but comfortable – place to eat. And that just about sums up the food too. Service makes you think that you're in the politest cafeteria in the world and the prices don't spoil the illusion. Although portion sizes and seasoning can vary, the food is freshly cooked and generally delicious. All of which meets with unqualified approval from a loyal band of sophisticated regulars.

The menu is divided into three main sections: soup noodles, wok noodles, and rice dishes. Take your pick and then add some side dishes. The chilli beef soup ho fun (£6.95) is a good choice. A large bowl full of delicate, clear, chilli-spiked broth which is then bulked out with yards of slippery ho fun – ribbon noodles like thin tagliatelle – plus slivers of beef and fresh coriander. The black bean seafood noodles (£6.95) are an altogether richer and more solid affair, made from egg noodles with prawn, mussels, squid and peppers. Rice dishes range from long-cooked pork and chestnuts (£6.50), to gong bao chicken with pine nuts (£6.95), and the simpler Szechuan aubergine (£5.50). The side dishes are great fun, with good spare ribs (£3.25); guo tie (£3.95), which are pan-cooked dumplings filled with either vegetables or pork; and onion cakes (£2), Beijing street food made from flat, griddled breads laced with spring onions and served with a dipping sauce.

Try the tea here, too. As well as offering Chinese and herbal teas, Jenny Lo has enlisted the help of herbalist Dr Xu who has blended two special therapeutic teas: long-life tea (£1.65) – described as "a warming tonic to boost your energy" – and cleansing tea (£1.85), "a light tea for strengthening the liver and kidneys". It tastes refreshing and faintly gingery, and is doubtless cleansing, too.

La Poule au Pot

231 Ebury St, SW1 ℡020 7730 7763   ⊖ Sloane Square

Daily 12.30–2.30pm & 7–11.15pm (Sun until 10.30pm)   All major credit cards

You are in trouble at the Poule au Pot if you don't understand at least some French. It is unreservedly a bastion of France in England and has been for more than three decades. What's more, several of the staff have worked here for most of that time, and the restaurant itself has hardly changed at all, with huge dried-flower baskets and a comfortable rustic atmosphere. The character of the place, however, is very different at lunch and dinner. The wide windows make it light at lunch, but by night candlelight ensures that La Poule is a favourite for romantic assignations.

A small dish of crudités in herb vinaigrette is set down as a bonne bouche. Different fresh breads come in huge chunks. The menu is deceptive, as there are usually more additional fresh daily specials than are listed. The patient waiters struggle to remember them all and answer your questions about the dishes. As a starter, the escargots (£6.75) deliver classic French authenticity with plenty of garlic and herbs. The soupe de poisson (£6.50) is not the commonly served thick soup, but a refined clear broth with chunks of sole, scallop, prawns and mussels. A main course of bifteck frites (£13.75) brings a perfectly cooked, French-cut, steak with red-hot chips. Ask for mustard and you get Dijon. The gigot aux flageolets (£13) is pink and tender with beans that are well flavoured and not overcooked. The pudding menu features standards like crème brûlée (£4.50), huge, served in a rustic dish, and classically good, and banane à sa façon (£4.50), lightly cooked with a caramel rum sauce and a scoop of ice cream – very rich. There is also a selection of good pudding wines: a glass of Monbazillac (£2.95) makes an excellent companion to the richness of the desserts.

If you are a Francophile, you'll find all your favourites, from French onion soup to boeuf Bourguignon, from quiche to cassoulet. And, such is the atmosphere of the place that, for a few hours at least, you forget that you are in England, particularly if you take advantage of the prix fixe lunch (£14.50 for two courses and £16 for three).

VICTORIA & WESTMINSTER ⓥ INDIAN

Quilon

41 Buckingham Gate, SW1 ⓒ020 7821 1899   ⊖ St James's Park

Mon–Fri noon–2.30pm & 6–11pm, Sat 6–11pm   All major credit cards

Quilon is about as swish as Indian restaurants get; as you'd expect when you learn that it is owned by the Taj Group who also run a dozen of India's most upmarket hotels. This elegant, modern, 92-seater opened in September 1999, and anyone who still has a mental block that unfairly pigeonholes all Indian restaurants as cheap and cheerful should pop along for a reality check. Quilon has the appearance of a sophisticated restaurant; you get the service you'd expect in a sophisticated restaurant; you get the quality of cooking you'd expect from a sophisticated restaurant. And unsurprisingly, you get the size of bill you'd expect from a sophisticated restaurant. Chef Sriram's menu, built around "Coastal Food", showcases the splendid cuisine of Kerala – lots of fish and seafood, fresh peppercorns, and coconut. The food is very good indeed.

Start with the Coorg chicken (£4.75) – chunky chicken with rich spicing and a hint of Coorg vinegar. Or pepper shrimps (£5.50) – prawns fried in batter with plenty of chilli and a touch of aniseed. In season there may be partridge masala (£4.75), cooked in really fresh spices. Moving on to the mains, seafood tempters include crab Calicut (£14.50) and prawns Byadgi (£17.95); the latter are enormous prawns grilled with the specially imported and pleasantly hot Byadgi chillies. Or try Southern Canara lamb curry (£12.25) – very, very rich with a clean and honest heat – or the guinea fowl salan (£12.50), cooked with coconut milk and yoghurt. These are all fairly spicy choices, but there is also gentler fare – plenty of chicken options, and several duck dishes. All the main courses come with a vegetable of the day, but the vegetable dishes themselves are worthy of note. Standouts include a coconut gravy made tangy by a hint of tamarind, and a Malabar vegetable stew (£5.95), made again with coconut milk but also with curry leaves.

In the middle of the dining room there is an outpost kitchen, where a busy chef works at an array of burners making fresh appams (£1.95), the feathery rice pancakes which are stunning hot and so-so cold. Here, having them cooked in front of you in the dining room, you get to taste them at their very best.

CENTRAL

£20–£60

Rhodes in the Square

Dolphin Square, Chichester St, SW1 ℰ020 7798 6767	⊖ Pimlico
Tues–Fri noon–2.30pm & 7–10pm, Sat 7–10pm	All major credit cards

Get him away from all that television hype, and Gary Rhodes is actually a very good cook. In his restaurants there is a real respect for genuine British ingredients, and the resulting dishes are always good to eat. It's hard to understand why restaurant critics tend to rank his food below that of his more French-inspired peers. Rhodes in the Square is the place to make up your mind – a large, plush dining room with dark-blue velvet and gleaming metalwork, it's very swish. This is not a cheap restaurant, though you could maybe console yourself by thinking of all the bond dealers tucking in at Gary's City restaurant – they're paying a bit more for the same quality. And, as always seems to be the case, this quality of food is most wallet-friendly at lunch: two courses for £16.50, and three courses for £19.50 is not so bad.

In the evenings, dinner is £31 for three courses, with only a couple of supplements. Starters are simple and stunning: seared tunafish with poached egg Benedict, pan-fried white pudding sausage with cabbage and crispy bacon, risotto of duck confit with prunes, finished with a sesame oil dressing. But the one starter every self-respecting hedonist must try is the lobster omelette thermidor (£2.80 supplement) – presented in its own little pan, this is a melting omelette with a rich sauce and chunks of lobster. Main courses are equally rich and reassuring: two salmons with sorrel-flavoured leeks and crème fraîche mashed potatoes, red wine beef "lasagne" with a chestnut mushroom cream sauce, steamed monkfish "scampi" with minestrone sauce, roast loin of lamb flavoured with bone marrow and anchovy. For pudding, you could pass up the famous Rhodes bread and butter pudding – though it is a signature dish – and try iced pear parfait with sweet kirsch cherries, or the frozen espresso mousse with bittersweet oranges.

The menu has become somewhat simpler since the early days in 1998 and, if anything, prices are lower. Anything that makes this kind of honest cooking more accessible is to be applauded.

£30–£70

Roussillon

16 St Barnabas St, SW1 ✆020 7730 5550   ⊖ Sloane Square/Victoria

Mon–Fri noon–2.30pm & 6.30–10.45pm, Sat 6.30–10.45pm   All major credit cards

www.roussillon.co.uk

The people who run Roussillon are brave and single-minded. When they opened a bar and restaurant called Marabel's on this site in 1998 they installed a very bright and very young French chef called Alexis Gauthier. Things did not go exactly as they wished and within six months they had closed it down. It reopened almost immediately as Roussillon, without the bar but still with Alexis, and most of the dishes that had won him acclaim still in place. If anything, the Roussillon menu reads even better than its predecessor, with dishes combining strong flavours and making good use of fine English ingredients. Why is the use of fine local produce both a natural thing for French chefs and a strategy that is rarely adopted by their British counterparts? To see the advantages of being season- and market-driven, try the terrific-value set lunch at Roussillon – £25 for two courses and £28.50 for three. Or splash out on one or other of the five-course showing-off menus – the vegetarian "Garden Menu" (£29) and the "Seasonal Menu" (£35/£38).

The menu changes four times a year and works on a prix fixe basis: two courses cost £35 and three courses £38, with supplements only rearing their head when foie gras, lobster or langoustine make an appearance. You can expect to start with good soups and risotti – perhaps the particularly good pumpkin risotto with veal jus; or a green pea consommé, royale of blonde liver and sautéed pea shoots; or maybe a salad of blue Bembridge lobster, with its consommé. Main courses are divided rather coyly into "the sea" and "the land", with four dishes to a section. Fish dishes may include sea bass, Swiss chard and chick pea beignet and flat parsley. The beef is organically raised Aberdeen Angus from Donald Russell. The eggs come from Torfrey Farm. The veal gets a commendable subtitle, "élevé sous la mère", and has much more flavour than factory-farmed veal. The third course divides into three: cheese, fruit and chocolate. All ambitious stuff.

At the bottom of the menu is written: "Our home-made breads are all prepared with organic yeast from Gloucestershire crab apple, grape and white wine." Now, that would be the height of pretension, were it not for the fact that they are very delicious breads indeed.

The Antelope

22–24 Eaton Terrace, SW1 ☎020 7730 7781

The Antelope's country-style charm attracts a massively varied mix of people, from Eaton Square wealthies to the Aussie crowd. Its interior, well worn by decades of solid drinking, gives it a genuinely local feel. Enjoy Tetley's, Marstons Pedigree, Adnams and various guest beers.

Fox & Hounds

29 Passmore St, SW1 ☎020 7730 6367

A tiny, sleepy local with a beer and wine licence only. Its size has kept it from being invaded by Sloanes and too many day-trippers. Regulars from the neighbourhood have been coming here for decades, however, which gives it a friendly atmosphere. The beer is from Young's brewery.

The Orange Brewery

37 Pimlico Rd, SW1 ☎020 7730 5984

SW1 is more than just the postcode at this large, comfortable pub. It's one of the beers brewed at the pub itself, along with a stronger one, SW2, and a thick, luscious, dark beer called Pimlico Porter. There aren't many pubs that brew, so it's worth a visit. If you ring ahead you may even get a trip round the tiny brewery.

Vino Veritas

44 Elizabeth St, SW1 ☎020 7730 5437

A modern cross between a pub and a wine bar, this polished, pale-wood venue attracts a very friendly younger crowd more for lager and wine than bitter. Beck's, Kronenbourg 1664 and John Smith's are favourites, but there's Theakston's XB as well. It's closed at the weekend.

Zander

45 Buckingham Gate, SW1 ☎020 7378 3838

A bright, very modern, and comfortable venue with what they claim to be the longest bar in Europe. Plenty of room to mix and mingle and enjoy some of the more innovative cocktails – perhaps a chocolate, cucumber or lychee Martini. A good range of wines and beers, though the latter are only served in half pints. The crowd is young, and tends to stay and play late.

Waterloo &
The South Bank

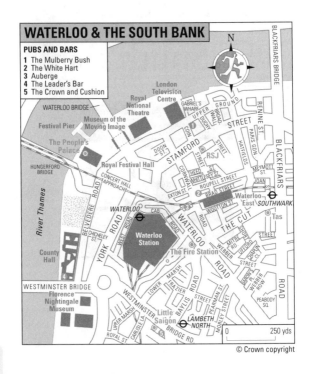

WATERLOO & THE SOUTH BANK

PUBS AND BARS

1 The Mulberry Bush
2 The White Hart
3 Auberge
4 The Leader's Bar
5 The Crown and Cushion

N

BLACKFRIARS BRIDGE

London Television Centre

Royal National Theatre

WATERLOO BRIDGE

Festival Pier

Museum of the Moving Image

The People's Palace

HUNGERFORD BRIDGE

Royal Festival Hall

CONCERT HALL APPROACH

River Thames

County Hall

WESTMINSTER BRIDGE

Florence Nightingale Museum

BELVEDERE ROAD

YORK ROAD

CHICHELEY ST.

B.

WEST SQ.

WATERLOO

CAB

Waterloo Station

The Fire Station

GABRIEL'S WHARF

UPPER GROUND

CORNWALL

DOON ST.

STAMFORD STREET

THEED

WHITTLESEY ST.

EXTON ST.

ROUPELL STREET

BRAD STREET

WOOTTON ST.

WATERLOO ROAD

RENNIE ST.

PARIS GDN.

HATFIELDS

RSJ

MEYMOTT ST.

JOAN

Waterloo East

BLACKFRIARS

SOUTHWARK

THE CUT

Tas

MITRE RD.

WEBBER STREET

UFFORD

CHURCH

BALDWIN

WEBBER ROW

FRAZIER STREET

MARSH

LOWER MARSH

BAYLIS

PEARMAN ST.

MORLEY STREET

ROAD

PEABODY SQ.

UPPER MARSH

Little Saigon

CARLISLE LA.

LAMBETH BRIDGE RD.

NORTH

ROYAL ST.

0   250 yds

© Crown copyright

The Fire Station

150 Waterloo Rd, SE1 ✆020 7620 2226   ⊖ Waterloo

Mon–Sat noon–2.45pm & 5.30–11pm,

Sun noon–9.30pm   Amex, Mastercard, Switch, Visa

When you arrive at The Fire Station it's hard to imagine that the food will be of much distinction. This is a big barn of a place with pumping music, and to get to the restaurant at the back you have to fight your way through noisy waves of colourful-drink-swillers. Decoration is scant, consisting mostly of red and cream paint and blackboards painted with popping champagne corks. At first glance, it looks exactly like a theme hamburger bar. But if you look a little closer you'll see an open-plan kitchen preparing good-looking food and a lot of happy diners. It's worth persevering.

The menu offers everything but hamburgers. It changes daily but there are some simple things that often feature – curried parsnip and yoghurt soup (£3.75), warm salad of chicken livers, black pudding, bacon, flat mushrooms, cherry tomatoes and balsamic jus (£6.25), braised lamb shank with creamed potatoes, curly kale, tomato and borlotti bean sauce, and gremolata (£11.50), and fillet of salmon with asparagus, spinach, new potatoes and a blood orange butter sauce (£11.50). But the daily changes give the kitchen a chance to have fun – first courses might feature chicory, Gorgonzola, walnut and cured tomato salad with Pommery dressing (£5.75), say, or Parma ham and toasted chorizo with a selection of fruit and a griddle cake (£5.95). For mains you might see ostrich steak with sweet potato hash, tropical fruit salsa and plantain crisps (£11.95), and Thai yellow marlin loin curry (£11.75). The cooking is accomplished and correct, and the service is friendly. The only problems are the tendency towards "sorlin" cooking (it's-all-in) and, though it seems churlish to comment on over-generosity, the gargantuan portions. Thankfully, puddings are simple, but there are four huge scoops for one helping of caramel ice cream with butterscotch sauce (£3.95). To wash it all down, there's a decent wine list with five reds and whites by the glass as well as a 50cl carafe.

There's a set menu available up to 7.30pm – two courses for £10.95, three for £13.50 – which makes it a sensible place to drop in to on the way to the Old Vic or the National Theatre. It's a little less frenetic then, as well.

£15–£35

Little Saigon

139 Westminster Bridge Rd, SE1 ℂ020 7207 9747	⊖ Waterloo/Lambeth North
Mon–Fri noon–3pm & 5.30–11.30pm,	
Sat & Sun 5.30–11.30pm	Amex, Mastercard, Visa

After ten years running a restaurant in Frith Street, the Long family had had enough. Soho rents were hitting the stratosphere and the lease was up for renewal. So Mr Long and his wife opened Little Saigon, just behind Waterloo Station, a homely restaurant serving good Vietnamese food from a comprehensive menu. Stick to the indigenous dishes and take the opportunity to get to grips with Vietnamese spring rolls – both the crispy deep-fried kind and the "crystal" variety. The latter are round discs of rice pastry like giant, translucent communion wafers, which you soak in a bowl of hot water until pliable and then roll around a filling made up of fresh salady things, interesting sauces, and slivers of meat grilled on a portable barbecue.

Run amok with the starters. Sugar-cane prawns (two for £3.20) are large prawn "fish cakes" impaled on a strip of sugar cane and grilled. Vietnamese Imperial spring rolls (£2.60) are of the crispy fried variety, but they are served cut into chunks and with lettuce leaves to roll them up in. Also good is the strangely resilient Vietnamese grilled squid cake (£3.50). Topping the bill are crystal spring rolls (four for £2.60); these are "pre-rolled" – delicate pancakes, thin enough to read through, filled with prawns and fresh herbs – and quite delicious. It's as if each of the starters comes with its own special dipping sauce, and the table is soon littered with an array of little saucers – look out for the extra-sweet white plum sauce and the extra-hot brown chilli oil. For mains, ha noi grilled chicken with honey (£5.30), special Saigon prawn curry (£6.40), and the house special fried crispy noodles (£4.80), can all be recommended.

Do try and master the "specialities" – an intermediate course where you soak your own crystal pancakes and use them to wrap crunchy salads and meats barbecued at the table. Soak the pancakes too long and they stick to the plate; not long enough, and they won't wrap. Grilled slices of barbecued beef (£12), and grilled slices of pork in garlic sauce (£12), are both splendid.

The People's Palace

Level Three, Royal Festival Hall, South Bank, SE1 ©020 7928 9999 ⊖ Waterloo

Daily noon–3pm & 5.30–11pm   All major credit cards

www.capitalgroup.co.uk

When this restaurant first opened, there were tales of diners who had finished their dinner late being locked into the Festival Hall and of others wandering for ages between levels. It is still not the most straightforward venue to find, but it has its own entrance now, opposite Hungerford Bridge. And it's worth seeking out. It's a very large place, run with the high standards you would hope for, considering that it is within the South Bank Centre and many diners are either pre- or post-concert, which makes timings crucial. The food is well presented and accurately cooked; there may not be too many culinary high jinks but the menu is composed of well-balanced, satisfying dishes at reasonable prices. Add the fabulous view overlooking the Thames, the sound service, a child-friendly policy (they're nice to kids, and provide highchairs and children's menus), and it all adds up to an attractive package.

The bargains at the People's Palace are its fixed-price menus. Lunch menus are available daily: £12.50 for two courses plus £4.95 for pudding (on Sunday, all day, it's £15.95 plus £4.95 for pudding). Pre-theatre is £15.50 and £20.45. For this, you choose from a good spread of daily selections. On the à la carte you'll find starters like goats' cheese, sweet pepper and basil parfait (£7), New England corn chowder (£5.75), and tarte fine of artichoke, onions and Dolcelatte cheese (£7.75). Mains include roast sea bass with spiced noodles, peppers, bean sprouts and coriander (£17.50); rump of lamb with shepherd's pie and baby onions (£15.50); fillet of cod with truffled creamed leeks and orzo pasta (£15.50), and honey-roast magret of duck with pot-roast vegetables (£14.25). Puddings (£4.95) are almost predictable – the sticky toffee pudding comes with vanilla ice cream, there's a passionfruit brûlée, and a tarte Tatin of pineapple with toasted coconut ice cream (£8.50 for two people).

It's worth figuring the Festival Hall's concert programme into your plans. On a popular night, you'll need to book for pre- or post-concert sittings. When you call to make a reservation, ask the receptionist, who will know just what's on and when it finishes.

£18–£45

RSJ

13a Coin St, SE1 ℃020 7928 4554	⊖ Waterloo
Mon–Fri noon–2.30pm & 5.30–11pm, Sat 5.30–11pm	All major credit cards

www.rsj.uk.com

Rolled Steel Joist may seem a curious name for a restaurant, but it is appropriate – there is an RSJ holding up the first floor if you really want to see it. What's more interesting about RSJ is that it's owned and run by a man with a passion for the wines of the Loire. Nigel Wilkinson has compiled his list mainly from wines produced in this region and it features dozens of lesser-known Loire reds and whites – wines which clearly deserve a wider following. Notes about recent vintages both interest and educate, and each wine is well described so that you know what you're going to get.

The menu is based on classical French dishes, but with a light touch and some very innovative combinations – a few from elsewhere. The starters might include wild boar rillette with apple chutney (£5.95), or a lobster risotto with wild rocket (£6.75), or warm smoked eel and bacon salad (£5.95), or a pan-fried duck egg with foie gras and toasted brioche (£8.95). Moving on to the main courses, typical choices might include turbot with stir-fried spinach and coriander (£16.95), fillet of beef with wild mushrooms, bacon and horseradish mash (£16.95), supreme of Challon duck confit with mash and braised lentils (£14.95), or calves' liver with crispy pancetta bacon, bubble and squeak, and sauce Diable (£13.95). The puddings can be the kind of serious stuff that you really should save room for – chocolate truffle cake with coffee custard (£5.25), warm pear and almond tart with vanilla ice cream (£4.25), or maybe panna cotta with rhubarb compote (£4.95).

Like the Peoples' Palace (see p.181), RSJ is situated close to the South Bank Centre's cinema, concert halls and theatres, and is clearly enjoyed by patrons. It appears to cater for both the early crowd and the late crowd who are not rushed in any way – always a good sign. The set meals at £14.95 for two courses and £16.95 for three represent jolly good value. Use the Web site to check out the RSJ Wine Company, whose list is a joy to anyone devoted to the fine wines of the Loire.

Tas

33 The Cut, SE1 ✆020 7928 1444   ⊖ Southwark

Mon–Sat noon–11.30pm, Sun noon–10.30pm   All major credit cards except Diners

Tas wears its colours on its sleeve. It's a bright and bustling Turkish restaurant where eating is cheap. The menu and the set menus have pro-liferated until there is an almost baffling choice. There is often live music. All of which explains why the place is heaving with office parties, birthday bashes, and hen nights every night of the week. The management is obviously alert to the possibilities of a modern restaurant serving Turkish dishes – the feel of this place is closer to a busy West End brasserie than to your standard street-corner Turkish grills. Expect colourful crockery, plenty of plants and an overdose of noise. If lively is what you like then Tas will do just fine.

The menu is a monster. Four soups, followed by twelve cold starters, twelve hot starters, ten salads, eight rice dishes, four side orders, six pasta dishes, ten vegetarian dishes, fourteen grills, ten casseroles (including mousakka which is stretching things a bit), fourteen fish and shellfish dishes, nine desserts. Overwhelmed? You should be, everyone else is. Which is probably why Tas also offers four set menus starting at three courses for £6.45 and peaking at a combo of six meze, a grill, dessert and a coffee at £17.95 (for a minimum of two people). Now you can see why the parties flock here. The first thing to say about the food is that it is well presented and tastes wonderfully fresh. From the cold starters, favour the zeytin yagli bakla (£3.25), which is a fine dish of broad beans with yoghurt; the patlican salatasi (£3.25), a rich aubergine purée; and the cacik (£2.75), a simple cucumber and yoghurt dip. The bread is very good. Stars of the hot starter menu are the borek (£3.25), which is filo pastry filled with cheese and deep-fried, and the sucuk izgara (£3.25), a Turkish garlicky sausage. Unless you have particular likes or prejudices to pander to, go on to the good, sound grills – bobrek izgara (£5.95) are lambs' kidneys, and tavuk shish (£6.95) is a chicken kebab. The fish dishes are accurately cooked and come in large portions – grilled halibut (£8.95) comes with tomato sauce, while the kalamari (£6.95) brings squid with a walnut sauce.

As the menu announces: "Tas is our traditional Anatolian cooking pot, used to prepare casseroles" – overlook the moussakka and turn instead to the bademi tavuk (£6.45), a casserole of chicken and almonds.

Auberge

1 Sandell St, SE1   ©020 7633 0610

This modern blue-and-yellow bar follows a French and Belgian theme with draught Stella, Leffe and Hoegaarden plus a massive range of strong bottled Trappist beers. Wines are French and New World and there is a pleasant cafe-bar atmosphere enjoyed by commuters heading to Waterloo station.

The Crown & Cushion

133–135 Westminster Bridge Rd,
SE1   ©020 7928 4795

A large one-room Free House, this wildly decorated pub attracts a lively local crowd for Fuller's London Pride, Green King IPA and Stone's Bitter. There are old advertising signs and number plates on the walls, other memorabilia both real and ersatz, a patio garden, and table football.

The Leader's Bar (also The Lounge Bar & The Library Bar)

County Hall, Embankment,
SE1   ©020 7902 8000

Once the HQ of the ill-fated GLC, now a hotel, County Hall has three bars which offer luxury with commensurate prices. For the full experience walk along the river before taking tea in the Library (3–6pm), gaze upon the stepped grass wedding cake in front of the hotel and then head to The Leader's Bar, with its portraits of past GLC heads. You could even drink a toast to the old pictures of Mayor Ken.

The Mulberry Bush

89 Upper Ground, SE1   ©020 7928 7940

This is a modern Young's pub, decorated in traditional style. Just across the road from the London Television Centre, it attracts a mixed crowd of locals and TV types, including the odd celeb. There's a quiet, conservatory-style area at the back and a bistro upstairs which isn't bad if your dining plans fall through.

The White Hart

29 Cornwall Rd, SE1 ©020 7401 7151

A neighbourhood local filled with people who have lived around here for years, this comfortable, traditional venue is bright and friendly. Favourites on tap are Fuller's London Pride, Staropramen and Hoegaarden.

City & East

Brick Lane & Spitalfields.....................................187

The City 197

Clerkenwell.....................................211

Docklands 221

Hackney & Dalston 229

Hoxton & Shoreditch.....................................239

Further East 247
   Forest Gate, Newbury Park, West Ham

Brick Lane
& Spitalfields

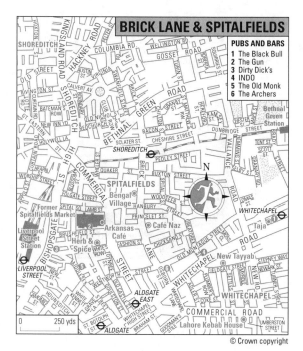

BRICK LANE & SPITALFIELDS

PUBS AND BARS
1 The Black Bull
2 The Gun
3 Dirty Dick's
4 INDO
5 The Old Monk
6 The Archers

© Crown copyright

Arkansas Café

Unit 12, Old Spitalfields Market, E1 ✆020 7377 6999	⊖ Liverpool Street
Mon–Sat noon–2.30pm, Sun noon–4pm	Mastercard, Visa

As you approach the Arkansas Café the glow from its steel-pit barbecue invites you in. Bubba Helberg and his wife Sarah claim that they serve the best barbecue this side of the pond, and they may just be right, for they are regularly in demand as the US Embassy's barbecue experts (they also open here for evening parties of twelve or more). Their food is fresh and simple, and Bubba only uses the highest–quality ingredients, choosing his own steaks individually from Smithfield market to make sure that the meat is marbled enough for tenderness. The provenance of his lamb and sausages is listed for all to see. He marinates and smokes his own beef brisket and ribs, and his recipe for the latter won him a soul food award back home. His secret home-made barbecue sauce is on every table, but he won't sell the recipe to anyone.

Decor is spartan – clean-scrubbed tables, canvas chairs and paper plates – but this does not intrude on the quality of the food. There are no starters, so you just get stuck in. Any of the steaks – Irish ribeye (£8.95), American ribeye (£12.25) – are good bets, barbecued with Bubba's special sauce and served with potato salad and a vegetable salad. Corn-fed French chicken (£6.25) is tender and full of flavour; a side order of chilli (50p) provides a spicy sauce-like accompaniment. USA beef brisket (£9.75) comes meltingly tender and smoky. Most of the other dishes on the menu are platters or sandwiches, the latter including choices like duck breast sandwich (£5), free range pork rib sandwich (£3.95) and, of course, hot dog (£3.25). Puddings (all £2) include New York-style cheesecake and New Orleans pecan pie. They are as sweet and as solid as they should be. The wine list is short and to the point, but the beer list is long, with a large selection of serious beers including Budvar and Budweiser (both £3.25), and the American Anchor Steam (£2.50).

Diners at Arkansas usually include expat Americans homesick for authentic barbecue, which has to be a good sign. Eat in and take an extra order home.

£8–£18

Bengal Village

75 Brick Lane, E1 ©020 7366 4868   ⊖ Aldgate East/Liverpool Street

Daily 6–11.30pm   All major credit cards

No doubt about it, Brick Lane is becoming more sophisticated. Where once all was BYOB restaurants serving rough-and-ready curries at bargain-basement prices to impoverished punters seeking chilli and all things familiar, you will now find a crop of slick new establishments serving authentic Bangladeshi cooking. The Bengal Village is one such place. There's a blonde wood floor and modernist chairs, but it's about more than just design. The menu touches all the bases; trad curryholics can still plough their way through more than a hundred old-style curries – korma, Madras, vindaloo – but now they can also try some more interesting Bangladeshi dishes, too.

Bucking what seems to be becoming the trend, starters are not the best dishes at the Bengal Village – the onion bhajis (£1.95) are, well, onion bhajis, and the chicken tikka (£2.10) is no more than sound. Move straight along to the Bangla specialities. Bowal mas biran (£5.80) is boal fish that has been deep-fried with a rich sauce. There are four shatkora curries. The shatkora is a small green fruit that has a delightful bitter citrus tang and goes very well with rich meats – lamb shatkora (£4.85), for example. Then there are ureebisi dishes, traditionally made with the seeds of a large runner-bean-like plant – in the UK butter beans are often substituted and nobody seems to mind. Try chicken ureebisi (£4.85). There are also some rather splendid vegetarian options: chalkumra (£3.95), subtitled "ash-ground", and supposed to be made with a pumpkin-like gourd, in practice turns out to be slices of marrow in a korma-ish sauce. The marrow kofta is a curry with large and satisfactorily dense vegetable dumplings floating, or rather sinking, in it. There are two thalis available, offering a complete meal (either vegetarian or non-vegetarian) for £6.75 or £9.70.

The wine list comes on a small card which makes splendid reading. "Bolinger Champaign – £39.95"; "Moet and Chandan – £40.95"; "Jacobs Greek (Red Wine) – £9.75". Go for Bangla Beer (£3.20) or follow the great Brick Lane tradition and take your own refreshment with you in a carrier bag.

Café Naz

46–48 Brick Lane, E1 ℂ020 7247 0234   ⊖ Aldgate East

Mon–Fri noon–midnight, Sat 6pm–midnight,

Sun noon–3pm & 6pm–midnight   All major credit cards

www.cafenaz.com

Café Naz dominates Brick Lane with its elegant facade, complete with an all-glass staircase and spacious upstairs dining room. "Contemporary Bangladeshi Cuisine" is what it says on the menu and generally speaking that is what you get, though you will find some of the Indian restaurant standards – a list of baltis and, of course, chicken tikka masala. The decor is certainly contemporary: bright colours, modern furniture and a gleaming open kitchen where you can watch the chefs at work. Prices are low – thirty curry restaurants within a stone's throw makes for serious competition – and service is attentive.

Start with the boti kebab (£2.95), either lamb or chicken, cooked in the tandoor and served with a plateful of fresh salad. Or there's adrok chop (£3.95), small pieces of lamb chop which have been marinated in ginger and garlic before getting the treatment in the clay oven. Fish cutlet (£2.95) brings pieces of a Bangladeshi fish called the Ayre, deep-fried and served with fried onions. These could be called goujons if they weren't so large and didn't contain a good many large bones. For main courses, the dhansak (£4.50) comes as either mutton or chicken and is very tasty – it's cooked with lentils and turns out at once hot, sweet and sour. Or how about palak gosht (£4.95), a simple dish of lamb and spinach? Then there's gosht kata masala (£5.95), a splendidly rich lamb curry; or chicken sour masala (£5.95), which is chicken in a very tomatoey tomato sauce sharpened with a little vinegar. Naan bread (£1.35) is freshly cooked, and wiped with butter – delicious. And there are a range of vegetable dishes (all £2.75) – niramish, mutter aloo, bindi, sag aloo, brinjal. Very sound and very good value.

Weekdays, the buffet lunch is an attractive option – a chance to go through the card for £7.95, sampling curries, tandoori chicken, rice dishes and a constant flow of hot naans. If you want to do this justice, pick a day when all is serene – a nap after such a lunch is obligatory.

Herb & Spice

11a Whites Row, E1 ✆020 7247 4050	⊖ Aldgate East/Liverpool Street
Mon–Fri 11.30am–2.30pm & 5.30–11.30pm	Amex, Diners, Mastercard, Visa

Do not let the tiny, rather gloomy dining room and huge swags of plastic flowers put you off this treasure of a curry house on Whites Row, a small road just off Commercial Street and tucked in behind Spitalfields. A loyal clientele from the City means that to secure one of the 22 seats you'll probably have to book! The menu here includes all the curry classics, plus one or two dishes you may not have spotted before, but what sets Herb & Spice apart from the pack is that the dishes are freshly cooked and well prepared and yet the prices are still reasonable. When the food arrives it will surprise you: it's on the hot side, with plenty of chilli and bold, fresh flavours.

It's not often that the popadoms grab your attention. They do here. Fresh, light, crisp popadoms (55p) are accompanied by equally good home-made chutneys – perky chopped cucumber with coriander leaf, and a hot, yellowy-orange, tamarind-soured yoghurt. The kebabs make excellent starters: murgi tikka (£2.75), chicken, very well cooked; shami kebab (£2.75), minced meat with fresh herbs; gosht tikka (£2.55), tender lamb cubes. For a main course you might try the unusual murgi akhani (£6.95), a dish of chicken cooked with saffron rice and served with a good, if rather hot, vegetable curry. Or there's bhuna gosht (£4.95), a model of its type – a rich, well-seasoned lamb curry with whole black peppercorns and shards of cassia bark. Murgi rezalla (£5.95) is chicken tikka in sauce: much hotter – and with more vegetables – than its cousin the chicken tikka masala. The breads are good, too: from the decent naan (£1.65) to the shabzi parata (£1.95), a thin, crisp wholemeal paratha stuffed with vegetables.

For a real tongue-trampler, try the dall shamber (£2.75), a dish of lentils and mixed vegetables which is often overlooked in favour of that popular garlicky favourite, tarka dhal. Traditionally served hot, sweet and sour, at Herb & Spice dall shamber comes up hot (very hot, with an almost chemical bite from the large amounts of chilli) and very, very sweet indeed. Not for the faint-hearted.

Lahore Kebab House

2 Umberstone St, E1 ©020 7481 9737	⊖ Whitechapel/Aldgate East
Daily noon–midnight	Cash or cheque only

The Lahore was for years something of a cherished secret among curry-lovers – a nondescript, indeed downbeat-looking, kebab house serving excellent, very cheap fare. Recent years, however, have seen a few changes. Gone are the sticky carpet and the bleak Formica table tops; there are no longer sacks of gram flour stacked inside the door; even the theatrical drama of the open kitchen has been tamed. Thankfully, the food is still good and spicy, the prices are still low, and the service brusque enough to disabuse you of any thoughts that the new round marquetry tables and posh shop front have taken the Lahore upmarket. What they do here, they do very well indeed – and if you need any further proof, look at all the other similarly named places which have sprung up all over town.

There is no elegant menu at the Lahore – merely a board on the wall listing half a dozen dishes. Rotis (50p) tend to arrive unordered, your waiter watching your eating patterns and bringing bread as and when he sees fit. For starters, the kebabs are standouts. Seekhe kebab (50p), mutton tikka (£2.50) and chicken tikka (£2.50) are all very fresh, very hot, and very good, served with a yoghurt and mint dipping sauce. The biryanis are also splendid – meat or chicken (£6), well spiced and with the rice taking on all the rich flavours. The karahi ghost and karahi chicken (£5.50 for a regular portion or £11 for a huge one) are uncomplicated dishes with tender meat in a rich gravy. The dal tarka (£3.50) is made from whole yellow split peas, while sag aloo (£3.50) brings potatoes in a rich and oily spinach purée. A sad loss from the menu is paya (an awesome dish of long-stewed sheeps' feet, thought by some to be the hallmark of any genuine Pakistani restaurant) – apparently it's impossible to get top-quality sheeps' feet nowadays. Much more palatable, if you want a very Lahore kind of delicacy, is the home-made kheer (£2). This is a special kind of rice pudding with cardamom.

This Lahore is unlicensed but happy for customers to bring their own beer or wine – and there's a nearby off-licence ready to oblige. You will certainly need some complement to the generally hot food – though note that alcohol isn't the best cooling agent. For that, you need to order a lassi.

£3–£10

New Tayyab

83 Fieldgate St, E1 ©020 7247 9543   ⊖ Whitechapel/Aldgate East

Daily 5pm–midnight   Cash or cheque only

Since the Tayyab first opened in 1974 it has continued to spread: after the initial cafe, there came the sweet shop, and now that the New Tayyab occupies what was once the pub there is an uninterrupted sweep of Tayyab enterprises on the north side of Fieldgate Street. Inside the New Tayyab (which is open only in the evenings) it looks as if someone has made a determined assault on the record for fitting the greatest number of chairs in the smallest possible space, while going for double points in the grotesque furniture category. The food is straightforward Pakistani fare: good, freshly cooked, served without pretension, and at prices lower than you would believe possible – something that is much appreciated by the hordes of impoverished students who make up a large proportion of the customers. Booking is essential and service is rough-and-ready. This is not a place to umm and err over the menu.

The simpler dishes are terrific, particularly the five pieces of chicken tikka served on an iron sizzle dish, with a small plate of salady things and a medium-fierce, sharp, chilli dipping sauce (£2). They do the same thing with mutton (also £2). Four lamb chops – albeit thin ones – cost £2.80. Sheekh kebab are 70p each; shami kebab, 60p each; and round fluffy naan breads, 60p. The karahi dishes are simple and tasty: karahi chicken – chicken in a rich sauce – costs £3.80 for a normal and £7.40 for a large portion. Karahi batera (quails) are £4 and £8. Karahi aloo gosht (£3) is lamb with potatoes in a rich sauce heavily flavoured with bay leaves. Or there's karahi mixed vegetables (£2.80). There is also a list of interesting daily specials. Surprisingly, 1999 saw the discontinuation of paya (fancy the dreaded, double gluey, sheeps' feet stew not appealing) – perhaps regulars were saving themselves for the splendidly named meat pillo (£3.50) served every Wednesday. Chunks of mutton slow-cooked in rice, it's a dish that's rich, satisfying, and seeded with whole peppercorns for bite.

The Tayyab is strictly BYOB if you want alcohol; to judge by its own offerings it is something of a shrine to Coca-Cola. But whether you're going for beer or Coke, make sure you try the Tayyab lassi anyway; a yoghurt drink served in a pint glass, it comes sweet or salted (£1.50), and with mango or banana (£2).

Taja

199a Whitechapel Rd, E1 ℂ020 7247 3866	⊖ Whitechapel
Mon–Wed & Sun 11am–midnight, Thurs–Sat 11am–12.30am	All major credit cards

www.cuisinenet.co.uk/taja

Taja's exterior of black and white vertical stripes certainly jolts the eye. Venture in and you find a dining area accommodating sixty covers across two floors. The counter is ultra-modern in stainless steel and the seating has recently been upgraded from stools to comfy chairs. From the ground floor large windows look out onto the hurly-burly of passing traffic just inches away. The food tastes very fresh, and is markedly cheap. So far so good. By now, those in the know will have recognised that the restaurant in question is a converted toilet in the Whitechapel Road. And, as if that is not novelty enough, Taja is a genuine rarity – a thoroughly modern Bangladeshi restaurant. The menu is both enlightened and lightened, with a host of vegetarian dishes balancing the traditional favourites.

Start with that great test of a tandoor chef, chicken tikka (£1.95): at Taja you get half a dozen sizeable chunks of chicken, cooked perfectly – not a hint of dryness – with the obligatory salad garnish (a waste of time) and a yellowish "mint sauce". Or try chotpoti (£1.95), described on the menu as "green peas and potatoes with spices, served with a tamarind chutney – high in protein". Move on to a biryani – mixed vegetable, lamb, chicken or prawn – all £4.95; a good-sized portion comes with a dish of really splendid vegetable curry by way of added lubrication. There are also a host of curry house favourites. Chicken bhuna (£4.29) is an outstanding choice, with a really fresh sauce, hot but not too hot, and lots of fresh herbs. Very good indeed. The naan breads – plain, peshwari or keema (£1.50) – are large, thick-rimmed and very fresh, as a naan should be. The Taja got its licence in 1999 but you can still bring your own for a small corkage. Healthier types will enjoy the fresh juices – orange and carrot (£1.95) is especially good.

Taja offers all sorts of set meals and deals. The "fast set snack – ready in five to ten minutes" weighs in at £5.50 for veggies, £6.50 for omnivores. Or you could splash out on the "All day and every day buffet eat as much as you like non-vegetarian and vegetarian £5.95 per person" (the "day" in question being restricted to 11am–6pm).

The Archers

42 Osborn St, E1   ℂ020 7247 3826

Brick Lane isn't well served with pubs, so this one provides welcome relief at the Aldgate end. Whitbread beers on tap. Look out for the irreligious motto, "a cask of ale works more miracles than a church full of saints".

The Black Bull

199 Whitechapel Rd, E1   ℂ020 7247 6707

A traditional Free House with unusual beers and guest ales. Nethergate's Suffolk County and Pitfield's East Kent Goldings are on offer, together with big-screen sports. Very convenient for the market outside.

Dirty Dick's

202 Bishopsgate, EC2   ℂ020 7283 5888

Done out like an old wooden sailing ship, this galleried theme pub serves Young's Bitter, AAA and Special. It's a bit touristy with its barrel tables, galleried upper bar and T-shirts for sale. But you get a good drop of beer and there's a lively, out-to-enjoy-themselves crowd of an evening.

The Gun

54 Brushfield St, Old Spitalfields Market, E1   ℂ020 7247 7988

Just as you'd expect, the Gun has a cannon motif on the carpet, real guns displayed on the wall and Charles Wells' Bombardier bitter on tap. Big, open and friendly, it's also the pub closest to the old market itself.

INDO

133 Whitechapel Rd, E1   ℂ020 7247 4926

By day, INDO – which used to be the Old Blue Anchor pub – is a coffee bar-cum-art gallery, with an interesting range of exhibitions and happenings. At night, it transforms itself into a groovy bar. The decor – scrubbed wooden floors and old church pews – is eclectic, as is the crowd, and there's Stella and Hoegaarden on tap.

The Old Monk

92–94 Middlesex St, E1   ℂ020 7247 1727

With nothing old about it at all, this themed lounge bar is actually a newish place, large and comfortable, with sofas and a relaxed atmosphere. It attracts a young, noisy crowd, more for the alcopops and bottled beers than the Courage Best, London Pride and Deuchar's Caledonian IPA. DJs on Thursday night.

The City

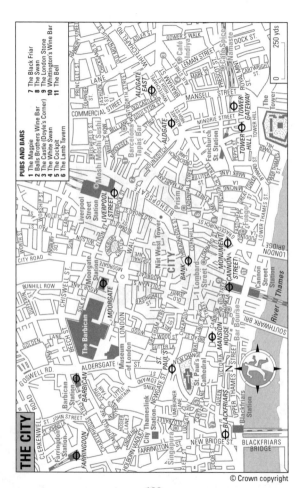

THE CITY

PUBS AND BARS

1 The Magpie
2 Balls Brothers Wine Bar
3 The Castle (Doyle's Corner)
4 The White Swan
5 The Cockpit
6 The Lamb Tavern
7 The Black Friar
8 The Swan
9 The London Stone
10 Whittington's Wine Bar
11 The Bell

0   250 yds

© Crown copyright

1 Lombard Street
The Brasserie

1 Lombard St, EC3 ⓒ020 7929 6611   ⊖ Bank

Mon–Fri 11.30am–3pm & 6–10pm   All major credit cards

The Brasserie at 1 Lombard Street was formerly a banking hall and the circular bar sits under a suitably imposing glass dome. This is a brasserie in the City, of the City, by the City and for the City. It is connected to Bloomberg – a sort of elitist Ceefax-cum-email system which keeps City traders in touch with each other, rather like passing notes at school – and messages flash in and out. "Can you confirm your reservation at 1 Lombard Street?"; "Yes. But we'll be ten minutes late." The brasserie menu is a model of its kind, long but straightforward with a spread of dishes that is up to any meal occasion – starters and salads, soups, egg and pasta, caviar, fish, crustacea, meat, puddings. It delivers on pretty much every front, serving satisfying dishes made with good fresh ingredients, and surprisingly it manages to be both stylish and unfussy at the same time. The bar, meanwhile, is like any chic City watering hole – loud, brisk and crowded, with simultaneous conversations in every European language.

The brasserie menu changes every couple of months, to ring the changes for its band of regulars, and in addition there are daily specials. The starters can be ambitious, like red mullet with Provençal vegetables (£9), or simple, like carpaccio of salmon (£9.95), while further down the menu there will be some even more comfortable options like a soft-boiled free-range egg (£8.25 or £11.95 main course) served with baked potato, smoked salmon, sour cream and chives. There's enough listed under crustacea to fuel even the wildest celebrations, including seared scallops with a fennel and Pernod velouté (£19.95), and clam stew (£8.50/£12). Then the meat section features a very well-made coq au vin à la Bourguignon (£14.95) plus steaks, sausages, liver and chops. During the season you may also find fricassee of pheasant in puff pastry (£18.95).

There is a smaller, forty-seater room at the back of the bar set aside for fine dining at fancy prices. It's interesting to note, however, that caviar is a brasserie dish – 50g of beluga served with blinis, steamed poatoes and sour cream will set you back £78.

Bar Bourse

67 Queen St, EC4 ©020 7248 2200	⊖ Mansion House
Restaurant Mon–Fri 11.30am–3.30pm	All credit cards except Diners

Anyone who says City people are boring hasn't been to Bar Bourse. As much bar as restaurant, it is run by Louise Mayo, herself an ex-City stockbroker. Her mission is to bring interesting food and fun to the bright-jacketed traders in the area, and as the pictures by the entrance attest, she and her staff do it well. Playing to the City beat, Bar Bourse offers a restaurant menu at lunchtime, but becomes a noisy and crowded bar after 6pm, filled with a youthful clientele intent on testing the cocktail menu and champagne list to destruction.

The bar snacks (Mon–Fri 6–9pm) are innovative. For £6 you get a baked-on-the-premises focaccia stuffed with fillings like smoked chicken, avocado and basil crema; salami, salad and pesto; crisp bacon, lettuce, plum tomato and mozzarella. There is a huge cocktail list as well, offering favourites like margaritas to classics like whisky sour or flavoured martinis. All are £6 and worth it. From the restaurant menu, which changes weekly, choose starters like carpaccio of tuna with sweet and sour cucumber (£7.75) or foie gras terrine with chutney and toasted brioche (£11.50). Main courses may include char-grilled ribeye or fillet of beef, chunky chips and herb butter (£15–£19); risotto with pesto (£7/£11); or pot-roasted gammon with chickpeas, smoked paprika and chorizo (£13), which sounds complex, but works well. On a plainer note there is fish and chips (£14.25), presented here as smoked haddock in a beer batter with pea purée and tartare sauce. There are some interesting salads too – try the green herb salad, or the wild rocket. You can have them for £3 as a side order or £5 as a starter. For pudding, try banana tart with prune and Armagnac or vanilla pod and redcurrant brûlée (both £5).

Wines range from thoughtfully priced "house" at £12 a bottle to more exotic items like Château Latour 1983 (£170) and Le Montrachet 1994 (£130). Champagnes run from J. Lemoine (£30) to Dom Perignon 1990 (£125), with Bollinger at £42 in between. It's not cheap, but Bar Bourse is good fun and a great place to mix with the City bonus boys and girls who thrive on a good spend.

£10–£25

Barcelona Tapas Bar

1a Bell Lane, E1 ✆020 7247 7014   ⊖ Aldgate

Mon–Fri 11am–11pm and usually Sun 10am–4pm

(but call to check!)   All major credit cards

www.barcelona/tapas.com

At the start of the East End, not a hundred yards from the towering buildings of the City, you find yourself among the market stalls of Petticoat Lane and Middlesex Street. On one of the less salubrious corners you'll see a banner bearing the legend "tapas". Note that the arrow points down. As you descend the stairs into a cramped basement which seats about twenty, try to still the thought that this is an inauspicious start to your lunch or evening. Barcelona is, in fact, one of London's best tapas bars. The range of snacks wouldn't be sniffed at in Barcelona or Madrid, and includes a fair few Catalan specialities – including the classic tomato-and-garlic-rubbed bread, a good accompaniment to any tapas session.

You'll find a number of tapas lined up in typical Spanish style along the back half of the bar – these are just a few of the selection on offer. The Barcelona has a vast (in more ways than one) menu written in Spanish and Catalan with English translations. Many are simple, like Serrano ham (£7.50), or queso Manchego (£3.95), or aceitunas (olives, £1.50–£2.50), and rely on the excellent quality of the raw ingredients. Then there are peasant dishes like fabada Asturiana (£3.25), a stew of white beans with chorizo. More skill is involved in creating the paellas; the paella Valenciana (£10.95 per person) is particularly good. And there is also a chicken brochette (£6.95). But, for those with meetings within 24 hours, avoid anything that advertises its garlic. The Spanish seem blithely unaware of the havoc they wreak with the social lives of unsuspecting diners. And here, as well as being delicious, the gambas al ajillo (£6.95) are pungent enough to give you heartburn and the kind of breath that gets you elbow room in a thronged rush-hour tube.

Unusually for such a small place with such a huge choice, there's no need to worry about freshness. There is a bigger, smarter, newer and less charming Barcelona nearby, and the apparent lull between ordering and receiving your dish may be because the girl is running around the corner to the other kitchen to fetch a portion.

Café Indiya

30 Alie St, E1 ℡020 7481 8288   ⊖ Aldgate East

Mon–Fri noon–midnight, Sat 6pm–midnight   All major credit cards

Café Indiya is a new-wave Indian restaurant – bright colours, jars of spotlit spices in alcoves, wooden floors, modern (and surprisingly comfortable) furniture. Perhaps best of all is the add-on menu of weekly specials. Batch-cooked food, evenly balanced spicing. Hallelujah! What a splendid idea. The food here is tailored to the clientele, who are predominantly City types breaking out for lunch. Indiya has always been keen to give some indication of the strength of curries (it must be hard to arbitrate when you are distracted by burning indigestion) but ironically it's only the chicken peri-peri, a tandoor dish that has no warning label, that gets anywhere near "really hot".

Start with childa (£2.25), savoury coriander and ginger pancakes, served with yoghurt, or murgh puda, which is a more conventional pancake wrapped around chunks of chicken. Or share the mixed kebab karaha (£9), a rainbow of grilled meats from the tandoor, going all the way from tandoori chicken to a decent, spicy chicken peri-peri, by way of sheekh kebab and suchlike. The main courses come in large portions, within attractive plain white serving bowls. Goan fish curry (£4.95) has a good concentrated sauce, while Nariel gosht (£7.15) is a welcome twist on korma with a rich coconut sauce. There's chicken xacutti (£6.60), too – said to be the most complex curry of all. The naan breads (£1.75) are good, and the lemon rice (£2.25) is amazing – with an intensely citrus fragrance. Of the side dishes, baingan (£2.90), stewed whole baby aubergines, has real star quality.

You have to approve of an Indian restaurant that offers live music (usually Thursday night). You also have to admire a sales line that links soul music and soul food. But it takes a truly affable diner to stomach the pun with which they once advertised this revelry – "Pappa dom preach!" . . .

Café Spice Namaste

16 Prescot St, E1 ✆020 7488 9242	⊖ Aldgate East/Tower Hill
Mon–Fri noon–3pm & 6.15–10.30pm, Sat 6.30–10pm	All major credit cards

www.book2eat.com

During the week this restaurant is packed with movers and shakers, all busily moving and shaking. They come in for lunch at 11.59am and they go out again at 12.59pm. Lunchtimes and even weekday evenings the pace is fast and furious, but come Saturday nights you can settle back and really enjoy Cyrus Todiwala's exceptional cooking. What's more, with the City "closed for the weekend", parking is no problem. It is well worth turning out, for this is not your average curry house. The menu, which changes throughout the year, sees Parsee delicacies rubbing shoulders with dishes from Goa, North India, Hyderabad and Kashmir, all of them precisely spiced and well presented. The tandoori specialities, in particular, are awesome – fully flavoured by the cunning marinades but in no way dried out by the heat of the oven.

Start with a voyage around the tandoor; the murg kay tikkay (£3.50/£7) tastes as every chicken tikka should, with yoghurt, ginger, cumin and chillies all playing their part. Or there's venison tikka aflatoon (£4.25/£8.50), which originates in Gwalior, and is flavoured with star anise and cinnamon. Also notable is the dahi kachori (£3.85), a Gujarati pastry case filled with moong beans and fried. For a main course, fish-lovers shouldn't stray past the fish cooked ambotik ani xit (£10.25) – hot and sour, with the tang of palm vinegar. Choose meat and you should try the beef xacutti (£10.25 including mushroom pulao rice), a most complex curry containing more than twenty ingredients. Breads are also excellent, while some of the accompaniments and vegetable dishes belie their lowly status at the back of the book-sized menu. French beans jeera (£3.95) are cooked with chopped shallots and roasted cumin seeds – simple and very good. Choney ani oemio chey ussal (£4.25) is a splendid Goan dish of chickpeas and mushrooms with coconut in the masala.

It's a good idea at Café Spice Namaste to do as the in-the-know diners do, and choose from the speciality menu that changes every week.

Fuego

1a Pudding Lane, EC3 ℰ020 7929 3366	⊖ Bank/Monument
Restaurant Mon–Fri 11.30am–4pm & 5.30–9.30pm	
Tapas bar Mon–Fri 11.30am–2am	All major credit cards
www.fuego.co.uk	

Fuego, a subterranean tapas bar and restaurant, is sited in Pudding Lane, where the first flickerings of the Great Fire of London started out on their path of destruction. A good many contemporary paths to destruction likely set out from these parts, too, as, unlike many City establishments, Fuego doesn't close mid-evening but braves it out until 2am on weekdays. As a result, and because of its good-value snacks and meals, it's a popular haunt for reckless City folk who don't care what time they go home. Typically, the clientele are suit-clad and arrive in single-sex groups. However, the segregation doesn't last long, as after 8pm, from Tuesday to Friday, Fuego transforms into a disco. For a more sophisticated atmosphere, you could try the lunchtime-only restaurant or come on a Monday night.

The menu is the same wherever in Fuego you choose to dine: typical tapas fare with hot and cold dishes ranging in price from £2.25 for sopa de pueras (onion and leek soup) to £4.95 for the more expensive meat and seafood dishes. A couple of these and some French fries or, better still, fiery tomato patatas bravas (both £2.35) make a good foundation. The gambas gabardinas (£4.95) – crispy, battered tiger prawns in garlicky paprika sauce – are particularly good. Or try pulpo encebollado (£4.35) – a generous plateful of octopus in a pink pepper sauce. After a bad day at the office, the albondigas en salsa (£3.25) – meatballs in tomato sauce – make reassuring comfort food. More lively are the chorizo y polenta (£3.45), with red wine sauce, and the rinones al Jerez (£3.25), or kidneys in sherry – and you should always look out for the weekly specials, which are often interesting. For the less adventurous, home-made hamburgers (£5.50–£5.95) and sizeable toasted sandwiches (£4.75–£5.95) are available with French fries. And if you're not drinking beer or sherry, there's a decent house wine at £9.50 a bottle.

As if things were not wild enough already, there is a happy hour in the tapas bar between 5pm and 7pm, after which intensive preparation the long haul to 2am becomes fairly intimidating.

Moshi Moshi Sushi

Unit 24, Liverpool Street Station, EC2 ©020 7247 3227   ⊖ Liverpool Street

Mon–Fri 11.30am–9pm   Mastercard, Visa

www.moshimoshi.co.uk

Moshi Moshi Sushi serves healthy fast food, Japanese style – its dishes circulate on a kaiten or conveyor belt. There are a dozen or so such places in London these days, but this one claims to have been the first. Its location, inside Liverpool Street railway station, meshes perfectly with the concept. With its glass walls and ceiling, and no-smoking policy, it is a great and very wholesome place to eat before setting off on a train journey. It is, however, much more than a refuelling stop for commuters and, reassuringly, you'll find both local office workers and Japanese diners enjoying leisurely meals. Either sit at the bar and watch your dinner circulate, or opt for table service, with some nice views of the old station arches. Set menus range from £4.90 to £11.50.

If you opt for a bar seat, the ordering system is child's play – just pluck your chosen dishes from the conveyer belt as they trundle past. You'll be charged according to the pattern on each individual plate you end up with. All the sushi is good and fresh, and there's a decent range of authentics – from the somewhat acquired taste (or texture) of uni (sea urchin, £2.90) through to flying fish roe (£2.90) – as well as some delicious California hybrids, combining avocado and crabstick with a sweet, sticky sushi rice rolled with sesame seeds. Regular sushi choices such as negitoro temaki, a seaweed-wrapped roll of tuna and spring onion (£2.90), or shakemaki (salmon roll, £2), are done well, too, as is the Nigiri sushi (£1.20–£2.90). Of the puddings, all £2.50, the custard pancake, or dorayaki, is good, as are the various ice creams. Unless you're a fan, avoid adzuki dishes, no matter how dark, sticky and mysterious they look, as they consist of oversweetened red bean paste – definitely an acquired taste.

Look out for the cartoons on the laminated cards, which give handy tips spelling out which sushi are best for beginners and which are "challenging". There are also helpful hints on just how to treat the fiery, ground wasabi which will clear your sinuses faster than anything else on the planet.

£30–£90

Prism

147 Leadenhall St, EC3 ℭ020 7256 3888   ⊖ Bank

Mon–Fri 11.30am–3.30pm & 6–10pm   All major credit cards

www.prismrestaurant.co.uk

The question we should ask ourselves is: where have all the bank's gone to? And the answer is probably that they have vanished into cyberspace behind hole-in-the-wall machines, leaving free all these tantalising banking halls with the kind of lofty ceilings and grandiose pillars that make restaurant designers drool. Prism, part of the Harvey Nichols plan for world domination, is an expensive City restaurant. Eating here is rather like being inside a towering, white-painted cube, very slick, and very much an old banking hall. The food is a well-judged blend of English favourites and modernist influences. There is the obligatory long bar, and the obligatory suave service. As a restaurant it has no pronounced character but rather leaves an impression of modernity – no bad thing in the stuffy old City.

Starters are well executed. Tempura of Whitby cod and pea purée (£7.50) is fresh and good, the sweet and minted purée making a nice foil for light and crisp fried fish. Aubergine parfait, spiced chickpeas and lavosh crispbread (£6.50) resembles a pâté devised for a vegetarian but it is well presented and well seasoned. When it comes to main courses, the menu splits half-fish and half-meat. On the fish side there are simple dishes like halibut chunk, Lyonnaise potatoes and Béarnaise sauce (£14.50), and more adventurous offerings like sea bass with fennel and rocket purée and crab beurre blanc (£15); the meat side offers Cumberland sausage, creamed potato and brown sauce with onions (£9.50), as well as pan-fried calves' liver, bubble and squeak, grilled streaky bacon and Madeira sauce (£12.50) – all the sauces are rich, smooth and seasoned properly. On a slightly more modern note there is also Cajun chicken with sweet potato purée, spring onion crème fraîche and mango salsa (£13.50), and roast loin of veal with creamed borlotti beans (£15). Puddings all cost £6 and include rum baba, warm cherries, vanilla ice cream, and sorbets.

The wine list is for bankers. There are a few bottles to be had for sensible prices but the main thrust is towards whatever the traffic will bear. Which is the best deal: a bottle of Krug for £130 or a magnum of Dom Perignon for £250? Simple – buy both.

£20–£40

Singapura

1–2 Limeburner Lane, EC4 ©020 7329 1133	⊖ Blackfriars/St Paul's
Mon–Fri 11.30am–3.30pm & 5.30–10pm	All major credit cards
www.singapura-restaurants.co.uk	

Not only has this large, modern restaurant just off Ludgate Hill won a succession of accolades as "London's most beautiful restaurant", but also it is one of just a handful of places outside Singapore where you can sample Nonya cuisine. Singapore boasts four great culinary traditions: Chinese, Indian, Malay, and Nonya. Nonya food, which belongs to the people once known as the "Straits Chinese", is a fusion of the Malayan and Chinese traditions and ingredients. It is generally (but not always) spicy, sweet, and characterised by a good deal of garlic, galangal and lime leaves. At Singapura it's very well done, if at some cost.

In many ways the starters are the stars here – and not just because you hit them with a fresh appetite. Siput (£5.95), described as "mussels stir-fried with lemon grass, lime leaves, chillies and ginger in a sherry sauce", resembles an Oriental moules marinières: small, sweet mussels are cooked in a broth that would make a delightful (if fiery) soup. Chicken satay (£5.75) comes juicy and with an assertive peanut sauce, while the Wantun udang (£5.95) is an indulgence – a marinated tiger prawn wrapped in a pastry blanket and cooked until crisp. From the main courses you might try babi tauceo (£7.50), which is made from crispy pork slices with the classic Nonya sauce based on yellow bean paste. Char kuay teow (£7.50) is Singapore street food: broad rice noodles, stir-fried with fairly pungent chunks of fishcake, eggs and prawns. In the vegetable section, choi sum (£4.95) is a supercharged version of the Chinese favourite "greens with oyster sauce": stronger, fishier, and packed with garlic and ginger. By the time the puddings come around, your tongue is probably only fit for the home-made ice creams, which come in moody varieties like Earl Grey, marmalade parfait, and brown bread – two scoops cost £4.50.

Maureen Suan-Neo, master chef of the Singapura restaurants, has introduced a list of speciality dishes with the emphasis on game – five starters and five mains – to titillate Western palates unused to the delights of such exotic ingredients as blachan. Blachan is made from dried, salted shrimps, and smells a bit like rotten fish. Surprisingly enough, it tastes yummy.

It's important to remember that many of these pubs and bars are not open at the weekend, when the City virtually closes down. Always call to check first.

Balls Brothers Wine Bar

158 Bishopsgate, EC2   ©020 7426 0567

An established City wine bar, this vast cavern of a place offers plenty of room, together with the famous Balls Brothers wine list. Excellent house champagne at £22.50 and brilliant clarets for less than £20 make this a wine lovers' favourite. You can also pick up a copy of their retail list, and buy direct.

The Bell

29 Bush Lane, EC4   no phone

Reputedly a tavern since before the Great Fire of London, this small, traditional pub has a friendly, local feel. It's used by a regular crowd who enjoy well-kept Courage Best and Directors.

The Black Friar

174 Queen Victoria St, EC4   ©020 7236 5650

With its church-like interior and relief sculptures of monks, this attractive, angular pub is very popular with younger City types and tourists. Expect Tetley's, Adnams, Brakspear and London Pride on tap and a noisy pavement bustle in summer. Easy to find and hard to leave.

The Castle (Doyle's Corner)

44 Commercial Rd, E1   ©020 7481 2361

A Free House with a loyal and regular clientele, The Castle has been in the Doyle family for forty years. John, the current owner, serves good Tetley's, London Pride and Courage Best together with Dublin Cask Guinness, which is brought over especially.

The Cockpit

7 St Andrew's Hill, EC4   ©020 7248 7315

Very tucked away, this tiny, regulars' retreat is worth searching out. It's quaint and charming, with curiously curved doors, and tends to be quiet when other pubs around are noisy. Friendly staff offer Courage Directors and Marstons Pedigree among the usual lagers and bottled beers.

Lamb Tavern

10–12 Grand Ave, Leadenhall Market, EC3   ©020 7626 2454

Huge and justifiably popular, this traditional Young's venue is right in the heart of the beautifully restored Leadenhall market. It's very busy at lunchtime, which is also when you get to see the Victorian tiled and vaulted basement bar. The two dartboards are always in use.

The London Stone

109 Cannon St, EC4   ©020 7626 8246

A theme venue in Gothic style with display cases of bubbling alchemics and glaring gargoyles all over the place. There's plenty of room to sit in panelled booths and enjoy a good range of bottled beers and alco-pops, with Courage Directors and Theakston on tap as well. Or why not try one of the cocktails named after the Seven Deadly Sins?

The Magpie

12 New St, EC2   ©020 7283 9484

Serving Timothy Taylor's Landlord, Wadworth's 6X and Fuller's London Pride, this well-kept old pub is probably the closest to Liverpool Street station's Broadgate entrance. It's also quiet and friendly, and seems to be off the City-suit circuit.

The Swan

Ship Tavern Passage, 77–80 Gracechurch St,
EC3 ©020 7283 7712

A cramped old pub with a narrow
ground-floor bar and a larger one
upstairs. Squeezing past the regulars
makes for quick friendships as a mixed
crowd enjoys Fuller's Chiswick, London
Pride, Honeydew Organic and ESB. A
good range of wines in the upstairs bar,
too.

White Swan

21–23 Alie St, E1 ©020 7702 0448

A pub since 1826, this Shepherd
Neame establishment offers Master
Brew Bitter, Bishop's Finger, Spitfire and
seasonal ales. The interior is much as it
was one hundred years ago, and you
really do feel as though you're stepping
back into London's past.

Whittington's Wine Bar

21 College Hill, EC4 ©020 7248 5855

Two hundred years of storing and serving wine have given this painted brick
cellar bar a genuine resonance.
Reputedly owned by Dick Whittington
himself, it's a hit-your-head-on-the-
ceiling venue, offering an exceptional
wine list in a charming atmosphere to a
mix of City types in suits.

Clerkenwell

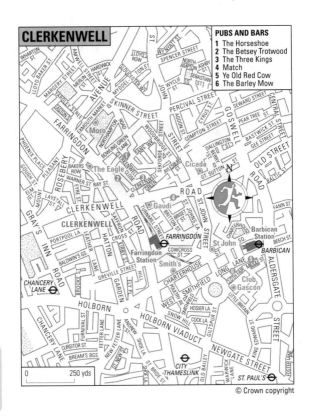

CLERKENWELL

PUBS AND BARS

1 The Horseshoe
2 The Betsey Trotwood
3 The Three Kings
4 Match
5 Ye Old Red Cow
6 The Barley Mow

© Crown copyright

0   250 yds

Cicada

132 St John St, EC1 ✆020 7608 1550	⊖ Farringdon
Mon–Fri noon–11pm, Sat 6–11pm	All major credit cards

Once Clerkenwell was where you went for printing and watch repairs. But it's fast becoming London's coolest City-fringe dormitory – a fact that is reflected in its growing choice of restaurants and bars. Cicada is one of a number catering to the growing local population. Part bar, part restaurant, it offers an unusual menu loosely based in Southeast Asia that changes three or four times a year and allows you to mix and match from small, large and side dishes. This suits a lot of modern tastes, as everyone can share dishes and different flavours.

To start, the Vietnamese chicken spring rolls, wrapped with lettuce and mint (£5), are a good opening move. They're delicious, fresh-tasting and at the same time crunchy, sweet and spicy. Or try the very savoury miso soup with clams (£4.50). The rest of the "small dishes" are, as the name implies, more complex than the usual run of starters. Chilli-salt squid comes with adjud sauce (£6), and there are Japanese gyoza dumplings (£4.75), and crispy fried fish with chilli, holy basil and lime leaf (£5.50). Moving on to the large dishes, how about a big bowl of ramen – vegetable, prawn, swordfish, chicken or beef (£7.95/£9.50)? Or prawn pad Thai (£8.25)? Or tempura cod with seaweed wrap, mirin and miso dressing (£9) – a dish that puts a new spin on London's most popular chip-shop fish. Other good choices might be the sweet ginger noodles (£2.50), a tasty bowlful; or the rare char-grilled beef salad with pungent nah jhim (£8.50). Puddings include tempting offerings like green tea cheesecake, spicy blueberry compote (£6), and a chocolate and lemongrass brûlée (£4.50). There is a good selection of mid-priced wines and beers, including Tiger beer (£2.80) if you want to go Oriental, and a house Sauvignon (£14.50) from the part of Mexico that is almost southern California – particularly good at a not-too-unreasonable £14.50 a bottle.

Cicada has a friendly bar-like atmosphere, and the staff are young and easy going. If the weather is good it's a great place to sit outside. It's set back from the main part of the street so the pavement tables give a degree of privacy. All in all, it makes a good bridge between going to a bar for a drink and going to a restaurant for a meal.

Club Gascon

57 West Smithfield, EC1 ©020 7796 0600   ⊖ Farringdon

Mon–Fri noon–2pm & 7–10pm, Sat 7–10.30pm   Mastercard, Visa

Club Gascon burst onto London's collective palate in 1998. Critics
swooned. Reviewers raved. Awards were dispensed. It remains shock-
ingly popular: if you want a booking, they advise calling two or three
weeks ahead, though you may strike lucky with a cancellation. Pascal
Aussignac is the chef here, and his cooking is that of the southwest of
France, tidied up a little but generally authentic. The menu is set out as
six sections and the portions are larger than some starters but smaller
than most mains, the idea being that you indulge in your very own
dégustation, trying several dishes – not the cheapest way of eating.

The sections are "La route du sel" – cured meats and charcuterie; "Le
potager" – vegetables and cheese; "Les foies gras"; "L'océan" – fish and
shellfish; "Les pâturages" – mainly duck and cassoulet; "Le marché" –
game and offal. There are forty different dishes. It's important to spread
your ordering and not just to pick from one section – no matter how
good, five consecutive foie gras dishes are bound to pall. Here are a
couple of promising combinations: farmhouse jambon de Bayonne
(£5.50), piperade Basquaise and stewed beans (£4), grilled foie gras of
duck with grapes (£9.50), crispy smoked eel with horseradish cream
(£6), beef fillet a la plancha, Madeira sauce and stuffed pimento
(£7.50), galette of potatoes and truffled sausage (£13.50). Or maybe
velouté of watercress and broad beans (£5.50), three oysters with grilled
chipolata (£4.50), le spécial Gascon en terrine (£7.50), and grilled fresh
scallops, cream of caviar and crispy potato (£9)? The problem with eating like this is that you can hit on a dish that is amazing and therefore
too small. You must have the time and confidence to order a second, or
even third, serving.

If you feel daunted there is a regional menu which changes monthly:
five courses for £30 (£50 with five glasses of wine). This tasting menu
must be ordered by everyone at the table and is a worthwhile experiment – the menu Toulousain, for example, typically leads you from
jambon de Bayonne to duck foie gras aux picquillos, roast tuna
andouille, and cassoulet Toulousain, finishing with ice cream and prunes
in Armagnac. A pretty good way to shed £30.

The Eagle

159 Farringdon Rd, EC1 ✆020 7837 1353	⊖ Farringdon
Meals served Mon–Fri 12.30–2.30pm & 6.30–10.30pm,	
Sat 12.30–3.30pm & 6.30–10.30pm, Sun 12.30–3.30pm	Cash or cheque only

The Eagle was for years a run-down pub in an unpromising part of London. Then in 1991 it was taken over by food-minded entrepreneurs who transformed it into a restaurant-pub, with an open kitchen turning out top-quality dishes. They were pioneers: there should be a blue plaque over the door marking the site as the starting place of the great gastro-pub revolution. In the years since, neither the food nor the decor has changed much, though they have opened an enterprising and interesting gallery upstairs. The Eagle itself remains a crowded, rather shabby sort of place – and the staff still have attitude. The kitchen is truly open: the chefs work behind the bar, and the menu is chalked up over their heads. It changes daily, even hourly, as things run out or deliveries come in. The food is broadly Mediterranean in outlook with a Portuguese bias, and you still have to fight your way to the bar to order and pay.

This is a pub with a signature dish. Bife Ana (£8.50) has been on the menu here since the place opened and they have sold tens of thousands of portions. It is a kind of steak sandwich, whose marinade has roots in the spicy food of Portugal and Mozambique, and it is delicious. The rest of the menu changes like quicksilver but you may find the likes of the famous caldo verde (£4.50) – the Portuguese chorizo and potato soup which takes its name from the addition of spring greens; or there may be a grilled, whole wild sea bass, with trevisse, broccoli, and chicory salad and anchovy dressing (£12); or a delicious and simple dish like roast free-range chicken with pancetta, tarragon, olives and oven potatoes (£9); or a full-blown paella Valencia with squid, clams, prawns, chicken, saffron, peppers and broad beans (£10). To finish, choose between a plate of fine cheeses – Manchego, cabrar del tietar fresca and muntanolya – served with toast and quince paste (£6), or the siren charms of those splendid small Portuguese cinnamony custard tarts – pasteis de nata – at £1 a piece.

Even with pavement seating providing extra capacity in decent weather, The Eagle is never less than crowded, the music is always loud, and the staff are busy and brusque. A great place, nonetheless.

Gaudí

63 Clerkenwell Rd, EC1 ✆020 7250 1057	⊖ Farringdon
Mon–Fri noon–2.30pm & 7–10.30pm	All major credit cards

Gaudí is a restaurant hidden within a nightclub – Turnmills – which in the past has meant it has kept rather strange opening hours. But as the stature of the restaurant has increased, so the opening hours have got less eccentric. Now they no longer ask everyone to leave in the middle of Friday night. This is a good thing, as chef Nacho Martinez serves some of the most interesting Spanish food in London. Not the sometimes weary food of the Costas and tapas bars, but high-flown, well-executed Modern Spanish cuisine. Do not allow the asymmetric, soft-shaped, flowing curves of the Gaudiesque interior put you off, even if you do expect Dr Who to step from behind a plaster-of-Paris boulder at any moment.

Chef Martinez changes his menu in line with the season, and perhaps for some simple linguistic reason his dish descriptions are sometimes exhaustingly lengthy. Start with ensalada de queso Manchego con requeson, membrillo y vinaigre de Jerez (£9.50) – a cheese salad with quince and a cream mousse; or perhaps patatas estrelladas con pimients del piquillo y su yema emulsionada (£8.50) – confit potatoes with scrambled egg whites and roast green peppers. The empanadas here are very good, if untraditional – empanadas rellenas de vieras y bouquet de escarola y comino (£10) are small pastries made with scallops and endive. Main courses are ambitious and largely successful – rodaballo al horno con mestra de verduritas, mejillones al vapor y salsa verde (£15) is roast turbot with mixed vegetables, steamed mussels and a coriander sauce. Or how about lomo de jabali mechado asado con cebolitas glasedas rellenas de berenjenas y nido de patatas con setars (£16) – loin of wild boar served with glazed onions filled with aubergines and wild mushrooms? If all these exotic descriptions make you nervous, and sound as if this is a chef who has gone well over the top, take heart. This is good food, and even the wildest flights of fancy tend to work well. Go on, don't be dull.

Puddings are all £5 – pastries, deep-fried ice cream, a mousse made from Manchego cheese – imaginative stuff, as you'd expect. There's a grand and expansive wine list with enough Spanish rarities to please even the most demanding Iberian oenophile.

Moro

34–36 Exmouth Market, EC1 ©020 7833 8336   ☉ Farringdon/Angel

Mon–Fri 12.30–2.30pm & 7–10.30pm   Amex, Mastercard, Visa

In its relatively short life Moro has scooped up a hatful of awards. This modern, rather stark restaurant typifies the new face of Clerkenwell and attracts a clientele to match. In feel it's not so very far away from the better pub restaurants, although the proprietors have given themselves the luxury of a slightly larger kitchen. This is also a place of pilgrimage for disciples of the wood-fired oven, and as the food here hails mainly from Spain, Portugal and North Africa it is both Moorish and moreish. There is also good Spanish drink: dry fino and manzanilla for an aperitif or to accompany a meal; sweet Pedro Ximenez to go with the puds. The only problem lies in Moro's popularity. It's consistently booked up, which places a bit of a strain on both kitchen and waiting staff. A relatively new development is the tapas menu which offers a good range of small dishes priced between £2 and £5.50 – a good way to test things out!

Soups are among Moro's best starters. They do a notable veal, farika and turmeric soup with almonds (£4.50). Depending on the season and the fresh produce in the markets you may also be offered starters such as pan-fried calves' liver with cumin, garlic and yoghurt (£6), scrambled egg with broad beans and jamon (£5.50), or piquillo peppers stuffed with salt cod and potato (£5.50). Or there's another classic combination of brandada, salt-cod purée with olive oil and potato, with toast made from the superb sourdough bread produced in the wood-fired oven, piquillo peppers and olives (£5). Main courses are simple and are often traditional combinations of taste and textures. As with the starters, it's the accompaniments that tend to change rather than the core ingredients. Look out for wood-roasted longhorn beef with roast potatoes, spring greens and garlic purée (£14.50), or perhaps wood-roasted belly pork with roast vegetables and quince aioli (£13). There is usually a tempting array of fish dishes, too, along the lines of charcoal-grilled monkfish with farika, dressed spinach and zhoug (£14).

Do not miss the splendid Spanish cheeses (£4) served with membrillo – traditional quince paste. And there's no excuse to avoid the Malaga raisin ice cream dowsed in Pedro Ximenez (£4).

£15–£40

Smiths, the Dining Room

CLERKENWELL ⑪ MODERN BRITISH

67–77 Charterhouse St, EC1 ✆020 7236 6666   ⊖ Farringdon

Cafe Mon–Fri 7am–5pm, Sat & Sun 10.30am–5pm

Restaurants Mon–Fri 11am–3pm & 6–11pm, Sat 6–11pm   All major credit cards

www.smithsofsmithfield.co.uk

Calling Smiths of Smithfield, which opened in May 2000, an ambitious project is like saying that pyramid-building calls for a large workforce. First take a Grade II listed warehouse overlooking Smithfield Market and gut it. Rebuild the inside in ultra-modern meets Bladerunner style and then open less than a year behind schedule with the two restaurants, two bars, private rooms, kitchens and whatever, spread over four floors. On the ground floor there is a bar and cafe serving an ocean of drink and good, sensible food from breakfast to bedtime. At the top is the area known as "Fine Dining" – a 75-seater which pays particular attention to quality meat with good provenance – and sandwiched in between is the 120-seater "Dining Room". The culinary mainspring is John Torode – the man who will be forever tagged with the honour "the chef who opened Mezzo" (see p.140).

The Dining Room is a large space around a central hole which looks down onto the smart bar area. Eating here is rather like sitting at the centre of a deactivated factory – a tangle of exposed pipes and girders. The menu is divided into Larder (ie starters), Soups, Mains, Grills, Extras, Lunch Daily Meat Market Specials, and Sweet Tooth. The way the prices are expressed, however, is coy and irritating – Larder "all at 4 1/2 Pounds"; "Extras 2 1/4 Pounds". Bah humbug. The starters are simple and good: smoked haddock, Old Spot bacon and mustard (£4.50), a rather fine salad with crisp Romaine and two cheeses (£4.50), pea and broad bean soup with sour cream (£3.50). Main courses show off the careful buying policy: crisp belly of pork with mashed potato and salsa verde (£9.50), rabbit leg with sage butter, peas and mash (£10.50), grilled turbot with capers, red chard and fennel (£10.50). The lunch specials are from the comfort-eating school, and feature such delights as shepherds pie (£9.50). Puds are good. Try the baked nectarine with a glass of sherry (£3.50).

There's a decent breakfast on offer in the cafe/bar/pub downstairs. And it is available all day, so Dr Johnson would have been happy.

218

St John

26 St John St, EC1 ✆020 7251 0848   ⊖ Farringdon

Mon–Fri noon–3pm & 6–11pm, Sat 6–11pm   All major credit cards

www.stjohnrestaurant.co.uk

One of the most frequent requests, especially from foreign visitors, is "Where can we get some really English cooking?". Little wonder that the promise of "olde English fare" is the bait in so many London tourist traps. The cooking at St John is genuinely English. It is sometimes old-fashioned, and makes inspired use of all those strange and unfashionable cuts of meat – and, in particular, offal – which were once commonplace in rural England. Technically the cooking is of a very high standard, while the restaurant itself is without frills or design pretensions to the point where it is almost uncomfortably bare. You'll either love it or hate it. But be forewarned: this is an uncompromising and opinionated kitchen, and no place to take a hard-core vegetarian.

The menu changes every session, but the tone does not, and there's always a dish or two to support the slogan "nose to tail eating". Charcuterie, as you'd imagine, is good: a simple rabbit terrine (£5.70) will be dense but not dry – well judged. Or, for the committed, what about a starter of roast bone marrow and parsley salad (£5.80)? Truly delicious. Or potted pig's head (£5). Or lamb and barley broth (£5.20). Be generous to yourself with the bread, which is outstanding; the bakery is in the bar, and you can purchase a loaf to take home. Main courses may include roast Middlewhite (a rare, traditional, breed of pig) with split peas (£14.80), or deep-fried skate with tartare sauce (£11.20). Maybe there will be pigeon and celeriac (£11.80), or a dish of Stinking Bishop – a wonderful, pungent Gloucestershire cheese with potatoes (£7) – perversely, in this den of offal, a veggie delight. Puddings are trad and well executed: rice pudding with plums (£5), or a slice of strong Lancashire cheese with an accompanying Eccles cake. Joy of joys, there is even a seriously good Welsh rarebit (£4.50).

St John has forged quite a reputation, and it's encouraging to see a party of Japanese businessmen sitting down to their pot roast beef and pickled walnut toast (£10.50) rather than the usual overcooked tourist diet of "roast beef of old England". Whatever your feelings about meat and offal cookery, St John serves English food at its most genuine.

CLERKENWELL

The Barley Mow

50 Long Lane, EC1   ©020 7606 6591

A buzzy, traditional pub with secluded alcoves for privacy and quiet. There are usually eight beers on tap, including Flowers IPA, Brakspear Special and Adnams Broadside. A wide mix of residents and local office people give it a "regulars' favourite" feel.

The Betsey Trotwood

56 Farringdon Rd, EC1   ©020 7253 4285

Life-size film character models bring this otherwise traditionally decorated pub to life. Stare Marilyn Monroe, Charlie Chaplin, Laurel and Hardy and Groucho Marx in the eye as you sup Shepherd Neame's Bishop's Finger and Spitfire. A determined crowd of local workers and journalists keep the atmosphere sparky.

The Horseshoe

24 Clerkenwell Close, EC1   ☏ 020 7253 6068

Tiny on the outside, but huge inside, this friendly Free House offers Tetley's, Greene King IPA and London Pride in ground-floor and upstairs bars. There's a large patio garden and two pool tables. It's also home to the Islington folk club, as the assorted beards and sandals testify.

Match

45–47 Clerkenwell Rd, EC1   ©020 7250 4002

If you like cocktails, this cool, dark bar is a great place to drink them. The list is well judged, with a good combination of classics balanced with new ideas, and prices are reasonable. Match is noisy and often packed, but nice with it. Brilliant martinis, and a Long Island Iced Tea to die for.

Three Kings

7 Clerkenwell Close, EC1   ©020 7253 0483

Despite its wildly eccentric papier-mâché decor, this is a traditional local. Smoke-filled and very friendly, it seems to be unaware of the passage of time. Beers include Old Speckled Hen and Fuller's London Pride. Outside, take a look at the best pub-name typography ever.

Ye Olde Red Cow

71 Long Lane, EC1   ©020 7606 0735

A small, modern, well-scrubbed Shepherd Neame pub with Spitfire, Best and Master Brew. A larger bar upstairs offers a wide choice of bottled beers and wines.

CITY & EAST

Docklands

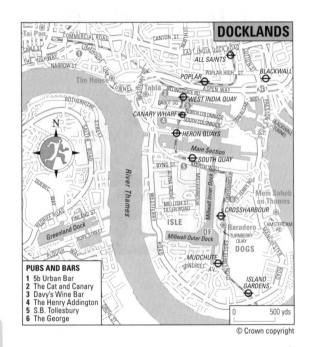

DOCKLANDS

Tai Pan

COMMERCIAL ROAD

CANTON ST.

EAST INDIA DOCK ROAD

ALL SAINTS

THE HIGHWAY

CABLE ST.

LIMEHOUSE

NARROW ST.

The House

LIMEHOUSE TUNNEL

ROTHERHITHE

SALTER STREET

The Cut

WESTFERRY RD

Tabla

POPLAR

POPLAR HIGH ST.

BLACKWALL

ASPEN WAY

A1261

BILLINGSGATE RD.

WEST INDIA QUAY

PRESTONS RD.

BLACKWALL TUNNEL

WEST FERRY RD.

CABOT SQ.

NORTH COLONNADE

CANARY WHARF

SOUTH COLONNADE

HERON QUAYS

N

Main Section

SOUTH QUAY

QUEBEC WAY

BYNG ST.

MARSH WALL

ALPHA GROVE

MILLHARBOUR

Millwall Inner Dock

Mem Saheb
on Thames

REDRIFF ROAD

FINLAND ST.

MELLISH ST.

TILLER ROAD

WESTFERRY

ISLE

CROSSHARBOUR

Baradero

AMSTERDAM RD.

MANCHESTER RD.

Greenland Dock

ROPE STREET

OF

Millwall Outer Dock

DOGS

TURNBERRY
QUAY

PLOUGH

ROAD

MUDCHUTE

SANDRIFT

AV.

ISLAND
GARDENS

PUBS AND BARS

1 5b Urban Bar
2 The Cat and Canary
3 Davy's Wine Bar
4 The Henry Addington
5 S.B. Tollesbury
6 The George

River Thames

0   500 yds

Baradero

Turberry Quay – off Pepper St, E14 ℗020 7537 1666	DLR Crossharbour
Mon–Fri noon–11pm, Sat 6–10.45pm	All major credit cards

Baradero is modern, light, tiled and airy. And, as far as the view of Millwall dock and proximity to the London Arena will permit, you could almost think yourself in Spain. Essentially a tapas bar, it offers main courses too – and both are of restaurant quality. Take a seat at the bar, or at one of the well-spaced tables, order yourself a bottle of Estrella beer or a glass of fino sherry, and set about the tapas. There is even a floor show of sorts in the form of the balletic automatic orange juicer, called a Zumm, which seems to wave the whole oranges about for inspection before squashing them for juice.

Start with an order of pan con aioli (95p) – good bread with a pot of fearsome but seductive garlic mayonnaise. Or pan con tomate (£1.30) – Catalan-style toast drizzled with olive oil and rubbed with garlic and tomato. Add some boquerones (£3.15), classic white anchovies sharp with vinegar and garnished with raw garlic slices, and jamon Serrano (£4.75), a large portion of dark, richly flavoured, dry-cured ham. Then follow up with hot tapas such as croquetas de pollo (£3.50) – whoever would have thought that croquettes could taste so good? Or pulpo a la Gallega (£4.95), octopus boiled and seasoned in Galician style. Or the particularly delicious fabada Asturiana (£4.95) – an Asturian bean stew loaded with chunks of sausage, black pudding and ham hock. Also lurking on the tapas menu is paella Valenciana (£16.50). This is the real thing, with chicken and shellfish, and it feeds two. If you can restrain your ordering, and do not end up crammed full of tapas, there is a further list of main courses which changes weekly – try chuletas de cordero al romero (£11.50), charcoal-grilled lamb cutlets, which are simple and good. Or maybe lubina al horno (£12.75) – baked sea bass with salted "Canary" potatoes and a Mediterranean salad. There is also a convenient special offer – prix fixe hot and cold tapas (£19.50 per person) – which runs all day.

As well as adding new tapas and main courses each week to keep regulars from getting bored, the proprietors of Baradero organise food festivals, during which visiting Spanish chefs prepare serious regional food – small lambs, suckling pigs, all manner of delights.

DOCKLANDS ⑰ MODERN BRITISH

House

27 Ropemaker's Field, Narrow St, E14 ℂ020 7538 3818   DLR Westferry

Mon–Thurs noon–3pm & 6.30–9.30pm, Fri–Sun 6.30–10pm   All major credit cards

House looks rather odd, stranded here among all the chic new apartments, trendy lofts and converted warehouses. Before its latest incarnation in 1999 it was called "the House they left behind" – a sort of backhanded compliment. Now it has been done up in modern fashion complete with stainless-steel bar, and is simply called House. The food, Modern British, makes good use of fresh ingredients. At lunch the menu is a touch more restrained than in the evening – beefburgers and sausages rather than steaks and lobster – and is correspondingly less pricey. With all those obviously wealthy people starting to congregate in E14, isn't it surprising that there are not more neighbourhood eateries as reliable as this one?

At lunch, starters may include dishes like a very genuine Caesar salad (£4.95), or a wild mushroom broth served with French stick (£3.50), or crispy duck with plum chutney (£4.95)? In the evening things escalate to feuillantine of lamb sweetbreads with rocket salad (£5.50) and salad of king prawns and haricots verts with roasted garlic and a mustard vinaigrette (£6.50). Service is cheerful and, while House is unlikely to win a Michelin star, it has certainly attracted a good crowd of grateful locals, so much so that in 2000 it doubled the number of covers – it now seats seventy. Main courses at lunchtime range from boar and apple sausages on mashed potato with onion gravy (£8.95) to penne served with slow-roast peppers, black olives, tomatoes, and fresh basil and Pecorino shavings. In the evenings things are different: perhaps grilled tuna steak, baked pale aubergine, roast cherry tomatoes and a balsamic yellow pepper sauce (£14.75)? Or grilled lobster on saffron couscous with wilted spinach and a clam sauce (£19.95)? Puddings range from apple and sultana strudel with whipped cinnamon cream (£4.95), to roast figs on a char-grilled peppered pineapple with coconut cream (£4.50).

House is an informal sort of place, but that doesn't stop it having an interesting wine list. Krug 1989 for £120 is a very Docklands sort of thing, but a bottle of Campofiorino 1996 Masi for £17 is a genuine bargain.

CITY & EAST

Mem Saheb on Thames

65–67 Amsterdam Rd, E14 ©020 7538 3008	DLR Crossharbour
Mon–Fri noon–2.30pm & 6–11.30pm, Sat & Sun 6–11.30pm	All major credit cards

Mem Saheb on Thames has certainly got an evocative address. "Amsterdam Road" conjures up pictures of old-fashioned docks and wharves, rolling fog banks and cheery East Enders. In practice this bit of Docklands is a lot like Milton Keynes: Amsterdam Road (along with nearby Rotterdam Drive and Rembrandt Court) are all new, not brand spanking new, but new enough for you to notice that some of the paintwork is starting to get chipped. The redeeming factor is the river. As the Thames sweeps round in a majestic arc, the flats at the end of Amsterdam Road and the Mem Saheb restaurant have a superb view across the water to the Millennium Dome. Mem Saheb is certainly "on-Thames". As a result there's a good deal of squabbling for the middle table in the non-smoking section (pole position as far as the view is concerned) – ultimately, however, the lucky winner must balance the delights of the twinkling lights of the Millennium folly with the piped-music speaker that hovers directly above the table.

Start by sharing a tandoori khazana (£8.95), which is a platter of mixed kebabs from the tandoor, including good chicken tikka. Or perhaps salmon samosas (£2.50)? Also tasty is the kabuli salad (£2.95), a winning combination of chickpeas and hard-boiled egg in a sharp tamarind dressing. Of the main courses, boal dopiaza (£6.95) teams meaty steaks of boal fish from Bangladesh with an onion-based sauce; chicken bemisal (£6.95) is sweet and sour with a welcome belt of green chilli; while prawn and pumpkin (£6.95) balances hot and sweet, although is rather let down by the small and undistinguished prawns. The breads and vegetable dishes are good (particularly the aloo chana – £4.50 – a simple dish of potatoes and chickpeas), and the chef is to be commended for avoiding artificial additives and colourings.

The spicy dhal (£4.50, £2.50 as a side dish) is made with yellow split peas and small, red, dried chillies. The chilli flavour infuses the dhal and this is a very successful dish . . . until the moment when the unwary diner bites into one of these little red booby traps: then the ensuing pain is enough to banish any calm induced by the restful river view.

£20–£50

Tabla

The Dockmaster's House, Hertsmere Rd E14 ©020 7345 0345	DLR West India Quay
Mon–Fri noon–3pm & 6–11pm	All major credit cards

info@tablarestaurant.com

Paradoxically, for a restaurant within a lunchtime's stroll from the ants' nest that is Canary Wharf, one of the salient features of this slick new Indian restaurant is its sixteen-space car park. Tabla is located in the Dockmaster's House at what was once the gate to the West India Dock but is now the hub of its own network of mini-motorways, flats and multi-plex cinema – in such a location a car park is handy. The food is good, modern and authentic, which seems to be something of a contradiction but works well. Take Goan-style haddock as an example. The restaurant is barely a quarter-mile from Billingsgate and the chef has taken the sensible decision to use fresh British fish rather than frozen Indian ones. Thus haddock supplants Kingfish in this Goan favourite, resulting in an accomplished dish that is wonderfully fresh.

The menu is written in English – no transliterated words here – with a short list of starters including pea and coriander soup (£3.95), smoked salmon samosas (£4.25), chicken tikka (£3.95), and crab cakes with coriander and chilli (£4.95). Then there's a selection of tandoori dishes (tandoor work is a speciality of the chef here): as well as classics like neck cutlets (£5.95/£11.95) there is salmon steak (£5.95/£11.95) and duck breast (£5.95/£11.95). Main courses are original and well spiced. There's the above-mentioned Goan haddock in a hot and spicy sauce (£11.50), shredded chicken tikka in a tomato and fenugreek sauce (£8.95) – reassuringly close to chicken tikka masala – lamb shank on the bone (£11.95), the admirably succinct hot South Indian chicken curry (£8.50), and pickled king prawns with chillies and whole spices (£12.95). The vegetable side dishes are also simple and delicious: green beans with coconut (£3.25), and black lentils slow-cooked with cream, aka dal Bukhara (£2.95). The breads are all good.

Good curry, Italian furniture, linen tablecloths, a demystified menu – all elements that will fill Tabla with lunchers cast adrift in the desert of Canary Wharf. In the evenings, however, the prospect of a place to park is what will really pack them in. You'd better book.

Tai Pan

665 Commercial Rd, E14 ©020 7791 0118 or 0119	DLR Limehouse
Mon–Thurs & Sun noon–11.15pm, Fri & Sat 6–11.45pm	All major credit cards

As anyone who has followed the adventures of Sherlock Holmes will know, Limehouse was London's first Chinatown, complete with murky opium dens. So, despite the well-intentioned efforts of the Docklands Development Board to promote the area, today's Limehouse seems pretty tame in comparison. It can, however, boast about the Tai Pan. This restaurant is very much a family affair – the ebullient Winnie Wan is front of house, running the light, bright dining room, while Mr Tsen commands the kitchen. He organises a constant stream of well-cooked, mainly Cantonese dishes, and slaves over the intricately carved vegetables which lift their presentation. He's a good cook, and as well as all the old favourites the menu hides one or two surprises.

After you've waded through the complimentary prawn cracker and seriously delicious hot-pickled shredded cabbage, start with deep-fried crispy squid with Szechuan peppercorn salt (£6.80), or fried Peking dumplings with a vinegar dipping sauce (£4.30), which are delicious. Or try one of the spare-rib dishes (£5.60), or the soft-shell crabs (£4.30 each), or the nicely done crispy fragrant aromatic duck with pancakes and the accoutrements (£15.50 for a half). Otherwise, relax and order the Imperial mixed hors d'oeuvres (£4.40 per person, for a minimum of two), which offers a sampler of ribs, spring rolls, seaweed and prawn and sesame toast, with one of the carrot sculptures as centrepiece. When ordering main dishes, old favourites like deep-fried shredded beef with chilli (£5.80), and fried chicken in lemon sauce (£5.30), are just as you'd expect. Fried seasonal greens in oyster sauce (£4.30) is made with choi sum and very delicious, while the fried vermicelli Singapore style (£5.20) will suit anyone who prefers their Singapore noodle pepped up with curry powder rather than fresh chillies.

Sometimes there are "specials" which don't feature on the main menu. They're generally worth trying. Hun tsui kau (£2.90) – green banana or plantain encased in minced prawn and deep-fried – is particularly popular. There are also some bargains to be had among the special lunch deals. Asking Winnie to recommend something is always a good idea. Sinking your teeth into the carved vegetables is not.

5b Urban Bar

27 Three Colt St, Limehouse,
E14 ☏020 7537 1601

Since it's been modernised, this old Docklands boozer, firmly planted on the Aussie circuit, pulls a ferociously bright crowd. Fuller's London Pride and Adnams Broadside on tap, plus Steinlager and Export Gold by the neck. The zebra-striped exterior is hard to miss, as are the piles of copies of *Southern Cross*.

The Cat & Canary

1–24 Fisherman's Walk, Canary Wharf,
E14 ☏020 7512 9187

A new venue kitted out with Victorian-style mirrors, this Fuller's pub offers ESB, Chiswick and organic Honeydew beers on tap. Though the crowd is brash, made up of City trader types, the place is large enough not to feel crowded. Outside tables and a traditional Docklands view.

Davy's Wine Bar

31–35 Fisherman's Walk, Canary Wharf,
E14 ☏020 7363 6633

An olde-worlde-style place with huge flagstones covered in real sawdust, this large, comfortable Davy's has an excellent selection of spirits as well as the usual wines and its own Ordinary Bitter and Old Wallop beers. The outside tables, and the view across the water to old Docklands buildings and cranes add to its appeal.

The George

114 Glengall Grove, E14 ☏020 7987 2954

The history of this 150-year-old pub is told in pictures on the walls. It started life as a three-storey hotel, but the top two floors were pulled down to avoid the window tax. There's a big conservatory, and a garden reputedly built on ground consecrated for a secret Masonic lodge. Old Speckled Hen, Ruddles Best and Courage Best on tap.

The Henry Addington

Mackenzie Walk, Canary Wharf,
E14 ☏020 7513 0921

Named after the founder of Canary Wharf, this was the first bar to set up in the regenerated area in 1993. It's open, airy and more for lager fans than beer drinkers: Grolsch, Staropramen, Carling, Caffrey's and Guinness Extra Cold are the main offerings. Outside tables and a dockside view.

S B Tollesbury

Millwall Inner Dock, Marsh Wall,
E14 ☏020 7363 1183

Probably the only pub to have been part of the Dunkirk evacuation, the Sailing Barge *Tollesbury* – a wooden vessel, built in 1900 – is now a fully fledged Free House with Real Ales like Adnams and Harvey's by the cask. You can sit outside on deck in summer.

Hackney
& Dalston

HACKNEY & DALSTON

PUBS AND BARS
1 The Hen and Chicken
  Theatre Bar
2 Lighthouse Bar
3 The Village
4 Maddigan's on Mare Street
5 The Fox
6 The Cat and Mutton

0   500 yds

© Crown copyright

Anatolya

263a Mare St, E8 ℭ020 8986 2223   BR London Fields/ ⊖ Bethnal Green

Daily 6am–11pm   Cash or cheque only

This small – five-table – diner has no menu other than the neon list, all in Turkish, above the counter. There are scores of such places in Hackney and on nearby Green Lanes, and there's not much, at first glance, to distinguish this from countless others. But, as the regulars know, the Anatolya stands out for its unbeatable combination of consistently good and absurdly cheap food, and extraordinarily friendly service. Waiters put everyone at their ease, patiently describing for non-Turkish speakers each dish on the mangal (grill). Anatolya takes the Turkish tradition of hospitality seriously, and, depending on the whim of the waiter, you may well find yourself plied with a sticky baklava, or a complimentary tea served in a delicate tulip-shaped glass.

Dishes change daily, but you can usually depend upon the lhamacun (£1.20), spicy minced lamb on feather-light charred flat bread enlivened with buttery juices, red peppers and herbs. For mains it's best to stick with the lamb, which comes in a variety of guises: et sote (£3.80), fried with chilli sauce, is a little rich, but the skewered minced lamb charred to perfection on the grill is flawless, the red peppers and flat-leaf parsley rounding off a good, robust flavour. It costs £4.40 before 3pm and £5.50 thereafter. Or try the barbecued chicken (£4/£5.50) – eight crisp-skinned wings piled onto a plate with bulghur and fresh salad. There are usually a couple of casseroles bubbling away, too; the sulu yemekler (literally "watery meal") can take a number of forms, usually entailing chunks of meat with soft-cooked carrots, potatoes and courgettes (£3.50). Side dishes, all £2, include the usual hummus and taramasalata, along with a punchy haydari, a kind of rough garlic paste with chopped parsley, and a creamy cacik, whose cool combination of cucumber, garlic and yoghurt makes a perfect accompaniment to the spicy grilled meats.

Even counting the three stools over the mangal, and the tiny bar at the back, Anatolya is often crowded, especially on weekend evenings, so it can be a good idea to book a table.

Centuria

100 St Paul's Rd, N1 ©020 7704 2345	BR Canonbury/ ⊖ Highbury & Islington
Mon–Fri 6–11pm, Sat 12.30–11pm, Sun 12.30–10.30pm	Mastercard, Switch, Visa

Centuria is a "new pub". It looks like a place that's had the windows re-glazed, the floors stripped, the clientele changed and a back-room restaurant added. And so it has, and is all the better for it. Where once a few glasses of stout and pork scratchings changed hands, now a lively Italian restaurant flourishes. The menu, chalked on huge boards, changes throughout the evening as ingredients run out – a sign of freshness and quality and also good entertainment, as the cooking is done behind an open counter. Modern as this Italo-gastro-pub might be, the giant pepper mill is alive and well at Centuria and portions are reassuringly huge.

Starters include traditional favourites like insalata tricolore (£4.50), funghi al aglio (£4.25), and calamari alla griglia (£5.50), but there are some more adventurous offerings. Try Mediterranean merguez, spicy sausages on a bed of rocket and served with toasted Tuscan bread and hummus, or the fegato di pollo con spinaci (£5.25), chicken livers fried with goats' cheese and spinach – very rich. There are five pastas on offer – among them fusilli al salmone (£7.50), penne Centuria (£6.50) with sun-dried tomatoes and broccoli, and tagliatelle al funghi (£6.50) – and twelve main courses. Grilled lamb steak with beans, ginger and mint sauce (£9.50) is very good; merluzza al forno (£9.50) is baked cod on a mussel risotto, and tonno alla Siciliana (£9.50) is served just-cooked with couscous and peperonata. A side order of bruschetta (£2.85) comes heaped with grilled vegetables and pesto. Puddings include the ubiquitous tiramisù (£3.25), banoffee pie (£3.25) and cheesecake (£3.25), and there's a rich bitter chocolate tart served with mascarpone (£3.25), which is everything that it promises and more. Wines are reasonably priced, with a very crisp Sauvignon Blanc Gato Negro going for £13.50.

Centuria, situated at a small road junction, is also the only pub in the immediate area. Both of which make it a focal point with a nice villagey feeling. It's a pleasant venue for young Islingtonians, making it a busy place, and if you drop in for a beer and hope to get a table in the restaurant you should make your play early. Better to book.

Faulkner's

424 Kingsland Rd, E8 ℂ020 7254 6152	⊖ Liverpool Street
Mon–Thurs noon–2pm & 5–10pm, Fri noon–2pm & 4.15–10pm,	
Sat noon–10pm, Sun noon–9pm	Cash or cheque only

Faulkner's is a clear highlight among the kebab shops and chippies that line the rather scruffy Kingsland Road: a spotless fish-and-chip restaurant, with a takeaway section next door. It is reassuringly old-fashioned with its lace curtains, fish tank, uniformed waitresses, and cool yellow walls lined with sepia-tinted piscine scenes, and it holds few surprises – which is probably what makes it such a hit. Usually Faulkner's is full of local families and large parties, all ploughing through colossal fish dinners while chatting across tables. It also goes out of its way to be child-friendly, with highchairs leaned against the wall, and a children's menu priced at £3.25.

House speciality among the starters is the fish cake (£1.30), a plump ball made with fluffy herby potato. Or there's smoked salmon (£3.95), which comes in two satisfying wads, or prawn cocktail (£3.25). If you fancy soup, you've got tomato (80p) or a more exotic French fish variety, peppery and dark (£1.90). For main courses, the regular menu features all the British fish favourites, served fried or poached and with chips, while daily specials are chalked up on the blackboard. Cod (£6.60) and haddock (£7.75, £7.95 on the bone) retain their fresh firm flesh beneath the dark, crunchy batter, while the subtler, classier sole – Dover (£12.50) or lemon (£9.95) – is best served delicately poached. The mushy peas (65p) are just right, lurid and lumpy like God intended, but the test of any good chippy is always its chips, and here they are humdingers – fat, firm and golden, with a wicked layer of crispy little salty bits at the bottom. Stuffed in a soft doughy roll, they make the perfect chip butty. Most people wet their whistles with a mug of strong tea (55p), but there are few bottles of wine on offer, including a Merlot (£7.20) and a Chablis (£17.25).

Though always lively, Faulkner's is particularly fun at Saturday lunchtime, when traders and shoppers take time out from the local market to catch up, gossip, and joke with the waitresses.

Huong Viet

An Viet House, 12–14 Englefield Rd, N1 ©020 7249 0877	BR Dalston Kingsland
Mon–Fri noon–3.30pm & 5.30–11pm, Sat noon–4pm & 5.30–11pm	Mastercard, Visa

Huong Viet is the canteen of the Vietnamese Cultural Centre which occupies a rather four-square and solid-looking building that was once one of Hackney's numerous public bath houses. It has long had a reputation for really good, really cheap food, and the regulars were understandably nervous when a refurbishment was announced at the beginning of 2000. Would the Huong Viet end up all bleached wood and modern art? Would it be transformed into Dalston's answer to Mezzo? Everyone can breathe a sigh of relief, however, as the new Huong Viet is pretty much like the old Huong Viet in every important respect. The food is still fresh, unpretentious, delicious and cheap. The service is still friendly and informal. And the building still looks a lot like an ex-council bath house.

Start with the spring rolls (£2.10) – small, crisp, and delicious. Or the fresh rolls (£2.80), which resemble small, carefully rolled-up, table napkins. The outside is soft, white and delicate-tasting, while the inside teams cooked vermicelli with prawns and fresh herbs – a great combination of textures. Ordering the prawn and green leaf soup (£2.30) brings a bowl of delicate broth with greens and shards of tofu. Pho is the most famous Vietnamese soup, but calling this meal-in-a-bowl soup seems to be selling it short. The pho here is formidable, especially the Southern white noodle soup, filled with pork and prawn (£4). Hot, rich, full of bits and pieces, it comes with a plate of herbs, crispy beansprouts and aromatics that you must add yourself at the last moment so none of the aroma is lost. The other dishes are excellent too. Look out for sautéed scallops with mushroom and bamboo shoots (£5.50) – this works exceptionally well as the earthy, musty taste of the mushrooms sets off the fresh sea-sweetness of the scallops. You should also run amok with the noodle dishes – choose from the stir-fried soft white noodle dishes, or the crispy fried egg noodles. The mixed seafood special (£5.50) brings a smoky, flavoursome dish of fine noodles with squid, scallops, and prawns.

All the food tastes fresh. It's obviously been freshly cooked and the chef has used spankingly fresh ingredients. There is a set lunch (£5) which comprises a starter and a main course, accompanied by jasmine tea, mineral water or sweet home-made lemonade.

Little Georgia

2 Broadway Market, E8 ☎020 7249 9070	⊖ Bethnal Green
Tues–Fri noon–3pm & 6.30pm–midnight,	
Sat 6.30pm–midnight, Sun noon–4pm	All major credit cards

You could be forgiven for thinking that the Little Georgia was just another pub which had been converted into a trendy restaurant. It is certainly bare. The tables and chairs are certainly resolutely ordinary. But then you clock the blackboards with their unpronounceable specials, and the greeting of the somewhat harassed maitre d' who approaches with a beaming smile. Even if you are not intimately familiar with Georgian and Russian food, spotting a genuine welcome is easy enough, and you'll find one here. You'll also find an interesting list of essentially peasant dishes. From the menu it would seem that Georgians live on walnuts, pomegranate and beetroot, and that in order to make something of such basics they are not averse to adding the occasional handful of spice.

The starters fall into two categories – cold (£3.80) and hot (£4). Among the colds there are some exciting dips, or phkalis, which are a kind of pounded mixture: choose beetroot and walnuts, or the one predominantly made of leeks, or the one made from spinach and walnuts. They are good, with strong flavours and interesting textures. Then there is the Russian salad; even if youthful encounters with the tinned, mass-produced variety have left you scarred for life, do try this, as it is terrific. The soups here are also very fine; there is usually a soup of the day, which could well be something imaginative like wild mushroom with red basil and red wine – a surprisingly successful meeting of flavours. Main courses veer from things you will have heard of, like shashlik (£9) and beef stroganoff (£8.50), to more obscure ethnic dishes like khingarli (£8.50). Order the latter and the front of house will gently enquire whether you had had them before – "they are," he will explain, "very … Georgian". When they arrive, khingarlis turn out to be large, solid dumplings stuffed with spicy minced meat and naked save for a knob of butter. Very tasty and very, very filling. There is also plenty of choice for vegetarians, and the puddings do not disappoint.

Finally, you should make a point of trying the Georgian red wines: unsubtle, tannic, rich, fruity, almost musty … and cheap!

HACKNEY & DALSTON ① FRENCH

Soulard

113 Mortimer Rd, N1 ℂ020 7254 1314	BR Dalston Junction
Tues–Sat 7–10.30pm	Mastercard, Visa

Squeezed improbably into the front room of a converted house on a residential street, Soulard pays homage to all those wonderful meals remembered from holidays in provincial France, and whisks you out of this Hackney/Islington no-man's-land – the oddly named enclave of De Beauvoir Town – to Provence or the Dordogne. Looking for all the world like some regional French country-hotel restaurant, with the dining room centred on a large brick chimney, Soulard is a great find, serving sound food at practical prices. Everyone's in a good mood here, from the solicitous patron, who will greet you and ask after your welfare throughout the night, to the well-dressed, special-occasion clientele.

The proprietors at Soulard are eager to keep things as simple as possible. Meals are prix fixe: three courses will cost you £17.95 (excluding wine), while two go for £16.50 (with dessert thrown in if you arrive between 7pm and 8.30pm from Tues to Thurs). The small, fine-tuned menu is supplemented by blackboard specials; all are written in French, but there's always someone hovering to translate. As you would hope, there's a considered wine list, including a classy selection of dessert wines. Of the starters, escargots come in a whimsical puff-pastry snail, which trails a creamy, garlicky sauce and is packed with nicely cooked molluscs. Specials may include grilled calamari salad, all primary colours, fragrant oil dressing and the tenderest charred squid. Main courses are rich; meat-lovers will favour the traditional duck confit. Various fresh fish dishes are also listed on the blackboard, and precisely cooked – be it in a creamy mushroom sauce or in a sea-salty broth.

Although soulard is French for "drunkard", you should try and stay sober for the desserts, which are Gallic to the hilt. Try to resist the bavarois aux framboises, light and delicate, or the inspired black-and-white chocolate mousse, the bitter chocolate top layer contrasting beautifully with the sweet-as-spun-sugar base. Once a month there is a Menu Gastronomique which provides more dedicated diners with five courses for £26.95.

CITY & EAST

PUBS & BARS

The Cat & Mutton

76 Broadway, E8 ☎020 8249 1224

Toby Bitter, Worthington's and Tennant's Extra on tap feed the enthusiastic crowd of football fans. The big-screen sports, darts players and pool sharks vie to make the most noise. There's an amazing collection of trophy football scarves.

The Fox

372 Kingsland Rd, E8 ☎020 7254 4012

Very lively, up-for-it venue with a cosy, characterful feeling. John Smith's and Websters Yorkshire Bitter are the favourites on tap. Live music at the weekend and karaoke on Thursday.

The Hen & Chicken Theatre Bar

109 St Paul's Rd, N1 ☎020 7704 2001

Boasting a 54-seat theatre upstairs, and a cellar bar, this traditional corner pub plays host to a raft of different events, from comedy on Sunday and Monday to fringe theatre, DJs and live music the rest of the week. Worthington Draught and Fuller's London Pride on tap.

Lighthouse Bar

382 Essex Rd, N1 ☎020 7288 0685

This relaxed, comfortable lounge-style bar, furnished with leather chesterfields and low tables, isn't a place for the elderly or the staid. The young, bottled-beer-drinking crowd enjoys quizzes on Monday, "Play Your Own CDs" on Tuesday, and DJs from Thursday to Sunday.

Maddigan's on Mare Street

255 Mare St, E8 ☎020 8985 7391

Comfortable venue with a very New York feel – all scrubbed brickwork, pine tables and draped-lady Deco lights. To drink, however, you'll get a good pint of Fuller's London Pride, organic Honeydew ale and Greene King IPA. There's a heated patio garden.

The Village

512 Kingsland Rd, E8 ☎020 7923 3657

A straightforward, welcoming pub with Caffrey's, Grolsch and Kronenbourg as the favourites. The new landlord has elbowed the DJs who used to play here, so it's probably one of the quietest pubs in the area.

Hoxton
& Shoreditch

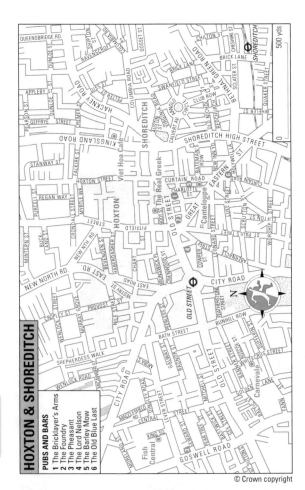

HOXTON & SHOREDITCH

PUBS AND BARS

1 The Bricklayer's Arms
2 The Foundry
3 The Pheasant
4 The Lord Nelson
5 The Barley Mow
6 The Old Blue Last

© Crown copyright

£30–£90

Canteloupe

35 Charlotte Rd, EC3 ✆020 7613 4411	⊖ Old Street/Shoreditch
Mon–Fri 12.30–3pm & 6.30–11pm, Sat 7–11.30pm	Mastercard, Switch, Visa

Property people keep saying that Shoreditch and Hackney are the "in" places to live, but until you visit somewhere like Canteloupe you may be forgiven for not believing them. It's been trading happily since 1996 and it's packed to the gunnels. Artistic-looking types swig beer from the bottle and wine from the glass in the front, nodding to each other and lip-reading – even on a quiet night you're pushed to do anything else – whilst snacking on a predictable but good tapas menu, running the gamut from basic – a Spanish tortilla (£2.75) – to wilder flights of fancy. But if you want a bit of peace and quiet, fight your way to the back of the warehouse-like building and you'll find the restaurant proper.

Though the food comes from the same kitchen wherever you eat it, the different menus bear little relation to each other. In the restaurant it changes every day, but always shows a bias towards Spain: spinach, roast garlic and almond soup (£3.50), or Spanish platter (£6), which consists of boquerones, Manchego cheese with quince jelly and three or four types of Spanish sausage. Main courses range widely: char-grilled saffron chicken with tabbouleh and harissa (£10.50), say, or Aberdeen Angus ribeye with peppers, anchovy and fried polenta (£12.50). Golf-ball shaped salmon and cod cakes, salade Niçoise, anchovy mayonnaise (£9) is very good, as is the "two potato" gratin with baby spinach, pine nuts and artichoke sauté (£8). There's a well-annotated wine list with a fair number of wines by the glass. Sadly though, for a happening place with pretensions to Spain, there are no sherries on the list at all.

This place is busy, so it's best to book. If not, you may have to wait with the groovy kids in the main bar. Those with sensitive ears should avoid Wednesday, Friday and Saturday nights, when DJs pump up the volume.

£11–£18

Carnevale

135 Whitecross St, EC1 ℗020 7250 3452	⊖ Old Street
Mon–Sat noon–3pm & 5.30–10.30pm	Delta and Switch only

This rather strange little restaurant is tucked into an ordinary shop-like space halfway along a scruffy street which is all street market by day and dingy grubbiness by night. Inside is a clean, light, if cramped space – blond wood tables and chairs – plus carefully selected, if not particularly original, prints on the walls and a faux garden to the rear. The interior has not so much been designed to the hilt, as is the current fashion, but rather put together in workable form to meet the needs of the customers. Mercifully, the enduring tendency of vegetarian restaurants to litter the premises with hippie references has been brought under control.

Instead, close attention seems to have been paid to the food, which is cooked with care. Take your time over some very good marinated Greek olives (£1.50) and bread dipped in nutty olive oil while you decide what you'll eat. The menu (which changes every couple of months), is not over-long – ten dishes in all – but is as varied as you could wish for, with starters ranging from warm Moroccan spiced bread with fried egg, buffalo mozzarella, rocket and chilli jam (£4.50) to celeriac seaweed roll with pickled vegetables, buckwheat noodles and pak choy in black bean dressing (£4.50). Home-made tagliatelle with trompettes de la mort, garlic leaves and Parmesan (£5.50 small, £8 main-course size) and a salad of asparagus, new potatoes and baked plum tomato (£4.50) are good enough to serve in many grander establishments. Main courses are equally well prepared. Smoked paprika and borlotti sausages in red wine sauce (£8.50) is a big, hearty, rib-sticking dish with plenty of depth of flavour. Butternut squash and spinach spring rolls with green peas and coconut laksa (£7.75) has all the zingy herbs and spices one would expect. There is a plentiful list of side orders, though given the size of the portions it is unlikely that you'll need any. If your stamina is up to them, puddings (£3.75) are good too – rhubarb and elderflower jelly with dairy-free vanilla cream or Pavlova with chocolate mousse, passionfuit and caramelised banana.

Service is relaxed, coffee is good, and there are a number of alternative drinks on offer. But if you are a wine drinker take care when grappling with the short list, and aim above the house selection (£9.75), which is pretty unforgiving.

Fish Central

151 King's Square, Central St, EC1 ℗020 7253 4970	⊖ Barbican
Mon–Sat 11am–2.30pm & 4.45–10.30pm	All major credit cards

The Barbican may appear to be the back of beyond – a black hole in the heart of the City – but perfectly ordinary people do live and work around here. Apart from the theatres and concert hall and the proximity to the financial district, one of the main attractions of the place is Fish Central, which holds its own with the finest fish-and-chip shops in town. Fish Central is also to be commended for its pricing policy. As each issue of this guide comes out prices move inexorably upwards, but the latest price rises here only apply to a handful of dishes and tend to be at a standard level – 15p! If only this were the case everywhere.

Though at first sight Fish Central appears just like any other chippy – a takeaway service one side and an eat-in restaurant next door – a glance at its menu lets you know that this is something out of the ordinary. All the finny favourites are here – from cod to rock salmon (both £3.70) – but there's a wholesome choice of alternatives, including grilled Dover sole (£8.90), and roast cod (£6.70) with rosemary and Mediterranean vegetables. Many of these dishes would not be out of place in much grander establishments. You can eat decently even if you are not in the mood for fish. Try the Cumberland sausages (£3.60) with onions and gravy, or the spit-barbecued chicken (£5.10 per half-bird – a very fair price). If you think your appetite is up to starters, try the prawn cocktail (£2.60) – the normal naked pink prawns in pink sauce, but genuinely fresh – or the seafood salad (£3.10), which puts all of those run-of-the-mill Italian restaurants to shame. Chips (£1.20) come as a side order, so those who prefer can order a jacket potato (£1.20) or creamed potatoes (£1.20). Mushy peas (£1.20) are . . . mushy, and Wallies (40p) – pickled gherkins to you – come sliced and prettily served in the shape of a flower.

Fish Central certainly pulls in a crowd of devoted regulars. On any given night, half the customers seem to know each other. Unusually for a chippy, it has an alcohol licence, which means there's a palatable dry Garrogny house white (£7.50) or, at a modest splash, champagne (£19.95) – the perfect partner for mushy peas.

The Real Greek

15 Hoxton Market, N1 ✆020 7739 8212	⊖ Old Street/Shoreditch
Mon–Sat noon–3pm & 5.30–10.30pm	Amex, Mastercard, Visa

This particular Real Greek is called Theodore Kyriakou, the able chef who launched the original Livebait behind Waterloo. Traditionally, Greek food has had a pretty rough deal in Britain: sure, there are quantities of restaurants which call themselves "Greek", but they are usually run by Greek Cypriots with a menu that concentrates on Cypriot food. Thus, for generations of Brits, Greek food has meant greasy, lukewarm moussaka, lurid pink cod's roe gloop, and pine-flavoured wine. Real Greek food is nothing like that, and showing off the authentic dishes of his homeland is the difficult mission Kyriakou has embarked upon.

The restaurant is small and comfortable, with the kitchen centre stage. The menu comes as a shock: the first section is mezedes and it explains that in Greece you would have small portions of a wide range of dishes. Here each platter has three or four components – chicken with walnuts accompanies dolmades, pan-fried hard cheese, and a yoghurt, cucumber and garlic dip (all for £6.70), while red wine-marinated octopus comes with home-salted cod and potato and garlic aïoli (£6.90). Or try Kalamata olives, yellow split-pea purée, a coarse salami from Levkas, warm salad of seasonal leaves, and a delicious feta cheese, which has been matured in oak barrels (£6.50). On to the small dishes, which could be either starters or sides: cuttlefish cooked in red wine and its own ink (£7), say, or lentils with smoked fish (£6.45). Main courses are a revelation: roast neck of lamb, smoked pork and spicy beef sausages served with bean casserole (£14.50), roast fillet of fish Spetsai style (£14.90), roast guineafowl served with Itz hilopites (a Greek noodle), cooked in gizzard broth with chestnuts and dressed with grated Kaseri cheese (£15), or Corfu-style pot roast of pork stuffed with kumquats (£14.80). Then there is a whole range of Greek cheeses and desserts – the honey doughnuts (£5) and the revani, a rich syrup-soaked cake (£5) are outstanding.

There is a genuine bargain set lunch and "early doors" dinner (5.30–7pm) which costs just £10 for two courses. The Real Greek has another surprise for you – the list of stunning wines at reasonable prices. Look out for the glorious pudding wine from the island of Patras, and the surprisingly sophisticated reds.

Viet Hoa Café

72 Kingsland Rd, E2 ☏020 7729 8293	⊖ Old Street
Daily noon–3.30pm & 5.30–11.30pm	All major credit cards except Amex

The Viet Hoa dining room is large, clean, light and airy, with an impressive golden parquet floor. The cafe part of the name is borne out by the bottles of red and brown sauce which take pride of place on each table. The brown goop turns out to be hoisin sauce and the red stuff a simple chilli one, but they have both been put into recycled plastic bottles on which the only recognisable words are "Sriracha extra hot chilli sauce – Flying Goose Brand". Apparently this has made all but the regulars strangely wary of hoisin sauce.

As befits a cafe, there are a good many splendid "meals in a bowl" – soups, and noodle dishes with everything from spring rolls to tofu. For diners wanting to go as a group and share, an appetiser called salted prawn in garlic dressing (£4.60) is outstanding: large prawns are marinated and fried with chilli and garlic. From the list of fifteen soups, pho (£3.10 or £4.15) is compulsory. This dish is a Vietnamese staple eaten at any and every meal – including breakfast. Ribbon noodles and beef, chicken or tofu are added to a delicate broth. It comes with a plate of mint leaves, Thai basil, and chillies, your job being to add the fresh aromatics to the hot soup – resulting in astonishingly vivid flavours. Main courses include shaking beef (£6.60) – cubes of beef with a tangy salad – and drunken fish (£6.50) – fish cooked with wine and cloud-ear mushrooms. Both live up to the promise of their exotic names. Bun bi (£4.15) is a splendid one-pot dish – noodles with shredded pork and moreish spring rolls, plus a side dish of "fish sauce" – light, chilli-hot, sharp, sweet, and fishy all at once. Also in one-pot-with-vermicelli territory you'll find bun nem nuong (£5) which features grilled minced pork, and that old favourite, Singapore noodles (£4.25).

This is a good restaurant in which to make a first foray into Vietnamese food. It is very much a family-run place, with the grandparents sitting at a table dextrously rolling spring rolls and the younger generations waiting the tables. They're very helpful to novices.

The Barley Mow

127 Curtain Rd, EC2   ✆020 7729 3910

A quiet and unspoilt little local. Adnams Broadside and Fuller's London Pride are the beers on tap, enjoyed by people who look as if they've been part of the furniture for decades. There's a real old-fashioned feeling to this place – quite delightful.

The Bricklayers Arms

83 Charlotte Rd, EC2   ✆020 7739 5245

One of the oldest pubs in the area, this Free House has kept its traditional char-acter as well as attracting the new media luvvies of Hoxton. Art exhibitions and DJs from Wednesday to Sunday drag down the age range, but Timothy Taylor's Landlord and Directors keep the old regulars happy. The odd Hoxton celeb also drops in.

Foundry

84–86 Great Eastern St, EC2 ✆020 7739 6900

This modern pub bar hosts art exhibi-tions downstairs and DJs playing what-ever they fancy upstairs. It's a Free House, and among other beers, the local microbrewery's Pitfield's Bitter is on offer. It's pretty fresh as well, as it is simply carried over from the brewery, conve-niently located just across the road.

The Lord Nelson

262 Old St, EC2   ✆020 7253 3558

Just a short walk from Old Street roundabout, this traditional pub has a friendly atmosphere. A mixed crowd of office workers and local residents enjoy Young's Bitter, Charles Wells' Bombardier and Greene King IPA. There are two pool tables in a separate room.

The Old Blue Last

38 Great Eastern St, EC2   ✆020 7739 5793

An unprepossessing corner site masks a cheerful Free House with Websters, Yorkshire and John Smith's on tap. At weekends a resident band, with varied guest singers, pulls a big crowd of locals down from their lofts and regulars from further afield.

The Pheasant

166 Goswell Rd, EC1   ✆020 7253 7429

This comfortable, modernised pub, with its big picture window, serves Tetley's, Adnams Broadside and Calders Cream Ale to business people by day and City University students of an evening. It's something of an oasis in an area not well served by pubs.

Further East

Forest Gate,
Newbury Park, West Ham

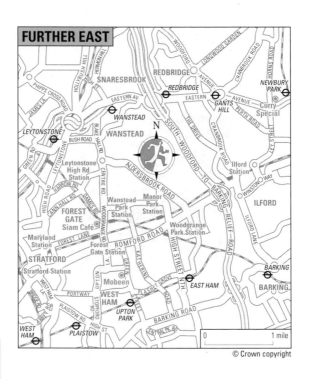

FURTHER EAST

HOLLYBUSH HILL
HERMON HILL
PHIPPS CROSS ROAD
JAMES LA
EASTERN AV
WOODFORD
LONGWOOD GARDEN
CRANBROOK ROAD
HORNS ROAD

SNARESBROOK
REDBRIDGE

REDBRIDGE
AVENUE
EASTERN
AVENUE

NEWBURY PARK

GANTS HILL
PERTH ROAD

Curry Special

LEYTONSTONE
WANSTEAD

WANSTEAD

BLAKE HALL RD
BUSH ROAD

N

THE DRIVE
CRANBROOK ROAD

LEYTONSTONE
GREEN SO
Leytonstone High Rd. Station
CENTRE RD

SOUTH WOODFORD TO BARKING

Ilford Station

LEY STREET

ALDERSBROOK ROAD
WINSTON WAY

ILFORD

CANN HALL RD
HARROW RD
JAMES ST
WOODGRANGE RD

Wanstead Park Station
Manor Park Station

Woodgrange Park Station

SOUTH WOODFORD TO BARKING RELIEF ROAD

ILFORD LANE

FOREST GATE
Siam Café

Maryland Station
FOREST LANE
ROMFORD ROAD
HIGH STREET

Forest Gate Station
KATHERINE RD

STRATFORD
Stratford Station

UPTON LA
GREEN ST
GROVE

BARKING
BARKING

Mobeen
PLASHET ROAD

EAST HAM

PORTWAY
STOPFORD RD
WEST HAM

WEST HAM
UPTON PARK

BARKING ROAD

WESTHAM LA
ABBEY RD
PLAISTOW RD
HIGH ST.

WEST HAM
PLAISTOW
CENTRAL PK. RD

| 0 | | 1 mile |

© Crown copyright

Curry Special

2 Greengate Parade, Horns Rd, Newbury Park,

Essex ©020 8518 3005   ⊖ Newbury Park

Tues–Sat 12.30–2pm & 6–11.30pm, Sun 6–11.30pm   All major credit cards

The tentacles of the Anand family (see The Brilliant, p.535) stretch far and wide, and their restaurants all serve a particular kind of Punjabi-meets-Kenyan food. Curry Special is the Eastern outpost in far-off Essex – when interrogated about why they picked Newbury Park when deciding to open a restaurant in 1982, the proprietors talk about "having friends and family in the area". Suffice to say they have had things pretty much to themselves and this restaurant has become a magnet for anyone out east who wants something a bit more interesting than the standard curry house menu. Rich flavours are achieved by long, slow cooking and carefully chosen spices; there are no instant fixes, no cream, no yoghurt, no handfuls of nuts.

Great pickles. Pause amongst the poppadoms to enjoy the carrot pickle, a genuinely Punjabi-hot super-crunch. Then go on to try the butter-fried chicken (half £6.50, whole £12), suitably, uncannily buttery, and something of a signature dish – as you'd expect, considering dynastic links with The Brilliant. There's also jeera (cumin) chicken at the same price and chilli chicken (half £7, whole £13): very tasty. The specials board is worth investigating – pili pili bogo (£3) is a dish of mixed vegetable pieces dusted in spiced flour and deep-fried. The curries are simple and rich – methi chicken (for one £6.50; half a chicken £16; and a whole £30), and a delicious palak lamb (£5). From the vegetables section, choose the tinda masala (£3). You will be asked (rather disconcertingly, as how hot is hot?) whether you want your curry mild, medium or hot. Perhaps the spicy Punjabi grub has shocked some previous Essex punters – for whatever the reason, medium here is pretty tame, and you may want to go for hot. Bread-wise, indulge yourself with a hot bhatura (£1.50), which could be subtitled "fried bread meets doughnut".

For all its suburban location opposite B&Q, and its strangely dated name, Curry Special is busy enough to make booking advisable even early in the week. Essex folk seem to know what they like.

Mobeen

222–224 Green St, E7 Ⓒ020 8470 2419   ⊖ Upton Park

Daily 11am–10pm   Cash only

If you have never been to West Ham, the whole of Green Street is likely to come as a surprise. It has the feel of Brick Lane and Southall, but everything is much, much cheaper – in the market here you can buy a whole goat for the price of a dozen lamb chops in the West End. Mobeen itself seems to operate at "factory gate" prices, offering a kind of 1950s Asian works-canteen ethos – with appropriate decor. As you go in, the kitchen lies behind a glazed wooden partition to your left, while to your right are cafe tables and chairs. The clientele hits this place like a breaking wave – it can be impressively busy at 11.50am.

The dishes and prices are listed above the servery hatches and the food is displayed below. You go up to the hatch, wait your turn and then order up a trayful, which will be reanimated in the microwave. Then it's off to another hatch for fizzy soft drinks and to yet another port of call to pick up cutlery and glasses. This is workmanlike food in large portions at basic prices. Most things are available in two sizes: chicken tikka (£2.50/£3.40) is red and hot, very hot. Sheekh kebabs are spicy and piping hot (thanks to the microwave). Meat samosas are just 55p each. Masala fish (£3.30) is rich and good. The biryani (£2.70/£3.50) is commendably ungreasy and may actually have benefited from being cooked and reheated. There's also spinach and meat curry (£2.60/3.20), a meat curry (£2.50/£3.20), and a bhuna meat curry (£2.60/£3.50). The breads are serviceable, although the bahtra (£1), a very thick, fried, stuffed paratha, will tip you over your cholesterol allowance for about a fortnight. This establishment is just up the road from West Ham's home ground – you have to wonder what Alf Garnett would have made of it all.

Mobeen is unlicensed and bringing your own is not allowed, but among the soft drinks and juices are some novelty items: for 50p you can try a fizzy mango juice in a lurid can. Just the thing to tempt a jaded palate.

Siam Café

103 Woodgrange Rd, E7 ✆020 8536 1870	BR Wanstead Park
Mon–Sat 7–10pm	Access, Visa

There is an inordinate number of outré hairdressing salons where Woodgrange Road turns the bend before the railway bridge, but it is still a mainish sort of main road, with shops and pubs interspersed with cafes. One of these is the Siam Café, cast very much in the mould of the late lamented Pie Crust Café. By day the Siam is a greasy spoon serving trad English greasy stuff, and by night it transforms into a family-run Thai eatery. This is one of the few restaurants in London where, after a solicitous enquiry as to whether this is your first visit, you may be treated to a short speech of welcome. The decor is fairly rugged and the lighting is neon – this is not one of your ultra-cool West End establishments. But the welcome is a warm one and the food carefully made, workmanlike, and cheap.

Starters here tend to hail from the fryer, and that includes the chicken satay (£4.50). The best are the crispy wonton (£3), and the steamed dumplings – a mix of prawn and pork (£3.80). The squid rings are crisp (£3.20). The rest of the menu falls into a series of categories – soups, red curries, green curries, stir-fries, and noodles – and all these dishes offer simple home cooking of a high standard. Spicing is accurate and everything tastes fresh. Soups are good value: tom yum kai (£3.25) is chicken soup. The sauces are good and clean-tasting. The stir-fries include chicken ginger (£4.60) and prawns with chilli and basil leaves (£5.75). The classic noodle dish, pud Thai, comes with chicken (£5.50) and king prawns (£6.50). Stir-fried noodles with egg, ground peanut, spring onion, dried shrimp, dried turnip and cabbage, it lives up to its billing on the menu – very tasty indeed.

You may bring your own drinks to the Siam Café, which is probably a very good thing as the jasmine tea (the high point of the drinks list) is neither redolent of jasmine or of tea, although it does come in a nice mug from that rustic collection given away by a leading petrol station.

North

Camden Town & Primrose Hill.....................255

Hampstead & Golders Green.....................265

Highgate & Crouch End.....................279

Holloway & Highbury.....................287

Islington.....................297

Maida Vale & Kilburn.....................309

St John's Wood & Swiss Cottage.....................317

Stoke Newington.....................325

Wembley.....................335

Further North.....................343
  Haringey, Hendon, Kingsbury, Willesden

Camden Town
& Primrose Hill

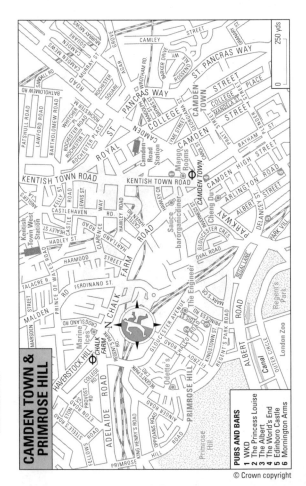

CAMDEN TOWN & PRIMROSE HILL

PUBS AND BARS
1 WKD
2 The Princess Louise
3 The Albert
4 The World's End
5 Edinboro Castle
6 Mornington Arms

© Crown copyright

Cheng Du

9 Parkway, NW1 ✆020 7485 8058	⊖ Camden Town
Daily noon–2.30pm & 6.30–11.30pm	Mastercard, Visa

When you walk into a Chinese restaurant and see not only designer ice buckets for your wine but also an espresso machine, your heart either sinks or soars. If you're on the side of the ice buckets, then you will enjoy Cheng Du, an elegant if slightly pricey place, improbably located in the busy bit of Camden Town. It bills itself as a Szechwan restaurant, but don't expect too much in the way of raw or fierce flavours, for dishes here seem to have been "civilised", perhaps a little too much so. Yet the flavours are delicate, platefuls are pretty, and if you want a few more pyrotechnics you can always order a saucer of chilli oil to sear the taste buds.

Steamed dumplings with Szechuan garlic dressing (£4 for eight dumplings) is a good starter – the dressing light and tasty. The deep-fried squid tossed with peppercorn salt (£5.00) is fresh and well cooked, too, as are the steamed fresh scallops with garlic dressing (£4.60 for two). Main courses are all in a similar vein – peasant dishes that are heavily reliant on garlic, chilli and Szechwan pepper, "tidied up" and made more accessible and more stylish. Try the steamed chicken with red dates, black funghi and golden lilies (£5.80), or the double-cooked pork (£5.70) in a rich sauce with capsicums, the ever-present spring onions and a red braising sauce – rich flavours predominate. The only real disappointment could be a dish of fried spring onions with black bean and green chilli (£3.90) – this carries a warning, "very hot" . . . but when it comes it isn't.

One section of the Cheng Du menu is outstanding – the steamed fish, served either with ginger and spring onions, or in a black bean sauce. There are plenty of these fishy options: Dover sole £16.20; turbot £12.80; and salmon £7. All these prices may vary seasonally and sea bass is always priced on a "per pound basis" – £12. It's hard to beat a whole sea bass – firm-fleshed, delicious and perfectly cooked, arriving on a platter in all its glory, and then meticulously filleted at the tableside by a waiter – unless, of course, your wallet will stretch to the same treatment for a Dover sole.

The Engineer

65 Gloucester Ave, NW1 ©020 7722 0950   ⊖ Chalk Farm

Mon–Fri 9–11.30am, noon–3pm & 7–11pm, Sat 9am–noon,

12.30–3.30pm & 7–11pm,

Sun 9am–noon, 12.30–3.30pm & 7–10.30pm   Mastercard, Switch, Visa

The Engineer is one of that burgeoning roster of gastro-pubs whose food side has grown and grown – it now has tables in the bar, a more formal restaurant, tables in the garden (for those occasional summer days), and a salle privée on the first floor. Wherever you end up sitting, you'll get offered the same menu (which changes every two weeks) and you'll pay the same price. The cooking is accomplished, with good strong combinations of flavours, and a cheerful, iconoclastic approach to what is fundamentally Mediterranean food. The latest development is that they open for breakfast seven days a week. When do they sleep?

Your hackles may rise at £1.75 for home-made bread and butter, but the bread is warm from the oven, with a good crust, and the butter is beurre d'Isigny, and, as they refill the basket after you've scoffed the lot, you end up feeling happier about paying. Starters are simple and good. There's soup (£3.75). There may be a summery salad such as feta cheese, dandelion leaf, watermelon and mint with an orange dressing (£5.95), or grilled asparagus with pocket poached egg and chive and truffle butter (£5.95). At lunchtime the mains will probably be quite light – eggs Benedict, eggs Florentine, a pan-fried organic beef burger. For dinner, expect dishes like leg of lamb with adoba sauce (roast chilli and honey), and a prune and pistachio couscous (£11.75), or a risotto of oyster mushroom, sage and fennel with rocket and Parmesan (£8.75). There's often a new twist put on an old favourite, so pan-fried duck breast comes with stir-fried greens, wok-fried black beans and a soy and honey sauce (£13.50). A very successful dish indeed. Do not miss out on a side order of baker chips (£2.25) – thick wedges of baked potato fried until crispy. Thanks to The Engineer's pub status, there is always a decent pint of beer to be had and the coffee is excellent, too – all in all, plenty of reasons why it's so busy, and plenty of reasons why you should book.

At the bottom of the menu it says proudly, "Please note that all our meat is free range and organic". Hurrah! They deserve your support.

Mango Rooms

10 Kentish Town Rd, NW1 ©020 7482 5065	☉ Camden Town
Mon 6pm–midnight, Tues–Sun noon–3pm & 6pm–midnight	Mastercard, Visa

Mango Rooms is an engaging place, although it does make you wonder why everyone in this part of London is striving so hard to be laid-back. Hereabouts the coolness seems a little forced, and the casualness somehow elaborate. No matter. This restaurant describes itself as offering "traditional and modern Caribbean cuisine", the walls are bright and shabby, the staff gentle, and cooking reliable. If there is a fault to be found, it would be that the spicing and seasoning is somewhat tame, as if the act has been cleaned up a bit – spookily enough, the identical criticism can be levelled at Cheng Du (see p.257), which is about a hundred yards away. Perhaps Camden's restaurateurs simply have an unusually good grasp of what their customers like? Mango Room is certainly very full, and everyone seems to be having a great time, in a laid-back, Camden-cool kind of way.

Traditional starters are the most successful, like the salt cod fritters with apple chutney (£3.80). Or crab and potato balls (£3.70) – the exception to the under-spiced rule. Ebony wings, marinated in chilli pepper, garlic and soya with a hot and sweet dipping sauce (£3.70) is a nice dish but not a hot one. For a main course, "Camden's famous curry goat with hot pepper, scallions, garlic, pimento and spices" (£7.80) is subtitled "A hot, spicy traditional dish", which it isn't. But it is very tasty: well presented and with plenty of lean meat. The West Indian permit (£8.50) is a small but solid fish, accurately cooked and served with a choice of different sauces. The side dishes are excellent – plantain (£1.70), rice and peas (£1.50), white and sweet potato mash (£2), and a very good, dry and dusty roti (£2.50). The cooking is consistent and the kitchen makes a real effort with the presentation. If you like your Caribbean food on the sweet side and without the fierce burn of lantern chillies or pepper sauce, you will have a great time here.

Puddings are good – the mango and banana brûlée (£3.50) sports an exemplary hard top – and the Mango Rooms special rum punch (£4.50) is sweet enough for most people to class it as a dessert. The bar here is lively and seems to be ever-expanding,

£8–£25

Marine Ices

8 Haverstock Hill, NW3 ©020 7485 3132	⊖ Chalk Farm
Restaurant Mon–Fri noon–3pm & 6–11pm, Sat noon–11pm, Sun noon–10pm	
Gelateria Mon–Sat 10.30am–11pm, Sun 11am–10pm	Mastercard, Switch, Visa

Marine Ices is a family restaurant from a bygone era. In 1947, Aldo Mansi rebuilt the family shop along nautical lines, kitting it out with wood and portholes (hence the name). In the half-century since, while the family ice cream business has grown and grown, the restaurant and gelateria has just pottered along. All for the good. That means old-fashioned service and home-style, old-fashioned Italian food. It also means that Marine Ices is a great hit with children, for, in addition to the good Italian food, there is a marathon list of stunning sundaes, coupes, ice creams and sorbets.

The menu is long: antipasti; salads; pastas and sauces; specialities and pizzas. Of the starters, you could try selezioni di bruschetta (£3.80), which combines one each of three well-made and fresh bruschetta – roast vegetables, sardines and tomatoes. Or go for the chef's salad (£3.95), a rocket salad with pancetta and splendid croutons made from eggy bread. Pasta dishes are home-made: casarecce Aldo (£6.80), from the specials list, has a tasty sauce of spring onions, spinach and ricotta – simple, and very good. Main courses range from pollo valdostana (£7.40) to scalloppa Milanese (£8.60) and fegato alla Veneziana (£8.90). Pizzas are immense, freshly made and very tasty, in whichever of their many guises you choose (£5.20–£6.50). And where others may be set on saving Venice, at Marine they support the Rebuild the Roundhouse fund; for every Roundhouse pizza (£6.50) – cheese, tomato, ham, mushroom, and fresh chilli – sold, they donate 50p.

When you've had your meal, take a breath and ask for the gelateria menu. There are sundaes, from peach melba (£2.40) to Knickerbocker Glory (£3.65). There are coppe, including Stefania (£4.40), one scoop each of chocolate and hazelnut ice cream, covered in nuts and hot fudge sauce. There are bombe, cassate, and, best of all, affogati (£4.20): three scoops of ice cream topped with Marsala or – even nicer – espresso coffee. Or create your own combo from fourteen ice creams and eight sorbets. They're £1.25 a scoop.

Odette's

130 Regent's Park Rd, NW1 ©020 7586 5486	⊖ Chalk Farm
Mon–Fri 12.30–2.30pm & 7–11pm, Sat 7–11pm	All major credit cards

Odette's is a charming, picturesque restaurant, ideally set in pretty Primrose Hill. The walls are crammed with gilded mirrors and hanging plants, there's a pleasant conservatory at the back (with a skylight open in warm weather), and candles flicker in the evenings. Add well-judged modern British food, the odd local celeb, and staff who always try to make you feel special, and you have all the ingredients for a very successful local restaurant. In summer, try to get one of the tables that spill out onto the villagey street.

The food makes commendable use of seasonal produce, so do not expect to find all the dishes listed every time you visit. However, the olive and walnut bread is a constant – warm and delicious. Starters, if you strike lucky, might include a delicate watercress soup with garlic tortellini (£3.50), or a warm salad of char-grilled Jerusalem artichokes, roasted tomatoes and rocket (£6.50). When in season, the Irish oysters (£7.50) are a good choice and well presented. Mains generally include at least one choice each of fish, meat, game and chicken. Pan-fried lemon sole comes with harissa, candied aubergines and globe artichokes (£13) – delicious. Cumin roast neck of new season lamb, soft polenta and spring greens (£12.50) is another good choice, as is the sauté of black-leg chicken, fresh pasta, new season peas and broad beans (£12). Monkfish wrapped in Parma ham, served on a bed of roasted red peppers and spring onions with warm vinaigrette (£13), is a great combination, while veggies might go for tarte Tatin of caramelised onions and goats' cheese (£9). Puddings (all £4.75) are wonderfully indulgent, and include chocolate espresso tart with crème fraîche, lemon curd parfait with strawberries, and an outstanding mango and stem ginger sorbet. The set lunch (Mon-Fri, £10) is worth noting.

Odette's has a very long wine list, with something to suit all tastes and purses. It's also nice to get such a large choice of wines by the glass and half-bottle. Try a glass of South African Chardonnay for £3.15, or a bottle of Sauvignon de Touraine for £8.25.

CAMDEN TOWN & PRIMROSE HILL ⑩ BRITISH

Sauce barorganicdiner

214 Camden High St, NW1 ℂ020 7482 0777   ⊖ Camden Town

Mon–Sat noon–11pm, Sun noon–4.30pm   Delta, Mastercard, Switch, Visa

If organic is the new rock'n'roll then Sauce is another band to listen to. Associated with the well-known Camden Brasserie (upstairs), Sauce (downstairs) is dedicated to wholesome tasty plates of organic food served all day. Sauce claims 95% of the ingredients are produced by farmers who care for the environment, and are free from chemicals, pesticides and preservatives. As for the "barorganicdiner" bit, Sauce offers a separate juice and cocktail bar and a bright, colourful restaurant. Juices and smoothies range from carrot, apple and ginger (£3.10) – and very perky it is, too – to cocktails like Margaritas (£4.25 glass, £15 pitcher). Newspapers and flyers for worthy causes provide food for the mind as well, and it's fine just to go for a beer or a coffee.

Start with corn fritter with roast vegetables and tomato salsa (£4.50) and you get a solid, almost meaty, fritter; or soup of the day (£3.50), perhaps red pepper; or crab cakes with sweet chilli sauce (£4.95) – very moreish. Main courses include an obligatory veggie burger with nuts, seeds, tomato relish and fat fries (£6.50), which is crisp and tasty, and a beef burger with tomato relish and fat fries (£7.50) – as good a burger as you'll get anywhere. There are also fine sandwiches and wraps – try the spicy black beans, rice, pepper and melted cheese in a tortilla wrap (£5.95), and, if you're hungry, add shredded chicken for an extra £1. Puddings include chocolate nut brownie with caramel sauce (£3.50); fresh fruit of the day over waffle plus maple syrup (£3.25), and baked banana with caramel sauce and vanilla ice cream (£3.25). There are organic teas, coffees and fruit tisanes, and you can choose dairy or soya cream – it must be said that, from a taste perspective, cows beat beans hands down when it comes to turning out cream. If you fancy something stronger, there's Freedom lager and a host of organic wines.

Sauce provides the security of well-chosen organic ingredients, served in a chic environment. If you want to eat this way (and you know it makes sense), then this place is a godsend.

NORTH

The Albert

11 Princess Rd, NW1   ✆020 7722 1886

There's a cosy country-pub feel to this small, bright little local. A large private garden at the back makes it very useful in summer, too. Much favoured by residents of the grander Primrose Hill houses, who enjoy the Fuller's London Pride and Greene King IPA.

Edinboro Castle

56 Mornington Terrace, NW1 ✆020 7255 9651

This huge bar has been well modernised with pale wood, stained glass and long communal tables. A large patio garden ensures plenty of atmosphere in summer and a predominantly young crowd enjoys Worthington and Staropramen. DJs play from time to time.

The Mornington Arms

3 Mornington St, NW1   ✆020 7383 4869

A real round-the-corner local, this rambling pub has a large conservatory and a small beer garden at the back. A traditional boozer, it's the sort of place where the landlord knows all his customers by name. Courage Best and John Smith's on tap.

The Princess Louise

22 Chalcott Rd, NW1   no phone

Below the scrubbed wooden ground floor lies a secret patio garden and bar. Open fires and big windows give this place a cheery, modern and relaxed feel. There are piles of newspapers to read and Adnams, London Pride and Stella to drink.

WKD

18 Kentish Town Rd, NW1   ✆020 7267 1869

A relaxed coffee lounge by day, by night WKD turns into a bright, loud cocktail bar with a late licence. A door policy operates after 10pm, with DJs playing soul and R&B to a cheerful crowd who favour mixer drinks and cocktails above beer. WKD? It stands for Wisdom, Knowledge, Destiny.

The World's End

174 Camden High St, NW1   ✆020 7482 1932

Reputedly the biggest pub in Europe, this colossal Free House is easy to get lost in. At the weekend, especially, a noisy crowd of Camden Lock shoppers swells the numbers and everyone seems to have a good time. There's a huge selection of lagers and alco-pops. The famous Goth club Underworld is, you guessed it, underneath.

Hampstead & Golders Green

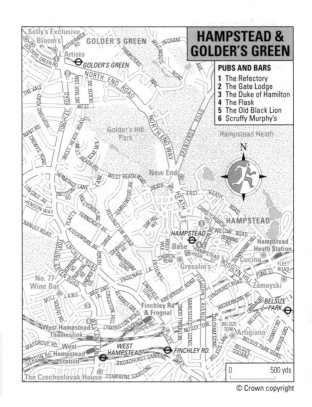

HAMPSTEAD & GOLDER'S GREEN

PUBS AND BARS

1 The Refectory
2 The Gate Lodge
3 The Duke of Hamilton
4 The Flask
5 The Old Black Lion
6 Scruffy Murphy's

0   500 yds

© Crown copyright

£16–£38

No.77 Wine Bar

77 Mill Lane, NW6 ℂ020 7435 7787	⊖ West Hampstead
Mon & Tues noon–11pm, Wed–Fri noon–midnight,	
Sat 1pm–midnight, Sun 1–10.30pm	Mastercard, Visa

The "77" has gone through a few changes. Fans of the place's old-style, ultra-casual, ultra-corny menu, with its resident 12oz burger "the Fat Bastard", will be more than a little shocked by the new chef's style. Grown-up food has finally made an appearance at this long-running party. The wine list is long, informed and offers good value. The menu changes monthly and marches in step with the seasons, the puns have gone the way of the old rough-and-ready dishes, and in their place are what could best be described as Modern British classics – if such a thing is possible.

Starters include soupe de jour (£3.95). Or how about a terrine of chicken leek and trompette mushrooms with yellow pepper vinaigrette and herbs (£5.95)? Then there is squid with noodles, black pudding and chorizo, poached egg and saffron cream (£5.75), and a confit duck salad with spring onions, garlic and rosemary emulsion (£4.75). Main courses also appeal: braised lamb shank, mashed potatoes, slow roast tomatoes and coriander jus (£10.50), roast cod, pea and mint purée, glazed baby onions, smoked pancetta and sherry vinegar jus (£10.95), pot roast chicken, celeriac Dauphinoise, braised red cabbage and jus of thyme (£9.95). The pud list also offers some classics – warm chocolate fondant pudding with bitter chocolate ice cream (£4.50), say, and that noblest pudding of them all – bread and butter (£4.50). "77" is also to be commended for offering a selection of English and French cheeses with accurate and educated tasting notes. What a very good idea.

Like the menu, the wine list changes as whim and stocks dictate, but look out for delights such as Amarone Classico della Valpolicella, Allegrini 1991 (£24.95) or Three Choirs Estate Reserve, lightly oaked, 1996 (£13.75). Anyone visiting Mill Lane for the first time should bear in mind that in this part of North London the busiest night of the week is Thursday, which is when the wine bar will be at its liveliest. They certainly know how to party in these parts.

Artigiano

12 Belsize Terrace, NW3 ℗020 7794 4288	⊖ Belsize Park

Mon–Sat noon–3pm & 6.45–11pm, Sun noon–3pm & 6.45–10pm

All major credit cards

This is one of London's more difficult-to-find restaurants, situated halfway up a dead-end street in the rabbit warren of Belsize Park. Nevertheless, tracking it down is well worth the effort. When you do find it, you will be confronted with a bright, airy restaurant, glass-fronted and with generous skylights. There's more chance of seeing a traffic warden than a passing car and the only disturbance from outside is the rustle of leaves. For such an out-of-the-way place the restaurant is surprisingly big, with more than 100 covers, and remarkably busy, full of thirty-something professionals who've sought it out for the same reasons you have – good food and service, convivial atmosphere, and an escape from the rat race.

The menu is longer than you'd expect in such a restaurant, with eight first courses and eight pastas – all of which can be ordered as starters or mains – followed by eleven main courses, but it seems that the kitchen can cope. There is an admirable tendency to use spanking fresh ingredients and to let them be themselves. A first course of marinated organic tomatoes (£5.50/£8.50) is served with little broad beans, sautéed onions and Parmesan croutons, dressed simply in top-quality olive oil. Ordering marinated spring vegetables (£5.50/£8.50) brings an interesting selection of vegetables, served with really good buffalo mozzarella. There's top-notch prosciutto (£7.50/£10.50), served with melon or mango in a way that somehow avoids naff, and a good beef carpaccio (£7.50/£10.50). Pastas are home-made and innovative. A fish version of spaghetti carbonara (£7.50/9.50) is better than it sounds, as is ravioli with buffalo ricotta and thyme (£6.50/£9). More substantial, the saltimbocca (£11.50), with spinach, Gorgonzola and sultanas, is splendid, as is the grilled swordfish with ratatouille (£12.50). The chocolate sorbet (£4) is seductive and the strawberries (£4.50) are marinated in spumante and balsamic vinegar.

Having weathered that risky first year Artigiano looks set fair. If you are able to make it at lunchtime, go for the set menu – £10.50 for two courses, £13.50 for three.

L'Artista

917 Finchley Rd, NW11 ©020 8731 7501	⊖ Golders Green
Daily noon–midnight	Mastercard, Visa

Situated opposite the entrance to Golders Green tube, and occupying an arch under the railway lines, L'Artista is hard to miss. With its pavement terrace, abundant greenery and umbrellas, this is a lively, vibrant restaurant and pizzeria that exercises an almost magnetic appeal to the young and not so young of Golders Green. At the weekend it is literally full to bursting and tables spill onto the terrace – a perfect spot to eat al fresco, providing the traffic isn't too heavy on the Finchley Road. Inside, the plain decor is enhanced by celebrity photographs; the waiters are a bit cagey if asked just how many of them have actually eaten here, but the proximity of the tables ensures that you get to rub shoulders with whoever happens to be around you, famous or otherwise.

The menu offers a range of Italian food with a good selection of main courses such as fegato Veneziana (£7.10), a rich dish of calves' liver with onion and white wine. The trota del pescatore (£6.90) is also good, a simple but effective trout with garlic. But L'Artista's pizzas are its forte. They are superb. As well as traditional thin-crust capricciosa (£5.90) with anchovies, eggs and ham, or quattro formaggi (£5.60), there are more unusual varieties such as mascarpone e rucola (£5.10), a plain pizza topped with mascarpone cheese and heaps of crisp rocket, which is actually very good. The calzone (£5.70) – a cushion-sized rolled pizza stuffed with ham, cheese and sausage and topped with Napoli sauce – is wonderful. Pastas are varied and, for a change, the penne alla vodka (£5.40) made with vodka, prawns and cream, is well worth a try. For something lighter, try the excellent insalata dell'Artista (£4.80), a generous mix of tuna, olives and fennel, with an order of equally good garlic pizza bread (£2.50).

L'Artista tries hard to bring something of the atmosphere of Naples to Golders Green. By a happy accident this ambience is enhanced by the Vesuvian tremors which occur whenever a Northern line train rumbles ominously overhead.

HAMPSTEAD & GOLDERS GREEN ⓜ MODERN BRITISH

Base

71 Hampstead High St, NW3 ©020 7431 2224   ⊖ Hampstead

Mon–Sat noon–2.30pm & 7–10.30pm, Sun noon– 2.30pm   All major credit cards

It's strange. In Hampstead the shops are smart, the houses are smart, the people are smart . . . but there are relatively few high-quality places to eat. Enter into this patchy restaurant scene a talented chef from the West End, one Pierre Khodja, and his cafe-restaurant on the high street. The double door reflects the origins of this establishment as two neighbouring shops; the right-hand door leads to the cafe and the left-hand door to the restaurant. At lunch the cafe heaves with people drawn in by the excellent pastries, sandwiches, soups and simple dishes. In the evening the restaurant makes a spirited attempt to serve high-class cuisine. Hampsteadians fill the place at the weekend, but you can get a table without much trouble earlier in the week. The decor is modern, the service is friendly and the stylish ambience is palpable. Even more important: Pierre Khodja is a really good cook.

When Khodja worked in the West End his menus harked back to North Africa, which was the gastro-fad of the moment. Here at his new base things are more straightforward, but there are still welcome flashes of inspiration. The fish cake (£7.95) on the lunch menu is very good, served with hollandaise sauce and a scattering of small chunks of chorizo for piquant contrast. At dinner starters may include a soup of the day (£4.50), grilled asparagus (£5.95), roasted scallops (£6.50), or goats' cheese crottin (£5.50). Mains range from roast salmon with lobster mash and lime jus (£14) and baked whole sea bass (£17) with potato, peppers and chilli, to duck breast (£15.50) – or rather, "salsify duck confit with ravioli and berry jus". Desserts are of a very high quality. (There is a steady takeaway trade at the cafe, as scores of Hampstead hostesses carry off the splendid lemon tarts.)

The menu occasionally features a dish called lobster tagine (£17). This may be served in a tagine, and the chef may have been born and bred in the Maghreb, but tagine it is not. The lobster is well cooked (ie not overcooked), and is balanced with the sweetness of chestnuts and a pleasing whiff of anise. Sophisticated cooking, and well worth trying.

Bloom's

130 Golders Green Rd, NW11 ℂ020 8455 1338   ⊖ Golders Green

Mon–Thurs & Sun noon–11pm, Fri 10am–2pm/3pm (winter/summer)

All major credit cards except Diners

Bloom's goes way back to 1920 when Rebecca and Morris Bloom set up the company to produce their great discovery – the original Veal Vienna. Since then "Bloom's of the East End" has carried the proud tag as "the most famous kosher restaurant in the world". Setting aside the indignant claims of several outraged New York delis for the moment, given its history it's a shame that the East End Bloom's was forced to shut, and that they had to retrench to this, their Golders Green stronghold, in 1965. Nonetheless, it's a glorious period piece. Rows of sausages hang over the takeaway counter, there are huge mirrors and chrome tables, and inimitable service from battle-hardened waiters.

So, the waiter looks you in the eye as you ask for a beer. "Heineken schmeineken," he says derisively. At which point you opt for Maccabee, an Israeli beer (£1.90), and regain a little ground. Start with some new green cucumbers (80p) – fresh, crisp, tangy, delicious – and maybe a portion of chopped liver and egg and onions (£4.20), which comes with world-class rye bread. Or go for soup, which comes in bowls so full they slop over the edge: beetroot borscht (£2.90), very sweet and very red; lockshen, the renowned noodle soup (£2.90); or kreplach, full of dumplings (£3.20). Go on to main courses. The salt beef is as good as you might expect (£12.90 a plate). In 1999 Bloom's was taken over by Jonathan Tapper (one of the fourth generation of the Bloom family), and there have been some changes – main courses now come with vegetables. But you can still order extra side dishes … those legendary dishes that have made the reputation of Jewish food .

Whatever else you try, don't leave without sampling the latkes (£1.90) – enormously solid and uncompromising potato pancakes. And the tzimmas (£1.90) – honeyed carrots so cloyingly sweet that they could claim a spot on the dessert menu. It's filling, wholesome, comforting food. Enjoy!

Cucina

45a South End Rd, NW3 ©020 7435 7814 ⊖ Belsize Park

Mon–Thurs noon–2.30pm & 7–10.30pm, Fri & Sat noon–2.30pm & 7–11pm,

Sun noon–2.30pm · All major credit cards except Diners

This single-fronted restaurant, next to a bakery near South End Green, looks like the archetypal traiteur or smart food shop. And that is what it is, at least downstairs, where the Hampstead literati feast upon a range of rather good meals to go. But if you enter and turn right up the stairs, you come to a large, brightly painted, wooden-floored, roof-lit dining room. Very modern, very fashionable, very chic. At lunch, all is relatively quiet and talk at the scattered tables is generally of business. Things hot up in the evening, however, when the à la carte menu takes over. This menu changes every two weeks or so and darts about between cuisines and continents, but wherever you alight you can be sure of well-presented dishes and service that is friendly and efficient (if sometimes a little too speedy).

Dinner-time starters may include char-grilled quail with chorizo risotto and chive oil (£5.50), deep-fried field mushrooms in chickpea batter with yoghurt and rocket (£5.25), baked goats' cheese terrine with ratatouille salsa (£5.50), or perhaps buffalo and green peppercorn sausages with apple, onion and thyme chutney (£5.25) – solid and meaty. Among the main courses there is always a fish of the day, often something interesting like mahi-mahi. Other fish dishes feature, too, such as char-grilled northern albacore with wasabi potatoes, seaweed aioli and soy dressing (£13.75). Then perhaps char-grilled guinea fowl with sag aloo, yoghurt and almonds (£12.95), or char-grilled rib of beef (for two) with frites (£24.95)?

In Cucina's early days the menu sometimes read better than the dishes themselves actually turned out, but it has since bedded in well and many of the more complex excesses of the formative period have been abandoned.

£12–£26

The Czechoslovak House

74 West End Lane, NW6 ©020 7372 5251   ⊖ West Hampstead

Tues–Fri 6–10pm, Sat & Sun noon–3pm & 6–10pm   Cash or cheque only

With its low prices, the kind of ambience where Harry Lime would feel right at home, and bafflingly retro decor, The Czechoslovak House is always filled with a happy mix of students and locals. It is situated in the old, established Czechoslovak National House (too good an institution to be sundered – or even to adapt its name), and its dining room is a class act. Genuine flock wallpaper gives a unique backdrop for some striking portraits: among them Václav Havel, Winston Churchill, and a very young-looking Queen Elizabeth II with her crown and regalia picked out in glitter powder.

Menu-writers across London should be forced to study here – it is hard to improve on the concision of "meat soup" (£2.50). Passing that dish by, try starting with tlacenka (£2.50), which is home-made brawn with onions. Or Russian egg (£4), egg mayonnaise with salad, ham and onions. Or the rather good rollmops (£2.20), again with onions. (You need to like raw onions to do well at the starters.) Main courses deliver serious amounts of home-made, tasty food. Beef goulash with dumplings (£7.70) is red with sweet paprika, and cooked long and slow until the meat is meltingly tender. Order smoked boiled pork knuckle, sauerkraut and dumplings (£8.70), and you will be served a vast and tasty ham hock, good (if rather sweet) sauerkraut, dumplings, plus a small jug of wildly rich pork gravy. If you don't fancy dumplings, the roast veal comes with creamed spinach and superb fried potatoes (£8.40). To drink, set your sights on beer – Gambrinus on draught is £2.20 a pint and there are a number of other bottled Czech beers, including one whose label is fetchingly decorated with a motorcycle and sidecar. There is a story behind this graphic, which the amiable bartender will explain – not that you will be able to remember the tale after drinking the stuff.

There is one pudding that will have any cholesterol-wary diner clutching at their pacemaker. Apricot dumpling (£3.50) is a cricket-ball-sized lump of dough with an apricot inside. It comes under a coat of sour cream, and sits in a sea of melted butter. The only concession to modern fresh food fads is the garnish of three grapes. It is awesome.

Gresslin's

13 Heath St, NW3 ⓒ020 7794 8386   ⊖ Hampstead

Mon 7–10.30pm, Tues–Sat noon–2.30pm & 7–10.30pm,

Sun noon–2.30pm   All major credit cards except Diners

Michael Gresslin's, a small, rather humble-looking restaurant on Hampstead's busy Heath Street, has stayed the course since opening in 1996. In 1999 it had a facelift – all glass, stainless steel and leather – but the menu follows the same star as before, and the cuisine is still Modern European. Here you'll find a succession of dishes all given an imaginative twist – very much in the modern idiom, where Mediterranean flavours meet Oriental flourishes – and presentation on the plate is taken very seriously. This combination has secured Gresslin's a considerable and devoted following.

The efficient French waiters are knowledgeable about the food, and happy to recommend something they think you'll like, but it is hard in any case to go far wrong. The seasonal menu is short and well thought out, underpinned by quality, fresh ingredients, and with a good balance of fish, meat and vegetarian options. Starters might include spicy tiger prawns with Oriental noodle salad (£7.50), or squid ink tagliatelle with fresh clams, chilli oil, and smoked cod roe (£6.50), or soup of Jerusalem artichokes with Stilton and truffle oil (£4). Everything is precisely cooked. For mains, you get a choice of ten or so dishes. Baby chicken pot au feu with mustard fruits (£12.95) appeals, as do the monkfish cheeks with green butter gratin, steamed pak choi, kay chay couscous and orange Puy lentils (£18.50). Or perhaps stir-fried vegetable torlino with mozzarella pine kernels (£12.50). Desserts are good, too: try the chocolate pecan brownies with hot chocolate fudge sauce and vanilla ice cream (£6.50), or the panettone, orange and prune trifle with mascarpone marsala (£4.50).

It's unlikely you'd visit Hampstead just to go to Gresslin's, but it's a real asset when you're there. Look out for the set menus, all of which offer a choice: dinner, served Monday to Thursday, is £14.95 for two courses and £17.95 for three; lunch, Tuesday to Saturday, is £12 for two courses including coffee. Sunday lunch gives you a choice of four starters, five mains and four desserts – £13.95 for two courses and £16.95 for three.

New End

102 Heath St, NW3 ℂ020 7431 4423   ⊖ Hampstead

Tues 6–11pm, Wed–Sat noon–3pm & 6–11pm, Sun 6–10.30pm   All major credit cards

www.thenewend.co.uk

New End is a spiffing restaurant – providing that you give up all dreams of parking anywhere within three days' march. As a consequence of enthusiastic yellow-liners Hampstead residents are even smugger than you might expect; not only do they have enough money to own a house in Hampstead but also they get residents' parking rights – a combination that makes them pretty unassailable. They like New End and fill it every night (though it's worth noting that Hampsteadians do not care to dine except at 8 sharp – lesser mortals have a better chance of getting a table at 7.30 or at 9). The room is pleasantly unfussy, the service is friendly, and the food is very good indeed.

The chef here is Tom Illic, and his menu changes to shadow the seasons. It's a well-written menu, and gloriously short. There are six starters (three fish, three meat), six main courses (again half-and-half), and a separate page of vegetarian dishes – two starters and two mains. Short menus work when, as is the case at New End, you fancy all the options. Starters like wild sea trout tartare with oyster and caviar (£9.50), smoked haddock tortellini (£7.50), and braised pig's cheek with garlic and parsley mash (£6.95) are beautifully presented and well flavoured. Mains are accomplished: baked fillets of sole come with asparagus and crab vinaigrette (£17), while the diver-caught scallops with apple and endive tarte Tatin (£18.50) are cooked just enough to taste sweet, but not so far as to become rubbery. Stuffed rabbit saddle with fresh peas and Serrano ham (£16.95) arrives as two small cylinders of meat wrapped in ham with a tiny rack of rabbit chops. Grilled veal cutlet with goats' cheese, anchovy and almond fondue (£18.50) is also very good. Throughout, the sauces are strongly flavoured and well balanced. Puddings are equally elaborate, from the fromage frais bavarois, with roast apricots and spiced Madeleines (£5.50) to the poached white peaches, berry compote and a sabayon (£5.50). The set lunch at New End gets you two courses for £15 and three for £18.50.

There are two wine lists. The one entitled "Fine Wine" may make you flinch – prices range from £48 to £125 a bottle. Luckily, the other list covers the territory between £14 and £50.

£16–£35

Solly's Exclusive

146–150 Golders Green Rd, NW11 ℂ020 8455 2121   ⊖ Golders Green

Sun–Thurs 6.30–10.30pm, Sat 8pm–1am   All major credit cards except Diners

What makes Solly's Exclusive so exclusive is that it is upstairs. Downstairs is Solly's restaurant, which is less exclusive – a small, packed, noisy place specialising in epic falafel, those crispy balls of minced chickpeas that are deep-fried and served with all manner of salads. You'll find Solly's Exclusive by coming out of Solly's Restaurant, turning left, and left again around the side of the building, and then proceeding through an unmarked black door. Upstairs, a huge, bustling dining room accommodates 180 customers, while a back room provides another 100 seats which lie in wait for functions, bar mitzvahs and so forth. The decor is interesting – tented fabric on the ceiling, multicoloured glass, brass light fittings – while waitresses, all of them with Solly's Exclusive emblazoned across the back of their waistcoats, maintain a brisk approach to the niceties of service.

The food is tasty and workmanlike. Start with the dish that pays homage to the chickpea – hoummus with falafel (£4.25) – three crispy depth charges and some well-made dip. Even the very best falafel in the world cannot overcome the inherent problems of eating chickpeas – their thunderous indigestibility – and as falafel goes Solly's are pretty good. Otherwise, you could try Solly's special aubergine dip (£3.25). Or the Moroccan cigars (£5), made from minced lamb wrapped in filo pastry and deep-fried. Solly's pitta (£1.25) – a fluffy, fourteen-inch disc of freshly baked bread – has more in common with a perfect naan than Greek restaurant bread. Pittas to pine for. For a main course, the lamb shawarma (£9.75) is very good, nicely seasoned and spiced, and served with excellent chips and a good, sharp-tasting mound of shredded cabbage salad. The barbecue roast chicken with the same accompaniments (£9.50) is also good. Steer clear of the Israeli salad (£2.75), however, unless you relish the idea of a large bowl of chopped watery tomatoes and chopped watery cucumber.

Solly's Exclusive is kosher and under the supervision of the London Beth Din, so naturally its opening days and hours don't follow the same rules as non-Jewish establishments. If you're not fully conversant with the Jewish calendar, check before setting out.

£12–£30

Zamoyski

85 Fleet Rd, NW3 ℂ020 7794 4792   ⊖ Belsize Park

Daily 5.30–11pm   All major credit cards

Zamoyski is a small, friendly place with a long menu, supplemented by various specials written on a mobile blackboard, and a list of vodkas that is longer still. Downstairs there's room for twenty in the bar, and upstairs there's a larger dining room. The staff are cheerful and prices are low – a combination which pulls in a broad spectrum of customers from middle-aged couples taking dinner à deux, to people enjoying an early-evening drink with a starter or two, to large parties (often from the nearby Royal Free Hospital) intent on laying into the vodka. The watershed here is about nine o'clock, by which point you'll need to start viewing the place through the bottom of a shot glass.

This is one of those Slavic/Polish restaurants where the starters have a distinct edge on the main courses; ordering three starters per person and sharing is a very attractive strategy. The management have spotted this trend and offer a "9 course Polskie Mezze" (£6.95) – an outrageously low price (sadly, it is not available after 7pm on Friday or Saturday). One daily special always worth including in your raft of starters is the soup (£2.20), which could be anything from sorrel to beetroot. Then try some herring: sledz wedzony (£4.75), smoked herring with horse-radish cream, or sledz w oleju (£4.75), the sweeter matjes fillet, both come with an accompanying shot of vodka. You might move on to placki losos (£4.50), little potato and walnut pancakes topped with smoked salmon. Among the main-course specials you might find kaszanka, which is home-made black pudding with mash (£8), or zywiecka, a tasty smoked garlic sausage (£8). And don't miss out on the pierogi rozne (£4) – small dumplings stuffed with potato and cheese, or mushrooms, or meat. Regular main courses are made of sterner stuff, their mission to be more filling than fanciful: kotlet cielecy (£9.50) is a veal escalope; kaczka z jabikami (£9.50) is a frazzled half-duck; and schab ze sliwkami (£8) is a tenderloin of pork stuffed with prunes.

Take a look at the barrels on the bar: they are full of bisongrass vodka. Feeling nervous? You should. Anywhere that serves vodka by the barrel deserves respect!

The Duke of Hamilton

23–25 New End, NW3   ℂ020 7794 0258

This friendly, 200-year-old local prides itself on a no-food and no-music policy. As the landlord says, "we make people talk to each other here". Fuller's ales, draught Czech Budweiser, and Biddenden Kentish Cider on draught.

The Flask

14 Flask Walk, NW3   ℂ020 7435 4580

The Flask is one of those rare places that captures the spirit of an area. It's very much Hampstead's signature pub and feels for all the world like a village inn. It greets a wide mix of locals and day-trippers out to shop, walk on the heath and enjoy Young's ESB on draught.

The Gate Lodge

622 Finchley Rd, NW11   ℂ020 8458 6258

Hidden in a parade of shops, this small, narrow Free House wins a cheerful and friendly crowd of regulars in an area not well served by drinking venues. It's more a bar than a pub, but there's a relaxed convivial atmosphere. Guinness and Fosters are the favourites on tap.

The Old Black Lion

295 West End Lane, NW6   ℂ020 7435 4389

A welcoming, traditional pub with acres of space and a comfortable beer garden. Distinctive for the "No Children" sign and beer-pump handles made from old tools. Great to have your Greene King Abbot ale hammered out.

The Refectory

911 Finchley Rd, NW11   ℂ020 8455 2020

A very lively, noisy venue with theme nights and a predominantly young crowd. There's pool, big-screen TV and a disco, Klub Extreme. Beck's and Kronenbourg 1664 are the on-tap favourites, with alco-pops in hot pursuit.

Scruffy Murphy's

283–285 West End Lane,
NW6   ℂ020 7794 7817

One of the better and older of London's Styrofoam Irish venues with chucklebutty pictures and mock packaging. Well-drawn Guinness, Guinness Extra Cold and Caffrey's enjoyed by a cheery crowd of regulars.

Highgate
& Crouch End

HIGHGATE & CROUCH END

PUBS AND BARS
1 The Maynard Arms
2 The King's Head
3 Harringay Arms
4 The Prince of Wales
5 The Flask

© Crown copyright

La Bota

31 Broadway Parade, Tottenham Lane, N8   ⊖ Finsbury Park/Turnpike Lane

℗020 8340 3082

Mon–Fri noon–3pm & 6–11.30pm, Sat noon–3.30pm & 6–11.30pm,

Sun noon–3.30pm & 6–11pm   Amex, Mastercard, Visa

This bustling tapas bar and restaurant enjoys a good evening trade – and with good reason. It's a Galician – northwest Spanish – place, and that's always a good sign, particularly for seafood. The best of its tapas fall into two categories: there are the "raw" ones like Serrano ham, which simply need careful buying and good bread as accompaniment, and there are the stews which have been made in the morning and reheated as necessary – thankfully, most of the rich, unfussy dishes of Galicia lend themselves well to this treatment. Your first decision is a crucial one: do you go all out for tapas (there are 21 on the menu, plus fifteen vegetarian ones, plus another eighteen or so daily specials chalked on a blackboard)? Or do you choose one of the main courses – Spanish omelette, paellas, steaks, chicken, fish and so forth? Perhaps the best option is to play to La Bota's strengths and order a few tapas, then a few more, until you have subdued your appetite and there's no longer a decision to make. In the meantime enjoy the air conditioning – and the house wine at a very reasonable £7.50.

Start with simple things. Boquerones en vinagre (£2.95) brings a plate of broad white anchovies with a pleasant vinegar tang. Jamón Serrano (£4.15) is thinly sliced, ruby red and strongly flavoured – perfect with the basket of warm French bread that is on every table. Then move on to hot tapas: mejillones pescador (£3.35) is a good-sized plate of mussels in a tomato and garlic sauce; quail Tio Pepe (£2.85) is a lone quail in a sherry sauce; rinones al Jerez (£2.75) is a portion of kidneys in another sherry sauce, rich and good. Duck a la pimienta (£3.25) is duck on the bone, cooked long and slow in rich gravy. Then there's egg tuna mayonnaise with potato salad (£2.70), rabbit cazuela (£2.85), chicken Riojana (£3.20), and patatas bravas (£1.85), the tasty dish of potatoes in a mildly spicy tomato sauce. Just keep them coming . . .

If you like squid, and don't mind looking at a whole one, opt for chipirones a la plancha (£3.85) – four squidlets grilled to tender perfection.

Fiction

60 Crouch End Hill, N8 ℂ020 8340 3403   ⊖ Finsbury Park/Highgate

Wed–Sat 6.30–10.30pm, Sun 12.30–4pm & 6.30–10.30pm   Mastercard, Visa

www.fiction-restaurant.co.uk

Opposite a hairdresser called Pulp sits Fiction. Fact. But the restaurant was there first, and named after the bookshop whose premises it took over. The hairdressers are the film buffs and named their place accordingly. And there's no gore in the tale, as Fiction is strictly vegetarian, although not in the missionary hair-shirt and holier-than-thou style. Rather, the idea is to rediscover the use of indigenous herbs and to cook, with plenty of wine, dishes that were popular in the days when people ate a lot less meat than they do now. All dishes and wines are marked as vegetarian, vegan and organic where relevant.

While Fiction's menu changes every six to seven weeks, there are a few signature dishes: black truffle pâté (£4.95), served with lemon olives and three-seed crostini, is one of them. It's very rich and very tasty. Or try herby onion polenta cake with a cream and sage sauce (£4.95), or cheesy sweetcorn and coriander fritters served with salad garnish and a delicious sweet chilli sauce (£3.95) – a bit like Thai crab cakes without the crab. The signature main courses are wood-roasted butternut squash (£9.45), and "The Good Gamekeeper's Pie" (£9.45) – the former described fulsomely as "a succulent 'steak' of squash filled with lemon-garlic mushrooms", the latter as "chestnuts, wild mushrooms, 'mock duck', leek, carrot and broccoli, prepared in an old English marinade of red wines, and baked in a puff pastry pie". Both are very nicely flavoured. There's also Irish stew and Bundorran sausages, a stew of carrot, turnip, potatoes, shallots and Murphy's stout served with cheese and leek sausages (£8.50). Side dishes include roast garlic mash with olive oil (£2.50), roast seasonal vegetables in butter and marjoram (£2.95), and the mini power plate – a salad of mixed leaves and organic freshly sprouted legumes and alfalfa (£2.95). The signature pudding is triple chocolate terrine with strawberry coulis (£3.95) – just one taste will tell you why it stays on the menu.

The large outdoor area, with its beautifully planted gardens helps make Fiction a summer favourite, but it is essential to book whatever the season may be.

Jashan

19 Turnpike Lane, N8 ☏020 8340 9880   ⊖ Turnpike Lane

Tues–Sun 6–11.30pm   All major credit cards

This elegant, bright and roomy Indian restaurant has a loyal local follow-ing, all of whom are in on The Secret. This secret – which isn't very well kept – is that the Jashan kitchens have a sideline in preparing ready meals for a number of the West End's more prestigious food halls. As to deciding which proud offerings of the foodie havens started life in N8, an intensive tasting programme is the only way you'll ever be quite sure. You're in for quite a treat, for, like other leading Indian restaurants, Jashan has recently added many authentic regional dishes to its repertoire.

Take a look at the menu – and look is meant literally. The management at Jashan have superimposed each list of dishes on a photograph of all those dishes laid out as if for a banquet. This is a dangerous strategy . . . what if your pomfret isn't as big as the one in the picture? It also makes for an intimidatingly long and glossy menu. A good point to start would be with the pakora (£2.75), an array of vegetables ranging from a slice of potato to a whole chilli and a spinach leaf, all mixed in a spicy gram flour batter and fried until crisp. Or go for the dehati chaas (£1.95), which is a glass of yoghurt that thinks it is a cheese, served either sweet or salty. Or share a tarah tarah ke kabab (£10.95), which presents a range of kebabs from the tandoor – the kebabs are very good here, well spiced, and precisely cooked. As a main course, try murg zaibunissa (£5.95), chicken in tasty-but-mild white gravy. Or gosht kesari (£5.95), lamb in a saffron sauce. That Rajasthani classic, dal bukhara (£2.95), lentils tempered with butter, is also good. And there's a long list of breads; make sure you try phudina parantha (£1.75), a flaky fresh paratha with a sprinkling of mint.

By the time you are contemplating the dessert course the pictorial menu seems less unusual. Affable waiting staff will quite understand cries of "the pink one". This is Jashan ka falooda (£3.75), made up of malai kulfi in a sea of bilious-pink, rose-flavoured, milk. Perhaps not.

£10–£25

O's Thai Café

10 Topsfield Parade, N8 ℂ020 8348 6898   ⊖ Finsbury Park

Mon 6.30–11pm, Tues–Sat noon–3pm & 6.30–11pm,

Sun noon–3pm & 6.30–10.30pm   Mastercard, Visa

O's Thai Café is young, happy and fresh – just like O himself. With his economics, advertising and fashion design background, and a staff who seem to be having fun, O brings a youthful zip to Thai cuisine. His cafe is fast and noisy, and the music is played at high volume. But that's not to say the food is anything less than excellent, and very good value too. Order from the comprehensive and well-explained menu or from the blackboard of specials which runs down an entire wall.

Of the many starters you can do no better than order the special (£7.95 for two), which gives you a taster of almost everything. Satays are tasty, prawn toasts and spring rolls are as crisp as they should be, and paper-wrapped thin dumplings really do melt in the mouth. Tom ka chicken soup (£3.75) is hot and sharp, with lime leaf and lemongrass. Main courses include Thai red and green curries – the gaeng kiew, a spicy, soupy green curry of chicken and coconut cream (£5.50), is pungently moreish – as well as an interesting selection of specials such as yamneau, aka weeping tiger (£9.50) – sliced, spiced, grilled steak served on salad with a pungent Thai dressing. If you like noodles, order a pad mee si iew (£5.50), a stir-fry of vermicelli with vegetables, soy sauce, peanuts and the main ingredient of your choice: chicken, beef, pork, king prawn or bean curd. Puddings include khow tom mud – banana with sticky rice wrapped in banana leaf (£1.95), Thai ice cream (£2.50), and fruit fritters served with golden syrup and ice cream (£2.50). There is a wide and varied wine list, with Budweiser, Budvar, Gambrinus and Leffe beers on draught. O's does takeaway too.

If you're new to Thai food, O's is a good place to learn, as the staff are happy to explain how it all works and you can specify how hot you like your food. Most main courses are around £6, which makes for very good value, and all of them are served with a delightfully moulded mountain of rice which is included in the price. They also offer a discount if you eat early and vacate your table by 8.30pm.

The Village Bistro

38 Highgate High St, N6 ©020 8340 5165	⊖ Highgate/Archway
Daily noon–3pm & 6–11pm	All major credit cards

Having served French food of varying fashionability for decades, The Village Bistro is something of an institution in Highgate. You can almost forget you're in London here; all is quaint and countrified in this narrow Georgian house approached by a corridor off Highgate's main road. Inside can be a bit of a squeeze, and the decor is all chintzy curtains and crooked paintings, but any sense that you're sitting in an old aunt's living room is swept away by the food, which is Modern French. Presumably this combination of ancient and modern is exactly what hits the spot in Highgate, as this restaurant is, and has been, consistently successful. Downstairs, the windows peek out onto the hilly High Street, while a spindly, winding staircase leads upstairs to the smokers' floor.

Come here hungry: sauces can be rich and dishes very filling. The menu, which changes every few months, includes a range of old stalwarts along with a sprinkling of more contemporary creations. A really tasty starter is goats' cheese wrapped in aubergine with grilled vegetables and spicy tomato dressing (£6.50). Also good is the Parma ham with marinated leeks, baby leaves and home-dried tomatoes, with a soft-boiled egg and Parmesan crisp (£6.95). Traditionalists might opt for the fine French onion soup with cheese croutons (£3.95), or, in season, asparagus with Hollandaise sauce (£6.50). There's a good choice of main dishes, and always two specials – dishes like a panaché of seafood with Parmesan, lemon and olive oil (£13.50). For a well-judged mix of flavours and textures, go for the escalope of veal with Parmesan mash, fried egg and capers (£12.50). Or you might try monkfish roasted with garlic, rosemary and preserved lemon on French beans and mussels (£13.95), or maybe peppered fillet steak with gratin Dauphinoise (£14.95).

Desserts (all £4.50) can be solid and formidable. The white chocolate parfait with dark chocolate truffle is not for anyone wearing tight clothing. The classic crème brûlée, and crêpe filled with vanilla ice cream and hot raspberry sauce, are wiser choices, although still satisfactorily self-indulgent. From Monday to Saturday there is a set lunch at £13.50 for two courses; on Sunday it's £14.95 for three.

The Flask

77 Highgate West Hill, N6   ✆020 8340 7260

With its rabbit warren of bars, Dick Turpin legend, stunning views and huge front courtyard, this ancient and quaint pub is justifiably popular. It's very much a refreshment point for walkers too. Bass Red Triangle, Adnams Broadside and Tetley's are favourites here. There's also a better than average wine selection.

Harringay Arms

153 Crouch Hill, N8   ✆020 8340 4243

Quiet, small and friendly, with a tiny white-walled garden and a hint of the Irish, the Harringay has been a popular local since 1851. Courage Best, Directors and Guinness are the draught favourites here.

The King's Head

2 Crouch End Hill, N8 ✆020 8340 1028

A very lively venue, popular with a young crowd out to party at the club downstairs. Pioneering comedy alternates with music down there, while Tetley's and Ind Coope's Burton ale are consumed upstairs.

The Maynard Arms

70 Park Rd, N8   ✆020 8341 6283

A vast bar that caters for Muswell Hill's younger set. Three pool tables, live bands and a beer garden are among the attractions, but most popular of all is the Toby Bitter at £1.10 per pint.

The Prince of Wales

53 Highgate High St, N6   ✆020 8340 0445

This villagey pub, largely left alone by the tourists, has a quiet and welcoming atmosphere. It opens at the back to Pond Square, which makes it popular in summer. Courage Directors and Best are the favourites on tap.

Holloway
& Highbury

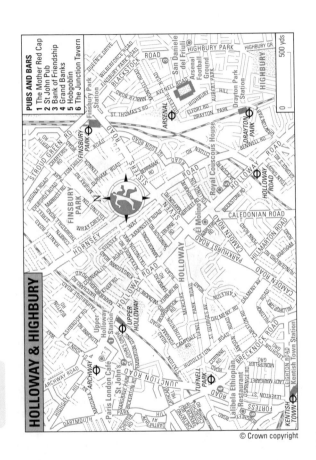

HOLLOWAY & HIGHBURY

PUBS AND BARS
1 The Mother Red Cap
2 St John Pub
3 Bank of Friendship
4 Grand Banks
5 Hobgoblin
6 The Junction Tavern

500 yds

© Crown copyright

Lalibela Ethiopian Restaurant

137 Fortess Rd, NW5 ©020 7284 0600 | ⊖ Tufnell Park

Mon–Thurs 6pm–midnight, Fri–Sun 6–11pm | All major credit cards except Diners

The real Lalibela is a twelfth-century Ethiopian church – carved, in the shape of a cross, from a huge outcrop of solid rock. Its namesake in Tufnell Park is remarkable for serving uncompromisingly authentic Ethiopian food and for its genuine understanding of hospitality. It has a slightly harassed, but still laid-back, feel that is a great comfort to the diner. And, however ignorant of Ethiopian cuisine and customs you may be, pure ungilded hospitality shines through. Upstairs, you will be seated on low, carved, wooden seats around traditional low tables (so that you can eat with your hands). If your knee joints won't take that kind of punishment, ask for a table downstairs and resign yourself to dripping sauce down your front.

Starters are few, but they banish any inkling that you may have about being in an odd kind of curry house. The lamb samosas (£3.25) have very dry, papery pastry and a savoury, spicy filling – delicious. The Lalibela salad (£3.25) is potatoes and beetroot fried together with a spicy sauce and served hot. Main courses are served traditionally, that is to say as pools of sauce set out on a two-foot-diameter injera bread. Injera is cold, made from fermented sourdough, and thin. You tear off a piece and use it to pick up something tasty. Portions are small, which makes prices seem high. But flavours are intense. If you prefer, you can have the dishes with rice or mashed potato. What goes on the injera? Wot – that's what . . . doro wot (£6) – a piece of chicken and a hard-boiled egg in a rich sauce; or begh wot (£5.85) – lamb with a bit more chilli. Lalibela ketfo (£7.50) is savoury mince and amazing, highly spiced, cottage cheese – delicious. King prawn special (£6.50) is prawns in a tomato, onion and chilli sauce.

Do try the Ethiopian traditional coffee (£5), which is not only delicious, but also something of a feast for the eyes. After parading a small wok full of smoking coffee beans through the restaurant, the staff bring it to you in a round-bottomed coffeepot on a plaited quoit.

El Molino

379 Holloway Rd, N7 ©020 7700 4312	⊖ Holloway Road
Mon–Sat 11am–11pm	All major credit cards

El Molino is a class tapas bar and restaurant – far better than you might be led to expect from its regulation bullfight posters and Spanish ceramics. Since opening in November 1992, owner Tino Risquez has built up a loyal clientele from Islington and the nearby University of North London. He offers robust Spanish food, fairly mildly spiced, and in generous portions that belie his explanation of tapas – "The Taste of Spain in Little Dishes" – in the window. Here, you can dine well on the tapas alone.

Good tapas – or starters – include a fine rinones al Jerez (£3.20), well-sherried and garlicky kidneys; escalivada (£2.75), a rich dish of fried aubergine, peppers and onions; a generous round of traditional Spanish tortilla (£2.75), made fresh and served hot straight from the pan, and albondigas (£3), Spanish meatballs in a thick tomato sauce. There are also the usual offerings of Serrano ham (£5), queso Manchego, a cheese from La Mancha (£3.20), and patatas bravas (£2.20), as well as more spicy dishes like octopus in oil and paprika (£5.20). Main courses are reasonably priced, too, with dishes such as pez espada provincial, a swordfish in tomato and garlic sauce (£5), and pollo riojana, chicken pieces in tomato, peppers, mushrooms and wine sauce (£5.45). Tino confirms that his paella is as authentic as it is possible get over here – the rice highly flavoured with peppers, mussels, chicken, and small and large prawns. It's properly prepared, fresh every order, so there's a 45-minute wait. Wines are reasonably priced, with the house wine coming in at £8.25. As to chilled beers, pick between San Miguel and the slightly stronger Estrella (£2.10). There is no minimum charge and customers are welcome to come in just for one dish, except on Friday and Saturday nights, when it's advisable to book.

Although anglicised, El Molino tries to stay as authentically Spanish as possible and Tino keeps a range of drinks behind the bar to remind him of home. Try Ponche in its distinctive silver bottle. It's brandy-based, vanilla-sweet, and just the thing for a night-cap.

Paris London Café

5 Junction Rd, N19 ☏020 7561 0330	⊖ Archway
Mon–Sat 8am–11pm, Sun 9am–10.30pm	Cash or cheque only

You have to get on a train to get good, reasonably priced French cooking. But forget the Eurostar, and hop instead onto the Northern line. Brothers Jérôme and Frédéric Boileau's Paris London Café is right opposite the exit from Archway tube station. The restaurant is small and tables are tightly packed, making for a bustling atmosphere that confirms you've made the right choice. Most of North London knows about the Paris London Café, so it's often very busy. They serve breakfast, lunch and dinner – and on Sundays there's "Frunch", a mixture of brunch and lunch that includes French roasts of the day.

Starters are classic. Soupe du jour (£2.25) is freshly made and so thick you could eat it with a fork. Cassolette d'escargots au beurre d'ail (half dozen £3.75, dozen £5.75) is all you would expect of snails and garlic butter, but with a hint of Pernod, too; make sure you have plenty of French bread and be prepared for a shiny chin. Among the mains, lapin à la Dijonnaise (£6.95) is rabbit cooked in a mild mustard sauce, while bourride Provençal (£6.95) is concisely described as a fish hotpot with a soup base. The magret de canard au poivre vert (£10.95) is a sophisticated dish, prepared with confidence and emblematic of the way in which the Paris London is building on its success. As for the side dishes, gratin Dauphinoise (£2.25) is as creamy, cheesy and garlicky as it should be, while petits pois à la Française are a must. Puddings are equally good. Tarte des demoiselles Tatin (£3.50) is sweet, tart and caramelised with solid chunks of buttery apple. Poire belle Hélène (£3.75) is a blast from the past – pear, ice cream, chocolate sauce. There is a good selection of wines that ranges from simple robust country choices at low prices to finer vintages.

The Paris London has gone from success to success, and in the process the menu has moved somewhat upmarket, though not outrageously so. There are still bargains to be had: the prix fixe menu at £9.95 for three courses; a menu des Gourmands, which at £15.95 for five courses offers even better value; and lunch express Monday to Friday (£6.95). All in all, this is a great place to eat, and to practise your French – and, yes indeed, les patrons mangent ici.

£10–£24

Royal Couscous House

316 Holloway Rd, N7 ©020 7700 2188   ⊖ Holloway Road

Daily 5–11pm   Cash and cheques only

Karim Menhal, the diffident young man dressed in immaculate whites, is billed as head chef here – he also manages to do the bills, run the bar, wait on tables and hold open the front door. Described as "handsome" in one of the many admiring restaurant review clippings that adorn the front window, he certainly has a way about him. His restaurant is long, and the tables are topped with oilcloth. The walls are lined with Moroccan tourist posters, cheap carpets (you have to hope they are cheap, as they've been nailed to the decorative wood cladding), and pretend firearms. The food is very fresh, very tasty, and very good value, and Mr Menhal keeps the service well up to scratch.

Begin with an array of starters and hot bread. The bread is particularly tasty. The aubergine dip (£1.90) is amazing, with chopped aubergines that have been cooked and cooked to concentrate the flavour. Smoked pepper (£1.80) is made with strips of roasted green peppers. Even the spicy olives (£1) are worthy of note – black and green olives with chunks of red chilli. Then there's the merguez salad (£3.50) – a few links of the small and spicy lamb sausages with a terrific tomatoey sauce and some salad. Main courses split into couscous and tagines. The laksour couscous (£7.95) is a combination of lamb, merguez and mixed vegetables, with light and nicely cooked couscous. Royal tagine (£6.50) is a classic Moroccan dish of lamb with prunes, sesame seeds and slices of boiled egg – sweet and rich. Tafraout tagine (£5.95) is made from chicken with olives and those wholly delicious brine-preserved Moroccan lemons. For pudding, try the ceffae (£2.50) – a mound of couscous cooked in butter, sugar, cinnamon and almonds. Finish with mint tea (£1.20) or Moroccan coffee (£1.20) – a kind of heavily spiced cappuccino.

You can BYOB and incur a corkage of just £1 per person, but the Moroccan wine list features eight honest wines (all reasonably priced at £8.49–£11.99) – a far cry from the days when the proud revelation of a bottle of Moroccan red was enough to strike fear into the heart of any dinner party guest.

£25–£50

San Daniele del Friuli

72 Highbury Park, N5 ✆020 7226 1609	⊖ Arsenal
Mon–Sat 6–11pm	Mastercard, Visa

Highbury Park is a strange place to find a football club. Lots of grand, renovated houses, wide streets, trees and, just a stroll around the corner, there's the Arsenal. Don't attempt to go to San Daniele on match days, when it will be full of happy, very respectable, middle-class footie fans loading up on Italian grub before braving the bitter wind to watch the Gunners. San Daniele opened in the summer of 1996, with a chef from Friuli – that bit of Italy in the extreme northeast around Trieste. The dining room is large and airy, and manages to combine echoes of the old, giant pepperpot-style Italian restaurants with the more spartan modern look. The service is family-style, both attentive and informal, and the dishes lean that way as well, being substantial and unfussy. The menu is a long one, so, unless nostalgia gets the upper hand and you are swept away on a wave of desire for whitebait or insalata tricolore, pay special attention to the "altri Friuliani" (regional delicacies) and to the chef's specials.

The cooking here scales no modern gastronomic heights, and it is not cheap, but portions are large and the hospitality wholehearted. Simple things are well presented, like the antipasto di prosciutto e salami (£5.80) – a large plate of salamis, cured meats, dried ham and some rather fine pickled vegetables. Or there's the pasticcio alla Friuliana (£5.80), a lasagne made with speck and Montasio cheese. There are also risotto and pasta dishes, which make up an extensive and usually pretty imaginative daily specials board. For a main course you can choose between a dozen different Neapolitan pizzas, fresh fish dishes, and lots of old favourites – the huge calves' liver (£10.50) comes in a classic butter and sage sauce and is accurately cooked to order. Veal chop (£10.50) comes with a Marsala and mushroom sauce.

For pudding there is an old-fashioned tiramisù (£3), rich with alcohol and mascarpone – delightfully different from the fluffy, faffy fakes that are all the rage in the W-fronted postcodes.

£12–£35

St John's

91 Junction Rd, N19 ©020 7272 1587 ⊖ Archway

Mon 6.30–11pm, Tues–Sat noon–4pm & 6.30–11pm,

Sun noon–4pm & 6.30–10.30pm | All major credit cards except Amex

Archway's unprepossessing Junction Road is an unlikely setting for this fine gastro-pub, where the emphasis is firmly on the gastro rather than on the pub. The food is broadly Mediterranean, with a passion for all things rich, earthy and flavoursome, and there's a real joie de vivre in the combinations of tastes, textures and colours. Not only that, the dining room, which lies beyond the pub itself, looks fabulous: all louche, junk-store glamour with its high, gold-painted ceiling, low chandeliers and plush banquettes. There's an open kitchen at one end of the room, while at the other a giant blackboard displays the long, daily changing menu. You get lots of food here, so make sure to come hungry.

As an opening move, friendly staff bring fresh white bread and bottles of virgin olive oil and balsamic vinegar. The food is robust and piled high on the plate: a starter of mussels and clams with chorizo and chilli, garlic and coriander cream (£5) is a substantial, lusty affair. As is the char-grilled mackerel with bruschetta, sauce vierge and tapenade (£4.75), which brings a big hunk of pleasantly smoky fish. Terrine of rabbit, pork, and black pudding with apricot chutney and toast (£5) is quite simply a triumph. Lighter options include soup, perhaps white bean and tomato with avocado salsa (£4), and at least one salad, such as rocket, endive, pear and fennel with Parmesan (£4.25). Main courses range from the traditional – char-grilled T-bone steak with roast tomatoes, horseradish, crème fraîche, home fries and watercress (£14) – to the adventurous – warm salad of duck confit, black pudding, pancetta, beetroot and roasted leeks (£9.50). The fish is invariably good – perhaps char-grilled monkfish with mash, salsa verde and Puy lentils (£11). You'll need to take a breather before venturing into pud territory (all £4.25). The rhubarb and raspberry crumble with ginger ice cream is good, but star turn must be the blissful strawberry and clotted cream fool with shortbread. The intelligent wine list includes eighteen varieties by the glass, with a Cava at £3.25.

St John's gets more crowded and more convivial as the night goes on, but it *is* possible to have a dîner à deux; just make sure you're ready to be romantic by 7.30pm, when you've a chance of getting a table. You should book, whatever time you come.

Bank of Friendship

224–226 Blackstock Rd, N5   no phone

A Courage pub with John Smith's and Directors on draught, the Bank of Friendship is a proper old-fashioned local. No juke box, no fruit machines, no television – just friendly people, a darts board and open fires. No one knows why the sign outside says Bureau de Change, incidentally.

Grand Banks

156–158 Fortess Rd, NW5   ℡020 7419 9499

A trendy lounge bar where bright young Kentish Townies enjoy one or two of the 75 cocktails or Stella, Hoegaarden, Leffe and Boddingtons on draught. Comfy old settees and low tables give the place a very relaxed, clubby atmosphere. Live music on Sunday, Monday and Tuesday.

Hobgoblin

274 Holloway Rd, N7   ℡020 7607 3743

A Wychwood Brewery pub with a very young and very noisy student crowd from the University of North London, the Hobgoblin delivers Dr Thirsty's Beetlejuice and a good pint of Dog's Bollocks. Big-screen TV, karaoke and live bands on Friday and Saturday keep it busy, fast and loud. A great place to meet if you're in a crowd or looking to meet one.

The Junction Tavern

101 Fortess Rd, NW5   ℡020 7267 1727

This panelled Courage house – the "JT" to locals – has a young clientele and a wide selection of beers. Fosters, Tetley's, John Smith's, Guinness, Kronenbourg, Stella and Carlsberg are all on tap. The two pool tables, conservatory and outside patio add to its popularity. Check out the library of old bottles.

The Mother Red Cap

665 Holloway Rd, N19   ℡020 7263 7082

You'll mix with a friendly Irish crowd in this classic pub with its big, old-fashioned mirrored walls. It's a Free House with Tetley's, Calders, and very cold, well-poured Guinness on draught. There's a pool table, sports TV and good music – if you can't hold on till dinner time you can fine-tune your appetite here with O'Malley's County Mayo Ham and Connemara chicken crisps.

St John Pub

91 Junction Rd, N19   ℡020 7272 1587

Modern pub with comfortable, stylish decor. There's a great selection of wines by the glass, good cappuccino and a relaxed, mixed crowd drinking Hoegaarden, Stella and Old Speckled Hen on draught and Beck's and Budvar by the bottle. Don't think you can stay and eat in the restaurant at the back unless you have had the foresight to book. It's busy and very good – see opposite.

Islington

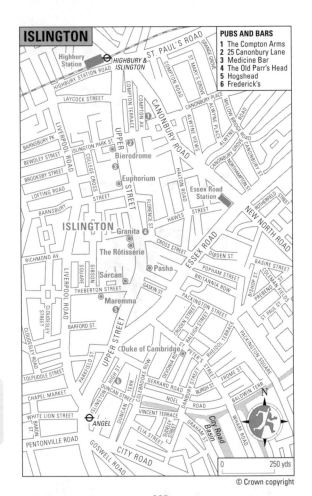

ISLINGTON

PUBS AND BARS
1 The Compton Arms
2 25 Canonbury Lane
3 Medicine Bar
4 The Old Parr's Head
5 Hogshead
6 Frederick's

Highbury Station
HIGHBURY & ISLINGTON

ST. PAUL'S ROAD

HIGHBURY STATION ROAD

LAYCOCK STREET

LIVERPOOL ROAD

BARNSBURY PK

BEWDLEY STREET

BROOKSBY STREET

LOFTING ROAD

BARNSBURY

RICHMOND AV.

CLOUDESLEY STREET

CLOUDESLEY ROAD

TOLPUDDLE STREET

CHAPEL MARKET

WHITE LION STREET

PENTONVILLE ROAD

COMPTON TERRACE

COMPTON AV.

ISLINGTON PARK ST.

COLLEGE CROSS

UPPER STREET

COMPTON RD

ST MARY'S GROVE

COMPTON ROAD

GRANGE GROVE

ST PETER'S GROVE

CANONBURY PLACE

CANONBURY ROAD

ALWYNE VIEWS

ALWYNE PLACE

ALWYNE VILLAS

WILLOW BRIDGE ROAD

CANONBURY GROVE

NORTHAMPTON ST.

CANONBURY ROAD

HALTON ROAD

Essex Road Station

FLORENCE ST.

HAWES STREET

CROSS STREET

ESSEX ROAD

NEW NORTH ROAD

NOTHERFIELD STREET

Bierodrome

Euphorium

ISLINGTON

Granita

The Rôtisserie

Sárcan

GIBSON SQUARE

LIVERPOOL ROAD

THEBERTON STREET

Maremma

BARFORD ST.

Pasha

DIBDEN ST.

POPHAM STREET

BRITANNIA ROW

PACKINGTON STREET

GASKIN ST.

CRUDEN STREET

RALEIGH STREET

BASIRE STREET

BISHOP ST.

COLEMAN ST.

PREBEND ST.

ST PAUL ST.

PACKINGTON SQUARE

UPPER STREET

BARNSBURY ST.

Duke of Cambridge

ST. PETER'S STREET

DOVE ROAD

RHEIDOL TERRACE

FROME ST.

HIGH ST.

COLEBROOKE ROW

GERRARD ROAD

NOEL ROAD

DANBURY STREET

BURGH ST.

BALDWIN TERR

ISLINGTON GRN

DUNCAN STREET

DUNCAN TERR

ANGEL

DUNCAN ST.

VINCENT TERRACE

ELIA STREET

SHRLEY

SURLEY

GRAHAM ST.

CITY ROAD

GOSWELL ROAD

WHARF ROAD

City Road Basin

N

0   250 yds

© Crown copyright

NORTH

298

£5–£55

Bierodrome

173–174 Upper St, N1 ✆020 7226 5835	⊖ Highbury & Islington
Daily noon–11pm	All major credit cards
www.belgo.restaurants.com	

Bierodrome is part of the Belgo empire (see p.32), and shares their emphasis on modernist and iconoclastic architecture. The long, low bar is a temple to beer, and with that beer you can eat if you wish. The menu introduces a change of pace from the other branches – yes, there is life after mussels! Here there are "tartines", or smart snacks, along with steaks, lobsters, croquettes and frites. Surprisingly enough, the beeri-ness runs amok in the dessert section, where, as well as a sorbet made from cherry beer, there is an ice cream made with Leffe blond beer. There's another Bierodrome in South London at 40–44 Clapham High St (✆020 7720 1118).

It is no surprise that when the Bierodrome first opened they found that the customers were walking off with the beer and wine list. It makes stunning reading, with more than 200 beers to pore over and ultimately pour out. At random, consider: a banana beer – Chapeau Tropical 25cl (£2.55), a very strong beer – Kasteel bier Ingelmunster 11% 75cl (£11.75), and a very big beer – La Veille Bon Secours 7.5% 1500cl (£635!). As you work your way through your delicious malty glassful, what you will need is some food. Croquettes make good starters; try the Trappist cheese with piccalilli (£4.95). Salads are tasty – Liègeoise (£5.50) teams bacon, tomatoes, French beans, onions, boiled egg and new potatoes. Then there are the famous Belgo mussel pots – a kilo pot with frites and mayonnaise (£9.95). Or half a spit-roast chicken with frites (£8.95). Steaks include a 6oz sirloin with frites, salad, tomatoes and garlic butter (£9.95). There are lunch bargains – sausages with frites and a bottle of mineral water costs £5. And the Bierodeal, available on weekdays (£12.95), gets you salade Liègeoise followed by a pot of mus-sels and a coffee.

The atmosphere is much as you'd expect with 200 strong beers on offer. And the huge Nebuchadnezzars containing fifteen litres of La Veille Bon Secours, at a thought-provoking £635 a pop? At the beginning of 2000 they were selling at the rate of one every couple of months.

£15–£35

Duke of Cambridge

30 St Peter's St, N1 ✆020 7359 3066	⊖ Angel

Mon–Fri 12.30–3pm & 6.30–10.30pm, Sat 12.30–3.30pm & 6.30–10.30pm,	
Sun 12.30–3.30pm & 6.30–10pm	All major credit cards

www.singhboulton.co.uk

In the canon of organic, things don't get much holier than this, the first gastro-pub to be certified by the Soil Association. Game and fish are either wild or caught from sustainable resources and the forty-strong wine list is 95% organic. There's a small bookable restaurant at the back, but most diners prefer to share the tables in the noisy front bar – the Duke is for the gregarious as well as the organic battalions.

The blackboard menu changes daily and you order from the bar. Robust bread with good olive oil and grey sel de mer is served while you wait. Starters include roast tomato soup (£4.50) and warm duck and rabbit salad with spinach, onions, pine nuts and sultanas (£7.50). The latter, more like a very rich stew on wilted spinach than a salad, would easily be enough for two all-in wrestlers. Main courses of grilled Barnsley lamb chop with Swiss chard, swede and carrot purée (£13) and seared scallops with pepperonata and roasted new potatoes (£10.50) are tasty and fulfilling. The Barnsley is a very meaty double lamb chop shaped like a butterfly. Portions are dauntingly huge – a million miles away from bar snacks. There are vegetarian choices too, like fennel and pesto risotto (£8). Puddings include apple crumble and cream, chocolate walnut cake, a good sherry trifle with a real old-fashioned taste (all £4.50), plus organic cheese (£6). The wines are well chosen and varied, with a Greek Domaine Spiropoulos Porfyros at £16 and New Zealand Te Aria Malbec at £21.

There are also many unusual bottled beers and non-alcoholic drinks, all organic. Connoisseurs will seek out the deliciously light and refreshing Eco Warrior ale or the Freedom Brewery's organic Pilsener. But the zenith of the beer list must be Singhboulton ale. The Pitfield Brewery brews this rich, organic beer exclusively for the Duke of Cambridge, and it is named after the owners, Geetie Singh and Esther Boulton.

Euphorium

203 Upper St, N1 ©020 7704 6909	⊖ Highbury & Islington
Mon–Sat 12.30–2.30pm & 6–10.30pm,	
Sun noon–3.30pm	Amex, Mastercard, Visa

This Islington restaurant – which serves Modern European food amid smart, minimalist decor – has been winning the praise of locals since it opened. The dining room is in a conservatory at the back and, despite being on the small side, manages to deliver a nice feeling of space, with large windows looking onto a courtyard and soft spotlights creating a mellow, comfortable atmosphere. Before eating, you might have a drink at the bar (which serves a good range of snacks throughout the day), where the modern glass front is perfect for taking in Upper Street's increasingly fashionable bustle. A big plus at Euphorium is the friendly, laid-back staff, who genuinely seem to enjoy themselves.

The bread is delicious – fresh from the ovens of the Euphorium bakery next door. The menu is short but varied and changes with the seasons. Starters might include prawns in butter and chilli oil (£6.50), or baby spinach, roast red peppers and goats' cheese (£5.50). The grilled asparagus, Parmesan and truffle oil also appeals (£7.50). For mains, you get a choice of around eight dishes, all bearing an eclectic European stamp. Calves' liver comes with spring-onion mash, capers and lemon zest (£13.50), while char-grilled peppered lamb comes with a butter bean purée that provides a good, contrasting texture (£13.95). Fish tends to be more simply handled: for example, a whole grilled sea bass accompanied by braised baby fennel and peppered potatoes (£17.50), or plaice, chips and mushy peas (£12.50). There's usually an imaginative veggie option, too, like field mushrooms stuffed with crumbs, garlic and Parmesan (£8.95). Leave room for pudding. Parfait of whisky and praline with almond biscuits, or figs in red wine and vanilla syrup with mascarpone and honey puffs (both £5), should induce an agreeable euphoria.

Following the comment in past editions about the beers listed (up from one to three in 1999), we can report that it is back down to two in 2000. If you don't fancy a Peroni or Budvar, have a look at the brief but well-chosen wine list instead. Euphorium Express delivers two courses for £12.50 at lunch and between 7pm and 8pm.

Granita

127 Upper St, N1 ✆020 7226 3222	⊖ Highbury & Islington/Angel
Tues 6.30–10.30pm, Wed–Sat 12.30–2.30pm & 6.30–10.30pm,	
Sun 12.30–3pm & 6.30–10pm	Mastercard, Visa

Architecturally minimalist, modern and very Islington, Granita is stark when empty at 7.30pm, but comes to life from 9pm when it fills with locals who look upon it as their local. Run by Vicky Leffman, front of house, and Ahmed Kharshoum, in the kitchen, it offers some interesting modern ideas with influences from the Mediterranean and beyond. The menu is short, with around six starters and five main courses, and changes weekly as, according to Vicky, Granita's customers visit often and seek variety.

A typical starter at Granita is a pressed Mediterranean sandwich: aubergine, red pepper, courgettes, olives, bufala mozzarella, basil, rocket (£5.95) delivers exactly that – a concentrated sandwich of Mediterranean flavours. Or you might find Thai-spiced cod wraps, with chilli and coriander dipping sauce (£5.50) – equally intensely flavoured. For the main course, new season's chump of lamb, char-grilled aubergine and red pepper salad (£12.95), or braised duck in red wine with sage, rosemary boiled potatoes and green beans (£12.50). Other main courses can include dishes like char-grilled calves' liver, with chickpeas, potatoes, tomatoes and rocket (£11.95), which demonstrates Granita's varied influences. There are no side dishes on offer, so whatever you order comes as complete as the descriptions promise. Puddings may feature a chocolate semifreddo with fudge sauce (£4.95), and orange and cardamom ice cream with Middle Eastern fruit salad (£4.95). There is an excellent selection of sweet wines, too, including Elysium black muscat (£3.75) from the USA, which is almost sherry-like in its density, and a luxurious Tokaji Aszu 5 puttonus – the sweetest of Hungary's Tokajis (£4.50). The wine list is equally cosmopolitan, though with more choices from the New World than the Old.

Tony Blair was a famed Granita habitué, prior to his ascension, and the place is still a favourite with North London's social intelligentsia. Set lunches of two (£11.95) and three (£13.95) courses are good value. It's advisable to book, whatever time you plan to eat.

Maremma

11–13 Theberton St, N1 ℗020 7226 9400	⊖ Angel
Tues–Fri 6–11pm, Sat & Sun noon–3pm & 6–11pm	All major credit cards

The white walls, architectural flower arrangements and flattering lighting could place this restaurant anywhere, but the healthy, deliberately dressed-down thirty- and forty-something clientele place Maremma definitely in the heart of Blairite Islington. These are customers who holiday in Chiantishire and who know best. They will not just nod and say "very nice" when asked. You're more likely to hear "it was fine but it could have done with a touch more salt" or "have you thought of adding a drop or two of truffle oil?" It's brave to open a top-class Italian restaurant in this neighbourhood, but Maremma is just that. It's been here since early 1999 and has bedded in splendidly.

The menu is formally set out and littered with chic Italian favourites – insalata caprese (£6.70), buffalo mozzarella with tomatoes and basil oil, cacciucco (£13.50), which is a Livorian fish stew, and risotto radicchio e Taleggio (£6.70), a successful combination of bitter radicchio and deliciously rich cheese. The minestrone (£4.20) is top-class: a simple vegetable soup enriched with pesto, uncomplicated by luxury ingredients, and, surprisingly, without pasta. Padellata di seppioline (£6.20) brings a plate of sautéed baby cuttlefish, cooked with tomato, peas and mangetout – perfectly cooked and strongly flavoured without being too rich. Of the excellent pastas, the mezzalune di melanzane (£5.90/£7.90), semicircular ravioli filled with aubergine and served with a sauce of sausage and red onion, is extremely good. The grilled scalopina di vitello, con funghi porcini (£11.90) – so easy to overcook – is well judged. Tiramisù (£4.50) is heaven, and sometimes they even have "zuppa Inglese" among the dolci – that's trifle to most of us.

Maremma hits just the right note. The wine list makes good reading – there's a good house wine at £10.50, but the sky's the limit. Plus there's a crèche at weekends so that smart Islington mums and dads can reminisce about long lunches in Tuscany pre-bambini.

£15–£30

Pasha

301 Upper St, N1 ©020 7226 1454   ⊖ Angel

Mon–Fri noon–3pm & 6–11.30pm,

Sat & Sun noon–midnight   All major cards except Switch

If you picture Turkish food as heavy and oil-slicked, think again. Pasha is dedicated to producing fresh and light authentic Turkish food that's more suited to modern tastes. Dishes are made with virgin olive oil, fresh herbs, strained yoghurts and fresh ingredients prepared daily. It doesn't look like a traditional Turkish restaurant either, being open and airy with only the odd brass pot for decoration. The management describe it as "Modern Ottoman". It has clearly adapted well to its Upper Street location – so well, in fact, that the wine list offers spritzer for £2.50.

For anyone new to Turkish cooking the menu is a delight. Dishes are clearly described so that you can try them on a no-risk basis. Staff are helpful and will encourage you to eat in Turkish style with lots of small "meze" dishes. There are set menus (minimum two people) of £10.95 for thirteen meze and £17.95 for a Pasha Feast, which gives diners ten meze plus main courses, dessert and coffee. Meze may include hummus, tarama, cacik, kisir – a splendid bulghur wheat concoction – falafel, courgette fritters, meatballs and a host more. Other noteworthy starters include aranavut ciger (£3.95), which is lamb's liver served with finely chopped onions and parsley. Main courses are more familiar – a selection of kebabs and the like – but, again, there is a better than usual choice. Try kilic baligi (£10.95), fillet of swordfish marinated in lime, bay leaf and herbs and served with rice; or istim kebab (£8.95), roasted aubergine filled with cubes of lamb, green peppers and tomatoes with rice; or yogurtlu iskender (£8.45), a trio of shish, kofte and chicken on pitta bread soaked in fresh tomato sauce, with fresh herbs and topped with yoghurt. Though meat undeniably dominates the menu, there are seven vegetarian and five fish selections. Puddings include the usual Turkish stickies, but once again are light and freshly made.

Wines are priced fairly, there is Efes beer from Turkey (£2.50), and that powerful spirit raki (£2.95) for a tongue-numbing blast of the real Middle East.

The Rôtisserie

134 Upper St, N1 ✆020 7226 0122	⊖ Highbury & Islington/Angel
Mon & Tues 6–11pm, Wed–Fri noon–3pm & 6–11pm,	
Sat noon–11pm, Sun noon–10pm	All major credit cards

The Rôtisserie is buzzing, brightly painted and unpretentious, with a commitment to quality underlying both food and service. Its South African owner makes regular trips to Scotland to lean on the farm gate and make small talk about Aberdeen Angus steers (which, if they did but know it, will soon be visiting his grill), and his menu claim, "Famous for our steaks", seems well earned. The kitchen also frets about the quality of their chips, which is no bad thing, as the classic combination of a well-grilled steak with decent frîtes and Béarnaise sauce is one of life's little luxuries. The restaurant's success is shared by two other branches, offering much the same menu, at 56 Uxbridge Rd, Shepherd's Bush, W12 (✆020 8743 3028), and 316 Uxbridge Rd, Hatch End, Middlesex (✆020 8421 2878).

Rôtisserie starters are sensibly simple: a good Caesar salad (£3.95), tiger prawns peri peri (£4.50), char-grilled vegetable salad with pesto (£3.95). Having brushed aside these preliminaries, on to the steaks: Scottish Aberdeen Angus – 10oz rump (£10.95); 12oz sirloin (£14.95); 8oz fillet (£14.95) – carefully chosen, carefully hung, carefully cooked. All of them (and all other main courses) come with a good-sized bowl of frîtes. Since the vanquishing of the fatuous beef-on-the-bone ban there is now a 14oz T-bone (£15.95). If you don't want steak, try one of the other rôtisserie items, such as the French, corn-fed chicken leg and thigh (£5.95); or the wonderful spit-roasted Barbary duck – half a duck with fruit chutney (£11.95). The rest of the menu covers the bases for non-meat eaters. There's a grilled fish of the day (£10.95), or vegetable brochettes with spiced rice (£7.95). Puddings are sound and range from apple and cinnamon cake with hot caramel (£3.50) to home-made ice cream (£3).

The South African influence is a constant lurking presence behind these chunks of grilled meat, so expect "monkey gland" sauce – rich and dark, made to a secret recipe rumoured to include both Coca-Cola and Mrs Ball's Chutney.

£10–£25

Sarcan

4 Theberton St, N1 ℰ020 7226 5489   ⊖ Angel/Highbury & Islington

Daily 11.30am–11.30pm   All major credit cards

Brash, basic and very busy, Sarcan drops a welcome pebble of reality into the maelstrom of trendy Islington. The food is Turkish, and reliable enough. The service combines bustle with charm and prices are low – perhaps all the competition round here helps keep them that way. The decor is predictable, with a sort of Turkish-tourist-board feel to it, and a couple of tables perched outside on the pavement when the weather is up to it. Be warned that it can get very full and pretty rowdy on a Saturday night.

The menu is something of a magnum opus. The score is as follows: cold hors d'oeuvres 17; hot hors d'oeuvres 11; salads 3; main courses 17; specials 7; vegetarian mains 10; seafood dishes 4; and finally 3 different set menus. One starter achieves "must-have" status, both on grounds of variety and value: the mixed meze (£4.95) is a triumph, a large round plate divided up into sectors like a wheel, and filled with a huge range of dips. Expect hoummus, kisir (a kind of tabbouleh with wheat, mint and parsley), zetinyagli mercimek (a stunning green lentil salad), enginar (artichoke hearts), pilaki (kidney beans), ispanak tere ture (spinach and yoghurt), and many more! All served with rather good, round, flat and substantial Turkish bread – pide not pitta. From the hot starters, go for hellim (grilled halloumi cheese) or borek (deep-fried cheese in filo parcels). If you haven't succumbed to the temptation to eat only starters, go for grilled meat, which is plainly cooked and served with both rice and salad. Beyti (£6.50) is made with round flat fillets of grilled lamb – surprisingly tender; or there's shish kofte (£5.50); or sucuk izgara (£4.95), which are spicy sausages. On the vegetarian menu you'll find melemen (£5.50), a Turkish-style omelette – rather like a Spanish tortilla without the potato. And there is also fish and chips – actually swordfish and chips, kilic baligi (£7.45).

You cannot really eat at a Turkish restaurant without trying some offal: Albanian liver (£2.75) is chopped and fried and, despite its name, a Turkish favourite. The uykuluk (£5.50) – sweetbreads – are very tasty too.

25 Canonbury Lane

25 Canonbury Lane, N1   ©020 7226 0955

Part cocktail bar, part wine bar, part lounge, this stylish new venue attracts a chatty crowd of younger locals and Upper Street shoppers. It's very easy-going and relaxed, and everyone is extremely friendly. There's an excellent wine list, plus bottled beers, spirits and a featured cocktail of the month.

The Compton Arms

4 Compton Ave, N1   ©020 7359 6883

A tiny local, tucked away, the Compton Arms is an unspoilt gem, managing to maintain a country-pub atmosphere so near to the hustle that is Upper Street. It's hard to find – that's how the fiercely loyal regulars like it – but well worth finding. Greene King IPA and Abbot ales and Martha Graham's Brewery ale are the signature draught beers.

Frederick's

Camden Passage, N1   ©020 7359 2888

This luxurious little bar, which fronts its own restaurant, welcomes non-diners. House champagne at £24 is enjoyed by happy groups of antique-hunters from the Camden Passage market nearby. The quietly restrained atmosphere is a bit formal, but the place as a whole is quite relaxed.

Hogshead

77 Upper St, N1   ©020 7359 8052

A "try before you buy" offer on all wines and beers encourages you to experiment in this spacious, comfortable pine-decorated bar. Try one of the many specialist Real Ales such as Nimmo's XXXX, Woodford's Wherry or Nethergate's Umber Magna.

Medicine Bar

181 Upper St, N1   ©020 7704 9536

The strict "no ties or officewear" policy defines this hip venue with its funky purple decor. It's relaxed by day, but very lively and hard to get into at night, when it fills with Islington's style leaders and a club crowd here for the DJs (after 9pm). Cocktails, wine, bottled beers and draught lagers including Kronenbourg 1664.

The Old Parr's Head

66 Cross St, N1   ©020 7226 2180

An excellent example of how to modernise an old pub while keeping its character intact, this very friendly Free House has a huge selection of drinks. The sixteen tequilas and fifteen whiskies lead the running, and cocktails are big, but there are also plenty of wines, beers and alco-pops to choose from.

Maida Vale
& Kilburn

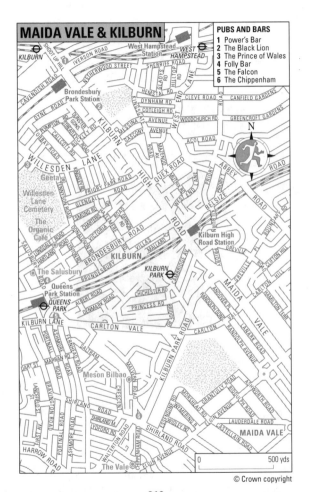

MAIDA VALE & KILBURN

PUBS AND BARS
1 Power's Bar
2 The Black Lion
3 The Prince of Wales
4 Folly Bar
5 The Falcon
6 The Chippenham

KILBURN
SHOOT UP HILL
West Hampstead Station
WEST HAMPSTEAD
IVERSON ROAD
CAVENDISH ROAD
NETHERWOOD STREET
SHERRIFF ROAD
Brondesbury Park Station
HEMSTAL RD
DYNHAM RD
COTLEIGH RD
AVENUE
WEST END LANE
CLEVE ROAD
CANFIELD GARDENS
WOODCHURCH RD
GREENCROFT GARDENS
DYNE ROAD
MESSINA
GASCONY
AVENUE
ACOL ROAD

N

WILLESDEN LANE
Geeta
PRIORY PARK ROAD
QUEX ROAD
WEST END LANE
ABBEY
ROAD
Willesden Lane Cemetery
BLENGAL
ESMONK RD
CHARTERS RD
VICTORIA RD
BELSIZE
ROAD
The Organic Café
BRONDESBURY ROAD
BRONDESBURY VILLAS
MALLARD
Kilburn High Road Station
GREVILLE
The Salusbury
KILBURN
KILBURN PARK
Queens Park Station
QUEENS PARK
ALBERT ROAD
CHICHESTER RD
PRINCESS RD
MAIDA VALE
DENMARK ROAD
KILBURN LANE
CARLTON VALE
CARLTON
RANDOLPH AVENUE
SALTRAM
KILBURN PARK ROAD
Meson Bilbao
CRESCENT
GRANTULLY ROAD
BIDDULPH ROAD
ASHWORTH ROAD
SHIRLAND ROAD
MORSHEAD RD
WYMERING RD
LAUDERDALE ROAD
CASTELLAIN ROAD
MAIDA VALE
HARROW ROAD
The Vale
ELGIN AVENUE
SHIRLAND ROAD

0   500 yds

© Crown copyright

Geeta

57–59 Willesden Lane, NW6 ©020 7624 1713	⊖ Kilburn
Mon, Tues & Sun noon–2.30pm & 6–10.30pm,	
Fri & Sat noon–2.30pm & 6–11.30pm	All major cards except Switch

Some years ago, this family-run vegetarian restaurant bit the bullet and installed a tandoor oven, and now the menu runs the gamut from South Indian vegetarian dishes to curry house favourites like beef Madras, before peaking triumphantly with "special tandoori dishes". But, diversify as they might, Geeta's strengths still lie in simple, unpretentious, South Indian vegetarian food, with decor and prices to match.

Start with masala dosai (£2), a crisp, twelve-inch pancake folded around a savoury potato stuffing – a great combination of textures and carefully spiced. There are also all the South Indian favourites – if it can be made out of rice or lentils, you'll find it here – including uttapam (£1.80), a kind of Indian pizza made from lentil dough, iddly sambar (£2.40), steamed rice and lentil cakes, and vadai (£1.20), a deep-fried lentil doughnut. Onion bhajis (£1.30) are interesting, taking the form of onion rings crisply fried in a gram flour batter, which makes them much less soggy than their cricket-ball counterparts. The vegetable samosas (£1.20) are also very good. Turning to more substantial matters, the menu offers a base of boiled rice (£1.20), fried rice (£1.50), lemon rice (£1.50), or coconut rice (£1.50); lemon rice is amazing – rich and lemony, speckled through with onion seeds, and thoroughly delicious. Bombay aloo (£1.90), or potato and green beans with coconut (£1.90), or black eyed beans (£1.90), are all good, while in the "spicy vegetable dishes (dry)" section, the green banana curry (£1.90) is a favourite with local customers – try it and you'll see why. Of the meat dishes, you'll find that the sag gosht (£3) is an accomplished lamb curry thickened and enriched with spinach, while the "newcomer" dishes from the tandoor – like the mixed grill (£6.90) – are fresh and tasty.

It is also worth mentioning how very rare it is to see a wine list where, if you avoid the extravagance of a £10 bottle of Chablis, everything is priced at £6.50 a bottle or less.

£10–£30

Meson Bilbao

33 Malvern Rd, NW6 ©020 7328 1744   ⊖ Queens Park/Westbourne Park

Mon–Thurs noon–2.30pm & 6–11pm, Fri noon–2.30pm & 7–11.30pm,

Sat 7–11.30pm   All major cards except Amex

Visiting this Basque restaurant-tapas bar is not so much an out-of-body experience as an out-of-country experience. The man in charge is José Larrucea, who has finally got his own restaurant after a career cooking for others. The pace here is gentle, and to confirm your sense of displacement this is probably the only restaurant in London where three out of five of the house specials are made with hake, while one of the others features dried cod! In good weather the dining tables invade the pavement, inside there's a focal-point bar and, just when you think you've got the measure of the place, you discover another large dining room in the basement.

There is an excellent-value set menu at £8.90 for a soup or starter, main course, ice cream and coffee. But for the best of Meson Bilbao come in a group and run amok with the tapas: king prawns in garlic sauce (£3.90), boquerones, those wonderful, nutty-tasting white anchovies (£2.75), mussels Bilbaina, spicy and tomatoey (£3.50), or chiperones en su tinta, stuffed squid in an ink sauce (£3.90). The patatas bravas (£2.50) are not overly bravas, but the chorizo Busturia (£3.90) is a triumph and should not be missed – it's a sandwich-style concoction with two slices of grilled aubergine acting as the "bread", and sliced, grilled chorizo serving as filling. Now you are at a turning point. You can either persevere with tapas, perhaps a plate of strongly flavoured jamón Serrano (£4.90), or switch to something more substantial. Such as the especialidad de la casa – "merluza a la koxkera" (£18 for two people). This is a round earthenware dish of hake cooked with clams, asparagus, king prawns and peas, and is something of a favourite with the regulars, judging by the number quietly tucking in. Or you could have your hake grilled (a la plancha – £8.90) or fried (rebozada – £7.50).

José Larrucea's passion is for the wines of Rioja, and the list here is more diverse than you'd expect. Furthermore, he has wines not on the list that are even more fascinating. Treasured bottles, wines from the vineyards of his friends – you only have to ask.

The Organic Café

21–25 Lonsdale Rd, NW6 ⓒ020 7372 1232   ⊖ Queens Park

Mon noon–5pm, Tues–Sun 9.30am–5pm & 7–10.30pm   Cash or cheque only

www.organiccafe.co.uk

The Organic Café is a real treat. Even for those whose heart sinks when confronted with such an obviously worthy establishment, this is a genuine neighbourhood gem in a quiet, semi-private road. When it is too cold to enjoy one of the pavement tables, enter instead the largish blue-painted dining room, decorated with branches of twisted fig and reclaimed chicken-wire light fittings, and relax. Though many Londoners still find the idea of a restaurant that serves wholly organic food a bit suspect, there is nothing alternative about the quality of the cooking here.

The menu changes sporadically and is divided traditionally into starters, mains and puds, with the addition of one-course dishes consisting of salads and pastas, but you can mix and match as you wish. Vegetarian choices are exceptionally good, but there is plenty for meat eaters as well. The cooking is reasonably classical and well grounded, with little that is unnecessarily fancy. Expect a couple of soups – chilled gazpacho perhaps, with a herb ice cube, or warm watercress soup (both £3.80), or a mixed platter of crostini made with the restaurant's own houmous, tapenade and caponata (£5.70). Galantine of wild rabbit with onion marmalade (£5.60) is exceptionally good: moist, flavoursome and a nice size for a first course. The wild Irish smoked salmon (£6.80) comes with a well-seasoned dill sour cream, while wild mushroom risotto (£9.80), made with vegetable stock, has more to it than you might expect. Chicken breast on bubble and squeak with red wine jus (£12.80) is good old-fashioned fare, and fillet of beef with sauce Béarnaise (£15.80) is one of the better steaks you'll get in London. Puddings (£4.75) are on the heavy side – chocolate and orange truffle cake, say, or glazed lemon tart with honey crème fraîche. The organic drinks list is short, but there is a range of wines, beers, spirits and juices.

Most of the customers (many of whom are families) are regulars. There is no music to disturb animated conversations, and service is informal but efficient. Lunchtime is brunchtime.

£16–£35

The Salusbury

50–52 Salusbury Rd, NW6 ℗020 7328 3286   ⊖ Queens Park

Mon–Sat 12.30–3.30pm & 7–10.30pm,

Sun till 10pm   All major credit cards except Diners

On the surface, the Salusbury is a straightforward pub in the middle of a parade of shops. It's fun and friendly and clearly a home from home for a table-hopping crowd who all seem to know one another. To get to the restaurant, you shoulder your way through the packed bar to find a quieter room filled with the kind of tables your mum had in her living room, stripped and scrubbed, with a display of eclectic art lining the walls.

The excellent and varied menu follows a mainly modern Italian theme rather than the more predictable Modern British bias of so many gastropubs. Starters include grilled prawns with chilli (£7), asparagus risotto (£6.50), and spaghettini with bottarga and marinated cod (£6.50). The prawns are crispy, grilled in their shells, and the spaghettini is tossed with cubes of potato to lighten the richness. Main courses of vignarola (braised spring vegetables; £8.50), pot-roasted guinea fowl with mascarpone and rosemary (£11), and roast tuna with balsamic vinegar (£11), are also delicious. The tuna is cooked slightly longer than is the current fashion – that is, it isn't totally raw – and the vignarola consists of what's in season. Perhaps such delights as small artichokes and tiny broad beans. Ricotta ice cream with candied fruits and dark chocolate (£3.95) is like a delicious cassata and, after the very large main course portions, quite enough to share. The wine list is not large, but is well chosen. There is a very good French Pinot Noir for £20 that tastes like it ought to cost a lot more. Bread and olive oil is served while you wait and most of the starters can be had as main courses, though with portions sized the way they are you'd be mad to want to.

The Salusbury serves a highly critical crowd with excellent food in stimulating surroundings. If there's one niggle it's that portion sizes can be daunting. In Yorkshire they call it being "over-faced", but if value is your thing you'll like the Salusbury a lot.

The Vale

99 Chippenham Rd, W9 ℗020 7266 0990	⊖ Maida Vale
Mon 7–11.30pm, Tues–Sat 12.30–3pm & 7–11.30pm,	
Sun 12.30–3pm & 7–10.30pm	Mastercard, Visa

There appears to be something of a restaurant boom in the maze of streets that makes up the ever-fashionable hinterland of Maida Vale/Kilburn/north Notting Hill – call it what you will. The Vale, situated in a large corner site with a pleasing aspect, is something of a glazier's dream, with windows whichever way you look. This makes it a very pleasant place to pass a peaceful sunny afternoon, and in the kitchens is Francesca Melman who used to wow them at the nearby Cow Dining Room. The exterior is somewhat deceptive, but venture in and you'll find yourself in a comfortable sage-green room with a handsome bar and a spiral staircase leading below. To one side there is a large conservatory, flatteringly lit, which is probably where you will be shown to a table.

The daily changing menu is ruled by the seasons and promises good gutsy Modern British stuff. Starters may include ham hock and tarragon choux farci with grain mustard sauce (£4.75), Thai chicken soup (£3.50), smoked haddock with mussel feuillete, leeks and saffron (£5), roast breast of wood pigeon with swede purée and red wine sauce (£5) – all simple and good. Main courses also travel around Britain for their inspiration – the poached fillet of salmon with asparagus, Jersey Royal potatoes and Hollandaise (£12) is a classic seasonal combo. Vegetarians can eat well here – the butternut squash and pine nut ravioli with Gorgonzola and marjoram sauce (£9.50), or the broad bean and wild garlic leaf risotto, with poached egg and truffle oil (£8.50) both appeal. Puddings are suitably self-indulgent – try the gratin of pear with vanilla ice cream (£4.75). The service is affable, and by virtue of the very size of the place you stand a good chance of picking up a table should you call in on spec. There are also set lunches to be had (Tues–Sat; £8.50 for two courses, £11.50 for three).

The spiral staircase that leads down to the loos also leads to the private members' bar – though it's not actually that private, seeing as membership is free and seems to be granted on request.

MAIDA VALE & KILBURN

The Black Lion

274 Kilburn High Rd, NW6 ✆020 7624 1520

Go, if only to look at the amazing rococo ceiling and bas-reliefs picked out in gold. A riot of Victoriana in a large, friendly and comfortable local. It's a Free House, but there's more Guinness consumed than anything else.

The Chippenham

207 Shirland Rd, W9 ✆020 7624 2270

A Victorian temple to booze, this large and comfortable pub offers Tetley's and Kilkenny to a mixed, mainly local crowd in a vaulted and beautifully tiled interior. There are a few B&B rooms.

The Falcon

341 Kilburn Lane, W9 ✆020 7624 1842

Customers are welcome to play the piano, otherwise it's hip live bands on a Friday and disco on Saturday in this traditionally decorated corner pub, which dates from the 1950s. There's plenty of room for friendly crowds of regulars to enjoy Greene King IPA and Toby Bitter.

The Folly Bar

53–55 Salusbury Rd, NW6 ✆020 7624 9153

The eclectic decor attracts a younger cocktail- and mixer-drinking crowd. There's Greene King IPA if you like, live jazz on Sunday and a very lively make-new-friends atmosphere.

Power's Bar

332 Kilburn High Rd, NW6 ✆020 7624 6026

Don't be fooled by the tiny frontage. This lively cocktail-oriented bar goes on forever. A mixed Aussie and local crowd cranks up the atmosphere, and it gets very frisky on a Friday night. Caffrey's, Staropramen and Grolsch keep the fans happy.

The Prince of Wales

101 Willesden Lane, NW6 ✆020 7624 9161

This big, comfortable Victorian alehouse – all frosted glass and mirrors – features big-screen sport, two pool tables and Saturday night karaoke. It divides conveniently into two main bars, one of which is far quieter than the other. John Smith's, Fosters and Kronenbourg are the favourite pints.

NORTH

St John's Wood & Swiss Cottage

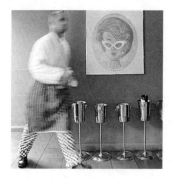

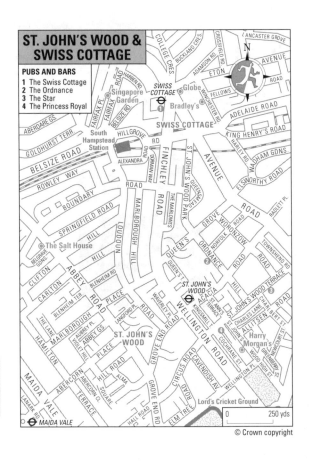

ST. JOHN'S WOOD & SWISS COTTAGE

PUBS AND BARS

1 The Swiss Cottage
2 The Ordnance
3 The Star
4 The Princess Royal

N

LANCASTER GROVE
COLLEGE CRES
BUCKLAND CRES
CROSSFIELD RD
ADAMSON RD
ETON
AVENUE
ROAD
HARBEN RD
FAIRFAX PL
FAIRFAX RD
BELSIZE RD
Singapore Garden
SWISS COTTAGE
Globe
WINCHESTER RD
FELLOWS
Bradley's
SWISS COTTAGE
ADELAIDE ROAD
KING HENRY'S ROAD
ABERDARE GS
GOLDHURST TERR.
South Hampstead Station
HILLGROVE RD
MARLEY RD
WADHAM GDNS
BELSIZE ROAD
ALEXANDRA
ORMAN WAY
ST. JOHN'S WOOD PARK
FINCHLEY ROAD
QUEENSMEAD
AVENUE
ELSWORTHY ROAD
ROWLEY WAY
ROAD
RADLET PL.
BOUNDARY
SPRINGFIELD ROAD
LOUDOUN
HILL
MARLBOROUGH HILL
THE MARLOWES
GROVE
WORONZOW
ROAD
TOWNSHEND RD
The Salt House
BELGRAVE GDNS
CLIFTON
CARLTON
ABBEY
BLENHEIM RD
BLENHEIM TER.
QUEEN'S
QUEEN'S
ORDNANCE
ROAD
NORFOLK
HILL
ROAD
ST. JOHN'S WOOD TERRACE
THE LANE
MARLBOROUGH PLACE
AUBREY PL.
ABBEY GS
LANGFORD PLACE
ROAD
WAVERLEY RD
ST. JOHN'S WOOD
ACACIA RD
ANN'S TERRACE
KINGSMILL
CHARLES LANE
CHARLBERT ST
ALLITSEN RD
Harry Morgan's
HAMILTON
MAIDA VALE
ABERCORN
VIOLET HILL
ST. JOHN'S WOOD
HILL ROAD
ALMA SQUARE
ABERCORN PL.
TERRACE
GROVE END ROAD
CIRCUS ROAD
WELLINGTON ROAD
CAVENDISH AV
WELLINGTON PL
COCHRANE ST
ST. JOHN'S
WOOD HIGH ST
MARCHBERT ST
LANARK RD
MAIDA VALE
LANK RD
HALL ROAD
GROVE END RD
ELM TREE ROAD
Lord's Cricket Ground

0   250 yds

© Crown copyright

NORTH

318

Bradley's

25 Winchester Rd, NW3 ℗020 7722 3457	⊖ Swiss Cottage
Mon–Fri noon–3pm & 6–11pm, Sat 6–11pm,	
Sun noon–4pm & 6–11pm	All major credit cards

Bradley's, tucked away in a side street behind Swiss Cottage, is hard to find – and you get the impression that the regular clientele would prefer to keep the secret to themselves. The food here is pretty impressive – but that's not all. The atmosphere is warm and inviting, the menu covers and (metal) plates are probably the heaviest in London, and the loos are definitely a must-visit. All of which forms a good backdrop for chef/proprietor Simon Bradley's cooking and presentation. Dishes revolve around a combination of fresh ingredients and are served with a view to making the most of the visual appeal. They can look terrific.

A starter of potato pancake with gravadlax, soured cream and lime chilli vodka (£7.50) is presented as a slim high tower, the frozen vodka in a tiny shot glass. Very fresh and tasty, and not too much dill either. Chargrilled squid with watercress, plum and chilli sauce (£5.50) is better than good. Tagliolini with lobster, prawns, mussels and basil (£6.90) would do well as a main course. Peppered venison with artichoke mash and onion gravy (£13.50) is rich, dark and delicious – the subtly flavoured mash makes a good foil for the richness of the venison. Other main courses include pan-fried veal with apple and sage Tatin and redcurrants (£12.50), herb-crusted rack of lamb with mushroom, potato and tarragon gratin (£15), and a good selection of fish. You don't need extra vegetables, but the cauliflower fritters with tomato chutney (£1.60) are too delicious to ignore. And if you are going for desserts, the chocolate pudding with marmalade ice cream (£5) is enough for two – the ice cream nicely tart with its caramel orange flavour.

Bradley's extensive wine list includes a large selection of unusual and higher-priced New World wines that are often hard to find. A lively, but full-flavoured biscuity house champagne at £27 is good value, too, and Bradley's is a fine venue for a celebration dinner. There is also a Sunday brunch menu at £14 for two courses and £17 for three.

Globe

| 100 Avenue Rd, NW3 ℂ020 7722 7200 | ⊖ Swiss Cottage |

| Mon & Sat 6–11pm, Tues–Fri noon–3pm & 6–11pm, | |
| Sun noon–3pm & 7–10pm | Amex, Mastercard, Visa |

The bright blue-and-yellow splash of colour tucked away behind Swiss Cottage underground station has a story attached to it. Quite simply, Neil Armishaw, owner and manager of Globe, brought back some unique hand-made blue and yellow plates from the USA and decorated the restaurant to match them. However idiosyncratic, the locals have taken to this friendly, buzzy place, where the food – an accomplished meld of modern and traditional, with Pacific influences – is in keeping with the decor.

Among the starters you'll find char-grilled squid, Oriental pilaw and sweet chilli sauce (£5.25), warm lamb confit salad with houmus and vanilla and mint dressing (£4.95), Malaysian vegetable laksa with crispy vermicelli (£3.95), and linguine with sweet pepper pesto and spring vegetables (£4.95). Main courses may include fillet of Scottish beef with bubble and squeak, mushroom and shallot sauce (£13.95), char-grilled sea bass bok choi and Oriental stir fry (£13.95), roast cod, red pepper and squash stew with Gruyère and leek sauce (£12.95), or marinated rump of lamb with crushed minted new potatoes and cranberry chutney (£12.95). Vegetarians are pretty well treated here – perhaps a porcini and Parmesan risotto with sautéed mushrooms (£10.50), or open ravioli of Mediterranean vegetables, mozzarella and pesto (£10.95)? Puddings include the ubiquitous crème brûlée, here with white chocolate and raspberries (£4.50), and a refreshing Campari and grapefruit sorbet with pink grapefruit salad (£4.50). But the star of the show is usually the rather good home-made ice cream – how about chocolate, caramel and honeycomb flavours, with butterscotch sauce (£4.50)? We are talking serious sugar intake here.

Globe is built like a conservatory, with a glass roof and sliding doors that pull open, and an open-front courtyard for al fresco dining. There is a popular weekday lunch at £14 for two courses and £15 for three, which sportingly includes a glass of house wine and a cup of coffee.

Harry Morgan's

31 St John's Wood High St, NW8 ✆020 7722 1869   ⊖ St John's Wood

Daily 11.30am–10pm   All major credit cards

In 1950, Harry Morgan, a successful butcher in Park Road, St John's Wood, started to cure his own salt beef. It proved so popular that he and his wife set up a restaurant to sell the delicacy. In 1962 the restaurant moved to its present site in St John's Wood High Street, where a couple of years ago it was taken over by a Mr Herschel. It was all change: out went the traditional little room with its handful of tables and the walls papered with pictures of famous clients . . . and in came a new large, airy room with acres of blond wood. The salt beef, nonetheless, has weathered all these storms remarkably well; prime Scotch beef is still boned-out and pickled on the premises, and sandwiches can be ordered lean or fat according to taste.

Harry Morgan's sells that most famous of Jewish cure-alls, chicken noodle soup – with dumplings (£3.80), or with everything (£3.95). It is very good – modestly described by Herschel as the "best soup in the world" – and the customers seem to agree; they sell 250 portions a day. Of the other starters, try the chopped liver (£3.50) – very rich and smooth – or the egg and onion (£3.50). Then go on to a salt beef sandwich on rye bread (£4.95); ask for horseradish, and don't be surprised when your sandwich comes with a ruby-red layer – Jewish horseradish is inextricably linked with beetroot. You could add a latka, a seriously weighty, fried potato pancake (£1.50), on the side. Or go your own way with any of the other specials. The menu lists everything from roast turkey (£7.50) to worsht (beef salami) and eggs (£6.50).

There is a real mystique to pickled cucumbers. What is described rather disdainfully as a "wally" in London fish-and-chip shops is elevated to an art form in Jewish cuisine. The subtlest is the "new green", fresh and crisp; then there's the "sweet and sour" – this one is large and knobbly; or there is the connoisseurs' choice, the "heimishe", intense and salty. And the price of all these delights? A modest £1.50 a portion.

ST JOHN'S WOOD & SWISS COTTAGE ⑪ BRITISH/PUB

The Salt House

63 Abbey Rd, NW8 ©020 7328 6626   ⊖ St John's Wood

Mon–Fri noon–3pm & 6.30–10.30pm,

Sat & Sun noon–4pm & 7–10.30pm   All major credit cards except Diners

The Salt House combines corner pub, bar, restaurant and flower stall. There is a paved area set back from the road with benches and tables for the few al fresco dining days. The restaurant is reached through a large pub-style bar, and the whole has a relaxed friendliness where women on their own can feel quite at home. In 1999 the Salt House was taken over by Adam Robinson of The Chiswick (see p.488) fame and the food follows his style. The menu is based on what's fresh and in season, prepared simply and with accompaniments designed to bring out the best in the main ingredients. So it is no surprise that the menu changes daily according to what is best on the markets.

The food is all carefully cooked, well presented and unfussy. Starters may include a rich and satisfying chorizo and white bean soup (£3.75), a warm salad of smoked undyed haddock, poached egg and smoked bacon (£4.50), or Parma ham with spring vegetables and mint (£4.75), which is fresh with new season's broad beans and peas. For a main course, try breast of chicken with boulangère potatoes and thyme (£8.25), roast cod with mash and salsa verde (£8.50), spiced aubergines with cumin, sour cream and spring onions (£6.75), grilled fillet of sea bass, with couscous and cherry tomatoes (£11), calves' liver with semolina gnocchi and sage (£8.75), or an onglet steak with chips and horseradish (£10.75). Puddings include raspberry tart (£4) – actually more of a crème brûlée with raspberries, and all the better for it – rhubarb fool and shortbread (£3.75) – pleasantly tart and creamy at the same time – and, for the unreconstructed sweet tooth, a chocolate pot (£4).

The food here is that superb combination of simple and stylish, the service is attentive and friendly, and there's a well-chosen wine list with a welcome absence of extravagant prices – but the real stars at the Salt House are the customers. Everyone seems to be enjoying themselves, and the mood is infectious.

NORTH

Singapore Garden

83a Fairfax Rd, NW6 ✆020 7328 5314	⊖ Swiss Cottage/Finchley Road
Daily noon–2.45pm & 6–10.45pm	All major credit cards

www.singaporegarden.com

Singapore Garden is a busy restaurant – don't even think of turning up without a reservation – and performs a cunning dual function. Half the cavernous dining room is filled with well-heeled, often elderly, family groups from Swiss Cottage and St John's Wood, treating the restaurant as their local Chinese and consuming crispy duck in pancakes, money bag chicken, and butterfly prawns. The other customers, drawn from London's Singaporean and Malaysian communities, are tucking into the squid blachan and the Teochew braised pig's trotters. So there are cocktails with parasols and there is Tiger beer. But it's always busy – and the food is interesting and good.

Start with a fresh crab fried in its shell (£12.75). It's a trade-off, to be honest, as frying (rather than baking) means that the leg and claw meat can be on the dry side, but also ensures that there are sublime crispy bits encrusting the brown meat. It comes with ginger and spring onions, Singapore chilli sauce, or black pepper and butter. If you're feeling adventurous, follow with a real Singapore special – the Teochew braised pig's trotter (£10), which brings half a pig's worth of trotters slow-cooked in a luxurious, black, heart-stoppingly rich gravy. Or try the claypot prawns and scallops (£12), which delivers good, large crunchy prawns and a fair portion of scallops stewed with lemongrass and fresh ginger on glass noodles. Very good indeed. From the Malaysian list you might pick a daging curry (£6) – coconutty, rich and not especially hot. You must also try the mee goreng (£5), because this is how this noodle dish should be – a meal in itself.

At the bottom of the menu you'll find the "healthy alternative" known as Steamboat (£31.50 per person, for a minimum of two). This is a kind of party game. Eager participants drop tasty pieces of fresh meat and seafood into a cauldron of broth, which bubbles away at the table, then experience agonies of frustration when they find that they haven't the dexterity to fish them out with chopsticks.

The Ordnance

29 Ordnance Hill, NW8   ©020 7722 0278

More a wine bar than a pub, this well-hidden and very relaxed venue caters for local well-heeled residents. Candles in the evening and an interesting wine list make you feel you've been invited into someone's home – and indeed, the outside looks more like a private residence than a public house. There's a separate restaurant on the premises as well, so if your dining plans fall through you could always try and eat here.

Princess Royal

11 Circus Rd, NW8   ©020 7483 9711

A comfortable, easy-going atmosphere marks out this pub – which was Charlie Chaplin's local – in an upmarket area not well served by them. Less music and TV than in most pubs makes for an agreeably quiet and peaceful drink. Bass, Worthington and Fuller's London Pride are the favourites on tap.

The Star

38 St John's Wood Terrace,
NW8   ©020 7722 1051

You'll find open fires and a genuine local community feeling here, with Bass and Worthington on tap. It's off the beaten track, and has resisted the games machines and pool table invasion. It's well worn from decades of care and regular use and has pavement tables for summer drinking.

The Swiss Cottage

98 Finchley Rd, NW3   ©020 7722 3487

This massive island site, popular with foreign-language students, comprises four huge bars – you'll need to specify one if you're meeting somebody. There's the Victoria & Albert, The Tap Room, a Members' Pool Club, and an outside patio that gets full in summer. Sam Smith's Sovereign, Old Brewery and Extra Stout are the signature beers on tap.

NORTH

Stoke Newington

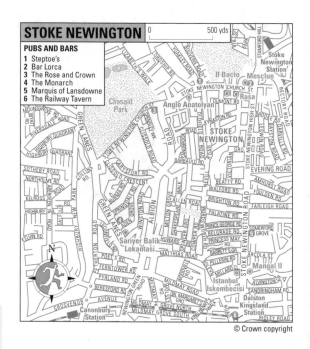

STOKE NEWINGTON

0   500 yds

PUBS AND BARS

1 Steptoe's
2 Bar Lorca
3 The Rose and Crown
4 The Monarch
5 Marquis of Lansdowne
6 The Railway Tavern

© Crown copyright

Anglo Anatolyan

123 Stoke Newington Church St, N16 ©020 7923 4349	BR Stoke Newington
Mon–Fri 5pm–midnight, Sat & Sun 1pm–midnight	Mastercard, Visa

The food is sound at the Anglo Anatolyan, the bills are small, and tables are so crowded that you get to meet all the other diners. But the most intriguing feature of the restaurant is the large and impressive royal crest which is engraved in the glass of the front door: under it, an inscription reads, "By Appointment to Her Majesty Queen Elizabeth II, Motor Car Manufacturers". Why? Do the Windsors slip up to Stoke Newington when they feel a new Daimler coming on? Predictably, asking the waiters for provenance doesn't help much: they look at you seriously and confide that they "got the door secondhand".

Royal warrants aside, the food at the Anglo Anatolyan is usually pretty decent. The bread in particular is amazing. Large, round flat loaves about two inches deep, cut into chunks, soft in the middle and crisp on the outside; it is baked at home by a local Turkish woman and is a far cry from the flat, hard, mass-produced pitta pockets of the supermarkets. To accompany it, start with ispanak tarator (£2.95), spinach in yoghurt with garlic. And a tremendous, coarse tarama (£2.45). And sigara borek (£2.95), crisp filo pastry filled with cheese and served hot. And arnavut cigeri (£2.95), cubes of fried lambs' liver. Dine mobhanded so that you can try more starters. The main courses are more easily summarised: 16 ways with lamb, 1 with quails, 2 with chicken, 1 with prawn, and 2 vegetarian dishes. Kaburga tarak (£6.25) is crisp, tasty lamb "spare-ribs"; iskander kebab (£6.75) is fresh doner on a bed of cubed bread and topped with yoghurt and tomato sauce; kasarli beyti (£6.75) is minced lamb made into a patty with cheese and grilled. They are all pretty good.

Like all the Turkish restaurants in this end of town, this is a very laissez-faire kind of place and standards can vary from visit to visit, but when you've eventually had your fill you'll be presented with a handwritten bill, at the bottom of which is printed "Another cheap night out". This, for once, is simply the truth.

Il Bacio

61 Stoke Newington Church St, N16 ℂ020 7249 3833   BR Stoke Newington

Mon–Fri 6–11pm, Sat & Sun noon–11.30pm   Mastercard, Visa

Opened in 1995 by Sardinian childhood sweethearts Luigi and Michela, Il Bacio has justly become one of the most popular fixtures on Stoke Newington's "restaurant row". The decor is upbeat – sunshine-yellow walls are lined with splashy modern canvases – and each (smallish) table has a vase of fresh flowers. Potted palms screen off a couple of tables for privacy, but, although *bacio* means "kiss", don't plan a romantic dinner here: this is a noisy place, loud with laughter and birthday parties.

If you feel you'll have room for a starter, the insalata di mare (£5.50) – packed with sea-fresh clams, calamari and prawns – or the grilled goats' cheese with poached pears (£5.50) – melt-in-the-mouth rounds of cheese perfectly set off by lightly poached fruit – work well. The garlic bread (£2.65) is good, though if you're having pizza as a main course bear in mind that this is simply a base without the topping. Perfectly judged main course pastas include gnocchi di patate (£6.50), in a confident tomato and basil sauce, and velvety penne al salmone (£6.95). But it's the colossal pizzas that keep Il Bacio full every night: spilling off the plate, they never fail to produce a shriek of amazement from first-timers. Bases are paper-thin, cooked expertly in a wood-burning oven, so there's none of the unpleasant greasy oozing prevalent in lesser pizzas. All but the pescatora (£6.95 – seafood, capers, parsley) are built on a sauce of tomato and mozzarella. The Sardegna (£6.50), with its aubergines and onion, and the Bacio (£7.50), topped with frankfurters and olives, both add a twist. Of the home-made desserts, the tiramisù (£3.50), a luscious, sozzled brick of sponge, cream and liquor, wins star prize.

In summer, French windows open out onto the pavement. It's a great place to survey the street life, but be warned that Il Bacio is opposite the local fire station. Sudden ear-shattering siren wails can send even the juiciest mozzarella morsel shooting down the wrong way.

£8–£25

Istanbul Iskembecisi

9 Stoke Newington Rd, N16 ℂ020 7254 7291	BR Dalston Kingsland
Daily noon–5am	All major credit cards

The Istanbul Iskembecisi is just across the road from Mangal II (see p.330), and at heart they are singing off the same sheet. Despite being named after its signature dish – Iskembe is a limpid tripe soup – the Istanbul is a grill house. Admittedly it is a grill house with chandeliers, smart tables and chairs, and upscale service, but it is still a grill house. And because it stays open late into the morning it is much beloved by clubbers and chefs – they are just about ready to go out and eat when everyone else has had enough and set off home. The grilled meat may be better over at Mangal II, but the atmosphere of raffish elegance at the Istanbul has real charm.

The iskembe (£2.50) – tripe soup – has its following. Large parties of Turks from the snooker hall just behind the restaurant insist on it – and you'll see the odd regular downing two bowlfuls of the stuff. For most people, however, it's bland at best, and even the large array of additives – salt, pepper, chilli (this is a dish that you must season to your personal taste at the table) – cannot make it palatable. A much better bet is to start with the mixed meze (£4.50) – good hummus and tarama, superb dolma, and the rest of the usual suspects. Then on to the grills, which are presented with more panache than usual. Pirzola (£6.50) brings three lamb chops; sis kebab (£5.75) is good and fresh; karisik izgara (£8.50) is a mixed grill by any other name. For the brave, there is also a whole section of offal dishes, among them kokorec (£5) – lamb's intestines – and arvnavaut cigeri-sicak (£4.50) – liver Albanian-style. Somebody, somewhere must be mourning two casualties of the BSE era which have been taken off the menu – kelle sogus, their "roasted head of lamb", and beyin salata, "boiled brain with salad".

Just when you think you're on safe ground with the desserts, there is still a surprise in store – kazandibi (£2.50), which is a "Turkish type creme caramel, milk based sweet with finely dashed chicken breast". Delicious.

Mangal II

4 Stoke Newington Rd, N16 ℃020 7254 7888   BR Dalston Kingsland

Daily noon–1am   Mastercard, Visa

The first thing to hit you at Mangal II is the smell: the fragrance of spicy, sizzling char-grilled meat is unmistakeably, authentically Turkish. This, combined with the relaxing pastel decor, puts you in holiday mood before you've even sat down. The ambience is laid-back, too – at slack moments, the staff shoot the breeze around the ockbasi, and service comes with an ear-to-ear grin. All you have to do is sit back, sink an Efes Pilsener (£1.50) and peruse the encyclopedic menu.

Prices are low and portions enormous. Baskets of fresh bread are end-lessly replenished, so it's just as well to go easy on the appetisers. With a vast range of tempting mezeler (starters), however, resistance is well-nigh impossible. The 23 options include simple hummus (£2.50) and dolma (£2.50); imam bayildi (£3), aubergines stuffed with onion, tomato and green pepper; thin lahmacun (£1.50), meaty Turkish pizza, and karisik meze (£4), a large plate of mixed dishes that's rather heavy on the yoghurt. There's a fair spread of salads (all £2.50–£3), too, though you get so much greenery with the main dishes that it's a wasted choice here. The main dishes (kebablar) themselves are sumptuous, big on lamb and chicken, but with limited fish and vegetarian alternatives. The patlican kebab (£7) is outstanding: melt-in-the-mouth grilled minced lamb with sliced aubergines, served with a green salad, of which the star turn is an olive-stuffed tomato shaped like a basket. The kebabs are also superb, particularly the house special, ezmeli kebab (£7), which comes doused in Mangal's special sauce. Or, if you don't fancy a grill, there's a choice of three freshly made and hearty "daily stews" (£3.50–£4).

After swallowing that lot, dessert might not be feasible, but after a long break – there's no pressure to vacate your table – you might just be tempted by a slab of tooth-achingly sweet baclava (£2). Alternatively, round off the evening with a punch-packing raki (£3) or a slap-in-the-face Turkish coffee, which will often be on the house, courtesy of the genial proprietor Okkes Torbas. And, for a final blast of Ottoman atmosphere, pay a visit to the bathroom – the no-frills facilities are a real taste of old Istanbul.

Mesclun

24 Stoke Newington Church St, N16 ℗020 7249 5029	BR Stoke Newington
Daily 6–11pm	Mastercard, Visa

Mesclun looks like a special-occasion kind of place, its stylish decor a tad incongruous on this careworn parade of cheap-and-cheerful ethnic restaurants. Small and elegant, with linen tablecloths, pine floor, and simple, dark-wood furniture, it seats about forty people. Most of them are relaxed thirty-something locals, quietly complacent that they're onto a good thing. For, despite all appearances, Mesclun is a bargain, serving astonishingly good-value, assured Modern European food.

Meals start with complimentary bread and a tapenade of rough-chopped olives, sun-dried tomatoes and capers. Irresistibly moreish, but take it easy: the portions coming are large. This is especially true of the starters, most of which could pass as main courses – like pan-fried chicken livers, balsamic reduction, baby spinach salad (£5), or beautifully prepared roast woodcock with a rich chorizo and bean sauce (£5). There are simpler choices, such as French onion soup (£3.50). One of the more elaborate (which should be ordered as soon as possible, as it is cooked to order and takes fifteen minutes to prepare) is the melted onion, Fontina cheese and oyster mushroom tart (£5). For a main course, consider the superb daily fish specials: choices may include roast cod with basil dressing or char-grilled tuna, depending on what's good at the market. Otherwise there's a judicious balance between meat (free-range/organic) and vegetarian options. The Mesclun risotto is made with brown rice, parsley, mixed vegetables and Parmesan (£7.50) and served with a green salad; the pan-fried calves' liver with smoked bacon, spinach and Dolcelatte sauce (£9.95) is meltingly good. All come with side veg: perhaps a satisfying trio of celeriac Dauphinoise, herby ratatouille and buttery beans. Desserts (all £3.25, except for the farmhouse cheeses at £3.95) are upper-crust comfort food: hot chocolate brownies with vanilla ice cream and hot chocolate fudge sauce; baked blueberry cheesecake; Muscat custard and mixed fruit compote; zabaglione and Amaretto semifreddo with butterscotch sauce.

Service at Mesclun is special – patient, attentive and humorous – and, though there can be long pauses between courses, it's simply too pleasurable an experience for anyone to mind much.

£12–£27

Rasa

55 Stoke Newington Church St, N16 ℗020 7249 0344	BR Stoke Newington
Mon–Fri 6–11pm, Sat & Sun noon–2.30pm & 6pm–midnight	All major credit cards

Rasa has built up a formidable reputation for outstanding South Indian vegetarian cooking. In fact, when diners stop arguing as to whether Rasa is the best Indian vegetarian restaurant in London they usually go on to discuss whether it is the best vegetarian restaurant full stop. As well as great food, the staff are friendly and helpful and the atmosphere is uplifting. Inside, everything is pink (napkins, tablecloths, walls), gold ornaments dangle from the ceiling, and a colourful statue of Krishna playing the flute greets you at the entrance. Rasa's proprietor and the majority of the kitchen staff come from Cochin in South India. As you'd expect, booking is essential.

This is one occasion when the set meal – or "feast" – (£15) may be the best, as well as the easiest, option. The staff take charge and select what seems like an endless succession of dishes for you. But, however you approach a Rasa meal, everything is a taste sensation. Even the pappadoms are a surprise: try the selection of crispy things served with six homemade chutneys (£3) – quite simply, a revelation. If you're going your own way, there are lots of starters to choose from. Mysore bonda (£2.50) is delicious – shaped like a meatball but made of potato spiced with ginger, coriander and mustard seeds. Kathrikka (£2.50) is slices of aubergine served with fresh tomato chutney. The main dishes are just as imaginative. Beet cheera pachadi (£3.75) is a colourful beetroot curry, zingy and tasty with yoghurt and coconut; moru kachiathu (£3.85) combines mangoes and green bananas with chilli and ginger. Or go for a dosa: paper-thin crisp pancakes folded in half and packed full with a variety of goodies – masala dosa (£4.75) is filled with potatoes and comes with lentil sauce and coconut chutney. Puddings sound hefty but arrive in mercifully small portions; the payasam (£2.25), a "temple feast", blends dhal with jaggery (raw sugar) and coconut milk – a fine end to a meal.

The word rasa has many meanings in Sanskrit: "flavour", "desire", "beauty", "elegance". It can also mean "affection" – something that the whole of northeast London feels for this wonderful restaurant.

Sariyer Balik Lokantasi

56 Green Lanes, N16 ✆020 7275 7681	BR Canonbury
Daily 5.30pm–late	Cash or cheque only

This is a restaurant which used to stretch the credulity of even the most adventurous diner. Until 1999, the outside looked as if it had been ineptly boarded up in the aftermath of some bomb outrage. Inside it was small and seriously shabby. Now there is a new frontage, new decor, and new owners – changes are expected. That said, as this edition goes to press, the menu remains the same, and thankfully so. The new regime would be unwise to change anything that works so well. This is a fish restaurant where the fish ends up either in a large frying pan on a domestic stove or on the large grill. Very fresh fish plainly cooked is a delight, and to pay such basic prices is very rare indeed.

The menu is a clear reflection of how diligent the chef has been in the markets. But the fish comes later. Start with the mezes you will see in serried ranks of china pudding basins in the chilled cabinet. They all cost £2. Best among them are the peynir ezmesi, a mix of walnut, cheese and chilli; the bakla, which is cold broad beans; and the ipanak tarator, a blend of spinach, garlic and yoghurt. Everything is served with chunks of toasted, thick-cut bread. Then there are the hot starters at £5. Try the deep-fried mussels, or perhaps the squid rings. Both arrive hot from the frying pan and are very good with a shake of salt and a squeeze of lemon. Main courses are fishy, and you will have to ask what is available, partly because it depends what is good at the market and partly because things run out – the wiser diner will book, especially if going mob-handed. There's usually salmon, halibut, anchovies, tuna – something for everyone. To accompany the feast it is hard to better a bottle of cold Efes beer. One warning: unless your sweet tooth is well in the ascendant, beware of the Turkish puddings.

From time to time, the restaurant serves the somewhat mysterious "mock sea bass". This is the name by which it is known at Billingsgate market, but on interrogation various rather sheepish London fishmongers confess that they have never heard of it. The importer says that he gets it from Canada, but whatever it is called you should try some. It is a firm, meaty, admirably bone-free fish, and it tastes simply terrific.

Bar Lorca

175 Stoke Newington High St,
N16   ☎020 7275 8659

One of London's favourite Latin club venues, Bar Lorca gets wonderfully crowded as the night draws on with a pack of sexy salsa dancers. Go just to see great dancing or to enjoy an exceptional range of Spanish and Latin cocktails, wines and beers. It's absolutely heaving with people on weekend evenings, when it's open late.

Marquis of Lansdowne

48 Stoke Newington Rd,
N16   ☎020 7254 1104

An unreconstructed old boozer, brimming with character and characters. It's large, comfortable and welcoming, full of friendly people happily enjoying Boddingtons, Guinness and Youngers Bitter. Live bands occasionally add to the bustle.

The Monarch

68–70 Green Lanes, N16   ☎020 7249 9109

A relaxed old pub with a friendly crowd of happy regulars who know that it's the only traditional pub for miles around. Tetley's, John Smith's and Stella are the favourites on tap.

The Railway Tavern

59 Kingsland High St, E8   ☎020 7254 5219

It's easy to miss this tiny pub right beside Dalston Kingsland railway station. Divided into two separate bars with a beer garden at the back, it's usually packed with bargain-hunters from the market opposite during the day. Stones and Toby Bitter are the most popular ales, with Guinness coming a close second.

The Rose & Crown

199 Stoke Newington Church St,
N16   ☎020 7254 7497

Newly refurbished with a flagstone floor and big panelled windows, this large corner pub has a comfortable, old-fashioned feel. There's a very good selection of wines plus Marstons Pedigree, Adnams Bitter and Ruddles County. Watch out for the aged dog, who likes to doze beneath the tables.

Steptoe's

102 Stoke Newington Church St,
N16   ☎020 7254 2906

A friendly local with polished wood decor, a relaxing front-room atmosphere, a pool table and a back terrace. Charles Wells' Bombardier and IPA are on tap, with Fargo as well. There's also a selection of fourteen single malt whiskies to enjoy by the large open fire.

Wembley

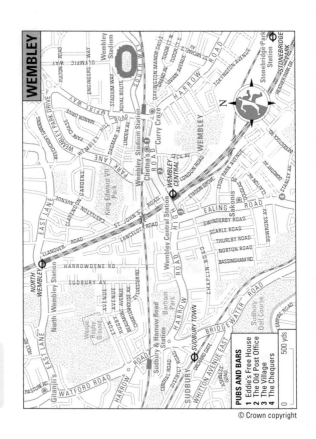

WEMBLEY

PUBS AND BARS
1 Eddie's Free House
2 The Old Post Office
3 The Village
4 The Chequers

0   500 yds

© Crown copyright

Chetna's

420 High Rd ℭ020 8900 1466	⊖ Wembley Central
Tues–Fri noon–3pm & 6–10.30pm, Sat & Sun 1–10.30pm	Mastercard, Switch, Visa

Chetna's is a remarkable Indian restaurant – busy enough to need a queuing system. You register your interest at the counter and get given a cloakroom ticket, and when your table is ready your number is called. The restaurant has smart wood tables and chairs, ceiling fans and some seriously ornate brass chandeliers, but despite these trappings it is still awesomely cheap. The food is very good indeed and the menu is a bit of a surprise, opening with a section headed "seaside savouries" – an odd claim in a vegetarian establishment – and moving through to Chetna's Pizza Corner, confirming once again that when Asians go out to dinner they often want a change from usual fare. The concept of a large "special vegetable hot pizza" (£5.20) cooked by an Indian chef and made with pure vegetarian cheese, onions, and special Chetna sauce – green pepper, corn, and hot green chillies – has undeniable charm.

Start with a truly amazing mouthful – Chetna's masala golgapa (£1.90); these are small, crisp golgapas filled with potatoes, onions, moong, chana, green chutney, sweet and sour chutney, and topped with sev. You load them into your mouth and as you chew different tastes and textures take over. It's an astonishing sensation. Order more portions than you think you'll need. Also try the kachori (£1.90) – a crisp coat encases a well-spiced ball of green peas. Then there are the karela, bhindi and tindora curries (£2.50). The karela dish, made from bitter melons, is genuinely bitter – very interesting and, word has it, very good for the blood. Or there's Chetna's crispy bhajia (£1.90) – slices of potatoes crisp on the outside with a batter containing bits of chilli and perfectly cooked. The most visually striking dish must be the paper dosa (£3), a giant chewy cone of nutty-tasting pancake with a vegetable sambhar and coconut chutney for dipping.

The award for most comprehensive dish must go to the Delhi Darbar thali (£6.10), which is served with one sweet, one farsan, three vegetables, chutney, vegetable biryani, dhal, raita, papadum and paratha. There's a minimum charge of £3.50 per person at Chetna's – presumably to stop a large family sharing one Delhi Darbar thali for dinner.

Curry Craze

8–9 The Triangle, Wembley Hill Rd ☏020 8902 9720   ⊖ Wembley Central

Mon 6–10.30pm, Wed–Fri 12.30–2.30pm & 6–10.30pm,

Sat 6–11pm   All major credit cards except Diners

You'll need to book to get into Curry Craze – not only on Wembley match days, when in-the-know football regulars fill the place to take advantage of the special pre- and post-match buffets, but also on normal week-ends, which can be pretty busy. This is no surprise, for, despite its unfortunate name, Curry Craze is a very good Indian restaurant indeed – a genuine and friendly family-run place that serves predominantly Pun-jabi food with a smattering of East African Asian dishes. And if some items on the menu have a familiar ring to them, that is because the Mal-hotras who run Curry Craze are related to the Anands – the dynasty responsible for the famed Brilliant and Madhu's Brilliant in Southall (see p.535 and p.537).

As at the Brilliants, you could do worse than start with a share of butter chicken, or any of its variants, jeera, methi or chilli chicken (£6.50 for a half-chicken). Or the sheekh kebab (four for £4.95) served as a sizzler on an iron dish and very tasty. Or chilli corn (£2.95) – corn on the cob given the hot sauce treatment. Main courses range from karahai dishes to old favourites like chicken tikka masala (£6.25), biryanis and pure veg dishes. Karahi prawns (£7.95) come in a good rich sauce. Tinda lamb (£5.95) is a delightful dry curry of lamb and tinda – a Punjabi vegetable which is a member of the squash family, something like what you'd expect of a tomato merged with a potato. Punjabi bhartha oro (£4) is a prince among side dishes: a roasted aubergine, mashed and cooked with onions and peas. Pakorian raita (£2.45) is very odd indeed, but provides a perfect change of texture – pea-sized balls of gram flour cooked and served cold in a tangy yoghurt sauce. To dip into all these dishes, there are bhaturas (£1) – deep-fried breads, like puffy savoury doughnuts, and not for dieters – and very delicious peshwari (£2.25) or plain (£1.20) naans.

One house speciality well worth trying is Mrs Malhotra's dall makhani (£4), a rich black lentil and kidney bean dhal. It is made by combining the dhal with a tarka containing onions, ginger and tomatoes cooked in ghee.

Geetanjali's

16 Court Parade, Watford Rd ✆020 8904 5353	⊖ Wembley Central
Daily noon–3pm & 6–11.30pm	All major credit cards

www.geetanjali-restaurant.com

There are a good many Indian restaurants in Wembley, and it would be easy to write off Geetanjali's as just one more of the same. On the face of it, for sure, the menu is pretty straightforward, with a good many old, tired dishes lined up in their usual serried ranks – chicken tikka masala, rogan josh, and so on and so forth. But Geetanjali's has a secret weapon, a dish that brings customers from far and wide. Word on the street is that this place serves the best tandoori lamb chops in North London. And when you have tasted them you'll agree.

This chop lover's haven has a large roomy dining room, and the service is attentive, if a little resigned when you pitch up and order a raft of beers and a few portions of chops – or as the menu would have it lamb chopp (£4.50). Of course the chops are good. Very good, thick-cut and exceedingly tender, and very nicely spiced. Accompany them with a luccha paratha (£2.50), warm and flaky and presented in the shape of a flower with a knob of butter melting into its heart. The alternative is the intriguingly named bullet nan (£2.50), which promises to be hot and spicy, and delivers in good measure. You have been warned. Even if you're not a complete chopaholic you can also do well here. Go for starters such as the good chicken tikka haryali (£4.50) – chicken breast marinated in green herbs like coriander and mint before being cooked in the tandoor. Rashmi kebab (£3.90) is also good – made from minced chicken and spices. Main courses include mathi gosht (£6.90), which is lamb with fenugreek, lamb bhuna (£6.50), and lamb badam pasanda (£6.90). And should this emphasis on bread and meat leave you craving some of the green stuff there's sag aloo (£4.50), or karahi corn masala (£4.50).

This is not the cheapest Indian restaurant in Wembley, but it does have a certain style, even extending to the sophisticated peppermint fondant mints that accompany your bill. And, it goes without saying, it does serve the best tandoori chops in North London.

£4–£10

Sakonis

127–129 Ealing Rd, Alperton ℗020 8903 9601	☖ Alperton
Mon–Thurs & Sun 11am–11pm,	
Fri & Sat 11am–midnight	Delta, Mastercard, Switch, Visa

Sakonis is a top-notch vegetarian food factory. Crowded with Asian families, it is overseen by waiters and staff in baseball caps, and there's even a holding pen where you can check out the latest videos and sounds while waiting your turn. From a decor point of view, the dining area is somewhat clinical, a huge square yardage of white tiling – easy to hose down. Nobody minds: the predominantly Asian clientele is too busy eating. The Indian vegetarian food here is terrific, but it's old hat to many of the Asian customers who dive straight into what is, for them, the most exciting section of the Sakonis menu – the Chinese dishes. These tend to be old favourites like chow mein and chop suey cooked by Indian chefs and with a distinctly Indian spicing. Unless curiosity overwhelms you, stick to the splendid South Indian dishes. There are two other branches: 6–8 Dominion Parade, Station Rd, Harrow (℗020 8863 3399), and 116 Station Rd, Edgware (℗020 8951 0058).

Sakonis is renowned for its dosas. Effectively these are pancakes, so crisp that they are almost chewy, and delightfully nutty. They come with two small bowls of sauce and a filling of rich, fried potato spiced with curry leaves; choose from plain dosa (£3.50), masala dosa (£4.50), and chutney dosa (£4.60), which has spices and chilli swirled into the dosa batter. Try the farari cutlets (£3.50): not cutlets at all, in fact, but very nice, well-flavoured dollops of sweet potato mash, deep-fried so that they have a crisp exterior. In fact, all the deep-fried items are perfectly cooked, very dry, with a very crisp shell, but still cooked through. A difficult feat to achieve. Also worth trying are the bhel puri (£3.30), the pani puri (£2.50), and the sev puri (£3.30) – amazingly crisp little taste bombs: pop them in whole and the flavour explodes in your mouth.

Some say that the juices at Sakonis are the best in London, and while that may be hyperbole they certainly are very good indeed. Try madaf (£2.50), made from fresh coconut, or melon juice (£2.25), which is only available in season, passion juice (£2.75), or the orange and carrot mix (£2.50), which is subtitled "health drink".

The Chequers

149 Ealing Rd, Alperton   ©020 8902 1329

This big, comfortable, 1950s pub is hard to miss, being right on a road junction. It's ideally placed for a drink after a day exploring the wonderful Ealing Road market with its Asian foods and clothes, and before going on to eat. Courage Best and John Smith's are the signature ales.

Eddie's Free House

412 Wembley High Rd   ©020 8795 2263

Dedicated to sport and karaoke on Saturday nights, this lively venue plays host to a mixed crowd who follow the matches. It's small, cosy, comfortable and, surprisingly, not very noisy. Tetley's, John Smith's, Guinness and Guinness Extra Cold are the favourite beers here.

The Old Post Office

397a Wembley High Rd   no phone

The counters of this sympathetically converted old post office now dispense Greene King IPA, Charles Wells' Bombardier, draught lagers and alcopops to a young and frantic crowd. There is a section to suit every mood. Even the pool table has its own little alcove.

The Village

529 Wembley High Rd   ©020 8795 5894

This big, comfortable place gets full and noisy at weekends. There's big-screen sport, live bands, karaoke and the occasional DJ. It's popular with a predominantly young crowd who enjoy Fosters, Carlsberg, Guinness and Guinness Extra Cold. As befits a pub in Wembley, the beer pumps are topped with footballs.

NORTH

Further North

Haringey, Hendon,
Kingsbury, Willesden

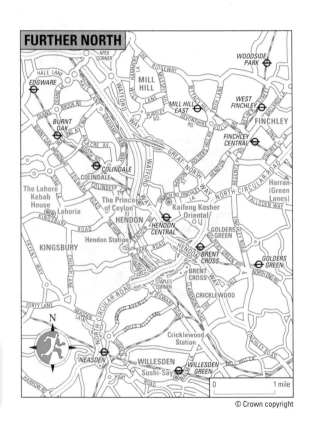

FURTHER NORTH

APEX CORNER
WOODSIDE PARK
HALE LANE
EDGWARE
MILL HILL
WEST FINCHLEY
WATFORD WAY
MILL HILL EAST
FINCHLEY
BROOK RD
DEANS
PURSLEY RD.
DEVONSHIRE RD.
HALE LANE
RIDGEWAY
HAMMERS LA
BITTACY HILL
GRAHAME PARK WAY
BURNT OAK
APACHE AV.
GREAT NORTH WAY
FINCHLEY CENTRAL
COLINDALE
COLINDALE
COLINDEEP LA.
WATFORD WAY
HENDON
NORTH CIRCULAR ROAD
Harran (Green Lanes)
FALLODEN WAY
The Lahore Kebab House
Lahoria
The Prince of Ceylon
Kaifeng Kosher Oriental
KINGSBURY ROAD
HENDON CENTRAL
GOLDERS GREEN
KINGSBURY
Hendon Station
PARK ROAD
BRENT CROSS
GOLDERS GREEN
CHURCH LANE
BROADWAY
HENDON WAY
BRENT CROSS WAY
NORTH END
BRENT CROSS
CHURCHLANE
STAPLES CORNER
CRICKLEWOOD
CLAREMONT RD
BRYANT WAY
FORTY LANE
NORTH CIRCULAR ROAD
NEASDEN LANE
DOLLIS HILL LANE
EDGWARE ROAD
FINCHLEY ROAD
N
Cricklewood Station
NEASDEN
WILLESDEN
WILLESDEN GREEN
MILL HILL LA.
HARROW RD.
Sushi-Say
HIGH ROAD

0   1 mile

© Crown copyright

NORTH

344

£8–£14

Harran

399 Green Lanes, N4 ✆020 8348 5434	⊖ Manor House
Daily 24hr	Cash only

For a small Turkish restaurant in Haringey, Harran certainly has an impressive waterfall. The back wall of the dining room is given over to a chunky rock face overflowing with water, topped with a clock surmounted by an eagle with wings akimbo. It all has a certain style, as does the large wood-fired oven, which is immensely solid, brick-built and looks just like a small cottage. You can only wonder why there are gutters at the bottom of the impeccably tiled roof. Though this establishment has been trading 24 hours a day since it opened in 1997, skirmishes with antiquated British licensing laws mean that the drinks licence may come and go (and on some occasions they cannot even allow BYO). When all is resolved, the friendly waitress announces, they will reprint the menu; in the meantime look at the takeaway menu board or ask. In a street lined with Turkish restaurants, Harran stands out because of the freshness of the food, the splendid baking, and sensibly modest prices.

Start with hunks of hot, fresh bread, lightly dusted with sesame seeds (50p). Perfect with the gloopy salads (all 50p), all of which make great starters – yoghurt and cucumber, yoghurt and salad, and a splendid "chilli" salad (a kind of super salsa). The grills are terrific, and very fresh indeed. Shish kebab (£6), adana kebab (£5.50), and iskender kebab (£7) all arrive with rice and salad. Then there are pizzas, and Turkish pizzas; lahmacun (£1.50), meaty pide (£4), egg pide (£4). And stews, like the rich bean stew with rice (£3.50). Puddings are something of a challenge. Keskul (£2), described as "rice pudding without the rice", comes as a small foil takeaway tray full of strange, very sweet, ground-rice pudding topped with walnuts; it has a strangely resilient and pliable skin.

Should you be in Harran at about 10pm, you will see the baker going into overdrive, plunging tray after tray of delightful little cheesy pastries into the little brick hut. He is gearing up for the rush. Between 1am and 6am, the restaurant offers a running buffet, salads, dips, grills and freshly baked pastries – both savoury and sweet. This is amazingly popular at the weekend, not surprisingly – it costs just £4 per person,

£20–£40

Kaifeng Kosher Oriental

51 Church Rd, Hendon, NW4 ℂ020 8203 7888

⊖ Hendon Central

Mon–Thurs & Sun 12.30–2.30pm & 6–11pm,

Sat 1hr after sunset–11pm (Sept–April only)

All major credit cards

www.kaifeng.co.uk

The Kaifeng Kosher Oriental restaurant is a one-off: an opulent Chinese restaurant that claims to be (and doubtless is) the only kosher Oriental establishment in Britain. According to the family tree on the wall, the most important family of Kaifeng's former Jewish community is named Chao Luang-Ching. The inscription adds, rather enigmatically, that "Ezekiel is probably Chao Lunang-Ching Gwlyn Gym". So now you know. The long, narrow dining room fills up fast with affluent locals, happy to pay smart North London prices which have more in common with the West End than the suburbs. But you get a decent deal, friendly and excellent service that almost justifies the fifteen percent surcharge, and fresh, well-cooked (if a trifle under-seasoned) dishes. If you're Orthodox Jewish, Kaifeng must make a welcome change; if you're not, then seeing how favourite dishes like sweet and sour pork, prawns kung po and so forth turn out kosher-style is a lot of fun.

Start with Capital spare ribs (£6.95), which is absolutely delicious, made from lamb instead of pork and arguably even better for it. Hunan chicken with lettuce wrap (£11.50) is also fresh and good, while the usual prawn and sesame seed toast becomes sesame chicken (£6.95). Of the main courses, the sweet and sour lamb (£11.95) is slightly less successful – a good, sharp sauce still makes no impression on fairly tough chunks of lamb. But there are some interesting and unfamiliar dishes like beef strips with pine seeds (£11.95), sliced mango chicken (£11.50), and mixed vegetables in coconut cream (£5.95). Shellfish dishes, meanwhile, turn into fish, usually sole, which is served in a variety of familiar styles including steamed with ginger and spring onion (£15.95), and drunken (£15.95), which is sliced and served in kosher rice wine.

Given its unique status, the Kaifeng is a pretty popular place and even early in the week it tends to fill quickly. So take the precaution of booking if you're travelling out here specially.

The Lahore Kebab House

248 Kingsbury Rd, NW9 ☏020 8905 0930   ⊖ Kingsbury

Daily 1pm–midnight   Cash or cheque only

This grill house was once a branch of the famous Lahore Kebab House in East London. Then, in 1994, Mr Hameed bought the business and with it the right to use the name "Lahore Kebab House of East London" anywhere within a five-mile radius of Kingsbury. Although completely independent of the Umberstone Street establishment (see p.193), this bare and basic restaurant remains faithful to the spirit of the original. Kebabs are cheap, freshly cooked and spicy, while the karahi dishes are also worth delving into. Recently the Lahore has gained the advantage of a drinks licence, so you can now purchase Tusker and Kingfisher beers without having to pop out to one of the neighbouring off-licences.

There's not much point in coming to the Lahore unless you're after some kind of kebab. If you just want a starter bite, there's seekh kebab (75p each). Or, for more serious eating, there's a list of kebabs all with five pieces per skewer – mutton tikka (£2.20); chicken tikka (£3); jeera chicken (£4.20); chicken wings (£4.20); lamb chops (£5). Everyone is very helpful here, and they are happy to make you up a platter for however many diners (three pieces of each kebab, for example), charging pro rata. Unusually, for such a stronghold of the carnivore, there's also a long list of vegetarian dishes all served in the karahi. Include a couple with your order – perhaps karrai dhal (£3.50), or karrai sag aloo (£3.50), which is particularly rich and tasty. Back with the meats, karrai ghost (£4.70) is a rich lamb curry, while the "chef's special" (£6), a hand-chopped keema made with both chicken and lamb, is a revelation – very tasty, with recognisable, finely chopped meat, and a far cry from the anonymous mince that forms the backbone of keema dishes in so many curry houses. It is thoroughly recommended. As are the breads – tandoori nan (90p) and tandoori roti (60p) – which are fresh and good.

The Lahore's weekend specials all appeal: karrai nehari (£7), slow-cooked lamb shanks; karrai bhindi (£4), or okra; and karrai karela (£4), made from bitter melons.

£8–£20

Lahoria

274 Kingsbury Rd, NW9 ✆020 8206 1129   ⊖ Kingsbury

Tues–Thurs 6–11.30pm, Fri & Sat 5.30pm–midnight,

Sun 3pm–midnight   Mastercard, Visa

The last edition of this guide went on a bit about the shabby, somewhat neglected decor of this Kingsbury stalwart. So much so that the proprietors have energetically set about things and now the room has new chairs and the walls are resplendent in several shades of pink. It's still small. It's still busy, particularly at the weekend. And, even taking into account the refurb, it's still true that nobody comes here for the ambience. There's also plenty of competition – half a dozen other Indian restaurants clustered on this stretch of road. But, quite simply, what makes the Lahoria stand out, what has kept it going from strength to strength, is the sheer quality of the food.

So, the food: it's fresh, not painfully hot (unless you want it to be), and well balanced. There are a lot of East African Asian specialities and dishes come by either the plate or the karai. Start with a plate of jeera aloo (£3.95), tasty, rich, soft, fried potatoes with cumin – a sort of Indian pommes Lyonnaise. Or have a plate of masala fish (£4), two fat fillets of tilapia cooked in a fresh green masala. You must try the chilli chicken (£5.75), nine chicken wings in a dark green, almost black, sludge that is rich with ginger, chillies, coriander and just a hint of tamarind sourness – triumphant but not so hot that it hurts. You can also try this sauce with potatoes (£4.25). Then there are the tandoori chops (£4), which are very good indeed. Also look out for the mari chicken (£5.75), which is chicken marinated in cracked black pepper. For a main course it is hard to praise the karai spring lamb (£5.75) highly enough: served on the bone, it is deliciously rich. Or try a simple classic like karai methi gosh (£5.75). The karai red kidney beans (£3.95), and karai bangan ka bartha (£4.50), based on aubergines and onions, are good bets, too.

On Friday, Saturday, and Sunday, Lahoria offers two notable specials – karai goat (on the bone, £5.75) and karai undhiu (£4.50), which is a dish of mixed vegetables. They also have a magnificent chiller full of bottled beers, including Beck's, Holsten, Carlsberg and Budweiser and – best of all – Tusker from Kenya. All at £2.20.

The Prince of Ceylon

39 Watford Way, Hendon, NW4 ©020 8203 8002   ⊖ Hendon Central

Mon–Fri noon–3pm & 6–11.30pm, Sat & Sun noon–11.30pm   All major credit cards

The Prince of Ceylon has been a mainstay of London's Sri Lankan community for the past twenty years, its quality and rarity (even now there are only a dozen Sri Lankan places in London) transcending its location. Watford Way, reminiscent of a Grand Prix pit lane, at least offers parking spaces. And once inside the restaurant, it's very welcoming – especially during the popular all-afternoon Sunday buffet. Eating Sri Lankan food, which is quite distinct from dining at most Indian places, is interesting. Whereas in an Indian curry house there's a tendency to choose a dish, and then some bread or rice to go with it, Sri Lanka turns this principle on its head. Breads, rices and staples are strange and delightful, forcing the curries, sambals and devilled meats and seafood into a supporting role.

Starters are deceptively named. Mutton rolls (£1.95) are delicious crispy spring rolls filled with spicy lamb and potatoes, served with a chilli-tangy tomato ketchup. The same sauce appears with the fish cutlets (£1.95) – spherical, lemony fish cakes. Or there's rasam (£1.50), a spicy soup, thin, almost gritty with aromatic spices, and with a wicked chilli kick. Moving on to the main courses, start by picking your staple. Hoppers (75p) are a must: thin, crispy, bowl-shaped breads. Or there are string hoppers (£2.75), cakes of vermicelli that come into their own dowsed with a bowl of kiri hodi (coconut milk curry). The kiri hodi also accompanies pittu (£3), a plain white cylinder that looks like a narrow roll of kitchen towel; it is made in a special steamer by packing the funnel with a mix of grated coconut and rice flour. Highlight among the breads is coconut roti (£2.25), a crisper, thinner kind of paratha. To lubricate these delights, pick from a range of curries and devilled dishes. The mutton curry (£4.95) is a good meat-and-gravy dish, while the unassumingly named "fried mutton onion" (£4.95) is even better. Good devilled dishes include the devilled prawns (£4.95), chilli-hot and piquant.

Whatever you order, be sure to get a side dish of seeni sambal (£2.25) – a spicy onion jam that adds flavour and texture. And leave room for a pud: either wattalappan (£1.95), Sri Lanka's second cousin to crème caramel, made with palm syrup, or (buffalo) curd and syrup (£3).

£20–£50

Sushi-Say

33b Walm Lane, NW2 ©020 8459 7512 or 2971   ⊖ Willesden Green

Tues–Fri 6.30–10.30pm, Sat & Sun noon–2.30pm

& 6.30–10.30pm   All major credit cards except Diners

Yuko Shimizu and her husband Katsuharu run this small but excellent Japanese restaurant and sushi bar. It has a very personal feel, with just ten seats at the bar and twenty in the restaurant, plus a private booth for five or six. Shimizu means pure water and the cooking is pure delight. It's a tribute to how sophisticated our palates have become that a restaurant like this can do well so far out of town. The menu offers a full classical Japanese selection, making it a difficult choice whether to limit yourself to sushi or go for the cooked dishes. Perhaps adapting the European style, and having sushi or sashimi as a starter and then main courses with rice, brings you the best of both worlds.

Sitting at the sushi bar gives you the chance to watch Katsuharu at work. With a sumo-like stature and the widest grin this side of Cheshire, his fingers magic nigiri sushi of exquisite proportions onto your plate. It's an accomplished show and the sleight of hand is impressive. In the lower price brackets you'll find omelette, mackerel, squid and octopus (£1.70). At the top end there's sea urchin, fatty tuna, and yellow tail (£2.70). In between there is a wide enough range to delight even the experts. Nigiri yoku (£15.70) brings you eleven pieces of nigiri and seaweed-rolled sushi and it's a bargain, heavy on the fish and light on the rice. Cooked dishes do not disappoint, either. Ebi tempura (£10.50) brings you crispy battered king prawns – the batter so light it's almost effervescent – and menchi katsu (£6.30) delivers a deep-fried oval shaped from minced beef and salad. There are set dinners for all tastes, priced from £17.50 to £27.50, mixed sashimi for £15.50, and home-made puddings such as Goma (sesame) ice cream (£1.90). There's also a selection of special sakes, which are served chilled, and even a half-frozen sake (Akita Onigoroshi) at £5.50. Less a slush puppy than a slush mastiff.

The menu is in English and the staff are very helpful, so dining at Sushi-Say gives you a good chance to develop your knowledge of Japanese food by trying something new.

South

Battersea 353

Brixton & Camberwell 361

Clapham & Wandsworth 369

Greenwich & Blackheath 379

Kennington & Vauxhall 385

Putney 393

Tower Bridge & Bermondsey 401

Wimbledon & Southfields 415

Further South 423
    Bromley, Croydon, Epsom Downs, Forest Hill,
    Herne Hill, Norbury, Tooting, West Dulwich

Battersea

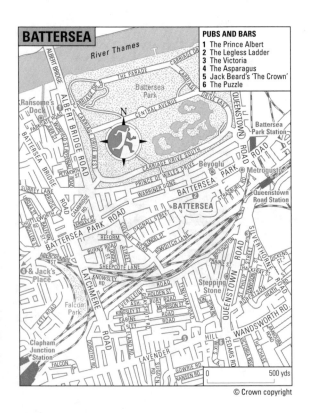

BATTERSEA

PUBS AND BARS

1 The Prince Albert
2 The Legless Ladder
3 The Victoria
4 The Asparagus
5 Jack Beard's 'The Crown'
6 The Puzzle

© Crown copyright

Beyoglu

50 Battersea Park Rd, SW11 ✆020 7627 2052	BR Battersea Park
Daily 6pm–midnight	Delta, Mastercard, Switch, Visa

www.londraturk.com.beyoglu.htm

Some years ago Beyoglu made the trek halfway across London – from Stoke Newington to Battersea – and on the way some of the more radical specialities of the Turkish grill house got left behind. You won't find those Turkish delicacies of brains, sweetbreads and so forth, and the grill has been tidied away out of sight in the depths of the kitchen. But the boast "all grilled dishes cooked on real wood charcoal" means the results are here for all to see: simple but tasty fresh food at reasonable prices. This is a formula that'll guarantee a full house in Stoke Newington, Battersea or anywhere between, and it's best to book before setting out. It is not a big place.

Dips and pitta always make good sense. At Beyoglu the fava (£2.80) is something of a star – broad beans are puréed with oil, onion, dill and a touch of garlic. Tarama (£2.50) is pinky and perky. Muska borek (£3.20) are triangular – like tiny samosas – very light, very hot pastry filled with melting feta and parsley. Venture towards the grilled meats, which all come with competent rice or chips and rather good fresh-cut salads of sliced onions, tomatoes and grilled mild chilli peppers. The special mixed grill (£10) comprises a quail, a slice of lamb (rolled best end of neck), a piece of lamb steak, and a lamb chop. The other combination platter is the karisik izgara (£9), which provides grilled chunks of lamb and chicken, adana kebab (made from mince), a kidney, and, seemingly, whatever else is to hand! If you pine for the more obscure and traditional grilled bits, the bobrek izgara (£6) delivers a portion of well-grilled and delicious lamb kidneys, while vegetarians will be pleased to find among the starters a good pilaki, made from white beans and potato with onions in a tomatoey sauce (£2.80).

The sucuk (£3.20) are described in the hot starters section of the menu as "char-grilled spicy Turkish sausages". They are imported from Cyprus and are very good indeed. Pleasantly spicy, they have an excellent texture – miles away from the usual gnarled and gristly items in a slick of suspect oil.

Jack's Place

12 York Rd, SW11 ©020 7228 8519	BR Clapham Junction
Tues–Sat 6–11pm, Sun noon–3pm (Sept to Easter only)	Mastercard, Visa

Jack's Place is a Battersea institution which dates back to the days when SW11 was not the kind of postcode that estate agents described as desirable. The restaurant occupies a long, dark room decorated with pictures of Positano (the restaurant's butcher, an old family friend, hails from there), the royal family, various high-ranking military officers, and American presidents. There's also a dusting of Chelsea FC memorabilia – and it is rumoured that if you have the indecency to admit to following Arsenal, standards of service and cuisine fall off markedly. Jack, his wife, his daughter Angela, and now her daughter Cindy, all work in the family business, and the family calling is to serve steaks. Customers come from far afield, and from all walks of life. They like the lack of airs and graces, they like the simple table settings and, if truth be told, they like the slightly old-fashioned feel to the place.

Jack's is an unrepentant and unreconstructed menu; dishes are as you remember them. "Retro" is more of a way of life here than the latest fad. Prawn cocktail (£4.75) is just lettuce, prawns and pink stuff, and there's also melon boat (£1.95) and stuffed mushrooms (£3.75) – home-made, like everything here. Steak-wise, there's entrecôte (£14.85) plain, Mexicaine, chasseur, or au poivre. Or fillet (also £14.85) plain, mignon or chasseur. The meat is good quality, and the cooking precise – rare means rare. Everything comes with six different veg plus potatoes, and the sauces taste just as they did in their heyday in the 1960s. Adventurous souls may want to try the gammon and pineapple (£11.50), or the large grilled Dover sole (£17.50) – fresh and good.

Jack's is certainly a place where drinking men feel at home. The bar is a real bar, which makes it all the more difficult not to be stunned by the sophistication (and terrific value) represented by the wine list. You could treat yourself to a very good bottle of Spanish red – Berberana Riserva 1988 – for £13.50. And for those with cash in their wallets, there are some splendid vintage ports – Graham 1960 or Offley 1960 at the tantalising come-on price of £88.50. Also 1976 Lanson Black Label champagne at £72.50.

Metrogusto

50 Battersea Park Rd, SW8 ©020 7627 2052	BR Battersea Park
Mon–Fri noon–3pm & 6.30–10.45pm, Sat noon–3.30pm & 6.30–10.45pm,	
Sun noon–3.45pm	Mastercard, Delta, Switch, Visa

Arriving at Metrogusto is not inspiring. It is hard to see inside without peering through the window, and entrance is through a solid, heavy, closed door. But once inside, you'll be faced with high ceilings, lots of natural light, and a partial view of the kitchen. Wooden tables and chairs lend the room an air of informality, while the modern art on the walls and around the room, sometimes light-hearted, sometimes more serious, adds interest.

The menu, which changes every month or so, is written in a wonderful mix that could only be called Italglish – you'll find gems like semolina scura al sugo bianco di smoked haddock (£6) and calf's liver con salsa di cacao with cubes of polenta gialla (£13.50). It's a sub-editor's nightmare and refuses to stick to any rules. The philosophy of the kitchen, however, is clearly entirely Italian. Starters range from a classic insalata de bufala (£6) and bresaola della casa all'olio (£7), to a more complicated, but very nicely made, panciarotta calda di asparagi e ricotta (£6). Pastas come as starters or main courses; there's a range of pizzas, plus four or five main dishes for good measure. Specials are chalked up on a blackboard above the kitchen. The cooking is competent, the portions large. A main course of gnoccheti sarda alla Matrice (£8.50) produces a bowl of accurately cooked, well-sauced pasta big enough to feed four; pizza del moro (£7.50), with aubergines, sultanas and pine kernels, tastes great and would satisfy a long-distance lorry driver. Puddings are on the heavy side, but the ice cream (£4) is heavenly, and the budino di cacao con crema di cioccolato bianco (£4), sinful and highly recommended. Gratifyingly, ordering cheese (£5.50) brings a selection of British cheese from Neal's Yard rather than anything from Italy. The all-Italian wine list is long and well chosen, but with no explanations. Thankfully, the managers know their way around it and will advise something sensible.

Metrogusto has a relaxed, friendly atmosphere. The food is good, the pricing fair and the customers – a mixture of locals going out for a bite to eat, families celebrating and clubbers preparing for a night on the tiles – all look happy. No wonder.

£16–£35

Ransome's Dock

35–37 Parkgate Rd, SW11 ℂ020 7223 1611	BR Battersea Park
Mon–Fri 11.30am–11pm, Sat 11.30am–midnight,	
Sun 11.30am–3.30pm	All major credit cards

www.ransomesdock.com

Ransome's Dock is the kind of restaurant you would like to have at the bottom of your street. It is formal enough for those little celebrations or occasions with friends, and informal enough to pop into for a single dish at the bar. The food is good, seasonal, and made with carefully sourced ingredients. Dishes are well cooked and satisfying, not fussy, the wine list is encyclopedic, and service is friendly and efficient. All in all, Martin Lam and his team have got it just right. Everything stems from the raw ingredients: they use a supplier in East Anglia for the smoked eels; they dicker with the Montgomerys over prime Cheddars; small producers stop by with their finest wines. The menu changes regularly, but the philosophy behind it does not. Look out for the bargain set lunch – two courses for £12.50.

Before rampaging off through the main menu, make a pit stop at the daily specials; if nothing tempts you, turn to the seven or eight starters. If it's on, make a beeline for the Norfolk smoked eel with warm buckwheat pancakes and crème fraîche (£8). Very rich, very good, and very large. Or there may be house-smoked pigeon breasts with celeriac remoulade (£6). Or Morecambe Bay potted shrimps with wholemeal toast (£6.25). Main courses are well balanced – Dutch calves' liver (£13.50) may come with Cumbrian smoked bacon, bubble and squeak and shallot sauce – delicious stuff. Sea bass might be accompanied by a girolle mushroom risotto and spinach (£16). Perhaps spinach, ricotta and pine nut filo pastry with a tomato pepper sauce (£10.50) tempts? Or there may be a "shorthorn" sirloin steak (£16.95) with mustard and tarragon sauce, roast tomatoes and big chips – not just any old steak, but one from a well-hung, Shorthorn steer. Puddings run from the complicated – a hot prune and Armagnac soufflé with Armagnac custard (£5.75) – to the simple – Greek yoghurt with honey and toasted pistachio nuts (£4.25).

The wine list makes awesome reading. Long, complex, arcane – full of producers and regions you have never heard of – with fair prices. Advice is both freely available and helpful.

Stepping Stone

123 Queenstown Rd, SW8 ©020 7622 0555   ⊖ Clapham Com/BR Queenstown Road

Mon noon–2.30pm & 7–10.30pm, Tues–Fri noon–2.30pm & 7–11pm,

Sat 7–11pm, Sun 12.30–3pm

All major credit cards

Although very much a neighbourhood restaurant, Stepping Stone deserves a wider public. Its commitment to using only the best ingredients, most of them organic and free-range, sourced direct from many small and individual suppliers, ensures a quality of taste in simple dishes that is very rewarding. Fish is bought from the port, meat from the farm, game from the shoot. There's a separate, large no-smoking room, the whole place is air-conditioned, and owner Gary Levy's policy is to encourage people to arrive early and stay late. In short, it's enlightened . . . and the food is consistently good.

As you would expect, the menu changes daily, being market-driven, and makes best use of what is available. For starters there might be diver-caught scallops, black pudding, potatoes, mustard vinaigrette (£7.50), or warm duck breast and poached pear salad (£6.50), or roast foie gras and apple tart (£7.75). The best advice is to favour the more seasonal dishes, like wild garlic potato and leek soup (£4.25). For main courses dive into smoked haddock, bubble'n'squeak, poached egg and grain mustard sauce (£11.75) – a rewarding and classic combination – or rare grilled tuna with sauce vierge and sautéed ratte potatoes (£13.50). The meat is carefully chosen here and when not from rare breed animals is usually well aged – try the ribeye steak, with horseradish mash and Bourguignonne sauce (£14.25). Puddings are worth saving room for. There's chocolate tart with blood orange sorbet (£4.75), rhubarb crumble with vanilla sauce (£4.50), or a selection of cheeses from Neal's Yard dairy, London's premier English cheesemonger (£5.50).

The wine list is divided by type – "zesty", "aromatic", "light and fruity", and so on – which helps match wine with food. Lunch specials get you two courses for £12.50 from the set menu, and there is an "Early Bird" deal served Monday to Friday (£15 for three courses; you have to be out by 9pm). A three-course Sunday lunch will set you back £16.50.

The Asparagus

1–13 Falcon Rd, SW11   ☏020 7801 0046

This is a large, comfortable, no-music pub with lots of nooks and corners and an unusually large drinks selection. In addition to Boddingtons, Theakston and Shepherd Neame's Spitfire on tap, you can taste a number of guest ales including Everard's Tiger and the Hop Back Brewery's Summer Lightning. The wine selection is also better than average. Popular with a mixed crowd of regulars and Real Ale aficionados.

Jack Beard's "The Crown"

102 Lavender Hill, SW11   ☏020 7228 8215

Reputedly the only real pub left on Lavender Hill, The Crown has been sympathetically updated with scrubbed tables and pine chairs. There's a pavement patio, too, and in addition to Courage Best a number of guest ales for the predominantly local regulars.

The Legless Ladder

339 Battersea Park Rd, SW11☏020 7622 2112

An ultra-friendly bar with long communal tables and benches to ensure mixing and matching. The bar staff encourage this and claim to chat to anything that moves. Greene King IPA, Young's Special and Shepherd Neame's Spitfire on tap. And do ask about the cat.

The Prince Albert

85 Albert Bridge Rd, SW11   ☏020 7228 0923

With its old prints, panels, mirrors and frosted glass, this traditional pub captures a real Victorian drinking house atmosphere. Its regulars seem to use it as a second home, enjoying Guinness, Fosters and Beck's on draught. There's a patio beer garden and no music.

The Puzzle

47–49 Lavender Hill, SW11   ☏020 7978 7682

A strict over-21s policy belies the ethos of this light, open, blond-wood bar – with its giant Connect 4 and Jenga games, board games and table football, it's actually for big kids. Bottled beers and alco-pops are the favourites with the youngish crowd.

The Victoria

166 Queenstown Rd, SW8   ☏020 7622 4117

Mr Steve Doubtfire runs the Vic with friendly concern for his customers' well-being. It's a straightforward, comfortable local with a warmer than average welcome for strangers from a landlord blessed with a sense of humour. Courage Best is the signature ale on tap.

Brixton
& Camberwell

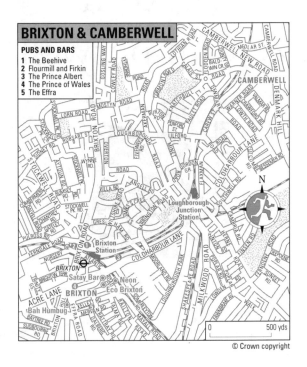

BRIXTON & CAMBERWELL

PUBS AND BARS
1 The Beehive
2 Flourmill and Firkin
3 The Prince Albert
4 The Prince of Wales
5 The Effra

© Crown copyright

Bah Humbug

The Crypt, St Matthews Church, Brixton Hill, SW2 ©020 7738 3184	⊖ Brixton
Mon–Fri 5pm–midnight, Sat 11am–midnight,	
Sun 11am–11.30pm	Mastercard, Switch, Visa
www.bahhumbug.co.uk	

Bah Humbug is underneath an active church. Hardened Presbyterians may feel a little peculiar eating, drinking and making merry below a place of worship, but there are more reasons for visiting than sheer perversity. Its subterranean location makes it naturally atmospheric, and the large space, divided by low vaults, feels remarkably intimate. There are comfortable sofas and chairs at the entrance, with a selection of newspapers to choose from, and the dining area is given a distinctly Gothic feel by velvet and tapestry. But there are no Goths here: just friendly, laid-back staff and people out to enjoy themselves.

The menu is mostly vegetarian, with a fish dish here and there. Die-hard carnivores may be disappointed, but the choice is innovative and interesting enough to satisfy everyone else. You could start with pumpkin and almond roulade with fresh basil pesto and cream cheese filling (£3.90), or perhaps deep-fried risotto cake with green chilli, leek and pine nuts served on coriander, red onion, chilli and lemon salsa (£3.90). Then progress through a selection of savoury crêpes (made with organic ingredients and, apparently, love). These are filled with interesting mixtures like refried beans, cheddar cheese and spring onions with tomato and coriander salsa (£5.80). There is a selection of main courses as well – poached organic salmon on a dill potato rosti with celeriac cream sauce (£12.90), and organic aubergine with wild ceps, smoked French garlic, and potato Dauphinoise (£9.60). Puds are simple but good, leading with a range of sweet crêpes (£3.80–£4.10).

At the weekend, Bah Humbug does a serious brunch. The perceptive set breakfasts are given appropriate titles, from the "somnambulist" (£7), which includes eggs Florentine, a cup of Horlicks and freshly squeezed lettuce and mango juice, to the "hedonist" (£11.60), which consists of buck's fizz, kedgeree and croissants, a cappuccino, and fresh strawberries and chocolate fondue.

Eco Brixton

4 Market Row, Brixton Market, Electric Row, SW9 ©020 7738 3021	⊖ Brixton
Mon, Tues & Thurs–Sat 8.30am–5pm	Mastercard, Visa

If you're in Brixton around noon, Eco (formerly Pizzeria Franco) is a must for your lunch break. Make your way to Brixton Market – London's first market with electric light – and don't be put off by the smell from the fishmonger's shop opposite. Once inside Eco, the whiff soon gives way to more appetising wafts of cooked cheese and coffee from your neighbour's table. Peruse the menu while you queue among the trailing shoppers, be prepared to share your table, then sit down to perhaps the best pizza in South London. Pizzeria Franco, now technically Eco Brixton, has the same menu as its sister, Eco on Clapham High Street (p.373), but this one closes at 5pm. It's small and popular, so things can get hectic. Still, the service is friendly, the pizzas crisp, the salads mountainous. Plus there is an identical takeaway menu, at the same prices.

All the famous pizzas are here: pleasingly pungent Napolitana (£5.50) with the sacred trio of anchovies, olives and capers; or quattro stagioni (£6.50), packed full of goodies. But why not try something less familiar, such as coriander-topped roasted red pepper and aubergine (£6.30) or enjoy la dolce vita (£6.50), where rocket, mushrooms and dolcelatte all vie for attention; or even the amore (£6.30), with its French beans, artichoke, pepper and aubergine? Or one of the calzone (all £6.70)? It's a difficult choice. For a lighter meal – lighter only because of the absence of carbohydrate – try a salad. Tricolore (£5.90) is made with baby mozzarella, beef tomato, avocado and olives, while antipasto pancetta (£7.80) includes avocado, prawns, chicken, buffalo mozzarella, pancetta and artichoke. Side orders like the melted cheese bread (£3.10) and mushroom bread (£3.50) are highly recommended, but be warned – one size fits two. For a quick sandwich, Eco also wins out; its focaccia are stuffed with delights like Parma ham and rocket (£5.90) or chicken and barbecue ham (£5.50).

You could also go for starters, but at lunchtime they seem a little surplus to requirements. There are just eight options, ranging from avocado vinaigrette (£3.60) to seafood salad (£4.90). Puddings are even fewer: pecan pie (£3.20), tiramisù (£3.50) and profiteroles (£3.20). As you'd expect from an Italian place, the coffee is good.

Neon

71 Atlantic Rd, SW9 ℂ020 7738 6576	⊖ Brixton
Mon–Fri 5.30pm–midnight, Sat 11.30am–midnight	Mastercard, Switch, Visa

Neon seems a strange name for this bar/restaurant – its signage is neon-free, as is the whole of the interior. In fact, both interior and exterior are remarkably dimly lit. So walk up Atlantic Street, past the debris left after the day's trading at Brixton Market, and look out for Neon on your left. You'll be greeted by a friendly, laid-back guy who'll lead you through the deep-red reception into the minimalist dining area, all black and white with a huge monochrome painting on one wall. Seating is on black lacquer benches; tables are black lacquer also.

The food menu, which changes every fortnight, offers a range of Italianate flavours. It's short, but the expediency of serving salads and pastas in two different sizes, starter and main, serves to bulk it out. Food here is more like good home cooking than fancy cheffy stuff. But occasionally that's exactly what you want, and at these prices it's fine. Dishes are no more or less than as described – bruschetta with grilled vegetables and smoked Provola cheese (£3.90) is toast covered with vegetables and melted cheese and a salad of rocket with walnuts. Taleggio cheese and pears (£3.80 starter, £5.80 main) could benefit from a touch of pepping up, but still passes muster. Pastas (£4.20–£4.40 starter, £6.20–£6.40 main) are cooked al dente and come with a variety of sauces. Main courses are simple but classic – chicken with olives and Marsala wine (£7.20), swordfish and rocket with parsley dressing (£7.40), aubergines with Parmesan cheese (£6.80). There's a bargain to be had in their excellent prosecco valdobiadenne at £13.90 a bottle, but beer drinkers find themselves with much more choice.

If you're quick off the mark, you can be part of the decision-making process at Neon – they hold free food tastings every evening before 7pm, when the chef tries out new dishes for forthcoming menus. History doesn't relate, however, if you would be in line for a refund should one of the experiments underperform.

Satay Bar

450 Coldharbour Lane, SW9 ℡020 7326 5001   ⊖ Brixton

Mon–Thurs noon–3pm & 6–11.30pm, Fri & Sat noon–2am,

Sun 1pm–midnight   All major credit cards

www.sataybar.co.uk

The Satay Bar, part of the regeneration of the heart of Brixton, is tucked away behind the Ritzy cinema. First impression of this lively restaurant and bar is one of fun, pure and simple. The term "laid-back" could have been invented for this place; the interior is dark and warm and the non-stop party atmosphere is bolstered by the thumping beat of the background music. Settle in, relax and take a look at the art. If you happen to like one of the many paintings adorning the walls, buy it; the restaurant doubles as a gallery for local talent, with exhibitions changing fortnightly.

Dishes are Indonesian with the chilli factor toned down (for the most part) to accommodate European taste buds. The menu is a testing one – at least when it comes to pronouncing the names of the dishes – but the food is well cooked, service is friendly and efficient and the prices are reasonable. Your waiter will smile benignly at your attempt to say udang goreng tepung (£5.95) – a delicious starter of lightly battered, deep-fried king prawns served with a sweet chilli sauce. Obvious choices, such as the chicken or prawn satay (£5.25), are rated by some as the best in London; or try the chicken wings (£4.45) with garlic and green chilli – no less appealing. The hottest dishes are to be found in the curry section. The medium kari ikan (£5.25), a salmon-based, Javanese fish curry, packs a punch even in its "medium" incarnation, while the ren-dang ayam (£5.25), a spicy chicken dish, is only cooled somewhat by the addition of a coconut sauce. For something lighter, the mee goreng (£4.45) is a satisfying dish of spicy egg noodles fried with seafood and vegetables; or there's gado-gado (£4.25), a side dish of bean curd and vegetables with spicy peanut sauce, which is almost a meal in itself.

If terminal indecision sets in and you find yourself pinned by the menu like a rabbit in the headlights, try the rijstafel (£11.95 per person, mini-mum order for two), a combination of seven specially selected dishes. This has a vegetarian option.

The Beehive

407–409 Brixton Rd, SW9   ©020 7738 3643

This bright and cheery Wetherspoons pub greets a very mixed crowd of market traders, shoppers and local residents. There's a chatty buzz and everyone seems to know everyone else. Guest ales include Rebellion Springer and Hayes Clever Endeavour as well as favourites like Theakston's Best. There's also a no-smoking area.

The Effra

38a Kellett Rd, SW2   ©020 7274 4180

A friendly local pub with real life and soul, as well as a relaxed and welcoming atmosphere. Favourites on tap are Red Stripe lager, Bass Red Triangle and Young's Bitter. In addition to good background music, there's live jazz on Thursday and Sunday.

Flourmill & Firkin

442–444 Brixton Rd, SW9   ©020 7737 4892

A huge barn of a place, this scrubbed wood and pine venue attracts a younger table football and mixer drinks crowd. It's roomy enough to get lost in, but fills up in the evenings. You'll find Marstons Pedigree, Wadworth's 6X and Bass Red Triangle on tap, but vodka and Red Bull are more the order of the day.

The Prince Albert

418 Coldharbour Lane, SW9 ©020 7274 3771

A very mixed crowd frequents this nicely modernised pub. It's long and narrow, with a cheery, welcoming feel. There's a small beer garden and a tucked-away pool table. Favourites on tap include Flowers Original, Whitbread Poacher and Hoegaarden White.

The Prince of Wales

467 Brixton Rd, SW9   ©020 7501 9061

The hip club flyers stacked by the door tell you that this is a younger and noisier than average venue. It's big, dark and comfortable by day, but gets very lively at night with techno DJs on Friday and Saturday until 1am. Favourites on tap include Staropramen, Grolsch, Carling and Fuller's London Pride.

SOUTH

Clapham
& Wandsworth

CLAPHAM & WANDSWORTH

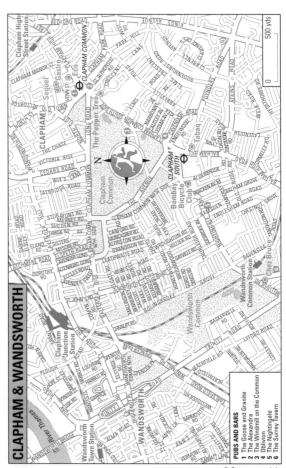

PUBS AND BARS
1 The Goose and Granite
2 The Alexandra
3 The Windmill on the Common
4 Oblivion
5 The Nightingale
6 The Surrey Tavern

© Crown copyright

Bombay Bicycle Club

95 Nightingale Lane, SW12 ©020 8673 6217	⊖ Clapham South
Mon–Sat 7–11pm	All major credit cards

Local estate agents talk lovingly of the "Nightingale Triangle" – that ever-so-select group of properties just off Clapham Common – and the residents probably acknowledge the Bombay Bicycle Club as one of the assets which helps justify the properties' premium prices. This establishment is not a typical curry house. It is light, airy and chic, and a glimpse of the vast bowl of white lilies in the centre of the room would make any upmarket florist rub their hands with glee. More importantly, the food is not run-of-the-mill, either. The menu changes regularly – classics are adapted, cultures mixed, liberties taken. Generally most of it works, and stylish food tallies with a stylish setting. This is not a cheap Indian restaurant, but nobody seems to mind – after all, it is in the "Nightingale Triangle"!

The starters range from the straightforward – vegetable pakora (£4); lamb samosa (£4) – to the more complex, like a brochette of monkfish cooked in the tandoor (£6.50). Tellicherry squid (£4.75) is a good opening move, sliced thin and fried crisp with a good dipping sauce. You can also get shish kebab Khybari (£4.50) and Cochin rajah prawns (£9.50), king prawns with garlic and butter. On to main course dishes. There's a Calicut fish curry (£9.50) and another interesting dish called gosht kata masala (£8), with a sauce made with onions, garlic, ginger, and garam masala. Or murgh Mangalore (£8) – a curry flavoured with aniseed and cardamom, which can be served with extra chilli on request. Or try a vegetarian dish. As well as a simple mixed vegetable curry (£8), there is a vegetable dopieaza, a veg selection in a light sauce with yoghurt and coriander (£8). Rice is basmati, but too pricey at "£3.75, serves two". "Daal of the day" is expensive, too, at £4.50, but the tarka daal made with whole pulses is certainly good. There is also a specials menu, which lists dishes that are even more closely tied to seasonal availability – something that is always to be commended. Breads are hot and good.

The wine list is long, well chosen, and takes a fearful hammering – empty wine bottles must mount up by the skipload. But then Bombay Bicycle Club isn't your usual Indian.

CLAPHAM & WANDSWORTH ⓣ FRENCH

Chez Bruce

2 Bellevue Rd, SW17 ⓒ020 8672 0114   BR Wandsworth Common

Mon–Thurs noon–2pm & 7–10.15pm, Fri & Sat 12.30–2.30pm

& 6.30–10.30pm, Sun 12.30–3pm   All major credit cards

When a restaurant gets its first Michelin star (as Bruce Poole's comfortable little restaurant in Wandsworth did in 1999) the regular customers who have been studiously keeping the place a secret cannot help but shudder. What will become of their favourite? Will the dishes grow more fancy? Will the number of small fiddly in-between courses multiply? In short, will the kitchen set off after a second and third star and leave behind everything that has made the place so outstanding? Good news. Chez Bruce is still delivering honest, unfussy, earthy, richly flavoured food. It is old-fashioned food, which avoids the latest gastro-trend, and often features the likes of pig's trotters, and rabbit, and mackerel. Dishes are sometimes rather laconically described on the menu. It is also a real bargain. The star has made one difference, however: the wine list has been extended and refined and is now winning prizes of its own. Prix fixe three-course menus offer lunch for £21.50 (Sun £23.50), and dinner for £25.

The menu changes from season to season and day to day. Generally, the lunch menu is a shortened version of the dinner menu. The kind of starters you can expect are cream of asparagus soup, or foie gras and chicken liver parfait with toasted brioche, or terrine of smoked and cured fish with beetroot and horseradish. Or there might be a classic lurking, perhaps vitello tonnato. Main course dishes are deeply satisfying. You could well find rump of lamb with galette Sarladaise, ratatouille and aioli, or roast cod with olive oil mashed potatoes, or roast belly of pork with crackling, lentils, girolles and salsa verde, or roast pigeon with fondant potato, mushroom duxelle and Madeira sauce. This is one of those places where everything on the menu tempts. It is also one of the last strongholds of offal (perhaps the reason why this restaurant is the favourite haunt of so many off-duty chefs?). Look out for sweetbreads, or perhaps calves' liver served with spinach and ricotta ravioli, sage beurre noisette and Madeira jus.

The sweets here are well-executed classics: proper crème brûlée, clafoutis of plums with clotted cream, tarte Tatin aux poires. No wonder Chez Bruce is booked every evening well in advance. Go for lunch instead – it'll make your day.

Eco

162 Clapham High St, SW4 ✆020 7978 1108   ⊖ Clapham Common

Mon–Fri noon–4pm & 6.30–11pm (11.30pm Fri),

Sat noon–5pm & 6–11.30pm, Sun noon–5pm & 6–11pm   All major credit cards

Eco is a seriously modern, seriously trendy pizzeria. It is a designer place: all sinuous curved wrought iron, simple banquettes, and a lot of plain wood. But for all that, it is friendly and welcoming. There's a pizza of the day written up on a big board and they do not blench when families turn up for lunch with a toddler in tow. In the evenings, however, things get a good deal more fashion-oriented and the music quite a bit louder. On the menu you'll find a note setting out an interesting approach to the lingering problem of table turning. Each party, it says, gets the use of the table for "an hour and a half" and if you want to take more time than that you have to prearrange things with the manager. Quite clever, that.

The whole operation, in fact, is a thoughtful one. There's a short list of starters – perhaps a tomato and anchovy salad (£4.50) – then pizzas, focaccia, calzone, oven-baked dishes and salads. Though they do a few pastas, most dishes go through the ovens, which makes a lot of sense – there are baked lemongrass prawns (£4.90) or goats' cheese and aubergine (£5.30). The pizzas come both classic – Margherita (£4.95), quattro formaggi (£6.90), American hot with pepperami (£5.80), quattro stagione with artichoke, ham, mushrooms, olives and anchovies (£6.90) – and not so classic – amore with roast red pepper and green beans (£6.90), smoked salmon and spinach (£7.90), La Dolce Vita, rocket and mushrooms (£6.90), and aubergine and sun-dried tomato (£6.20). They are all generous-sized, freshly cooked, and well made. Delicious, in a word. The focaccia are good, too: sandwiches made with pizza bread, and including simple favourites like mozzarella and avocado (£5.90), or Parma ham and rocket (£6.50). Then there are the calzone, which are a kind of folded-up pizza: tradizionale (£6.90) combines ham, artichoke, mushrooms, mozzarella, olive oil, garlic and herbs. But with pizzas as good as these, why fold them up?

Eco's coffee is good, too, and the puddings simple but satisfying – like tiramisù (£4.20) or raspberry chocolate truffle (£4.50).

£13–£18

Gastro

67 Venn St, SW4 ©020 7627 0222   ⊖ Clapham Common

Daily 8am–midnight   Cash or cheque only

You're not allowed to book at this attractive little bistro off Clapham Common and, somewhat annoyingly, they restrict the tables at the front to parties of four and regulars. So if there are just two of you, you are likely to be shown through to the corridor-like room on the side or to places at the communal table at the back. Cheer up, though – the big table is a jolly affair. You will be able to see what everybody else orders, which always helps when trying to make up your own mind, and you will have a perfect view of the kitchen, a room so small that the mind boggles at the thought of producing dinner for eight in there, let alone for a restaurantful. It also means that you don't have to try and resist the fantastic-looking French patisserie – the likes of tarte aux fraises or bavarois vanille et cassis – on offer at the bar counter. These are cunningly priced at £1.75 during the day and £3.95 in the evening.

The staff are French and the menu lists all the Gallic favourites. Judging by the mistranslations, it was obviously written by a Frenchman. The food is inexpensive and generously portioned. Think yourself back to your last French holiday and enjoy. There are oysters sold in sixes (95p each), an assiette de charcuterie (£6.45), or moules à la marinière (£5.95) to start; lapin chasseur (£9.85) and andouillette grillée (£7.45) to follow. The fish soup (£3.95) arrives steaming, with all the trimmings. A pissaladière (£3.95), the traditional southern tart of onions, olives and anchovies, comes with crumbly, perfectly cooked pastry that looks and tastes as though they make it themselves, though, given the size of the kitchen, it would seem unlikely. Perhaps a plain entrecôte (£11.75) tempts? Or half a lobster (£16.95)? And there is always "Confit de canard, haricot en salade" (£10.95), which is as good and as simple as it sounds.

House wine is served by the glass, carafe and bottle. The red is better than the white, but not by much. If funds are sufficient, delve further into the short list of five whites and five reds, or do the sensible thing and order a bottle of top-class French cider (£6.25).

The Pepper Tree

19 Clapham Common South Side, SW4 ©020 7622 1758	⊖ Clapham Common
Mon noon–3pm & 6–10.30pm, Tues–Sat noon–3pm & 6–11pm,	
Sun noon–10.30pm	Mastercard, Visa

Situated on the seemingly endless south side of the Common, just a stone's throw from the tube station, this open-fronted Thai eatery serves no-nonsense, short-order dishes. This kind of spicy Thai food is perfectly in tune with the clientele, which is predominantly made up of twenty-somethings – as will be instantly apparent from both the crowds and the hubbub. 1999 saw a thorough refurbishment here, and resulted in new loos, bar, floor, lighting and tables. Thankfully, the food is still well cooked in a pleasantly straightforward sort of way and prices have not risen unduly.

You can build your meal in stages, rather like you would a Greek meze. Vegetable rolls (£2.25) are made with vermicelli noodles, shaved carrots and Chinese mushrooms wrapped in filo pastry. Egg-fried rice (£1.75), is just that; or there's a stir-fry of mixed seafood (£4.50), which is tossed with fresh chillies, garlic and sweet basil. Green prawn curry (£3.95) is simmered in coconut milk with Thai aubergines, lime leaves and sweet basil, and comes medium-hot. Big tum chicken noodles (£4.75) are thick, yellow and fried with chillies and sweet basil. Among the salads, the Pepper Tree (£3.95) combines marinated grilled slices of beef with lemon juice, coriander, spring onions and chilli. Many dishes use the same ingredients but ring the changes in terms of balance and preparation techniques. Sweet things include stem ginger ice cream (£1.95) and bananas in coconut milk (£2.50) sprinkled with sesame seeds. Sticky rice with mango (£2.50) is described on the menu as mango with sticky rice, which seems a model of accuracy.

The Pepper Tree churns out simple spicy food, which is distributed by cheerful staff and sold at affordable prices. Even the drinks are reasonable – you can get a mug of tea for under a quid, and there are bottles of house reds and whites at £7.95. There's also Argentine Norton Merlot (£11.95), which is a real bargain.

Sequel

4 Venn St, SW4 ✆020 7622 4222	⊖ Clapham Common
Mon–Fri 6–11.30pm, Sat 10.30am–4.30pm & 6–11.30pm,	
Sun 11.30am–5.30pm	All major credit cards

Venn Street seems to have turned itself into something of a gastronomic Mecca in Clapham, and Sequel, one of the latest to join its ranks, is already proving to be a hit. If you arrive for an early dinner, you'll find the place a little quiet, but the place hots up as the evening moves on. There's a pleasant bar at the front of the premises, but for dinner you should make your way to the back where you'll find a small mezzanine restaurant area.

The food is of the modern eclectic variety, with plenty of lateral thinking and fusion ideas. Fusion food may have fallen from the very pinnacle of fashion, but when it's done well, as it is here, it's worth seeking out. The menu is divided by price, with two dishes at £4.50, one at £5, two at £5.50 and so on, right up to £12.50, and there is no distinction between expensive small dishes and inexpensive larger ones. If you are in any doubt the staff, who are very keen to talk about the food, will be happy to help. There are nineteen dishes in all, with flavours and ideas imported from around the world. Some are simple, based on classics – roasted nashi pear with Parma ham-wrapped cashel blue cheese and honey mustard dressing (£5.50) – but most are a little more complicated. Try the adobo-rubbed tiger prawns with mizuna, feta, chickpeas and avocado salsa (£7). The kitchen has searched hard for unusual ingredients: paperbark-roasted Northern albacore, green mango pickle (£11), arborio-crusted shark with lemon conserve (£10.50). In other hands these dishes could be disappointing, but here they work, for the most part, very well. There may be the odd dish that isn't ideal – too rich or too spicy for its main ingredient – but they are mostly good, original and interesting, showing passion and enthusiasm.

There are only about thirty seats in the restaurant, so you'd be wise to book. Should you arrive before your companions (or become bored with them) you can gaze upon the large screen above the bar, which shows classic movies – Life is Beautiful, Rear Window etc – with the sound down.

Tabaq

47 Balham Hill, SW12 ©020 8673 7820   ⊖ Clapham South

Mon–Sat noon–2.45pm & 6pm–midnight   All major credit cards

www.tabaq.co.uk

The owners of Tabaq used to drive up from the suburbs to work in a smart West End restaurant. On the way they would travel up Balham Hill and past Clapham Common. They had set their sights on having a restaurant of their own – a restaurant where they would serve traditional Pakistani specialities. So, when signs went up outside 47 Balham Hill they took the plunge. They named their restaurant after the tabaq – a large serving dish – and set about dishing up authentic Lahori fare. Plaudits soon arrived: in 1998 they won the Best Pakistani Restaurant in the UK and National Curry Chef awards.

The menu comes with a multitude of sections – appetisers, grills, seafood, curries, specialities, rice, breads, vegetables, plus another sheet of "cuisine specials" – chicken, lamb, side orders, charga. Best not to worry about the soups and appetisers. Go instead straight for the tandoor and grill section, which features some of the best dishes on the menu. Seek kabab Lahori (£5.50) is made from well-seasoned minced lamb, and shish kabab lamb (£5.50) is delicious. The king-size prawns cost £10 for five, and if you find yourself wondering whether any prawn could be worth £2 you should try them. As an accompaniment order raita (£1.95), yoghurt with cucumber, herbs and spices, and maybe a naan-e-Punjabi (£2), heavy, butter-rich bread from the tandoor, with kachomer (£1.95), a kind of coarse-cut Asian salsa. At this stage of your meal you may well be tempted to simply order more grills or charga dishes. If you don't succumb, try palak gosht (£6.50), lamb with spinach, or gurda masala (£6.50), a dish of lambs' kidneys, or the ultra-mild murgh moglai (£6.50).

Charga dishes are a speciality here. They are cooked using a "steam roasting" technique peculiar to Lahore, in which the meat goes on a platform over a water tray and then into the oven. The meat retains more moisture cooked this way – and it's a healthy option, too, producing less fat. Choose from charga kababs (£5.50), a whole chicken (takes 30min, £13), or a leg of lamb (24hrs notice, £35).

The Alexandra

14 Clapham Common South Side,
SW4   ✆020 7627 5102

Pine-clad pub decorated with an entertaining mish-mash of advertising signs, junk and ephemera. The youngish crowd enjoy Fosters and Kronenbourg 1664 on tap, along with a good range of wines and alco-pops.

The Goose & Granite

196–198 Clapham High St,
SW4   ✆020 7498 4931

Stones Bitter at bargain basement prices makes this a very popular venue. You can get Fuller's London Pride and Bass Red Triangle, too. It's a roomy and comfortable old pub with several bars and lots of comfy nooks and corners. The exterior is mock Tudor and there's a huge beer garden at the back with elegant herbaceous borders. One of the bars has a conservatory glass roof, and is bathed in an appealing yellow glow.

The Nightingale

97 Nightingale Lane, SW12   ✆020 8673 1637

This small, cosy local is welcoming and comfortable. But it's the sheltered and heated back garden, and the hop-decorated conservatory, which guarantee its popularity. That and the fact it's a Young's pub with the whole range of Young's bottled beers: Acclaim, Ram Rod, Extra Light, Light Ale, Double Chocolate and Special London Ale, as well as the ales on tap.

Oblivion

7–8 Cavendish Parade, SW4 ✆020 8772 0303

Outside, giant blue lamps and a pavement patio beckon. Inside, Gothic sculptures and broken mirrors welcome a young and noisy crowd for the £10 per jug Happy Hour cocktails (which are called things like Woo Woo, or Bacon and Tomato Sandwich). There are live DJs Thursday through Saturday, and twenty shooters at £2.50 a pop.

The Surrey Tavern

226 Trinity Rd, SW17   ✆020 8672 5880

A great place to stop for refreshment after a walk on the common, this big, traditional corner pub hosts a mixed crowd of sports and pool fans. Sky TV and three pool tables keep them happy. There is pavement seating in summer, and strict prohibitions on taking your beer glass across to the common. Favourite drinks are Boddingtons and Guinness.

The Windmill on the Common

Clapham Common South Side,
SW4   ✆020 8673 4578

The Windmill, right on the common, has three huge bars. It's traditional in feel with carpets, leaded lights and a beer garden. Young's Bitter, Special and AAA are the favourites on tap, and there is a very good wine selection, which may have something to do with the fact that the place is also a hotel and a restaurant.

Greenwich
& Blackheath

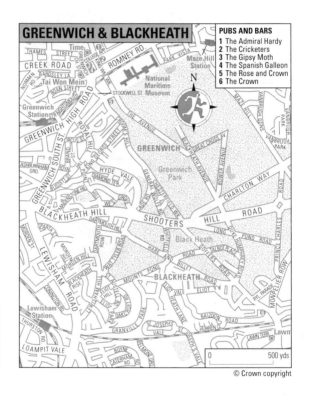

GREENWICH & BLACKHEATH

PUBS AND BARS
1 The Admiral Hardy
2 The Cricketers
3 The Gipsy Moth
4 The Spanish Galleon
5 The Rose and Crown
6 The Crown

© Crown copyright

Lawn

1 Lawn Terrace, SE3 ⓒ020 7379 0724	BR Blackheath

Mon–Thurs 6–10.30pm, Fri 6–11pm, Sat 11am–2.30pm & 6–11pm,

Sun 11.30am–5.30pm All major credit cards

www.lawnrestaurant.com

Lawn is to be found on the premises of an old print works. The presses and inks have long gone, but the austere brick exterior, exposed beams and pipework give clues to its past. The restaurant is located upstairs, along with a bar and greeting area, and the industrial decor is enlivened by aquatic blue walls and blond-wood floors. Dining is loosely divided into three zones: there's the main restaurant, and two smaller semi-private areas in an atrium and a mezzanine level. The high ceilings and vault-like feel make the main dining area seem noisy but this adds to the buzzy ambience. This is Greenwich's trendiest restaurant, and the long menu brings with it strong echoes of the Bank group (see p.31) of which Lawn is now a part.

The menu changes slightly every two to three weeks but maintains a modern European feel. You'll find starters from all over – fish soup with croutons and rouille (£4.50), smoked salmon platter (£8.50), duck terrine with apple and plum chutney (£7.50), rocket with Parmesan and roast cherry tomatoes (£5.95) – along with the likes of crab linguine (£8.50/£11.50), or Thai spiced fish and crab cakes with sweet chilli sauce (£6.50). Main courses are reassuringly solid, with dishes such as grilled ribeye, sauce Béarnaise and fat chips (£15.50), chicken breast, bubble and squeak, and green mustard sauce (£10.50), and, reflecting the Bank group's fishy heritage, fish and chips with tartare sauce (£12.95). Puddings are creative – pistachio crème brûlée (£4.50), say, or lemon and lime baba with a vanilla yoghurt sorbet (£4.50). The comprehensive wine list gives good descriptions by weight and taste, with prices to suit all pockets. There's a bustling brunch at the weekends, and a good-value set lunch and "early" dinner – two courses £11.95 and three for £15.50.

In its previous incarnation – pre-takeover it was known as One Lawn Terrace – Lawn was one of the sharp new arrivals south of the river. Happily the advent of big business and the stock-exchange-friendly Bank group has not spoilt the place.

Tai Won Mein

49 Greenwich Church St, SE10 ©020 8858 1668   ⊖ Cutty Sark Gardens

Daily 11.30am–11.30pm   Cash or cheque only

With the masts of the tea clipper *Cutty Sark* providing an impressive backdrop, Tai Won Mein's simple signs urge you to "eat fast food" – and the stark interior with its long, low benches reinforces the message. But, while quality is often sacrificed for speed of service, that is certainly not the case here, probably because the menu is so well tailored to the demands made on it. Good-quality food, together with extraordinarily reasonable prices, mean that this place is always busy. Not quite Japanese subway-type busy, but at the weekend, when the nearby markets are in full swing, you must expect to wait for a seat. This will give you a chance to get to know your prospective table-neighbour while you queue. Hang on in there – it is all well worth it.

Table decoration is sparse and your placemat doubles as the menu. Starters include spring rolls (£3.10) and fried spare ribs (£3.10). Make sure you ask for the chilli sauce. Main courses are divided into rice, noodles and ho fun (which are a kind of ribbon-like noodle, flatter and softer than the usual); the noodle section is then subdivided into fried noodles and soup noodles. The house special soup noodle (£3.65) is served in an enormous bowl, a steaming vat of egg, prawn, beef, squid, crabmeat, mussels, fresh greens and, finally, noodles. Less colourful, but certainly no less satisfying, is pork with noodles in soup (£3.10). The fried noodle dishes are equally imposing – huge plates piled high with such delights as mixed seafood (£3.65). Then there's ho fun with king prawn in soup with vegetables (£3.65), and fried ho fun with roast pork and duck (£3.65). Rice dishes – chicken with curry sauce (£3.10) or ribs with black bean sauce (£3.10) – are equally popular. Sadly, Tai Won Mein is a pudding-free zone.

You can wash down the main courses with Sapporo (£2.80), a crisp Japanese beer. For the health-conscious how about the mixed fruit juice (£1.50) – a blend of apple, orange and carrot. Looks odd, tastes great, but did Brussels make the carrot a fruit without telling us?

Time

7a College Approach, SE10 ©020 8305 9767   ⊖ Cutty Sark Gardens

Mon–Fri noon–2.30pm & 7–10.30pm, Sat 7–11pm All major credit cards except Diners

www.timerestaurant.com

A boatswain's hail from the Cutty Sark, and anywhere within range of the Dome, is not promising territory for a food lover – this is tourist terrain, where the restaurants don't need to work very hard to pull in the punters. Thankfully, Time is an exception. First impressions are no great shakes, mind you – beyond the impressive doorway, entrance is gained up a flight of insignificant stairs to the right. And when you reach the first level, you'll be confronted with a noisy bar with little sign of dining. But simply glance onwards and upwards, and you will see a dining room above. Work your way to the back of the bar and up another set of stairs, and you'll suddenly feel very comfortable. Here is a small (just 35 or so seats), appealing dining room, with roomy tables and an elegant clientele over-looking the merry mayhem below.

The menu is not a long one, with just eight starters and eight main courses, but it offers plenty of choice, celebrating flavours borrowed from around the world. The tariff is set at £23.50 for three courses and £19.50 for two. First courses vary from smoked haddock and baby leek terrine with coriander and lemongrass relish to an interesting and well-constructed salad of duck confit with celeriac and light chilli plum sauce. On the way you might find a competent Puy lentil and oyster mushroom salad with grilled peppered goats' cheese. Main courses range from a stalwart roast salmon with mixed seafood risotto and parsley sauce to the more unusual Szechwan rack of lamb flavoured with lemongrass and served with a lemon-scented jus. Among each eight choices are two vegetarian options; these are well thought out and more interesting than the norm. Expensive ingredients are littered throughout – truffles, foie gras and langoustine all make an appearance. Portions are generous but not oppressively so. Desserts are substantial rather than froufrou.

Visit mid-week, and you'll probably be entertained by some light jazz, but whether there is music playing or not you'll find the place both friendly and lively, and the service agreeable. Booking is essential.

The Admiral Hardy

7 College Approach, SE10   ©020 8858 6452

One of Greenwich's quieter pubs, this Free House backs onto the covered market and offers a great range of guest specialist Real Ales in addition to many flavoured vodkas. Expect names like Eccleshaw's High Duck, Blakeney's No 1 and the locally brewed O'Hanlon's.

The Cricketers

22 King William Walk, SE10   ©020 8858 3630

An old-fashioned local, the Cricketers has somehow managed to retain a haven-like atmosphere in the tourist storm. It's cosy and relaxing, with a good range of beers including Toby and Brain's Bitters, Worthington Draught, Marstons Pedigree and a number of guest ales.

The Crown

49 Tranquil Vale, SE3   ©020 8852 0326

You get pavement tables, a view of Blackheath and a well-kept traditional atmosphere in this T & J Bernard pub. There's also a no-quibble replacement policy for the many Real Ales on offer. Expect to find specials like Brain's The Rev James Ale and Hardy and Hansons Vintage 1832 Ale in addition to Greene King IPA and Abbot.

The Gipsy Moth

60 Greenwich Church St, SE10   ©020 885 0786

With a view of the Cutty Sark and the river itself, this nautically themed pub attracts its fair share of tourists. It's roomy and comfortable with a conservatory, beer garden and traditional pub decor. Tetley's, Adnams and Fuller's London Pride are the signature ales.

The Rose & Crown

1 Croom's Hill, SE10   ©020 8293 1898

There's been a pub here since Elizabeth I passed this way, but it's been renovated a few times since. The current incarnation has big open windows and more local regulars than many Greenwich pubs. Courage Best and Directors are the ales on tap and there's a good wine list with house champagne at £22.50.

The Spanish Galleon

48 Greenwich Church St,
SE10   ©020 8858 3664

A large, conventional Shepherd Neame pub with fewer nautical accoutrements than its name implies. The lively atmosphere attracts younger visitors as well as tourists, and it can get crowded. In addition to Bishop's Finger and Spitfire, expect to find Oranjeboom and Hurliman lagers on tap.

Kennington
& Vauxhall

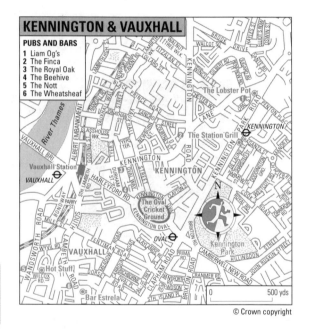

KENNINGTON & VAUXHALL

PUBS AND BARS

1 Liam Og's
2 The Finca
3 The Royal Oak
4 The Beehive
5 The Nott
6 The Wheatsheaf

© Crown copyright

Bar Estrela

111–115 South Lambeth Rd, SW8 ✆020 7793 1051   ⊖ Stockwell

Daily 8am–midnight   All major credit cards

Bar Estrela operates on various levels – literally. In the basement there are tables for football and pool, on the ground floor there's a cafe-bar and tapas counter, and on the mezzanine floor there's the restaurant. Visiting Estrela is very like being in Portugal – if you can overlook the weather and South London streets outside. The wines are Portuguese; the beers are Portuguese; and the TV is tuned to a Portuguese channel. The menu is long, and the dishes are simple, honest and . . . very Portuguese!

Start with caldo verde (£1.60) – this is the famous green cabbage soup, much enlivened here by chunks of rather good sausage, which help overcome a suspicion that it might be somewhat under-seasoned. Gambas Estrela (£4.50) make a brave attempt to impersonate the ones you enjoyed while sunning yourself on holiday. The buttery sauce is particularly good, with a touch of piri piri that makes it pleasantly spicy. Then you can choose from about forty different main courses. These include most of the Portuguese favourites – indeed, more than you'll find in most restaurants in Portugal. They do a good arroz de marisco (£9) – the Portuguese version of paella – an equally nice feijoada de marisco (£8), which is bean stew with seafood, and arroz de polvo (£7.50), a tasty dish of octopus and rice. Bacalhau con batata, grão e ovo (£7.50) is typical of the heartier main courses: set out on the plate is a chunk of cooked salt cod, a ladleful of boiled chickpeas topped with sliced raw onion, a large boiled potato and a hard-boiled egg – you make your own dressing from the oil and vinegar supplied. Or you could try the classic carne de porco a Alentejana (£7.50), a terracotta bowl filled with the surprisingly delicious combination of chunks of fried pork, fried potato and tiny clams in their shells. The portions, as in Portugal, are family-sized, and a couple of starters and one main should keep most couples happy.

The cooking at Estrela is all the better for being pleasingly unsophisticated, while the wine list allows you to conduct a masterclass in Vinho Verde – the perfect accompaniment to hearty Portuguese food. The four different ones on offer are all young, fresh and tart, and range from a wholly reasonable £11 to a bargain £8.50 a bottle.

SOUTH

Hot Stuff

19 Wilcox Rd, SW8 ℰ020 7720 1480	⊖ Vauxhall
Mon–Sat noon–10pm	Amex, Mastercard, Visa

This tiny restaurant, run by the Dawood family in south Lambeth, is something of an institution. It has only eighteen seats and offers simple and startlingly cheap food to an enthusiastic local following. The food is just what you would expect to get at home – always presuming that you live in Nairobi and are part of the Asian community. Trade is good and has been the catalyst for a refurb – the place is newly done in soft blues and greens.

The starters are sound rather than glorious, so you'll do best to dive straight into the curries. There are eight different chicken curries and nine different meat dishes – all £3 or under. The most expensive dish in the house is the king prawn biryani, which costs £6.25 – not much more than you would pay for a curried potato in the West End. It is hard to find any fault with a curry that costs just £3! The portions aren't monster-sized and the spicing isn't subtle, but the welcome is genuine and the bill is tiny – a gratifying combination. Arrive before 9.30pm and you can sample the delights of the stuffed paratha (£1), which are light and crispy with potato in the middle, and taste seriously delicious. Chickpea curry (£2.20), daal (£2.20) and mixed vegetable curry (£1.80) all hit the spot with vegetarians. For meat-eaters, the chicken Madras (£2.90) is hot and workmanlike, while the chicken bhuna (£2.95) is rich and very good. However, the jewel in the crown of the Hot Stuff menu is masala fish (£3.50), which is only available on Wednesday, Thursday and Friday. Thick chunks of tilapia are marinated for 24 hours in salt and lemon juice before being cooked in a rich sauce with tomatoes, coriander, cumin and ginger.

Hot Stuff closes prudently before the local pubs turn out, and part of the fun here is to watch latecomers – say a party of three arriving at 9.50pm – negotiating with the indomitable chef and matriarch, Beley Dawood, to secure some dinner. Promising to eat very quickly and to order only the simplest dishes seems to do the trick. This restaurant is driven by the principles of hospitality and it puts many more pretentious establishments to shame.

The Lobster Pot

3 Kennington Lane, SE11 ℡020 7582 5556   ⊖ Kennington

Tues–Sat noon–2.30pm & 7–11pm   All major credit cards

You have to feel for Nathalie Régent. What must it be like to be married to – and working alongside – a man whose love of the bizarre verges on the obsessional? Britain is famed for breeding dangerously potty chefs, but The Lobster Pot's chef-patron Hervé Régent, originally from Vannes in Brittany, is well ahead of the field. Walk down Kennington Lane towards the restaurant and it's even money as to whether you are struck first by the life-size painted plywood cutout of Hervé dressed in oilskins, or the speakers relaying a soundtrack of seagulls and melancholy Breton foghorns. Inside, portholes allow you a glimpse of swimming fish, while in the upstairs bar there's a ship's wheel to play with while you await your table.

The clues all point towards fish, and doubtless Hervé will appear to greet you in nautical garb, moustache bristling, and guide you towards his best catches of the day. The fish here is pricey but it is very fresh and very well chosen. Starters range from well-made, very thick, traditional fish soup (£6.50) to a really proper plateau de fruits de mer (small £10.50, large £21). The main course specials feature strange fish that Hervé has discovered on his early-morning wanderings at Billingsgate. Mahi mahi from the Indian Ocean might arrive in a thick tranche with a "skin" of smoked salmon, accompanied by fresh samphire (£18.50) – delicious. Simpler, and as good in its way, is la sélection de la mer à l'ail (£14.50), which is a range of fishy bits – some monkfish tail, an oyster, a bit of sole, tiny squid, and so on – all grilled and slathered in garlic butter. Or you might opt for a perfect pairing of monkfish with wild mushrooms (£16.50). The accompanying bread is notable, a soft, doughy "pain rustique", and, for once, le plateau de fromage "à la Française" (£6.50) doesn't disappoint.

The Lobster Pot's weekday set lunch for £15.50 – which could get you moules gratinées à l'ail, followed by filet de merlan sauce créole, and crêpe sauce à la mangue – makes lots of sense. And for a serious beano there is an eight-course surprise menu (three fish, one meat and so on, for £45 per person). In any case, whatever you plan on eating, do not venture here without your sense of humour.

£18–£32

The Station Grill

2 Braganza St, SE17 ©020 7735 4769	⊖ Kennington
Tues–Sat 6–10pm, Sun 12.30–2.30pm	Mastercard, Visa

In 1962 the Station Grill, a steak house, opened for business, and proceeded over the next 37 years to build up a steady trade. Then in December 1999, the proprietor's son – Erkin Mehmet – took up the baton. All change at the Station. In came a new dining room, a new kitchen and new chefs. Mehmet switched from the kitchen to front of house and the Station Grill greeted 2000 as a surprisingly good French restaurant. Erkin's new chefs spent their formative years in the kitchens of the Roux Brothers catering division, and now the Station's menu (which changes monthly) offers tasty, well-presented, "bourgeois" French food that combines two blissful attributes – really good cooking and really low prices.

The menu is broadly seasonal and very ambitious. It costs £14.95 for two courses, £19.95 for three, but it's hard to see how the prices can go on being so low when the food is this good. Astonishingly, whatever the kitchen tries for, they seem to bring it off in some style. As a starter, smoked eel and leek tartlet with olive, radish and red pepper salad is triumphant – good short pastry, rich creamy leeks, chunks of eel fillet and a salad crisp enough for contrast. The grilled fillet of mackerel with wilted red Swiss chard and dill and beetroot vinaigrette is also good, as is the ballotine of foie gras with pear chutney (£2 supplement). Main courses are also stellar, and everything looks really elegant on large white plates. Confit duck leg (delicious, ungreasy, and full of flavour) may come with a perfect disc of rosti potato and a sublime mixture of cabbage, cream and bacon. Roast wood pigeon is teamed with a thyme and garlic potato cake and a white onion jus. Sautéed fillet of red snapper comes with spinach and tomato linguine and a chive cream sauce. Puddings are top-notch, too. Anyone for double baked chocolate soufflé?

Very good stuff. And even when under pressure the service never loses its smile. The people working here care. The Achilles heel is the wine list, which owes more to the steak house heritage than the splendid French food that they are serving now. Ignore it and concentrate on the food.

390

The Beehive

51 Durham St, SE11   ✆020 7582 7608

A very lively after-work crowd descends on this traditional wood-panelled pub from their offices by the river. There are two bars, pool, a secluded beer garden and Young's Bitter along with Courage Best.

The Finca

185 Kennington Lane, SE11   ✆020 7735 1061

Latin sounds and drinks are the order of the day at this lively venue. It's salsa or Gypsy Kings for the ears and Estrella, Corona, Negra Modelo and Dos Equis beers for the tongue. There are also Spanish brandies from £2.50 to £5 a shot, Spanish wines and sherries, and a happy hour from 5pm to 7pm. Keen dancers can take salsa lessons at the club upstairs.

Liam Og's

140 Newington Butts, SE1   ✆020 7735 1973

This Irish-themed, two-storey venue greets its lively, youngish crowd with a mix of good background music, Guinness, Tetley's and Calders Cream ale. There are a number of hidden nooks and crannies and "The Gods" upstairs if you crave somewhere quiet to talk and chill.

The Nott

257 Wandsworth Rd, SW8   ✆020 7720 7243

Formerly the Nottingham Castle, this Free House has been revamped to attract a younger, mixed clientele. Today it's bright and cheerful, all blond wood and cane chairs. Pool, big-screen TV and music keep the punters happy, and John Smith's, Flowers IPA and Fosters are the favourites on tap.

The Royal Oak

355 Kennington Lane, SE11   ✆020 7735 1984

Rebuilt in 1891, this ancient, tiny, corner pub offers a glimpse of what pubs used to be like. The friendly regulars have clearly enjoyed its quiet charms for many decades. Guinness and Bass Red Triangle are the favourites.

The Wheatsheaf

126 South Lambeth Rd, SE11   ✆020 7622 3602

Landlord Brian Day keeps this traditional 1800s pub in good condition for his mixed crowd of local regulars and after-work drinkers. It's friendly, but with a sharp South London attitude. Charles Wells' Bombardier, Courage Best and John Smith's on tap.

Putney

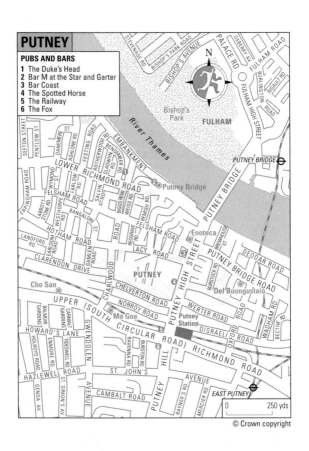

PUTNEY

PUBS AND BARS

1 The Duke's Head
2 Bar M at the Star and Garter
3 Bar Coast
4 The Spotted Horse
5 The Railway
6 The Fox

© Crown copyright

Cho-San

292 Upper Richmond Rd, SW15 ℂ020 8778 9626 | BR Putney

Tues–Fri 6.30–10.30pm,

Sat & Sun noon–2.30pm & 6.30–10.30pm | All major credit cards

Too many Japanese restaurants use extremely high prices and ultra-swish West End premises to keep themselves to themselves – as a European adventurer basking in the impeccably polite and attentive service, it's hard not to feel a little anxious. What should you order? How do you eat it? Will it taste nice? How much does it cost? If you have ever been assailed by these worries you should pop along to Cho-San in Putney. This small, unpretentious, family-run restaurant opened in 1998 and has gradually built up a mixed trade. As well as a host of knowledgeable Japanese drawn by the good fresh food and sensible prices there are interested Londoners tucking into sushi with gusto – on one occasion these devotees included a twelve-year-old girl, who, judging by her uniform, had dropped in for dinner on the way home from school.

The menu is a book. And it is one that is worth reading. This is your chance to try all those dishes you have never had, and without wounding your pocket. The sushi is good. The sashimi is good. A giant boat of assorted sushi and sashimi, with miso soup and dessert costs £15.90. But why not try some more obscure sushi? The prices of the fancy ones range from £2.60 to £5 for two pieces. Or if you prefer your fish cooked, choose the perfect cuttlefish (£5.60) – a stunning achievement, its batter light enough to levitate. And then there's always the kushiage – dishes where something is put onto a skewer, gets an egg and breadcrumb jacket and is treated to a turn around the deep-fryer. Ordering tori kushiage (£3.90) gets you two skewers, each of which holds two large lumps of chicken and a chunk of sweet onion. Delicious. Or opt for tempura seafood and vegetable (£8.60), king prawn (£8.60), or vegetable pancakes (£5.60). Then there are meat dishes, the fish dishes, the rice dishes, the soba noodles, the udon noodles . . . and the hot sakes, cold sakes, and beers. You could eat your way to a good understanding of Japanese food here. Ask the charming, helpful staff and get stuck in.

If decision-making isn't your forte, take the easy option – there is a profusion of seven-course set meals costing between £15.80 and £16.80.

PUTNEY • ITALIAN

Del Buongustaio

283 Putney Bridge Rd, SW15 ©020 8780 9361   ⊖ East Putney

Mon 6.30–11pm, Tues–Sat noon–3pm & 6.30–11pm,

Sun 12.30–3.30pm & 6.30–10.30pm   Amex, Mastercard, Visa

On the first day of each month it's all change at Del Buongustaio as they unleash a new menu on the appreciative residents of Putney. The menu here features well-cooked, authentic food, with a sprinkling of less familiar dishes from the Cinderella regions like Puglia and Piedmont, as well as some painstakingly researched gems that once graced tables in Renaissance Italy. The dining room is light and airy and pleasantly informal. The cooking is good, with authentic dishes and friendly service. Take time to study the wine list, which is particularly strong on classy bottles from the less well-known provinces.

Who knows what the next menu will bring? But you can hazard a guess that there will be interesting pasta dishes. Such as a splendid spaghetti integrale alle vongole e capesante (£5.70 starter, £7.90 main) – wholewheat spaghetti with fresh clams, chillies and spring onions. Or perhaps girello rustica con rucola, spinaci e provola affumicato (£7.90) – pasta sheets rolled around a mixture of spinach, rocket and cheese, and served with a chunky sauce made from chopped tomatoes and basil. Thoroughly delicious. The piatto pizzicarello (£6.90), described with disarming modesty as a "plate of savouries", is a regular starter option. And then there is the torta rinascimentale di fave, ricotta e prosciutto (£5.50 starter, £7.90 main) – an amazing multi-layered cake of broad beans, prosciutto, ricotta and fontina cheese which comes with a rocket and egg sauce. Main course dishes may include lamb, sea bass, veal, pork, chicken, guinea fowl, cod, or perhaps a Swiss chard and ricotta pudding. Costolette d'agnello con inslatina di taccole, peperoni e asparagi (£11.35) is a typical offering – lamb chops with leaves and asparagus and a rosemary pesto. Look out for the "dal campo" side dishes, particularly the puré di patate alla parmigiana (£2.80), silky mashed potato with Parmesan cheese.

There are eight splendid pudding wines by the glass – including Vin Santo 1994 (£4.25), the befuddlingly alcoholic Aleatico di Puglia (£3.75), and a 1991 Recioto della Valpolicella (£3.75). There is also a huge selection of merciless grappas.

Enoteca

28 Putney High St, SW15 ℰ020 8785 4449   ⊖ Putney Bridge

Mon–Fri 12.30–2.30pm & 7–11pm, Sat 7–11pm   All major credit cards

If you like your Italian food a little more adventurous than the usual, then it is worth making the journey to Putney and Giuseppe Turi's restaurant. Enoteca has been in the forefront of modern Italian cooking for some years now, and always has interesting new twists on traditional favourites. Everything is based on fresh ingredients and, like some other notable venues, Enoteca offers a very personal version of good Italian regional cooking. Giuseppe himself hails from Apulia, and many dishes are based on recipes from this area. Wines are a special feature, with a monumental list of more than ninety specialist Italian wines in categories from "light" to "great wines". In addition there is a separate by-the-glass menu with eleven Italian regional offerings, an excellent way to educate the palate. Exploring regional Italian wines is something of a hobby for Turi; he has bought many, many of them and laid them down for future drinking.

As for the food, you'd do well to start with the very moreish sardine marinate con pinoli ed uvetta (£6.50) – fried sardines that have been marinated with pine nuts and raisins. Also good are the calamari in padella con borlotti e cipolle rosse (£7.50), pan-fried squid with warm borlotti beans and red onions, and the proscuitto d'anatra con rucola e Parmigiano (£8.50), a home-cured duck leg with rocket. Pasta choices may include ravioli con rape rossi e semi di papavero (beetroot ravioli, basically – £7/£8.50), and tagliolini ali frutti di mare (£9.40/£10.90), fine black and white pasta with a tasty mix of seafood. Main courses include coniglio con finocchio e salsa rosmarino (£12.50), roast rabbit with Parmesan baked fennel. There is always fresh fish of the day and a dish of the day. Desserts will test your mettle – go for the torta di cioc- colata con nocciole (£4.95), a blockbusting chocolate and hazelnut cake, or perhaps the particularly good, authentic tiramisù (£4.75).

Though there are many good restaurants in this area, Enoteca has a loyal following and, except for Monday and Tuesday nights, it is essential to book. If you're more of a wine bluff than a wine buff you'll be grateful for the discreet numbers printed beside each dish on the menu – they represent the recommended wines, all of which are available by the glass.

£12–£25

Ma Goa

244 Upper Richmond Rd, SW15 ©020 8780 1767	BR Putney/ ⊖ East Putney
Tues–Sat 6.30–11pm, Sun 12.30–3pm & 6–10pm	All major credit cards

www.magoa.co.uk

Despite the stylish ochre interior, complete with fans and blond wooden floor, despite the cafe-style chairs and tables, and the computer system to handle bills and orders, the overwhelming impression you are left with when you visit Ma Goa is of eating in somebody's home. It's the inspired home cooking that does it. And that all the staff are related helps. This place is as far as you can possibly get from the chuck-it-in-a-frying-pan-and-heat-it-through school of curry cookery. The food is deceptively simple, slow-cooked, and awesomely tasty. And it is authentically Goan into the bargain.

The menu is fairly compact: half a dozen starters are followed by a dozen mains, while a blackboard adds a couple of dishes of the day. Stuffed papards – papards are jolly close to popadoms – are served as a parcel, the papard wrapping up spiced potatoes (£3.75). Sorpotel (£3.95) is made from lambs' liver, kidney and pork in a sauce rich with roast spices, lime and coriander. The Goan sausage is, well, a sausage . . . also rich, with palm vinegar, cinnamon and green chillies (£3.95). All starters come with pitta bread. Main courses are amazing. The spices are properly cooked out by slow-cooking, which makes lifting the lids of the heavy clay serving pots a voyage of discovery. Porco vindaloo (£8), sharp with palm vinegar, is enriched with lumps of pork complete with rind. Hara masala pomfret (£8.75) is a pomfret that has been pan-fried with garlic, coconut, chilli and a rich Goan green masala. Delicious. Or there's Robi's beef fry (£8.25), which is beef marinated in mustard oil, garlic and ginger, and cooked with onions, black pepper, lime juice, crushed coriander seeds and fried potatoes – it's complex, and very rich. Vegetarians are equally well served. Chickpea chaat (£3/£5.50) is tasty with roasted spices and tamarind, while turi (£3/£5.50) is courgettes with tomatoes and mustard seed. The rice here is excellent.

On the specials board you might be lucky enough to find lamb kodi (£7.25), described as "lamb with cloves, garlic, and chilli". On the electronic message winging its way to the kitchen this is shortened to "Bella's lamb" – dishes here really are made from family recipes.

Putney Bridge

The Embankment, SW15 ✆020 8780 1811   ⊖ Putney Bridge

Tues–Sat noon–2.30pm & 7–10.30pm, Sun 12.30–3pm   All major credit cards

www.putneybridge.com

For a relative newcomer to the scene, Putney Bridge has already been through its fair share of changes. The elegant modern building has deservedly won plaudits from the great and the good in the world of architecture, but the grub has struggled to live up to the surroundings. The latest chef is Anthony Demetre, who favours a full-on approach – amuse-gueules and pre-desserts, accomplished presentation, a wine list that leads you gently through the expensive classics. Can it just be coincidence that these are the kind of attributes reputed to be most highly prized by Mr Michelin and his band of inspectors? The food is good. Flavours are well balanced, everything looks attractive and there is plenty of inspiration. Then you pay. This is not a bargain bite – unless, of course, you are very well heeled. Entry level is a set lunch at £19.50, and a two-course set dinner for £32. Thereafter the price increases to £39.50 for three courses (with a good many supplements), or £50 for a five-course Menu Gourmand.

The menus change to reflect what produce is available. A typical summer set lunch would start with new season courgette flowers filled with crab and basil mousse, then warm "carpaccio" of salmon with grilled vegetables and young leaves, followed by a chocolate and banana fondant. Very nice too. Venturing on to the à la carte (at £39.50) you might start with red mullet "bécasse de mer" sauté of fennel, artichoke and tomatoes – this is challenging stuff. Or there's foie sautéed with pain d'épice, quince purée and Maury syrup. For mains there are four fish and four meat, all elegant: maybe a roast sea bass with crushed potatoes and olive oil jus, or rack and confit shoulder of lamb, with young vegetables, jus and tapenade. All ingredients are top-quality and the sauces very well made. The wine list must be taken seriously by both you and your wallet.

Even if you can avoid the allure of a very good French cheeseboard (supplement £3), you won't be able dodge the baked meringue and rhubarb "Alaska", or the zingy blood orange sorbet.

PUTNEY

Bar Coast

50–54 Putney High St,
SW15   ✆020 8780 8931

This bright bar attracts a noisy and up-for-it young crowd for the DJs and 1am licence from Thursday to Saturday. They're also keen on the jugs of cocktails, which cost from £10 upwards. £14 gets you a jug of vodka and Red Bull, and there's Staropramen, Caffrey's and Grolsch for pint drinkers.

Bar M at the Star & Garter

4 Lower Richmond Rd,
SW15   ✆020 8788 0345

Tables overlooking the river give this American-looking bar a romantic and glamorous feel. Modern cane furniture and pale wood sets the tone. Tetley's, Caffrey's and Guinness are the signature draughts popular with the younger drinkers.

The Duke's Head

8 Lower Richmond Rd,
SW15   ✆020 8788 2552

One of the oldest taverns in Putney, this well-kept and traditional Young's pub has a pleasant, time-stands-still atmosphere. There's a river view from the back bar and Young's Special, Ordinary, AAA, Export lager and Pilsener to enjoy.

The Fox

167 Upper Richmond Rd,
SW15   ✆020 8788 1912

A modern pub with a lively and friendly atmosphere, this venue attracts a young-couplish crowd of local after-work drinkers.There's Fuller's London Pride, Boddingtons and Flowers Original for the beer fans and a better than average wine list as well.

The Railway

202 Upper Richmond Rd,
SW15   ✆020 8788 8190

Look up when you go in, and you'll see an amazing model railway running just below the ceiling. Most people seem unaware of it in the nicely modernised, but still traditional-feeling, bar. There are some unusual pints pulled here, including Bateman's Dark Mild and Weston's Old Rosie Scrumpy Cider on draught. The latter is at 7.5% ABV, so do your looking up before you drink it.

The Spotted Horse

122 Putney High St, SW15   ✆020 8788 0246

Wonderful Elizabethan-style brickwork and leaded light windows give this traditional Young's pub a delightful, old-fashioned country feel. It's narrow, but goes on forever, with some comfortable bars at the back. There's also a good selection of Young's bottled beers.

SOUTH

Tower Bridge
& Bermondsey

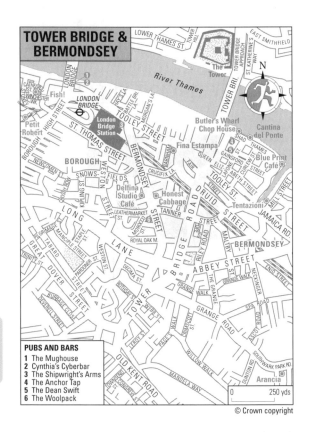

TOWER BRIDGE & BERMONDSEY

River Thames

LOWER THAMES ST · TOWER HILL · TOWER BRIDGE APPROACH · ST. KATHERINE'S WAY · EAST SMITHFIELD

The Tower

TOWER BRI.

N

CATHEDRAL ST · Fish! · LONDON BRIDGE · DUKE ST. HILL · BATTLE BRI. · MORGAN'S LA.

Petit Robert

HIGH STREET · BOROUGH · NEWCOMEN ST · CROSBY ROW · KIPLING ST.

LONDON BRIDGE · London Bridge Station

ST. THOMAS STREET · SNOWS · FIELDS · WESTON STREET

TOOLEY STREET

Butler's Wharf Chop House · SHAD · THAMES · Cantina del Ponte

Fina Estampa · QUEEN · GAINSFORD · LAFONE ST. · CURLEW STREET · Blue Print Café

BOROUGH · FARNHAM · BERMONDSEY · CRUCIFIX · FAIR

Delfina Studio Café · Honest Cabbage · MOROCCO · LEATHERMARKET ST. · TANNER STREET

ABETH STREET · TOOLEY ST. · DRUID STREET · Tentazioni · MILL STREET · JAMAICA RD.

LONG LANE · STAPLE STREET · WESTON STREET · DECIMA ST. · ROYAL OAK M.

BRIDGE ROAD · RILEY ROAD · MALTBY STREET · BERMONDSEY

ST. GRIMAGE · TABARD · TRINITY ST. · GREAT DOVER STREET · MANCIPLE STREET · PARDONER ST.

ABBEY STREET · THE GRANGE · GRANGE WALK · NECKINGER · ENID STREET

BURBAGE CLOSE · NEWELL STREET · TOWER · WEBB ST · ROUEL RD. · GRANGE WALK · GRANGE ROAD · SPA ROAD

OLD KENT ROAD · PAGES WALK · KINGSCOTE ST. · LEROY ST. · WILLOW WALK · DUNTON RD. · SOUTHWARK PARK RD.

TOWNSEND · CONGREVE ST. · MANDELA WAY · Arancia

0 — 250 yds

© Crown copyright

PUBS AND BARS

1. The Mughouse
2. Cynthia's Cyberbar
3. The Shipwright's Arms
4. The Anchor Tap
5. The Dean Swift
6. The Woolpack

Arancia

52 Southwark Park Rd, SE16 ℗020 7394 1751	BR Bermondsey
Daily 7–11pm	Mastercard, Visa

Gentrification is spreading through this part of town, where the neat rows of rather nice old terraced houses have been spotted by people toiling in the City of London – people who are quite smart enough to value short-ening their trip to work. Arancia is a product of these changing times; ten years ago this patch was all pie and mash and car chases. Now sensible and authentic Italian food is quite acceptable – and the proprietors of Arancia are to be congratulated on keeping the food cheap enough to attract the long-term residents, while at the same time good enough to ensnare newcomers. Success on all fronts. This is an old-fashioned, reg-ularly changing, seasonally inspired menu. At Arancia they manage to offer a three-course set meal for £7.50, a bargain whether you are bour-geois or Bermondsey.

On a hot day starters might include sopa di Toscana (£2.70), a well-seasoned and satisfying chilled soup made with peppers, tomatoes and bread with basil oil and croutons. Or you might have a big helping of spaghettini ariabbiata (£3.80). Fritelle di baccalà (£4.10) turns out to be small flying-saucer shaped discs of salt cod and chickpeas fried until crisp and served with a salad made from cherry tomatoes. In fact, in the course of a meal, this restaurant could radically change your perception of salt cod – among the main courses there's a really stunning baccalà alla Napoletana (£8.60), a large chunk of home-salted cod served with a slab of crisped polenta and a sauce made from tomatoes, olives and pine nuts. You can also bank on the maiale arrosto (£8.90), cold roast loin of pork with pickled cabbage and grape chutney, and the agnello alla griglia (£8.90), which is marinated lamb cutlets with new potatoes, roast pepper and walnut relish. The puddings are adventurous; perhaps a rather good chocolate semifreddo (£3), or fried pecorino parcels with cinnamon honey (£3.50), or that quintessentially Italian pud, ice cream terrine (£3).

The pursuit of bargain prices rather rebounds on you when you arrive at the wine list, which is all Italian. They are certainly bargains, they are all drinkable, but if you're after something really splendid you'll be out of luck. The proprietors of Arancia also run an outside catering busi-ness: with food as simple and as good as this, it should be worth investigating.

Blue Print Café

TOWER BRIDGE & BERMONDSEY ⑰ MODERN BRITISH

Design Museum, Shad Thames, SE1 ℂ020 7378 7031	⊖ Tower Hill/London Bridge
Mon–Sat noon–3pm & 6–11pm, Sun noon–3pm	All major credit cards
www.conran.com	

On the first floor of the Design Museum you'll find the Blue Print Café – the oldest of Sir Terence Conran's gastrodome restaurants. It has since acquired his Pont de la Tour, Butler's Wharf Chop House (see opposite) and Cantina del Ponte (see p.406) as neighbours, but the Blue Print has an identity that borrows from no one. It can turn out pricier than you might expect from a cursory look at the menu, and the service can be a bit uptight, but the cooking is honourable, the dishes imaginative, and the setting and views are as good as London gets.

Starters are a must. You might find three Arab salads with flatbread (£6), or salted breast of Hereford duck with redcurrant jelly (£7.50), or a simple fennel and parsley soup (£5), but they will have one thing in common – top-quality ingredients, strong flavours and pleasing combinations of textures. Mains also aim for simplicity, like the tart of ossau per brebis, potatoes and baby artichoke (£11), rich with the famous ewes' milk cheese; or the onglet with mustard and watercress (£12.50), or sea bass with potatoes, salsify and truffles (£16). These are all dishes which appeal to diners who know their food, as are the braised peppered duck leg with herbs (£12), and the loin of rabbit with morcilla, parma ham and cabbage (£16). Side orders include a light and airy mash (£2.50) – an indispensable accompaniment to any of the fish dishes. Puddings are unmissable, too, including favourites like crème brûlée (£5) – thinly crusted with slightly soft crème brûlée, just as it should be – or chocolate, mascarpone and coffee trifle (£6.50), or even chocolate brownie with fudge sauce and vanilla cream (£6.50). The eclectic wine list has many unusual offerings as well as a particularly good house champagne (£29.95) – and the Blue Print is a fine place to celebrate.

The Blue Print has superb river views, and as evening falls the lights of the city skyline opposite, and those of Tower Bridge, make London almost beautiful. Book in advance and ask for a table near a terrace window – or, when it's open (and they are reluctant on all but midsummer days and nights), out on the terrace itself.

SOUTH

Butler's Wharf Chop House

36e Shad Thames, SE1 ℡020 7403 3403   ⊖ Tower Hill/London Bridge

Restaurant Mon–Fri & Sun noon–4pm & 6–11pm, Sat 6–11pm

Bar Mon–Sat noon–11pm, Sun noon–4pm   All major credit cards

www.conran.com

Butler's Wharf Chop House – another Conran creation – really deserves everyone's support. For this is a restaurant that makes a genuine attempt to showcase the best of British produce. There's superb British meat, splendid fish, and simply epic British and Irish cheeses. What's more, the Chop House wisely caters for all, whether you want a simple dish at the bar, a well-priced set lunch, or an extravagant dinner. The dining room is large and airy and the view of Tower Bridge a delight, especially from a terrace table on a warm summer's evening.

Lunch in the restaurant is priced at £19.75 for two courses and £23.75 for three. The menu changes regularly but tends to feature starters such as roast tomato soup with cheese straw; or Loch Fyne smoked salmon; or peppered chicken livers on toast. Mains will include dishes like wild boar and apple sausages with sage and onion mash, as well as the house speciality of spit roasts and grills. They do a flawless roast rib of beef with Yorkshire pudding and gravy, and excellent double lamb chop, rocket, new potatoes and mint. After that you just might be able to find room – and an extra £4 – for a pud like Cambridge burnt cream with marinated raspberries. Dinner follows the same principles but is priced à la carte and features more complex dishes. Thus, there may be starters like roast scallop, salmon and horseradish terrine (£8), or a rocket, apple and bacon salad (£6.50). Mains may include slow-roast belly pork, prunes and cider (£14); Dover sole with parsley butter and chips (£21); or steak and kidney pudding with oysters (£15). There's also steak and chips, priced by size – £16.50 for an 8oz sirloin to £25 for a 12oz fillet.

The bar menu is appealing – two courses for £8, three for £10 (Mon–Fri). You might choose Loch Fyne herrings, beetroot and potato salad, then spit-roast gammon with mustard and honey sauce, followed by chocolate and orange mousse – a pretty good tenner's worth. There is also a serious weekend brunch menu in the bar, which costs £13.95 for two courses and £16.95 for three.

£10–£35

Cantina del Ponte

Butler's Wharf, Shad Thames, SE1 ✆020 7403 5403	⊖ Tower Hill/London Bridge
Mon–Sat noon–3pm & 6–11pm, Sun noon–3pm	All major credit cards

www.conran.com

Jostling for attention with its more renowned neighbour, and considerably pricier Conran cousin, the Pont de la Tour, the Cantina del Ponte does not try to keep up, but instead offers a different package. Here you are greeted with the best earthy Italian fare, presented in smart Conran style. The floors are warm terracotta, the food is strong on flavour and colour, the service is refined, and the views are superior London dockside. There are many Italian restaurants around town within the same price range, but this is one of the better ones – if only for the setting, which rivals a fair few Italian cities. Book ahead and bag a table by the window or, better still in the summer, brave the elements and sit under the canopy watching the boats go by. Inside is OK but less memorable and the low ceilings a bit claustrophobic if you're seated at the back.

The seasonal menu is a meander through all things good, Italian-style, with a tempting array of first courses, pasta and risotto, pizzas and mains as well as side orders, pudding and cheese. If you can't meet the minimum order of £10 per head from this little lot, then you must be exceptionally choosy. Perfect for balmy evenings is the Piedmontese pepper with iman bayaldi and mint yoghurt (£6.25). Imaginative and vegetarian to boot, there may be pumpkin and ricotta cannelloni with creamed walnut, garlic and parsley (£8.50), while the risotto made with porcini mushrooms, confit rabbit and tarragon is a more substantial affair (£9). Pizzas are equally filling, and feature imaginative toppings like marinated swordfish (£8). Main courses range from £13.50 to £14.95 for serious meaty and fishy dishes. The highlights include a grilled fillet of beef with porcini mushrooms, parsley and olive oil (£14.95). It's a tall order, but if you can manage it try a pudding of chocolate panettone bread and butter pudding (£5.50): dark, bitter and indulgent. A lighter, but no less delicious, option is the pannacotta with blueberry compote (£5.50).

If you fancy live music while you eat, book a table for Friday evening, after 8.30pm. On summer nights this is a hard act to beat.

Delfina Studio Café

50 Bermondsey St, SE1 ©020 7357 0244	⊖ London Bridge
Mon–Fri noon–3.30pm (lunch)	All major credit cards

www.delfina.org.uk

Bermondsey has long been a centre for London's antique trade, but in recent years it has been changing character, with art galleries moving into the old warehouses around the wharves. Delfina Studio is at the hub. It houses a gallery and artists' studio space as well as a dining room, and if you're in southeast London checking out the art scene then there is no better place to come for lunch. Originally a cafe attached to a gallery (it still functions as such outside lunchtime hours), Delfina's is now a serious restaurant – bright and modern, both in its appearance and in the food it serves, with a mix of tastes created from light, fresh ingredients by head chef Maria Elia. It's moved well beyond cafe prices these days, but the quality of ingredients and cooking justify a bit of a splurge. And it's a lot cheaper than buying a painting in these parts.

The menu is astutely written, presenting a range of dishes that are perfectly judged for lunchtime. For starters you might find dishes like char-grilled vegetables with beetroot pesto and pecorino (£4.75), or octopus with new potatoes in lemongrass dressing (£5.75), or carrot and star anise soup with crème fraîche (£3.75). They are all good, and deliver crisp flavours that blend well. Main courses are equally satisfying: pan-fried monkfish with mango and beurre blanc (£13), or perhaps char-grilled lamb cutlet with thyme risotto (£13.95)? Char-grilling is something of a passion here. But the kitchen also turns out some pretty decent vegetarian options – try, for example, the baked field mushrooms, stuffed with herbs, pumpkin and dolcelatte (£9.95). Puddings, all at £4.25, are deceptively simple. Depending on season, they might include a chocolate mousse cake, a sticky toffee pudding, or goats' cheese with oatcakes. The wine list offers excellent wines at reasonable prices. A good Gamay (Domaine Charmoise 1997) costs £14.25, and the house wines from Delfina's own vineyards in Spain are £10.95 a bottle for very decent Iberian red, white or rosé.

At its own exhibition times, Delfina extends opening hours (ring for details), but a thriving outside catering business and functions within the gallery itself conspire to make the restaurant a lunchtimes-only affair.

TOWER BRIDGE & BERMONDSEY ⓦ PERUVIAN

Fina Estampa

150 Tooley St, SE1 ©020 7403 1342   ⊖ London Bridge

Mon–Fri noon–2.30pm & 6.30–10.30pm,

Sat 6.30–10.30pm   All major credit cards

While London is awash with ethnic eateries, Fina Estampa's proud boast is that it is the capital's only Peruvian restaurant. Gastronomy may not be the first thing that springs to mind when one thinks of Peru, but the husband-and-wife team running the place certainly tries hard to enlighten their customers and bring a little downtown Lima to London Bridge. With its fresh bright-yellow interior and throbbing rhythms (live music on Friday and Saturday nights), Fina Estampa has a warm and bright ambience, and the attentive, friendly staff add greatly to the upbeat feel.

The menu is traditional Peruvian, which means there's a great emphasis placed upon seafood – this is reflected in the starters, with such offerings as chupe de camarones (£6.95), a succulent shrimp-based soup; cebiche (£5.95), a dish of marinated white fish served with sweet potatoes; and jalea (£9.50), a vast plate of fried seafood. Ask for the salsa criolla – its hot oiliness is a perfect accompaniment. There is also causa rellena (£4.95), described as a "potato surprise" and exactly that: layers of cold mashed potato, avocado and tuna fish served with salsa – the surprise being how something so straightforward can taste so good. Main courses – the fragrant chicken seco (£10.95), chicken cooked in a coriander sauce; or the superb lomo saltado (£12.95), tender strips of rump steak stir-fried with red onions and tomatoes – are worthy ambassadors for this simple yet distinctive cuisine. Perhaps most distinctive of all is the carapulcra (£10.95), a spicy dish made of dried potatoes, pork, chicken and cassava – top choice for anyone seeking a new culinary adventure.

One particularly fine, and decidedly Peruvian, speciality is the unfortunately named Pisco sour (£3.50). Pisco is a white grape spirit and the Peruvian national drink, not dissimilar in taste and effect to tequila. Here they mix Pisco with lemon, lime and cinnamon, then sweeten it with honey, add egg white, and whip it into a frothy white cocktail, which is really rather good.

SOUTH

Fish!

Cathedral St, SE1 ✆020 7234 3333	⊖ London Bridge
Mon–Sat 11.30am–3pm & 5.30–11pm	All major credit cards

www.info@fishdiner.co.uk

You feel like a fish at Fish!. The restaurant's huge windows and glass ceiling contribute to a tank-like feeling. They also contribute to high noise levels and a general party ambience. The restaurant is large and there's a courtyard for al fresco eating, plus bar seating for armchair chefs who like to watch the real ones at work.

The menu is place-mat style, so you get sat down and start reading. On one side there are Fish! homilies that explain: the restaurant's ethic; kids' menus and games; highchairs; GM-free fish; takeaway; a Web site; a nutrition section – so much, in fact, that you're loath to turn over and read the real menu. This is equally innovative. On the one card is a smallish selection of dishes, wines and accompaniments. But the main reason for coming to Fish! is the self-selection menu. From a printed list of 22 contenders there are nine kinds of fresh fish, which change daily depending on the markets. You select your favourite, choose whether you want it steamed or grilled, and then choose salsa, hollandaise, herb butter, olive oil dressing or red-wine fish gravy to go with it. Create your own combo. Prices range from £8.50 for mullet to £15.95 for Dover sole. Portions are huge and the fish is as good and fresh as you'd expect. The traditional menu offers starters like prawn cocktail (£6.95), unreconstructed and with a properly pink, ketchupy sauce. Main dishes include fish cake (£7.80), made with salmon and smoked haddock, spaghetti tuna Bolognaise (£8.50), with fresh tomatoes and minced tuna, or fish and chips with mushy peas (£11.80). And for poor lost carnivores who have rather missed the point there is even a grilled free-range chicken breast (£11.50). If you like a traditional approach to fish, Fish! won't disappoint. Puddings include stalwarts like lemon sponge pudding and custard (£3.95), plus bread and butter pudding (£3.95), the latter rich with double cream. The house white, a Sauvignon de Touraine (£9.90), is light, crisp and a bargain.

Fish!'s menu adds interest to eating, with information that makes sense. There's also a Fish! shop next door for wet fish and sauces and a touch-screen recipe machine.

£12–£40

Honest Cabbage

99 Bermondsey St, SE1 ✆020 7234 0080	⊖ London Bridge
Mon–Wed noon–3pm & 6.30–10.30pm,	
Thurs–Sat noon–3pm & 6.30–11pm, Sun noon–4pm	Mastercard, Visa

The Honest Cabbage is heralded by a beguiling picture of a cabbage crowned with a halo, which sticks out into Bermondsey Street like an inn sign. Without the sign, the restaurant would be difficult to spot – there is long-term scaffolding next door, hiding the Cabbage from the view of the oncoming traffic. Once found, the place is a welcome lesson in simplicity – dark wooden tables and chairs are dotted around a medium-sized plain room. At the far end is a small bar and counter, but the whole of the shopfront is sheet glass, giving a spacious and well-lit feel – decoration is provided by glass jars of pulses along the windowsills.

The menu is chalked up on a segmented blackboard, though if you can't quite see it they have a printed version as well. There is a choice of ten or eleven dishes, with no division between first and main courses. It follows a simple formula of a soup, a sandwich, a salad, a pasta, a pie dish, a vegetarian dish, etc. The menu changes every day broadly in line with the seasons and what the markets have to offer. So you might choose from cream of mushroom soup (£3) or a steak and melted onion sandwich (£5), either of which would make a satisfying light lunch. And then there are the fresh meat and fresh fish options (these cost between £7 and £10), which might be a large portion of calves' liver with sweetbread – which is cooked pink and served with two vegetables – perhaps mangetout and carrots, plus mash or chips. Or grey mullet, grilled and dressed with an aromatic mixture of fresh thyme, olive oil and garlic. Puddings are straightforward – like a good lemon meringue pie (£4).

A short but considered drinks list not only provides a couple of organic wines but also a succession of bottled and draught beers. The Cabbage's strengths lie in its attitude and pricing, so, as you would expect, it is consistently busy. There's a serious brunch on Sunday morning. The Cabbage has a new sibling – The Honest Goose, 61 The Cut, SE1 (✆020 7261 1221).

£15–£35

Petit Robert

3 Park St, SE1 ℗020 7357 7003   ⊖ London Bridge

Mon–Sat noon–4pm & 6–10pm   All major credit cards

www.petit-robert.co.uk

Robert Didier's dad was also called Robert, so to his family he has always been "petit Robert". In later life he has got his own back by using the same name for his small, and somewhat eccentric, French restaurant. Petit Robert, one of the first foodie colonists of this strange net of streets around the Borough Market, serves straightfoward French food to a loyal local clientele. What makes Petit Robert really notable, however, is the astonishing Armagnac list. Quite simply, they have the best range of Armagnacs in Britain, including what is allegedly the last bottle of the world's oldest Armagnac – a bas Armagnac Baron de Lustrac 1830, since you ask, modestly priced at £165 for a double.

The food is French bistro food, with some unusually good patisserie and a competitive cheeseboard. There is a menu prix fixe (on offer until 7pm) with three or four choices in each section – £8.50 for two courses and £10.50 for three. You'll find simple dishes like lobster bisque or guinea fowl terrine to start with; then grilled shark fillet with braised fennel, duck stuffed with apricots, or lamb cassoulet; and finally the cheeseboard, a cheesecake, or apple and raspberry cobbler. The à la carte is more elaborate with starters like cuisse de grenouille à l'ail (£6.25), king scallop with saffron and basil sauce on a bed of pasta (£6.25), or goats' cheese baked in hazelnuts on salad dressed with vinaigrette (£5.75). Mains range from brill and salmon on a bed of leeks with a white wine sauce (£13.95) to pork loin with morel mushrooms sauce (£14.95) and sweet potato and spring onion cakes with a spicy tomato sauce (£11.25). The wine list extends to 200 bins and there are often bargains for the knowledgeable.

Back to the Armagnacs, which represent almost every year between 1900 and 1985.These are listed together with salient events to put them into context, so here's a quiz: which dates go on the following bottles? Tenarze Magnol 42% (£5.50), the year Man landed on the moon; Domaine Boingnères 48% (£14.50), the year President Kennedy was assassinated; H Dartigalongue 40% (£22), the year Germany was split into East and West. All prices per 50cl.

£10–£20

Tentazioni

2 Mill St, SE1 ✆020 7237 1100   ⊖ Bermondsey/Tower Hill

Mon & Sat 7–10.45pm, Tues–Fri noon–2.30pm & 7–10.45pm   All major credit cards

www.tentazioni.freeserve.co.uk

This small, busy and rather good Italian restaurant has crept up behind Sir Terence Conran's Thameside flotilla of eateries and is giving them a good run for their money. The food is high-quality peasant Italian, with strong, rich flavours and simple quality. The pasta dishes are good here, as are the stews, and the wine list is interesting. They also offer a "Menu Degustazione", which gets you five courses for £35. This serious little Italian restaurant now has siblings all over town: as well as the notable Grano (see p.491), there's also another outpost in Turnham Green – Riso, 76 South Parade, W4 (✆020 8742 2121).

The starters here are all priced at £7 or £8, unless you choose to have one of them as a main course, when the price goes up to £9. The menu changes to reflect the seasons and the markets, so you may find choices such as tagliolini neri freddi con vongole e broccoli, an unusual dish of black tagliolini served cold with clams and broccoli, or the tasty pappardelle quaglie e piselli, which is pappardelle with quails and peas, or mozzarella di bufala con caponata di verdure – buffalo mozzarella with vegetable caponata. In season there is a good deal of game on the menu, and often a particularly good traditional pasta with a richer-than-rich sauce made with hare or the like. Main courses offer hammer blows of flavour – bocconcini di coniglio impanati con carcofini (£15), which is described as a breaded navarin of rabbit with artichokes; or triglie con cicoria, fave e pecorino (£14.50) – pan-fried red mullet with chicory, broad beans and pecorino. Or an unusual dish like filetto di manzo al vapore con verdurine, salsa verde e mostarda (£16.50), which is steamed fillet of beef given vibrant colour from the salsa verde and a hit of flavour from the mustard-pickled fruits. For pudding it is hard to better the torta alle prugne e pere con gelato alla vaniglia (£6), a delicious prune and pear tart with vanilla ice cream.

The "Degustazione" provides an interesting and very tempting option. How does this sound? First, vitello tonnato, then agnolotti di patate e menta con peperoni, then the red mullet mentioned above, then a rabbit dish, and finally panna cotta alla grappa con arance caramellate. Pretty convincing.

The Anchor Tap

20a Horselydown Lane,
SE1   ℂ020 7403 4637

A short walk from the riverside, this regulars' local has a separate games room (slot machines and pool table), an upstairs bar, and a secluded patio overlooking Brewery Square. It's not over-touristy and there's a cosy, comfortable atmosphere. Sam Smith's Old Brewery Bitter is the favourite ale on tap.

Cynthia's Cyberbar

4 Tooley St, SE1   ℂ020 7403 6777

Tucked underneath London Bridge, this acid-blue cocktail bar employs Britain's first robot barmaid. Yes, she actually does make the cocktails, and it's amazing to watch. There are many metal-floored rooms in this warren of a place, which has a children's licence up to 9pm and a late club licence afterwards. Space-themed cocktails with charming names like Alien Vomit are the order of the day.

The Dean Swift

32 Lafone St, SE1   ℂ020 7357 0748

With its big, clear windows and clean simple lines this venue has a lounge-bar atmosphere. It's relaxed and friendly, with newspapers to read and lots of people sitting quietly and chatting. Wadworth's 6X and Fuller's London Pride are the favourites.

The Mughouse

1 Tooley St, SE1   ℂ020 7403 8343

It's all sawdust and old beams in this dark "olde worlde" cellar wine bar. Frequented by City types and medical staff from the nearby Blackfriars hospital, it offers a huge selection of wines and Davy's own-brew beers – 1870 lager, Ordinary Bitter and Old Wallop. Their excellent house champagne is £24 a bottle.

The Shipwright's Arms

88 Tooley St, SE1   ℂ020 7378 1486

This big, comfortable Real Ale pub boasts a huge selection of guest ales that change with each barrel. Expect brews like Avalon Springmore, Monkey Town Mild, Milton Brewery's Pegasus, Hop Cross Bunny, Snow White, Bellringer, Fireball and other curiously named beers, all of them being tried by a happy crowd of young fans.

The Woolpack

98 Bermondsey St, SE1   ℂ020 7357 7116

This is one of just a few pubs in the area, so it gets busy with antique dealers and shoppers from the surrounding market. It's noisy and friendly, with big-screen football, and there's a patio rear garden to get away from the crowds. Enjoy Courage Best, Deuchar's Caledonian IPA and Guinness Extra Cold.

Wimbledon
& Southfields

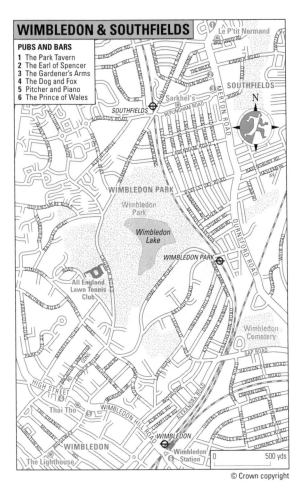

WIMBLEDON & SOUTHFIELDS

PUBS AND BARS

1 The Park Tavern
2 The Earl of Spencer
3 The Gardener's Arms
4 The Dog and Fox
5 Pitcher and Piano
6 The Prince of Wales

Le P'tit Normand

SOUTHFIELDS

Sarkhel's

SOUTHFIELDS

AUGUSTUS ROAD

REPLINGHAM ROAD

MERTON ROAD

N

WIMBLEDON PARK

Wimbledon
Park

QUEENSMERE ROAD

Wimbledon
Lake

DUNSFORD ROAD

WIMBLEDON PARK

All England
Lawn Tennis
Club

Wimbledon
Cemetery

GAP ROAD

HAYDON PARK ROAD

CROMWELL ROAD

HIGH STREET

Thai Tho

WIMBLEDON HILL ROAD

ALEXANDRA ROAD

QUEENS ROAD

WIMBLEDON

WIMBLEDON

Wimbledon
Station

The Lighthouse

0   500 yds

© Crown copyright

SOUTH

Lighthouse

75–77 The Ridgway, SW19 ©020 8944 6388	⊖ Wimbledon
Mon–Sat noon–2.45pm & 6–10.30pm,	
Sun 12.30–3.15pm & 6.30–9.30pm	All major credit cards except Diners

Lighthouse is a strange restaurant to find marooned in leafy suburbia – you would think that its modern, very eclectic menu and clean style would be more at home in a city centre than in a smart, quiet, respectable neighbourhood. Nevertheless it seems to be doing well. The restaurant, which opened in late 1999, has found its feet and the local clientele quite obviously enjoy it and keep coming back for more. First impressions always count and a light, bright interior – cream walls and blond wood – plus genuinely friendly staff make arriving at Lighthouse a pleasure.

At first glance the menu is set out conventionally enough in the Italian style: antipasti, primi, secondi, contorni and dolci. But that's as far as the Italian formality goes – the influences on the kitchen here are truly global. Dishes range from a salad of buffalo mozzarella, celery, anchovy, rocket and croutons (£5.20), to chump of lamb with broccoli, merguez, guindilla, almonds and tahini dressing (£14.50), via dem miso duck on pickled cabbage salad with roast tamarillo (£6.60). It would be very easy to get this sort of cooking wrong, but in fact Lighthouse does it remarkably well. Carpaccio of organic salmon with enoki mushrooms and ponzu dressing (£6.90) is made with absolutely fresh, top-quality fish. Deep-fried prawn ravioli with sautéed porcini, oyster mushrooms and grilled nori (£6.90) is a wonderful and unusual contrast of textures and flavours. Main courses of annoto marinated chicken on bonniato mash with peppers and spring onion relish (£13.70) and monkfish with grilled endive, bok choy, red wine jus and tarrator bruschetta (£13) are difficult – trying to harmonise and rein in so many different ingredients would challenge any chef. Perhaps the cooking is a little overcomplicated, but it's well executed and certainly intriguing. Puddings take us back to Italy with passionfruit and raspberry semifreddo (£4.75), and almond cantucci with a glass of vin santo (£6.50).

Someone has had a lot of fun choosing the wine list – a selection of about fifteen each of whites and reds which crosses as many frontiers as possible, If you want a bargain, go for lunch – a steal at £12.50 for two courses.

£10–£20

Le P'tit Normand

185 Merton Rd, SW18 ℡020 8871 0233   ⊖ Southfields

Mon–Thurs & Sun noon–2pm & 7–10pm, Fri & Sat 7–10.30pm   All major credit cards

Everything about this restaurant, from the red gingham cloths and the polished copper jugs, to the silk sunflowers on the tables and the framed Van Gogh reproduction shouts "French bistro". The menus are written entirely in French and the staff have some of the finest accents in London. In other hands this could be irritating and over the top, but at Le P'tit Normand it's artlessly charming.

The food is as Gallic as you could wish for. The main menu includes a full complement of old favourites – soupe à l'oignon (£3.50), cassoulette d'escargots (£4.25), côte de veau Normande (£9.75), carré d'agneau provençale (£9.50) – but there are also daily specials, chalked up on blackboards scattered around the room. These range from terrine maison (£3.95) to cassoulet maison (£10.75). Cream abounds and there is little choice for non-meat eaters, but the cooking is a true retro treat and the portions substantial. A starter of feuilleté de champignons (£4.75), a mixture of wild mushrooms and cream with a five-inch square slab of puff pastry, is well flavoured, but so rich it leaves you wondering where to put the main course. Boudin noir aux pommes (£3.95) is proper French black pudding, sweet and fruity, served with sautéed, caramelised apple. Both magret de canard (£9.50) and entrecôte aux cinq poivres (£9.25) are cooked to order, each of them with enough cream to dismay the arteries. There is a typically French attitude to vegetables – you don't get any unless you ask for them. If you do, the potatoes will inevitably be "Dauphinoise". Desserts can disappoint – there is less lavish use of butter in tarte Tatin (£3.95) than there should be, but the cheeseboard, with about twenty cheeses on offer (all French, naturellement) is excellent. The wine list is mercifully concise, well annotated and well priced, with a couple of special offers.

You may well need a digestif after such a meal. Have a Calvados (£3.95–£14). There are forty different vintages to choose from, going back to 1926. Le P'tit Normand is popular in the evening, so you would be wise to book. Lunch is grand value at £6 for two courses and there's a laid-back Sunday lunch at £12.95.

Sarkhel's

199 Replingham Rd, Southfields, SW18 ⓒ020 8870 1483   ⊖ Southfields

Tues–Thurs 6–10.30pm,

Fri & Sat 6–11pm, Sun noon–2.30pm   Amex, Mastercard, Visa

www.sarkhels.com

Before opening his own place in SW18, Udit Sarkhel was heading the kitchens of the famous Bombay Brasserie in the West End, where he had all the latest kit and a large brigade of chefs. Moving to Sarkhel's in Southfields must have been like resigning as conductor of an orchestra and setting up a one-man band, but it is certainly a huge asset to South London. And South London has certainly responded; the dining room seems to be enlarged at least once a year. Today Sarkhel's is a large, elegant restaurant, serving well-spiced food with a number of adventurous dishes scattered through the menu – the Chettinad dishes are particularly fine, hot and fresh. Moreover, it's a pleasant, friendly, family-run place offering good cooking at prices, which, though not cheap, certainly represent good value. Particularly on Friday, Saturday and Sunday lunchtimes, when you can get a bargain set lunch for £9.95. Booking is recommended.

Start by asking Udit or his wife if there are any "specials" on. These are dishes which change depending on what the markets have to offer. You might be offered a starter of crab (£5.95) cooked Malabari style, with some added Chettiyar spicing – a hint of sour tamarind, a whiff of chilli. Quite delicious. Or a shrimp balchao (£5.95), chilli-hot and served with mini popadoms. The chicken tikka (£6.50) is as good as you'll find anywhere. For main course dishes, check the specials again – it might be something wonderful like a prawn pulao (£6.95), cooked slowly in a pot. On the main menu, try the chicken korma narangi (£6.50) rich and citrussy, made with orange juice and preserved orange peel, or the achar gosht (£6.50), which is lamb cooked slowly in a sealed pot "dum phukt" style; or perhaps the jardaloo ma gosht (£6.50), a sweet and sour lamb dish made with apricots. All are delicious, without even a hint of surface oil slick.

Be sure to add some vegetable dishes. Both the baigan bhurta (£5.50), char-grilled aubergines mashed with spices, and the bhindi Jaipuri (£5.50), a small haystack of slivered okra and onions deep-fried until crisp, then served dusted with mango powder, are addictively good.

£15–£25

Thai Tho

20 Wimbledon High St, SW19 ✆020 8946 1542   ⊖ Wimbledon

Daily 11.30am–11.30pm   Mastercard, Switch, Visa

What looks like a small intimate restaurant as you walk through the door stretches way back behind the bar, giving Thai Tho a huge capacity. The front part of the restaurant is for non-smokers and is much cosier; if you are a smoker it may be worth foregoing your pre-prandial puff to sit there. The back room somehow seems to swallow up customers. Parties of six or more walk into the Tardis and vanish. The decoration is predictable but simple and rather welcoming – stripped-wood floor with Thai lamps and embroidered Thai cloths on the walls. Service is friendly, and presentation (so often over the top in Thai restaurants) is restrained, even elegant.

There is no set menu, so take two minutes over a spicy bowl of prawn crackers (£1.65) while you choose. Everybody's favourite Thai dishes are on offer here, from spring rolls (£4.25–£4.50) to green curry (£6.25), but there's plenty more besides. Portions are generous, so curb the tendency to over-order. You could play safe and order a mixed starter platter (£7.50), which includes spring rolls, chicken satay, chicken wings, sesame prawns on toast, and paper prawns (£4.95), or perhaps the tod man pla (£4.95), which are Thai fish cakes – but some of the deep-fried food here can be a tad greasy. Try instead the excellent tom yum soups (£4.50–£5.95), which are clear, well flavoured and spicy without being searing. There's a small selection of spicy main course salads, dressed with hot and sour sauce – yum woon-sen (£6.25), for example, a dish of grass noodles, pork and prawns – but thankfully they've forsworn the mouth-stripping green papaya salad. The curries are unexceptional, so it is worth being slightly more adventurous. Gai pad kee mun (£6.25), which is chicken with chilli, sweet basil and beans, is wonderfully aromatic, while the mee khom lad nah (£6.95), crispy noodles with vegetables and whichever principal ingredient you choose, is good enough to warrant a return visit. There's a decent, ungreedy wine list and a selection of beers to wash it all down.

Thai Tho certainly stands out among the pizza parlours, chain restos and cafes of Wimbledon High Street. Its slogan "The Best Thai Food in Town" may not be wholly justified, but as a local Thai restaurant which also does takeaway it's certainly better than average.

The Dog & Fox

24 High St, Wimbledon Village,
SW19   ©020 8946 6565

This big, old-fashioned pub with scrubbed wooden tables and panelling is right in the heart of the village and feels just like a country pub. Young's Ordinary, Special and AAA are the signature ales, and there's a Finches wine bar attached if you need more variety.

The Earl of Spencer

262 Merton Rd, SW18   ©020 8265 5103

Lively, loud pub with two pool tables, table football and – although they enforce a strictly over-21 policy –a younger than average crowd. Guinness, Guinness Extra Cold and Woodpecker Cider are the favourites on draught, and there's an enclosed pavement patio for summer drinking.

The Gardener's Arms

288 Merton Rd, SW18   ©020 8874 7624

No pool table, no jukebox and a no-children policy makes this nice old Young's local a quieter, more talk-oriented and friendlier pub than many. There's a dartboard in regular use. A small pavement patio gives some additional summer space.

The Park Tavern

212 Merton Rd, SW18   ©020 8355 8933

Roomy bars, mid-tone wood panelling and well-polished tables give this traditional local a home-from-home feeling. It's quiet in the day, but gets busy at night with regulars who favour Charles Wells' Bombardier, Wadworth 6X and spirits at £2 a double.

Pitcher & Piano

4–5 High St, Wimbledon Village,
SW19   ©020 8879 7020

This comfortable, medium-sized member of the popular chain is a favourite with local shoppers. Friendly staff serve a wide range of drinks from wine and mineral water to beer and coffee. Bank's Bitter is the ale on tap, but wine by the glass seems to be the favourite here.

The Prince of Wales

2 Hartfield Rd, SW19   ©020 8946 5369

Conveniently situated opposite the underground station, this big, comfortable pub has a huge selection of drinks. In addition to the usual wine, lager and alco-pops on offer there is a furious turnover of weekly guest ales. You never know what you might find, but there's a good chance of a Tisbury Natterjack, Thwaites Blooming Ale, and Wychwood Fiddler's Elbow.

Further South

Bromley, Croydon, Epsom Downs,
Forest Hill, Herne Hill, Norbury,
Tooting, West Dulwich

FURTHER SOUTH

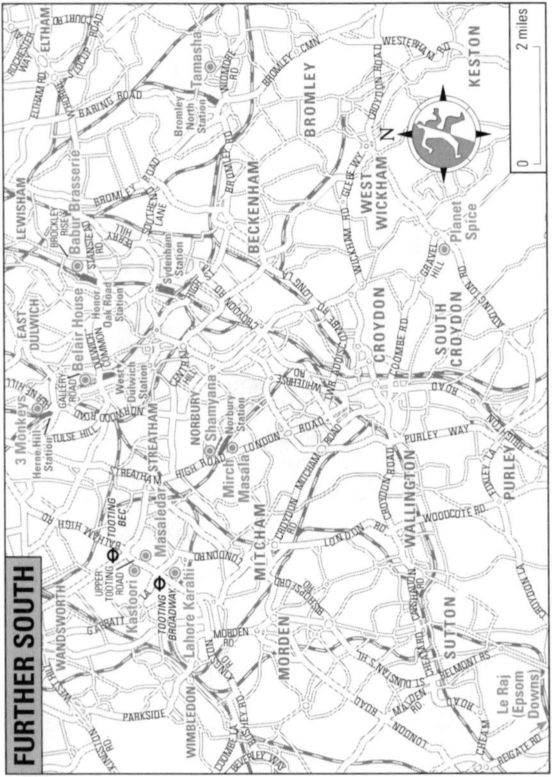
ELTHAM
LEWISHAM
EAST DULWICH
WANDSWORTH
Kastoori
UPPER TOOTING ROAD
TOOTING BEC
TOOTING BROADWAY
Lahore Karahi
Masaledar
STREATHAM
3 Monkeys
Herne Hill Station
Belair House
West Dulwich Station
Honor Oak Road Station
Babur Brasserie
Sydenham Station
Tamasha
Bromley North Station
BROMLEY
KESTON
NORBURY
Shamyana
Norbury Station
Mirch Masala
BECKENHAM
WEST WICKHAM
MITCHAM
MORDEN
WIMBLEDON
CROYDON
SOUTH CROYDON
Planet Spice
WALLINGTON
SUTTON
PURLEY
Le Raj (Epsom Downs)
N
0
2 miles

© Crown copyright

Babur Brasserie

119 Brockley Rise, Forest Hill, SE23 ©020 8291 2400	BR Honor Oak Park
Daily noon–2.30pm & 6–11.30pm	All major credit cards

The Babur Brasserie is a stylish and friendly restaurant serving elaborate and interesting dishes which bear no resemblance to run-of-the-mill curry house fare – an unexpected find in SE23. The food is both subtle and elegantly presented and, while it does cost a touch more than most sub-urban Indian restaurants, you are still paying a great deal less than you would in a French or Italian place of similar quality. There is a buffet lunch on Sunday (£8.95) at which children eat free if they are less than eight years old . . .

How nice to be faced with a list of appetisers and see so few familiar dishes. Patra (£2.95) is a Catherine wheel sliced off the end of a roll of avial leaves which have been glued together with chickpea paste and deep-fried. The result is crispy and very tasty. Aloo choff (£2.95) is a grown-up potato croquette with vegetables and spices coated in ground cashew nuts. Prawn bulchao (£4.70) is a Goan dish, agreeably hot, while murgh tikka lasania (£3.95) gets you a plate of yoghurt-coated chunks of chicken cooked in a tandoor and delightfully juicy inside. Main courses are just as good. Try jalfrezi (£6.95) – lamb with onions, ginger and capsicums. Or caldine (£8.75) – monkfish in a sauce that mixes coconut milk with cumin and coriander. Chicken peri peri (£7.50) is served in a seriously hot Goan red chilli sauce, while the sole fillets in patrani machli (£8.25) are marinated in coconut, yoghurt and spices, and served in a patra leaf. Then there are ten fresh vegetable dishes – vegetarians will applaud the option of picking four from the list with raita, rice and a naan bread for an inclusive price of just £11.75. On the subject of bread, try the lacha parata (£2.10) – a flaky paratha made with ghee. The dessert menu is more extensive and more elabo-rate than usual, too, running the gamut from Viceroy's banana pie (£2.95) to kulfi (£2.35), that dense and tasty Indian ice cream.

Hing, or asafoetida, is a spice which has not only a distinctive flavour but also a rude name. In oonbhariu (£4.75) – a dish from the vegetables section – it is blended with lovage and cumin to accompany bananas, sweet potato, baby aubergines and shallots. Particularly delicious, and not stinky at all.

£6–£18

Belair House

Gallery Rd, Dulwich Village, SE21 ℂ020 8299 9788	BR West Dulwich
Mon–Sat noon–2.30pm & 7–10.30pm,	
Sun noon–3pm & 7–9.30pm (lunch only in winter)	All major credit cards

www.belairhouse.co.uk

Belair House is a large, pale Georgian house, standing alone in Dulwich Park. A Grade Two listed building, it has been sensitively and painstakingly restored. In the summer the two terraces do sterling service, one filled with diners and the other with drinkers. This establishment is already justly popular with locals, and Sunday lunch in particular is booked up well ahead. With its head start of tall, well-proportioned rooms and a sweeping staircase, the decor is both elegant and surprisingly bright – research shows that, when built, the interior of the building would have been painted in the lurid colours fashionable at the time. The kitchen makes use of whatever is best from the markets to produce a regularly changing menu.

The good-value set lunch offers starters like Parma ham stuffed with aubergines and capers, and mains such as pan-fried John Dory or double cutlet of lamb; desserts include indulgent frozen white chocolate and pistachio mousse. The prix fixe is priced in an enlightened way – £14.50 for any two courses, £17.50 for three courses, Monday to Saturday. There's a set dinner served Monday to Thursday for £24.95, which is also the cost of the Sunday lunch. The à la carte, which is available at both lunch and dinner, offers smarter dishes at smarter prices. They might include starters of smoked trout salad and pike brandade (£5.95), celery and apple soup with blue cheese croutons (£5.50), and smoked ham and wood pigeon terrine (£7.75). Mains may range from fillet of cod with leek and mussel pie, mash, and parsley purée (£16.95); to English lamb cutlet and home-made lamb sausages with flageolet beans (£16.95). Puddings are often adventurous – just try the blood orange soufflé (£5.95) – and there is always the tasty option of British cheeses with onion compote (£7.50).

Look carefully in the toilets downstairs and you will spot vestiges of a former incarnation of Belair House – it used to act as a changing room for children using the surrounding playing fields.

Kastoori

188 Upper Tooting Rd, SW17 ✆020 8767 7027   ⊖ Tooting Broadway

Mon & Tues 6–10.30pm, Wed–Sun 12.30–2.30pm & 6–10.30pm   Mastercard, Visa

Anyone who is genuinely puzzled that people can cope on – and indeed enjoy – a diet of vegetables alone should try eating at Kastoori. Located in a rather unpromising-looking bit of Balham, Kastoori is a "Pure Vegetarian Restaurant". Gujarati food is leavened with East African influences and is so delicious that you could invite even the most hardened carnivore and be pretty sure that they will be as entranced as everybody else. The large and cavernous restaurant is run by the admirably helpful Thanki family – do be sure to ask their advice, and act on it. Recently Kastoori underwent a facelift: the decor may have changed from pink to blue and yellow but thankfully the quality of the food has stayed the same.

First onto the waiter's pad (and indeed first into the mouth, as they go soggy and collapse if made to wait) must be dahi puri (£2.50) – tiny crispy flying saucers filled with a sweet/sour yoghurty sauce, potatoes, onions, chickpeas and so forth. You pop them in whole; the marriage of taste and texture is a revelation. Samosas (three for £1.80) are excellent, but also in the revelation category are the onion bhajis (five for £2.10) – bite-sized and delicious, a far cry from the ball-of-knitting variety served in most high-street curry emporia. Then make sure that someone orders the vegetable curry of the day (£4.25), and others the outstanding cauliflower with cream curry (£4.25) and the special tomato curry (£4.25) – a hot and spicy classic from Katia Wahd. Leave room for the chilli banana (£4.50), bananas stuffed with mild chillies – an East African recipe – and mop everything up with generous helpings of puris (60p) and chapatis (60p).

The smart move is to ask what's in season, as the menu is littered with oddities which come and go. For example, you might find rotlo – millet loaf (£2.50, served only on Sunday). Or the dish called, rather enigmatically, "beans of the day" (£4.25). Another interesting and esoteric dish is drumstick curry (£4.50). Drumsticks are thin, green, Asian vegetables about eighteen inches long and twice as thick as a pencil. You chew the flesh from the stalk. This is a place where it pays to experiment.

Lahore Karahi

1 Tooting High St, SW17 ✆020 8767 2477   ⊖ Tooting Broadway

Daily noon–midnight   Cash or cheque only

Though the bright neon spilling onto the pavement beckons you from Tooting High Street, spiritually speaking, the Lahore Karahi is in Upper Tooting Road. It's a busy place, which has increased the number of seats to cope with the ever-growing swell of customers, and now even boasts air conditioning. Behind a counter equipped with numerous bains-marie stand rows of cooks, distinguishable by their natty Lahore Karahi base-ball caps, turning out a daily twelve-hour marathon of dishes. Prices are low, food is chilli-hot, service is speedy. Don't be intimidated: simply seat yourself in a Habitat chair, don't worry if you have to share a table, and start ordering. Regulars bring their own drinks or stick to the exotic fruit juices – mango, guava or passion . . . all at just 80p.

Unusually for what is, at bottom, an unreconstructed grill house, there is a wide range of vegetarian dishes "prepared under strict precautions". Karahi karela (£2.95) is a curry of bitter gourds; karahi saag paneer (£3.50) teams spinach and cheese; and karahi methi aloo (£2.95) brings potatoes flavoured with fenugreek. Meat-eaters can plunge in joyfully – the chicken tikka (£2.25), seekh kabab (50p), and tandoori chicken (£1.75) are all good and all spicy-hot, the only fault being a good deal of artificial red colouring. There are also a dozen chicken curries and a dozen lamb curries (from £3.50 to £3.95), along with a dozen special-ities (from £4.50 to £7 for king prawn karahi). Those with a strong constitution can try the dishes of the day, like nihari (£4.50), which is lamb shank on the bone in an incendiary broth, or paya (£3.95), which is sheep's feet cooked until gluey. Breads are good here: try the jeera nan (60p) or the tandoori roti (60p).

The Lahore Karahi comes into its own as a takeaway, and there's usually a queue at the counter as people collect their considerable banquets – not just chicken tikka in a naan, or portions of curry, but large and elab-orate biryanis as well – meat (£3.25), chicken (£3.25), prawn (£4.95), or vegetable (£2.95). For wholesome, fast-ish food, the cooking and the prices here are hard to beat.

Masaledar

121 Upper Tooting Rd, SW17 ✆020 8767 7676   ⊖ Tooting Bec/Tooting Broadway

Daily noon–midnight   Mastercard, Visa

What can you say about a place that has two huge standard lamps, each made from an upturned, highly ornate Victorian drainpipe, topped with a large karahi? When it comes to interior design, Masaledar provides plenty of surprises – and a feeling of spaciousness that's the very opposite of most of the bustling Indian restaurants in Tooting and Balham. This establishment is run by East African Asian Muslims, so no alcohol is allowed on the premises, but that doesn't deter a loyal clientele, who are packing the place out. Along with several other restaurants in Tooting Road, Maseladar has had to expand, and has added another 25 covers. The food is fresh, well spiced and cheap – there are vegetable curries at under £3 and meat curries for less than £4 – and, to cap it all, you eat it in an elegant designer dining room.

As starters, the samosas are sound: either two meat (£1.40) or two vegetable (£1.25). Or try the chicken wings from the tandoor (five pieces £1.75), or the very tasty lamb chops (four pieces £3.25). You might move on to a biryani – chicken or lamb (£4.25) – which are tasty and rich. Or perhaps try a karahi dish like karahi methi gosht (£4.25). This is strongly flavoured and delicious, although guaranteed to leave you with fenugreek seeping from your pores for days to come. Then there's the rich and satisfying achar gosht (£4.25). The masaledar daal (£2.95) is a less successful dish, unless you like your dhal runny. The breads, however, are terrific – especially the wonderful thin rotis (60p). Look out for the lunch special – a thali with curry, naan, rice, plus coffee and ice cream for £2.95.

Sometimes the brisk takeaway trade, and the fact that all dishes are made to order, conspire to make service a bit slow, but you can always lean back and enjoy your surroundings. And, despite or because of the absence of alcohol, you can have an interesting evening's drinking. Mango shake (£1.75 a large glass, £4.50 a jug) is rich, very fruity and not too sweet; order one before your meal, however, and greed will ensure that you have finished it by the time your food comes. Both the sweet and salty lassi (£1.25, or £3.75 for a large glass) are very refreshing, as is the fresh passion juice (£2.50 a large glass, £6.95 a jug), which is perhaps the best bet for accompanying your meal.

£6–£16

Mirch Masala

1416 London Rd, Norbury, SW16 ©020 8679 1828 BR Norbury

Daily noon–midnight All major credit cards

You'll find Mirch Masala just up London Road from Norbury station. It may not look much from the outside, but it deserves a place on any list of London's top ten Indian restaurants – something South London's Asian community appear to have cottoned on to. As befits such a culinary temple, the chefs take centre stage; the kitchen is in full view and you can watch the whole cooking process, which culminates, as likely as not, in a chef bringing the food to table. They are certainly prone to wandering out while you are enjoying the last of your starters to ask if you're ready for your main course. What's more, at the end of the meal they are also happy to pack up anything you don't finish so that you can take it home. Take advantage, over-order and try a lot of different dishes; this is a very friendly place serving spectacular food at low prices. Both the food and the service are unpretentious in the extreme, which makes for very contented diners indeed.

Start with a stick each of chicken tikka (£2.50) and lamb tikka (£2.50), crusted with pepper and spices on the outside, juicy with marinade on the inside. Very good indeed. Or try the butter chicken wings (£3), cooked in a light, ungreasy sauce laden with flavour from fresh spices and herbs. Then move on to the karahi dishes, which are presented in a kind of thick aluminium hubcap. The vegetable karahi dishes are exceptional. Go for the butter beans and methi (£3.50) – an inspired and delicious combination of flavours – and karahi valpapdi baigan (£4), aubergines cooked with small rich beans. Among the best meat dishes are the karella gosht (£5), lamb with bitter gourd, and the deigi saag gosht (£5), spinach, lamb and a rich sauce. Even something simple like karahi ginger chicken (£5) proves how good and fresh-tasting Indian food can be. Rice (£1.50) comes in a glass butter dish complete with lid. Breads include a good naan (70p) and an indulgent deep-fried bhatura (60p) that will provoke greed in anyone who has ever hankered after fried bread.

A meal at Mirch Masala will be a memorable one. As they say on the menu, "Food extraordinaire. You wish it – we cook it."

Planet Spice

88 Selsdon Park Rd, Addington, South Croydon ✆020 8651 3300	Croydon Tramway
Mon–Sat noon–2.30pm & 6.30–11.30pm,	
Sun 12.30–3.30pm & 6–11.30pm	All major credit cards

Planet Spice is a fish out of water. Even the presence of the latest transport innovation – the much vaunted new tramway – cannot prepare you for the surprise you get when you arrive here. The restaurant (a sister establishment to the Babur Brasserie; see p.425) is located at the junction of two major roads and in premises that have been used for everything from a Greek restaurant to a dance school. Today the building houses an Indian restaurant of a very high order indeed – if Planet Spice were in the West End it would be showered with critical acclaim.

The chefs have had to make certain compromises. The takeaway side of things is still dominated by old-style dishes – korma, Madras, chicken tikka masala – and any sit-down customers who look perplexed at the main menu can opt for these. The main menu, however, is agreeably ambitious and really is the one you should work from. Start with lobster samosas (£4.95), which are very delicate, or calamari balchao (£3.75), which is squid in a rich pungent sauce. The ragda pattice (£3.25), a freshly made potato cake with a tasty chickpea curry, is also good. Main courses are distinguished by accurate and well-balanced spicing and unusually careful cooking. Try the green fish curry from Goa (£7.75); it varies from day to day, but could well be a perfectly cooked salmon in an amazing, velvety, creamy sauce. Team it with the lime and cashew nut rice (£1.95). Or there's an exemplary duck xacuti (£8.25), the duck breast pink and smokey and cooked separately from the sauce, which is dark and rich with flavour. Or try chicken Chettinad (£6.95), a South Indian dish famous for its fieriness (although it is somewhat tamed here).

These are ambitious dishes, handled well. It's probably due to there being not one but two able chefs in the kitchen: the ex-chef to the president of India and a South Indian specialist from the Indian Taj Group of luxury hotels! However did they find their way to Addington?

£12–£25

Le Raj

211 Fir Tree Rd, Epsom Downs, Surrey ©01737 371371 | BR Epsom Downs

Daily noon–2.30pm & 5.30–11pm | All major credit cards

www.leraj.com

Le Raj was always a distinctive restaurant, and its proprietor and chef Enam Ali was always a good cook. Following a major refurbishment in 1999, and a new menu, this seventy-seater is now outstanding. This is not the food of the high-street curry house, but a fresh-tasting, thought-provoking cuisine. Granted, Mr Ali's obsession with presentation is still to the forefront and you will sight both domes and triangular black plates, but overlook that, and the piped music, and you will have a great time. Ingredients are first-rate, flavours are exciting, and you'll wait as happily for each course as you would in a good French restaurant. The wait means that each of your dishes is being cooked with care.

From the starters, try chot poti (£2.95) – this is a cone of masala popadom filled with chickpeas cooked in cumin, chilli and coriander. Delicious. Or tikka kerkere (£3.50), a superb chicken tikka variant, made with tender meat with a very thin, crisp coat. Or esa puri (£3.50), a well-flavoured fried puri wrapped around spiced prawns. Everything looks elegant but, more importantly, everything tastes good. Main courses include some excellent Bangladeshi dishes – maacher tarkari (£11.50) is made with boal, a meaty fish in a light tomatoey and creamy sauce. It's delicious, and gratifyingly bone-free. Enam Ali is not afraid to add to dishes, and the chicken naga (£6.95) is a perfect example; the chicken, cooked with nutmeg and fresh herbs, is also tempered with hot African chillies. For good, intense flavours, order the kacchi (£9.95), a traditional Dhaka biryani, where the rice and lamb are cooked together in the pot slowly. The side dishes are good, as well. There's laau bhajee (£3.50), a very rich curry of pumpkin with bay leaf. And a first-class dhal (£3.50). Even the simple things are good, like the naans (£1.95) and rotis (£1.75).

Indian restaurants often proclaim their intention of crashing the barrier and becoming the first to gain Michelin recognition. Le Raj might just make it and deserves encouragement, not least for being a showcase for genuine and sophisticated Bangladeshi food.

Shamyana

437–439 Streatham High Rd, SW16 ✆020 8679 6162	BR Norbury
Daily noon–midnight	Amex, Mastercard, Visa

The rather good Indian food that you'll find in Tooting is gradually making its way south. At the forefront of this diaspora was the peerless Mirch Masala (see p.430); Shamyana followed suit and opened a few hundred yards up the road. What all these successful restaurants seem to have in common is well-made, unfussy, spicy food. Indeed, Shamyana even goes so far as to claim the ultimate in endorsements, that their head chef was "trained in Lahore". And there's no doubt that this kind of (often fiercely spicy) Punjabi food has become the first option of the Asian community. The restaurant has obviously done service as a banqueting hall in the past and there is a vast upstairs room with a sweeping staircase. But for the moment all the action is on the ground floor, where customers are lured to marvel at the brass ceiling. Ignore the decor and concentrate instead on the food, which is cheap and good.

Start with chilli chicken wings (£2.50) or chicken tikka (£2.55) – tandoori dishes that are well spiced and well cooked. They're not at all dried-out; the man on the marinades knows his stuff. As you move on to main courses there is an imposing array of vegetarian dishes – over a dozen to choose from (between £3.45 and £3.75). Then there is an assortment of Punjabi favourites: ginger chicken (£4.50), or desi methi chicken (£5.20), rich with fenugreek. Another very good dish is the masala karella gosht (£4.50); the pundits will tell you that the flesh of the karella, or bitter melon, is very good for the blood and has a cleansing effect. But, medicinal or not, this is certainly an addictively good flavour – the lamb and karella curry is a real winner. The biryanis can disappoint, but the "special" pilau (chicken on Thursday and Friday; lamb Saturday and Sunday) are terrific, as is the special karahi gosht (£16 for what is rather optimistically described as a "portion for four people" and turns out to be a rather good lamb curry on the bone that may feed three).

The rotis are grand here. And there's an intriguing side dish you must order: mixed fried ginger, chilli and onion (£1) lives up to its description exactly and is very handy for adding to rice or eating on its own with bread. Shamyana is a bring-your-own, so feel free.

£8–£20

Tamasha

131 Widmore Rd, Bromley, Kent ©020 8460 3240 · BR Bromley South

Mon–Sat noon–2.30pm & 6–11pm,

Sun noon–2.30pm & 7–10.30pm · All major credit cards

www.tamasha.co.uk

Tamasha, very roughly translated, means "a bit of a do", and this is a great place to come when you decide to push the boat out. From the moment you are greeted by the doorman, dressed in authentic costume, and shown into the mock-colonial interior, you know that this is no run-of-the-mill suburban curry house. Tamasha has a style all of its own, over the top and down the other side – as you can tell from its Polo bar, a cosy intimate setting perfect for aperitif or cocktail. The dining rooms – called Victorian, Raj and India Club – are light and airy, and there's a less formal room upstairs. The food lives up to these surroundings and is quite moderately priced (there's an all-in bargain Sunday buffet at £8.95). To wash it down, both ice-cold Cobra beer and Dom Perignon have a strong local following.

The menu lists dishes from all over India. Starters include well-known dishes such as seekh kebab (£3.95) and king prawn puri (£4.95) – both good – and extend to unusual delights such as utthapams (£3.95) – a South Indian ground rice pancake cooked with onion, green pepper and coriander, then served with creamy green coconut chutney. The chicken manchoori (£7.95) is fiery with green chilli and tomatoes, although not overpoweringly so, and the Goan fish curry (£8.50) is sweetened with coconut. Vegetarian dishes such as navratan masala (£6.95), mushrooms with cream and nine dried tropical fruits, provide a sweeter, fresher alternative to the more highly spiced and richer prawn-based raja jhinga silchari (£10.95) – apparently, this was a very popular dish with East India Company officials. To round off your meal, try the Tamasha coffee (£4.50 per person, minimum four people). It sounds expensive, but the theatre of the preparation alone – caramelised glasses, grapefruit peel, brandy and lots of flames – is worth the price. And the coffee isn't bad either.

If the thought of the journey home seems too daunting, why not stay in one of rooms the Tamasha has maintained from its previous incarnation as an hotel? A double room costs £55 including breakfast – pukka English, of course.

Three Monkeys

136–140 Herne Hill, SE24 ℗020 7738 5500	BR Herne Hill
Mon–Sat 6–11pm, Sun noon–3pm & 6–11pm	All major credit cards

www.3monkeyseating.com

In the West End and the City, cool restaurateurs are forever buying up old banks, ripping the insides out, slapping on a coat of ultra-chic frosted glass and reopening as the latest thing in slick designer restaurants. It's just a bit of a shock to see such an establishment – complete with a gangplank bridge over the basement bar – in sleepy old Herne Hill. And if that doesn't rock your imagination back on its heels, let's just add that Three Monkeys is an Indian restaurant. Albeit an unusual one. The well-written menu steers firmly away from clichéd Indian food. All this style does not come cheap, however, and some of the prices are on the high side, but this is such a brave and extravagant enterprise you could almost turn a blind eye.

Starters range from shammi kebab (£4.95) – minced lamb rissoles the size and shape of a hockey puck – to a brilliant, messy-looking dish, palak palodi chat (£4.75) – small cubes of spinach mixture deep-fried until crisp and served with plenty of chunky raw veg and two sauces, sharp tamarind and creamy yoghurt. Very nice. As is the vogue, there is an open kitchen, and the grills and bread are all well made. The main courses run from simple dishes like rojan gosht (£8.95) to dishes like chicken makhni (£8.95), which many curryologists assert is the parent of chicken tikka masala. Look out for a range of good fish dishes, and do not be put off by the fact that most of the curries have names unfamiliar to British curry houses; they are authentic for all that. The prices are steepest anywhere you find the words "large" and "prawn". Large prawns peri peri (£14.75) is described as large prawns pan-fried with a spicy Goan masala. They taste OK; it's up to you whether you wish to pay nearly £3.50 for each prawn. Also in the good-but-expensive category is bhindi Jaipuri – a dish of okra cut very fine and deep-fried before being served with a seasoning of sour dried mango powder (£5.50).

Three Monkeys is a slick, fashionable, modern Indian restaurant serving commendably authentic food at prices that have to be taken seriously. It's not the monkeys' fault that they're in Herne Hill.

West

Barnes & Sheen 439

Chelsea 447

Ealing & Acton 461

Earl's Court 471

Fulham 477

Hammersmith & Chiswick 485

Notting Hill 495

Richmond & Twickenham 515

Shepherd's Bush & Olympia 525

Southall 533

Further West 543
    Greenford, Hampton, Surbiton

Barnes & Sheen

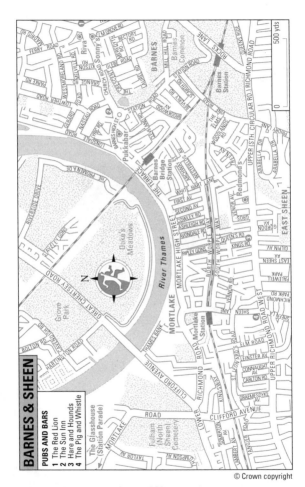

BARNES & SHEEN

PUBS AND BARS

1 The Red Lion
2 The Sun Inn
3 Hare and Hounds
4 The Pig and Whistle

The Glasshouse
(Station Parade)

© Crown copyright

The Glasshouse

14 Station Parade, Kew Gardens, Surrey ©020 8940 6777	⊖ Kew Gardens
Mon–Sat noon–2.30pm & 7–10.30pm, Sun 12.30–3pm	All major credit cards

Despite the boom of recent years, opening restaurants is still a precarious business. The Glasshouse, however, which opened in 1999, seems not only to have lived up to its admirable pedigree – chef Anthony Boyd honed his craft at the Michelin-bedecked Square (see p.90) and Chez Bruce (see p.372) – but also to have survived that difficult "be-patient-just-opened" period. What's more, the restaurant is on the doorstep of Kew Gardens underground station, which makes it easy for anyone who can get onto the District line. The interior has a clean-cut, modern feel to it and the chairs are worthy of lavish praise – they are blissfully comfortable, an aspect of dining which is all too often overlooked. The food is good. Very good. Boyd's style, which combines Square's sophistication and the rich flavours of Chez Bruce, is a sure-fire winner.

The menu is a simple one, which changes daily and usually makes you choose from seven starters, seven mains and seven puds. At lunch two courses cost £17.50 and three £19.50; for dinner the price is £25 for three courses, and £23.50 for two. This is a snatch-their-hand-off bargain. The cooking, imaginative and straightforward, owes much to French cuisine. Starters range from Rossmore oysters with gazpacho jelly through mussel risotto with crisp mackerel and ravigote butter to deep-fried goujons of plaice with tartare sauce – half a dozen perfectly cooked fingers of plaice with a dollop of rich, almost chunky, tartare. Main courses vary from a classically inspired blanquette of veal with morels and truffled mashed potatoes to fillet of cod with a cèpe crust, leeks and pearl barley. The roast guinea fowl with boudin blanc and grain mustard is good. Puddings have a deft touch and include old favourites like rum baba and savarin. The pear and almond tart with a poire William custard is particularly fine. The wine list is short and thoughtfully drawn up, with one or two unusual selections.

Service at Glasshouse is masterful, and will leave you feeling thoroughly cosseted. However, it's just as well to note the small print at the bottom of the menu which warns "Please order taxis at least 25 minutes before they are required".

Pukkabar

21 Barnes High St, SW13 ℂ020 8878 7012 — BR Barnes Bridge

Daily 12.30–2.30pm & 6.30–10.30pm — All major credit cards

Pukkabar, or "The Pukkabar and Curry Hall" to spell out its more fulsome title, started life in Sydenham. It was the brainchild of Trevor Gulliver, the mastermind behind that HQ of nose-to-tail cuisine – St John in Clerkenwell (p.219). Mr Gulliver's quaint theory was that curry is a very British dish, and that this British perspective is the one from which it is best approached. The Pukkabar offers well-made, well-spiced, good-value food in clean surroundings and with the minimum pretension and fuss. Curries are batch-cooked and the rest of the menu is made up of fresh food from the tandoor and a range of tasty Indian street food for starters. As with so many kinds of food, when it comes to curry simple is good and, despite its English antecedents, the Pukkabar has ended up having a good deal more in common with Southall or even Delhi than most high-street curry houses.

The menu changes regularly, but you can expect to find about eight starters listed, several of which are suitable for vegetarians. From the tandoor there's chicken tikka (£3.75) – well cooked and tender – or tandoori salmon (£4.95), or tandoori peppered lamb (£3.95). The presentation is accomplished here. Also on the starters menu is chot poti (£3.50) – a puri topped with a savoury mix of pan-fried chickpeas, onion and pumpkin, this is one of those dishes that is at its most delicious when straight out of the kitchen. In addition to the mixed tandoori (£7.95, chicken, lamb and salmon), the main courses are curries: lamb chilli curry (£5.95); Goan prawn coconut curry (£7.95); a hot Bengal fish curry (£6.25); a mild aromatic lamb curry with yoghurt (£5.95); and even that all-British favourite, chicken tikka masala (£5.95). Rice dishes and breads are good; check out the cheese naan (£2). For pud there are Hill Station ice creams (£3) – better a reputable bought-in ice cream than a poorly made one from the kitchen.

Lunch at Pukkabar is something of a bargain. They offer a light dish – tandoori chicken salad, say, or the Goan prawn curry – with rice and either a glass of house wine or a Cobra beer for just £8.50.

Redmond's

170 Upper Richmond Rd West, SW14 ℭ020 8878 1922	BR Mortlake

Mon–Fri noon–2.30pm & 7–10.30pm, Sat 7–10.30pm,

Sun noon–2.30pm	Delta, Mastercard, Switch, Visa

Redmond Hayward is an improbably good cook to be found in a small neighbourhood restaurant. The key to this conundrum is that this is his own small neighbourhood restaurant, a pretty, fifty-seater in Sheen. They tweak the menu on a daily basis, so it reflects the best of what the season and the markets have to offer. The dinner menu is not particularly short – about eight starters and mains – and proves astonishing value at £22 for two courses and £25 for three. There are also two lunch menus – the "express" at £10 for two courses and £12.50 for three, or the wider menu at £16.50 for two courses or £21.50 for three. What's even more astonishing is that the list is not splattered with supplements or cover charges; in fact, a "discretionary" service charge (a meagre 10%) is added to the bill, but only when your party numbers six or more. And the food here really is very good indeed: well seasoned, precisely cooked, immaculately presented.

If the terrine of chicken and foie gras is available when you visit, pounce – it's delicate, multi-layered, multi-textured, superlative-inducing in every way. There may also be a crab and mussel broth with lemongrass and ginger, or razor clams marinière, or perhaps a Taleggio and Swiss chard tart with green salad. Main courses combine dominant flavours with elegant presentation. Corn-fed chicken breast comes with "A"-class mash, wild mushrooms and parsley oil – marvellously, the chicken tastes just how chicken is supposed to taste. Roast rump of lamb comes with a warm salad of minted new potato, green beans and shallots, and grain mustard dressing. Lemon, parsley and garlic couscous partners char-grilled scallops. The puddings are wonderful, too. Praline millefeuille of crème brûlée and poached peach with raspberry sauce makes an imposing tower out of luxurious dollops of vanillaey crème brûlée, peach segments and craquelin. The strawberry, raspberry and elderflower jelly comes with a delicate vanilla cream.

The short wine list is littered with interesting bottles at accessible prices – there are halves, magnums, pudding wines, and just plain bargains. Splash out on the splendid Gigondas at £25, a perfect partner for the impressive all-British cheeseboard.

£25–£45

Riva

169 Church Rd, SW13 ✆020 8748 0434	BR Barnes
Mon–Fri noon–2.30pm & 7–11pm, Sat 7–11.30pm,	
Sun noon–2.30pm & 7–9.30pm	Amex, Mastercard, Visa

When Andrea Riva opened his doors some years ago, Hammersmith Bridge allowed easy access to devotees north of the Thames who doted on his straightforward Italian cooking. Then the bridge closed; then it reopened; and it is a testament to the pulling power of the kitchen that throughout this prolonged spell of planning blight the restaurant continued to be busy. It just goes to show – people will put themselves out for good food. Inside, this is a rather conservative-looking restaurant, with a narrow dining room decorated in a sombre blend of dull greens and faded parchment, and chairs which have clearly seen service in church. As far as the cuisine goes, Riva provides the genuine article, so first-time customers are either delighted or disappointed. The menu changes regularly with the seasons.

Starters are good but not cheap: the frittelle (£8.50) is a tempura-like dish of deep-fried Mediterranean prawn, salt cod cakes, calamari and artichoke, with a balsamic dip. If it is on the menu, you must try bocconcini di bufala – buffalo mozzarella with roasted peppers, red onions, cherry tomatoes and capers (£7), vibrant and deliciously oily. The brodetto "Mare Nostrum", a chunky saffron-flavoured fish soup (£7), is also superb – a delicate alternative to its robust French cousin. Serious Italian food fans, however, will find it hard to resist the sapori Mediterranei (£19 for two), which gets you crab and fennel salad; baccala mantecato and polenta; poached pike in salsa verde; and eel in tomato sauce – a combination that is unlikely to be found on many menus outside the Po valley. Among the main courses, branzino al rosemary (£15) is a splendid combination of tastes and textures – a fillet of sea bass with rosemary and shallots is served on a potato tortino with fava beans. Battuta di pollo – chicken breast marinated in thyme and balsamic vinegar with spinach and pumpkin gratin (£12.50) – delivers a finely balanced blend of flavours.

If there's anybody out there who still thinks that pizza and pasta are the Italians' staple diet, Riva's uncompromising regional menu proves otherwise. The house wines are all priced at a very accessible £10.50. Of the whites, the pale-coloured Tocai is crisp, light and refreshing.

Sonny's

94 Church Rd, SW13 ©020 8748 0393	BR Barnes Bridge
Mon–Sat 12.30–2.30pm & 7.30–11pm,	
Sun 12.30–3pm	All major credit cards

If the scientists are to be believed, we must evolve or die, and if they're looking for corroborating evidence they will find it at Sonny's. This is one of those restaurants people describe as a "neighbourhood stalwart" and for once the term is not inappropriate. Barnes-ites have been supporting Sonny's since Modern British cuisine was just a twinkle in a telly chef's eye. The interior is modern but gratifyingly unthreatening and there is a busy, casual feel about the place. Sonny's shop next door sells a good many of those little delicacies that you would otherwise have to make the dangerous journey to the West End to procure. Leigh Diggins is chef here and he has a good grasp of just what his customers want. The menu is modern but not aggressively so, dishes are interesting but not frightening, and you will find the occasional flash of innovation.

The menu changes on a regular basis to reflect the seasons, so you might find starters like watercress soup with Jersey Royals and truffle oil (£4.25), or chicken and sweeetbread terrine with mixed leaves and sweet pickle (£6.50), or even, on a more whimsical note, maple-roasted quail with apple and red wine risotto (£6.75). Main courses may take classic combinations like pan-fried calves' liver with pancetta, and then add crushed new potatoes, button onions and garlic leaves (£11.50). There tend to be some attractive fish dishes, too: steamed fillet of halibut with Jersey Royals, broad beans and langoustine dressing (£14), say, or roasted wild sea trout with fresh pasta, grilled ceps and fresh peas (£12.50). Or you could go much more trad and much more hearty with the grilled fillet of beef, bone marrow and mustard glaze, fondant potato and asparagus (£15.50). The service is welcoming and the wine list provides some sound bottles at sound prices.

Puddings are comfortable: sorbets, jellies, baked Alaska with raspberries (£5.25). If Barnes is your neighbourhood, you will be glad that it has a restaurant like this, especially as there is a set lunch during the week – £12 for two courses, £15 for three. If Barnes isn't your neighbourhood, you could try one of Sonny's siblings – Parade, in Ealing (p.467), or The Phoenix, 162 Lower Richmond Rd, SW15 (©020 8780 3131).

Hare & Hounds

216 Upper Richmond Rd West,
SW14   ✆020 8876 4304

Right on the main road, this cheery, welcoming Young's pub has a massive interior with leaded roof lights and a huge, well-kept beer garden with children's play area. There's a full-sized snooker table in a separate room too, but it gets booked well in advance. All Young's draught and bottled beers are on offer.

The Pig & Whistle

86 Sheen Lane, SW14   ✆020 8878 7785

A mixed crowd of local regulars enjoys this nice traditional pub with all the usual trimmings – sport on TV, games machines, and the like. Favourite ales on tap include Courage Best and Directors.

The Red Lion

2 Castelnau, SW13   ✆020 8748 2984

This is a big, old-fashioned, family local. It's child-friendly, with a play area in the large patio garden where huge canvas umbrellas shield the tables and heaters. Inside, the darts board gets a lot of serious use. It's a Fuller's pub, so you get London Pride, ESB and Chiswick Bitter.

The Sun Inn

7 Church Rd, SW13   ✆020 8876 5256

Hugely popular old pub with a lovely view of Barnes Common and the duck-pond – it's almost like being in the countryside. Inside, low ceilings and a country-kitchen feel make it wonderfully cosy. Beers on tap include Tetley's, Adnams and Ind Coope Burton Ale. It gets very crowded at weekends.

Chelsea

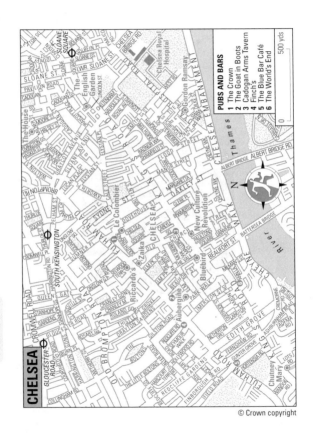

CHELSEA

PUBS AND BARS

1 The Crown
2 The Goat in Boots
3 Cadogan Arms Tavern
4 Finch's
5 The Blue Bar Café
6 The World's End

0   500 yds

© Crown copyright

Aubergine

11 Park Walk, SW10 ✆020 7352 3449   ⊖ South Kensington/Earl's Court

Mon–Fri noon–2.30pm & 7–10.30pm, Sat 7–10.30pm   All major credit cards

William Drabble deserves a prolonged burst of applause. It's not so long ago that he took up the challenge of filling the shoes of the very lively Gordon Ramsay (p.454) at Aubergine. In his five-year tenure Ramsay had brought notoriety and accolades to the restaurant in roughly equal measure, becoming a walking embodiment of the phrase "hard act to follow". All of which didn't bother Mr Drabble one bit. He took over, wrote his own menu, and gained his own accolades. Aubergine has a pretty, elegant, airy dining room and serves very good French food with panache and élan. This is top-drawer dining. The set lunch at £16 for two courses and £19.50 for three is an outrageous bargain. No wonder that, as in Ramsay's day, bookings at Aubergine are becoming hard to come by.

A lunch that comprises pan-fried red mullet with escabeche followed by daube of beef in its own juices with pomme purée doesn't read, look or taste like £15's worth. Even at full throttle the main menu offers three courses for £42.50 which is not so very fierce for cooking of this calibre. Starters may include seared scallops with pea purée; mousse of foie gras with girolles; warm salad of truffled vegetables with asparagus purée, or boudin of pigeon with foie gras, caramelised turnips, and truffle juice. Main courses, which appeal greatly, include dishes like roasted sea bass with sauté of peppers, artichokes and rocket with basil oil; saddle of venison with creamed confit cabbage and Madeira jus; veal sweetbreads with celeriac fondant, braised lettuce and truffled jus; pot-roast chicken with a casserole of ceps and bacon. Well-conceived, well-executed dishes, beautifully presented. It would be hard to suggest improvements. The Menu Gourmand at £55 will spin the experience out by presenting seven pixie portions and so allow you to appreciate more of Mr Drabble's skills. Desserts are equally accomplished – figs marinated in red wine and port with fromage blanc mousse and sorbet; hot chocolate fondant with clementine sorbet. The service is accomplished and unobtrusive.

The only cautionary note relates to the wine list, where the prices bolt swiftly out of reach for all but the most special of special occasions.

£20–£40

Bluebird

350 King's Rd, SW3 ©020 7559 1000	⊖ Sloane Square
Mon–Fri noon–3pm & 6–11pm, Sat 11am–3.30pm & 6–11pm,	
Sun 11am–3.30pm (brunch) & 6–10pm	All major credit cards
www.conran.com	

This is a slick place. If you like slick places, you'll like it a lot. Conran's Bluebird complex is large and sprawling: there is a food hall, a kitchenware shop, a cafe, a flower stall, a members-only club and the restaurant itself. The dining room is large with a central bar and manages to be both crowded as well as light and airy. The food is modern – Modern European, if that is in any way a meaningful description – and the Oriental twist to dishes which was a feature when the Bluebird started out has been tempered as the restaurant has matured. The service is professional to a T and the prices look fair – although when all is finally added up you may be surprised how high the total can be. There is, however, a good-value set lunch – two courses for £12.75, three courses for £15.75 – which also does service as a pre-theatre option, before 7pm.

You might start with goat ricotta, olives and peppers (£6.25), or perhaps something more sophisticated like rare tuna with pickled ginger, cucumber and wasabi (£8.25). Wood-roast sardines, olives, capers and tomato (£7.50) makes good use of the vaunted wood-fired oven. The main courses are divided into fish/shellfish, pasta/risotto, meat, grill/rôtisserie, wood roast, and dishes for two, which can make working through the menu a mission that demands your full attention. The monkfish with sweet and sour sauce and jasmine rice (£18.50) appeals, as does the potato gnocchi with Italian sausage and peas (£11.50). The equipment-led sections are also worth browsing; the rôtisserie turns out pretty good corn-fed poussin with wild mushrooms and garlic (£15), while the wood-fuelled oven contributes organic pork loin with bean ragout (£12.75), and a pizza with ratte potatoes, Fontina and thyme (£9.50). Enlist an accomplice and you can have Chateaubriand with matchstick fries and watercress (£39 for two).

Puddings – champagne jelly with raspberries and an almond biscuit (£5.25), or fig tart with vanilla ice cream (£5.50) – are generally successful.

Chutney Mary

535 King's Rd, SW10 ✆020 7351 3113	⊖ Fulham Broadway
Mon–Thurs 12.30–2.30pm & 7–11.30pm, Fri & Sat 12.30–2.30pm & 6.30–11.30pm,	
Sun 12.30–3pm & 7–10.30pm	All major credit cards
www.chutneymary.com	

For such a large, well-designed, elegant restaurant, the food at Chutney Mary is remarkably close to tasting home-made – which is perhaps the greatest compliment you can pay an Indian meal in London. Dishes here are not cheap, but the food is freshly prepared and the spicing is always authentic. The menu combines regional Indian specialities with Anglo-Indian dishes from the days of the Raj – so this is an opportunity to try curiosities like "Country Captain". About four dishes change each quarter, but the restaurant hosts a succession of festivals which focus on the food of a particular region, when you will find fifteen to twenty regional specialities in pride of place on the menu. You will have to book in the evening and for the very popular jazz brunch on Sunday, which comes in at the wholly reasonable price of £15 for three courses.

Starters are split into vegetarian and non-vegetarian, and can be conveniently ordered as a selection (£6/£7.50). The former brings samosas, papri chat and veggie kebabs; the latter, crab cake, papri chat and lobster samosa. Both are tempting options, as is the spicy calamari stir-fried with Malabar spices (£6.25). For mains, turn to the regional dishes, which tend to be complex and interestingly spiced – green chicken curry from Goa, for instance, with fresh coriander, green chilli, mint and tamarind (£11.50), or a fiery Mangalore prawn curry cooked in an earthenware pot (£15.75), or Osmani korma, a classic Hyderabadi lamb curry made with sandalwood, rosebuds and saffron. All of these dishes come with aromatic Basmati rice. As a side dish, look out for crisp-fried okra and banana (£3.75) from Chettinad and Madras. Breads are also worth ordering – particularly the parata stuffed with spicy mashed potato with lime and herbs (£2.50).

The brunch menu features one or two plain but delicious dishes. Akuri (spicy scrambled eggs served with granary toast) is one of them, and shredded lamb and potatoes fried in roasted spices is another.

Le Colombier

145 Dovehouse St, Chelsea Square, SW3 ℅020 7351 1155	⊖ South Kensington
Mon–Sat noon–3pm & 6.30–11pm,	
Sun noon–3.30pm & 6.30–10.30pm	All major credit cards

From outside on Dovehouse Street you can see that Le Colombier was once a pub. It occupies the classic corner site and, despite rather more tables and chairs outside than tends to be the norm given the British weather, it doesn't look alien to Chelsea. But it is. This is a French place: it is run by Monsieur Garnier, who has spent most of his career at the exalted end of the London restaurant business, but Le Colombier is without doubt very, very French.

The menu is French, the cooking is French, the service is French and the decor is French. When the bill comes, you tend to be surprised that a) it is no larger and b) that they ask for pounds not francs. The cooking is about as good as you would have found in a smart Routier in rural France during the 1970s – before such places became hard to find. Starters include such bistro classics as oeufs pochés meurette (£5.80), soupe de poissons (£5.30), and feuilleté d'escargots à la crème d'ail (£6.80). Also oysters, goats' cheese salad, duck liver terrine, and tomato and basil salad. Listed under "les poisssons" there is rouget vinaigrette de tomate (£14), a simple dish made with red mullet, and coquilles St Jacques aux champignons sauvages (£14.80), which is scallops with wild mushrooms. Under "les viandes" there is steak tartare pommes frites (£14.80) and côte de veau (£15.90). Moving on to "les grillades", these are steaks and chops. Puddings include crêpes suzette (£4.90) and omelette Norvégienne pour deux (£12), which is described as "baked Alaska", something of a geographical conundrum.

Service is as French as the menu itself, but Le Colombier is not some trendy retro caricature. None of the atmosphere is posed: if this seems like a provincial French eatery, that is because that is what it is. The fact that it is located in Chelsea makes the set menu for lunch and early diners – two courses and first cup of coffee for £13 – all the more remarkable.

The English Garden

10 Lincoln St, SW3 ✆020 7584 7272   ⊖ Sloane Square

Mon–Sat noon–3pm & 6–11pm   All major credit cards

When Searcy Corrigan Restaurants went shopping in Chelsea during the autumn of 1999, this is one of the places they bought (the other being The House; see p.455). The English Garden got the full makeover treatment: a maple-wood bar, lashings of soft creamy and biscuity tones, and a judicious use of grey British slate. The new kitchen is headed up by Malcolm Starmer who worked with Richard Corrigan for five years at the Lindsay House, and before that in the Barbican. The service is slick, the room is comfortable, and Starmer's food is good. There are echoes of the Lindsay House, but only faint ones; this is well-conceived Modern British food which relies on good combinations of strong flavours.

The menu changes twice a day. For lunch there is a three-course set lunch at the derisory price of £19.50, including half a bottle of wine. Less than £20 for roasted sweetbread, green beans, shallots and rosemary, followed by fillet of monkfish, white asparagus, blood orange and basil, and then lemon cream, mixed berries, caramel crunch, plus half a bottle of wine? This is a stellar bargain. Or perhaps baked duck's egg with brioche, Serrano ham, and Taleggio (a baked egg with a cheese and ham toastie to dip into it!), followed by roast rump of lamb, merguez, pea purée and roast garlic, and finishing with poached pears mascarpone and basil? In the evening the duck egg combo appears on the starters list (£7); or you could have butter poached lobster with fennel, apples and shellfish juices (£8), or parfait of foie gras, rabbit rillettes, and fig chutney (£8). Mains include belly and shoulder of pork with pea purée and crubeens (£16) – a very well-executed dish, rich and savoury. Or roast rump of veal with artichoke, Taleggio and ceps (£15). Or spatchcock pigeon with macaroni, Bayonne ham, Parmesan and truffles (£18). Or lasagne of fennel, goats' cheese, tomato and green olives (£14).

Elsewhere in the garden there are two elegant private rooms which can be joined together, creating space for parties of ten, twenty or thirty.

CHELSEA ⊕ FRENCH

Gordon Ramsay

68–69 Royal Hospital Rd, SW3 ©020 7352 4441   ⊖ Sloane Square

Mon–Fri noon–2pm & 6.45–11pm   All major credit cards

Things have calmed down a bit for Gordon Ramsay, the wunderkind ex-footballer chef for whom in 1999 the media spotlight burnt a little brighter than he would have wished. Meanwhile his restaurant (which is still thought of by many as the place where La Tante Claire used to be) struggled to settle. Latterly it seems to be achieving greater consistency, and you can only hope that the prospect of yet another television series doesn't get between Mr Ramsay and the stoves. The dining room has a modern and spacious feel with glass screens; the service is certainly three-star; and the food – well, there's no doubt that this is three-star. And thankfully the prices are not as high as you might fear. There are two fixed-price cartes (lunch and dinner) – £55 for three courses, £70 for seven – and a steal of a set lunch at £28 for three courses. Even if you add £5 for a glass of good house wine, this represents accessible, great cooking.

The menu here is constantly evolving and changing as inspired by the kitchen's creativity and season's imperatives, though a good number of Ramsay favourites have made the journey from Aubergine (see p.449): cappuccino of haricots blancs with sautéed girolles and grated truffle, braised shin of beef, and vanilla crème brûlée with jus Granny Smith, to name just three. Look out (on the main menus) for a wonderful ravioli of lobster poached in lobster bisque served with a fine basil purée and confit tomatoes – solid, satisfying, light and fresh all at the same time. Or the pigeon from Bresse poached in a bouillon of ceps served with choux farcis. But really you're in safe hands here – pick a dish or even an ingredient you like and see how it arrives (demanding something made from Bramley apples, however, would not be considered particularly tactful). You won't be disappointed. This is a class act through and through, and the puddings and petits fours are just as classy.

You will have to book at Gordon Ramsay, but sensibly enough reservations are taken only a month in advance, avoiding a potentially huge backlog necessitating booking on your wedding day for the first anniversary! Book now, and count the days.

WEST

The House

3 Milner St, SW3 ✆020 7581 3002	⊖ Sloane Square
Mon–Fri noon–3pm & 6–11pm, Sat 6–11pm	All major credit cards

Until 1999 this chintzy, tweedy, fussy little restaurant went under the sobriquet of "The English House", at which point in swept Searcy Corrigan Restaurants and everything changed . . . except the chintzy, tweedy, fussy decor. There is nothing fussy or remotely old-fashioned, however, about chef/patron Graham Garrett's food, which is strongly flavoured, well seasoned, straightforward and British. And after dining here you have to admit, albeit grudgingly, that the warren of little rooms and the "country-house-naff" wallpaper have a certain charm.

The menu changes on a weekly basis to keep pace with what the markets have to offer. It costs £23 for three courses at dinner, and there's a set lunch at a giveaway £14.50. In winter you could expect hearty starters like black pudding on potato pancake, poached egg and mustard Hollandaise; lamb sweetbreads with braised baby gem lettuce, pea cream and pancetta; salt cod and potato fritters with pickled vegetable relish; or ham hock, foie gras and artichoke terrine. The kitchen does a lot of home curing and home salting, and sensible regulars make a beeline for the resulting dishes. Main courses range from the super-straightforward – fried wing of skate with shrimp beurre noisette; risotto of asparagus with poached egg and Parmesan cheese; pan-fried rump skirt, garlic spinach and sauce Bercy – on to more adventurous stuff like saddle of rabbit stuffed with goats' cheese and green olives with braised artichokes, or roast breast and confit leg of Norfolk chicken with a liver and bacon sauce. Puds are modern: pineapple tarte Tatin with black pepper ice cream; Sauternes and almond cake with marinated prunes; caramelised banana, vanilla waffle, maple syrup ice cream. But sometimes modern can be good!

The wine list is thoughtful. The front of house team is well established and know just what they are doing. The cooking is accomplished and dishes have a remarkably satisfying quality about them. But you must either overlook or enjoy the decor. As well as owing ultimate allegiance to Richard Corrigan (p.144), The House has a sister restaurant nearby in Chelsea – The English Garden (p.453).

New Culture Revolution

305 King's Rd, SW3 ℂ020 7352 9281   ⊖ Sloane Square

Daily noon–11pm   All major credit cards

This is one of the latest in a series of noodle-bar chains to target London, and arguably among the best. New Culture Revolution brings Londoners noodles and dumplings in soup, with a North Chinese spin. They have recently changed the booking policy and now take reservations for parties of more than four people. If you haven't booked you may have to queue, but for only five or ten minutes – tables turn around pretty fast. Once settled in, take time to peruse the menu, which gives you a chance to catch up with the philosophy of Northern Chinese cooking. There are a number of Confucius-like comments about the herbs and spices used, plus explanations about how wholesome this food is for the body. You'll find you feel better already.

The menu itself is divided into several sections – starters "specially chosen to stimulate good digestion and cleanse the palate", and various combinations of soup, dumplings, noodles and rice dishes. Stimulate the juices with grilled prawns with chilli and garlic (£4.70), a "refreshing and energising" raw juice (£2.50 – a blend of carrot and apple), or the steamed qing kou (£4.50) – New Zealand greenlipped mussels. The main courses are filling stuff. The vegetarian tong mein (£4.90) is thick with writhing noodles at the bottom of a huge bowl of "mellow home-made" stock, together with enough vegetables to feed a small terracotta army. A Revolution extra chow mein with sha sha spices (£5.80) brings fried noodles and vegetables with a combination of beef, chicken and seafood – a good deal better than anything the local Chinese takeaway can deliver. Duck enthusiasts will find xiang su ya (£6.90) a happy solution – seasoned rice with crispy duck pan-fried with herbs and spices.

After 45 minutes you'll find yourself out on the street again, much to the relief of those waiting. It's not that you'll have been hurried or been made to feel unwelcome; rather that your tolerance of the lime-green walls and uncomfortable seats will be running out. Good design feature, that.

Riccardo's

126 Fulham Rd, SW3 ✆020 7370 4917   ⊖ South Kensington

Mon–Fri 11am–3pm & 6pm–midnight, Sat noon–3.30pm & 6.30pm–midnight,

Sun noon–3.30pm & 6.30–11pm   All major credit cards

The Riccardo in question here is Riccardo Mariti, whose father was a successful restaurateur in the 1970s. Their Fulham Road site has seen a few changes in recent decades – like all good establishments it has evolved. There is still a large area of pavement seating (suitably walled in by canvas and heated during the winter), there is still old-fashioned and courtly Italian service, and there is probably even a giant pepper mill hidden away somewhere. Thereafter things have changed. Riccardo has introduced a "spuntino" menu, which is rather like an Italian tapas or meze – you are encouraged to have several courses and this is made easier by small portions. Prices are fair but the cost of your dinner can mount, as you can find yourself eating rather more than you had intended. The food is very simple, very delicious and very Tuscan.

This is a relaxing, self-indulgent way to eat, and one which seems to suit the laid-back denizens of Chelsea. The menu lists – and "lists" is the right word – some 45 different dishes, priced between £1.25 (bread and butter) and £8.75 (minute steak tagliata with sautéed radicchio and chicory). In between there are soups, bruschetta, fish dishes, pastas, risotti, polenta, antipasti – a glorious array of this and that. It is essentially simple, peasant food, very delicious and with good strong flavours. Some of the star choices are gnocchi di polenta al Gorgonzola (£5.25); insalata di spinaci (£4.25), a spinach salad with prosciutto, avocado and Parmesan; sarde "alla Diavolo" (£5.25), grilled sardines; ravioli de melanzane (£5.25), ravioli with aubergine and ricotta cheese butter and sage; carpaccio (£6.30), slivers of raw beef fillet with Parmesan; and salsiccia con lentiche (£6.40), Italian sausages with lentils. Oh, and you'll even find that old warhorse prosciutto melone (£5.25), Parma ham and melon. There really is something for everyone, however world-weary their palate.

On the back of the menu the imposing wine list is exclusively Italian but for half a dozen famous-name champagnes. The list repays investigation, as there are a good many interesting bottles from Tuscany and the lesser-known Italian wine regions: the offerings go all the way from house wine (£10.95) to Sassicaia (£95).

Zaika

259 Fulham Rd, SW3 ©020 7351 7823   ⊖ South Kensington

Mon–Fri noon–2.30pm & 6.30–10.30pm, Sat 6.30–10.30pm,

Sun 12.30–2.30pm & 6.30–10pm   All major credit cards except Diners

Even given the fierce cut and thrust that passes for normality on the Indian restaurant scene, Vineet Bhatia had a pretty turbulent 1999. In and out of more restaurants than a busy critic, he ended up chef-patron at Zaika. This is an upmarket Indian restaurant that gives the lie to any snobs who still maintain that Indian food can never amount to anything. Thankfully, Zaika manages to be unpretentious: the food is wholesome; it looks good and tastes good; and though your bill will not be a small one it will not be a West End wallet-breaker either. There are novel dishes to be sampled, but they sit alongside classics – you can still enjoy an impeccable rogan josh served on the bone. Zaika marched straight onto the shortlist of London's exceptional Indian restaurants.

Start with the dhungar machli tikka (£5.95). It is hard to praise this dish highly enough: a well-marinated chunk of salmon, cooked in the tandoor, and served when just right. Wonder of wonders, not over-done! Or there are good murg shammi (£4.95), chicken patties; and seekhe murghabi (£5.50), which are minced duck rolls. Some thought goes into the main courses. This is not a seasonal menu in the strictest sense of the term, but in the summer the grey mullet will give way to sea bass and the cauliflower will be changed for broccoli. The nariyal jhinga (£11.95), made from prawns cooked in a coconut masala tempered with lime leaves, stands out. Or there's lal mirch murg (£9.50), a spicy chicken dish made with fennel and coriander seeds. The koh-e-rogan josh (£9.75) is very good. Jungli murghi dalcha (£11.50) is most interesting. This is a black cardamom- and cinnamon-smoked guinea fowl breast, served with black lentil sauce and lemon rice. Inspirational stuff. The simpler dishes are also good – try the dubkiwale aloo (£4.25), a straightforward dish of potatoes with cumin. And the breads are splendid: try the malai nan (£2.50) with your starters – it's cheesy, sticky, self-indulgent.

On the dessert menu you may find the chocomosa (£3.95). This is a dish that Vineet Bhatia has been toying with for a good while now, and one which finally seems to have come right: crisp samosas containing an admirably bitter melted chocolate.

The Blue Bar Cafe

451 Fulham Rd, SW10   ✆020 7352 8636

It's as easy to get a coffee or an elder-flower tea as a beer or cocktail in this light, modern, wood-floored bar. On two floors, it serves a mix of local residents and Fulham Road shoppers who relax with papers and magazines – which are obligingly left out for them. Beers on offer include Leffe, Stella and Marstons Pedigree. There's a small patio garden as well.

Cadogan Arms Tavern

298 King's Rd, SW3   ✆020 7352 1645

Done out in country-barn style with massive old beams, this dark and comfy pub welcomes a mix of local residents and King's Road day-trippers. There's a separate games room upstairs. Beers on offer include Theakston's SB, Courage Best and Directors.

The Crown

153 Dovehouse St, SW3   ✆020 7352 9505

A friendly place where people chat to strangers, this small corner pub has been attracting a local clientele for years. It's been refurbished a couple of times, but keeps its comfortable charm. Beers on tap include Adnams, Fuller's London Pride and Hoegaarden.

Finch's

190 Fulham Rd, SW10   ✆020 7351 5043

This beautifully tiled traditional pub has been updated very well, keeping all the old character, but adding things like huge doors to open up the front and make it light and accessible. A very nice atmosphere in which to enjoy Youngers Bitter, Special and all the Young's bottled beers.

The Goat in Boots

333 Fulham Rd, SW10   ✆020 7352 1384

More of a lively bar than a pub, this venue offers jelly vodka shots and flavoured vodkas (including toffee and banana). A cocktail bar downstairs puts on special promotions every night, and if you like beer there's Courage Directors and Morland's Old Speckled Hen, so all tastes are catered for. Close to the Kartouche club, it gets quite lively later on.

The World's End

459 King's Rd, SW10   ✆020 7376 8946

There's been a tavern on this site since the 1700s, although this isn't the original. It's big and light, with outside tables, and a library where you can borrow books. The beers on tap, from the Badger Brewery, include Tangle Foot, Champion, Dorset Best and Hofbrau lager.

Ealing & Acton

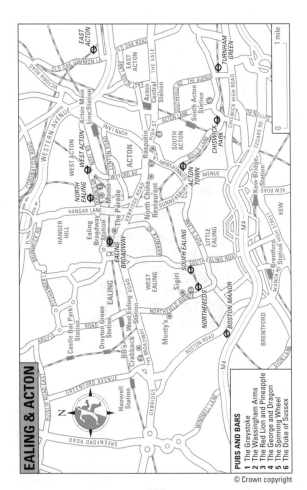

EALING & ACTON

WEST

PUBS AND BARS

1 The Greystoke
2 The Wassingham Arms
3 The Red Lion and Pineapple
4 The George and Dragon
5 The Spinning Wheel
6 The Duke of Sussex

© Crown copyright

BB's Crabback

3 Chignell Place, West Ealing, W13 ©020 8840 8322   ⊖ Northfields

Mon–Sat 6.30–11pm   Mastercard, Visa

Brian Benjamin (the eponymous chef at BB's) is from Grenada, but his food encompasses the whole Caribbean – classic dishes from Jamaica jostle those from Trinidad, as well as Grenada itself. The restaurant, hidden away behind the Uxbridge Road, can appear a rather charming backwater, an impression enhanced by the laid-back staff. But it is not undiscovered territory. The walls are papered with awards from various "salons culinaires" – and in 1999 Benjamin added the Afro-Caribbean Chef of the Year award. This restaurant has a remarkable repertoire and everything is played in tune. Be sure to book if you want a table on a Friday or Saturday night.

Start with ackee salt fish (£4.25). This is the classic Jamaican dish served with "bakes", which are like a kind of fried dumpling. Or try BB's crabback (£5.25) – a crabback is nothing more complicated than a crab shell filled with crabmeat and coated in a cheesy, creamy sauce. Or there's devilled salt fish balls (£4.25) – spicy, irregular fish cakes. Or callaloo and okra soup (£4.25). Main courses all come with a choice of rice and peas, plain rice, or saffron rice. The rice and peas here is a revelation, dark and spicy without being chilli-hot – very rich, with a waft of cloves. The saffron rice is good too, yellow and buttery. The main courses are half fish and half meat dishes – steak River Antoine (£12.95) is a sirloin steak flamed in Grenadian rum with a sweet relish sauce, while scampi Ashley (£11.95), named after Benjamin's son, has a sauce made with mushrooms, saffron and cream. Or there's Spice Island jerk chicken (£10.50), which is hot and spicy with a dozen herbs. Side dishes are good fun. Go for fried or boiled plantain (£3.25); dasheen (£3.25), a root vegetable like a well-mannered parsnip; roti skins, which brings wafer-thin, dry, delicious bread (£4.50); or jumbie umbrellas (£3.25), which translates as mushrooms!

If you're in inflammatory mood, try a dessert of banana flamed in rum and lemon (£5.20), which arrives at table quite seriously on fire. And to really indulge, finish with a cool slipper coffee (£5.95), described as "with cognac and a hint of rum. Topped with cream." It's enough to make the Irish look to their laurels.

EALING & ACTON ⓉⒿ JAPANESE

Momo

14 Queen's Parade, West Acton, W5 ⓒ020 8997 0206   ⊖ West Acton

Mon–Sat noon–2.30pm & 6–10pm   All major credit cards

www.lamms.com

The opening of a Japanese school in Acton led to widespread Nipponification of the local shops and services – there are Japanese food shops, estate agents, and even a mysterious Aladdin's cave called the Japanese Recycling Shop, which has shelf after shelf of repaired and refurbished electronic gadgetry – everything from rice cookers to typewriters. Nearby on Queen's Parade is this restaurant, a small establishment with 28 seats – it's a good idea to book. Service is smiling and helpful, and the long menu gives every opportunity to explore those less familiar dishes which may make you nervous in more intimidating, formal establishments.

If you don't feel up to extensive menu exploration, go for the set menus – three or four dishes culminating in dessert may be had for prices ranging from £7.30 to £16 (lunch) or £15 to £25 (dinner). Assembling a meal yourself, you might start with yakitori (£3.80), three small, very good chicken kebabs; or kanisu (£6.30), a bowl of crabmeat and cucumber marinated in rice vinegar, which is delicate and fresh. Soups are very intriguing, especially dobin-mushi (£3.80), which comes in a small teapot with a tiny cup on top – a rich broth with chunks of shrimp and chicken to fish out with your chopsticks. Then there's buta shogayaki (£6.90) – thin strips of belly pork grilled with ginger and soy and served with a mound of ultra-thin coleslaw. If you want to try a grandstand dish, nigiri-zushi (£16) brings a box with a dozen pieces of assorted fish sushi, complete with gari – the amazingly delicious pickled ginger. Lovers of eel bow to the una jyu (£16.50), which is a box of rice topped with fillets of eel grilled with kabayaki sauce.

The operators at British Telecom's directory enquiries specialise in confusing this establishment with the larger, North African, restaurant of the same name in the West End (see p.111). Fortunately the staff here have the number of the other Momo and politely ask callers whether they want Momo W1 or Momo W5; the most frequent response, of course, is that the caller doesn't know.

WEST

Monty's

54 Northfield Ave, Ealing, W13 ©020 8567 6281	⊖ Northfields
Daily noon–2.30pm & 6–11.30pm	All major credit cards

www.montys.uk.com

Once upon a time the now defunct Ealing Tandoori held West London curry lovers in thrall – it was the undisputed first choice. Then, in the late 1970s, the three main chefs left to open their own place, which they called Monty's, on South Ealing Road. As business boomed, two of the chefs moved on to set up independently – but as all three co-owned the name Monty's, they all use it, and that is why there are now three different Monty's, all fiercely independent but each with the same name and logo. Unlike many small Indian restaurants these are "chef-led", which is a key factor in making Monty's in Northfield Avenue an almost perfect neighbourhood curry house. You won't find banks of flowers or majestic staircases; the tables are too close together; and you may be crowded by people waiting for a takeaway. But the cooking is class, the portions are good, and prices are fair. This is a restaurant which has a fine grasp of what its customers want. And apparently they want more of it – Monty's Northfield has a new sibling on Ealing Broadway (©020 8576 4646).

A complimentary plate of salady crudités arrives with any chutneys and popadoms ordered, but starters are the exception rather than the rule here – perhaps because of the well-sized main course portions. Trad tandoori dishes are good, like the tandoori chicken (£4.50 for two pieces). Or there is hasina, lamb marinated in yogurt and served as a sizzler (£6.15). The boss here remembers introducing the iron plate sizzlers at the Ealing Tandoori years ago and claims that his were the first in Britain. As you'd expect with a good tandoor chef, breads are delicious – pick between nan (£1.50) and Peshwari nan (£2.25). But the kitchen really gets to shine with simple curry dishes like methi ghosht (£6.95) – tender lamb (and plenty of it) in a delicious sauce rich with fenugreek – and chicken jalfriji (£6.95), which is all the dish should be. Vegetable dishes are also made with more care than is usual – both brinjal bhaji (£3.75) and sag paneer (£3.50) are delicious.

Monty's is one of very few local curry houses to serve perfectly cooked, genuine, basmati rice. So the plain boiled rice (£1.95) – nutty, almost smoky, with grains perfectly separate – is worth tasting on its own.

North China Restaurant

305 Uxbridge Rd, Ealing Common, W3 ℗020 8992 9183   ⊖ Ealing Common

Daily noon–2.30pm & 6–11.30pm (midnight Fri & Sat)   All major credit cards

www.northchina.co.uk

The problem with "special" dishes that must be ordered 24 hours in advance is that you tend to notice them only when you read the menu (rather than the requisite 24hrs before). The North China has such a dish. The restaurant itself has a 24-carat local reputation: it is the kind of place people refer to as "being as good as Chinatown", which in this case is spot-on, and the star turn on the menu doesn't disappoint. It is crispy Peking duck – but unlike all upstart crispy ducks, this Peking duck comes as three separate courses. Firstly there is the skin and breast meat served with pancakes, shreds of cucumber and spring onion plus hoisin sauce. Then there is a fresh stir-fry of the duck meat with beansprouts, and finally the meal ends with a giant tureen of rich duck soup with lumps of the carcass to pick at. It is awesome. And so is the price – £42. It's even more awesome, though, when you consider it as three courses for four people – which works out at just over £3 per person per course.

So what goes well with duck? At the North China the familiar dishes are well cooked and well presented. You might start with barbecued pork spare ribs (£4.90), or the whimsically named lettuce puffs (£3.40 per person, minimum two), which turn out to be our old friend "mince wrapped in lettuce leaves". For a supplementary main course, prawns in chilli sauce (£7.25), although not very chilli, is teamed with fresh water chestnuts and very good. Singapore fried noodles (£4.10) is powered by curry powder rather than fresh chilli, but fills a gap. Hidden among the familiar on the menu are a few more interesting dishes. One such is grilled chicken Peking style (£5.15). This is a breaded chicken escalope that is served with quite a sharp, vinegary sauce that is redolent of pickled cabbage.

The genuinely friendly service at the North China stems from the fact that it is a family restaurant. If the genuine Peking duck does not appeal perhaps you should consider the North China's other high-ticket item. When lobsters are good at market they go onto the menu at a seasonal price – about £22.50 per lobster.

Parade

18–19 The Mall, Ealing, W5 ℭ020 8810 0202	⊖ Ealing Broadway
Mon–Sat 12.30–2.30pm & 7–11pm,	
Sun 12.30–3.30pm	All major credit cards except Diners

People who live in the better parts of Ealing drive Jaguars and live in million-pound houses. These are the sophisticated and leafy suburbs, but until the arrival of Parade in 1999 there was not a single proper restaurant to while away those evenings when the television disappoints. So when Parade opened (on a site that formerly hosted a rather arch Indian restaurant) you could hear the sighs of relief echoing around the neighbourhood. A sister restaurant to Sonny's in Barnes (see p.445), this is a modern, clean, keen sort of place, where neither the food nor the service will let you down. If you plonked this eatery down in the West End it would be run-of-the-mill, but here it deserves star billing. That's why it is so amazingly busy every night of the week; nowadays locals bemoan the fact that they cannot get in without booking.

At lunchtime – when the restaurant is under a lot less pressure – there's a very decent set lunch, which costs £12 for two courses and £15 for three. In the evening the ante goes up to £19.50/£23.50. The menu changes regularly and is seasonally based. Starters are eclectic but well conceived, as the kitchen understands what the customer wants. Perhaps you'll find farfalle with asparagus, wild mushrooms and truffle oil; Thai squid salad with peanuts, lime and coriander; snail and artichoke Pithivier in red wine, garlic and herbs; or pig's trotter fritter with confit of belly pork, arracina beans and mustard. Mains are grown-up versions of the starters with dishes like osso bucco with mashed potatoes, artichokes and gremolata; roast halibut with curried mussel broth and cucumber raita; rare grilled swordfish with red pepper risotto, oregano and olive salsa. The cooking is sound and the dishes are well presented. Service is generally slick, but has been known to creak under the intense pressure.

Parade's puddings are good. Especially the pastrywork – sable of poached pear with clotted cream and butterscotch sauce; hot chocolate pudding and blood orange sorbet; pecan pie, banana sorbet and caramelised banana. Strangely, an apple and prune clafoutis, with nutmeg ice cream, is so very Ealing.

£10–£25

Rasputin

265 High St, Acton, W3 ©020 8993 5802	⊖ Acton Town
Daily 6–11.30pm	Mastercard, Visa

You'll find the "Rasputin Russian Restaurant and Wine Bar" up at the Ealing end of Acton High Street. The restaurant is a cave of dark-red felt, filled with English tearoom tables and chairs, and loud Russian background music which seems to alternate between Soviet covers of Boney M and Val Doonican. It's all very jolly, and the Russian specialities are homely and delicious. And all this is before you have made any inroads into the twenty different vodkas, which come both as single shots and – take care here – "by the carafe".

With the menu comes a plate of cucumber, cabbage, green tomatoes and peppers, all markedly salty and with a good vinegary tang. For a starter, try pierogi – rich little dumplings that come stuffed with a choice of potato and cheese, meat, or sauerkraut and mushrooms; they are all priced at £3.85 a portion. The blinis (small buckwheat pancakes) are also good – try them with smoked salmon and sour cream (£4.50), or, if you enjoy the special thrill of finding a bargain, with 40g of Russian Sevruga caviar (£12.50). Sledzie is also delicious – pickled herrings with sour cream, apples, gherkins and dill (£3.45). At Rasputin they are constantly tinkering with the menu and there usually seem to be several versions extant at once. Hold out for the golubtsy (£7.50), which is permanently under threat of banishment from the menu – this is a simple but satisfying dish of cabbage leaves stuffed with meat and rice. Very wholesome and very good. Or there's kotley po Kievsky (£7.95) – a chicken Kiev made with tarragon butter. Fish fans may want to try the losos (£9.95), which is a fillet of salmon cooked with artichoke hearts, capers and a white wine sauce.

One of the desserts is an old favourite. "Charlotka" (£2.95) is none other than a classic dish, the Charlotte Russe – a mousse cake surrounded by sponge biscuits . . . welcome back. Also interesting is the Russian tea served in a glass and holder. It is made with tea, lemon and a splash of vodka (£1.95), with a small bowl of honey alongside for sweetening.

Sigiri

161 Northfield Ave, W13 ⓒ020 8579 8000	⊖ Northfields
Tues–Sun 6.30–11pm	Mastercard, Visa

www.sigiri.com

On the menu it says, "One of the main ingredients in Sri Lankan cuisine is coconut" – presumably in response to the duty of care which has been imposed on restaurateurs, who must now save their customers from the dangers of nut allergies. In one respect it's sound advice, for if you are not partial to coconut you should think about eating elsewhere. Behind the somewhat industrial brick facade this restaurant is surprisingly spacious, the food is authentic and the service is charming. This is a very gentle place, and it seldom seems very busy, but you will often hear Sigiri being praised within the Sri Lankan community.

The menu is long and complicated. For starters it is hard to oppose that Sri Lankan cousin of the masala dosa, the appa or hopper – bowl-shaped rice pancakes which are usually served with a sambol to add zing and flavour. Choose from plain (£1.50), egg (£1.60), or one with a dollop of coconut cream in the bottom (£1.60). The sambols are fun – pol sambol (£1.50) is made from onion and coconut with a seasoning of Maldive fish, while seeni sambol combines a kind of spicy onion jam with a sprinkle of dried fish. Very tasty. Also good is the malu miris (£3), which is a large, very mild, chilli stuffed with minced lamb and deep-fried. For main courses the fish dishes are good here: seer fish (£4.50) comes in rich tomatoey gravy. The basic curries are also splendid – chicken with potato (£4.50) is much richer and less austere than it sounds. The fried mutton (£5.50) is something of a disappointment, however, turning out a little on the greasy side; much better to leave room for some of the excellent vegetarian dishes like the green banana (£3) or the mallum (£3), which is finely shredded cabbage cooked with spices and coconut. The pickles are notable – try the achcharu pickle (80p), a red-hot combo of little pickled onions and little pickled chillies, and the amberella chutney, which is very like Italian mustard fruits.

Staff at Sigiri are very concerned that the food should not be too hot for you (perhaps they have had trouble with some of the more tooth-melting dishes). Be brave: there are real flavours riding tandem with the chillies!

The Duke of Sussex

75 South Parade, W4   ✆020 8742 8801

Overlooking the green, this large pub is traditional and comfortable. Dedicated to a regular local crowd of sports enthusiasts, it has three pool tables and table football. There's also a big beer garden and a "no kids in the bar" policy. Favourites on tap include Stella, Castlemaine XXXX and Guinness.

The George & Dragon

183 Acton High St, W3   ✆020 8896 9666

The exterior tells you this pub has been here for at least three centuries. Low ceilings and beams confirm its venerable status inside, where it's cosy as well as friendly. Expect to find Fosters, Guinness and John Smith's. There's also a live music venue tacked onto the back, so it gets lively at weekends.

The Greystoke

7 Queens Drive, Queens Parade,
W5   ✆020 8997 6388

Bargain-hunters get a good deal in this nicely panelled and friendly local. At 6pm and 9pm they spin a Wheel of Fortune and you get discounts on whatever the pointer lands on. Will it be 50p off Miller, or 30p off John Smith's? Only the wheel can say . . .

The Red Lion & Pineapple

281 Acton High St, W3   ✆020 8896 2248

There's been a pub, or pubs, on this site since 1751 and this latest is an agglomeration of past Red Lions and Pineapples. It's busy, big and bright, with large windows and lots of different groups each claiming an area for themselves. Drink Courage Directors, Morland's Old Speckled Hen or Fuller's London Pride.

The Spinning Wheel

227 Northfield Ave, W13   ✆020 8567 8348

This lively music venue/pub is an oasis in an area not well served by them. No surprise, then, that it attracts a young noisy crowd for the Tetley's, Boddingtons and Guinness as well as the live pub-rock bands. There's even draught wine on tap, with varietal types like Tempranillo and Chenin Blanc.

The Walsingham Arms

128 The Broadway, Uxbridge Rd,
W13   ✆020 8579 6978

The only pub for miles around, this big, busy, traditional pub hosts a happy crowd of local workers and residents. There's a large beer garden, big-screen TV and live music from Friday to Sunday with everything from jazz to pub rock. Enjoy Flowers Original and Boddingtons.

Earl's Court

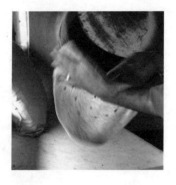

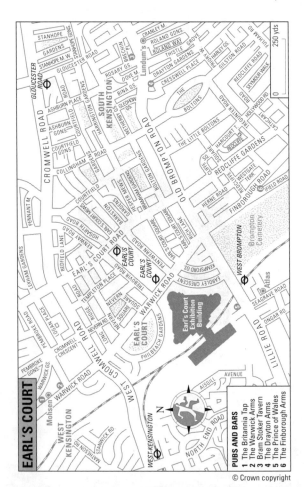

EARL'S COURT

WEST

PUBS AND BARS
1 The Britannia Tap
2 The Warwick Arms
3 Bram Stoker Tavern
4 The Drayton Arms
5 The Prince of Wales
6 The Finborough Arms

© Crown copyright

The Atlas

16 Seagrave Rd, Fulham, SW6 ✆020 7385 9129	⊖ Earl's Court
Mon–Sat 12.30–3pm & 7–10.30pm,	
Sun 12.30–3pm & 7–10pm	Mastercard, Switch, Visa

Once upon a time pubs were for boozing. You got sarnies maybe, and pickled onions if you were lucky. The Atlas is as far away from that kind of place as it is possible to get. In a lively and informal atmosphere, brothers Richard and George Manners serve the kind of innovative Mediterranean-inspired food that many full-blown restaurants would be proud of. George is the chef and he trained at gastro-pub HQ, The Eagle in Farringdon (see p.215). The flavours come mainly from Spain and North Africa and huge strings of dried peppers and bundles of cinnamon sticks vie for attention in the kitchen. But there are no concessions. The menu is chalked on a board twice daily, depending on what's in supply and George's inspiration. You read, you remember, and you order at the bar.

Starters include crostini of grilled courgette salsa, boquerones with gremolata, prosciutto and pear (£5) – very delicious, the courgette salsa is destined to become a classic – or spring onion and garlic soup with Parmesan and fried spring onion tops (£3.50), which is creamy and rich. Main courses range from grilled Tuscan sausages, fennel and black pepper, caponata of aubergines and red peppers, celery and pine nuts (£8), to grilled swordfish steak, salmonoglio of oregano, cous cous salad with mint and almonds (£10). Penne with spinach, ricotta, molasses-cured pancetta, butter and Parmesan (£7) brings a generous bowl of pasta, well seasoned and with plenty of chunky pancetta, while grilled rib eye steak with Puy lentils, parsley and balsamic vinegar (£9) is a great dish, the lentils rich and earthy and the steak cooked precisely as requested. A major outcry by the sweet-toothed has changed the house rules, and puddings (which once were served only at the weekends) are available during the week . . . if George has had time to make them.

The wine selection is also chalked up, and there are some unusual offerings served by the glass, which makes The Atlas a good venue for wine-lovers in search of a bit of impromptu tasting. Everyone else will be pleased to have found an eatery where you can get a decent pint. The Atlas is busy, noisy, friendly and young, and the food is good into the bargain. You're likely to end up sharing a table, so get there early.

£25–£65

Lundum's

119 Old Brompton Rd, SW7 ℡020 7373 7774   ⊖ Gloucester Road/South Kensington

Mon–Sat 10am–11pm, Sun (brunch) 10am–4pm   Amex, Mastercard, Visa

In 1999 the Lundum family (this is a genuine family restaurant – four of them work in the business) took over this site on the Old Brompton Road and set about turning it into London's premier Danish restaurant. The Lundums would be the first to admit that there is not a lot of competition; in fact this may well be London's only Danish restaurant, which gives them something of a head start. There's nothing particularly Danish about the room, which is pleasantly light and airy with huge mirrors and a sky-light, much the same as in previous incarnations – there has been some kind of a restaurant here for decades. What has changed for the better is the atmosphere. Now, all is fervent enthusiasm; they proudly produce interesting (and delicious) dill-flavoured aquavit, which is specially imported just for them. They also import the Danish sausages and all manner of other delicacies. The food is elegantly presented, competently handled and . . . Danish. At lunchtime it's trad Danish, in the evening modern Danish. You cannot help but be swept along by the tidal wave of commitment and charm – remember, there is a whole family working on you.

At dinner (£17.25 for two courses and £21.50 for three) the menu, which changes seasonally, reads like a lot of other menus – smoked salmon gravad lax, roast guinea fowl, steamed lemon sole. Best, then, to visit at lunch when there are more Danish dishes on offer; the set lunch is priced at £12.50 for two courses and £15.50 for three. Go à la carte and try the shoal of herrings (£3.25/£5.25) – simply marinated, or spicy, or lightly curried, or sour with dill. There are a dozen open sand-wiches (£4–£7.75): salt beef; smoked eel with scrambled eggs and chives; gravad lax with mustard dressing. There are two platters – Dan-ish delicacies (£12.50), or all fish (£14.50). Or try the Medisterpolse, Danish sausage, with creamed cabbage (£7.25). Desserts are indulgent and the aquavit deadly.

"Gamle Ole – Danish Old cheese (18 months) served on rye bread and lard with onions, aspic and rum dripping" (£4.50). At first glance this dish, on the lunch menu, doesn't read well. But persevere, because it is really good, with tasty strong cheese and a seductive combination of tastes.

Mohsen

152 Warwick Rd, W14 ©020 7602 9888	⊖ Earl's Court
Daily noon–midnight	Mastercard, Visa

Just suppose that you are visiting Homebase on the Warwick Road. As the traffic thunders past, spare a thought for the people who still live here. For indeed, across the road you will see signs of habitation – two pubs, one a Young's house, the other selling Fuller's beer, and between them Mohsen, a small, busy Persian restaurant. This shouldn't come as a complete surprise, as you are not so very far from the nest of Iranian shops run by Mr Reza on Kensington High Street, but for somewhere so hidden away Mohsen tends to be gratifyingly busy. There is nothing better than a loyal core of knowledgeable Middle Eastern customers to keep up standards in a Middle Eastern restaurant.

In the window is the oven, where the bread man works to keep everyone supplied with fresh-from-the-oven sheets of bread. This bread (80p) is terrific: wholemeal, large and flat, but not too flat, with a perforated surface and a sprinkling of sesame seeds that gives a nutty crunch. The waiters conspire to see that it arrives in a steady stream and never has a chance to get cold. The starters list is largely made up of things to go with the bread. You must have sabzi (£2.30), which is one of the most delicious and health-oriented starters in the world. It is a basket containing a bunch of fresh green herbs – tarragon, flat parsley and mint – plus a chunk of feta. Eat it with your bread. Or there's koo koo sabzi (£1.80), which is rather like an under-egged Spanish omelette made with a bumper helping of parsley, dill, coriander, barberries and walnuts. Very tasty. Humous (£1.80) is good. There's also a grand selection of mixed salty pickles – torshee (£1.60) – and a splendid, warm, smoky purée of aubergines called mirza ghassemi (£2.50). The main courses tend to revolve around grilled meat – joojeh kabab (£6.20), for example, is a poussin, jointed, marinated, grilled and served on rice. Then there is chellow kabab-e-barg (£6.90), which is outstanding – a tender fillet of lamb flattened and grilled. It is traditionally accompanied by an egg yolk (50p extra).

Look out for the dish of the day – on Wednesday it is kharesh badenjan (£6), a stew of lamb and aubergines. And always be sure to finish with a pot of aromatic Iranian tea (£2.50), which is served in tiny, elegant, gilded glasses.

Bram Stoker Tavern

148 Old Brompton Rd, SW5   *©020 7373 2818

Dracula-meets-Frankenstein seems to be the theme of this Gothic venue with its fantastical horror decor. Brightly coloured cocktails named after the seven deadly sins are the order of the day. Lust is tequila, blackcurrant and orange juice, Sloth is Amaretto, Bailey's, vodka, Kahlua and cream. Great fun, but not a place for a quiet night out.

The Britannia Tap

150 Warwick Rd, W14   *©020 7602 1649

A small, comfortable, wood-panelled pub that caters mainly for locals and the nearby office crowd. The fire is real rather than gas, there's a small patio garden, it's friendly and lively at the same time, and there's the full Young's range from Double Chocolate bottled beer to AAA in summer and Winter Warmer when it's cold.

Drayton Arms

153 Old Brompton Rd, SW5   *©020 7835 2301

Big, plain windows and scrubbed wooden tables and chairs in this bar-pub. Hoegaarden, Grolsch and Staropramen are the favourites on tap. Drawing a local crowd, the Drayton gets busy in the evenings with bright, young Hoorays.

Finborough Arms

118 Finborough Rd, SW10   *©020 7373 2631

Sit in the corner window seat and watch the traffic jams while you enjoy Flowers Bitter or Original Strong Ale in this friendly, narrow local. You can book seats for the fringe theatre that runs from the same venue.

The Prince of Wales

14 Lillie Rd, SW6   *©020 7385 7441

Decorated with old pots and casks, this comfortable traditional pub has patio beer gardens at both the front and rear, with heaters and pergolas for protection against the elements. Courage Directors and John Smith's are the signature ales, enjoyed by a mixed local crowd.

The Warwick Arms

160 Warwick Rd, SW6   *©020 7603 3560

Exposed brickwork, dangling brass musical instruments and a variety of jugs, pots and ephemera decorate this nice, old-fashioned local. Beers on tap include Adnams Bitter, Fuller's London Pride and ESB.

Fulham

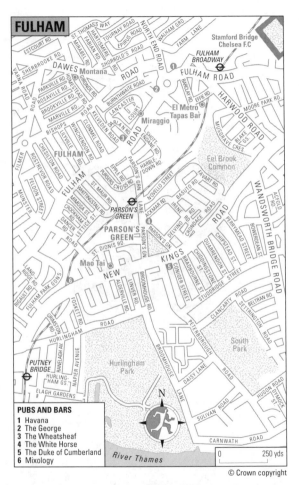

FULHAM

PUBS AND BARS

1 Havana
2 The George
3 The Wheatsheaf
4 The White Horse
5 The Duke of Cumberland
6 Mixology

© Crown copyright

Mao Tai

| 58 New King's Rd, SW6 ©020 7731 2520 | ⊖ Parsons Green |

Mon–Fri noon–3pm & 7–11.30pm, Sat 12.30–2.30pm & 7–11.30pm,

| Sun 12.30–2.30pm & 7–11pm | All major credit cards |

Mao Tai is much more Chelsea than Chinatown, both in appearance and in the kind of food it serves. It's a pretty restaurant, cleverly lit, well-decorated, and with brisk efficient service. The food is Szechwan – sophisticated but with a satisfactory chilli burn and a nice scattering of old favourites. The clientele is just what you would expect from an area that is the very apple of any estate agent's eye. Such surroundings – and, to be fair, such food – do not come cheap. Still, you'll leave well fed and well looked after: both the cooking and service are slick and chic.

Start with steamed scallops (£7.85 for two). These are usually a pretty good indication of things to come and at Mao Tai they are well cooked – just firm without having become rubbery. Salt and pepper prawns (£7.85 for six) are very fresh but somewhat disconcertingly fried in their shells, so the lovely crispy bits end up on the side of the plate. Fire-cracker dumplings with Chinese chives (£6.20) are terrific – innocent-looking Shanghai-style dumplings with a reassuring belt of chilli lurking to surprise the unwary. Also good in the starters section are the salt and pepper soft-shell crabs (£6.50 each). For main courses, you have a choice of more than fifty dishes. Do not be too daunted: order Szechuan squid in a hot bean sauce (£9.20) – tender squid and, as it says, a hot beany sauce. No disappointments here. Also good is the tangerine peel chicken (£7.85), a delightful and delicate dish. Or General Tseng's chicken (£7.85), which is diced chicken and peppers in Ma La sauce. "Tigers Whiskers" (£7.50) is made from pork shreds in sea spice sauce, while braised "Mao Tai" duck (£9.50) is a variant of duck in plum sauce: this one is boneless and very tasty indeed, the ubiquitous chilli making only a small guest appearance.

In the vegetable section there's a choice of braised lettuce or broccoli in oyster sauce (£5.50) – opt for the lettuce. The still-crisp furls of cos are nicely wilted and make the perfect match for oyster sauce. Very good indeed. Alternatively, you can opt out of the decisions and order the Mao Tai feast – £23.70 per person for a minimum of two.

£8–£18

El Metro Tapas Bar

10–12 Effie Rd, SW6 ℂ020 7384 1264   ⊖ Fulham Broadway

Daily 9am–midnight   All major credit cards except Diners

More taverna than tapas bar, El Metro resurrects memories of days spent island-hopping around the Aegean when atmosphere was the only consideration in choosing somewhere to eat. Pretentious it ain't. Asked about the origins of the pulpo a la gallega – "fresh octopus cooked in sea water" (£3.95) – the waiter replied in hushed tones, "Chelsea harbour". And as for the sea water? "It isn't." El Metro is a popular place, which means that reservations are essential to secure yourself a table, and even then you'll probably find yourself waiting; an amiable barman serving Cruz Campo Spanish beer (£2.50), or even a nostalgic glass of San Miguel (£2.70), and live music help pass the time. Full-blown mayhem surrounds the narrow dining area, which is presided over by a rather imposing bull's head.

The menu begins on an unintentionally authentic note with that Costa delicacy – the full English breakfast. Choose from egg, bacon, sausage, baked beans, tomato and toast (£3.95), or savour them with a nice cup of tea (£4.25). Generally accepted as the first meal of the day, breakfast here is served until 5pm. If you're ready for lunch or dinner, you can either go mainstream with a cheeseburger (£5.95) or lean towards the Spanish specialities – perhaps start with sopa de ajo, a spiced garlic soup with poached egg (£3.45). Or plunge straight into the calamares fritos, crispy fried flour-coated squid rings (£3.95), which are deliciously tender to the bite. The albondigas (£6.45) – meatballs cooked in spicy sauce – are sound; the tortilla (£2.95) is solid and filling, and they do a nice dish of vieras gratinadas – grilled scallops and prawns, topped with Hollandaise sauce (£11.25). Desserts (£2.75–£3.25) consist mainly of flans and ice creams . . . more fond memories of the Costas.

House red and white Rioja Vega (£9.95) is reasonably priced, but most parties (for which this makes an ideal venue) prefer Sangria (£9.95 per large jug), which makes a dangerously high-octane short-cut to merriment. You'll find more of the same at El Metro's other branch – which is usefully, if a little bizarrely, sited inside the underground station at Hammersmith – El Metro, The Metropolitan Arcade, Beadon Rd, W6 (ℂ020 8748 3132).

£15-£40

Miraggio

510 Fulham Rd, SW6 ℡020 7384 3142   ⊖ Fulham Broadway

Tues–Thurs 12.30–3pm & 7.30–11pm, Fri 12.30–4pm & 7.30–11pm, Sat 12.30–4pm

& 7.30–10.30pm, Sun 12.30–4pm   All major credit cards except Diners

Bright cafe-style gingham tablecloths and a simple rustic air belie the quality behind this family-run establishment. Your first sign of this is the appetising display of antipasti in the window. There are mouthwatering wafer-thin strips of char-grilled courgette and aubergine, nutty little boiled potatoes with virgin olive oil and roughly chopped flat-leaf parsley, strips of grilled peppers, small and large mushrooms and an aubergine and tomato bake with tiny melted mozzarella cheeses. It's enough to stop even the most jaded foodie in their tracks.

For starters choose the antipasti misti della casa (£8.50) and you'll get the window dishes. Otherwise, try sauté vongole (£11), sweet little clams sautéed until they are just open, or carpaccio di manzo (£8), a paper-thin raw beef fillet. Pastas include the usual suspects, with some less familiar dishes like rigatoni funghi e salsiccia (£8), which is rigatoni with sausages and mushrooms, or gnocchi crema scampi (£8.50). There are plenty of meat and fish choices, too, including spigola al forno con patate (£18), which is oven-baked sea bass with potatoes; calamari fritti (£15), a dish of perfectly cooked deep-fried squid; abbacchio scottadito (£9), simple grilled lamb; and filetto spinaci e patate (£15), a carefully cooked fillet steak with spinach and potatoes. If you're not already having spinach with your main course, try a side order of spinaci burro e Parmigiano (£4). Popeye would faint with pleasure. Puddings include what is claimed to be the best tiramisù in the area (£4) and zocolette (£4.00), a home-made profiterole with a Nutella filling. The kitchen is open to the dining room, so you can see your food being cooked, which makes for great entertainment. You can also be assured that ingredients like fish are fresh because Miraggio goes one step further than a lot of places and has the confidence to mark the few items that are frozen (like king prawns) with an asterisk.

Also remarkable is that Miraggio is currently a bring-your-own-bottle establishment, so your choice of wine is very wide indeed. This is a delightfully straightforward place, and a welcome addition if you want to enjoy good home-style Italian cooking in Fulham.

FULHAM ⊕ AMERICAN SOUTHWEST

Montana

125–129 Dawes Rd, SW6 ℗020 7385 9500	⊖ Fulham Broadway
Mon–Thurs 7–11pm, Fri 7–11.30pm,	
Sat noon–11.30pm, Sun noon–10.30pm	All major credit cards except Diners

For atmosphere alone, Montana deserves the credit for livening up an otherwise dull corner of SW6. Hidden away down Dawes Road, it is certainly out on its own. An easy-going sort of restaurant with live jazz in the evenings (Wed–Sun), Montana serves quirky Southwestern food that has gained much praise despite a stream of critics pointing out that the dishes have little if anything to do with Montana (which in any case is not in the Southwest USA). The decor is all ragwash and cowskin, and – like that of its siblings, Dakota in Notting Hill, Canyon in Richmond, Utah in Wimbledon and Idaho in Highgate – would be more at home in *Twin Peaks* than West London. Captured in two early sepia prints, Sitting Bull broods over the assembled diners – whatever would he have made of this "Southwestern American" dining experience?

Your opening move is to sample the two fresh house breads, which are strongly flavoured with herbs and chilli. Then perhaps a wholehearted chilli relleno (£6.55), or wild boar and butternut squash quesadilla (£6.75), or even the Rhode Island smoked scallop, mussel and fennel chowder (£6.25) – Southwestern via New England. The menu changes with the seasons but is always on the adventurous side. There may be a pecan- and mustard-crusted rump of lamb (£14.75), or seared tuna (£13.25), which sounds simple enough but is accompanied with citrus and pinto bean salad, tobacco shallots and a red wine and cumin dressing. Vegetarians get similar complexity: the vegetarian selection (£11.50) comprises picos blue tamales, asparagus and mushroom flautas, wild rice and pecan-stuffed potato. Desserts can also prove exotic: how does a caramelised black cherry chimichanga sound? It comes with Brasil nut praline ice cream.

Montana has an interesting and wide-ranging wine list with bottles starting at around £12. There is a serious three-course set dinner priced at £25, but it is only available for parties of twelve or more, and contrary to most current trends Montana has discontinued its other set meal deals. Brunch, served on Saturday and Sunday until 4pm, is serious stuff.

WEST

Duke of Cumberland

235 New Kings Rd, SW6   ✆020 7736 2777

The outside is festooned with greenery and the inside is beautifully finished in this classic Young's pub. There's light wood panelling, decorative tiling and a very open atmosphere.

The George

506 Fulham Rd, SW6   ✆020 7736 4505

Traditional pub nicely cluttered with pictures and ephemera and a mix of velvet banquettes and wooden chairs. It has a real lived-in local feel and a regular crowd. Courage Best and Directors.

Havana

490 Fulham Rd, SW6   ✆020 7381 5005

Brilliant colours on the walls and leopardskin and zebra-stripe furniture mark out this cocktail bar. Solo singers perform on Sunday; for the rest of the week the place is pounding to a Latin beat. The young, lively crowd enjoy cocktails, mixer drinks, Fosters and Kronenbourg 1664 on tap. It's roomy and friendly, but noisy.

Mixology

108–110 New Kings Rd,
  SW6   ✆020 7731 2142

"Shakers" are the thing in this bright modern bar. For £10 you get a cocktail shaker of five shots of spirits shaken with fruit juice and ice, and shot glasses to drink it all from. Or you can stick to conventional cocktails or jugs of the same. Fosters, Miller and Kronenbourg 1664 are on tap for beer lovers. Watch out for the mirror tiles as you make your way to the loo.

The Wheatsheaf

582 Fulham Rd, SW6   ✆020 7384 1509

The Wheatsheaf's mock Tudor "ye olde oake beame" theme is slightly at odds with the games machines and big-screen sport. People feel very at home here, and more than a few even use it as an office. Greene King IPA and Abbot ales on tap, along with Morland's Old Speckled Hen.

The White Horse

1–3 Parson's Green, SW6   ✆020 7736 2115

Real Ale lovers don't need to die and go to heaven; they can just come to the White Horse (also known as the Sloaney Pony. . .) for the huge selection of ales – Harvey's Sussex Bitter, Highgate and Walsall Dark Mild, Hop Back Thunderstorm, and many more. They also host themed beer festivals here, and offer more than fifty bottled beers. It's huge and traditional, with attractive pale wood decor and a large outdoor section.

Hammersmith
& Chiswick

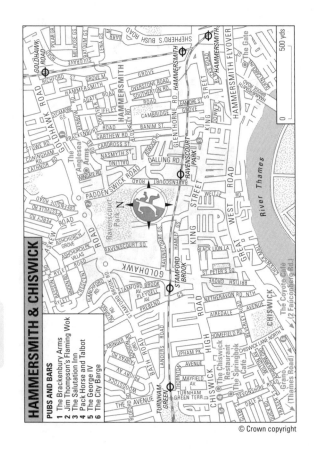

HAMMERSMITH & CHISWICK

PUBS AND BARS

1 The Brackenbury Arms
2 Jim Thompson's Flaming Wok
3 The Salutation Inn
4 Pack Horse and Talbot
5 The George IV
6 The City Barge

© Crown copyright

The Anglesea Arms

35 Wingate Rd, W6 ℗020 8749 1291   ⊖ Ravenscourt Park

Food served Mon–Fri 12.30–2.45pm & 7.30–10.45pm, Sat 12.30–3pm &

7.30–10.45pm, Sun 1–3.30pm & 7.30–10pm   All major credit cards except Amex

Do not make the mistake of pigeonholing this establishment as merely a pub. The Anglesea serves very good food indeed, with a kitchen the envy of many more mainstream restaurants. The chef-proprietor is Dan Evans, a seasoned campaigner who was head chef at several of the brightest eateries of the 1990s. At The Anglesea, Dan runs the kitchen, while his wife Fiona runs the bar and front of house. The menu changes at least twice a day, dishes are crossed out as they run out, and, when you've achieved "favoured local" status, you can ask for something simple that's not even on the board – if they have the ingredients you can have the dish. Pitch up early, claim a seat and, not only will you dine well, but you'll leave feeling good about the bill.

Who knows what Dan will have chalked up on the blackboard when you visit? How about a starter like foie gras and pigeon terrine with brioche and onion marmalade (£5.50) – not a dish you'd usually see at this price. Or there may be tomato, sweet basil and crab soup (£3.95), or home-cured gravadlax with horseradish blinis and beetroot (£4.95). Main courses may include sautéed lamb sweetbreads with fresh pappardelle, peas and mint (£8.50); or a compendium dish like large warm salad of duck breast and livers, chorizo, small potatoes, flat beans and Cabernet Sauvignon (£8.75). Or something simple like Gloucester Old Spot ham, egg and chips (£8.50). To round things off, there is always one British cheese in perfect condition – like St Andrew's, a cow's milk cheese served with black grapes (£5).

As befits food such as this, there's a wine list to match. A dozen wines are on offer by the glass, and the choice is thoughtful. Not very many restaurants, and very few pubs, offer a range of pudding wines by the bottle, half-bottle and glass. Among them is a delicious pudding wine called de Pacherence from Southwestern France (£16.50 a bottle, £4.50 a glass) – a far cry from the builders' overalls and pints of Guinness that once ruled the roost here.

The Chiswick Restaurant

131 Chiswick High Rd, W4 ℂ020 8994 6887   ⊖ Turnham Green

Mon–Fri 12.30–2.45pm & 7–11pm, Sat 7–11pm,

Sun noon–3pm   All major credit cards except Diners

The menu here changes twice a day. Not completely – the puddings will probably stay the same and two or three dishes will carry over – but there's always something fresh for the large number of local regulars. And they're a lucky lot, for The Chiswick is quite simply one of the best neighbourhood restaurants in London. It serves delicious, well-presented dishes that major in strong flavours. Service is informal but with a steely edge of competence. Pricing is enlightened, with a lunch and early-evening menu (7–8pm) that costs £9.50 for two courses and coffee, or £12.95 for three. This goes up, but not extravagantly, to £12.95 for two courses and £15.50 for three after the witching hour of 8pm. You might get something along the lines of vine tomato soup and chicken confit and mash; or Greek salad and grilled mackerel and salsa verde. No wonder the place is packed.

Everything here is driven by the seasons and the markets, and with a twice-daily changing menu it's hard to make very firm suggestions. The cuisine, particularly in the starters list, is perhaps a little more British than Modern. Given the chance, start with the potato pancake, wood pigeon and onion marmalade (£6.50), the warm salad of pork confit, dandelion and poached egg (£6.50), the porcini and potato soup (£4), or the terrific plate of charcuterie (£6.25), each element of which is teamed with a different home-made pickle or chutney. The inspiration for the main courses seems more widely spread. Roast halibut may be teamed with olive oil mash and red wine sauce (£12.75); calves' liver comes with melted onions and crisp sage (£11.75) and is very delicious indeed. The neck fillet of lamb with couscous, hummus and mint (£12.25) is surprisingly light and fresh-flavoured, while a fillet of sea bass (£15) may come with a simple salad Niçoise. The wine list has plenty of good choices in the middle price range.

Among the puddings, keep an eye out for banana bread and chocolate malt ice cream (£4.50): a nostalgic delight for anyone old enough to remember Horlicks and Ovaltine.

The Coyote Café

2 Fauconberg Rd, W4 ℂ020 8742 8545	⊖ Chiswick Park
Mon 5–11pm, Tues–Sat 11am–11pm, Sun 11am–10.30pm	Amex, Mastercard, Visa

The proprietor here, John Wasilko, was so impressed when he visited The Coyote Café in Santa Fe that he bought the rights to use the name in Europe. Now Southwest America has a firm foothold in Chiswick, and the natives seem to be enjoying it. The bar and restaurant is packed, making booking a must, and on sunny days the crowd spills out onto pavement seating. The best Southwestern cuisine, as presented here, is more delicate, intense and refined than your run-of-the-mill Tex-Mex; the chilli flavours may prove hot but the tastes are also discernibly sweet, sour, fruity and rich. If you are not familiar with this kind of food, you should leave your preconceptions behind.

As well as the regular menu there is also a sheet of specials which changes weekly. You might start with something genuinely out of the ordinary: how does Cajun angels in devil's blankets (£6.75) sound? It's a satisfying dish of five large shrimps wrapped in bacon and blackened. From the appetisers try the Santa Fe Caesar salad (£6.25 or £7 with chicken), which delivers a good, fresh mound of crisp leaves, croutons and Parmesan. Or there's a nice wild mushroom quesadilla with roast corn salsa (£5.25); or Gulf Coast crab cakes with creamed Creole sauce (£6.95). On the entrées list, you'll see some Tex-Mex favourites. Blackened ribeye steak with chipotle gravy, skinny fries and tobacco onions (£11.95) is worth having for the chipotle gravy, which is a kind of tomatoey, tangy, fruity chilli sauce. The Howlin' chilli burger (£7.95) is large and delicious, topped with a ladleful of splendid chilli. Turn to the specials for even wilder and more exciting dishes – like grilled halibut with peanut chipotle sauce (£10.25), or roasted venison with green chillies and wild boar bacon (£9.75).

The Coyote Café is famed for its Saturday and Sunday brunch: corn beef hash (£6.95); Creole eggs Benedict (£6.95); Texas ham'n'eggs Alexander (£6.55); huevos rancheros (£6.25); American pancakes with molasses (£3.55). Good enough to make you howl, which will not endear you to the residents of Chiswick Park – unless, of course, they too are dining and howling.

£14–£30

The Gate

51 Queen Caroline St, W6 ✆020 8748 6932   ⊖ Hammersmith

Mon–Fri noon–2.45pm & 6–10.30pm, Sat 6–11pm   All major credit cards

www.gateveg.co.uk

The extraordinary thing about The Gate, which is tucked away behind the Labatt's Apollo, is that you hardly notice that it's a vegetarian restaurant. This is enjoyable dining without the meat. It's not wholefood, it's not even healthy – indeed, it's as rich, colourful, calorific and naughty as anywhere in town. The clientele is a quiet and appreciative bunch of locals and pilgrims – it's unlikely that anyone could just stumble across this hidden-away, former artists' studio, which has been leased from the nearby church. The airy decor and the high ceiling give it a serene loft feel – which may be The Gate's only nod to veggie solemnities.

The short menu changes monthly, but starters are always great. There's usually a tart – like porcini and artichoke (£4.90) – which elsewhere, with its sophisticated salad, would be served as a main course. Also excellent are the sweet corn fritters (£4.50), crisp and well presented. Portions are invariably hearty, so it's a good idea to share starters in order to pace yourself and sample all the courses. The mains are generally well executed. Tortillas (£9.25) come stuffed with roasted butternut squash and re-fried beans, and served with chilli sauce, guacamole and sour cream. Or there's gumbo (£9.50), which teams a stew made with okra and sweet potato with a mix of long grain and wild rice, and a salad made from baby corn. Puddings are splendid: there may be rhubarb and plum crumble (£4.25), or the pressed chocolate torte (£4.50), which is a thinking person's death-by-chocolate. Those without a sweet tooth should go for the English cheeses (£5), where quince chutney and oat-cakes accompany farmhouse varieties.

The drinks list is extensive, with all manner of freshly squeezed juices (£1.75), herbal teas (£1.25) and coffee (£1.25–£1.75), while the wine list tops out at just over £20 and has something for everyone: vegan, vegetarian, organic and carnivore alike. Pud-lovers will enjoy a glass of Vinoix (£2.75) – this walnut-infused wine makes a pleasant change from the usual "stickies" and is the perfect complement to such formidable desserts.

£23–£60

Grano

162 Thames Rd, Chiswick, W4 ©020 8995 0120   ⊖ Gunnersbury

Mon–Sat 7–10.30pm, Sun noon–2.30pm   All major credit cards

Grano burst onto the scene at the end of 1998. One moment the mere thought of a journey to far-off outer Chiswick was enough to give restaurant reviewers a nosebleed, and the next there was a queue of taxis to get there. Not such a surprise when you take into account that Grano is run by Mauro Santaliquido and Alessio Brusadin, the duo behind Tentazioni (see p.412) and also Riso, 76 South Parade, W4 (©020 8742 2121). Design-wise the restaurant is more casual and neighbourhood than slick West End. This is an award-winning place where the food stands centre stage. Booking is essential in the evenings.

This is a place where the menu changes regulary. The kitchen's strengths are fish, game and pasta and whatever is best at the markets. Seasonality is king and the food is all the better for its reign. There is a simple pricing regime – two courses cost £19 and three courses £24. Starters might include tortino di funghi e indivia con insalata d'anatra, a mushroom and chicory tart that comes with a duck salad, or cestino di vegetale con mozzarella e ricotta, a tasty dish of mixed vegetables with ricotta and mozzarella cheese. All the home-made pasta are available as starters: look out the tagliolini nero con polpa de granchio e cipollotti – black tagliolini with crabmeat and shallots (£2 supplement). Main courses can be spectacular: look out for tagliata di tonno con puré di spinaci e cipolle rosse, a tuna steak with spinach purée and red onions; or nodino di vitello con patate e lardoni (£5 supplement), a veal chop with pancetta. There is a short, well-chosen list of interesting, regional Italian wines, good but not cheap.

For dessert, there is the omnipresent tiramisù, and the wonderful tortino di mandorle e nocciole con goccio di cioccolato fondente e salsa all' arancia – an almond and hazelnut tart with dark chocolate and orange sauce. Just goes to prove how much more romantic things sound when described in Italian.

The Springbok Café

42 Devonshire Rd, W4 ℗020 8742 3149	⊖ Turnham Green
Mon–Sat 6.30–11pm	Mastercard, Switch, Visa

As their customers have started to get used to the idea of a South African restaurant, Peter and Chantelle Gottgens have been able to drift the menus towards more ambitious and exotic dishes. The Springbok Café is small and informal, with the open-plan kitchen centre stage. What's more, Peter – who trained as a chef in South Africa and Italy – is passionate about both the quality and authenticity of his ingredients. He gets his fish from Mossell Bay or Port St John's and all the biltong, game and fresh herbs are flown in from South Africa. Due to EC regulations he can no longer import ostrich, but he does make sure to source English ostrich of South African stock.

The menu changes monthly, but you might start with smoked snoek pasta with sugar snap peas, char-grilled peppers and fresh basil (£4.95), zebra samosas with a rocket and herb salad (£5.25), or Cape Malay pickled fish (£4.50). For the main course, indulge yourself and try something that you have probably never had before – how about roast rack of wildebeest with sautéed vegetables and a Pinotage sauce (£12), or maybe crisp warthog belly with morogo, elgin apple, and rooibois tea compote (£11.50). The fish is particularly good here: try filleted Cape linefish with a mielie meal crust, baby mielies, green beans and butternut squash (£11.25). The side orders are original too: sweet potato and spring onion mash (£2), roast pumpkin with Acacia honey (£2), sweetcorn, chilli and dahnia fritters (£2.25). By the time puddings come round, see if you have room to share a prickly pear with peri-peri ice cream (£4.50), or a pot of moerkoffie (£1.25) with a side order of koeksusters (£1) – a kind of gingery doughnut soaked in syrup.

If you're the kind of person who only ever orders something that you are sure to like, perhaps consider having your meal elsewhere. Dining at the Springbok Café is a whole load of fun if you are interested in food; it is a place for "you'll never know until you've tried it". Take a few risks and discover something new.

The Brackenbury Arms

163 Goldhawk Rd, W12   ©020 8740 9458

The clack of pool balls from the central table will be the only thing to disturb you in this straightforward, convenient pub. Very much a regulars' local. Favourites include Fosters, Guinness and Guinness Extra Cold.

The City Barge

27a Strand on the Green, W4 ©020 8994 2148

Built as the Navigator's Arms in 1484, the City Barge become so known when the Lord Mayor of London's barge was moored nearby. It's a beautiful, original and authentic riverside pub with more character than most. Real fires in winter and towpath tables in summer make it very popular. Enjoy Courage Directors, Greene King IPA and Morland's Old Speckled Hen, but take care at high tide as the towpath can flood. It's a minute's walk from Grano, and around ten minutes from The Coyote Café.

The George IV

185 Chiswick High Rd, W5   ©020 8994 4624

Cool, dark and panelled, this traditional Fuller's pub is roomy and comfortable. Frosted-glass screens divide it into sections and there's a secluded sun-trap beer garden. The black granite bar and the black-and-white tiled floor give it a rather grand air. Enjoy Fuller's ESB, Chiswick, Bitter or seasonal ales like Winter Warmer.

Jim Thompson's Flaming Wok

243 Goldhawk Rd, W12   ©020 8748 0229

You can buy the pewter statues and carved wooden boxes that decorate this over-the-top Oriental-themed bar. Thai carvings and coloured bowls dangle from the ceiling, and the bar is fronted with mosaics. Theme nights get everyone up and jumping. Marstons Pedigree, Greene King IPA and Hoegaarden are the favourites on tap.

Pack Horse & Talbot

145 Chiswick High Rd, W5   ©020 8994 0360

This big, light pub plays host to a younger crowd of sports fans. A large, separate room houses three pool tables, Sky TV and games machines. Pavement tables allow you to watch the traffic crawl past. Courage Best and Directors are the signature ales on tap.

The Salutation Inn

154 King St, W6   ©020 8748 3668

Worth visiting for its glazed blue tiled exterior alone, this traditional Fuller's pub has been an institution here for more than two hundred years. It has a sheltered beer garden. Enjoy Fuller's ESB, Chiswick and seasonal ales. And look out for the beautiful tiled script that advertised the pub in 1910.

Notting Hill

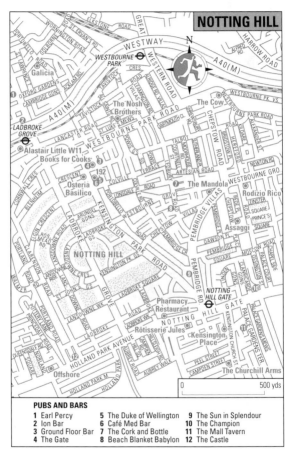

NOTTING HILL

PUBS AND BARS

1 Earl Percy	**5** The Duke of Wellington	**9** The Sun in Splendour
2 Ion Bar	**6** Café Med Bar	**10** The Champion
3 Ground Floor Bar	**7** The Cork and Bottle	**11** The Mall Tavern
4 The Gate	**8** Beach Blanket Babylon	**12** The Castle

WEST

192

192 Kensington Park Rd, W11 ⓒ020 7229 0482	⊖ Notting Hill Gate/Ladbroke Grove

Mon–Fri 12.30–3pm & 6.30–11pm, Sat 12.30–3.30pm &

6.30–11pm, Sun 12.30–3.30pm & 7–11pm   All major credit cards

192 is a pretty restaurant and wine bar that attracts a young, monied crowd of local media, literary and music folk (Virgin staff treat the place as a house cafe), most of whom seem to know each other. This makes for a friendly atmosphere with much kissing and table-hopping, and you may well find yourself in conversation with singers fresh from their recording session seated at the next table. The bar section is always busy, and has a lively, clubby atmosphere.

The menu offers the kind of food that seems simple but is very hard to do well. It is based on best-quality fresh ingredients with little interference, and changes daily to reflect what is in season and at the markets. Things are basically set out as à la carte but there are a couple of deals – two courses and coffee for £11.50 from Monday to Friday and £12.50 on Sunday. Starters may include seared foie gras with potato rosti and artichokes (£8.50), and crab, bacon, pousse and avocado salad (£8). Both are very, very good – the foie gras slightly pink and the crab salad made with large chunks of fresh white meat. Main courses include tagliatelle with tuna bottarga (£6/£8), braised oxtail with parsnip purée and ceps (£12.75), seared marlin with tomato, red onion and potato gratin (£13), and baked sea bass with samphire, lemon and chive beurre blanc (£12.50). These are exactly what you want them to be, with flavours and textures all perfectly judged. Presentation is excellent at 192, with an eye for garnishes that enhance your anticipation. Leave room for pudding, as there are delights like coconut and pineapple millefeuille (£4.45), which features baked pineapple in a thin biscuity pastry with coconut sorbet, and bitter chocolate tart with honey ice cream (£4.25).

192 is owned by the Groucho Club and the wine list features some of the club's wines – so if you can't wangle an invite to the Dean Street establishment, you can at least come here to see how the other half drinks.

£20–£50

Alastair Little W11

136a Lancaster Rd, W11 ℗020 7243 2220   ⊖ Ladbroke Grove

Mon–Fri noon–2.30pm & 6.30–11pm,

Sat noon–3pm & 6.30–11pm   All major credit cards

Alastair Little is a name that commands respect among restaurant-goers in London. Back in the 80s, he was one of the main pioneers of the Anglo-Italian movement, a man without a professional catering background who wanted to serve real food – clean, fresh cooking, with home-made pastas and terrines – of the style and type that we all wish we could serve at home. Following the success of his clean-cut site in Frith Street (see p.131), he opened this much less expensive sibling in 1996. Notting Hill trendies rushed in hordes to try it out, but they have since moved on, returning Alastair Little to the foodies. Forget the trends: this is a top-class place and one that, even after a modest refurb and repaint, feels extremely comfortable.

The daily changing menu is short and sweet at lunchtime and middle-sized and sweet for dinner. At lunch the price is fixed at £5 for first courses, £8 for pastas, £12 for mains and £5 desserts – extraordinarily inexpensive for this quality. In the evening you'll find the same dishes plus some others – two courses cost £23.50, three £27.50. Starters might be the likes of baked new season's garlic soup with quail's egg, or pear and Parmesan with wild rocket. Or there may be a chicken liver and foie gras parfait and toast, which is good enough to put a grin on the face of any normal, greedy person. Pasta dishes to follow might include tagliatelle with rabbit or rigatoni al sugo with buffalo mozzarella – an astonishing plateful, rich with braised beef. Or how about a wild mushroom risotto? Genuine comfort food. Mains are of the order of pan-fried skate wing with beurre noisette, spinach and Roseval potatoes; or corn-fed chicken with morel sauce and mash; or the extremely tempting slow-roasted shoulder of pork with braised red cabbage and roast potatoes. But it is the simple pasta dishes that are Alastair Little's real strength: don't miss out on them.

Desserts are the kind of rich, indulgent things that are so good you almost feel embarrassed to be seen choosing. How about Italian chocolate brownie? A mixed idiom maybe, but utterly delicious.

WEST

Assaggi

39 Chepstow Place, W2 ✆020 7792 5501	⊖ Notting Hill Gate
Mon–Fri 12.30–2.30pm & 7.30–11pm,	
Sat 1–2.30pm & 7.30–11pm	All major credit cards

Assaggi is a small, ochre-painted room above The Chepstow pub. It's generally full at lunch and booked well in advance in the evenings. The prices are unforgiving, and on the face of it paying so much for such straightforward dishes could raise the hackles of any sensible diner. But the reason Assaggi is such a gem, and also the reason it is always full, is that self-same straightforwardness. The menu may appear simple, but it is littered with authentic and luxury ingredients and the cooking is very accomplished indeed. Prepare yourself for a meal to be remembered.

You'll find a dozen starters – with the option to have the pastas as main courses, as well – and half a dozen main courses. Start with pasta – tagliolini con bottarga (£8.95), maybe, which is a dish of perfectly cooked fine pasta strands with the elusive and subtle flavour of smoked grey mullet roe. Or there's the Assaggi pasta loaf (£6.95/£8.95), a pinwheel of pasta with a well-flavoured filling. Or there may be a dish like capesante con puré di finocchi e vinaigrette d'acighe (£10.75) – a simple plate of perfectly cooked, splendidly fresh scallops – or bresaola Punta d'Anca (£6.95). Main courses are even more pared-down: calves' liver (£12.95), a plainly grilled veal chop (£17.95) with rosemary, fish of the day (£17.95), or filletto di manzo con galletti (£18.95) – a fist-sized lump of fillet steak with a mound of chanterelle mushrooms. All are memorable, while the side salad of tomato, rucola e basilico (£4.75) is everything you would wish for. Puddings change daily and cost £5.25. Look out for panacotta – a perfect texture – and the beautifully simple dish made from ultra-fresh buffalo ricotta served with "cooked" honey. To accompany, the short wine list features splendid and unfamiliar Italian regional specialities.

Assaggi is known for its bread. This is the famous carta di musica, very thin, very crisp and very delicious. It's like a kind of Italian popadom, only better. The name came about because, when well made, the papery texture is reminiscent of the sheets of vellum on which music was first written.

£10–£15

Books for Cooks

4 Blenheim Crescent, W11 ✆020 7221 1992   ⊖ Ladbroke Grove/Notting Hill Gate

Mon–Fri noon–1.30pm, Sat (sittings) noon & 1.45pm   All major credit cards

www.booksforcooks.com

This cookery bookshop is an extraordinary little place – a Mecca for foodies throughout London and beyond. Even at 11am on a Monday morning you will find a herd of gastronomes snuffling through the literary undergrowth, seeking inspiration for something or other. The knowledgeable, friendly staff know their stock and will tell you, through experience, not only which recipes will work but also where to look for further information. They test and try all sorts of cuisines and dishes in the kitchen at the back of the shop, and that's where a dozen diners can enjoy a good lunch at a bargain price. At Books for Cooks the proof of each pudding is in the eating.

Though the style of cooking changes from one day to the next, depending on whether today's cookery book is by the very English Gary Rhodes or the Sugar Club's Peter Gordon, the formula is always the same. There's a soup (£4) followed by two or three main courses (£8), one of which will be vegetarian and another meat-based. You'll also get a choice of two or three desserts (£3). They start serving at noon and carry on until they run out of food – usually around 1.30pm. The cooking will always be competent and the food served will reflect the nature of the cookery book used rather than the temperament of the person behind the stove. Sometimes you can eat food of genius, sometimes not, but it'll never be dull. And if you are deeply impressed by your squid pie or chocolate and almond torte, not only can you discuss its preparation with the chef, you can buy the book it came from. The one problem with Books for Cooks is that word is out and it has become essential to book; to be certain of getting in you should call a week in advance.

As if it wasn't already enough of a bargain, Books for Cooks have instituted a three-course set lunch for just £12. On Saturday – Portobello Market day – they do two sittings. Book for the second sitting if you can, and drop in earlier to find out what's on the menu. The staff love it when customers bring their own wine, relax and talk about food.

The Churchill Arms

119 Kensington Church St, W8 ©020 7792 1246	⊖ Notting Hill Gate
Mon–Sat 12.30–2.30pm & 6–9.30pm, Sun noon–2.30pm	Mastercard, Visa

In the ever-expanding field of pub restaurants The Churchill is something of an old stager. It was possibly one of the first in London to offer Thai food. Do you wonder why we see so few eating houses selling Indian food, incidentally? Or Chinese food? Could it be because of the grand profit margins on Thai cuisine? Well, whatever the motivation behind it, The Churchill has nurtured its clientele (who are largely students and bargain hunters) over the years by the simple expedient of serving some of the tastiest and most reasonably priced Thai food in London. The main dining area is in a back room featuring acres of green foliage, but don't despair if you find it full (it fills up very quickly) – meals are served throughout the pub. Service is friendly, but as the food is cooked to order be prepared to wait – it is worth it. If you really can't wait, pre-cooked dishes such as chicken with chillies (along with that other well-known Thai delicacy, Stilton ploughman's) are also available.

Dishes are unpronounceable, and have thoughtfully been numbered to assist everybody. The pad gai med ma muang hin-maparn (no. 15 – £5.50) is a deliciously spicy dish of chicken, cashew nuts and chilli served with a generous helping of fluffy boiled rice. Kwaitiew pad kee mao (no. 16 – £5.25) is pork, chicken or beef cooked with flat Thai noodles heated with red and green chillies – hot, but not unbearably so. The same cannot be said for khao rad na ga prao (no. 5 – £5.50), which is described as very hot. Not an understatement. This prawn dish with fresh chillies and Thai basil is guaranteed to bring sweat to the brow of even the most ardent chilliholic. For something milder, try the pad neau nahm man hoi (no. 17 – £5.25), beef with oyster sauce and mushrooms, or the khao rad na (no. 3 – £5.25), a rice dish topped with prawns, vegetables and gravy. Both are good. Puddings are limited in choice and ambition, but for something sweet to temper the heat try apple pie (£2.50) – a strange accompaniment to Thai food, but surprisingly welcome.

At lunchtime you'll get the same dishes for about 10 per cent less than in the evening, when waitress service for drinks is available. The best thing about The Churchill Thai Kitchen is you get restaurant-standard food with drinks at pub prices, and they even do takeaways in traditional foil trays.

Cow Dining Room

89 Westbourne Park Rd, W2 ℗020 7221 5400   ⊖ Westbourne Park

Mon–Fri 7–11pm, Sat noon–2.30pm & 7–11pm,

Sun 12.30–3.30pm & 7.30–10.30pm   All major credit cards except Diners

The Cow is something of a conundrum. On the one hand it is a genuine pub – a proper pub, with beer and locals – and on the other it has become something of a meeting place for Notting Hill's smarter residents. Downstairs all is fierce drinking and cigarette smoke, while upstairs you'll find an oasis of calm and, at its epicentre, a small dining room. It is a good place to eat. The atmosphere is informal but the food is accomplished. Towards the end of 1999 a new chef took up the reins here – the estimable Juliet Peston who had previously run the kitchens at Lola in Islington. The menu changes on a daily basis and delivers fresh, unfussy, seasonal food.

Starters put together delicious combinations of prime ingredients such as grilled asparagus with Parmesan (£6.50), carpaccio, broad beans and pecorino (£6.50), and roast new season's garlic goats' cheese with Parma ham, tomatoes, tapenade and sourdough toast (£6.75). Even without mentioning a main course dish of skate, Jersey Royals, French beans and salsa verde (£15.50), the menu is so resolutely seasonal that you will have gathered that all the dishes mentioned so far were served on a day in May. Other main courses include roast monkfish with bacon, peas and spring onions (£14.50); chicken saltimbocca with new potatoes, rocket and artichokes (£14.50); lamb cutlets, merguez, Greek salad, hummus and flatbread (£14.50); or, for something a little more Notting Hill in tone, roast lobster, chips, mayonnaise and green salad (£20). Puddings are suitably desirable: lemon tart (£5), chocolate brownie, vanilla ice cream and fudge sauce (£5), affogato al caffe (£5). Or you could go for cheese, which in this instance is well chosen and well kept – Colston Basset Stilton, with bitter leaf, apple and walnut salad (£5).

Probably the most complicated thing on the menu at the Cow Dining Room is the Cow Cocktail – "Prosecco di Conegliano e Valdobbiadene with wild cherries or strawberries" (£4.50). But the staff will happily fetch you a glass of the excellent De Koninck beer from downstairs if that doesn't tempt.

Galicia

323 Portobello Rd, W10 ©020 8969 3539   ⊖ Ladbroke Grove/Westbourne Park

Tues–Sun noon–3pm & 7–11.30pm   All major credit cards

As you walk up the Portobello Road it would be only too easy to amble straight past Galicia. It has that strange Continental quality – even when it is open it looks shut, and when it's shut it's invisible. Only make it through the forbidding entrance, and inside Galicia opens out into a bar (which is in all probability crowded), which in turn opens into a small 25-seat restaurant (which is in all probability full). The tapas at the bar are straightforward and good, so it is no surprise that quite a lot of customers get no further than here. One regular once confided that some of the best Spanish dishes he had ever sampled were given to him as tapas in the bar while he was waiting for a seat, and that when he finally got the elusive table he had eaten so much that he was forced to surrender it to someone in greater need. So, first secure your table . . .

. . . then cut a swathe through the starters – jamón (£4.25) is a large plate of sweet, air-dried ham; gambas a la plancha (£5.95) are giant prawns plainly grilled; and pulpo a la Gallega (£5) is a revelation – slices of octopus grilled until bafflingly tender and powdered with smoky pimenton. Galicia does straightforward grilled fish and meat very well indeed. Look for the chuleto de cordera a la plancha (£8.10), which are perfect lamb chops, or lomo de cerdo (£7.25), which are very thin slices of pork fillet in a sauce with pimenton. Or there's the suitably stolid Spanish omelette, tortilla (£4.90). And you should have some chips, which are very good here – thick and yet chewy, they taste just like those superior chips you get in Spain. The wine list is short and to the point, but also full of opportunities for exploration – you may find yourself the proud possessor of a Vega Grand Riserva for just £17.90. Or then again that bin may have run out.

Galicia is a pleasant place without pretension, though the waiters are all old-school – quiet, efficient to the point of brusqueness and with a slight tendency to grumpiness. The overall feel is of a certain stilted formality. The clientele is an agreeable mix of Notting Hill-ites and homesick Iberians, both of which groups stand between you and that table reservation – book early.

£18–£50

Kensington Place

201–207 Kensington Church St, W8 ©020 7727 3184	⊖ Notting Hill Gate
Mon–Sat noon–3pm & 6.30–11.45pm,	
Sun noon–3pm & 6.30–10.15pm	Amex, Mastercard, Visa

The first thing to know about Kensington Place is that it is noisy. The dining room is large, echoing, glass-fronted and just plain noisy. It's the racket of hordes of people having a good time. Rather than background music there's the busy hum of confidences, shrieks of merriment, and the clamour of parties. The service is crisp, the food is good and the prices are fair. The menu changes from session to session to reflect whatever the market has to offer, and there is a set lunch which offers a limited choice of three good courses for £14.50 during the week and £16.50 on Sunday. (By way of example: you might have chicken liver crostini with truffle paste and rocket, followed by wild sea trout with capers and lemon, then poached mirabelles with vanilla cream.) This is fine value for money. Regulars claim that the set lunch menu is the key to knowing just when head chef Rowley Leigh is cooking in person – apparently his handwriting is very distinctive!

Rowley Leigh's food is eclectic in the best possible way. The kitchen starts with the laudable premise that there is nothing better than what is in season, and goes on to combine Mediterranean inspirations with classic French and English dishes. Thus you may find (in due season) starters like fish soup with croutons and rouille (£5.50), griddled foie gras with sweetcorn pancake (£9.50), tagliarini with crayfish and baby leeks (£6), or omelette fines herbes (£4.50). These are sophisticated dishes, and well-chosen combinations of flavours. Main courses might be smoked haddock Monte Carlo (£13.50), spiced grilled quails (£14), roast guinea fowl with tajine vegetables and saffron (£13.50), or cod with parsley sauce (£12.50).

The dessert section of the menu offers what may be one of London's finest lemon tarts (£5), with well-made ice creams (£4.50) and traditional favourites with a twist: bread and butter pudding made with pannetone (£6), panna cotta made with coffee and mascarpone (£5.50). And for hardened pudding addicts there is the ultimate challenge – the grand selection (£10). Indulge yourself (or share) and take a glass of Tokaji Aszu 5 Puttonyos (£5) alongside.

The Mandola

139–141 Westbourne Grove, W11 ©020 7229 4734   ⊖ Notting Hill Gate

Mon 6–11pm, Tues–Sun noon–11pm   All major credit cards

The food at The Mandola is described as "urban Sudanese", and as that means foregoing the doubtful pleasures of some of the more traditional Sudanese delicacies – strips of raw liver marinated in lime juice chilli and peanut butter springs to mind – it seems like a pretty good bet. This would be a small, seriously informal, neighbourhood restaurant, but for the fact that it attracts people from all over town with its sensible pricing and often strikingly delicious dishes, so now they have not only had to buy the shop next door and expand to a respectable 74 covers but also to institute two sittings a night. Despite such minor irritations there's much to praise. The staff are so laid-back as to make worriers self-destruct on the spot. The restaurant is unlicensed, so everything from fine wine to exotic beer is available – if you choose to bring it with you. Or you could try the deep-red, citrus-sharp hibiscus tea, which the proprietor describes as "sub-Saharan Ribena".

To start there is a combo of dips and salads, rather prosaically listed as "mixed salad bar" for two (£8.95). There are a few Middle Eastern favourites here, given a twist and all strongly and interestingly flavoured. Salata tomatim bel gibna (£3.50) is made from tomatoes, feta and parsley; salata tahina (£3.25) is a good tangy tahini; salata aswad (£4.20) is a less oily version of the Turkish aubergine dish iman bayeldi; salata daqua (£3.50) is white cabbage in peanut sauce; and tamiya (£4.75) is Sudanese falafel. All are accompanied by hot pitta bread. As for main courses, samak magli (£8.95) shows just how good simple things can be – fillets of tilapia are served crisp and spicy on the outside, fresh on the inside, with a squeeze of lime juice. Chicken halla is cooked in a rich, well-reduced tomato sauce that would be equally at home in a smart Italian eatery (£8.50). Lovers of the exotic can finish with the Sudanese spiced coffee, scented with cardamom, cinnamon, cloves and ginger – your own flask and coffee set, enough for nine tiny cupfuls, for £4.

It is lucky that the bowl for the crushed green chilli with lime, onions and garlic(£1.75) is stainless steel, as the contents must be one of the hottest things in the known universe.

£20–£40

Nosh Brothers

12 All Saints Rd, W11 ©020 7243 2808	⊖ Westbourne Park
Mon 7–11pm, Tues–Sat noon–3pm & 7–11pm,	
Sun noon–4pm	All major credit cards except Diners
www.thenoshbrothers.com	

Once upon a time All Saints Road was nothing more than a small, dark side street near Portobello Road. Today, however, it is illuminated by many restaurants, and Nosh Brothers is one of the brighter lights. The restaurant is small and modern, almost stark, which means that little gets in the way of the cooking and eating, which is quintessentially simple and good. Lunch is either £15 for two courses or £18 for three, while dinner is à la carte with starters between £4 and £8 and main courses from around £10 to £15. The menu changes daily, and favours seasonal excellence.

To start you might have to choose between gazpacho; Greek salad; grilled asparagus risotto with fresh peas, parmesan and mint; air-dried beef with a salad of baby artichokes, green olives and rocket; smoked (undyed) haddock salad with bacon, new potatoes, chives and a poached egg; and a delicious dish of steamed, pan-opened mussels and clams plus fresh spaghettini with garlic parsley and tomato. The spaghettini is freshly cooked, then tossed with shellfish that has just been shown a hot pan. Combinations in every dish are very good. Typical main course offerings are tagliatelle with roasted cherry vine tomatoes, buffalo mozzarella, pine nuts and basil; grilled sea bass on a new potato and horseradish salad; a sweetly salty dish of just-cooked cod wrapped in Bayonne ham with artichokes, clams, peas and bacon; pan-fried duck breast with a white bean, parsley and roasted pepper salad; or roasted rump of lamb with cous cous, harissa spiced jus and a date and cumin relish – a well-judged dish in which the pinkly cooked lamb is not overpowered by the harissa. Puddings include summer pudding with clotted cream; raspberry crème brûlée; chocolate and pecan tart with mascarpone; home-made sorbets and ice creams; and Cashel blue and Wigmore cheeses with quince jam.

The wine list has been compiled with the same eye for quality and distinction as the food, with offerings from £13.50 for a good house wine to £85 for a Batard Montrachet 91.

Offshore

148 Holland Park Ave, W11 ℂ020 7221 6090   ⊖ Holland Park

Daily noon–3pm & 6.30–11pm   All major credit cards

www.offshore.uk.com

In this world of telly chefs and kitchen stars, it seems somehow inevitable that stardom would beckon anyone with a name like Sylvain Ho Wing Chong. Add the salient fact that he is a very able Mauritian fish cook and you can probably fill in the rest of his biog for yourself. Famous restaurants in North London, followed by a disastrous flirtation with the West End, culminated in Offshore, his latest establishment, in Holland Park. The menu is dauntingly long. There's a seasonal à la carte, plus l'arrivage de la semaine, plus catch of the day, plus set luncheons. The tone of the place is one of engaging eccentricity combined with a genuine (and very un-British) passion for all things fishy.

The fish dishes are of a consistently high standard, precisely judged and with a cheerful Franco-Chinese anarchy about the saucing. To start there may be a three-fish carpaccio "arôme des îsles" (£8.50), or crisp tuna bang bang (£8), or the Mauritian octopus curry (£9), which is very good. Alternatively, leave choosing the starters to the chef and opt for "picky picky" (£12.50 for two). Main courses include red snapper à la Créole (£16); vaqcua fillet with sauce Grand-Mère (£18), which is made from green peppercorns and Jalapeno chillies; grilled sea bass with a lemongrass butter (£21); and pave de Bourgeois farci aux pétoncles, papillote d'épinards (£19.50) – a wonderfully meaty fish stuffed with cockles and wrapped in spinach. From the more exotic reaches of the list, how about giant tiger prawns in a tamarind and coconut milk sauce (£20); or a whole lobster sleeping on a bed of spicy Chinese noodles (£28)? There are three non-fish dishes on the menu – chicken supreme, Scottish rib eye, herb-crusted poussin – but you'd be missing out not to order fish here. Puddings rush off in any direction that makes use of tropical fruit – roast baby pineapple, ginger-cinnamon toffee, and ice cream (£5)! Service is accomplished and French in tone, and the dining room is light and modern without being oppressively trendy.

Having said all of which, life would be a little easier were you to order the set lunch (£9 for one course, £13.50 for two courses, £16.50 for three courses). Good luck.

£10–£30

NOTTING HILL ⑪ ITALIAN/PIZZA

WEST

Osteria Basilico

29 Kensington Park Rd, W11 ©020 7727 9372   ⊖ Ladbroke Grove/Notting Hill Gate

Mon–Fri 12.30–3pm & 6.30–11pm, Sat 12.30–4pm & 6.30–11pm,

Sun 12.30–3.15pm & 6.30–10.30pm   Amex, Mastercard, Visa

Long before Kensington Park Road became the borough's hottest spot for outdoor dining, there was always a restaurant on this corner. When Duveen closed, the restaurant cat stayed on to have the next establishment named in its honour – Monsieur Thompson. Then, in its turn Monsieur T became Pizza by Numbers. Then in 1992 came Osteria, which has flourished ever since. Daytime stargazing is enlivened by arguments between parking wardens, clampers and their victims, while the traffic comes to a standstill for the unloading of timber lorries and for a constant stream of mini-cabs dropping off at the street's numerous restaurants. At dusk you get more of the same, with the streetlights struggling to make the heart of Portobello look like the Via Veneto.

Inside, pizza and pasta are speedily delivered with typical chirpy Italian panache to cramped, scrubbed tables. Go easy on the baskets of warm pizza bread, as the antipasti (£4.80) – various grilled and preserved titbits arranged on the antique dresser – are a tempting self-service affair. Of the other starters, frito di calamari e gamberi (£4.90) and spinaci e salsiccia con aceto balsamico (£4.90) – a rough Italian sausage served with spinach – are both delicious. Specials change daily and have no particular regional influence. Old favourites include fegato di vitello alla Veneziana (£9.50) and gamberoni alla griglia (£12.50): classic, well-prepared veal and prawn dishes. Among the permanent fixtures, linguine allo scoglio (£6.80) comes with mixed seafood, while fresh tomato and carré d'agnello al forno con patate e rosmarino (£9.80) is an oven-baked rack of lamb roasted with potatoes and rosemary. Pizzas vary in size depending on who is in the kitchen: perhaps staff with shorter arms throw the dough higher, resulting in a wider, thinner base, but all are on the largish size. Pizza diavolo (£6) comes with mozzarella and a good spicy pepperoni sausage.

House wines are served by the carafe, but it's much better to opt for the Montepulciano d'Abruzzo (£11), a pretty decent wine at a pretty decent price.

Pharmacy Restaurant

150 Notting Hill Gate, W11 ©020 7221 2442	⊖ Notting Hill Gate
Mon–Fri noon–2.45pm & 6.45–10.45pm,	
Sat & Sun noon–3pm & 6.45–10.45pm	All major credit cards

www.pharmacylondon.com

Ferociously trendy, almost impossible to get a booking in, and with its own secret VIP reservation number, Jonathan Kennedy's Pharmacy dominates the Notting Hill scene. Its shop-like exterior lights up the area. The ground-floor decor is that of a pharmacy, with shelves of pills, potions and lotions, and a sign advertising prescriptions. Upstairs Damien Hirst's butterflies adorn the walls and a stunning revolving hanging mobile by Danny Chadwick transfixes as you dine. But at the end of it all, Pharmacy is a restaurant. And one that's worth the trip for the grub alone. The dishes are based on simple but sophisticated ingredients and a "light" cooking style, with natural reductions, seasonal ingredients and well-balanced combinations.

Typically the à la carte menus offer eight starters and eight mains at lunch, rising to twelve and twelve in the evening. Dishes draw their inspiration from all over Europe, so you may find rare Spanish charcuterie and preserved lemons among the starters, and Dorset lamb and skordalia in among the mains. To start there may be a carpaccio of white fish with ginger, sesame oil and soya sauce (£9.75); sweetcorn soup with garlic butter (£5); roast sweet potato capelletti with pesto and pine nuts (£8.50); or tripe in the Roman style (£6.75). About half the main courses are usually fishy, thus you might be offered baked whole sea bass with charlotte potatoes and salsa verde (£22); seared tuna with red pepper coulis and potato gnocchi (£17); or poached organic salmon, little gem lettuce and bottarga (£15.50). On a meatier note, perhaps spit-roast suckling pig, braised fennel and apples (£16.50); crispy whole pigeon, beetroot purée and curly kale (£22.50); or char-grilled aged fillet with matchstick fries (£19)? For such an aggressively trendy establishment, the wine list bears investigation – the Pharmacy choice offers half a dozen bottles that are priced between £11.50 (vin de pays Chardonnay) and a Montagny premier cru from Buxy at £24.

If you're a people-watcher, then you're probably already a regular. The fun and the famous have made Pharmacy their own. Persevere – you'll get a table . . . eventually.

£18–£25

Rodizio Rico

111 Westbourne Grove, W2 ℂ020 7792 4035   ⊖ Notting Hill Gate/Bayswater

Mon–Fri 6.30pm–midnight, Sat 12.30–4.30pm & 6.30pm–midnight,

Sun 12.30–11pm   Amex, Mastercard, Visa

If you're a lover of smoky grilled meat, Rodizio Rico will come as a god-send. In the south of Brazil this restaurant would be pretty run-of-the-mill stuff, but in W11 "churrascarias" are the exception rather than the rule. Rodizio can be a puzzling experience for first-timers. There's no menu and no prices – but no problem. "Rodizio" means "rotating" and refers to the carvers who wander about the room with huge skewers of freshly grilled meat from which they lop off chunks on demand – rather like the trolleys of roast beef at Simpson's in the Strand. You start by ordering and then help yourself from both the salad bar and hot buffet to prime your plate. As the carvers circulate they dispense cheerfulness and bon-homie as they cut you chunks, slivers and slices from whichever skewer they are holding. You eat as much as you like, of whatever you like, and then you pay the absurdly reasonable price of £16.50 a head.

When you're up helping yourself to the basics, look out for the tiny rolls, no bigger than a button mushroom, called pão de queijo – a rich cheese bread from the south of Brazil. Also bobo, a delicious kind of bubble and squeak made from cassava and spring greens. Return to your seat and await the carvers – they come in random order, but they keep on coming. There's lamb, and ham, and pork, and spare ribs, and chicken, and silverside beef (grilled in a piece and called lagarto after a similarly shaped iguana!). Then for offal aficionados there are grilled chicken hearts. But the star of the show is picanha – the heart of the rump, skewered and grilled in huge chunks. Taste it and the arguments over the relative merits of rump and fillet are over forever – the "rumpers" would win by a landslide. Brazilians seem to revere the crispy bits, but if you want your meat rare you only have to ask.

South Americans rate the impossibly sweet soft drink Antartica Guar-rana (£1.70) very highly. "Just like the guarana powder you can get in the chemist's shop", they insist. If the lure of alternative rainforest stimu-lants doesn't appeal, house wines start at a reasonable £9.90 a bottle. And, as you would expect of a Brazilian establishment, the coffee is very good indeed.

Rôtisserie Jules

133a Notting Hill Gate, W11 ©020 7221 3331	⊖ Notting Hill Gate
Daily noon–11.30pm	All major credit cards
www.rotisseriejules.com	

This rôtisserie is one of three set up by the eponymous Jules – the others are at 6 Bute St, SW7 (©020 7584 0600) and 338 King's Rd, SW3 (©020 7351 0041). They are all admirably consistent: comfortable, modern dining rooms with the kitchen open and on show, and the rôtisserie always a star. They operate a free delivery service, too, and have a constant stream of people calling in for meals to take home, but somehow they manage to avoid a takeaway atmosphere. Rôtisserie Jules makes the proud claim on the menu that, except for the bread and ice cream, everything is prepared on the premises from scratch and without using frozen ingredients. It seems believable.

There is no evidence of wild flights of fancy on this menu. It has been simplified and now, rather than a separate starters section, you'll find side dishes and salads: corn on the cob (£2.50/£4.50), ratatouille (£2.50/£4.50), Caesar salad (£4.50), gratin Dauphinoise (£2/£3.75), rather good fries (£2/£3.75). All are fair enough. But what to put with them? You are probably here for the chicken. Careful timing is the key and the best time to visit is plumb in the middle of service, when things are at their busiest. That way you'll get your chicken freshly roasted and hot off the spit. There is nothing nicer. The chickens weigh about 3lb, and the pricing is complex: chicken (leg and thigh) with one side dish is £4.95; chicken (breast and wing) with one side dish is £6.25. A whole chicken, on its own, is £9.75. As well as chicken you could have tranche de gigot (lamb steak; £5.50); or a whole roast duck (£16), which weighs in at around 5lb (this feeds three or four people and they require half a day's notice); or, even better, a whole leg of lamb (£23), which weighs some 4¼lb (feeds between three and four, needs two hours' notice). Confused? Don't worry – the key factor is honest food at reasonable prices.

The dessert menu is short: chocolate mousse (£2), apple tart (£3.25), and Ben and Jerry's ice creams (£4.75). Rôtisserie Jules has that rare combination of simple food and sensible prices – impressive for an establishment that is both a regular restaurant and upscale takeaway,

Beach Blanket Babylon

45 Ledbury Rd, W11   ©020 7229 2907

The brilliant Gothic decor has attracted a cocktail-drinking crowd of celebrities and bright young things. It's more wine and mixer drinks than beer and, though expensive, is a great meeting place, as the wild interior gives everyone something to talk about.

Cafe Med Bar

184a–186 Kensington Park Rd,
W11   ©020 7221 1150

Banquettes and coffee tables in this cool cafe-lounge bar. It's a regular read-the-papers-and-meet-your-mates place for younger Notting Hill-Billies. Wine, mixer drinks and bottled beers are the favourites.

The Castle

100 Holland Park Ave, W11   ©020 7313 9301

This well-reconstructed pub with its distinctive tiled exterior has an open and modern feel. It pulls a mixed crowd of local residents and people walking around Holland Park. Signature beers include Fuller's London Pride, Staropramen and Grolsch on tap. The house wine, Chapel Hill, is a bargain at £9.

The Champion

1 Wellington Terrace, Bayswater Rd,
W2   ©020 7243 9531

Blond wood and a light airy feel make this corner pub very welcoming and relaxing. Attracting a mixed crowd in age and type during the day, it becomes predominantly gay in the evenings. Bar staff are friendly, young and stylish.

The Cork & Bottle

17 Needham Rd, W11   ©020 7229 1550

A friendly, traditional neighbourhood pub where a crowd of local regulars enjoy the home-from-home atmosphere. Well-poured pints of Brakspeare's Bitter and Marstons Pedigree are the favourites here.

Duke of Wellington

179 Portobello Rd, W11   ©020 7727 6727

Very busy on market days, this well-restored Young's pub fills with market traders and dealers who congregate for a refreshing pint of Special, Bitter or seasonal ale. There's a cafe-style atmosphere, with beautiful panelling and pavement tables.

The Earl Percy

226 Ladbroke Grove, W10   ©020 8960 3522

A huge, rambling old boozer, this neighbourhood local has three separate bars. Oddly, access between them – getting to the loos, for example – is through half-height hatches in the walls, meaning that you have to bend and stoop as you edge your way through. Enjoy William Youngers' Tavern Bitter or John Smith's before you bang your head.

The Gate

14 Blenheim Crescent, W11   ©020 7727 8802

A traditional neighbourhood pub in the middle of trendy Notting Hill Gate. It's smoky, friendly and full of local flavour and character. Drink Flowers Original or Wadworth's 6X.

Ground Floor Bar

186 Portobello Rd, W11   *©020 7243 0072*

Clubby and lounge-like, with leather chesterfield sofas and velvet banquettes, this big venue is favoured by a young crowd who meet in groups to chat and gossip. Favourites on tap include Red Stripe and Kirin beer.

ION Bar

161–165 Ladbroke Grove,
W10   *©020 8960 1702*

More like a hotel lobby than a pub, this modern bar attracts a younger crowd of clubby drinkers and people who just want to sit and chill on the leather couches and pouffes. An unpressurised place in which to enjoy Staropramen. Grolsch and Caffrey's on draught.

The Mall Tavern

71–73 Palace Gardens Terrace,
W8   *©020 7727 3805*

Ornate and ultra-Victorian in style, this delightful corner pub has a dozen different upholstery patterns on display. There's also a real old bar billiards table for those who can remember how to play. Signature ales on tap include Flowers Original, Fuller's London Pride and Morland's Old Speckled Hen.

The Sun in Splendour

7 Portobello Rd, W11   *©020 7313 9331*

This is a favourite for anyone planning to head down Portobello Road. It's small and comfortable, with a secluded patio beer garden and a better than average selection of bottled beers including Tiger, Freedom lager, Leffe and Czech Budweiser.

Richmond
& Twickenham

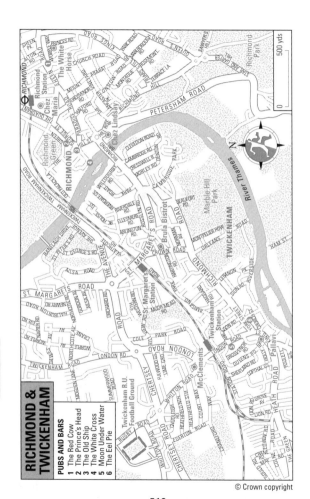

RICHMOND & TWICKENHAM

PUBS AND BARS

1 The Red Cow
2 The Prince's Head
3 The Old Ship
4 The White Cross
5 Moon Under Water
6 The Eel Pie

WEST

Brula Bistrot

43 Crown Rd, St Margarets, Surrey ✆020 8892 0602	BR St Margarets
Tues–Fri 12.30–2pm & 7–10pm, Sat 7–10pm	No credit cards

In 1999 two friends who worked in smart central London restaurants decided that the time had come to open their own place. They chose St Margarets as a locale, and as they were called Bruce Duckett and Lawrence Hartley they called their restaurant Brula. It had a tiny, yellow-painted, dining room about as wide as a railway carriage and an equally modest kitchen. It was very much a family affair. By spring 2000 Brula had become so outrageously successful that they were forced to move across Crown Road into larger premises. Now the Brula Bistrot (the name has been enlarged in keeping with the new premises) is no longer a cramped affair. There are large windows and a profusion of rather elegant stained glass. Thankfully, the food and philosophy have stayed the same – well-cooked bistro French food; limited choice; low, low prices.

You have to admire anyone who has the good sense not to mess with something that works really well. Lunch at Brula Bistrot will cost you £8 for one or two courses and £10 for three. Extra veg (should you want any) costs a further £1.50; an espresso to finish is £1. The menu changes on a weekly basis, so you might face a choice of pistou soup, chicken liver terrine with onion marmalade, or a salad of red peppers, anchovy and grated egg. Then on to roast chicken with tarragon and mash, fish of the day with curried aubergine, or gratin of new potatoes, courgette, crème fraîche and Parmesan. Finally, tart of the day, dark chocolate mousse, or cheese and biscuits. All very French, and all rather nostalgic, evoking that dimly remembered rural France when you could pitch up at any bistro de gare and be sure of a good, cheap, satisfying meal. In the evenings they add an extra dish to make four choices for each course – perhaps belly pork with soy sauce, ginger and garlic – and the restaurant goes à la carte. Starters usually cost under £5 and the notional limit for main courses is £10. Puds are around £4.

The Frenchness even extends to the list of suggested apéritifs at the top of the evening menu: kir (£3) or Pilsener (£2.50), Bellini or kir royale (£4.50). How very civilised.

Chez Lindsay

11 Hill Rise, Richmond, Surrey ℗020 8948 7473	⊖ Richmond
Mon–Sat 11am–11pm, Sun noon–10pm	Mastercard, Visa

At first glance Chez Lindsay looks rather like Chicago in the 1920s – all around you people are drinking alcohol out of large earthenware teacups. The cups are in fact traditional Breton drinking vessels known as "bolées", the drink is cider, and Chez Lindsay lists a trio of them, ranging from Breton brut traditionnel to Norman cidre bouché. This small, bright restaurant has had a loyal local following for a good many years. Most people are attracted by the galettes and crêpes, though the menu also includes a regularly changing list of hearty Breton dishes – especially fish. It's a place for Francophiles: both the kitchen and the front of house seem to be staffed entirely by Gauls, which in this instance means good service and tasty food.

Start with palourdes farcies (£5.95), where nine small clams are given the "snail butter" treatment – lots of garlic. Or the moules à la St Malo (£5.25), which are cooked with shallots, cream and thyme. Then you must decide between the galettes or more formal main courses. The galettes are huge buckwheat pancakes, large and lacy, thin but satisfying. They come with an array of fillings: egg, cheese and ham (£5.30); scallops and leeks (£7.95); Roquefort cheese, celery and walnuts (£5.95); and "Saisonnière" (£7.95), a mixture of egg, artichoke heart, mushrooms and lardons. The other half of the menu is very Breton, featuring a good steak frites (£12.75) and lots of fish and shellfish. The cotriade (£13.75) is an interesting dish: seriously meaty chunks of fresh halibut, cockles, queen scallops, shrimps and a large langoustine piled on top of a mound of potato slices cooked in a saffron fish stock, all served in a soup bowl. Very good indeed. Ask the amiable staff about off-menu goodies, which, depending on the market, might be anything from exotic fish to roast grouse.

At lunch the menu de midi delivers two courses – a salad and a galette – for just £5.99, and there is always a three-course prix fixe at £9.99. Real pud enthusiasts will save themselves for the chocolate and banana crêpe (£3.95), topped with a scoop of gin and lavender ice cream (£1.30), a bizarre-sounding combination which turns out to taste strangely delicious.

Chez Maria

5a Princes St, Richmond Market, Surrey ⓒ020 8948 1475	⊖ Richmond
Tues–Sat 6.30–11pm	Cash or cheque only

Michel de Ville has won his share of battle honours in his forty years in the catering industry, and his certificates and medals adorn the walls of this tiny restaurant he runs with Maria, his wife. The insignia of the Chevaliers de Tastevin is on one side and the gold medal he won as executive chef of the Playboy Club in America is on the other. This place is a "bistro du marché" of the kind that you would find in France, and they have added a particular quirk of originality – lunches are exclusively fish. Michel sees to the cooking; Maria, the service. You fetch your own wine from a nearby off-licence or wine merchant – Chez Maria is strictly BYO. There's also a sensibly simple pricing structure – £17.50 for two courses and £18.50 for three, with no charge for corkage. As there are only thirty seats you would be wise to book, especially at the weekend.

Maria is Portuguese and the menu claims that the restaurant offers "French and Portuguese Specialities", but the French side seems to have the upper hand. Michel cooks the kind of food that he is completely at home with – a sort of frozen-in-time bistro-favourites selection, but one where the dishes have been chosen to make the most sense of a single-handed kitchen. The pastrywork is good –try the tian des crevettes à la sauce Aurore et basilic, a sort of mini-quiche with prawns and a classic cream and tomato sauce. Fish of the day "façon du chef" is generally reliable. Or there might be a roast duck breast on a bed of braised cabbage. Recipes are traditional and none the worse for that; lamb could be paired with a rich haricot bean dish. This is good, honest, very unpretentious French food. Puddings continue the theme: tarte au citron, terrine au chocolat, and crème brûlée. Modernist gastronomes will not approve, but people who fondly remember cheap eats in France will feel pleasantly nostalgic. Here you can enjoy something very rare indeed in a world crowded with lattes, Americanos and tall-skinny-capps – a good cup of ordinary coffee for £1.

Michel is not above the occasional gastro-jest. To celebrate Burns night, you might be offered "Champignons farcis au Haggis et herbes fraîches", which somewhat gives the lie to the philosophical observation that life is too short to stuff a mushroom.

£28–£50

McClements

2 Whitton Rd, Twickenham, Middlesex ℗020 8744 9610 — BR Twickenham

Mon–Sat noon–2pm & 7–10pm — All major credit cards except Diners

McClements is a small, comfortable restaurant whose menu runs through all sorts of luxury ingredients. It also makes something of a feature of set menus, which combine a procession of dishes with matched glasses of wine. The decor and service, like the cooking, are very civilised and a strong local following seems very happy to use McClements for all those birthday and anniversary treats rather than make the voyage to the West End. This is a successful local restaurant, so much so, in fact, that the dining room recently had to be extended to seat 100 people. The cooking is trad French and rich, generally of a high standard, with elegant presentation and plenty of sightings of offal – up to and including the pig's trotter.

The menu changes periodically, but starters may be sea bass served with roast lobster and caviar beurre blanc (£8), or warm potato tart topped with smoked salmon, crème fraîche and caviar (£7), which takes the tried and tested blinis combination up a notch. The mixed hors d'oeuvres (£9.50) provides pixie portions of six starters presented with considerable élan. The main courses, all of which are priced between £14 and £15, follow the litany of turbot-steak-lamb-duck-monkfish and, just when you feel cosy . . . wham! There's cassoulet, or pig's trotter with a lump of sweetbread, or a rather good osso bucco. To follow, the plate of six little puddings is obviously such a hit that it has driven everything else off the dessert menu except the hot soufflé with Calvados sauce, and the selection of mature French cheeses. All desserts cost £4.50.

The set menus operate from Monday to Friday – £25 gets you a glass of champagne with canapés, a choice of three starters with a glass of Chablis, of four mains with a glass of claret, and pudding. Or, for £50, you could have a seven-course menu including a glass of wine with each course. Both are good value. The meals start with an amuse-gueule – actually four different ones – three canapés and a tablespoonful of rich lobster bisque in a coffee cup, and wind their way through to a giant plate of petits fours.

Pallavi

1st Floor, 3 Cross Deep Court, Heath Rd, Twickenham,

Middlesex ✆020 8892 2345 | BR Twickenham

Tues–Sun noon–3pm & 6–11pm | All major credit cards

This is a small outpost of an Indian restaurant empire which also includes Malabar Junction (see p.8) – an impressive pedigree. Pallavi, the simplest and the cheapest, started its days as a large takeaway counter with just a few seats. Now they have moved over the road from the original site to these smart new premises. The cooking has travelled well, and still deserves the ultimate compliment – it is genuinely home-style. Unpretentious dishes and unpretentious prices. True to its South Indian roots there is an impressive list of vegetarian specialities, but the menu features just enough meat and fish dishes to woo any kind of diner.

Start with that South Indian veggie favourite, the Malabar masala dosa (£3.50). The huge, crisp, pancake is made with a mixture of ground rice and lentil flour and is a perfect match for the savoury potato mixture and chutney. There's also a meat masala dosa (£3.95), described on the menu as a "non-vegetarian pancake delicacy" – full marks for accuracy there. Or try the delightfully named iddly (£3.50), a steamed rice cake made with black gram, which is eaten as a breakfast dish in India. Whatever you open with, have some cashew nut pakoda (£2.95), a kind of savoury peanut brittle made with cashew nuts, which is wholly delicious. The main dishes are simple and tasty, and are served without fuss. For unrepentant carnivores, chicken Malabar (£3.95), keema methi (£3.95) or kozhi varutha curry (£3.95) all hit the spot. But there are also most interesting fish dishes, including the fish moilee (£5.95). Veggies are good too: parippu curry (£2.25), split lentils with cumin, turmeric, garlic, chillies and onions; kalan (£2.50), a traditional sweet and sour dish of mango, yam, coconut and spices; cabbage thoran (£2.15), sliced cabbage with carrots, green chillies and curry leaves. The pilau rice, lemon rice, and coconut rice (all £2.20) are tasty, and parathas are even better. Try a green chilli or a sweet coconut paratha (both £2.50).

In this posh new incarnation Pallavi is fully licensed, so you are no longer obliged to bring your own carryout. Thankfully, the lassi (£1) is still just as good.

The White Horse

Worple Way, Richmond, Surrey ⓒ020 8940 2418   ⊖ Richmond

Mon–Sat noon–3pm & 6.30–10pm, Sun noon–4pm   Amex, Mastercard, Switch, Visa

All over town brave entrepreneurs are taking pubs away from the traditional breweries and transforming them into gold mines, but in this instance Fuller's brewery can be congratulated for encouraging quality themselves. The White Horse is a dark, spartan, bar-restaurant with good large tables that are well spread out – no sitting in your neighbour's pocket here. The food and pricing is also spot-on, as is confirmed by a steady trade and a note on the menu saying "we are now taking bookings for both lunch and early evening meals".

The menu is a short one, and all the better for it – five starters and five main courses, which change twice a day to accommodate whatever is best from the market. There might be a rocket, poached egg and Parmesan salad (£4.75), with perky rocket and a suitably runny egg yolk. Or a fish soup with rouille (£3.50), or cured salmon with cucumbers, oranges and horseradish cream (£4.75), or steamed mussels with chickpeas, tomatoes, parsley and garlic (£5). Main courses are also simple and well executed, like the Angus ribeye steak with chips, mustard and chilli Hollandaise (£9.75) – great chips – or the fried plaice fillet with broad beans, almond and coriander (£9) – fresh fish, well cooked and well presented. Or a caponata-stuffed pepper (£6.75), perhaps, or penne with bacon, Parmesan and parsley (£7). The wide-ranging wine list tops out at £22 for a smart American Pinot Noir. What's more, there is the intelligent option of a 250ml glassful of a dozen different wines (from £3.20 to £3.70). Puds are also seasonal, so you might enjoy strawberries with mascarpone, balsamic vinegar and toasted panettone (£4); coffee caramel and raspberry cream pots (£4); or grilled pineapple and toasted coconut ice cream (£4).

The last item on The White Horse's dessert section is Vivian's cheeses with wafers, oatcakes and chutney (£5). The cheese in question has made the short journey from Vivian's, the superb delicatessen a few doors down the road – call in there for all manner of goodies, including top olive oils on draught. The White Horse cheeseboard proves how much more satisfying it is to sample two or three cheeses in perfect condition than to be faced with a huge selection of the unripe and overripe.

The Eel Pie

9–11 Church St,
Twickenham   ℃020 8891 1717

An authentic old local, part of which used to be an undertaker's, this venue has become a sort of rugby shrine. Illustrations of famous players and photos of old games line the walls and the talk is of little else. Though it's packed at game time and at weekends, there's room enough for everyone, and the natives are friendly. Beers on tap, from the Badger Brewery, include Tangle Foot, Champion, Dorset Best and their Hofbrau lagers.

Moon Under Water

53–57 London Rd,
Twickenham   ℃020 8744 0080

Part of the J D Wetherspoon chain, this standard offering is big and comfortable. There's a "no dogs and no children" policy and the signature ales are all reasonably priced. You get a choice of Theakston's Bitter, Courage Directors and Shepherd Neame's Spitfire. Guest ales are on offer too, at slightly higher prices.

The Old Ship

3 King St, Richmond   ℃020 8940 3461

The Old Ship has been here since 1735, when it was a stopping post for stagecoaches. It's been sympathetically revamped since then and, unsurprisingly, has a quasi-nautical theme. It's nice and friendly with regulars who enjoy the Young's selection – Bitter, Special, AAA in summer, Winter Warmer in winter – as well as the great bottled beers.

The Prince's Head

28 The Green, Richmond   ℃020 8940 1572

This traditional pub attracts a mixed crowd of tourists and locals. It overlooks Richmond Green and backs onto little alleyways filled with antique shops. It's also convenient for the famous Richmond Playhouse theatre. It's a Fuller's pub, so customers can enjoy London Pride, Chiswick and ESB.

The Red Cow

59 Sheen Rd, Richmond   ℃020 8940 2511

A five-star hotel as well as a pub, this traditional local welcomes strangers, although it's obviously a regulars' retreat, too. Young's ales on tap and a better than average selection of wines. Book early for the bedrooms, though, as there are only four, at £80 a night each.

The White Cross

Riverside, Richmond   ℃020 8940 6844

Right on the river path, with a delightful view, this Young's pub has a comfortable lounge-like atmosphere. Outside, the balconies and river patio are a big hit in summer. Popular with tourists and also the rugby crowd, The White Cross gets very busy.

Shepherd's Bush
& Olympia

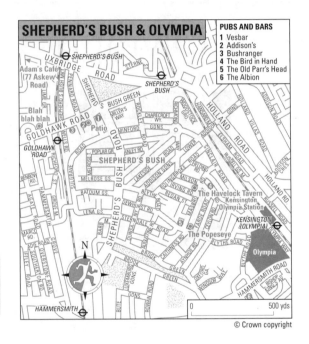

SHEPHERD'S BUSH & OLYMPIA

PUBS AND BARS

1 Vesbar
2 Addison's
3 Bushranger
4 The Bird in Hand
5 The Old Parr's Head
6 The Albion

SHEPHERD'S BUSH

Adam's Café (77 Askew Road)

UXBRIDGE ROAD

SHEPHERD'S BUSH

Blah blah blah

GOLDHAWK ROAD

Patio

GOLDHAWK ROAD

SHEPHERD'S BUSH

HOLLAND ROAD

The Havelock Tavern

Kensington Olympia Station

KENSINGTON (OLYMPIA)

The Popeseye

Olympia

HAMMERSMITH ROAD

N

HAMMERSMITH

0   500 yds

© Crown copyright

WEST

526

Adam's Café

77 Askew Rd, W12 ⓒ020 8743 0572	⊖ Ravenscourt Park
Mon–Sat 7–11pm	All major credit cards

Frances and Abdel Boukraa live a dual life. Each morning they run a respectable workers' cafe, and every evening they transform it into a North African restaurant. Bacon and eggs for breakfast; fish, grills, couscous and tagines for dinner. The kitchen here is run by a Tunisian chef with a Moroccan assistant, so all manner of North African delicacies are on offer – and the easy-going prices reflect the cafe heritage. You pick between three menus: rapide (£9.95 for a main course or two starters and mint tea or coffee); gourmet (£12.95 for main course and starter or dessert); or gastronomique (£14.95 for starter, main course and dessert). All exclude service, which you'll certainly want to reward. House wines start at £8, or you can bring your own (£1.50 corkage per person).

The Tunisian for amuse-gueule is "kemia" – complimentary saucers of wonderful home-made pickles and small meatballs and harissa, which arrive with the bread. As well as good home-made soups (fish, or the Moroccan spicy chickpea harira), you'll find that the starters are dominated by "briks" and "ojjas". Briks are deep-fried filo parcels filled with egg and herbs, egg and tuna, or peppers, mushrooms and potatoes. Ojjas are even more delicious. They come about when a pan of scrambled egg runs headlong into a pan of ratatouille: they are served with either merguez – a spicy sausage – or shrimps. There are also briwattes – filo parcels of seafood. For a main course, you choose between grills (mostly brochettes – kebabs), couscous and tagine. The couscous arrives, as it should, with a tureen of vegetables in sauce, and a choice of meats (or veg). If you like a little fire, mix some of the red-hot chilli sludge – harissa – into a spoonful of the sauce and pour it over the couscous. Tagines, which hail from Morocco, are casseroles cooked and served in the eponymous pot with a conical lid: try the chicken with preserved Moroccan lemons. For puddings, place your faith in the Moroccan assistant chef; she produces brilliant almond and lemon tarts.

Beware, however, of the Tunisian digestifs. Thibarine is an aromatic liqueur made from dates which tastes of mothballs, while Boukha is an eau de vie made from figs which is faintly reminiscent of petrol.

Blah blah blah

78 Goldhawk Rd, W12 ℗020 8746 1337

⊖ Goldhawk Road

Mon–Sat 12.30–2.30pm & 7–11pm

Cash or cheque only

The outside of Blah blah blah doesn't engender great excitement. It has a decent-sized shopfront, but the closed door and half-closed Venetian blinds over the windows make it look like a cross between a betting shop and a funeral parlour. Appearances can be deceptive: open the door and the first thing that hits you is the noise. There is nothing in the room to absorb the sound – the floors, tables and chairs are wooden, there are blinds rather than curtains, and the only decoration of note is wood, drift-wood and old iron lamps. Add wallpaper music and the noise becomes formidable. This is the restaurant where Paul McCartney asked for the music to be turned down. Pricing is simple – at lunch starters go for £2.95–£3.95, and mains £5.95. Then at dinner starters go up to £3.95–£4.95 and mains to £7.95, with one "special" at £8.50. Puddings are £4.50.

The little kitchen at the back of the room knows what it is doing. The mushroom gougère – a choux pastry ring doughnut filled with wild mushroom purée and Gruyère – is well made, properly seasoned and attractively presented. Californian sushi rolls are as good as you could hope to find outside a specialist establishment. The aubergine and goats' cheese crust turns out to be a core of goats' cheese, wrapped in thin lay-ers of goats' cheese, breadcrumbed and deep-fried; it is served with a potato and panzanella salad. The roast fennel, Pernod and ricotta pie has something of the coulibac about it, a large parcel served with tomato and thyme sauce. Main courses arrive on the huge side of large, but are moderately priced and obviously cooked to order. The desserts are ambitious and delicious: if it's on the list try the buttermilk and cinna-mon torta with frozen vanilla custard, an unusual and crispy cake which is surprisingly light.

Blah blah blah offers well-prepared food that just happens to be vegetar-ian, rather than the kind of heavy, wholemeal and meaningful fare you would expect from a more "in-your-face" vegetarian restaurant. It is unlicensed, so bring your own. There is a very reasonable corkage charge of £1.25 per person.

The Havelock Tavern

57 Masbro Rd, W14 ✆020 7603 5374   ⊖ Shepherd's Bush

Food served Mon–Sat 12.30–2.30pm & 7–10pm,

Sun 12.30–3pm & 7–9.30pm   Cash or cheque only

The Havelock is one of those pubs marooned within a sea of houses, in this instance the sea of houses just behind Olympia. It's a real pub, with a solid range of beers as well as an extensive wine list. What is most attractive, though, is the attitude that lies behind the menu, which is chalked up daily on the blackboard. As the chef half of the proprietorial partnership says, "We're in the business of feeding people." And that's just what they do, serving up seasonal, unfussy food – the kind of fresh, interesting wholesome stuff you wish that you could get around to cooking for yourself. The bar seats 75 and during the summer there's a terrific garden complete with vines and a pergola. Service involves stepping up to the bar and ordering what you want, so there's no service charge to bump up what are very reasonable prices indeed.

The menu is different every session, but at lunch there are more "one-hit" dishes, as most customers are pressed for time. Starters might be vegetable and white bean soup with harissa (£3.50); salt cod and smoked haddock fritters, tartare sauce and lemon (£5); or chicken galantine, toast and chutney (£5.50). Main courses range from penne with spicy sausage and tomato sauce with Parmesan (£7) to monkfish saltimbocca with spinach, garlic and olive oil mash (£10). The lunch menu might feature a plate of Italian salami, Parma ham, olives and pickles (£6), or a pan-fried leek and goats' cheese risotto cake stuffed with buffalo mozzarella, rocket and baked tomatoes (£5.50). For dinner you may find a char-grilled ribeye steak, blue cheese butter, chips and salad (£11) that has grown out of lunchtime's ribeye steak sandwich, horseradish, mustard chips and salad (£7.50). Puddings are equally reliable – try the pear and apple crumble with custard (£4).

A great deal of effort goes into selecting slightly unusual, and often bargain, wines for the blackboard wine list . . . but the biggest seller is still a glass of the house red. Popular rumour has it that the Havelock is one of Simon Hopkinson's favourite eateries. No wonder.

Patio

5 Goldhawk Rd, W12 ⓒ020 8743 5194   ⊖ Goldhawk Road/Shepherd's Bush

Mon–Fri noon–3pm & 6pm–midnight, Sat & Sun 6pm–midnight   All major credit cards

The ebullient Eva Michalik (a former opera singer) and her husband Kaz have been running this Shepherd's Bush institution for more than a decade. It's not hard to see why the show is still on the road: at Patio you get good, solid Polish food in a friendly, comfortable atmosphere – for a relatively small amount of money. This little restaurant is a people-pleaser; you can just as easily come here for an intimate tête-à-tête as for a raucous birthday dinner. The food is always reliable and sometimes it's really excellent. There are two floors; downstairs feels a little cosier and more secluded.

The set menu (available at lunch and dinner) is Patio's trump card. For £10.90 you get a starter, main course, petits fours and fruit . . . and a vodka. The menu changes daily – ask Eva to tell you what's new in the kitchen and you could get something that's not yet listed – and a dozen or so starter and main course choices are available on the set menu. Starters include plump and tasty blinis with smoked salmon; wild mushroom soup; Polish ham with beetroot horseradish; and herrings with soured cream. Everything is fresh and carefully prepared. For mains, there's a good selection of meat, fish and chicken dishes – the scallops in dill sauce, when available, are outstanding. Or you might try a Polish speciality such as golabki (cabbage stuffed with rice and meat), which is also available as a vegetarian dish; or chicken Walewska (chicken breast in fresh red pepper sauce); or sausages à la Zamoyski (grilled sausages with sautéed mushrooms and onions). Main dishes come with a hearty selection of vegetables – roast potatoes, broccoli, red cabbage. Be prepared, too, for high-octane puds, such as the Polish pancakes with cheese, vanilla and rum – the fumes alone are enough to send you reeling. Also good are the walnut gateau, and the hot apple charlotka with cream. For those after more variety, including a scattering of non-Polish dishes, the à la carte offers further choice, and for not a great deal more.

Patio is a good night out. The piano crammed in near the entrance is often put to use by a regular customer, and there are frequent sightings of a roving gypsy quartet.

£16–£50

The Popeseye

108 Blythe Rd, W14 ✆020 7610 4578	⊖ Hammersmith
Mon–Sat 6.45–10.30pm	Cash or cheque only

Just suppose you fancy a steak. A good steak, and perhaps a glass (or bottle) of red wine to go with it. You're interested enough to want the best, probably Aberdeen Angus, and you want it cooked simply. The Popeseye is for you. This quirky restaurant is named after the Scottish word for rump steak, and every week the proprietor buys his meat not from Smithfield or a catering butcher, but from the small butcher his family uses in the north of Scotland. The meat, of course, is Aberdeen Angus and the restaurant is a member of the Aberdeen Angus Society. The dining room is small, things tend to be chaotic, and the atmosphere is occasionally pretty smoky. As to the food, there is no choice: just various kinds of steak and good chips, with home-made puddings to follow. Oh, and the menu starts with the wine list. You choose your drink, and only when that's settled do you choose your steak – specifying, of course, the cut and the size (and they come very big here), and how you want it cooked. This winning formula is repeated at a second Popeseye at 227 Upper Richmond Rd, SW15 (✆020 8788 7733).

There are those times when, for nearly everyone, only a large piece of meat will do. You may have curry days, fish days, or pasta days, but for red meat days the Popeseye really hits the spot. Now, about these steaks. Popeseye comes in 6oz, 8oz, 12oz and 20oz (at £9.45, £11.45, £15.45 and £20.45). Sirloin also comes in 6oz, 8oz, 12oz and 20oz (£11.45, £14.45, £18.45 and £23.95). Fillet also comes in 6oz, 8oz, 12oz and 20oz (£13.45, £17.45, £21.45 and £29.95). All prices include excellent chips, and a side salad is an extra £3.45. Puddings are priced at £3.95 and come from the "home-made" school of patisserie – such delights as apple crumble, sticky toffee pudding and lemon tart.

The wine list is an ever-changing reflection of what can be picked up at the sales and represents good value. There are eighteen clarets, half a dozen wines from Burgundy, others picked from the Rhône, Spain and Argentina – and there are also two white wines on offer for people who have lost the plot. Ask advice. People have been seen here happily drinking Château Palmer 1987 for £53 a bottle, which, despite being a tidy sum, is also a bargain.

WEST

Addison's

45a Goldhawk Rd, W12   no phone

Hidden behind a small courtyard, this barn of a venue serves vast quantities of cheap beer to a cheery crowd of merrymakers. There's masses of room, communal tables and a meet-new-people atmosphere. Boddingtons, Caffrey's and John Smith's are the favourite beers here; the four-pint jugs of Fosters at £4.60 and Stella at £7.80 are popular too.

The Albion

121 Hammersmith Rd, W14 ©020 7603 2826

This friendly, busy little two-storey pub caters mainly for the Olympia exhibition crowd from across the road, and the clientele varies widely depending on what's on. Beers on tap include Courage Directors, Theakston and regular guest ales.

The Bird in Hand

88 Masbro Rd, W14   ©020 7603 2417

A cosy, authentic local, this is a friendly family-run establishment with an Irish flavour. Daughter Jenny Taafe will tell you about the Irish County and sporting prints on the walls while serving a good pint of Guinness, Fuller's London Pride or whatever takes your fancy.

The Bushranger

55 Goldhawk Rd, W12   ©020 8743 3016

Bush for Shepherd's Bush and Ranger for Queen's Park Rangers make this a pub to avoid on match days if you're wearing anything other than the obligatory light blue. At other times this QPR pub is welcoming enough, however, and it offers Fuller's London Pride, Marstons Old Speckled Hen and Wadworth's 6X.

The Old Parr's Head

120 Blythe Rd, W14   ©020 7371 4561

A large, comfortable corner local with a lively crowd of regulars from the surrounding offices and flats. There's a secluded garden patio and a good wine list as well as Fuller's London Pride, Bass Red Triangle, Staropramen and Hoegaarden on tap. Very busy at lunchtime, when they serve good Thai food.

Vesbar

15–19 Goldhawk Rd, W12   ©020 8762 0215

Modern, stylish bar with zinc-topped tables, sofas and a raised, non-service bar. Venetian blinds and full-length windows make it very bright and young in feel, but it's actually a very mixed crowd enjoying mixer drinks and beers like Leffe, Stella and Hoegaarden on tap.

Southall

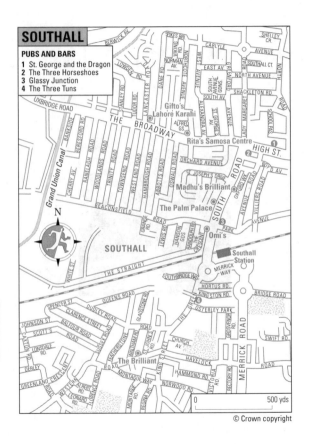

SOUTHALL

PUBS AND BARS

1. St. George and the Dragon
2. The Three Horseshoes
3. Glassy Junction
4. The Three Tuns

© Crown copyright

The Brilliant

72–76 Western Rd, Southall, Middlesex ©020 8574 1928	BR Southall
Tues–Fri noon–2.30pm & 6pm–midnight,	
Sat & Sun 6pm–midnight; closed Aug	All major credit cards

www.brilliantrestaurant.com

The Brilliant is a Southall institution. For more than twenty years the Anand family business has been a non-stop success and is now a bustling 250-seater – for 25 years before that, the family's first restaurant, also called the Brilliant, was the toast of Kenya. The food at The Brilliant is East African/Asian and very good indeed. D.K. Anand (known as Gulu) rules the kitchen with a rod of iron and, to quote him, "there's no frying-pan cookery here". A relatively small number of dishes are freshly cooked in bulk and if a curry needs to be simmered for three hours then that's what happens. The resulting sauces are incredibly rich and satisfying – and yet Gulu won't countenance any cream, yoghurt, nuts or dried fruit.

To start with, you must try the butter chicken (£8 half, £16 full). A half-portion will do for two people as a starter. This dish is an enigma: somehow it manages to taste more buttery than butter itself – really delicious. There's also jeera chicken (£8/£16), rich with cumin and black pepper. And chilli chicken (£9/£18), which is very hot. If you're in a party, move on to the special meals section – these come in two portion sizes, suggested for three people and five people. Methi chicken (£17.50/£32), masaladar lamb (£17.50/£32), and palak chicken (£17.50/£32) are all winners. Alternatively, choose from among the single-portion curries – which include masala talapia (£9), a fish curry of unimaginable richness with good firm chunks of boneless fish. Well-cooked basmati rice is £3.50 and, as well as good rotis (£1), the breads list hides a secret weapon – the kulchay (£1). This is a fried, white-dough bread, for all the world like a very flat doughnut. Hot from the kitchen they are amazing – it's best to order a succession so that they don't go cold.

Ask to try Gulu's pickles – carrot, sharp mango and hot lime. They are splendid. Also try the Kenyan beer Tusker (with its label rather engagingly designed like a bank note; £2.50). Unfortunately, enjoyable though it may be, it doesn't cut much ice with the chilli chicken!

Gifto's Lahore Karahi

162–164 The Broadway, Southall, Middlesex ©020 8813 8669   BR Southall

Mon–Thurs noon–11.30pm, Fri–Sun noon–midnight   All major credit cards

www.gifto.com

In Southall they know a good thing when they taste it. Gifto's Lahore Karahi specialises in freshly grilled, well-spiced meats and exceptionally good breads, backed up by a few curries and one or two odd dishes from Lahore. They do these superbly well and consistently. No money has been wasted on decor and certainly none is wasted on frills. Cafe tables are lit by mind-boggling chandeliers. Plates are heavy. A row of grinning chefs seem to juggle with the three-foot skewers as meat goes into the tandoor caked in a secret marinade and comes out perfectly cooked and delicious. Despite having 85 seats downstairs and more than a hundred upstairs, there is a still a queue outside at the weekend.

Whatever else you order, you need some bread. Peshwari nan (£1.20) is a triumph, hot from the oven, flavoured with garlic and fresh herbs, liberally slathered with ghee and sesame seeds . . . it's hard to imagine it bettered. To accompany it, you might start with an order of chicken tikka (£3.50), which is juicy and strongly spiced. Or go straight for a portion of five lamb chops, encrusted in tandoori pastes and grilled until crisp (£4.90). Or try pomfret fish from the tandoor – a worthwhile extravagance (£6.80). Curries include sag gosht – chunks of lamb in a dark-green, velvety spinach base (£4.90); and, more unusually, batera curry (quail – £5.90); nihari lamb, cooked slowly on the bone in a rich gravy (£5.90); and paya (£5.90), which the menu describes as "lamb trotters in thick gravy" – a gravy created by three hours' cooking in a pot with ginger, onions and garlic. For specialists only, perhaps. Very delicious, and supposed to "purify the blood", is the karela gosht (£5.50), a telling combination of bitter melon and lamb. The side dishes will tempt all comers, especially the tarka dhal (£3.50), which is rich and buttery.

You can specify your seasonings for all the Lahore's dishes – mild, medium or hot. Hot is very hot and will have you calling for a large mango shake (£2). All drinks at the Lahore are soft, though you can bring your own beer or wine (no corkage).

WEST

Madhu's Brilliant

39 South Rd, Southall, Middlesex ✆020 8574 1897	BR Southall
Mon & Wed–Fri 12.30–3pm & 6–11.30pm,	
Sat & Sun 6-11.30pm	All major credit cards

In the beginning was the Brilliant Restaurant and Nightclub in Nairobi; then there was The Brilliant restaurant in Western Road, Southall, run by the Anand brothers (see p.535), and then their nephew Sanjay set up Madhu's Brilliant, which is in South Road. These are the dynastic entanglements behind the continuing debate as to whether the original Brilliant or Madhu's serves the better food. Madhu's is a tad more sophisticated than The Brilliant, with more marble, and fancier service. But the East African/Punjabi food served at both has always been stunningly good and a real eye-opener to those accustomed to more standard curry house fare.

As at The Brilliant, you'll find all the Anand family signature dishes – butter chicken (£6.50 half-portion, £12 whole), jeera chicken (flavoured with cumin, £6.50 and £12), and chilli chicken (hot as Hades, £7 and £13). Also very good at Madhu's is the masala fried tilapia (£3) – chunks of fresh fish fried in a wonderfully exotic batter. On the chef's speciality list there are some interesting dishes, such as boozi bafu (£18). This is a cauldron of thin lamb chops, stewed for a long while in an improbably rich curry gravy. It is cooked and served on the bone, which means that not only does the sauce improve tenfold, but there are all those delicious bones to suck. Machuzi kuku (full, for up to six people, £30; half, for three people, £16) applies the same principle to chicken. From the single-portion curries list, the chicken curry with methi (£6.50) is well spiced, and there's a very respectable chicken tikka masala (£6.50) if you're feeling unadventurous. Breads are exemplary, the keema nan (£2.50) being particularly delicious.

Choosing between The Brilliant and Madhu's Brilliant remains a challenge. They both have their strengths: they are both streets ahead of your average run-of-the-mill curry house, and they can both be wholeheartedly recommended. Visit both and decide for yourself.

£5–£12

Omi's

1 Beaconsfield Rd, Southall, Middlesex ✆020 8571 4831 | BR Southall

Mon–Thurs 11am–9pm, Fri & Sat 11am–9.30pm | All major credit cards

Omi's is a small, no-frills eatery with a kitchen that seems at least as spacious as the dining area. The reason for this is next door, where you'll find one of Southall's larger banqueting and wedding halls. Omi's is a thriving outside catering operation and has never been purely a restaurant; until some years ago the food shared a counter with a van-rental business. Now you'll find tasty, Punjabi/Kenyan-Asian dishes, lots of rich flavours and great value. The dining room is hardly prepossessing, and the menu one of those back-lit neon display boards, but, as the notices proudly boast, it is "Fully Licensed". Don't miss out on a bottle of Ambari – a Goan beer for £3 – this sports an intriguing injunction on the back label, "For real fun drink chilled". This is one restaurant where your wallet will enjoy the trip as much as you.

The food is cooked by a formidable line-up of chefs in the back, doubtless knocking up dishes for diners with one hand while masterminding the next Indian wedding for 800 with the other, and, while you eat, a constant stream of people come and go to pick up their takeaways. Start with some of the starters, which are behind the counter. Chicken tikka (£3) is good and spicy. Aloo tikka (50p) is a large and savoury potato cake, rather like a fish cake without the fish, fried until delightfully crisp on the outside. Or try the masala fish (£2.75), a large slab of cod thickly encrusted with spices. Go on to sample a couple of the specials – aloo methi (£3.50), potatoes cooked with fenugreek, is very moreish indeed. The chilli chicken at Omi's shows influences from what is the second most popular cuisine on the Indian subcontinent – Chinese. The flavours are a kind of Punjabi sweet and sour. All the curries are commendably oil-free, strongly flavoured, and thrive on the cook-and-reheat system in operation here, and they are best eaten with breads – paratas (£1), rotis (40p) and bhaturas, the mega-indulgent puffy fried breads (50p), are all fresh and good.

If you feel a sudden tightening of your fist, you'll warm to the multicourse set meal on offer here – it costs a miserly £4, either vegetarian or non-vegetarian. West End emporia please note these prices!

Palm Palace

80 South Rd, Southall, Middlesex ✆020 8574 9209 | BR Southall

Mon, Wed & Thurs noon–3pm & 6–11pm,

Fri, Sat & Sun noon–3pm & 6pm–midnight | All major credit cards

The Palm Palace may be short on palms, and it is not palatial by any manner of means; but the food is great. This is the only Sri Lankan restaurant among the restaurant turmoil that is Southall, and the menu features a great many delicious and interesting dishes. As is so often the case with Sri Lankan food, the "drier" dishes are particularly appealing, and there is a good deal of uncompromising chilli heat. The dining room is clean and comfortable in a sparse sort of way, and service is friendly and attentive.

Starters are very good here. Try the mutton rolls (£1.50), long pancake rolls filled with meat and potatoes. Or there's the fish cutlets (£1.50), which are in fact spherical fish cakes very much in the same style as those you find in smart West End eateries, but better spiced and a tenth of the price. Move on to a "devilled" dish: mutton (£4.50), chicken (£4.50) or, best of all, squid (£4.95). With a dark tangy-sweet sauce with chilli bite, these dishes combine spices with richness very well. There was a time when every curry house in the land featured Ceylon chicken, usually just a standard chicken curry with an additional dollop of coconut milk. Here you'll find a short list of real "Ceylon" curries including mutton (£3.95); they're good, if straightforward. Try the chicken 65 (£4.50), whose name is said to refer to the age of the chicken in days. Whatever the provenance, it is a name worth noting, getting you delicious chunks of chicken with a rich and spicy coating. The hoppers (Sri Lankan pancakes) are good fun – string hopper (£2.50); egg hopper (£1.25); milk hopper (£1). Try a simple vegetable dish as well – the saag aloo (£2.50) gets you fresh spinach and thoughtfully seasoned, well-cooked potato, with *no* pool of surplus oil.

Beer-lovers must order a big bottle of Lion Stout (£3.50), which is dark, dangerous and delicious. As well as 8% alcohol, it brings with it a ringing endorsement from Michael Jackson, the "beer hunter" himself. Look at the back label and you will find not only his portrait, but also a short eulogy – "chocolatey, mocha, liqueurlike" and so forth. This beer is surprisingly good with spicy food.

Rita's Samosa Centre

112 The Broadway, Southall, Middlesex ©020 8571 2100	BR Southall
Daily 11am–10.30pm	Cash or cheques over £20

www.ritas.org.uk

Your first trip to Rita's will be memorable. The TV blares out Indian programmes, the neon strip-lights flicker over the lurid murals, the plastic-covered tables are busy with families eating dinner, teenagers pausing for snacks. Bedlam and mayhem are all around. Both the front windows of the restaurant are fenced off and each has become a separate little shop, one selling paan leaves with their aromatic fillings for chewing after dinner, and the other selling kebab rolls. If you are a shy, retiring type, this isn't a place for you – indeed, you probably won't get served. To eat here you must go up to the counter where all the dishes are set out in giant trays, choose your meal, pay, and then seat yourself. The food will eventually arrive. There's no sign of a system but everything seems to turn up in the end.

The dishes are divided into sections – curries, bread and rice, chaats (street food) and snacks. Snacks make good starters, as do chaats. Try an onion bhaji (£1) – huge, and opened out flat so that it's all the crisper. Bhel puri (£2.25), alu tikki (£2) and dahi puri (£2.50) are all street-food items – tasty and good value. Or how about half a pound of chicken tikka for £3.50? Or a superb fish tikka – also £3.50 for half a pound? They both eclipse the samosas (40p each), after which this diner is named. Main course curries are rich and simple. Try lamb (£4.50); or lamb saag (£4.50); or a deadly chilli lamb or chilli chicken (£5.50), both of which arrive scatter-bombed with halved fresh green chillies.

You can take your own beer or wine to Rita's, but it is much more fun exploring the (non-alcoholic) drinks section. A pint of salty lassi (£2) is wonderfully cold and pleasantly sharp, with a savoury dusting of fine-ground cumin seed. And then there's faluda. Faluda is very thin, very soft vermicelli which comes in a glass of milkshake. The sensation of these "worms" slithering up the straw and into your mouth is most disconcerting. Furthermore, you can have faluda with a scoop of ice cream in it (£2). What a way to end a meal.

Glassy Junction

97 South Rd, Southall ✆020 8574 1626

Punjabi pub with Lal Toofan and Cobra beers on draught, and Punjabi signs and pictures of the Punjab all over the walls. It's very much a home-from-home to the young Punjabi crowd who enjoy the three pool tables and live music at weekends.

St George & the Dragon

33 High St, Southall ✆020 8813 9429

This comfy old pub is short on frills, but long on welcome. It's relaxed and relaxing, full of regulars, and unpretentious. Favourites on tap here include John Smith's, Fosters, Holsten and Guinness.

The Three Horseshoes

2 High St, Southall ✆020 8574 2001

The bar staff are extra-friendly and saucier than usual in this large, traditional pub. It pulls a predominantly younger crowd who enjoy Flowers IPA, Wadworth's 6X and Bass Red Triangle among others. There's a patio beer garden, big-screen TV and the usual games machines.

The Three Tuns (Punjabi Junction)

45 The Green, Southall ✆020 8574 6216

Although Punjabi in character – the big-screen TV beams out more Bollywood than sport – this is a mixed, friendly local. There's a small beer garden. Favourites on tap include Cobra, Heineken and Guinness, with bottled Tusker and White Cap also popular.

Further West

Greenford, Hampton, Surbiton

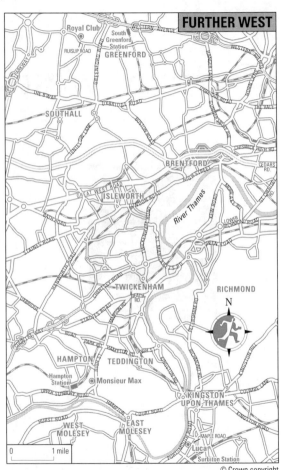

FURTHER WEST

Royal Club
South Greenford Station
GREENFORD
RUISLIP ROAD
WESTERN AVENUE
WESTERN
PARKWAY
THE B'WAY
UXBRIDGE ROAD
UXBRIDGE ROAD
THE VALE
SOUTHALL
CHISWICK HIGH RD
BRENTFORD
CEDARS RD.
GREAT WEST ROAD
HIGH STREET
ISLEWORTH
River Thames
LOWER RICHMOND RD
STAINES ROAD
NEW RD
QUEEN ROAD
TWICKENHAM
RICHMOND
N
HEATH RD.
HAMPTON
TEDDINGTON
PARK RD
HAMPTON RD
Hampton Station
Monsieur Max
UPPER SUNBURY ROAD
COOMBE LANE
HAMPTON COURT ROAD
KINGSTON UPON THAMES
HURST ROAD
KINGSTON ROAD
WEST MOLESEY
EAST MOLESEY
MAPLE ROAD
Luca
Surbiton Station

0   1 mile

WEST

Luca

85 Maple Rd, Surbiton, Surrey ©020 8399 2365	BR Surbiton
Tues–Sat 6.30–10.30pm, Sun noon–2.30pm & 6.30–10pm	Mastercard, Visa

Think Surbiton, and be prepared for your mind to fill with images of commuterland that would do Tony Hancock proud. Whatever you do conjure up, it is a fair bet that Annie O'Carroll is unlikely to feature. To say that her elegant restaurant is out of place here is something of an understatement; Ms O'Carroll was previously sous chef (and right-hand woman) to that arch-iconoclast Peter Gordon, and the eclecticism that stands him in such good stead makes a strange mainspring for Luca out here in the sticks. The sheer quality of the dishes has earned O'Carroll something of a local following. Regulars are no longer quite so amazed and nervous when she matches curried eggs with an obscure Australian fish, or teams rhubarb with venison. They have learned to trust the menu (despite its obvious eccentricities), which is a good thing as it changes weekly and there is very little on it that is comfortable and familiar. Good food is good food wherever you find it, even when that involves a journey to Surbiton.

The formula is a simple one, and relies on what specialist suppliers have to offer. The weekly changing menu provides a choice of six starters and six mains. How about spiced sweet potato and carrot soup with sun-dried tomato and pumpkinseed relish (£4)? Or, if that is not wild enough for you, dishes like red curry-marinated guinea fowl on refried beans with peanut dressing (£5.20)? To convince yourself that these are valid and interesting combinations of taste and texture, just try them. Go on to a main course like roast sirloin of venison with garlicky greens, chicken livers and ginger-braised rhubarb (£13.80), or one of the exotic fish dishes Luca does so well – pan-fried Australian Mullaway on roasted beetroot, courgettes, caramelised cauliflower and salsa rossa (£13.60). The side dishes may be as delightful as a simple rocket and Parmesan salad (£2.50), or as delicious and self-indulgent as the stunning horseradish mash (£2.50). Puddings hit the spot.

There is an amazing "early doors" offer – if you order before 7pm Tuesday to Thursday, three courses will cost you £15.95, two courses £12.95.

£15–£30

Monsieur Max

133 High St, Hampton, Middlesex ℗020 8979 5546	BR Fulwell
Mon–Fri noon–2.30pm & 7–10.30pm, Sat 7–11pm,	
Sun noon–2.30pm & 7–9.30pm	All major credit cards

You know those tabloid stories about people being trapped in the wrong bodies? Well, Max Renzland is a Frenchman trapped inside an Englishman. Monsieur Max is the latest – and most critically acclaimed – in a succession of restaurants from which Max and his late twin brother Mark struggled to dispense authentic French food and Gallic culture to appreciative Londoners. It embodies all the best bits of those legendary small French restaurants. Service is cheerful and unashamedly biased towards regulars. The short menu changes every day. Dishes range from stunningly simple to French classics. And, joy of joys, Monsieur Max is in London – well, nearly.

Max is also a bit of a bargain. Dinner (or Sunday lunch) is £24.50 for three courses; the midweek lunch is £14 for two courses or £17 for three. Starters range from the simple – finest Cantabrian anchovies, cured and served with shallots, or home-made rillettes of pork and duck – to the more complex – terrine of dill-marinated salmon layered with crème fraîche and cucumber salad. For a main course, if it's on the menu, you should jump at the poulet de Bresse in two services (for two). This takes 25 minutes: first you get the breast – simply roasted, with potato Dauphinoise and a vin Jaune and morel cream sauce – and then the legs, with a mixed leaf salad and truffle jus. Max has a new source of French chickens that supplies exclusively to this restaurant. He is very picky about his chickens, and once you taste one you'll see what all the fuss is about. His fish, duck and Scotch beef offerings are equally impressive. Puddings are of the order of rum baba, or an old-fashioned rice pudding with Madagascan vanilla, Agen prunes and cognac caramel. Push them aside and go for the cheeseboard – twenty French farmhouse cheeses in perfect condition. As for wine, there are about 250 bins – enough for the choosiest oenophile.

If you are a West London Francophile, you're probably already a regular here and will be unfazed by the minor eccentricities of the menu and service.

Royal Club

116–118 Ruislip Rd, Greenford, Middlesex ©020 8578 3255	BR Northolt
Daily noon–2pm & 6pm–midnight	Amex, Diners, Mastercard, Visa

To look at, this is such a straightforward, in-your-face curry house that the slighty more sophisticated menu comes as something of a surprise. As to provenance, the team here served in such curry stalwarts of the past as the Ealing Tandoori, and the Wembley Tandoori (which took over the torch after 1985). During the 1970s and 1980s, when curry around London was unremittingly rugged, these restaurants were famous for their genuine spicing and for taking some care over their cookery. Now Wembley's loss is Greenford's gain. The white-painted restaurant with lofty columns and well-spaced tables looks just like a curry house, only cleaner and smarter. The deal here is simple: you get curry that is a cut above the average; portions that are large; and service that is efficient and friendly. Sound spicing meets good pricing.

Even if you are nostalgic for old-style curry, you must try a dish that virtually counts as Indian home cooking: the wonderfully unpretentious aloo chat (£2.50). Perhaps the idea of spicy fried potato doesn't sound like a whizzy starter, but in practice it is very simple, and very good. Chicken tikka (£5.10) is tasty here, as is tandoori chicken (two pieces £3.90). Go on to the specialities, which are curry-house-meets-Punjabi: jeera chicken special (£6.75), rich with cumin, or tandoori butter chicken (£7.95), served on the bone and with a rich chicken tikka masala-ish sauce. For unreconstructed curryholics there is also a very sound lamb Madras (£4.50), hot and sharp. Side dishes include a good tarka dhal (£3.40), which comes with fresh green chillies, and a grand aloo chana (£3.50), which is a simple and spicy dish of chickpeas with potatoes. Breads are also good.

On the specials menu you'll find the Royal Chicken Dinner (£7.20), which will come as something of a shock to anyone who sees such things in terms of roast chicken, two vegetables and gravy – in Greenford this is a whole, marinated chicken breast, fried with cabbage and served in an ultra-rich white sauce made creamy with yoghurt and ground almonds. It is also a good enough dish to catch on at Sunday lunchtime.

Index

Index of restaurants by name 551

Index of restaurants by cuisine 568

Index of pubs and bars...579

Index of restaurants by name

A–Z note: The Avenue appears under A not T; Le Versailles under V and El Molino under M. Stephen Bull is an S, Chez Gérard is a C. Well, you have to have rules.

1 Lombard Street, The Brasserie   199

1 Lombard St, EC3
✆020 7929 6611
Modern French

192   497

192 Kensington Park Rd, W11
✆020 7229 0482
Modern British

Abu Ali   95

136–138 George St, W1
✆020 7724 6338
Lebanese

Adam's Café   527

77 Askew Rd, W12
✆020 8743 0572
North African

Al Waha   122

75 Westbourne Grove, W2
✆020 7229 0806
Lebanese

Alastair Little   131

49 Frith St, W1
✆020 7734 5183
Modern European

Alastair Little W11   498

136a Lancaster Rd, W11
✆020 7243 2220
Modern European

Alounak   121

44 Westbourne Grove, W2
✆020 7229 0416
Iranian

Anatolya   231

263a Mare St, E8
✆020 8986 2223
Turkish

Andrew Edmunds   132

46 Lexington St, W1
✆020 7437 5708
Modern British

The Anglesea Arms   487

35 Wingate Rd, W6
✆020 8749 1291
Modern British/Pub

Anglo Anatolyan   327

123 Stoke Newington Church St, N16
✆020 7923 4349
Turkish

Arancia   403

52 Southwark Park Rd, SE16
✆020 7394 1751
Italian

Ard Ri   71

At The O'Conor Don, 88 Marylebone Lane, W1
✆020 7935 9311
Irish

Arkansas Café   189

Unit 12, Old Spitalfields Market, E1
✆020 7377 6999
North American/Steaks

Aroma II   19

118 Shaftesbury Ave, W1
✆020 7437 0370
Chinese

Artigiano   268

12 Belsize Terrace, NW3
✆020 7794 4288
Italian

L'Artista 269

917 Finchley Rd, NW11
☎020 8731 7501
Pizza/Italian

Assaggi 499

39 Chepstow Place, W2
☎020 7792 5501
Italian

The Atlas 473

16 Seagrave Rd, Fulham,
SW6
☎020 7385 9129
Mediterranean/Pub

Aubergine 449

11 Park Walk, SW10
☎020 7352 3449
French

The Avenue 105

7–9 St James's St, SW1
☎020 7321 2111
Modern British

Babur Brasserie 425

119 Brockley Rise, Forest
Hill, SE23
☎020 8291 2400
Indian

Il Bacio 328

61 Stoke Newington
Church St, N16
☎020 7249 3833
Pizza/Italian

Bah Humbug 363

The Crypt, St Matthews
Church, Brixton Hill, SW2
☎020 7738 3184
Mostly Vegetarian/Modern
British

Bank 31

1 Kingsway, cnr of
Aldwych, WC2
☎020 7234 3344
Modern British

Bar Bourse 200

67 Queen St, EC4
☎020 7248 2200
Modern British

Bar Estrela 387

111–115 South Lambeth
Rd, SW8
☎020 7793 1051
Portuguese

Baradero 223

Turberry Quay - off Pepper
St, E14
☎020 7537 1666
Spanish

**Barcelona Tapas
Bar** 201

1a Bell Lane, E1
☎020 7247 7014
Spanish

Base 270

71 Hampstead High St,
NW3
☎020 7431 2224
Modern British

BB's Crabback 463

3 Chignell Place, West
Ealing, W13
☎020 8840 8322
Caribbean

Belair House 426

Gallery Rd, Dulwich
Village, SE21
☎020 8299 9788
French

Belgo Centraal 32

50 Earlham St, WC2
☎020 7813 2233
Belgian

Bengal Village 190

75 Brick Lane, E1
☎020 7366 4868
Indian

Beyoglu 355

50 Battersea Park Rd,
SW11
☎020 7627 2052
Turkish

**Bibendum Oyster
Bar** 159

Michelin House, 81
Fulham Rd, SW3
☎020 7589 1480
Shellfish

Bierodrome 299

173–174 Upper St, N1
☎020 7226 5835
Belgian

Bistro Daniel 96

26 Sussex Place, W2
☎020 7723 8395
French

Blah blah blah 528

78 Goldhawk Rd, W12
☎020 8746 1377
Vegetarian/British

Bloom's 271

130 Golders Green Rd,
NW11
☎020 8455 1338
Jewish

Blue Print Café 404

Design Museum, Shad
Thames, SE1
☎020 7378 7031
Modern British

Bluebird 450

350 King's Rd, SW3
☎020 7559 1000
Modern European

Boisdale 167

15 Eccleston St, SW1
☎020 7730 6922
Scottish

**Bombay Bicycle
Club** 371

95 Nightingale Lane,
SW12
☎020 8673 6217
Indian

Books for Cooks 500

4 Blenheim Crescent, W11
☎020 7221 1992
Modern British

La Bota 281

31 Broadway Parade,
Tottenham Lane, N8
☎020 8340 3082
Spanish

Bradley's 319

25 Winchester Rd, NW3
☎020 7722 3457
Modern British

The Brilliant 535

72–76 Western Rd,
Southall, Middlesex
☎020 8574 1928
Indian

Brula Bistrot 517

43 Crown Rd, St
Margarets, Surrey
☎020 8892 0602
French

busaba eathai 133

106–110 Wardour St, W1
☎0800 316 9950
Thai

**Butler's Wharf Chop
House** 405

36e Shad Thames, SE1
☎020 7403 3403
British

Café des Amis 33

11–14 Hanover Place, off
Long Acre, WC2
☎020 7379 3444
Modern French

Café España 134

63 Old Compton St, W1
☎020 7494 1271
Spanish

Café Indiya 202

30 Alie St, E1
☎020 7481 8288
Indian

Café Naz 191

46–48 Brick Lane, E1
☎020 7247 0234
Indian

Café Pacifico 34

5 Langley St, WC2
☎020 7379 7728
Tex-Mex

Café Spice Namaste 203

16 Prescot St, E1
☎020 7488 9242
Indian

Calabash 35

The Africa Centre, 38 King
St, WC2
☎020 7836 1976
African

RESTAURANTS A–Z INDEX

Canteloupe 241

35 Charlotte Rd, EC3
℡020 7613 4411
Mediterranean

Cantina del Ponte 406

Butler's Wharf, Shad
Thames, SE1
℡020 7403 5403
Italian

Le Caprice 106

Arlington House, Arlington
St, SW1
℡020 7629 2239
Modern European

Caravan Serai 72

50 Paddington St, W1
℡020 7935 1208
Afghan

Carnevale 242

135 Whitecross St, EC1
℡020 7250 3452
Vegetarian/Fusion

Centrale 135

16 Moor St, W1
℡020 7437 5513
Italian

Centuria 232

100 St Paul's Rd, N1
℡020 7704 2345
Italian/Pub

Cheng Du 257

9 Parkway, NW1
℡020 7485 8058
Chinese

Chetna's 337

420 High Rd, Wembley
℡020 8900 1466
Indian/Vegetarian

Chez Bruce 372

2 Bellevue Rd, SW17
℡020 8672 0114
French

Chez Gérard 5

8 Charlotte St, W1
℡020 7636 4975
French

Chez Lindsay 518

11 Hill Rise, Richmond,
Surrey
℡020 8948 7473
Very French

Chez Maria 519

5a Princes St, Richmond
Market, Surrey
℡020 8948 1475
French

China City 20

White Bear Yard, 25a Lisle
St, WC2
℡020 7734 3388
Chinese

**The Chiswick
Restaurant** 488

131 Chiswick High Rd, W4
℡020 8994 6887
Modern British

Chor Bizarre 83

16 Albemarle St, W1
℡020 7629 9802
Indian

Cho-San 395

292 Upper Richmond Rd,
SW15
℡020 8778 9626
Japanese

**The Churchill
Arms** 501

119 Kensington Church St,
W8
℡020 7792 1246
Thai/Pub

Chutney Mary 451

535 King's Rd, SW10
℡020 7351 3113
Indian

Cicada 213

132 St John St, EC1
℡020 7608 1550
Pacific Fusion

Circus 136

1 Upper James St, W1
℡020 7534 4000
Modern British

Club Gascon 214

57 West Smithfield, EC1
✆020 7796 0600
Very French

Le Colombier 452

145 Dovehouse St,
Chelsea Square, SW3
✆020 7351 1155
Very French

Cow Dining Room 502

89 Westbourne Park Rd,
W2
✆020 7221 5400
Modern British

The Coyote Café 489

2 Fauconberg Rd, W4
✆020 8742 8545
American Southwest/
Tex-Mex

**The Criterion
Brasserie** 107

224 Piccadilly, W1
✆020 7930 0488
Modern French

Cucina 272

45a South End Rd, NW3
✆020 7435 7814
Modern British

Curry Craze 338

8–9 The Triangle,
Wembley Hill Rd, Wembley
✆020 8902 9700
Indian

Curry Special 249

2 Greengate Parade, Horns
Rd, Newbury Park, Essex
✆020 8518 3005
Indian

**The Czechoslovak
House** 273

74 West End Lane, NW6
✆020 7372 5251
Czech/Slovak

Daquise 160

20 Thurloe St, SW7
✆020 7589 6117
Polish

Defune 97

61 Blandford St, W1
✆020 7935 8311
Japanese

Del Buongustaio 396

283 Putney Bridge Rd,
SW15
✆020 8780 9361
Italian

Delfina Studio Café 407

50 Bermondsey St, SE1
✆020 7357 0244
Modern British

**Diwana Bhel-Poori
House** 47

121 Drummond St, NW1
✆020 7387 5556
Indian/Vegetarian

Al Duca 108

4–5 Duke of York St, SW1
✆020 7839 3090
Italian

Duke of Cambridge 300

30 St Peter's St, N1
✆020 7359 3066
Modern British/Pub

The Eagle 215

159 Farringdon Rd, EC1
✆020 7837 1353
Mediterranean/Pub

**Ebury Wine Bar and
Restaurant** 168

139 Ebury St, SW1
✆020 7730 5447
Modern European

Eco 373

162 Clapham High St,
SW4
✆020 7978 1108
Pizza

Eco Brixton 364

4 Market Row, Brixton
Market, Electric Row, SW9
✆020 7738 3021
Pizza

The Engineer 258

65 Gloucester Ave, NW1
✆020 7722 0950
Modern British/Pub

The English Garden 453

10 Lincoln St, SW3
✆020 7584 7272
Modern British

Enoteca 397

28 Putney High St, SW15
✆020 8785 4449
Italian

Euphorium 301

203 Upper St, N1
✆020 7704 6909
Modern British

O Fado 161

45–50 Beauchamp Place, SW3
✆020 7589 3002
Portuguese

Fairuz 73

3 Blandford St, W1
✆020 7935 9311
Lebanese

Faulkner's 233

424 Kingsland Rd, E8
✆020 7254 6152
Fish & Chips

Fiction 282

60 Crouch End Hill, N8
✆020 8340 3403
Vegetarian/Modern British

The Fifth Floor 63

5th Floor, Harvey Nichols, Knightsbridge, SW1
✆020 7235 5250
Modern British

Fina Estampa 408

150 Tooley St, SE1
✆020 7403 1342
Peruvian

The Fire Station 179

150 Waterloo Rd, SE1
✆020 7620 2226
Modern British

Fish! 409

Cathedral St, SE1
✆020 7234 3333
Fish

Fish Central 243

151 King's Square, Central St, EC1
✆020 7253 4970
Fish & Chips

Fortnum's Fountain 109

181 Piccadilly, W1
✆020 7973 4140
British

French House Dining Room 137

49 Dean St, W1
✆020 7437 2477
Modern British

Fuego 204

1a Pudding Lane, EC3
✆020 7929 3366
Spanish

Fung Shing 21

15 Lisle St, WC2
✆020 7437 1539
Chinese

Galicia 503

323 Portobello Rd, W10
✆020 8969 3539
Spanish

Gastro 374

67 Venn St, SW4
✆020 7627 0222
Very French

The Gate 490

51 Queen Caroline St, W6
✆020 8748 6932
Vegetarian/Modern British

Gaudí 216

63 Clerkenwell Rd, EC1
✆020 7250 1057
Spanish

Geeta 311

57–59 Willesden Lane, NW6
✆020 7624 1713
Indian/Vegetarian

Geetanjali's 339

16 Court Parade, Watford Rd, Wembley
✆020 8904 5353
Indian

Gifto's Lahore Karahi 536

162–164 The Broadway, Southall, Middlesex
☎020 8813 8669
Indian

The Glasshouse 441

14 Station Parade, Kew Gardens, Surrey
☎020 8940 6777
French

Globe 320

100 Avenue Rd, NW3
☎020 7722 7200
Pacific Fusion

Gordon Ramsay 454

68–69 Royal Hospital Rd, SW3
☎020 7352 4441
French

Granita 302

127 Upper St, N1
☎020 7226 3222
Mediterranean

Grano 491

162 Thames Rd, Chiswick, W4
☎020 8995 0120
Italian

Great Nepalese 49

48 Eversholt St, NW1
☎020 7388 6737
Nepalese

The Greenhouse 84

27a Hay's Mews, W1
☎020 7499 3331
British

Gresslin's 274

13 Heath St, NW3
☎020 7794 8386
Modern European

The Hard Rock Café 110

150 Old Park Lane, W1
☎020 7629 0382
Burgers/Tex-Mex

Harran 345

399 Green Lanes, N4
☎020 8348 5434
Turkish

Harry Morgan's 321

31 St John's Wood High St, NW8
☎020 7722 1869
Jewish

The Havelock Tavern 529

57 Masbro Rd, W14
☎020 7603 5374
Modern British/Pub

Herb & Spice 192

11a Whites Row, E1
☎020 7247 4050
Indian

Honest Cabbage 410

99 Bermondsey St, SE1
☎020 7234 0080
Modern British

Hot Stuff 388

19 Wilcox Rd, SW8
☎020 7720 1480
Indian

House 224

27 Ropemaker's Field, Narrow St, E14
☎020 7538 3818
Modern British

The House 455

3 Milner St, SW3
☎020 7581 3002
British

Hunan 169

51 Pimlico Rd, SW1
☎020 7730 5712
Chinese

Hung Toa 123

51 Queensway, W2
☎020 7727 5753
Chinese

Huong Viet 234

An Viet House, 12–14 Englefield Rd, N1
☎020 7249 0877
Vietnamese

INDEX

Ibla 74

89 Marylebone High St, W1
☎020 7224 3799
Italian

Ikkyu 6

67a Tottenham Court Rd, W1
☎020 7636 9280
Japanese

India Club 36

143 Strand, WC2
☎020 7836 0650
Indian

Iran the Restaurant 98

59 Edgware Rd, W2
☎020 7723 1344
Iranian

Istanbul Iskembecisi 329

9 Stoke Newington Rd, N16
☎020 7254 7291
Turkish

The Ivy 37

1 West St, WC2
☎020 7836 4751
British

J. Sheekey 38

28–32 St Martin's Court, WC2
☎020 7240 2565
Fish

Jack's Place 356

12 York Rd, SW11
☎020 7228 8519
British/Steaks

Jashan 283

19 Turnpike Lane, N8
☎020 8340 9880
Indian

Jen 22

7 Gerrard St, W1
☎020 7287 8193
Chinese

Jenny Lo's Teahouse 170

14 Eccleston St, SW1
☎020 7259 0399
Chinese /Noodles

Joe Allen 39

13 Exeter St, WC2
☎020 7836 0651
North American

Kaifeng Kosher Oriental 346

51 Church Rd, Hendon, NW4
☎020 8203 7888
Chinese/Jewish

Kastoori 427

188 Upper Tooting Rd, SW17
☎020 8767 7027
Indian

The Kerala 7

15 Great Castle St, W1
☎020 7580 2125
Indian

Kettners 138

29 Romilly St, W1
☎020 7734 6112
Pizza/Burgers

Khan's 124

13–15 Westbourne Grove, W2
☎020 7727 5420
Indian

Kulu Kulu 139

76 Brewer St, W1
☎020 7734 7316
Japanese

Lahore Karahi 428

1 Tooting High St, SW17
☎020 8767 2477
Indian

Lahore Kebab House 193

2 Umberstone St, E1
☎020 7481 9737
Indian

The Lahore Kebab House 347

248 Kingsbury Rd, NW9
☎020 8905 0930
Indian

Lahoria 348

274 Kingsbury Rd, NW9
℡020 8206 1129
Indian

Lalibela Ethiopian Restaurant 289

137 Fortress Rd, NW5
℡020 7284 0600
Ethiopian

Lawn 381

1 Lawn Terrace, SE3
℡020 7379 0724
Modern British

Lee Ho Fook 23

4 Macclesfield St, W1
℡020 7734 0782
Chinese

Lighthouse 417

75–77 The Ridgway, SW19
℡020 8944 6388
Modern European

Little Georgia 235

2 Broadway Market, E8
℡020 7249 9070
Russian

Little Saigon 180

139 Westminster Bridge Rd, SE1
℡020 7207 9747
Vietnamese

Livebait Restaurant & Bar 40

21 Wellington St, WC2
℡020 7836 7161
Fish

The Lobster Pot 389

3 Kennington Lane, SE11
℡020 7582 5556
Very French

Luca 545

85 Maple Rd, Surbiton, Surrey
℡020 8399 2365
Pacific Fusion

Lundum's 474

119 Old Brompton Rd, SW7
℡020 7373 7774
Danish

Ma Goa 398

244 Upper Richmond Rd, SW15
℡020 8780 1767
Indian

Madhu's Brilliant 537

39 South Rd, Southall, Middlesex
℡020 8574 1897
Indian

Malabar Junction 8

107 Great Russell St, WC1
℡020 7580 5230
Indian

The Mandalay 99

444 Edgware Rd, W2
℡020 7258 3696
Burmese

Mandarin Kitchen 125

14–16 Queensway, W2
℡020 7727 9012
Chinese/Fish

The Mandeer 9

8 Bloomsbury Way, WC1
℡020 7242 6202
Indian/Vegetarian

The Mandola 505

139–141 Westbourne Grove, W11
℡020 7229 4734
Sudanese

Mangal II 330

4 Stoke Newington Rd, N16
℡020 7254 7888
Turkish

Mango Rooms 259

10 Kentish Town Rd, NW1
℡020 7482 5065
Caribbean

Mao Tai 479

58 New King's Rd, SW6
℡020 7731 2520
Chinese

Maremma 303

11–13 Theberton St, N1
✆020 7226 9400
Italian

Marine Ices 260

8 Haverstock Hill, NW3
✆020 7485 3132
Italian/Ice Cream

Masaledar 429

121 Upper Tooting Rd,
SW17
✆020 8767 7676
Indian

Mash 10

19–21 Great Portland St,
W1
✆020 7637 5555
Modern European

McClements 520

2 Whitton Rd,
Twickenham, Middlesex
✆020 8744 9610
French

Mem Saheb on Thames 225

65–67 Amsterdam Rd,
E14
✆020 7538 3008
Indian

Mesclun 331

24 Stoke Newington
Church St, N16
✆020 7249 5029
Modern European

Meson Bilbao 312

33 Malvern Rd, NW6
✆020 7328 1744
Spanish/Basque

El Metro Tapas Bar 480

10–12 Effie Rd, SW6
✆020 7384 1264
Spanish

Metrogusto 357

50 Battersea Park Rd,
SW8
✆020 7627 2052
Italian

Mezzo 140

100 Wardour St, W1
✆020 7314 4000
Modern British

The Mirabelle 85

56 Curzon St, W1
✆020 7499 4636
French

Miraggio 481

510 Fulham Rd, SW6
✆020 7384 3142
Italian

Mirch Masala 430

1416 London Rd, Norbury,
SW16
✆020 8679 1828
Indian

Mobeen 250

222–224 Green St, E7
✆020 8470 2419
Indian

Mohsen 47

152 Warwick Rd, W14
✆020 7602 9888
Persian

El Molino 290

379 Holloway Rd, N7
✆020 7700 4312
Spanish

Momo 111

25 Heddon St, W1
✆020 7434 4040
Moroccan

Momo 464

14 Queen's Parade, West
Acton, W5
✆020 8997 0206
Japanese

Monsieur Max 546

33 High St, Hampton,
Middlesex
✆020 8979 5546
Very French

Montana 482

125–129 Dawes Rd, SW6
✆020 7385 9500
American Southwest

Monty's   465

54 Northfield Ave, Ealing,
W13
☏020 8567 6281
Indian

Moro   217

34–36 Exmouth Market,
EC1
☏020 7833 8336
Spanish/North African

Moshi Moshi Sushi   205

Unit 24, Liverpool Street
Station, EC2
☏020 7247 3227
Japanese

Mr Kong   24

21 Lisle St, WC2
☏020 7437 7923
Chinese

Mulligan's   86

13–14 Cork St, W1
☏020 7409 1370
Irish

Neon   365

7 Atlantic Rd, SW9
☏020 7738 6576
Italian

**New Culture
Revolution**   456

305 King's Rd, SW3
☏020 7352 9281
Chinese/Noodles

New End   275

102 Heath St, NW3
☏020 7431 4423
Modern European

New Tayyab   194

83 Fieldgate St, E1
☏020 7247 9543
Indian

New World   25

1 Gerrard Place, W1
☏020 7734 0396
Chinese/Dim Sum

No.77 Wine Bar   267

77 Mill Lane, NW6
☏020 7435 7787
Modern British

Nobu   87

19 Old Park Lane, W1
☏020 7447 4747
Japanese

**North China
Restaurant**   466

305 Uxbridge Rd, Ealing
Common, W3
☏020 8992 9183
Chinese

Nosh Brothers   506

12 All Saints Rd, W11
☏020 7243 2808
Modern British

O's Thai Café   284

10 Topsfield Parade, N8
☏020 8348 6898
Thai

Odette's   261

130 Regent's Park Rd,
NW1
☏020 7586 5486
Modern British

Offshore   507

148 Holland Park Ave,
W11
☏020 7221 6090
Mauritian/Fish

Omi's   538

1 Beaconsfield Rd,
Southall, Middlesex
☏020 8571 4831
Indian

L'Oranger   112

5 St James's St, SW1
☏020 7839 3774
French

The Organic Café   313

21–25 Lonsdale Rd, NW6
☏020 7372 1232
British

Organic Veg   162

8 Egerton Gardens Mews,
SW3
☏020 7584 7007
Chinese/Vegetarian

Orrery 75

55 Marylebone High St, W1
☎020 7616 8000
French

Osteria Basilico 508

29 Kensington Park Rd, W11
☎020 7727 9372
Italian

Osteria d'Isola 64

145 Knightsbridge, SW1
☎020 7838 1099
Italian

Pallavi 521

1st Floor, 3 Cross Deep Court, Heath Rd, Twickenham, Middlesex
☎020 8892 2345
Indian

Palm Palace 539

80 South Rd, Southall, Middlesex
☎020 8574 9209
Sri Lankan

Parade 467

18–19 The Mall, Ealing, W5
☎020 8810 0202
Modern British

El Parador 48

245 Eversholt St, NW1
☎020 7387 2789
Spanish

Paris London Café 291

5 Junction Rd, N19
☎020 7561 0330
French

Pasha 304

301 Upper St, N1
☎020 7226 1454
Turkish

Passione 11

10 Charlotte St, W1
☎020 7636 2833
Italian

Patio 530

Goldhawk Rd, W12
☎020 8743 5194
Polish

The People's Palace 181

Level Three, Royal Festival Hall, South Bank, SE1
☎020 7928 9999
Modern British

The Pepper Tree 375

19 Clapham Common South Side, SW4
☎020 7622 1758
Thai

Le P'tit Normand 418

185 Merton Rd, SW18
☎020 8871 0233
Very French

Petit Robert 411

3 Park St, SE1
☎020 7357 7003
French

Pétrus 113

33 St James's St, SW1
☎020 7930 4272
French

Pharmacy Restaurant 509

150 Notting Hill Gate, W11
☎020 7221 2442
Modern European

Pizza on the Park 65

11 Knightsbridge, SW1
☎020 7235 5273
Pizza

Place 504

201–207 Kensington Church St, W8
☎020 7727 3184
Modern British

Planet Spice 431

88 Selsdon Park Rd, Addington, South Croydon
☎020 8651 3300
Indian

Pollo 141

20 Old Compton St, W1
☎020 7734 5917
Italian

The Popeseye 531

108 Blythe Rd, W14
✆020 7610 4578
Steak

La Poule au Pot 171

231 Ebury St, SW1
✆020 7730 7763
Very French

**The Prince of
   Ceylon** 349

39 Watford Way, Hendon,
NW4
✆020 8203 8002
Sri Lankan

Prism 206

147 Leadenhall St, EC3
✆020 7256 3888
Modern British

Pukkabar 442

21 Barnes High St, SW13
✆020 8878 7012
Indian

Punjab 41

80–82 Neal St, WC2
✆020 7836 9787
Indian

Putney Bridge 399

The Embankment, SW15
✆020 8780 1811
French

Quaglino's 114

16 Bury St, SW1
✆020 7930 6767
Modern British

Quilon 172

41 Buckingham Gate, SW1
✆020 7821 1899
Indian

R.K. Stanley 13

6 Little Portland St, W1
✆020 7462 0099
Modern British

**Raavi Kebab
   Halal Tandoori** 50

125 Drummond St, NW1
✆020 7388 1780
Indian

Le Raj 432

211 Fir Tree Rd, Epsom
Downs, Surrey
✆01737 371371
Indian

Randall & Aubin 142

16 Brewer St, W1
✆020 7287 4447
Seafood/Rôtisserie

Ranoush Juice Bar 100

43 Edgware Rd, W2
✆020 7723 5929
Lebanese

Ransome's Dock 358

35–37 Parkgate Rd, SW11
✆020 7223 1611
British

Rasa 332

55 Stoke Newington
Church St, N16
✆020 7249 0344
Indian/Vegetarian

Rasa Samudra 12

5 Charlotte St, W1
✆020 7637 0222
Indian/Fish

Rasa W1 88

6 Dering St, W1
✆020 7629 1346
Indian/Vegetarian

Rasputin 468

265 High St, Acton, W3
✆020 8993 5802
Russian

The Real Greek 244

15 Hoxton Market, N1
✆020 7739 8212
Greek

The Red Fort 143

77 Dean St, W1
✆020 7437 2115
Indian

Redmond's 443

170 Upper Richmond Rd
West, SW14
℃020 8878 1922
Modern British

**Rhodes in the
Square** 173

Dolphin Square,
Chichester St, SW1
℃020 7798 6767
Modern British

Riccardo's 457

126 Fulham Rd, SW3
℃020 7370 4917
Italian

**Richard Corrigan at The
Lindsay House** 144

21 Romilly St, W1
℃020 7439 0450
British

**Rita's Samosa
Centre** 540

112 The Broadway,
Southall, Middlesex
℃020 8571 2100
Indian

Riva 444

169 Church Rd, SW13
℃020 8748 0434
Italian

Rodizio Rico 510

111 Westbourne Grove,
W2
℃020 7792 4035
Brazilian

The Rôtisserie 305

134 Upper St, N1
℃020 7226 0122
Rôtisserie

Rôtisserie Jules 511

133a Notting Hill Gate,
W11
℃020 7221 3331
Rôtisserie

Roussillon 174

16 St Barnabas St, SW1
℃020 7730 5550
Modern French

Royal China 76

40 Baker St, W1
℃020 7487 4688
Chinese/Dim Sum

Royal Club 547

116–118 Ruislip Rd,
Greenford, Middlesex
℃020 8578 3255
Indian

**Royal Couscous
House** 292

316 Holloway Rd, N7
℃020 7700 2188
North African

RSJ 182

13a Coin St, SE1
℃020 7928 4554
French

Rules 42

35 Maiden Lane, WC2
℃020 7836 5314
Very British

Sakonis 340

127–129 Ealing Rd,
Alperton
℃020 8903 9601
Indian/Vegetarian

The Salt House 322

63 Abbey Rd, NW8
℃020 7328 6626
British/Pub

The Salusbury 314

50–52 Salusbury Rd, NW6
℃020 7328 3286
Italian/Pub

**San Daniele del
Friuli** 293

72 Highbury Park, N5
℃020 7226 1609
Italian

Sarcan 306

4 Theberton St, N1
℃020 7226 5489
Turkish

Sariyer Balik Lokantasi 333

56 Green Lanes, N16
☏020 7275 7681
Turkish/Fish

Sarkhel's 419

199 Replingham Rd,
Southfields, SW18
☏020 8870 1483
Indian

Sartoria 115

20 Savile Row, W1
☏020 7534 7000
Italian

Satay Bar 366

450 Coldharbour Lane,
SW9
☏020 7326 5001
Indonesian

Satay House 101

13 Sale Place, W2
☏020 7723 6763
Malaysian

Sauce barorganicdiner 262

214 Camden High St, NW1
☏020 7482 0777
British

Sequel 376

4 Venn St, SW4
☏020 7622 4222
Fusion

Shamyana 433

437–439 Streatham High
Rd, SW16
☏020 8679 6162
Indian

Siam Café 251

103 Woodgrange Rd, E7
☏020 8536 1870
Thai

Sigiri 469

161 Northfield Ave, W13
☏020 8579 8000
Sri Lankan

Simply Spice 51

53 Calthorpe St, WC1
☏020 7833 9787
Indian

Singapore Garden 323

83a Fairfax Rd, NW6
☏020 7328 5314
Singaporean

Singapura 207

Limeburner Lane, EC4
☏020 7329 1133
Singaporean

Smiths, the Dining Room 218

67–77 Charterhouse St,
EC1
☏020 7236 6666
Modern British

Soho Soho 145

11–13 Frith St, W1
☏020 7494 3491
French

Soho Spice 146

124–126 Wardour St, W1
☏020 7434 0808
Indian

Solly's Exclusive 276

146–150 Golders Green
Rd, NW11
☏020 8455 2121
Jewish

Sonny's 445

94 Church Rd, SW13
☏020 8748 0393
Modern British

Sotheby's Café 89

34–35 New Bond St, W1
☏020 7293 5077
Modern British

Soulard 236

113 Mortimer Rd, N1
☏020 7254 1314
French

Spiga 147

84–86 Wardour St, W1
☏020 7734 3444
Italian

La Spighetta 77

43 Blandford St, W1
☏020 7486 7340
Italian

The Springbok Café 492

42 Devonshire Rd, W4
☏020 8742 3149
South African

The Square 90

6–10 Bruton St, W1
☏020 7795 7100
French

St John 219

26 St John St, EC1
☏020 7251 0848
Very English

St John's 294

91 Junction Rd, N19
☏020 7272 1587
Mediterranean/Pub

The Station Grill 390

2 Braganza St, SE17
☏020 7735 4769
French

Stepping Stone 359

123 Queenstown Rd, SW8
☏020 7622 0555
Modern British

Sticky Fingers 55

1a Phillimore Gardns, W8
☏020 7938 5338
Burgers/Tex-Mex

The Sugar Club 148

21 Warwick St, W1
☏020 7437 7776
Pacific Fusion

Sushi Wong 56

38c-d Kensington Church
St, W8
☏020 7937 5007
Japanese

Sushi-Say 350

33b Walm Lane, NW2
☏020 8459 7512
Japanese

Tabaq 377

47 Balham Hill, SW12
☏020 8673 7820
Indian

Tabla 226

The Dockmaster's House,
Hertsmere Rd, E14
☏020 7345 0345
Indian

Tai Pan 227

665 Commercial Rd, E14
☏020 7791 0118
Chinese

Tai Won Mein 382

49 Greenwich Church St,
SE10
☏020 8858 1668
Japanese/Noodles

Taja 195

199a Whitechapel Rd, E1
☏020 7247 3866
Indian

Tamasha 434

131 Widmore Rd, Bromley,
Kent
☏020 8460 3240
Indian

La Tante Clare 66

Wilton Place, SW1
☏020 7823 2003
French

Tas 183

33 The Cut, SE1
☏020 7928 1444
Turkish

Teatro 149

93–107 Shaftesbury Ave,
W1
☏020 7494 3040
Modern British

Tentazioni 412

2 Mill St, SE1
☏020 7237 1100
Italian

The Terrace 57

33c Holland St, W8
☏020 7937 3224
Modern British

Thai Tho   420

20 Wimbledon High St,
SW19
✆020 8946 1542
Thai

Three Monkeys   435

136–140 Herne Hill, SE24
✆020 7738 5500
Indian

Time   383

7a College Approach,
SE10
✆020 8305 9767
Fusion

Tokyo Diner   26

2 Newport Pl, WC2
✆020 7287 8777
Japanese

The Toucan   150

19 Carlisle St, W1
✆020 7437 4123
Irish

The Vale   315

99 Chippenham Rd, W9
✆020 7266 0990
Modern British

**Vasco and Piero's
Pavilion**   151

15 Poland St, W1
✆020 7437 8774
Italian

Veeraswamy   116

Victory House, 101 Regent
St, W1
✆020 7734 1401
Indian

Viet Hoa Café   245

72 Kingsland Rd, E2
✆020 7729 8293
Vietnamese

The Village Bistro   285

38 Highgate High St, N6
✆020 8340 5165
French

Villandry Foodstore   14

170 Great Portland St, W1
✆020 7631 3131
Modern British

Wagamama   15

4 Streatham St, WC1
✆020 7323 9223
Japanese/Noodles

The White Horse   522

Worple Way, Richmond,
Surrey
✆020 8940 2418
Modern British/Pub

Wódka   58

12 St Albans Grove, W8
✆020 7937 6513
Polish

Woodlands   78

77 Marylebone Lane, W1
✆020 7486 3862
Indian/Vegetarian

Xios   126

47 Moscow Rd, W2
✆020 7243 0606
Greek

Yo!Sushi   152

52 Poland St, W1
✆020 7287 0443
Japanese

Zafferano   67

15 Lowndes St, SW1
✆020 7235 5800
Italian

Zaika   458

259 Fulham Rd, SW3
✆020 7351 7823
Indian

Zamoyski   277

85 Fleet Rd, NW3
✆020 7794 4792
Polish

Zilli Fish   153

36–40 Brewer St, W1
✆020 7734 8649
Italian/Fish

Index of restaurants by cuisine

Categories below are pretty self-explanatory, though note that "Indian" includes Bangladeshi, Indian and Pakistani restaurants. The area names are the neighbourhood sections by which this book is arranged.

Afghan

Caravan Serai 72
Marylebone

African

Calabash 35
Covent Garden & Holborn

East African

Lalibela Ethiopian Restaurant 289
Holloway & Highbury

The Mandola 505
Notting Hill

North African

Adam's Café 527
Shepherd's Bush & Olympia

Momo 111
Piccadilly & St James's

Moro 217
Clerkenwell

Royal Couscous House 292
Holloway & Highbury

South African

The Springbok Café 492
Hammersmith & Chiswick

Belgian

Belgo Centraal 32
Covent Garden & Holborn

Bierodrome 299
Islington

Brazilian

Rodizio Rico 510
Notting Hill

British

Blah blah blah 528
Shepherd's Bush & Olympia

Butler's Wharf Chop House 405
Tower Bridge & Bermondsey

Fortnum's Fountain 109
Piccadilly & St James's

The Greenhouse 84
Mayfair & Bond Street

The House 455
Chelsea

The Ivy 37
Covent Garden & Holborn

Jack's Place 356
Battersea

The Organic Café 313
Maida Vale & Kilburn

Ransome's Dock 358
Battersea

Richard Corrigan at The Lindsay House 144
Soho

Rules 42
Covent Garden & Holborn

The Salt House 322
St John's Wood & Swiss Cottage

Sauce
barorganicdiner 262
Camden Town & Primrose Hill

Modern British

192 497
Notting Hill

Andrew Edmunds 132
Soho

The Anglesea Arms 487
Hammersmith & Chiswick

The Avenue 105
Piccadilly & St James's

Bah Humbug 363
Brixton & Camberwell

Bank 31
Covent Garden & Holborn

Bar Bourse 200
City

Base 270
Hampstead & Golders Green

Blue Print Café 404
Tower Bridge & Bermondsey

Books for Cooks 500
Notting Hill

Bradley's 319
St John's Wood & Swiss
Cottage

The Chiswick
Restaurant 488
Hammersmith & Chiswick

Circus 136
Soho

Cow Dining Room 502
Notting Hill

Cucina 272
Hampstead & Golders Green

Delfina Studio Café 407
Tower Bridge & Bermondsey

Duke of Cambridge 300
Islington

The Engineer 258
Camden Town & Primrose Hill

The English Garden 453
Chelsea

Euphorium 301
Islington

Fiction 282
Highgate & Crouch End

The Fifth Floor 63
Knightsbridge & Belgravia

The Fire Station 179
Waterloo & The South Bank

French House
Dining Room 137
Soho

The Gate 490
Hammersmith & Chiswick

The Havelock
Tavern 529
Shepherd's Bush & Olympia

Honest Cabbage 410
Tower Bridge & Bermondsey

House 224
Docklands

Kensington Place 504
Notting Hill

Lawn 381
Greenwich & Blackheath

Mezzo 140
Soho

No.77 Wine Bar 267
Hampstead & Golders Green

Nosh Brothers 506
Notting Hill

Odette's 261
Camden Town & Primrose Hill

Parade 467
Ealing & Acton

The People's Palace 181
Waterloo & The South Bank

Prism 206
City

Quaglino's 114
Piccadilly & St James's

R.K. Stanley 13
Bloomsbury & Fitzrovia

Redmond's 443
Barnes & Sheen

Rhodes in the
Square 173
Victoria & Westminster

Smiths, the Dining
Room 218
Clerkenwell

Sonny's 445
Barnes & Sheen

Sotheby's Café 89
Mayfair & Bond Street

St John 219
Clerkenwell

Stepping Stone 359
Battersea

Teatro 149
Soho

The Terrace 57
Kensington

The Vale 315
Maida Vale & Kilburn

Villandry Foodstore 14
Bloomsbury & Fitzrovia

The White Horse 522
Richmond & Twickenham

Burmese

The Mandalay 99
Paddington & Edgware Road

Caribbean

BB's Crabback 463
Ealing & Acton

Mango Rooms 259
Camden Town & Primrose Hill

Chinese

DS = dim sum specialist

Aroma II 19
Chinatown

Cheng Du 257
Camden Town & Primrose Hill

China City 20
Chinatown

Fung Shing 21
Chinatown

Hunan 169
Victoria & Westminster

Hung Toa 123
Queensway & Westbourne Grove

Jen 22
Chinatown

Jenny Lo's Teahouse 170
Victoria & Westminster

Kaifeng Kosher Oriental 346
Further North - Hendon

Lee Ho Fook 23
Chinatown

Mandarin Kitchen 125
Queensway & Westbourne

Mao Tai 479
Fulham

Mr Kong 24
Chinatown

New Culture Revolution 456
Chelsea

New World DS 25
Chinatown

North China Restaurant 466
Ealing & Acton

Organic Veg 162
South Kensington

Royal China DS 76
Marylebone

Tai Pan 227
Docklands

Czech/Slovak

The Czechoslovak House 273
Hampstead & Golders Green

Danish

Lundum's 474
Earl's Court

Fish/Seafood/Shellfish

Bibendum Oyster Bar 159
South Kensington

Faulkner's 233
Hackney & Dalston

Fish! 409
Tower Bridge & Bermondsey

Fish Central 243
Hoxton & Shoreditch

J. Sheekey 38
Covent Garden & Holborn

Livebait Restaurant & Bar 40
Covent Garden & Holborn

Mandarin Kitchen 125
Queensway & Westbourne Grove

Offshore 507
Notting Hill

Randall & Aubin 142
Soho

Rasa Samudra 12
Bloomsbury & Fitzrovia

Sariyer Balik Lokantasi 333
Stoke Newington

Zilli Fish 153
Soho

French

1 Lombard Street, The Brasserie 199
City

Aubergine 449
Chelsea

Belair House 426
Further South - Dulwich

Bistro Daniel 96
Paddington & Edgware Road

Brula Bistrot 517
Richmond & Twickenham

Café des Amis 33
Covent Garden & Holborn

Chez Bruce 372
Clapham & Wandsworth

Chez Gérard 5
Bloomsbury & Fitzrovia

Chez Lindsay 518
Richmond & Twickenham

Chez Maria 519
Richmond & Twickenham

Club Gascon 214
Clerkenwell

Le Colombier 452
Chelsea

The Criterion Brasserie 107
Piccadilly & St James's

Gastro 374
Clapham & Wandsworth

The Glasshouse 441
Barnes & Sheen

Gordon Ramsay 454
Chelsea

The Lobster Pot 389
Kennington & Vauxhall

McClements 520
Richmond & Twickenham

The Mirabelle 85
Mayfair & Bond Street

Monsieur Max 546
Further West - Hampton

L'Oranger 112
Piccadilly & St James's

Orrery 75
Marylebone

Paris London Café 291
Holloway & Highbury

Le P'tit Normand 418
Wimbledon & Southfields

Petit Robert 411
Tower Bridge & Bermondsey

Pétrus 113
Piccadilly & St James's

La Poule au Pot 171
Victoria & Westminster

Putney Bridge 399
Putney

Roussillon 174
Victoria & Westminster

RSJ 182
Waterloo & The South Bank

Soho Soho 145
Soho

Soulard 236
Hackney & Dalston

The Square 90
Mayfair & Bond Street

The Station Grill 390
Kennington & Vauxhall

La Tante Clare 66
Knightsbridge & Belgravia

The Village Bistro 285
Highgate & Crouch End

Fusion

Carnevale 242
Hoxton & Shoreditch

Sequel 376
Clapham & Wandsworth

Time 383
Greenwich & Blackheath

Greek

The Real Greek 244
Hoxton & Shoreditch

Xios 126
Queensway & Westbourne Grove

Indian

Bangladeshi, Indian and Pakistani restaurants

Babur Brasserie 425
Further South - Forest Hill

Bengal Village 190
Brick Lane & Spitalfields

Bombay Bicycle Club 371
Clapham & Wandsworth

The Brilliant 535
Southall

Café Indiya 202
City

Café Naz 191
Brick Lane & Spitalfields

Café Spice Namaste 203
City

Chetna's 337
Wembley

Chor Bizarre 83
Mayfair & Bond Street

Chutney Mary 451
Chelsea

Curry Craze 338
Wembley

Curry Special 249
Further East-Newbury Park

Diwana Bhel-Poori House 47
Euston & King's Cross

Geeta 311
Maida Vale & Kilburn

Geetanjali's 339
Wembley

Gifto's Lahore Karahi 536
Southall

Herb & Spice 192
Brick Lane & Spitalfields

Hot Stuff 388
Kennington & Vauxhall

India Club 36
Covent Garden & Holborn

Jashan 283
Highgate & Crouch End

Kastoori 427
Further South - Tooting

The Kerala 7
Bloomsbury & Fitzrovia

Khan's 124
Queensway & Westbourne Grove

Lahore Karahi 428
Further South - Tooting

Lahore Kebab House 193
Brick Lane & Spitalfields

The Lahore Kebab House 347
Further North - Kingsbury

Lahoria 348
Further North - Kingsbury

Ma Goa 398
Putney

Madhu's Brilliant 537
Southall

Malabar Junction 8
Bloomsbury & Fitzrovia

The Mandeer 9
Bloomsbury & Fitzrovia

Masaledar 429
Further South- Tooting

Mem Saheb on Thames 225
Docklands

Mirch Masala 430
Further South - Norbury

Mobeen 250
Further East – West Ham

Monty's 465
Ealing & Acton

New Tayyab 194
Brick Lane & Spitalfields

Omi's 538
Southall

Pallavi 521
Richmond & Twickenham

Planet Spice 431
Further South - Croydon

Pukkabar 442
Barnes & Sheen

Punjab 41
Covent Garden & Holborn

Quilon 172
Victoria & Westminster

Raavi Kebab Halal Tandoori 50
Euston & King's Cross

Le Raj 432
Further South - Epsom Downs

Rasa 332
Stoke Newington

Rasa Samudra 12
Bloomsbury & Fitzrovia

Rasa W1 88
Mayfair & Bond Street

The Red Fort 143
Soho

**Rita's Samosa
  Centre** 540
Southall

Royal Club 547
Further West - Greenford

Sakonis 340
Wembley

Sarkhel's 419
Wimbledon & Southfields

Shamyana 433
Further South - Norbury

Simply Spice 51
Euston & King's Cross

Soho Spice 146
Soho

Tabaq 377
Clapham & Wandsworth

Tabla 226
Docklands

Taja 195
Brick Lane & Spitalfields

Tamasha 434
Further South - Bromley

Three Monkeys 435
Further South - Herne Hill

Veeraswamy 116
Piccadilly & St James's

Woodlands 78
Marylebone

Zaika 458
Chelsea

Indonesian

Satay Bar 366
Brixton & Camberwell

Iranian

Alounak 121
Queensway & Westbourne
Grove

Iran the Restaurant 98
Paddington & Edgware Road

Irish

Ard Ri 71
Marylebone

Mulligan's 86
Mayfair & Bond Street

The Toucan 150
Soho

Italian &
Pizzerias

Arancia 403
Tower Bridge & Bermondsey

Artigiano 268
Hampstead & Golders Green

L'Artista 269
Hampstead & Golders Green

Assaggi 499
Notting Hill

Il Bacio 328
Stoke Newington

Del Buongustaio 396
Putney

Cantina del Ponte 406
Tower Bridge & Bermondsey

Centrale 135
Soho

Centuria 232
Hackney & Dalston

Al Duca 108
Piccadilly & St James's

Eco 373
Clapham & Wandsworth

Eco Brixton 364
Brixton & Camberwell

Enoteca 397
Putney

Grano 491
Hammersmith & Chiswick

Ibla 74
Marylebone

Kettners 138
Soho

Maremma 303
Islington

Marine Ices 260
Camden Town & Primrose Hill

Metrogusto 357
Battersea

Miraggio 481
Fulham

Neon 365
Brixton & Camberwell

RESTAURANTS ⊕ CUISINE INDEX

INDEX

Osteria Basilico 508
Notting Hill

Osteria d'Isola 64
Knightsbridge & Belgravia

Passione 11
Bloomsbury & Fitzrovia

Pizza on the Park 65
Knightsbridge & Belgravia

Pollo 141
Soho

Riccardo's 457
Chelsea

Riva 444
Barnes & Sheen

The Salusbury 314
Maida Vale & Kilburn

San Daniele
del Friuli 293
Holloway & Highbury

Sartoria 115
Piccadilly & St James's

Spiga 147
Soho

La Spighetta 77
Marylebone

Tentazioni 412
Tower Bridge & Bermondsey

Vasco and Piero's
Pavilion 151
Soho

Zafferano 67
Knightsbridge & Belgravia

Zilli Fish 153
Soho

Japanese

Cho-San 395
Putney

Defune 97
Paddington & Edgware Road

Ikkyu 6
Bloomsbury & Fitzrovia

Kulu Kulu 139
Soho

Momo 464
Ealing & Acton

Moshi Moshi
Sushi 205
City

Nobu 87
Mayfair & Bond Street

Sushi Wong 56
Kensington

Sushi-Say 350
Further North - Willesden

Tai Won Mein 382
Greenwich & Blackheath

Tokyo Diner 26
Chinatown

Wagamama 15
Bloomsbury & Fitzrovia

Yo!Sushi 152
Soho

Jewish & Kosher

Bloom's 271
Hampstead & Golders Green

Harry Morgan's 321
St John's Wood & Swiss Cottage

Kaifeng Kosher
Oriental 346
Further North - Hendon

Solly's Exclusive 276
Hampstead & Golders Green

Lebanese

Abu Ali 95
Paddington & Edgware Road

Al Waha 122
Queensway & Westbourne Grove

Fairuz 73
Marylebone

Ranoush Juice
Bar 100
Paddington & Edgware Road

Malaysian

Satay House 101
Paddington & Edgware Road

Mauritian

Offshore 507
Notting Hill

Mediterranean & Modern European

Alastair Little 131
Soho

Alastair Little W11 498
Notting Hill

The Atlas 473
Earl's Court

Bluebird 450
Chelsea

Canteloupe 241
Hoxton & Shoreditch

Le Caprice 106
Piccadilly & St James's

The Eagle 215
Clerkenwell

Ebury Wine Bar and Restaurant 168
Victoria & Westminster

Granita 302
Islington

Gresslin's 274
Hampstead & Golders Green

Lighthouse 417
Wimbledon & Southfields

Mash 10
Bloomsbury & Fitzrovia

Mesclun 331
Stoke Newington

New End 275
Hampstead & Golders Green

Pharmacy

Restaurant 509
Notting Hill

St John's 294
Holloway & Highbury

Nepalese

Great Nepalese 49
Euston & King's Cross

North American & Burgers

Arkansas Café 189
Brick Lane & Spitalfields

The Coyote Café 489
Hammersmith & Chiswick

The Hard Rock Café 110
Piccadilly & St James's

Joe Allen 39
Covent Garden & Holborn

Kettners 138
Soho

Montana 482
Fulham

Sticky Fingers 55
Kensington

Pacific Fusion

Cicada 213
Clerkenwell

Globe 320
St John's Wood & Swiss Cottage

Luca 545
Further West - Surbiton

The Sugar Club 148
Soho

Persian

Mohsen 475
Earl's Court

Peruvian

Fina Estampa 408
Tower Bridge & Bermondsey

Polish

Daquise 160
South Kensington

Patio 530
Shepherd's Bush & Olympia

Wódka 58
Kensington

Zamoyski 277
Hampstead & Golders Green

Portuguese

Bar Estrela 387
Kennington & Vauxhall

O Fado 161
South Kensington

Pubs

The Anglesea Arms 487
Hammersmith & Chiswick
Modern British

The Atlas 473
Earl's Court
Mediterranean

Centuria 232
Hackney & Dalston
Italian

The Churchill Arms 501
Notting Hill
Thai

Duke of Cambridge 300
Islington
Modern British

The Eagle 215
Clerkenwell
Mediterranean

The Engineer 258
Camden Town & Primrose Hill
Modern British

**The Havelock
Tavern** 529
Shepherd's Bush & Olympia
Modern British

The Salt House 322
St John's Wood & Swiss
Cottage
British

The Salusbury 314
Maida Vale & Kilburn
Italian

St John's 294
Holloway & Highbury
Mediterranean

The White Horse 522
Richmond & Twickenham
Modern British

Rôtisserie

Randall & Aubin 142
Soho

The Rôtisserie 305
Islington

Rôtisserie Jules 511
Notting Hill

Russian

Little Georgia 235
Hackney & Dalston

Rasputin 468
Ealing & Acton

Scottish

Boisdale 167
Victoria & Westminster

Singaporean

Singapore Garden 323
St John's Wood & Swiss
Cottage

Singapura 207
City

Spanish

Baradero 223
Docklands

**Barcelona Tapas
Bar** 201
City

La Bota 281
Highgate & Crouch End

Café España 134
Soho

Fuego 204
City

Galicia 503
Notting Hill

Gaudí 216
Clerkenwell

Meson Bilbao 312
Maida Vale & Kilburn

**El Metro Tapas
Bar** 480
Fulham

El Molino 290
Holloway & Highbury

Moro 217
Clerkenwell

El Parador 48
Euston & King's Cross

Sri Lankan

Palm Palace 539
Southall

**The Prince of
Ceylon** 349
Further North - Hendon

Sigiri 469
Ealing & Acton

Steaks

Arkansas Café 189
Brick Lane & Spitalfields

Jack's Place 356
Battersea

The Popeseye 531
Shepherd's Bush & Olympia

Tex-Mex

Café Pacifico 34
Covent Garden & Holborn

The Coyote Café 489
Hammersmith & Chiswick

The Hard Rock Café 110
Piccadilly & St James's

Montana 482
Fulham

Sticky Fingers 55
Kensington

Thai

busaba eathai 133
Soho

The Churchill Arms 501
Notting Hill

O's Thai Café 284
Highgate & Crouch End

The Pepper Tree 375
Clapham & Wandsworth

Siam Café 251
Further East – Forest Gate

Thai Tho 420
Wimbledon & Southfields

Turkish

Anatolya 231
Hackney & Dalston

Anglo Anatolyan 327
Stoke Newington

Beyoglu 355
Battersea

Harran 345
Further North - Haringey

Istanbul Iskembecisi 329
Stoke Newington

Mangal II 330
Stoke Newington

Pasha 304
Islington

Sarcan 306
Islington

Sariyer Balik Lokantasi 333
Stoke Newington

Tas 183
Waterloo & The South Bank

Vegetarian

Blah blah blah 528
Shepherd's Bush & Olympia
British

Carnevale 242
Hoxton & Shoreditch
Fusion

Chetna's 337
Wembley
Indian

Diwana Bhel-Poori House 47
Euston & King's Cross
Indian

Fiction 282
Highgate & Crouch End
Modern British

The Gate 490
Hammersmith & Chiswick
Modern British

Geeta 311
Maida Vale & Kilburn
Indian

The Mandeer 9
Bloomsbury & Fitzrovia
Indian

Organic Veg 162
South Kensington
Chinese

Rasa 332
Stoke Newington
Indian

Rasa W1 88
Mayfair & Bond Street
Indian

Sakonis 340
Wembley
Indian

Woodlands 78
Marylebone
Indian

Vietnamese

Huong Viet 234
Hackney & Dalston

Little Saigon 180
Waterloo & The South Bank

Viet Hoa Café 245
Hoxton & Shoreditch

Index of pubs and bars

In the index below the area names **are the neighbourhood sections by which this book is arranged.**

5b Urban Bar 228
Docklands

25 Canonbury Lane 307
Islington

38 43
Covent Garden & Holborn

A

Addison's 532
Shepherd's Bush & Olympia

The Admiral Hardy 384
Greenwich & Blackheath

The Albert 263
Camden Town & Primrose Hill

The Albion 532
Shepherd's Bush & Olympia

The Alexandra 378
Clapham & Wandsworth

Alphabet 154
Soho

The Anchor Tap 413
Tower Bridge & Bermondsey

The Antelope 175
Victoria & Westminster

The Archers 196
Brick Lane & Spitalfields

The Asparagus 360
Battersea

Auberge 184
Waterloo & The South Bank

B

Balls Brothers Wine Bar 208
City

Bank of Friendship 295
Holloway & Highbury

Bar Coast 400
Putney

Bar Lorca 334
Stoke Newington

Bar M at the Star and Garter 400
Putney

Bar Oz 127
Queensway & Westbourne Grove

Bar Soho 154
Soho

The Barley Mow 220
Clerkenwell

The Barley Mow 246
Hoxton & Shoreditch

The Barley Mow 102
Paddington & Edgware Rd

Beach Blanket Babylon 512
Notting Hill

The Beehive 367
Brixton & Camberwell

The Beehive 391
Kennington & Vauxhall

The Bell 208
City

Bentley's Cabin 117
Piccadilly & St James's

The Betsey Trotwood 220
Clerkenwell

The Bird in Hand 532
Shepherd's Bush & Olympia

The Black Bull 196
Brick Lane & Spitalfields

The Black Friar 208
City

The Black Lion 316
Maida Vale & Kilburn

The Blue Bar Cafe 459
Chelsea

The Blue Posts 154
Soho

The Brackenbury Arms 493
Hammersmith & Chiswick

Bram Stoker Tavern 476
Earl's Court

The Bricklayers
Arms 246
Hoxton & Shoreditch

Britannia Tap 476
Earl's Court

The Bunch of
Grapes 163
South Kensington

The Bushranger 532
Shepherd's Bush & Olympia

C

Cadogan Arms
Tavern 459
Chelsea

Cafe Med Bar 512
Notting Hill

The Carlisle 154
Soho

The Carpenter's
Arms 102
Paddington & Edgware Rd

The Castle 208
City

The Castle 512
Notting Hill

The Cat and Canary 228
Docklands

The Cat and Mutton 237
Hackney & Dalston

The Champion 512
Notting Hill

The Chequers 117
Piccadilly & St James's

The Chequers 341
Wembley

The Chippenham 316
Maida Vale & Kilburn

The City Barge 493
Hammersmith & Chiswick

The Clachan 154
Soho

Claridge's Bar 91
Mayfair & Bond Street

The Coach and
Horses 91
Mayfair & Bond Street

The Cockpit 208
City

The Collection 163
South Kensington

The Compton Arms 307
Islington

The Cork and Bottle 27
Chinatown

The Cork and Bottle 512
Notting Hill

The Crescent Wine
Bar 163
South Kensington

The Cricketers 384
Greenwich & Blackheath

The Cross Keys 43
Covent Garden & Holborn

The Crown 360
Battersea

The Crown 459
Chelsea

The Crown 43
Covent Garden & Holborn

The Crown 384
Greenwich & Blackheath

Crown and Anchor 52
Euston & King's Cross

The Crown and
Cushion 184
Waterloo & The South Bank

The Crown and
Sceptre 16
Bloomsbury & Fitzrovia

Crusting Pipe 43
Covent Garden & Holborn

Cuba 59
Kensington

Cynthia's Cyberbar 413
Tower Bridge & Bermondsey

D

Davy's Wine Bar 228
Docklands

The Dean Swift 413
Tower Bridge & Bermondsey

Dirty Dick's 196
Brick Lane & Spitalfields

The Dog and Duck 154
Soho

The Dog and Fox 421
Wimbledon & Southfields

Drayton Arms 476
Earl's Court

Duke of Cumberland 483
Fulham

Duke of Hamilton 278
Hampstead & Golders Green

The Duke of Kendall 102
Paddington & Edgware Rd

The Duke of Sussex 470
Ealing & Acton

Duke of Wellington 512
Notting Hill

The Duke's Head 400
Putney

E

The Earl of Spencer 421
Wimbledon & Southfields

The Earl Percy 512
Notting Hill

Eddie's Free House 341
Wembley

Edinboro Castle 263
Camden Town & Primrose Hill

The Eel Pie 523
Richmond & Twickenham

The Effra 367
Brixton & Camberwell

The Elephant and
Castle 59
Kensington

F

The Falcon 316
Maida Vale & Kilburn

The Fifth Floor Bar 68
Knightsbridge & Belgravia

Finborough Arms 476
Earl's Court

The Finca 391
Kennington & Vauxhall

Finch's 459
Chelsea

The Flask 278
Hampstead & Golders Green

The Flask 286
Highgate & Crouch End

Flourmill and Firkin 367
Brixton & Camberwell

The Folly Bar 316
Maida Vale & Kilburn

Foundry 246
Hoxton & Shoreditch

The Fox 237
Hackney & Dalston

The Fox 400
Putney

Fox and Hounds 175
Victoria & Westminster

Frederick's 307
Islington

The Friend at Hand 52
Euston & King's Cross

G

The Gardener's Arms 421
Wimbledon & Southfields

The Gate 512
Notting Hill

The Gate Lodge 278
Hampstead & Golders Green

The George 228
Docklands

The George 483
Fulham

The George and
Dragon 470
Ealing & Acton

The George IV 493
Hammersmith & Chiswick

The Gipsy Moth 384
Greenwich & Blackheath

Glassy Junction 541
Southall

The Gloucester 68
Knightsbridge & Belgravia

The Goat in Boots 459
Chelsea

The Golden Eagle 79
Marylebone

The Golden Lion 117
Piccadilly & St James's

The Goose and
Granite 378
Clapham & Wandsworth

Grand Banks 295
Holloway & Highbury

Grape Street Wine Bar 16
Bloomsbury & Fitzrovia

The Grenadier 68
Knightsbridge & Belgravia

The Greystoke 470
Ealing & Acton

INDEX

Ground Floor Bar 513
Notting Hill

The Gun 196
Brick Lane & Spitalfields

H

Ha Ha Bar 16
Bloomsbury & Fitzrovia

Hare and Hounds 446
Barnes & Sheen

Harringay Arms 286
Highgate & Crouch End

Havana 483
Fulham

The Hen and Chicken Theatre Bar 237
Hackney & Dalston

The Henry Addington 228
Docklands

Hobgoblin 295
Holloway & Highbury

Hog in the Pound 91
Mayfair & Bond Street

The Hogshead 27
Chinatown

The Hogshead 307
Islington

The Hoop and Toy 163
South Kensington

The Horseshoe 220
Clerkenwell

I

The Imperial 27
Chinatown

INDO 196
Brick Lane & Spitalfields

The Intrepid Fox 154
Soho

ION Bar 513
Notting Hill

J

Jack Beard's "The Crown" 360
Battersea

Jamie's 16
Bloomsbury & Fitzrovia

Jim Thompson's Flaming Wok 493
Hammersmith & Chiswick

Jimmies Wine Bar 59
Kensington

The Jolly Gardeners 52
Euston & King's Cross

The Junction Tavern 295
Holloway & Highbury

K

The King's Head 27
Chinatown

The King's Head 286
Highgate & Crouch End

L

Lamb Tavern 208
City

Latest Rumours 43
Covent Garden & Holborn

The Leader's Bar 184
Waterloo & The South Bank

The Legless Ladder 360
Battersea

The Leinster 127
Queensway & Westbourne Grove

Liam Og's 391
Kennington & Vauxhall

The Library Bar 184
Waterloo & The South Bank

Lighthouse Bar 237
Hackney & Dalston

Lobby Bar, No 1 Aldwych 43
Covent Garden & Holborn

The London Stone 208
City

The Lord Nelson 246
Hoxton & Shoreditch

The Lounge Bar 184
Waterloo & The South Bank

M

Maddigan's on Mare Street 237
Hackney & Dalston

The Magpie 208
City

The Mall Tavern 513
Notting Hill

Marquis of
Lansdowne 334
Stoke Newington

The Mason's Arms 16
Bloomsbury & Fitzrovia

The Mason's Arms 102
Paddington & Edgware Rd

Match 220
Clerkenwell

The Maynard Arms 286
Highgate & Crouch End

Medicine Bar 307
Islington

Millennium
Knightsbridge 68
Knightsbridge & Belgravia

Mixology 483
Fulham

The Monarch 334
Stoke Newington

Moon Under Water 523
Richmond & Twickenham

The Mornington
Arms 263
Camden Town & Primrose Hill

The Mother Red Cap 295
Holloway & Highbury

The Mughouse 413
Tower Bridge & Bermondsey

The Mulberry Bush 184
Waterloo & The South Bank

The Museum Tavern 16
Bloomsbury & Fitzrovia

N

The Nag's Head 68
Knightsbridge & Belgravia

The Nightingale 378
Clapham & Wandsworth

The Nott 391
Kennington & Vauxhall

O

The O'Conor Don 79
Marylebone

Oblivion 378
Clapham & Wandsworth

The Old Black Lion 278
Hampstead & Golders Green

The Old Blue Last 246
Hoxton & Shoreditch

The Old Coffee
House 154
Soho

The Old English
Gentleman 102
Paddington & Edgware Rd

The Old Monk 196
Brick Lane & Spitalfields

The Old Parr's Head 307
Islington

The Old Parr's Head 532
Shepherd's Bush & Olympia

The Old Post Office 341
Wembley

The Old Ship 523
Richmond & Twickenham

Opera Terrace Bar 43
Covent Garden & Holborn

The Orange Brewery 175
Victoria & Westminster

The Ordnance 324
St John's Wood & Swiss
Cottage

P

Pack Horse and
Talbot 493
Hammersmith & Chiswick

The Park Tavern 421
Wimbledon & Southfields

The Pheasant 246
Hoxton & Shoreditch

The Pig and Whistle 446
Barnes & Sheen

Pitcher and Piano 421
Wimbledon & Southfields

The Pontefract Castle 79
Marylebone

Power's Bar 316
Maida Vale & Kilburn

The Prince Albert 360
Battersea

The Prince Albert 367
Brixton & Camberwell

INDEX

Prince Alfred 127
Queensway & Westbourne Grove

Prince Arthur 52
Euston & King's Cross

The Prince Edward 127
Queensway & Westbourne Grove

The Prince of Wales 367
Brixton & Camberwell

The Prince of Wales 476
Earl's Court

The Prince of Wales 286
Highgate & Crouch End

The Prince of Wales 59
Kensington

The Prince of Wales 316
Maida Vale & Kilburn

The Prince of Wales 421
Wimbledon & Southfields

The Prince Regent 79
Marylebone

The Prince's Head 523
Richmond & Twickenham

The Princess Louise 263
Camden Town & Primrose Hill

The Princess Louise 43
Covent Garden & Holborn

Princess Royal 324
St John's Wood & Swiss Cottage

The Puzzle 360
Battersea

R

The Railway 400
Putney

The Railway Tavern 334
Stoke Newington

The Rat and Parrot 59
Kensington

The Red Cow 523
Richmond & Twickenham

The Red Lion 446
Barnes & Sheen

The Red Lion 117
Piccadilly & St James's

The Red Lion 117
Piccadilly & St James's

The Red Lion 155
Soho

The Red Lion and Pineapple 470
Ealing & Acton

The Redan 127
Queensway & Westbourne Grove

The Refectory 278
Hampstead & Golders Green

The Ritz 117
Piccadilly & St James's

The Rose and Crown 384
Greenwich & Blackheath

The Rose and Crown 334
Stoke Newington

Rowley's 52
Euston & King's Cross

The Royal Oak 391
Kennington & Vauxhall

S

S B Tollesbury 228
Docklands

The Salutation Inn 493
Hammersmith & Chiswick

Scruffy Murphy's 278
Hampstead & Golders Green

The Shakespeare 127
Queensway & Westbourne Grove

The Shakespeare's Head 155
Soho

The Shipwright's Arms 413
Tower Bridge & Bermondsey

The Sols Arms 52
Euston & King's Cross

The Spanish Galleon 384
Greenwich & Blackheath

The Spinning Wheel 470
Ealing & Acton

The Spotted Horse 400
Putney

St George and the Dragon 541
Southall

St John 295
Holloway & Highbury

The Star 324
St John's Wood & Swiss Cottage

Steptoe's 334
Stoke Newington

The Sun in
Splendour 513
Notting Hill

The Sun Inn 446
Barnes & Sheen

The Surrey Tavern 378
Clapham & Wandsworth

The Sussex 43
Covent Garden & Holborn

The Swan 209
City

The Swiss Cottage 324
St John's Wood & Swiss Cottage

T

The Three Horseshoes 541
Southall

Three Kings 220
Clerkenwell

The Three Tuns 541
Southall

The Turk's Head 68
Knightsbridge & Belgravia

Two Floors 155
Soho

V

Vesbar 532
Shepherd's Bush & Olympia

The Victoria 360
Battersea

The Village 237
Hackney & Dalston

The Village 341
Wembley

Vino Veritas 175
Victoria & Westminster

W

The Walsingham
Arms 470
Ealing & Acton

The Warwick Arms 476
Earl's Court

Waxy O'Connors 27
Chinatown

West Central 27
Chinatown

The Wheatsheaf 483
Fulham

The Wheatsheaf 391
Kennington & Vauxhall

The White Cross 523
Richmond & Twickenham

The White Hart 184
Waterloo & The South Bank

The White Horse 483
Fulham

White Swan 209
City

Whittington's Wine
Bar 209
City

The William Wallace 79
Marylebone

The Wilton Arms 68
Knightsbridge & Belgravia

The Windmill 378
Clapham & Wandsworth

Windows at the
Hilton 91
Mayfair & Bond Street

WKD 263
Camden Town & Primrose Hill

The Woodstock 91
Mayfair & Bond Street

The Woolpack 413
Tower Bridge & Bermondsey

The World's End 263
Camden Town & Primrose Hill

The World's End 459
Chelsea

Y

Ye Grapes 91
Mayfair & Bond Street

Ye Olde Red Cow 220
Clerkenwell

Z

Zander 175
Victoria & Westminster

The Zetland Arms 163
South Kensington

Zilli Bar 155
Soho

Zoe 79
Marylebone

ROUGH GUIDES: Travel

Amsterdam	Greek Islands	Provence & the
Andalucia	Guatemala	Côte d'Azur
Australia	Hawaii	The Pyrenees
Austria	Holland	Romania
Bali & Lombok	Hong Kong	St Petersburg
Barcelona	& Macau	San Francisco
Belgium &	Hungary	Scandinavia
Luxembourg	India	Scotland
Belize	Indonesia	Sicily
Berlin	Ireland	Singapore
Brazil	Israel & the Palestinian	South Africa
Britain	Territories	Southern India
Brittany & Normandy	Italy	Southwest USA
Bulgaria	Jamaica	Spain
California	Japan	Sweden
Canada	Jordan	Syria
Central America	Kenya	Thailand
Chile	Laos	Trinidad & Tobago
China	London	Tunisia
Corfu & the Ionian	London Restaurants	Turkey
Islands	Los Angeles	Tuscany & Umbria
Corsica	Malaysia, Singapore &	USA
Costa Rica	Brunei	Venice
Crete	Mallorca & Menorca	Vienna
Cyprus	Maya World	Vietnam
Czech & Slovak	Mexico	Wales
Republics	Morocco	Washington DC
Dodecanese	Moscow	West Africa
Dominican Republic	Nepal	Zimbabwe & Botswana
Egypt	New England	
England	New York	
Europe	New Zealand	
Florida	Norway	
France	Pacific Northwest	
French Hotels &	Paris	
Restaurants 1999	Peru	
Germany	Poland	
Goa	Portugal	
Greece	Prague